A SWEET AND ALIEN LAND

Also by Henri and Barbara van der Zee

WILLIAM AND MARY

A Sweet

Alien

THE STORY OF
BY HENRI AND

THE VIKING PRESS   NEW YORK

and
Land

DUTCH NEW YORK
BARBARA VAN DER ZEE

First published in 1978 by The Viking Press
625 Madison Avenue, New York, N.Y. 10022

LIBRARY OF CONGRESS CATALOGING IN PUBLICATION DATA
Van der Zee, Henri.
A sweet and alien land:
the story of Dutch New York.
Bibliography: p.
1. New York (State)—History—Colonial period, ca. 1600–1775.
2. Dutch Americans—New York (State)—History.
I. Van der Zee, Barbara, joint author.
II. Title.
F122.1.V22   974.7′02   76–50665
ISBN 0–670–68628–x

Printed in the United States of America
Set in Videocomp Janson

Grateful acknowledgment is made to Barnes & Noble Books:
From *Narratives of New Netherland: 1609–1664*, edited by J.
Franklin Jameson, 1909, reprinted 1959. Reprinted by permission of Barnes & Noble Books (a division of Harper & Row
Publishers, Inc.).

To Ninka

ACKNOWLEDGMENTS

The authors gratefully acknowledge the assistance and encouragement they have received from numerous friends, colleagues and experts during the research and the writing of this book. They would like particularly to thank their editors, Alan Williams and Alida Becker in New York, and Caroline Hobhouse in London, for their keen interest and constructive criticisms; and Jackie Baldick for her never-diminishing enthusiasm.

Henri van der Zee wishes to express once again his deep gratitude to Henri Goeman-Borgesius, Editor of *De Telegraaf* in Amsterdam, whose indulgence made possible the writing of this book.

CONTENTS

List of Ilustrations   *xiii*

Chronology   *xv*

1   The Best Buy   *1*

2   Settling Down   *10*

3   Never So Good   *19*

4   First Rights   *29*

5   A Pilgrimage   *41*

6   Drunken Fools   *48*

7   Crowding On   *61*

8   A New Threat   *72*

9   Doubtful Neighbors   *83*

10   The Dutch Babel   *97*

11   A Very Mean Fellow   *109*

12   The English Savior   *123*

13   The Israelites   *137*

14   Another Father   *150*

15   A Bad Start   *161*

16   New Brooms   *168*

17   The Freedom Fighters   *180*

18   The Duke of Muscovy   *193*

19   Trouble in the North   *203*

20   Losing Ground   *212*

21   Total War   *225*

22   Turncoats   *235*

23   Danger from Abroad   *246*

24   Exit Nueva Suecia   *258*

25   The Peach War   *271*

26   Pastoral Problems   *280*

27   Heretic Confusion   *290*

28   The Failure of Amsterdam   *300*

29   Clash with Boston   *312*

30   The Esopus War   *320*

31   Here to Stay   *333*

32   A Brave Place   *341*

33   Law and Disorder   *351*

34   Homage in Verse   *359*

35   Reconnaissance   *374*

36   Annexation on Paper   *385*

37   Twice Tricked   *394*

38   War at Wiltwyck   *403*

39   Desperate Diplomacy   *413*

40   President Scott   *426*

41   Mad for War   *435*

42   The Duke's Invasion   *445*

43   The Fall of the City   *455*

44   The Birth of New York   *465*

45   Return of a Patriot   *473*

Epilogue   *482*

Notes   *495*

Bibliography   *532*

Index   *543*

ILLUSTRATIONS

The Dream

FOLLOWING PAGE 40

Willem Usselinx
"Figurative Map on Vellum"
Dutch ship
West India House
Mont Albaan's Tower
Letter to the States General
"Privileges and Exemptions," a pamphlet

The First View

FOLLOWING PAGE 108

The Hartgers drawing of New Amsterdam
A map dating from 1647
New Amsterdam's Coat of Arms
Drawing probably made by Augustine Heerman

Dutch Pioneers

FOLLOWING PAGE 192

David de Vries
Everardus Bogardus
Augustine Heerman
Cornelis Steenwyck

The Stuyvesants

FOLLOWING PAGE 332

The Peter Stuyvesant mansion
Peter Stuyvesant
Peter Stuyvesant's signature
Bayards' homestead in Alphen aan de Rijn, Holland
Nicholas Willem Stuyvesant

Changing Hands

FOLLOWING PAGE 444

James II, Duke of York
Johan de Witt
John Winthrop, Jr.
John Winthrop, Sr.
Cornelis Evertsen
View of New Amsterdam
City Hall in 1679

ILLUSTRATIONS

CHRONOLOGY

New World	1492	Old World
Columbus discovers the New World.		
	1524	
Giovanni da Verrazano discovers the Hudson River.		
	1579	
		Dutch Republic of Seven United Provinces founded, while involved in a war of liberation with Spain.
	1602	
Bartholomew Gosnold lands in Massachusetts Bay.		Dutch East India Company founded.
	1606	
		Virginia Charter ratified in England.
	1607	
Permanent settlement begins in Virginia.		
	1609	
Henry Hudson discovers Manhattan Island for the Dutch East India Company.		Truce of twenty-one years between Spain and Holland.

New World		Old World
	1610/1611	
		Peter Stuyvesant born in Peperga (Friesland).
	1614	
		New Netherland Company founded.
	1618	
		Charter of New Netherland Company expires.
	1620	
		The New England Council formed. *Mayflower* sets sail from Plymouth, England.
	1621	
		End of truce between Spain and Holland. Charter for Dutch West India Company ratified, under British protest.
	1623	
		First official settlers sail to New Netherland.
	1625	
Fort Amsterdam built on Manhattan.		Treaty of Southampton.
	1626	
Peter Minuit arrives in New Netherland as first director. First clashes with Indians. Manhattan bought for 60 guilders.		
	1627	
Secretary Isaack de Rasières travels to New Plymouth as representative of New Netherland.		
	1629	
		Massachusetts Bay Company incorporated.
	1630	
John Winthrop arrives in New England. Boston founded. Domain of Rensselaerswyck established.		
	1632	
Peter Minuit recalled to Holland. The *Eendracht* captured by English at Plymouth, setting off the first clash between Dutch and English over possession of New Netherland.		

CHRONOLOGY

	New World	Old World	

Wouter van Twiller arrives as new director general in New Amsterdam and establishes House of Good Hope on Connecticut River.	1633	
Massachusetts claims Connecticut. First English colonists arrive in Maryland.	1634	
	1635	Peter Minuit founds Swedish-Dutch Company for trade to New World.
Roger Williams establishes colony at Providence (Rhode Island). Saybrook (Connecticut) founded by John Winthrop Jr.	1636	
Pequot Indians decimated by English.	1637	First Swedish ships leave for Delaware.
Fort Christina founded at New Sweden on the Delaware. Settlement of English begins at New Haven. Willem Kieft succeeds Wouter van Twiller as director general of New Netherland.	1638	
Governor Kieft taxes Indians for the first time.	1639	
Uprising of Indians in New Netherland is followed by slaughter. Dutch buy Long Island. First serious clashes between Dutch and English at Connecticut River.	1640	
Connecticut's offer to buy House of Good Hope refused by Dutch. First church built in New Amsterdam.	1642	Prince Willem II of Orange marries Mary Stuart, daughter of King Charles I. Start of Civil War in England.

	1643	
Second Indian War in New Netherland. New Amsterdam numbers 400 inhabitants. United Colonies of New England constituted in Boston.		
	1645	
Peace treaty between Indians and settlers in New Netherland.		
	1647	
Peter Stuyvesant becomes director general of New Netherland. Kieft perishes while returning to Holland.		
	1648	
		Peace between Spain and Holland. Peace of Westphalia.
	1649	
John Winthrop Sr. dies and is succeeded by John Endicott as governor of Massachusetts.		End of Civil War in England. Charles I decapitated. Oliver Cromwell assumes power. *Remonstrance of New Netherland* published in Holland.
	1650	
Peter Stuyvesant travels to Hartford for meeting with United Colonies to form provisional agreement on boundaries (Hartford Treaty).		Prince Willem II dies. Willem III born.
	1651	
Stuyvesant builds Fort Casimir on the Delaware. Stuyvesant builds his bouwery.		Navigation Act ratified in England.
	1652	
First City Council in New Amsterdam.		First Anglo-Dutch War.
	1653	
First Provincial Assembly in New Netherland.		
	1654	
Connecticut seizes House of Good Hope. English fleet arrives at Boston with intention of invading New Netherland. Swedes capture Fort Casimir on the Delaware from the Dutch.		Peace between England and Holland. West India Company loses Brazil to Portugal.

New World	Old World

──────────────── 1655 ────────────────

Stuyvesant imprisoned by English at Barbados, but allowed to return to New Amsterdam. Dutch subdue Swedes at Delaware. Peach War at New Amsterdam with Indians. First Negro slaves from Africa arrive in New Amsterdam.

──────────────── 1656 ────────────────

Amsterdam buys Delaware and founds New Amstel.

──────────────── 1657 ────────────────

New Amsterdam introduces Burgher-recht (municipal freedom).

Sir George Downing becomes ambassador to Holland.

──────────────── 1659 ────────────────

First Latin School in New Amsterdam. Maryland tries to conquer Dutch colonies on the Delaware. New Haarlem founded.

──────────────── 1660 ────────────────

Esopus War with Indians. New Amsterdam now numbers 1,500 citizens.

Restoration in England. Charles II becomes King.

──────────────── 1661 ────────────────

Second Navigation Act accepted by Parliament. Dutch conclude peace with Portuguese. Charles II marries Catherine of Braganza.

──────────────── 1662 ────────────────

Connecticut receives its charter. English invasion of Long Island.

Treaty of friendship between England and the Dutch Republic.

──────────────── 1663 ────────────────

Earthquake in Canada, New England, and parts of New Netherland. Indian war at Wiltwyck. Stuyvesant to Boston to meet Commissioners of United Colonies. Second Provincial Assembly in New Netherland.

Staple Act accepted by Parliament.

──────────────── 1664 ────────────────

English fleet captures New Amsterdam.

──────────────── 1665 ────────────────

Stuyvesant summoned back to Holland to justify loss of New Netherland.

Second Anglo-Dutch War.

New World		Old World
	— 1666 —	
		Great Fire of London. Plague hits England and Holland.
	— 1667 —	
		Dutch sail up the Thames. End of Second Anglo-Dutch War.
	— 1668 —	
Stuyvesant returns to New York.		
	— 1672 —	
Stuyvesant dies.		Third Anglo-Dutch War.
	— 1673 —	
Dutch recapture New York for 15 months.		
	— 1674 —	
		End of Third Anglo-Dutch War, and return of New York to England.

A SWEET AND ALIEN LAND

THE

BEST BUY

High and Mighty Lords: Yesterday arrived here the ship Arms of Amsterdam, *which sailed from New Netherland, out of the River Mauritius, on 23 September. They report that our people are in good heart and live in peace there. . . . They have purchased the Island of Manhattes from the Indians for the value of 60 guilders; 'tis 11.000 morgens in size.* [1]

With these few words Peter Jansen van Schagen, the delegate of the States General in the Dutch West India Company, announced on November 5, 1626, the acquisition of Manhattan, the island in the mouth of the Hudson River, now the heart of New York. The government in The Hague was not impressed by what would later be described as "the best buy in the world." In its minutes the States noted dryly: "Received a letter from Mijnheer Schagen, written at Amsterdam the 5 inst., containing the advice of the arrival of a ship from New Netherland, which demands no action."[2]

The Dutch statesmen could not, however, deny that it was an excellent start to an enterprise for which they had never shown much enthusiasm. According to Van Schagen's letter, not only had some of the women in the province borne children and the first harvest been a success, but the *Arms of Amsterdam* had also brought back 8,250 furs, 7,246 of them beaverskins, valued at forty-five thousand guilders. After deducting the twenty thousand guilders that the company had spent on equipping the first pioneers, it was left with a handsome profit—an important point for the Dutch, who, with so many trading settlements all over the world, considered the purchase of one more island of little importance.

It was in May 1626 that Peter Minuit (in Holland called Minnewit) had made his bargain with the Canarsie Indians on Manhattan. Since gold and silver meant nothing to them, he paid with some beads and trinkets, following his instructions from Holland: ". . . in case the said Island is inhabited by some Indians . . . these should not be driven away by force or threats, but should be persuaded by kind words or otherwise by giving them something, to let us live amongst them."[3]

Minuit, a man of French parentage, had left his birthplace, the German town of Wesel, after its capture by the Spanish in 1624. When he embarked from Amsterdam on December 19, 1625, he had a commission from the West India Company to establish its colony in North America. His ship, the *Meeuwken* ("Seagull"), was delayed by winter storms, and not until January 9, 1626, was he able to sail from Texel, the large island off northern Holland that was the springboard for all Dutch marine adventurers. In May he arrived at New Netherland as the company's first representative to carry the title of director general—a grand name for the governorship of a community of two hundred people scattered among trading posts along the Hudson, Delaware, and Connecticut rivers, where they bartered with the Indians for furs. His first task was to bring them all together in one place, where they could be protected against attack by the original inhabitants of this Dutch corner of America, the Indians.

Manhattan Island was the most obvious choice. Measuring twenty-two square miles, with deep bays on north and south that made excellent harbors after the long and dangerous Atlantic crossing, it was "like a great natural pier ready to receive the commerce of the world." Its hilly countryside was covered with woods full of game and green meadows, while its soil was perfect for farming. The origin of its name is a mystery—Manahata, Manahatin, Manhattes, Manhates, Manadoes, and Mennades were just a few names for what the Dutch officially called Manhattan, probably the Indian word for "island of the hills."[4]

The first to mention this name (written as Manna-hata) was Robert Juet, the English mate of Henry Hudson, whose discovery

A SWEET AND ALIEN LAND

of the island in 1609 gave the Dutch their first possession in North America. Hudson, whose grandfather was one of the founders of the English Muscovy Company, had made two voyages to the Arctic searching for a northerly route to the Spice Islands. The Dutch East India Company, founded in 1602 with a virtual monopoly of the immensely profitable spice trade, knew of only two routes, both of them lengthy: southwest via the Magellan Strait, and southeast past the Cape of Good Hope. If there was a shortcut, they were as anxious as their commercial rivals to find it. And Dutch geographers, among them the famous Dominie Plancius, were of the opinion that if one could crash the ice barrier at 66°, one would find a northeast passage through the open seas.

Hudson had developed this idea, believing that if he could reach 83° north, he could turn east to the Indies. The Dutch East India Company heard about his theory, invited him to Amsterdam, and offered a contract: they guaranteed him eight hundred guilders, and an extra two hundred for his wife should he not return. On April 6, 1609, Hudson left Texel with the seventy-ton *Halve Maen* ("Half Moon"), hoping to head for the Far East by way of Nova Zembla, an island in the Barents Sea.

Emanuel van Meeteren, who as Dutch consul in London later talked to Hudson's crew, reported that the Englishman had found the sea around Nova Zembla so full of ice that he lost all hope "of effecting anything during the season." The cold was too much for the crew, and after violent disputes Hudson decided to try a route that a friend, Captain John Smith from the English colony of Virginia, had mentioned to him—"a sea leading into the western ocean, by the north of the southern English colony."[5]

He reached the American coast in July, and sailing along it, discovered on September 12 at 40°45′ a "good entrance between two headlands." Entering, he saw "as fine a river as can be found . . . with good anchoring grounds on both sides." Hudson had arrived at the spot that the Italian explorer Giovanni da Verrazano, sailing under the French flag, had described eighty-five years earlier as "a very pleasant situation among some steep hills, through which a very large river, deep at its mouth, forced its way to the sea."[6]

Like Verrazano, Hudson sailed on upriver and anchored at last at 42°40′, where he found a "friendly and polite people, who had an abundance of provisions, skins and furs," which they traded

THE BEST BUY

amicably with the crew. Juet tells in his journal how surprised the Anglo-Dutch sailors were to find a country so "full of great and tall oakes," inhabited by natives dressed in "Mantles of Feathers, and some in skinnes of diverse sorts of good Furres." Some of the women, to the amusement of the crew, were smoking from "red Copper Tobacco Pipes."[7]

A further exploration of the river, named by Hudson the Great River of the Mountain, was a less pleasant experience—one member of the crew was killed by an arrow through his throat. Hudson at once called back his sailors, then invited some of the chiefs to his cabin, giving them "so much wine and Aqua Vitae, that they were all merrie. . . . In the end one of them was drunke . . . and that was strange to them; for they could not tell how to take it." In spite of the first hangover any Indian could have had, this party at once improved relations with the Indians, who brought Hudson more tobacco and beads, and a "great Platter full of Venison." The Englishmen, however, after other unpleasant incidents with tribes living higher up the river, decided to return to the bay, where the *Halve Maen* rode quietly at anchor for some days, before "that side of the river that is called Manna-hata."[8]

"More could have been done if there had been goodwill among the crew," wrote Consul Van Meeteren plaintively from London. But Hudson, afraid of his unwilling sailors, who had several times threatened mutiny, thought it wiser to return to Europe. After a fast crossing, "on the seventh day of November, being Saturday: by the Grace of God we safely arrived in the range of Dartmouth," sighed Juet in his journal.[9]

The Dutch East India Company had to be patient a long time before it learned news of Hudson's voyage. Contrary winds made contact between England and Holland impossible for weeks, and when in January 1610 the Dutch could at last summon Hudson to report, the English had discovered his "betrayal" and refused to let him go. They had been slow off the mark in the transatlantic race, but during the reign of Elizabeth, and now of James I, England had become fascinated by the possibility of colonizing North America. "It was thought probable that the English themselves would send ships to Virginia to explore the aforesaid river," noted the well-informed Van Meeteren.[10]

The *Halve Maen* returned to Amsterdam in July under another captain. Hudson sailed again a month later, this time in the service

A SWEET AND ALIEN LAND

of his own country. It was his last voyage. In June 1611 a mutinous crew put him and his son into a small boat near Newfoundland and they were cast off, never to be seen again.

The members of the East India Company in Amsterdam were understandably disappointed by the results of Hudson's adventure. He had defied their instructions not to take any "other way or passage excepting the . . . ones north and north-east above Nova Zembla," and since England's James I had confiscated his journals and maps, they could only piece together a few sparse facts, with the help of the Dutch consul. Hudson's discovery of the Great River was of no interest to them. In their eyes, it was simply another dead end.

However, a small group of Amsterdam fur traders, who depended for their supplies on the French fur center at Rouen, was keenly interested in Van Meeteren's details of a rich harvest of beaver skins. The French King had banned the Dutch from trading in his new colony in Canada, and Hudson's discovery might give them the chance to develop their own hunting grounds.

The historian and geographer Johannes de Laet, who later played an important role in the West India Company, wrote that in 1610 a ship was again sent to the river "which was called Manhattes." The results of this expedition were not recorded, but thirteen fur traders in Amsterdam and Hoorn must have thought the risk worthwhile, for in 1613 they equipped no less than five ships to send to America. The two most important were the *Fortuyn*, sailed by "the worthy Hendrick Christiaensz of Cleves," and the *Tyger*, under the command of Adriaen Block. While the first went up to the mouth of the Fresh or Delaware River, Block sailed up the Great River, which by now had been renamed the Riviere van der Vorst Mauritius. Block's expedition nearly ended in disaster when his ship went up in flames, but with help from the Indians he built the first ship in America, the *Onrust* ("Restless"). With this vessel he explored Long Island Sound, naming one little island after himself; mapped the Stated Baai, now known as Cape Cod Bay; discovered the Connecticut River; and finally returned to the mouth of the Hudson River, where he met Christiaensz, who took him back to Holland.[11]

They left behind the *Onrust* and a small redoubt called the Fort Van Nassoueen (or Nassau) on Castle Island, near present-day Albany. According to tradition, it was built on top of a fortification left there by the French in 1540, fifty-eight feet square and surrounded by an eighteen-foot moat. The Dutch equipped it with two cannon and eleven guns, but had to build another fort three years later when the first was flooded out by the river. It was certainly not very impressive, but Fort Nassau was Holland's first foothold on American soil.[12]

Block and Christiaensz returned with a load of furs and—better still—a map of the American coast near Manhattan and Long Island, the famous "Figurative Map on Vellum," an excellent example of Dutch navigational expertise. This not only assured future sailors a safe passage to the Hudson River; it also earned for the thirteen merchants a much-coveted monopoly of trade with North America. The United New Netherland Company, formed after much squabbling, received from the States General on October 11, 1614, the exclusive right "to resort to, or cause to be frequented, the newly discovered countries situate in America between New France and Virginia . . . now named New Netherland." The patent was for four voyages to be made in three years, and any trespasser was to be punished with a fine of fifty thousand ducats.[13]

It was the start of an intensive and profitable trade, for which Christiaensz paid with his life. In 1619, while his ship the *Swarte Beer* was lying in the Hudson River, he was murdered by Orson, one of two Indians he had taken to Holland and back. The other founders of the United New Netherland Company had tried to renew their patent when it expired in 1618, but by that time the States General had other plans for New Netherland.[14]

As early as October 1606 the powerful Council of Amsterdam had proposed the founding of a West India Company, to have the trading monopoly along the West Coast of Africa as far south as the Cape of Good Hope, as well as in the Americas. A well-known Amsterdammer called William Usselinx had played an important role in the development of this idea. Born in 1567 in Antwerp, he had traveled extensively in Spain, Portugal, and the Azores before settling in Amsterdam, where he was known as one of the richest men in the province. During his travels he had learned a great deal about the Spanish and Portuguese colonies, and in 1600 he launched his first *Vertoogh* ("Remonstrance"), an eloquent piece of propaganda in which he attempted to convince his countrymen that newly-discovered countries could be exploited by coloniza-

A SWEET AND ALIEN LAND

tion. Instead of simply setting up trading posts, as was the practice of the Dutch merchants, he argued that they should send over farmers and families and found permanent settlements.

The Dutch initially listened with skepticism to his proposals, but when he dwelt on the possibility of injuring the Spanish, with whom they were at war, by robbing them of their colonies in the western hemisphere, their minds were made up. The province of Zeeland was the first to see the use of such a company. Amsterdam followed, and Usselinx developed his thoughts in a new *Vertoogh*. It was all too beautiful to be true. Before his eyes rose a vision of rich colonies in Guyana, "where more than 600 thousand miles of healthy, fertile and good soil" waited for the pioneers. To these "colonias and new republics" people would come from all over Europe, towns would be built, mines dug. God-fearing dominies would convert the natives, who, when they had attained to higher civilization and greater prosperity, would become eager consumers of Dutch goods.[15]

The creation of Usselinx's Eldorado had to be delayed; and it was never in fact to exist. In 1609, after forty years of war against Spain, the Protestant Dutch finally made a twenty-one-year truce with their Catholic foes. The chief architect of this truce was Pensionary Johan van Oldenbarneveld, and he saw in the proposed West India Company a threat to the fragile relationship with Spain —which still claimed all of America. The disappointed Usselinx turned his energies to a project nearer home, the draining of the Beemstermeer, a lake near Amsterdam, for use as farmland. It was a venture that lost him all his money.

The merchants of Amsterdam, however, continued to be highly interested in the New World, where, in the words of Van Meeteren, "good skins and furs . . . were to be got at a very low price." They had never been in favor of a truce with Spain, for what they had lost during the war in honorable trade, they had more than got back by privateering. Never had the aging Van Oldenbarneveld been more unpopular. His opposition to the projected West India Company was, for Amsterdammers, another bone of contention, and when in the middle of the truce a violent quarrel arose between two factions in the Dutch Calvinist Church, the Remonstrants and the stricter Contra-Remonstrants, Amsterdam watched with delight the fall of the Pensionary. He had sided with the Remonstrants, and in 1618 he was summoned for trial by the

Contra-Remonstrants who, with the support of the Dutch Stadholder Prince Maurits, got the upper hand. They trumped up a charge of high treason, and in May 1619 the old man, leaning heavily on his stick, walked to the scaffold.[16]

The death of Van Oldenbarneveld was more than a victory for orthodoxy; it was a triumph for the war party, the merchant oligarchs of Amsterdam who had been eager to end the detested truce so that their God-fearing—and profitable—war against Spain could be renewed. And with that war, the formation of a West India Company became once more a much desired possibility.

"After the change in government (as one might say) the old idea of sailing to the West Indies has been revived," wrote Cristofore Suriano, the Venetian ambassador at The Hague, when he learned of Van Oldenbarneveld's arrest. "The merchants are talking about it, and promise themselves large profits, thinking to damage heavily the King of Spain." A month later, in October 1618, he was able to tell the Doge that some of the Amsterdammers had asked him if the Venetians would care to invest capital in the new company. He had declined.[17]

Barely two months after the truce ended, in June 1621, the charter for the West India Company was completed. It was similar in most aspects to that for the highly successful East India Company. Like its big sister, now nineteen years old, the Geoctroyeerde West Indische Companie received the right to exercise government and administer justice in its territories, make alliances with the natives, erect forts, and declare war and peace with the consent of The Hague. Its trading grounds stretched south down the coast of Africa from the tropic of Cancer to the Cape of Good Hope, and along the coast of America from the north to the Magellan Strait, and beyond New Guinea.

Its organization was divided into five chambers, established in different towns, but, as was usual in the United Provinces, the wealthy Chamber of Amsterdam was the most important. It shouldered four-ninths of all the costs, and regarded New Netherland as its special protégé. It was, of course, the strongest in the governing body of the company, the Heeren XIX, or the nineteen Lords Directors, of whom one represented the States, while eight (later nine) were sent by Amsterdam. Among these was Johannes de Laet, the early historian of the company; the Amsterdam jeweler Kiliaen van Rensselaer, whose role in the development of New

A SWEET AND ALIEN LAND

Netherland was to be of immense importance; and Samuel Bloemaerts, who as Commissary of Sweden in Holland later double-
crossed his company and his country.[18]

While negotiations about the charter were going on, Usselinx
returned from exile in Zeeland, where he had fled his many creditors after the collapse of the disastrous Beemster-polder venture.
Deeply disappointed by the treatment the Dutch regents had ac-
corded his pet project, he warned them that the company could not
survive on trade and plunder alone. Colonization and the conversion of the savages were just as important. Like other critics, he
was dismayed, too, by the dictatorial powers the directors were to
be given. Future colonists would, he predicted, "fall under the
worst kind of slavery." But protest was useless. The West India
Company was clearly destined to be run by what one Dutch historian has described as "a number of the most selfish, greedy and
profit-seeking businessmen in Holland."[19]

THE BEST BUY

SETTLING DOWN

In April 1623 the first official settlers selected for the new province sailed from Texel with a vessel of 260 tons appropriately christened the *Nieu Nederlandt*. The West India Company, having settled its organizational problems, had arranged to send out just five or six colonists as the nucleus of the settlement, but when the vessel left, there were thirty families—almost all Walloons—on board. Nicolaes van Wassenaer, a physician in Amsterdam with a journalistic curiosity, reported in his *Historisch Verhael* ("Historic Relation") of 1624 that "the West India Company being chartered to navigate these rivers, did not neglect to do so, but equipped in the spring a vessel of 130 last . . . whereof Cornelis Jacobsz Mey of Hoorn was skipper."[1]

The departure had not gone unnoticed. The English, having commissioned the *Bonnie Bess* to carry planters to Virginia and explore the Hudson River, heard of it, and gave orders to expel "any such strangers as Hollanders or others, which is thought this year to venture there." The *Bonnie Bess* never got as far as the Hudson, but when Mey and the colonists reached the mouth of the Great River, they discovered a French ship. Its captain intended to erect there the arms of France, "but the Hollanders would not permit it," Van Wassenaer reported. With the help of some Dutch fur traders, they "caused a yacht of two guns to be manned" and convoyed the Frenchman off the Hudson. It was the only time that

France tried to intrude on the Dutch possession in America.[2]

One of the Dutchmen Mey found in New Netherland was Adriaen Jorisz Thienpont, an old hand in the fur trade, who was instructed by him to sail up the river with some of the colonists. They halted at the small ten-year-old Fort Nassau on Castle Island, by this time completely derelict. "They forthwith put the spade in the ground," Van Wassenaer reported, and not much later a new fort was ready, now called Fort Orange.[3]

Sixty years later one of the women who traveled with Mey, Caterina Trico of Paris, remembered "that four women came along with her in the same ship . . . which four women were married at sea" and that they and their husbands stayed about three weeks at the mouth of the Hudson River before sailing up to Fort Orange. According to her slightly wavering memory, there were eighteen families on board. The other twelve had gone to the Delaware and the Connecticut rivers, while eight men had been left on Manhattan "to take possession."[4]

Adriaen Thienpont, who had instructions from the company to get the precious fur trade under way, lost no time in establishing friendly relations with the Indians around Fort Orange. "As soon as they had built themselves some huts of bark, the Mahikanders or River Indians came and made Covenants of friendship with Arien Jorise there Commander, bringing him great presents of Beaver or oyr Peltry and desired that they might come and have a constant free trade," reported Caterina Trico.[5]

At the same time, Mey sailed on to the South River, where at the site of present-day Gloucester, on the eastern bank of the Delaware, he built another trading fort. Like the first one on the Hudson, it was called Nassau.

All seemed to be going extremely well. In Holland the first news from the colonists arrived in December 1624. "Everything was in good condition," Van Wassenaer was told. "The colony began to advance bravely, and to live in friendship with the natives." In the words of Caterina Trico, the Indians "were all as quiet as Lambs." For the West India Company, there was even more delightful news to come. When Thienpont sent his son back to Holland after a winter of bartering with the Indians, the young man carried five hundred otter skins and five hundred beaver skins with him, "which were sold for twenty-eight thousand, some hundred guilders."[6]

SETTLING DOWN

The story of the beaver trade—the great object of the West India Company in North America—has an almost fabulous quality. The pelts were the most sought after, but throughout the ages people believed strongly that other parts of the animal were just as useful. In his *Description of New Netherland* (1656) the Dutch lawyer Adriaen van der Donck quoted the assertion of Pliny, the great Roman naturalist, that the limbs of the beaver ("whereby he means the testicles") had all kinds of medicinal properties. And that the animals "sought by the hunters for their testes, and closely persued, would castrate themselves with their teeth and leave the parts for the hunters, which the creatures knew to be the price sought after." Other scientists were convinced that the tail of the beaver was fish.

Van der Donck rejected these tales but he believed in the versatile curative powers of beaver testicles. "The smelling of beaver-cods will produce sneezing and cause sleep . . . rubbed on the head of a drowsy person, it will produce wakefulness. Taken in water it serves to remove idiocy." Beaver oil—containing acetyl acid—was good for dizziness, trembling, rheumatism, lameness, and pain in the stomach. It even cured toothaches, and could restore "the sharpness of sight." Finally, "those who have the gout, should wear slippers and shoes made of beaver-skins."[7]

The West India Company would not have survived long if its beaver skins had only been bought by those who suffered from the gout. There was, in fact, an enormous European demand for the pelts, particularly in Germany; and in Russia they were the prestige fur. "There the skins are used for mantle linings," says Van der Donck. "Whoever there has the most and costliest fur trimmings is esteemed the greatest."

Even after the hair was completely worn away, the beaver skin had a market value: it was made up into hats, "before which it cannot be well used for this purpose for unless the beaver has been worn and is greasy and dirty it will not felt properly." The same use could be made of beaver skins that the Indians had worn as coats "until the same have become foul with sweat and grease."[8]

The settlers in New Netherland were free to trade for furs with the Indians or even to go hunting themselves, but the West India Company kept the valuable monopoly of sales outside America. The traders exchanged kettles, knives, beads, and later guns for furs, while the thick woolen duffel cloth, especially woven for the

A SWEET AND ALIEN LAND

company in Leiden, was soon so prized by the Indians that their overlords promptly forbade the colonists to produce their own textiles.⁹

To feed the settlers, New Netherland needed farms and flocks of cattle, and of these, too, the company intended to keep a firm control. When Commis (Commissary) William Verhulst arrived in the spring of 1625 to replace Mey, he had orders to lay out the first six farms on Manhattan. Until then, this island had only been used as a watering place for ships. There were a few goats and plenty of rabbits, whose ancestors had been brought over and let loose on the island years earlier by Hendrick Christiaensz, at the request of the old United New Netherland Company. But the West India Company decided to tackle the question of provisions more radically, and in 1628 it was reported to Samuel Bloemaerts, one of the members of the Amsterdam Chamber, that the soil on Manhattan had been ploughed eight times since 1624. "The six farms, four of which lie along the River Hellgate, stretching to the south side of the island, have at least 60 morgen [120 acres] of land ready."¹⁰

Cattle had been sent over at the beginning of 1625, followed by more settlers; and ships bound for New Netherland were freighted with stock for the company farms: "one with horses, the other with cows, and the third with hay," according to Van Wassenaer. "Two months later a fly-boat* was equipped carrying sheep, hogs, wagons, ploughs and all other implements of husbandry." The cattle were first off-loaded on Nut Island (now Governor's Island), where they remained two days. "There being no means of pasturing them there, they were shipped in sloops and boats to the Manhates." This Noah's Ark voyage of 103 head of livestock had been organized with the greatest care by a certain Pieter Evertsen Hulft: each animal had "its own respective servant" and a separate stall on the ship. And although twenty of the cows died soon after arrival on Manhattan—"the opinion is that they had eaten something bad from an uncultivated soil"—the rest settled down happily. By autumn they were thriving, and Hulft could breathe again.¹¹

The settlers themselves seemed pleased with their new home-

*Flyboats, used for bulk transport of freight, were first built in Holland in 1595. Lighter than galleys and needing only a small crew, their pointed sterns and bows, with a curved hull, afforded more loading space.

SETTLING DOWN

land. In 1624 a Zutphen minister, Dominie Baudartius, had a lyrical account from one of them, possibly a former parishioner: "We were much gratified on arriving in this country: Here we found beautiful rivers, bubbling fountains flowing into valleys, basins of running waters in the flatlands, agreeable fruits in the woods. . . . There is considerable fish in the rivers, good tillage land; here is, especially, free coming and going, without fear of the naked natives of the country."[12]

That the fifty-year-old clergyman declined the accompanying invitation to come over himself is, however, hardly surprising. The exchange of his comfortable vicarage in Zutphen for the "hutts of bark" the settlers lived in cannot have seemed very appealing at his age. These huts were in fact square trenches dug six or seven feet deep in the ground, the earth sides cased with timbers, the floor covered with wooden planks, and a roof made of branches covered with turf or bark.[13]

The makeshift huts began to be replaced by proper houses when a number of builders arrived in 1625 along with Hulft's cattle. They were headed by an Amsterdam engineer, Crijn Fredericks, who carried with him plans for a new and more solid fort at the mouth of the Hudson River. According to his grandiose design, the fort was to be pentagonal in shape, 1,050 feet in circumference, surrounded by a moat 54 feet wide and 8 feet deep. Two gates in the surrounding walls were to be connected by a street. In the center there was to be a marketplace, and around it houses for the council and notables, as well as a schoolhouse, church, and hospital all under one roof. His instructions urged that "as many people as possible, builders, ship crews and settlers," work on the job so that "Fort Amsterdam" would be finished quickly.[14]

Verhulst, who had been ordered to pick the best site for this fort, in July 1625 chose Manhattan. Van Wassenaer reported soon afterward that "a fort has been staked out by master Kryn Frederycks . . . it is planned to be of large dimensions." It was the birth of New York.[15]

The first design of Fort Amsterdam and its surroundings laid down a pattern that can still be traced today. Pearl Street, Broad Street, Beaver Street, and Whitehall Street in modern Lower Manhattan follow almost precisely Fredericks' original ground plan, and until recently houses No. 2 and 4 on Stone Street, and No. 19 and 21 on Bridge Street, stood on the site of the first stone houses

A SWEET AND ALIEN LAND

in Manhattan. Broadway, Park Row, the Bowery, and Fourth Avenue all follow the lines in Fredericks' plan.[16]

When the engineer returned to Holland in September 1626, the fort was unfinished but fast taking shape. Isaack de Rasières had been sent over by the company as its chief commercial agent and secretary of the province in 1626, and already in July he was able to write back that his ship "dropped anchor in the river before the Fort Amsterdam." And Van Wassenaer, who never actually set foot in New Netherland but was always well posted on the latest news, described it optimistically in November 1626 as "very large." The counting house, he went on, "is in a stone building covered with reed, the other houses are still of bark." But by the time the first buildings were standing, money seems to have run out, and plans for building a church were temporarily shelved. Instead, Francis Molemaecker, who was building a horse mill, agreed to add on to it "a spacious room, sufficient to accommodate a large congregation" on the first floor. The wooden church tower, next to the mill, carried nine bells, a trophy of the Dutch conquest of Puerto Rico in 1625.[17]

The congregation had to wait (perhaps not very impatiently) until April 7, 1628, before it could attend the first service. On that day Johannes Michaëlius arrived. The forty-four-year-old dominie (his name was latinized from Michielse) had been picked for his experience in Brazil and Guiana. The voyage out with his family had been appalling, through constant storms, "which fell hard upon the good wife and children." The food on board had been "very poor and scanty" due to a "wicked cook . . . but especially by reason of the captain himself, who daily walked the deck drunk." Seven weeks after his arrival, the minister suffered a fresh blow when his wife—"a virtuous, faithful and altogether amiable yoke-fellow" for sixteen years—died suddenly, leaving him with three small children.[18]

But grief did not stop him from looking about him, and he liked what he saw. His first letters to his colleagues in Europe were full of the progress the province was making, in spite of the first troubles with the Indians.

These troubles had started soon after Commis Verhulst was replaced by Director General Peter Minuit, who arrived with instructions to gather all the settlers together in Fredericks' fort. It was one of the wiser decisions of the Heeren XIX, and designed

SETTLING DOWN

to protect the colonists from the Indians on the mainland, "a bad race of savages," as De Laet explained, "who have always been very obstinate and unfriendly towards our countrymen." The move left only twenty-five traders at Fort Orange, the center of the fur trade, but it made the town that grew up around Fort Amsterdam, with its 270 souls, the largest settlement in North America after New Plymouth.[19]

How wise the move was became clear a few months later, when horrifying news from Fort Orange reached Manhattan. The commander in the north, Daniel Crieckenbeeck, together with three of his men, had been murdered by the Indians. One of them had been eaten by the savages, "after having well roasted him." In defiance of his instructions, Crieckenbeeck had become involved in a war raging between two neighboring Indian tribes, the Mohicans and the Mohawks, and it took all the diplomatic skill of one of the company's traders to restore peace and normal commerce with the Mohawks.

Near Fort Amsterdam itself there was another incident at about the same time that was a forewarning of possible future clashes. Three Indians of the Wecquaesgeek tribe, coming to sell some skins, were attacked by three of Minuit's men, who killed one of them. The young nephew of the victim fled, vowing to take vengeance one day—a vow he fulfilled many years later.[20]

Neither of these incidents had immediate consequences for Manhattan, but they gave new impetus to the building of the fort. De Rasières reported in 1628 that Manhattan would soon be a "superb fort, to be approached by land only on one side"; and Michaëlius related the same year that the "new fortress is in course of construction," praying in another letter: "May the Lord . . . watch over our walls."[21]

The euphoria of the first years of colonial life was, however, disappearing rapidly. The settlers had begun to quarrel among themselves, and Peter Minuit, far from controlling his small settlement, was often himself at the center of the storm. Company funds were being misapplied by officials, who were abusing their position to line their own pockets. Secretary De Rasières was eventually sacked and recalled to Holland and Jan van Remunde was sent out to replace him. But the change brought no improvement, and in September 1630 Kiliaen van Rensselaer received a disturbing account from Simon Pos, his representative at Fort Amsterdam:

A SWEET AND ALIEN LAND

I cannot help advising your honour of the disputes which exist in this small settlement of not more than 200 to 300 people. Now the director and Jan Remunde are very much embittered against one another. Here is all left to drift as it will; they let trade slip away and do not exert themselves to increase it . . . but are very diligent in bringing exorbitant suits and charges against one another. . . . The minister Jonas Michielsz [Johannes Michaëlius] is very energetic here stirring up the fire between them. [22]

Michaëlius had been more energetic than Pos knew. The dominie had made Minuit one of his elders, but the two men had soon fallen out, and not content with attacking Minuit to his face, the dominie wrote bitter complaints of his mismanagement back to Amsterdam: "We have a governor who is most unworthy of his office; a slippery man who under a treacherous mask of honesty is compound of all iniquity and wickedness." It is clear that in his critics' eyes at least, Minuit hardly fitted the role in which the West India Company liked to cast their governors: "that he is as a father, and not as a brute bully, guiding the people with a gentle hand."[23]

In spite of these distractions, the company did well during Peter Minuit's directorship. The war between the Mohicans and the Mohawks around Fort Orange had had an adverse influence on fur supplies, but exports nonetheless trebled between 1626 and 1632, when furs valued at 125,000 guilders reached Holland. Goods received from the company had grown in value from 20,000 guilders to more than 30,000. In the years between 1624 and 1632 the company received 63,000 skins, worth 454,000 guilders, and the harvests on Manhattan in these nine years had been excellent. Minuit had even ventured to build another ship, also called the *Nieu Nederlandt,* which, according to jealous English sources, was of 600 "tunnes." The company, however, was irritated by this extravagance, and added it to a swelling list of grievances against Minuit.[24]

By 1631 this list was complete. The complaints of De Rasières and Michaëlius, of Pos and Van Remunde, were quite enough to make the Lords Directors in Amsterdam forget what handsome profits Minuit had helped them make, and for most of them his record proved that colonization—which many had argued against all along—simply would not work. They had made the point already to the States General in 1629, complaining that while the trade in furs with New Netherland had been advantageous, "the people conveyed by us thither . . . have not been any profit." Minuit's enemies had added weight to their argument, and in August 1631 orders for his recall left the company's office (a former slaughterhouse) on the Heerengracht in Amsterdam.[25]

Early in 1632 an embittered Peter Minuit sailed on the *Eendracht* ("The Unity") for Holland. It was an incongruous name for a vessel that was also carrying Dominie Johannes Michaëlius and Secretary Jan van Remunde back to Holland. A fellow traveler, the fifteen-year-old son of one of the colonists, noted: "The officers there not able to get along together, they all came back and other arrangements will be made in order that the colony may be better managed and promoted, as otherwise through their disorder it would be entirely ruined."[26]

A SWEET AND ALIEN LAND

NEVER

SO GOOD

In matters of commerce the fault of the Dutch
Is giving too little and asking too much.[1]

This little English rhyme characterized perfectly the attitude of
the Dutch in the seventeenth century, and they were not ashamed
of it. Trade and plunder had been their road to freedom. By 1630
their war of liberation against Spain had been going on for sixty
years, and only commerce had made it possible to finance this long
struggle. It is thus hardly surprising that the West India Company
was far from enthusiastic about colonizing New Netherland. It
would certainly cost a lot of money to begin with, and what they
were after was a quick profit.

Nor were the Dutch people themselves any more enthusiastic
about leaving their country, other than for long trading voyages.
The whole idea of settling down on foreign soil at the other side
of the world, in an unknown country peopled by naked savages,
must have seemed madness to most Dutch, who were perfectly
content with their home country. The United Provinces, under
their Stadtholders the Princes of Orange and the States General,
formed one of the most powerful nations in the world; rich and
adventurous, they covered the oceans with a merchant navy that,
in 1637, was "judged to surpass those of the great kingdoms of
Spain, France, England and all the others."[2]

Why leave a country that in the words of the Venetian ambassador Girolamo Trevisano considered "the whole world as its territory" and which "enjoys everything that is elsewhere available." Dutch ships carried almost all the Baltic grain, half of the Baltic timber, half of the traffic in Swedish metal—and the North Sea itself, with its herring, cod, and haddock, was another source of wealth. In those centuries before refrigeration, salt and spices were among the world's most profitable commodities: the Dutch shipped most of the salt that went from France and Portugal to the Baltic, and they had a virtual monopoly of the spice trade, thanks to their energetic and predatory East India Company. In 1621 the formation of the West India Company had opened up trade routes to the rich coasts of Africa and the Americas. With Spain tottering through a destructive war, France weak and divided, and England impoverished, the Dutch had little to fear from their competitors. The world was indeed their market.[3]

The roving Dutchmen came home to a crowded country—and a small one. "There is no place from where one cannot reach the border within six hours," wrote Trevisano; and especially in the most important province, Holland, "on every five to six Italian miles one finds a town with 30, nay 50 thousand souls." But the Dutch were inventive. If Willem Usselinx had been unlucky in polder building, others were not. By 1640 the Hollanders and their neighbors in Zeeland had gained eighty thousand morgen of new land. "To dry these lakes and turn them into farmland, they use windmills," reported an admiring Trevisano. "As these mills stand close together and work at the same time, one sees a miraculous spectacle." He had visited a polder. "It seems incredible, when one tells it, a land dry and ploughed that shortly before was a deep and large lake."[4]

With the same energy and ingenuity, the Dutch fought against the sea, which gave them such wealth through trade and fishery but which was a constant threat since most of Holland and Zeeland was below sea level. They did this with dikes "made from seaweed, dried and mixed with a little earth, which sticks together amazingly well and defeats all storms."[5]

Behind these dikes the Dutch lived well, and the national prosperity was enjoyed by almost everyone, not just a privileged few. There was still poverty in parts of the seven provinces, and famines and plague killed thousands at irregular intervals; but to a

A SWEET AND ALIEN LAND

foreigner, the well-being of the Dutch was astounding. "It is true that in this country there is no-one who cannot live with ease according to his rank: nobody begs, and those who want to give alms, would not know to whom," wrote Trevisano.[6]

Most of the people lived simply, without spending lavishly on clothes, servants, or coaches. Their chief extravagances were enormous banquets—"sumptuous and solemn," according to a Frenchman—and their houses. The elegant brick exteriors and richly-furnished interiors recorded for us by Jan Vermeer and Pieter de Hoogh were the pride of the polishing and scrubbing Dutch housewives, but their zeal was not always admired by everyone. Usselinx, a bachelor, pitied their husbands who "do not dare to use a chair or stool, yes, do not go into a room, but shoeless, so as not to start a row." Unfortunately the Dutch housewives' obsessive cleanliness did not extend to their own persons. Their aversion to bathing was notorious, and a contemporary speaks with much disdain of their "filthy faces behind shiny stoops."[7]

Clean or not, the Dutch were an open-minded people. "The trans-ocean trade brought more than profit: it made windows into the mind," wrote the historian J. H. Plumb, and this was certainly true when it came to religious tolerance. "Everybody lives in his house with the religion which he has chosen," related the Venetian ambassador. "Although Calvinism is the principal religion, one closes the eyes for others and in Amsterdam alone there are every day 12 to 14 masses secretly read. No-one stops this, although everybody knows."[8]

The war with Spain had begun as a war for religious liberation, and the Dutch never forgot it. They would tolerate other opinions on one condition: that they did not endanger the economic development of the nation. As Pieter de la Court wrote in his *Interest of Holland:* "Next to the freedom to worship God, comes the freedom for all inhabitants to make one's living."[9]

Amsterdam, a haven for all sects, throve on this attitude of easygoing tolerance. The city had grown in a few decades from 20,000 to over 115,000 inhabitants, and it did not even possess a natural harbor. It owed its prominence mainly to the fact that its biggest North European competitor, Antwerp, was still in the hands of the Spanish and blockaded by the Dutch. Many of the wealthiest of the Antwerp merchants had fled to Amsterdam, taking their trade and their customers with them. Amsterdam's port was difficult of access, and the shallow waters made it necessary to use lighters in loading and unloading ships. But the port had great natural advantages too: it was easy to defend against any attack, and was connected to the rest of the country, to France, and to Germany by a complete system of canals and rivers. Best of all, it had the drive of the Dutch themselves.[10]

Within a few years of the opening of the seventeenth century, they had set up in Amsterdam a Chamber of Assurance, a Stock Exchange, a special Grain Exchange, a Bank of Exchange, a lending bank, and the great East and West India trading companies. Amsterdam became the financial center of Europe, and Dutch capital was soon flowing all over the world, even into places where it should not have gone. Jan Pietersz Coen, the Dutch governor of the East Indies, warned his compatriots against investing their florins in France, England, and Spain, as this would help those nations to "suppress the Dutch even more." But the flow was unstoppable. Neither the state nor the merchants could absorb so much surplus money, and it was Dutch guilders that subsidized the development of the grain fields of Russia, the vineyards of France and the Rhineland, the stock farming of sheep in Spain, the tobacco harvest of New England, and the sugar culture of Brazil and Barbados.[11]

There was so much money around that the Dutch, careful though they were, often succumbed to the urge to speculate, in cod liver oil, spices, or grain. Most of the time it was a fairly harmless form of gambling, but in 1636 it reached the dimensions of a national catastrophe when the speculators fell for the latest fashion —tulips. Initially they bought only for their own gardens, but in that year the "colleges of florists" became gambling dens. Decent citizens went mad and paid out huge prices for the following year's crop. In one town alone sales of more than ten million guilders were registered, and enormous profits were made . . . on paper. One Dutchman was lucky. For a single bulb, the legendary Black Tulip, he received two loads of wheat, four of rye, four oxen, four pigs, twelve sheep, two barrels of wine, four of beer, two casks of butter, a thousand pounds of cheese, a bed, a suit and a silver mug —to a total cash value of twenty-five hundred guilders. In February 1637 reason suddenly returned. Within days, the bottom fell out of the market and thousands of speculators were reduced to the begging bowl.[12]

But only rarely did the sturdy Dutch lose their heads—and their money—so easily. Usually they stood with both feet on their soggy soil, and they had no intention of risking the security of their own country for an uncertain future in New Netherland. The colonization of America by the Dutch was thus from the beginning virtually doomed.

The American historian Dixon R. Fox has remarked that "the failure of New Netherland is a testimony to the successful organization of life in the old Netherlands." For the Dutch there was no place like home. There was no pressing need to consider the colony in America.[13]

To the comfortable burghers of the Republic, the prospect of the voyage to New Netherland was almost sufficient deterrent in itself. The long crossing—graphically described in settlers' letters home or by returning travelers—was an ordeal in summer and hell in winter. The transports commonly used were the pinnaces of the West India Company, big sturdy vessels that could do double duty as war and merchant ships. Since hostilities were frequent, the convenience of the passengers was often sacrificed to the need for crowding as many guns as possible onto the upper decks.

These pinnaces were beautiful ships. In contrast to the ships of other countries, they were hardly decorated, apart from an uncrowned Dutch lion on the big curved bow and a carved or painted image of the ship's name on their distinctively flat stern, known as the *tafereel* ("taffrail," a word still used by the English). Three great sails, supplemented by a smaller bow chaser, gave them an impressive turn of speed, enhanced by the streamlined sides.[14]

But comfort on board was virtually nonexistent. There were one or two cabins for the elite who could afford a fare of one guilder (twenty stuivers) a day, and a few more intolerably cramped and scruffy little cubbyholes for those who could afford twelve stuivers. But most of the passengers were crammed into the dark stinking confines of the between decks, for which accommodation they were initially charged eight stuivers a day, though this was later cut to seven when the West India Company attempted to stimulate emigration in 1652.[15]

The travelers shared their damp, ill-ventilated home with chick-

NEVER SO GOOD

ens, pigs, and sheep. They cooked, ate, slept, and were seasick in one wretched crowd. During the endless weeks at sea, provisions rotted and drinking water became first stagnant and then foul.

The stench was unendurable, and one traveler complained that "the gunnen deck where they lodged was so beastly and noysome . . . as would much endanger the health of the shipps." Another Dutchman commented that "the pigs and dogs in our country get a better lodging." Even the frequent sprinkling of boiling vinegar —a favorite sanitary measure of the time—could not defeat the smell of rotting food, unwashed humanity, train oil, and polluted bilge water.[16]

Not surprisingly, sickness and infection were rife, and the ships' barber-surgeon had neither the training nor the resources to cope. Scurvy carried off both crew and settlers alike; dysentery and tropical fevers were predictable; typhoid fever was so common at sea that it was often known as "ship fever"; and any infection brought aboard soon swept through the between-decks. Burials at sea were a normal feature of the trip. When New Netherland's last governor, Peter Stuyvesant, sailed to the colony in 1647, 18 of the passengers died; in another ship, carrying 150 men, 39 died during the crossing, including the skipper.[17]

Many of the settlers took their own medicine chests with them —syrups, balsams, unguents, suppositories, pills, and quack remedies for seasickness picked up at fairs. Those officials and traders who had to cross frequently took special care to be well equipped. John Winthrop Sr. wrote his wife from Boston to be sure "to be warme clothed, and to have store of fresh provisions, meale, egges put in salt or grounde malt, butter, peas and fruits . . . a large frying panne, a small stewinge panne, and a Case to boyle Pudding in, store of linnen," and not to forget "sacke to bestowe amonge the saylors." Seasickness was difficult to combat, but he had found a remedy in Doctor Wrightes' *Electuarium lenitium,* to be drunk with the juice of "scurvy grasse" at five or six in the morning.[18]

Another seasoned traveler, John Josselyn, was one of the few who, long before the discovery of vitamin C, advised the use of juice of lemon "to cure or prevent scurvy." Other important ingredients for health were "conserves of Rose, Clove, Gilliflowers, Wormwood, Green-ginger, Burnt Wine, English Spirits, prunes to stew, Raisons of the sun, Currence, Sugar. . . ." He, too, had discovered something to cure seasickness—apart from conserve of

A SWEET AND ALIEN LAND

wormwood. "First make a paste of Sugar and Qum-Dragant mixed together, then mix with a reasonable quantitie of the powder of cinnamon and Ginger, and if you please a little Musk also." This had to be made "into Roules of several fashions, which you may gild." They were to be taken only "according to discretion."[19]

But the most effective medicine in the world could not shorten the frightful journey, which in the most favorable summer conditions took up to six or eight weeks, and in winter at least three months.

The trials of the trip began almost before the vessels had left behind the Schreierstoren (Weeping Tower) at Amsterdam. They had to negotiate the sandbank at the mouth of Het Y, around the little island of Pampus, and then cross the sand barrier at Texel, which separated the Zuyder Zee from the North Sea. Sometimes they waited weeks for a favorable wind before they could leave the Frisian Islands behind. The North Sea and the Channel were treacherous waters, and often exacted their toll of shipping, as in the winter of 1656–1657, when a small convoy of three ships, carrying 172 settlers to the Delaware, was beaten apart by a heavy storm that wrecked the sails of the largest ship, almost killing seven sailors. Entire ships disappeared in violent gales, which could scatter a whole convoy and add days or weeks to the crossing.

Enemy ships and pirates were another hazard, and when the councillor-poet Nicasius de Sille made his crossing in 1653, his pinnace had to battle three times with the English. Sometimes the emigrants were more fortunate and arrived triumphantly in New Amsterdam with a prize in tow.

But despite all these tribulations, the ships went inexorably on their long journey, beating down past Dover, across to the Caribbean Sea, with an occasional call at Guiana or Curaçao, and then "towards the mainland of Virginia, steering across, in fourteen days, leaving the Bahamas on the left and the Bermuda on the right hand." From Virginia, they followed the coast up to New Netherland, where New Amsterdam was surely a most welcome sight. They must have felt the same incredulous delight as John Winthrop Sr. when at last he touched land—"and there came a smell of the shore . . . like the smell of a garden."[20]

Those who made the effort to cross liked what they saw. Jacob Steendam, one of New Netherland's three poets, says it as a poet should:

New Netherland, Thou noblest spot on earth
Where bounteous Heaven ever poureth forth
The fulness of His gifts, of greatest worth.[21]

Letters to Holland from the earliest settlers were full of appreciation. "Whatever we desire in the paradise of Holland is here to be found," read Dominie Baudartius in Zutphen. "The country here is in general like Germany," wrote Dominie Johannes Megapolensis in 1644. "The land is good and fruitful in everything . . . the country is very mountainous, partly soil, partly rocks, and with elevations so exceeding high that they appear to almost touch the clouds." In this amazing country, so different from the damp and monotonous flatness of Holland, there were forests of firs, oaks, alders, beeches, elms, and willows. "The ground on the hills is covered with bushes of bilberries or blueberries: the ground in the flat land near the river is covered with strawberries, which grow so plentifully in the fields, that one can lie down and eat them." The grapes were enormous, and made an excellent wine.

There was plenty of animal life—deer and turkeys "as large as in Holland"; the all-important beaver; panthers, bears, wolves, foxes, and snakes. "Amongst others there is a sort of snake, which we call rattlesnake . . . they make way for neither man nor beast, but fall on them and bite them and their bite is very poisonous, and commonly even deadly too."[22]

The climate was agreeable, despite the sudden changes of cold and heat. Summers on Manhattan were hot, but "a southerly breeze usually sets in on the flood-tide . . . which blows over a cool element, and brings refreshment with it." It rained frequently, but only for two or three hours, "after which it will blow from the northwest, and be succeeded by fine cool weather: so that within an hour the clouds will appear as if they would spew cats, and in another hour scarcely a cloud will be seen." The winters were "fierce and severe and continue fully as long as in our country," but there was plenty of wood for fires, and plenty of furs "to cover one's self."[23]

Nicasius de Sille, another of New Netherland's three poets, found the weather important enough to praise it in rhyme:

But heat and sunshine now—a bright and genial sky
Infuse in me new life and nourishment supply.[24]

A SWEET AND ALIEN LAND

The Dutch in Europe were used to a constant struggle with the sea, but for New Netherlanders this problem did not exist. It was wonderfully relaxing for them to know that "the country is not subject to great floods and inundations," and that even the lowlands, which were sometimes inundated in the spring, "suffer but little."

The rivers and seas around the island were full of fish—salmon, sturgeon, codfish, halibut, herring, mackerel, and plenty of colossal shellfish. There is a tradition that there were only ten species of fish known to the Dutch when they discovered America, and that when they caught the shad, they named the fish Elft (eleventh); the bass Twaalft (twelfth), and the drum Dertienen (thirteenth).[25]

In one thing the Dutch were to be disappointed. The West India Company had high hopes that precious minerals would be found in New Netherland. Their colonists were instructed to look for diamonds, rubies, gold, silver, and copper. Anything found was to be brought at once to the director, but the finder would receive a tenth of the yield for six years. Nothing was found for years, and then at last in 1645 hope soared. In the course of peace negotiations with an Indian tribe at Fort Grange their interpreter began to paint his face with a lump of metal. Willem Kieft, then governor, asked him curiously what it was, and the Indian handed it over. Kieft studied it carefully, and with mounting excitement judged that "the lump contained some valuable metal." It was placed in a crucible, put on a fire, and the result was two pieces of gold worth three guilders. The experiment was kept secret, and later a small expedition sent by Kieft into the mountains returned to New Amsterdam with a bucketful of what looked like the same metal. Specimens were twice shipped off to Holland, but on both occasions the ship sank. Finally, the tantalized Lords Directors in Amsterdam sent over a team of mineralogists to the colony. They might have saved themselves the trouble: the gold turned out to be pyrites.[26]

From the beginning of the colony efforts were made to introduce the growth of tobacco, already such a valuable export from neighboring Virginia. The energetic Kiliaen van Rensselaer was especially interested. He even tried to engage "an English runaway boy named Rutger Morris," who, as he had heard in Holland, was not only an excellent drummer, but "understands tobacco

NEVER SO GOOD

planting" as well. Nothing came of Van Rensselaer's plans, though later trials on Manhattan were more successful.[27]

Yet another fantasy was that of a booming silk production. In 1652 someone pointed out to the Lords Directors in Amsterdam that New Netherland was rich in mulberry trees—the very thing for the cultivation of silkworms. Five years later Peter Stuyvesant, then director general, at last received a small box of silkworm eggs. He reported back to Amsterdam: they were rotten. Undeterred, the Lords Directors recommended that he obtain a fresh supply from his English neighbors in Virginia. Stuyvesant declined to waste his time: the mulberry trees of New Netherland, he irritably replied, were growing wild and sparse, "so that the silk will be difficult to cultivate."[28]

Slowly it became evident that the main sources of profit from New Netherland would remain furs and timber. The colonists had high hopes, expressed by the great seventeenth-century Dutch poet and playwright Joost van der Vondel, that New Netherland would replace Poland as the granary of Holland, but these were never fulfilled. Despite the discouragements, it was clear that New Amsterdam was a marvelous natural harbor and center for shipping, surrounded by rich country, and that the colony had enormous potential if it were properly exploited.

It was a fact that had not gone unnoticed. The Dutch province was squeezed in between New England in the north and Virginia in the south. In the days of Director General Peter Minuit, contacts between the colonies were rare, but by the time he sailed back to Holland in 1632, the English were very much aware of what they called the "intruders upon his Majesties most hopefull country of New England." If the Dutch had any illusions that they would be allowed to live there in peace, they would soon know better.[29]

The Hudson Valley and Manhattan itself were already, in the eyes of their English neighbors, who were struggling with the glacial soil of the northeast, "the garden of New England . . . a place exceeding all yet named." They were not impressed by the argument of a Dutch colonist, David Pietersz de Vries, that even the crabs of New Netherland "showed sufficiently that we ought to people the country, and that it belongs to us"—"their claws are the colour of the flag of our Prince, orange, white and blue."[30]

A SWEET AND ALIEN LAND

FIRST RIGHTS

On April 7, 1632, the States General in The Hague received an urgent message from the associate delegate to the Heeren XIX, Mijnheer Van Arnhem. The West India Company ship *Eendracht* had been seized by the English authorities while sheltering from storms in Plymouth harbor. As well as "a number of persons with their wife and children," and ex-Director Peter Minuit, the ship carried a cargo of furs, and according to the English, duties had to be paid on these since they had been procured in their colonies. The English had further accused the Dutch of having "appropriated some countries belonging to the king." Van Arnhem asked the States to act swiftly, and make it clear to the English that the West India Company had every right to trade "at such places in New Netherland, to wit between the North and South River; which had always been in the peaceable and uncontroverted possession of the Company."[1]

Their High Mightinesses hesitated. They were always anxious to keep relations with their neighbor across the North Sea as smooth as possible, and they saw no point in making a major issue out of what was to them hardly more than a remote and tiny trading post on the other side of the Atlantic. Accordingly, the Dutch ambassador in London, Albert Joachimi, was simply instructed to demand the release of the *Eendracht*. He traveled at once to Newmarket, where Charles I was attending the race meeting.[2]

The King received Joachimi with his usual courtesy, but he was visibly more fascinated by the horses than by this tiresome Anglo-Dutch incident. "He did not know what the circumstances were," he told the ambassador evasively, "and would inform himself further of it." Joachimi pressed him for a decision. The King sidestepped again: before he took any action, he told the Dutchman, he was first "desirous to obtain information of his right."[3]

On reading their ambassador's report, the members of the States General realized that if the West India Company's operations in North America were not to be constantly obstructed by the English, they must make a firm stand and assert their rights in New Netherland. They had, they felt, an excellent case, and Joachimi was instructed to put it to the King in the strongest possible terms, so that "the West India Company in future will be saved from all similar annoyance."[4]

Joachimi had to wait until Charles' return from Newmarket before he could make a move; but on May 23 he was received for another audience. He spoke forcefully. "The subjects of their Lordships the States," he told Charles, "have for a long time traded in the River Manathans, now called Mauritius . . . and had purchased from the native inhabitants and paid for a certain island called also Manathans."[5]

He had earlier sent the King—and he now reminded him of it —the Deduction of the West India Company in which the Heeren XIX demonstrated that Hudson's discovery in 1609 for the East India Company of that part of America between the 39th and the 41st parallel made it indisputably Dutch. Moreover, he pointed out, in the charter that James I had given the colonies of Virginia and New England in 1606, it was expressly stated that they should remain "one hundred miles apart from each other." The English charter had spanned the country from the 34th to the 38th parallel, and from the 41st to the 45th, and it had contained a caveat: the English companies could only take possession when "the said premises hereinbefore mentioned . . . be not actually possessed or inhabited by any other Christian Prince or Estate."[6]

Charles put up a flimsy defense against the right by purchase. It was not sure, he asserted, "whether the Indians from whom Minuit had bought Manhattan were *possessores bone fidei* of those countries . . . their residence being unsettled and uncertain." He disposed much more forcefully of the argument from first arrival.

There was no doubt that it had been the English, as was proved "by the concessions and letters patent they have had from our Sovereigns." Moreover, he reminded Joachimi, when eleven years earlier the English ambassador to The Hague, Sir Dudley Carleton, had objected officially to the Dutch fur trade "into that plantation," the States General had answered that "they knew nothing of that enterprise." And at about the same time, "a good number of families, inhabiting the United Provinces, were then soliciting him to procure them a place in the said country where they might settle among his Majesty's subjects"—according to him, fresh proof of the English rights. The King wound up the audience with a grand gesture. He offered that those Dutch still in America might remain as long as they were ready "to submit themselves to his Majesty's government."[7]

Having made his point, the King decided that no further action was necessary. When four days later Joachimi met the Lord High Treasurer and complained again about the unreasonable treatment of the *Eendracht*, he heard to his surprise that the ship would be released, but "without prejudice to his Majesty's rights." The Council of New England, at whose instigation the *Eendracht* with the "pretended Dutch governor" on board had been detained, sent a warrant to Plymouth from their Holborn headquarters for the release of the ship and its cargo.[8]

The incident of the *Eendracht* was one more pinprick in a cushion stuffed with needles. Relations between the English and the Dutch had become more and more strained over the last thirty years, and the cause was largely jealousy on the part of England. The success story of the small Dutch nation was followed with dismay and fear by its competitors on the other side of the North Sea.

The English were particularly impressed and worried by the Dutch commercial and fishery fleet. At the beginning of the seventeenth century Sir Walter Raleigh had already warned them that the Netherlands owned more vessels than eleven Christian nations together. An English traveler in Holland reported in 1609 that the Dutch fleet was twenty thousand ships strong. According to a Spanish source, the number was 16,289; and a German observer said that Holland had more ships than houses. These were exaggerated estimates, but more reliable sources calculated that the Dutch fleet around 1610 consisted of no less than 4,300 vessels—1,750 of the merchant navy, 2,000 fishing boats, 250 whalers, and about 300 vessels in the East and West Indies.[9]

This enormous power admitted hardly any competition; but the English had a more burning grievance against the Dutch, which can be summed up in one word—fish. According to the terms of ancient treaties, the Dutch enjoyed the right to fish the coastal waters of England and Scotland, and did so with energy. The Dutch fishing industry was a massive one, employing half a million people—a fifth of the total inhabitants of the Republic. Amsterdam was reckoned to be built on the bones of English herring, and the trade was central to Holland's prosperity. As Sir George Downing later put it: "The herring trade is the cause of the salt trade, and the herring and salt-trade are the causes of this country having, in a manner, wholly engrossed the trade of the Baltic Sea."[10]

The English themselves profited at least indirectly from the Dutch activities in what they thought of as their sea. Great Yarmouth, for instance, had forty brewers kept in business by the thousands of Dutch fishermen landing for its big fish market. But all their efforts to build up a rival English fishing industry had failed. Even an order of Queen Elizabeth that made Wednesday, Friday, and Saturday into fish-eating days could not turn the English into fishermen.

King James I tried another tack. The Venetian ambassador in London mentioned in 1609 that the herring industry infuriated the King more than anything else. "They [the Dutch] sent out every year to the coast of England 1700 vessels, in which perhaps 30,000 men are employed," he wrote the Doge. That year the Dutch had concluded their truce with Spain, and although James professed great "love and esteem" for them as a result, he made it clear that he did not desire "a further increase of their greatness" and published a proclamation in which he gave note "to all the world that our express Pleasure is, that from the beginning of the month of August next coming, no person of what nation or quality soever, be permitted to fish upon any of our Coasts and Seas." This was the signal for a long and involved diplomatic wrangle, from which the Dutch, appealing to their treaty rights, emerged victorious.[11]

In 1614 another conflict disrupted the uneasy peace. James I, in an attempt to restore England's position as principal exporter of cloth to the Baltic—from which the Dutch had successfully driven

A SWEET AND ALIEN LAND

the English—forbade the export of undressed cloth to Holland (undressed cloth was normally dressed in Middelburg, then reexported to the Baltic). The Dutch hit back by stopping all imports of cloth from England, dressed or undressed, and more than five hundred bankruptcies in the English cloth trade were the result. A furious Secretary of State, Sir Ralph Winwood, wrote to Ambassador Carleton in The Hague that as a reprisal, "His Majesty ought to forbid the Hollanders, by a fresh revival of former proclamations, to continue their yearly fishing on our coasts."[12]

But the Dutch knew, as James knew, that with his enormous debts and empty treasury, he had no way of enforcing such a prohibition. Instead he demanded that the Dutch pay a regular tax on the fishing—which the "bloodsuckers of his realm," of course, refused to pay.

As if all this were not enough, a third and fourth issue divided the two nations and, so the English felt, humiliated them. There was the whale fishery near Greenland, on which England claimed a monopoly because of her discovery of Spitzbergen in 1553—a claim the States General coolly rejected and the Dutch whale fishers consistently ignored. And then there was the lucrative Spice Islands trade, from which the Dutch had almost completely succeeded in excluding the English, often by force of arms. "There is nothing in the world," argued one of the Dutch East India Company's leading administrators, "that gives one a better right, than power and force added to right." To add insult to injury, the Dutch in the East Indies were in the habit of representing their Prince of Orange "as a great King and Lord," while holding James I up as no more than "a little kinglet."[13]

In the year 1621 the Dutch added another "intrusion" to the King's long list of grievances, but failed to treat the English protests against it as a serious threat. It was the colonization of their small part of North America.

Two years earlier the English captain Thomas Dermer, exploring the coast of the New World "from Cape Charles to Cape Codd up Delaware River and Hudsons River," had found "divers ships of Amsterdam and Horna who yearly had there a great and rich trade for furs."[14]

Dermer alerted the Council of New England, and its leader, Sir Ferdinando Gorges, protested to the Dutch, telling them that "the right of our Patent forbad them the place, as being by his Majesty

FIRST RIGHTS

appointed to us." The Dutch had apologized—"They understood no such thing," they added smoothly, "nor found any of our nation there, so that they hoped they had not offended"—and stayed.[15]

The English ambassador to The Hague, Sir Dudley Carleton, was instructed by James in December 1621 to make an official protest. The King complained angrily that despite the fact that he had granted by patent the coast of New England "unto particular persons; nevertheless we understand that the years past the Hollanders have entered upon some parts thereof and there left a Colony and given new names to the severall portes." He told Carleton to represent "these things unto the States Generall" and to stop the departure of the six or eight ships, which were on the point of leaving Holland to supply the Dutch colony.[16]

Carleton made careful inquiries, but he "could not find either by such merchants with whom I have acquaintance at Amsterdam, or by the Prince of Orange and some of the States . . . any more in the matter, but that about four or five years since two particular companies of Amsterdam merchants began to trade into those parts betwixt 40° and 45°, to which after their manner they gave their own names of New Netherlands . . . whether they have ever since continued to send ships of 30 or 40 lasts at the most to fetch furs." He reassured London that there were no plans for a colony —possibly his merchant friends included the anticolonial lobby of the newly-formed West India Company—but he nonetheless asked for an audience with the States General so that he could lodge an official protest.[17]

On February 9, 1622, he handed them the King's Memorial, which affirmed that the English, having taken possession of Virginia and "the northern part of the said country [Nova Anglia] gave H.M. incontestably the right to said country *jure primae occupationis.*" At the same time, he demanded not only that "the ships already equipped . . . be stopped, but also that the ulterior prosecution of said plantation may be expressly forbidden."[18]

The States General in its charter for the West India Company had never claimed specific areas of North America: it simply gave the company the exclusive rights to trade in the region of New Netherland for twenty-four years. Moreover, the members had at this time an urgent reason for being conciliatory to the English: the alarming possibility of a match between James' son Charles and the Infanta Donna Maria, sister of Philip IV of Spain, which

A SWEET AND ALIEN LAND

would unite the Royal Houses of Habsburg and Stuart, and could well turn England from a neutral neighbor into an active ally of their archenemy Spain, with whom they had just resumed war. So the ambassador received an equivocal reply. In the *Book of Resolutions of the Council of New England* a note of 1622 states that "upon complaint of Sir Dudley Carleton . . . it was answered there was no plantation or settlement to impeach the English right."[19]

The States General thus handed the English an excellent argument for aggression, which Charles I employed for the first time eleven years later during the conflict about the *Eendracht*, and which would pursue the Dutch for many decades.

The English based their claim to the whole eastern coast of North America on the exploratory voyage of Jean and Sebastian Cabot, who had sailed from Bristol in 1497 in the service of England's vigorous King Henry VII, to explore the New World discovered by Columbus five years earlier. The Cabots had staked no claim for the monarchy, as the English still accepted the papal division of the New World by the Treaty of Tordesillas, which allotted North America south of the 44th parallel to Spain. But Protestant Elizabeth I later rejected such airy claims as nonsense. She refused to accept "any title by donation of the Bishop of Rome" and denied Spanish rights to any place "other than those they were in actual possession of."[20]

In 1584 Richard Hakluyt in his *Discourse on Westerne Planting* set out to prove once and for all that the title of the "insatiable Spaniards" to the "West Indies" was unlawful, and that the only just title was "her Majesty's and of her noble progenitors." According to him, the English had every right to "if not all, yet at least to that part of America which is from Florida beyond the Arctic Circle." As proof, he cited the legendary voyages of a Welsh prince, Madoc ao Owen Gwyneth, in 1170, the fact that Columbus had initially offered his services to the English Queen, and finally the voyage of the Cabots.[21]

In the year of Hakluyt's best-seller, Raleigh set out, armed with Elizabeth's patent, "to discover, search for, find out, and view, such remote, heathen and barbarous lands . . . not actually possessed by any Christian princes, nor inhabited by Christian people. . . ."[22] Attempts to settle colonies in Carolina and Virginia followed almost at once. And in 1602 a small group of English traders under Bartholomew Gosnold landed in Massachusetts Bay, christened it Cape Cod, built a little fort, and went back to England. Some of these traders, attracted by the excellent cod fishery and the precious sassafras trees—the roots of which played an important role in medicine and as flavoring in contemporary cooking—returned the next year for an exploration that took them up to the shores of Maine, and as far south as Plymouth harbor.

These journeys attracted little attention in England, but when in 1605 a pamphlet appeared describing the voyage of a certain George Waymouth, who had brought five Indians back with him, interest suddenly sharpened. One of the people who came to meet the Indians was Sir Ferdinando Gorges, then still a young man but already glimpsing the possibilities of a continent that was to fascinate and preoccupy him for the rest of his life. He gathered together a group of fellow venturers and petitioned James I for a charter incorporating two companies, one for London and the other for the wealthy, important shipping center of Plymouth.

In April 1606, with the King's consent, the two Virginia companies were formed. The London Company and the Plymouth Company, as the Dutch later pointed out, were to remain one hundred miles apart from each other—leaving a vacuum into which the Dutch neatly slotted their claim.

After two disastrous expeditions, Gorges was still enthusiastic enough to send out an exploratory expedition in 1619—whose captain, Dermer, had warned him of the Dutch presence. He subsequently asked the King for a much larger grant, and in November 1620 a new patent made him "the sole proprietor of a huge undivided domain, extending from the 40th to the 48th parallel"—from sea to sea. New England was born.[23]

It was an act that contradicted several previous grants, and disregarded completely the fact that the Dutch had been settled in the Hudson Valley for eleven years. Elizabeth's argument against the Spanish claim—"mere discovery of a country, not followed by actual possession, confers no title"—never struck the English as valid against their own appropriations.[24]

The Gorges grant, and the founding of the New England Council, were only a beginning. More grants, to him and to others, followed rapidly, and the American historian Charles Andrews has remarked that "one wonders if any of the crown-lawyers or chancery-officials ever consulted the old patents in making out a

A SWEET AND ALIEN LAND

new one, or ever studied the geography of the regions they so easily gave away."[25]

America had seized the imagination of the English, and fantastic schemes were proposed. A certain Captain Bailey went so far as to suggest the making of a plantation "by which the Kingdom may annually be rid of 3000 poor . . . the prisons may be emptied, and much blood saved as well as relief given by sending them thither."[26]

The first settlers in New England were not, however, criminals but a group of high-minded and respectable people with "a great need and inward zeal" to advance the kingdom of Christ in a remote part of the world. They were Separatists, religious extremists who rejected all form of state intervention in church affairs and episcopal control.[27]

It is perhaps ironic that many of these Puritans came from England by way of Holland, where in 1608 they had found at Leiden and Amsterdam refuge from persecution in their own country. They had received a kindly welcome from the tolerant Dutch, and at first settled down happily. But they detested the "strange and uncouth language" of their hosts; they found it difficult to make a living; and they were discouraged by the little good they "did, or were likely to do, to the Dutch in reforming the Sabbath."[28]

Boldly, they decided to leave Europe and cross the Atlantic to create their own New World. They offered themselves to the Virginia Company in London, and in 1619 were granted a patent. But while business negotiations dragged on, their leader in Leiden, the Reverend John Robinson, was considering another possibility. He had heard of Dutch activities on the Hudson, and approached some of the Amsterdammers involved, bringing with him a glowing reference from the burgomaster of Leiden: "These English have lived among us now this twelve years, and yet we never had suit or accusation come against them."[29]

The Dutchmen he talked to were already involved in plans for the West India Company, with trading settlements on the Hudson, and they warmly recommended these ideal colonists to the States General. An English clergyman from Leiden, they stated, "well versed in the Dutch language," wanted to move to New Netherland with four hundred families, "to plant, forthwith, everywhere

FIRST RIGHTS

there the true and pure Christian religion, to instruct the Indian." They suggested that the English be allowed to go and settle on the North River, especially since the eyes of "his Britannic Majesty" were already roving over "your petitioners' possessions and discoveries."[30]

The request was seconded by the Stadholder, Prince Maurits, but the States rejected it all the same on April 11, 1620, fearing— not without reason, as it turned out—that English settlers in America were likely to be more loyal to the English Crown than to the States General. By this time, in any case, the Pilgrims had accepted a patent secured for them by a group of London backers. On July 21, 1620, they sailed from Delftshaven on the *Speedwell* to Southampton, and thence, in the 180-ton *Mayflower,* to Cape Cod. Exactly five months after leaving the United Provinces they came to their journey's end at New Plymouth.

There was in hospitable Leiden another group of religious refugees with an interest in the New World. They were Protestant Walloons, who had fled from the Spanish Southern Netherlands. Led by the forty-five-year-old Jesse de Forest, a wool merchant from Avesnes, fifty-six heads of families signed a round robin requesting permission to emigrate to Virginia, armed with which De Forest called on Sir Dudley Carleton at The Hague. A few months later he sent him a formal petition, explaining that the request was for a total of three hundred people.[31]

Carleton duly passed on the document, but the Virginia Company reacted with indifference, thinking it "not expedient that the said families" should settle together. Like the States, the English did not favor a massive invasion of foreigners. The De Forest petition, however, provided another useful debating point for the English in future arguments about Dutch rights in North America. As King Charles later told Ambassador Joachimi, they had been approached from Holland by "a considerable number of families . . . to procure them a place of habitation among his Maties subjects." If they had had the choice of living under Dutch rule, the English argued, they would certainly not have asked to "mingle with strangers."[32]

As it turned out, the Walloon refugees did finally live in America under Dutch rule. Jesse de Forest never made it himself: disappointed in his hopes to go to the Virginias, he had approached the West India Company and received permission to go to the West

Indies, but died on the voyage out. The other *péres de familles* and their households were more fortunate. They were among the first settlers who in April 1623, guided by Cornelis Jacobsz Mey, left the Republic on the *Nieu Nederlandt,* and reached the Dutch province safely.

FIRST RIGHTS

The

Dream

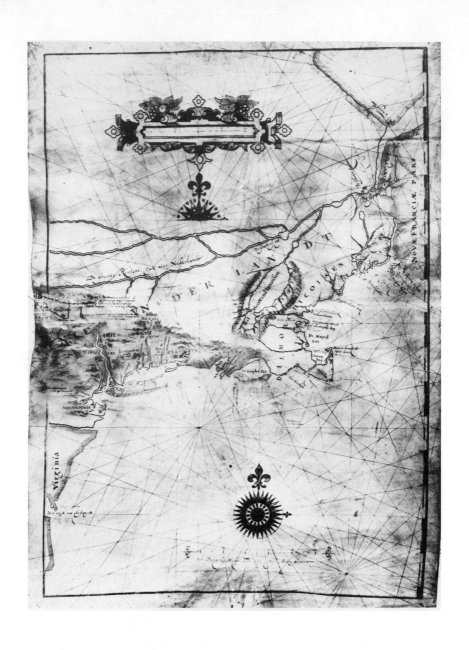

The *"Figurative Map on Vellum,"* which gave a group of Dutch merchants
the first monopoly of trade to North America in 1614.

*One of the ships that took
the adventurous Dutch around the globe.*
MUSEUM OF THE CITY OF NEW YORK

West India House, the headquarters of the company in Amsterdam.
MUSEUM OF THE CITY OF NEW YORK

*A view in Amsterdam, showing West India House on the left
and Mont Albaan's Tower in the middle.*
COURTESY OF THE LONG ISLAND HISTORICAL SOCIETY, BROOKLYN, N.Y.

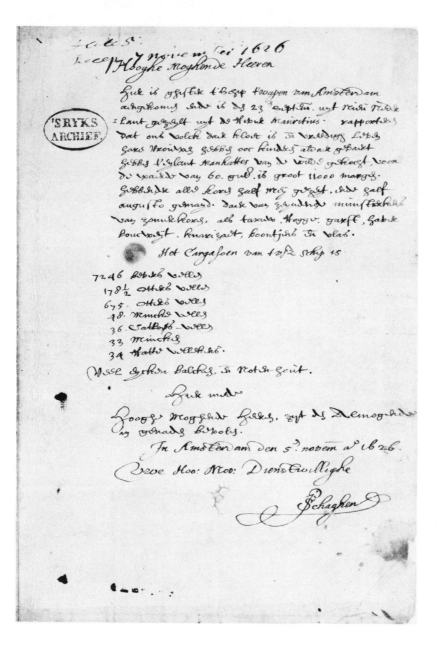

Letter to the States General, recording the purchase of Manhattan.
"... They have purchased the Island of Manhattes from the Indians for
the value of 60 guilders. ..." It was the best buy the Dutch
could have made but it was little appreciated.
ALGEMEEN RIJKSARCHIEF

VRYHEDEN

By de Vergaderinghe van de Negenthiene vande Geoctroyeerde West-Indische Compagnie vergunt aen allen den ghenen / die eenighe Colonien in Nieuw-Nederlandt sullen planten.

In het licht ghegheven

Om bekent te maken wat Profijten ende Voordeelen
aldaer in Nieu-Nederlandt , voor de Coloniers ende der
selver Patroonen ende Meesters, midtsgaders de
Participanten , die de Colonien aldaer
planten , zijn bekomen.

Westindsen Kan syn Nederlands groot gewin.
Verkleynt sviands Macht brengt silver-platen in.

T'AMSTELREDAM,

Voor Marten Iansz Brandt Boeckverkooper / woonende by
de nieuwe kerck / in de Gereformeerde Catechismus. Anno 1630.

The first document to be published about New Netherland,
"Privileges and Exemptions," a pamphlet to attract colonists.

A PILGRIMAGE

The close ties the Pilgrim Fathers and the Dutch had formed in the Republic were forgotten as soon as both set foot in America. The people of New Plymouth had to pay off enormous debts to their London backers before they could begin to feel independent, and beaver was their one hope. With anger and frustration they heard about the rich beaver trade the Dutch were operating with the Indians at Manhattan and Fort Orange, and they met other Dutch furtraders poaching very near their own preserve, at Buzzards Bay.

"The Dutch planted nere Hudson Bay . . . are likely to overthrow the trade," they complained to London in 1624. The answer sent back to Plymouth was brisk and brief: "We rather commend them, than condemne them for it"—a generous tone that would not be heard again.[1]

It was three years later that the first official contacts were made between the two colonies, and even then it was the Dutch who took the initiative. Unaware of the fears the Pilgrims had expressed, and assuming that they would be disposed to friendliness after their long stay in Holland, Isaack de Rasières, the secretary of New Netherland, wrote a letter from Fort Amsterdam to William Bradford, the governor of "Nieu Pliemven." The occasion of his letter was a festive one.

Since the collapse of the Anglo-Spanish marriage negotiations in Madrid, from which Prince Charles and the reigning English favorite Buckingham had returned to London in humiliated rage, English foreign policy had gone abruptly into reverse. It was now aggressively anti-Spanish, and Charles had married Henrietta Maria, the sister of Louis XIII of France. A wave of sympathy and friendship for the plucky little Dutch—staunch opponents of the haughty Spanish for so long—swept England, and at its crest the two countries signed the Treaty of Southampton of September 1625, an offensive and defensive alliance to last for fifteen years unless "the King of Spain will refrain from attacking the freedom of the United Provinces." But even a common hatred of Spain was not enough to make the English and Dutch see eye to eye on matters like the herring and whale fishery, or the spice trade. And the most persuasive and charming diplomat the Dutch could send to London in 1627, Jacob Cats—known as the People's Poet—achieved nothing in five months except a knighthood for himself.[2]

News of this cooling off had still not reached America when De Rasières congratulated Bradford in 1627 on the "new union" between their two nations. He began his letter with a string of "superfluous titles," commented Bradford later, but knowing the Dutch, he took it in the right spirit, "it being their maner to be full of complementall titles." De Rasières offered the Pilgrims "commodities and merchandise" in exchange for beaver, otter, and other wares, an offer that Bradford in his answer of March 19 readily accepted.[3]

The English governor, in his turn, rejoiced at the new Anglo-Dutch understanding, which would be "sufficient to unite us together in love and good neighbourhood in all our dealings." He had indeed not forgotten the "good and courteous entreaty" the Brownists had received in Holland, but nonetheless he added a reminder to De Rasières that the Dutch were trespassing on his Majesty's territory, though he reassured him that "for our parts, we shall not go about to molest or trouble you in any thing."[4]

The Dutch found the reminder of the so-called English rights worrying enough to send a delegate to New Plymouth. On August 7, 1627, Jan van Wieringen arrived in the little town carrying a "rundlet" of sugar, two Holland cheeses, and an official letter for the governor from Director General Peter Minuit and his Council. The letter was friendly but, as Bradford reported to the Council

A SWEET AND ALIEN LAND

for New England, it was also firm, "maintaining their rights and liberty to trade in those parts." According to the Englishman, Minuit made it clear that "as we had authority and commission from our King, so they had the like from the States of Holland, which they would defend." The letter ended with an invitation to Bradford to come and visit the Dutch at Fort Amsterdam; but he had to refuse—"one of our boats is abroad and we have much business at home." He apologized for sending Jan van Wieringen back empty-handed—"not having any thing to send you for the present that may be acceptable."[5]

A week later he sent the Dutch another letter, this time of firm but friendly warning. He would be unable to do anything for them, he said, "if you light either in the hands of those of Virginia" or of New England. "They will make prize of you, if they can, if they find you trading within those limits." He repeated somewhat impatiently the English arguments against the Dutch claim to have been trading in this region for twenty-six years: "You must understand that her Majesty Queen Elizabeth, of famous memory, hath begun to navigate and plant in these lands well nigh forty years ago." And he gave them a piece of excellent advice—to ask the States General to conclude an agreement with England about New Netherland "before any inconvenience befall." Finally he invited the Dutch to send an envoy for further talks.[6]

Two months later, in October, Isaack de Rasières left Fort Amsterdam for the first diplomatic mission in North American history. He set sail in the bark *Nassau*, crossed Rhode Island Sound, and arrived accompanied "by trumpeters and some other attendants" at Manomet (now Monument Beach), the Pilgrims' trading post north of Buzzards Bay. From there he sent a message to Bradford asking him to send a small boat. Jan van Wieringen had told him that the journey from Manomet to Plymouth took only six hours overland, "but I have not gone so far this three or four years; wherefore I fear my feet will fail me. . . ."[7]

The governor of New Plymouth was kind enough to send a boat able to navigate the cross-country tracery of streams and rivers, and De Rasières, honorably attended "with a noyse of trumpeters," finally reached New Plymouth. The trumpeters made the point De Rasières was to reaffirm: the Dutch were not mere petty traders poaching on English territory, but proud and considerable inhabitants of an important Dutch settlement.

A PILGRIMAGE

Bradford and De Rasières got on well. "A man of a fair and genteel behaviour," Bradford afterward said of the Dutchman. And De Rasières in turn was much impressed by the achievement of the Brownists.

The Pilgrims had visibly overcome their initial problems. They had been able—thanks to the mediation of an English-speaking Indian, Squanto—to conclude a treaty of friendship with the neighboring Indians that was to give them peace for more than half a century. Squanto, who had learned his English when he was taken to London to be sold as a slave—a fate he escaped with the help of Sir Ferdinando Gorges—had done more. He had shown the settlers "both the maner how to set (the corne) and after how to dress & tend it. Also he told them except they got fish and set with it (in these old grounds) it would come to nothing." And by the time of De Rasières' visit, the farms, "although not so good as ours, because they are more stony," were producing enough maize to give the Pilgrims a surplus for trade with the Indians.[8]

The Dutchman liked New Plymouth. The town, sited on the slope of a hill that stretched east to the seashore, was dominated by a large hilltop house with a flat roof on which six cannon were mounted. Down from this fortress ran the wide main street, "about a cannon-shot of 800 feet" long, and crossed by one other street. At the ends of the streets were gates in the hefty stockade that surrounded the place. Inside these walls, the houses were built of timber and—according to an amazed De Rasières, used to the straggling, disorderly building in and around Fort Amsterdam— very neatly arranged with tidy little gardens at back and sides.

He was solemnly received in the governor's house in the center of town, a sturdy building "before which is a square stockade upon which four patereros [pebble guns] are mounted so as to enfilade the streets." There was no church yet, but the Pilgrim congregation assembled every Sunday in the lower part of the fort. And De Rasières soon discovered that these Brownists had lost nothing of their religious fervor—he was struck by the "stringent laws and ordinances upon the subject of fornication and adultery, which laws they maintain and enforce very strictly indeed." His hosts even attacked the Dutchmen because they had heard from "the savages that we live so barbarously in these respects, and without punishment."[9]

His curiosity satisfied, De Rasières got down to the business that

A SWEET AND ALIEN LAND

had brought him to New Plymouth. He offered Bradford a treaty of trade and commerce. As a token of goodwill, he had brought "some cloth of three sorts and colours and a chest of white sugar," but Bradford was evasive, saying that he wished "it had been sooner propounded before we sent our factor into England and Holland." The reason for his hesitation was simply fear of those who opposed the Dutch presence in America. "We well knew . . . that this dealing and friendship with the Dutch . . . would procure us envy from others," he admitted later. Nevertheless he and his people entertained the Dutch secretary and his company with warm hospitality and friendliness, and when De Rasières left, the *Nassau* was empty. The Pilgrims had bought all his "Commodities."[10]

They bought more than duffel cloth and white sugar. De Rasières had offered to sell Bradford fifty fathoms of wampum and Bradford eagerly agreed. Wampum—or seawan, as the English called it—was the Indian currency, which the Dutch had found in common use by all the tribes along the Hudson River. The Indians strung the tiny black and white beads made from certain shells and cockles on hennep thread and afterward wove them into belts, valuing "these little bones as highly as many Christians do gold, silver or pearls."[11]

The source of these shells was the beaches on the Dutch end of Long Island, and on the nearby mainland, a handy location that had given the Dutch a monopoly of the wampum industry. De Rasières had heard that the Pilgrims had built a shallop at Manomet so that they could go and look for the valuable little shells themselves. If they succeeded, it would be a dire blow to the Dutch fur trade, which was New Netherland's *raison d'être*, and one of the objects of De Rasières' visit was to discourage English wampum-hunting expeditions by offering them a supply himself.[12]

Most of the Puritan New Englanders were disgusted by the introduction of the Indian currency, and called it the "Devil's Work and Money," but Bradford, more practically, regarded De Rasières' visit as a success for that reason especially. This first load of wampum was, he wrote, "the beginning of a profitable trade with us and the Indians."

De Rasières returned to Fort Amsterdam armed with expressions of friendship, and a letter in which Governor Bradford once more warned the Dutch to clear the "title of your planting in these

A PILGRIMAGE

parts" with the King of England. "We persuade ourselves that now may be easily and reasonably done, which will be harder and with more difficulty hereafter, and perhaps not without blows," he wrote with foresight. De Rasières also took back with him an alarming impression of the English settlers' determination to stand on their rights: Bradford had not hesitated to demand that the Dutch stop trading at Buzzards Bay, although the secretary had painted a highly deceptive picture of Dutch strength and numbers in Manhattan.[13]

Minuit was sufficiently concerned by the secretary's account of his visit to send off a request to the West India Company for a company of forty soldiers; the company, in turn, appealed to the States General. "The last letters from New Netherland bring word, that the English of New Plymouth threaten to drive away those there, or to disturb them in their settlement and little colony. . . ." But the directors were not enthusiastic about fighting the matter out: "We would rather see it secured by friendly alliance," they told the States. The States General accordingly sent no troops —and shelved the request for a friendly alliance.[14]

Much more concern was felt in London when the Council for New England read the report that Governor Bradford had dispatched to them after De Rasières' visit. He told them of the friendly approach, and asked for instructions on how to deal with the Dutch, warning that "for strength of men and fortification they far exceed us, and all in the land." The report reached the English capital at the same time as the publication of the widely-read *Planters' Plea*, in which the Dutch colony on the Hudson River was lauded: "the men whom they carrie, though they be not many, are well chosen, and known to be useful and serviceable." Life in New Netherland sounded utopian, since, according to the author, the settlers were as cherished by the company "as their own families," regularly supplied, and "knowne to subsist in a comfortable manner."[15]

The Dutch living in Manhattan would have laughed bitterly if they could have read this pamphlet—and Bradford might have spoken differently if he had accepted Minuit's invitation for a visit. At the time the Dutch were in the middle of their trouble with the governor and his officials, New Amsterdam was still only a clutter of unfinished buildings around an unimpressive fort, and little progress was being made: "the English . . . will in the meantime

A SWEET AND ALIEN LAND

drive us out of the trade since we go to work so slowly and are so slack," wrote Simon Pos unhappily to his employer Kiliaen van Rensselaer.[16]

It was fortunate for them that the English had a different impression. In particular, Sir Ferdinando Gorges was following with indignation the growth of the Dutch colonies in the middle of his patent, and in November 1631, with Bradford's report in his hand, he urged the Council for New England to petition the King. It should be made clear to the Dutch that they "should forthwith either relinquish it or become subjects of the King."[17]

The petition evidently impressed the King and the weather came to Sir Ferdinando's help by forcing the *Eendracht* into the harbor of Plymouth. That the vessel was eventually released after long negotiations hardly mattered to him. The great point was that the King of England had at last warned off the Dutch in person, after careful inquiries into "the nature of his right." He had committed himself completely, with a solemn declaration that North America was his. If the Dutch proposed to stay without his permission, "they shall impute it to themselves if hereafter they suffer."[18]

DRUNKEN FOOLS

The intervention of England's King Charles I in the *Eendracht* incident of 1632 had more than political repercussions. It had painful practical consequences for New Netherland. The West India Company, afraid that other vessels bound for the province would meet the same fate, suspended for the time being the dispatch of supply ships, and "the colonists there suffered greatly from want of grain and other necessaries, which they expected from Holland."[1]

The hungry and wretched settlers were by this time under the supervision of Bastiaen Jansz Krol, who had been appointed by the Lords Directors to replace Minuit. Krol, thirty-seven years old, hard-working, and ambitious, had started life as a textile worker in Friesland. In 1624 he came to New Netherland as a "comforter of the sick"—a church officer below the rank of minister. He had worked hard to reach this position, teaching himself to read and write before the church Classis of Amsterdam considered him worthy to "console and instruct all sick" and to read the Bible for the pious. The Classis made it clear to him that he—like all the "sieckentroosters" it sent abroad—was not to administer the sacraments, and gave him the generous salary of thirty-four guilders a month.[2] Seven months later he protested to the directors that since "there were many pregnant women whose children ought to be christened," the province needed a dominie, and reluctantly the

Classis gave him permission to baptize and marry people.[3]

His drive was not lost on the Heeren XIX, and shortly afterward in 1625, they made Krol "commis" or commander of Fort Orange. Four years later, when Krol returned for a short visit to Amsterdam, the good impression he had made caused him at once to become involved in an important new venture in New Netherland, the patroon project.

For years after its beginning, the colony was far from self-sufficient. The setting up of the farms on Manhattan, the six bouweries, had been one effort to cut down on the company's expense, but since, by 1629, costs had still not noticeably dropped, the West India Company devised a system of grants of land to the settlers to encourage them to grow more of their own food.

More important, however, was the reluctant approval given at the same time to another, more far-reaching scheme, the "Privileges and Exemptions of Patroons, Masters, and Private Individuals." Grandiose in conception, this new order virtually sanctioned the creation of colonies within the colony. Any member of the company who was prepared, at his own expense, to send out fifty settlers for not less than a year could claim rights over a territory stretching sixteen miles along the coast of sea or river, or eight miles along both sides of a river. The company reserved Manhattan and the precious fur trade for itself, but the "patroons" of these semi-independent domains would enjoy all gaming and fishing rights, milling rights, a tenth of the harvest, civil and criminal jurisdiction, and the power to appoint their own magistrates. They would pay certain duties to the company, but in order to promote the scheme, the Heeren XIX promised not to tax the tenants of a patroon for ten years, and to supply him, if possible, with African slaves.[4]

The scheme was greeted with enthusiasm by Kiliaen van Rensselaer, a founder-member of the West India Company who had always been an ardent advocate of greater agricultural development in the province. The fifty-year-old Dutchman, descendant of an old Gelderland farming family and now a wealthy businessman and jeweler in Amsterdam, had recently begun an ambitious scheme for the reclamation of the Crailo marshland, near Amsterdam. Wishing to diversify his interests, he looked across the Atlantic, where there was land to be had for the asking. From the start he and Usselinx had pressed unsuccessfully for the establishment

DRUNKEN FOOLS

of a full-fledged colony instead of a mere trading settlement, and he was one of the three commissaries for New Netherland that year, together with Samuel Bloemaerts and Samuel Godyn. He now grasped eagerly at this chance to realize, if only partially, his dream of turning New Netherland into the granary of the Republic, and in January 1629 he sent over for a report.[5]

By the time the States had approved the scheme in July, all three commissaries had staked their claims, and Bloemaerts and Godyn had already purchased their domain from the Indians. It was a tract of land on the southwest side of the Delaware, which they called Swanendael, near present-day Lewes.[6]

Van Rensselaer proceeded more cautiously. He had received encouraging reports about the land around Fort Orange, but he wanted someone reliable to see the transaction through for him. In the circumstances Krol was the perfect choice. Not only was he just then available in Amsterdam for discussion, but he was the West India Company's own commander at Fort Orange. The two men soon came to an agreement, and on Krol's return to New Amsterdam, he had detailed instructions from the jeweler. He was to purchase for him land lying on the west side of the Hudson, from the native Mohican and Mohawk Indians. "He will extend, if he is able, the limits so high and large above Fort Orange as they want to cede like below the Fort, so that it will stretch five miles above and below and as far inland as is possible." Krol had special orders to give no reason for dissatisfaction to the Indians, and to make payment in front of the whole tribe, after which he was to escort the chief to Manhattan, where the purchase would be ratified by the director general and his Council.[7]

On April 18 Krol carried out his instructions, and not much later the first farm was built at Rensselaerswyck. Four months later another agent of the company, Gillis van Hoossett, bought more land for Van Rensselaer which, together with a tract on the east bank of the Hudson and later acquisitions, made the Dutch jeweler "Lord of the Manor" over a country forty-eight miles long and twenty-four miles wide (a total of seven hundred thousand acres now lying in Albany, Rensselaer, and part of Columbia counties).[8]

As Van Rensselaer had ordered, Krol traveled to New Amsterdam in August, where Peter Minuit signed the deed. It was not the first one. Another patroon, Michiel Pauw from Utrecht, had bought land on the west shore of the North River, across from

A SWEET AND ALIEN LAND

Manhattan, called Hobocan Hacking (now Hoboken), and had the purchase ratified on July 12, 1630. His deed for the colony he called Pavonia is the oldest document preserved in the archives of the state of New York.[9]

Having dealt with Van Rensselaer's affairs successfully, Krol went back to look after company business at Fort Orange. But not for long. Minuit's recall to Holland in 1632—influenced in part by the company's view that he had signed away some of the best land to the patroons—made it necessary to look for a replacement. And Van Rensselaer, although he had resigned as a commissioner for New Netherland the previous year, still had enough influence to have Krol appointed "kommandeur" of the province.[10]

Krol took over at a difficult time. Apart from the slow arrival of provisions for the colony, a new incident with the Indians had greatly shocked the small community on Manhattan. It occurred at Swanendael, the domain of Bloemaerts and Godyn at the South River, where a small party of Dutch colonists had settled in 1631 under the supervision of the company's commissary, Gillis van Hoossett. As usual, the Dutch had erected the arms of the United Provinces on the day of their arrival, painted on a piece of tin they stuck to a pole upon the bank of what they called the Hoerekill. A few days later this token of their sovereignty disappeared— removed by an Indian chief who thought he could use it for a pipe. Van Hoossett protested so strongly at this "national insult" that the Indians hastily executed their chief and showed him the bloody remains. The commissary regretted they had gone that far, but it was too late—both for the chief and for the Dutch community. The execution of their chief had aroused some of the tribe to such fury that one day, while most of the settlers were at work in the fields, they took their revenge.

Three Indians, pretending to come for trade, turned up at the farm, where they found Van Hoossett and another sick Dutchman. They slaughtered both men on the spot. The massive bulldog chained to the house demanded more effort—twenty-five arrows were shot at him before he died. In the meantime a horde of savages attacked the other thirty-two colonists in the fields and murdered them, completing their revenge by burning the house and stockade to the ground.[11]

It was a month before the massacre was discovered. In December 1632 one of the Swanendael shareholders, Captain David Piet-

DRUNKEN FOOLS

ersz de Vries, arrived with his ship the *Eeckhoorn* ("Squirrel") to inspect his domain. A sinister silence reigned over the bones of the settlers.

De Vries was a French-born Dutchman whose taste for adventure had taken him from Newfoundland to the Mediterranean and the East Indies, involved him in fights with Turkish pirates, and enlisted him in the service of the French. He was a man of the world, intelligent and humane, and his experience was particularly useful at this juncture. Against the general clamor for revenge, De Vries argued its futility, and instead invited the Indians for talks. The result was a peace treaty sealed by a present of Dutch axes, bullets, and duffel cloth.[12]

Krol could not have had a better representative than De Vries in dealing with this bloody affair. He himself was engaged at Fort Amsterdam in a legal wrangle that eventually cost him his job. Two of the company's tenant farmers wanted to return to the Fatherland. The patroon's agent, Simon Pos, was anxious to get hold of more cattle for Rensselaerswyck, and wrote to his employer of the farmers' plans to leave. Van Rensselaer at once urged him to get hold of their livestock and take it up to Fort Orange. Krol, acting for the company, refused permission and violent disputes followed, all of which were reported back to Van Rensselaer, who, considering Krol's action one of great disloyalty in a former protégé, wrote gleefully in July 1632 to tell him that his role as "kommandeur" of New Netherland would soon be ended. The company, which had this time been at pains to exclude the jeweler from its decision making, had nominated his nephew, Wouter van Twiller, as the new director general of New Netherland.[13]

Van Twiller left late in 1632 for his post, but the Dutch settlers very nearly lost their new overlord before his arrival. His ship the *Soutberg* ("Mountain of Salt") ran into Turkish pirate galleys, and only escaped thanks to the presence on board of 104 soldiers—the first to be sent to New Netherland. Another encounter at sea was more profitable: when the *Soutberg* finally anchored before Manhattan, she had a rich prize in tow—a Spanish vessel, the *St. Martyn*, loaded with sugar.[14]

The nomination of Van Twiller had surprised his uncle, and it was now New Netherland's turn. The Dutch settlers, waiting to greet their new director general on the Strand outside Fort Amsterdam, studied him with astonishment as he disembarked and

A SWEET AND ALIEN LAND

marched at the head of his soldiers to the company's warehouse. They had expected their new governor to be a seasoned man of experience. Instead they saw a relatively young man (Van Twiller was twenty-seven) with an amiable and vacuous face. Until the time of his appointment, they learned, he had been a clerk in the West India Company's head office in Amsterdam. They wondered how he had climbed so fast—unless it had been with the help of his uncle, Van Rensselaer. And they would soon have plenty of cause to question the wisdom of the Lords Directors in making this appointment.

Van Rensselaer himself seems never to have had much hope of this nephew, sending him at one time a list of eight moral rules "to refresh his memory." Among them were warnings "to be zealous, to be carefull with all things and people, to be humble and patient, to be religious and to be modest in the use of food and drink." If he lived according to this list, Van Rensselaer suggestively added, "a curse would become a blessing, and slander would turn into honour." It never became obvious that the young man heeded his uncle's advice.[15]

De Vries, coming with the *Eeckhoorn* to Fort Amsterdam with a load of furs and corn from Swanendael, was one of the first witnesses of Van Twiller's inadequacy. De Vries arrived only days after the *Soutberg* dropped anchor, and the governor came out of the fort to welcome this prominent colonist. They chatted amicably for a while, then De Vries was called away on business. Two days later they met again, this time in less friendly circumstances.

An English ship, the *William*, had just docked in the East River. Sent over by three London merchants to bring back furs from the Hudson, it had a former West India Company employee, Jacob Eelkens, on board. The ship's captain, William Trevor, invited Van Twiller to come on board, and the director, after some dithering, finally accepted. De Vries went with him and looked on with dismay and disgust while Van Twiller—already "the sport of the people"—drank himself into a stupor with his officials. The captain, seeing his opportunity, told Van Twiller the object of his voyage. But drunk or not, Van Twiller refused to let him sail on, a furious row broke out, and the Dutch officials, noted an outraged De Vries, "got into such high words that the Englishman could not understand how it was that there should be such unruliness among the officers of the Company."

DRUNKEN FOOLS

Trevor waited a week to see if Van Twiller might change his mind. When he did not, the English captain coolly announced his intention of continuing up the Hudson. He reminded the director that the country belonged to the English, having been discovered by a certain "David Hutson." Van Twiller answered that Hudson had sailed in the service of the Dutch and that the river now named Mauritius was therefore Dutch. Trevor ignored him, hoisted anchor, and sailed upriver.

As Trevor had calculated, Van Twiller was a man of lethargic reaction. Only after De Vries and others put pressure on him did he finally assemble the people—and then in the way he thought would please them most. He had "a cask of wine brought out, filled a bumper and cried out for those who loved the Prince of Orange and him, to do the same as he did, and protect him from the outrage of the Englishman." The crowd grinned, drank, and went home, saying that the English were their friends.

De Vries thought it outrageous that the English should be allowed to get away with their raiding, and dining with Van Twiller that day, he strongly protested the governor's inaction. "I told him that he had committed great folly, as the Englishman had no commission." Van Twiller should have shot him with "beans from the eight-pounders," and De Vries warned the director that he had to teach the English a lesson; "otherwise one cannot control this nation, for they are so proud a nature, that they thought everything belonged to them."[16]

Eelkens had already pitched his tent a mile from Fort Orange when Van Twiller, prodded by De Vries, at last gave orders to Krol—still waiting for a ship back to Holland—to follow him with some soldiers. The Spanish prize, the carvel *St. Martyn*, was equipped, and Krol sailed up to the fort, where he discovered to his amazement that Eelkens had found an ally in no less a person than the company's commissary at Fort Orange. Hans Jorissen Van Houten had come to New Amsterdam with Van Twiller, taking up his post only a few weeks earlier. His appointment had been very much opposed by Van Rensselaer, but the company had pointed to his experience in the region—in fact, the worst argument they could have used. Van Houten was despised and hated by the Indians, who had not forgotten his behavior toward one of their sachems a few years earlier. After taking him prisoner, Van Houten had accepted a ransom—and then had him castrated, which treatment the chief had not survived.[17]

Van Houten had no intention of taking orders from Krol in his own territory, and he came on board the *St. Martyn* to tell Krol arrogantly that he would do better to return to New Amsterdam. "As long as Hontom was there, he himself would manage."[18] Krol, powerless to act without Van Houten's cooperation, stayed on nonetheless and was disgusted to see that Eelkens and Van Houten had become the best of friends, dining and drinking together. But soon the friendship turned sour. The Indians remembered Eelkens, who spoke their language, and the furs were piling up on his ship. It became clear even to Van Houten that the main business of the company was in danger, and at last he forbade the English to come near the fort to trade. One of them later recounted how he was bundled away by one of Houten's men, who "dranke bottle of strong waters of three or fower pints and were very merrye."[19]

Eelkens was unmoved, so Van Houten came and pitched a tent next to the English. Seeing their enemy, the Indians ran off, threatening "to stone him to death if they ever got the chance."[20] While tension mounted, Van Houten watched Eelkens' prospering commerce with growing jealousy. Finally he could bear it no longer and decided on action. His former friend had gathered three hundred to four hundred skins, and Van Houten could not risk losing a load of seven thousand, which was expected in a month's time. Calling on Krol for the help of his soldiers, he tore down the English tents and chased the crew back to the *William*. "And as they were carryinge them aboard, sounded theire trumpet in the boate, in disgrace of the English, and beate twoe Indians, which came and broughte others with them to trade," an English witness told later.[21]

The *William* returned to New Amsterdam, where Van Twiller in the meantime had pulled himself together and instructed his people that unless they wanted to lose "theire head and all their wages" they must refuse to deal with the English. For his part, he tried to confiscate the load of furs, but the *William* sailed before he could do anything.[22]

Transatlantic communications were leisurely—the round trip to Europe could take up to six months—and it was another year before the trouble with the *William* had repercussions in Europe. In the summer of 1634—two years after the *Eendracht* incident—Albert Joachimi, Dutch ambassador to London, warned the States

DRUNKEN FOOLS

General that the three merchants who had backed the *William* expedition were demanding reparation after complaining to the King. They claimed to have lost at least four thousand pounds. The English saw it as yet another good pretext to "pick a quarrel . . . about the possession of New Netherland," wrote Joachimi, who had this from "a noble Lord, who regrets to perceive that there is any misunderstanding between the Dutch and English nations." He advised the States to handle the case carefully, "as the King's jurisdiction is mixed up in it."[23]

The States acted accordingly. When the London merchants presented a claim for damage to the States, they passed it on to the West India Company, which refused to pay, pointing out that since the English had traded upon their territory, it was they who ought to pay reparations to the company. The Dutch, as the directors wrote to the States, had actually suffered far greater damages than the merchants. Krol, who finally arrived in Amsterdam in April 1634, had told the dismayed Lords Directors that just before he left Fort Amsterdam in July 1633, a Mohican called Dickop (Fathead) had brought news to Manhattan that the Indians had burned a company yacht and killed all the cattle around Fort Orange. "The injurious seed of discord hath been sown between the Indians and our people," the directors now complained. It was the Indians' revenge on Van Houten for the murder of their sachem and for his interference with their profitable trade with the English.[24]

On the diplomatic front the incident had slighter consequences. The English for the moment did not pursue the matter, and on a request from the West India Company to use this opportunity to settle at last the border question in America, the States answered coolly that they preferred to let the matter "take its own course."

By the time the *William* was at length chased away, Captain De Vries had already left New Amsterdam for his return to Holland. But not before Van Twiller had given a fresh display of crassness. He insisted on inspecting the cargo of De Vries, who in his position as patroon refused. Van Twiller then gave order to train the guns of the fort on the *Eeckhoorn*, but the captain was not so easily frightened. He stormed up to the governor and asked him furi-

A SWEET AND ALIEN LAND

ously "whether the land was full of fools. If they wished to shoot anything, they should have shot at the Englishman, who was violating the river." Van Twiller insisted on his right of search and sent twelve musketeers to arrest De Vries. They watched helplessly under the "shouts and jeers" of a crowd of bystanders as the captain was rowed away to his vessel.

Before he sailed, a boat arrived with letters the governor wanted to send to Holland, brought by Van Twiller's cousin, Coenraed van Notelman, and the secretary, Jan van Remunde. Van Remunde spotted some skins being loaded on the *Eeckhoorn* and wanted to confiscate them, but Notelman thought it too much effort and hinted that a good glass from the best cask would be preferable. De Vries sneered that "water was good enough for them, for they might otherwise fall overboard." He added, bitterly, that he had never seen such a bunch of "fools who know nothing except to drink," and parted with the prophetic words that the "Company by such management must come to naught."[25]

De Vries just missed a scene that would have confirmed his opinion. Hardly had he left than a skipper from Virginia, Captain Stone, arrived in New Amsterdam. With a shipful of cattle, he had lost his way in the tricky waters of the sound—De Vries, in fact, had met this old acquaintance and lent him a pilot—and he wanted to take on water. In the harbor he spotted a pinnace from New Plymouth against whose captain he had an old grudge. Van Twiller's reputation as a heavy drinker had already reached Virginia, so Stone invited the governor on board, plied him with excellent wine, and explained that he wanted to seize the Plymouth ship. Van Twiller, who was by that time in such a "drunken fitte . . . so as he could scarse speake a right word," gave his consent. Stone seized his chance, hurried some of his crew aboard the pinnace while its own crew was ashore, and carried it off.

"But diverse of the Dutch sea-men," so Bradford related happily, "who had been often at Plimoth and kindly entertained ther, said one to another, Shall we suffer our friends to be thus abused, and have their goods carried away, whilst our governor is drunke?" They followed the Virginian prize in two boats and rescued it. Van Twiller meanwhile sobered up enough to beg the master of the pinnace, "one of the council of Plymouth," to forget the whole incident.[26]

DRUNKEN FOOLS

But nobody did forget, nor was it possible to do so. In these first few weeks, Van Twiller had already created an image of drunken incompetence that lasted till the end of his directorate. And at this time it seemed that this end could not be far off. David de Vries, on returning to Holland, had given the Lords Directors a hair-raising account of affairs under Van Twiller. His uncle, Van Rensselaer, who was having his own differences with the company on the subject of patroons, was not helped by this disastrous family scandal, and wrote begging his nephew to be more careful. De Vries was campaigning against him, he warned, and "such a shameful pot has been on the fire for you, that I in all my life never would have believed that one could find men base enough to plan it." In defense of the family honor, he went so far as to single out one of Van Twiller's critics in the middle of crowded Dam Square in Amsterdam and went for him "in such a way . . . that he will not soon forget it."[27]

The secretary, Jan van Remunde, sacked by Van Twiller after a blazing row, had also joined the chorus of critics, writing to his wife in Holland long accounts of the governor's drunken inepti-tude, which she spread with alacrity. These reports dwelt particu-larly on the bitter quarrels that had arisen between Van Twiller and the new pastor of New Amsterdam, Everardus Bogardus. Following the example of his predecessor Michaëlius with Minuit, Bogardus—two years younger than the governor—had almost at once fallen out with him.

The dominie had traveled over with Van Twiller on the *Sout-berg*. He had some colonial experience already, having worked as a "comforter of the sick" in Guinea, and like Van Twiller, he was a bachelor with no fear of the bottle. Drunken brawls were inevita-ble, and on one occasion Van Twiller was seen running after Bogardus with "a naked sword" through the muddy streets of New Amsterdam, both of them under the influence of drink. The dominie's reaction was equally spirited, but on paper. In a letter he described the director as "a child of the devil; an incarnate villain," and promised to give him the next Sunday "such a shake . . . from the pulpit, as would make him shudder."[28]

Not everyone approved of Bogardus' behavior—he was accused of behaving like "a heathen, much less a Christian letting alone a preacher of the Gospel"—but the undignified row was added to a lengthening list of grievances against Van Twiller. Only the inter-

A SWEET AND ALIEN LAND

vention of his uncle Kiliaen Van Rensselaer saved him from a humiliating recall, "for believe me freely," warned the patroon, "had your honour not had me here, they would have summoned you home with an affront."

Van Rensselaer was powerless to save another nephew, Schout (sheriff) Coenraed van Notelman, one of the most blatant drunkards in the colony; and when the *Eendracht* sailed from Holland in April 1634, carrying the patroon's stern letter to Van Twiller, one of the passengers on board was Lubbertus van Dincklage, a replacement for the disgraced Notelman. Van Dincklage, who had been picked on the special recommendation of Van Rensselaer, was a doctor-in-law—"for such people can see deeper into a matter than those who have not studied and could be trusted as an adviser." In spite of his wealth, the patroon was still a naive man.[29]

At his arrival, Van Dincklage found a city that looked more prosperous than ever before, despite its director's drunken bouts. Van Twiller had been generous with company funds (yet another grievance in Amsterdam) and had made an effort to finish the fort. At least one bastion was rising, while the walls were almost completely repaired. His own house looked quite impressive, standing next to a guardroom "with lattice work" and the barracks for the 104 soldiers.

Outside the walls, the streets were messy and disorderly, crowded with people, hogs and chickens. But at least the town could now boast a bakery, a smithy, a cooper, and a midwife, while Adam Roclantsen, who had arrived at the same time as Van Twiller, had opened a school for boys and girls. His differences with Bogardus had not stopped Van Twiller from having a house built for the dominie, with its own stables, and on the north side of Pearl Street the governor had put up a little wooden church so that the pious need no longer climb to the first floor of the horse mill.[30]

The harbor of Manhattan hummed with activity.* In 1633, the company had given New Amsterdam "staple right," which empowered the city to request that all shippers either unload their vessels or pay certain duties. Ships from Holland, England, and the neighboring English colonies rode at their anchors in the Hud-

*In 1633 the population of New Amsterdam numbered between four hundred and five hundred.

DRUNKEN FOOLS

son, while in the taverns of the city the crews fraternized and the masters traded.

Prospects for the company looked good: in 1633 it had received from the province products to the value of more than ninety thousand guilders, a profit that was to rise in 1635 by another forty-three thousand guilders.[31]

Unfortunately for New Amsterdam, Van Rensselaer's plan to allow the province to supply directly the company's other colonies in Brazil and the West Indies had been rejected by the Lords Directors, who feared they might lose too much of their own export to these territories. They were still as "contrary minded" as always, sighed the patroon.[32]

CROWDING ON

"There is enough land. We should be good neighbours." With these words Sir John Harvey, governor of Virginia, welcomed Captain David de Vries when the Dutchman arrived at Jamestown, the capital of the English Crown colony, on his way to New Amsterdam in March 1633.

The governor had greeted him most impressively on the beach with an honor guard of musketeers and halberdiers, asking him from what place he came. De Vries, who had just concluded his depressing three-month stay at the devastated Swanendael, told him "from the South-bay in New Netherland," just thirty miles away. Sir John invited De Vries to his own house, where with glasses of Seck in their hands, the two men bent over a map. The governor realized at once that De Vries was talking about what he called the "Delwaerts Bay," which, he pointed out, was the King's territory. The Dutchman stoutly contradicted him, revealing the existence of Fort Nassau, built there by the Dutch in 1623. The governor shrugged his shoulders and declared that he would not trouble himself about it; to be good neighbors with the Dutch was more important to him. It was the end of the conversation, and the day closed in perfect friendship over a splendid dinner.[1]

Two years later the Virginians had changed their minds. In the summer of 1635 a fugitive turned up in New Amsterdam asking for the director general. He told Wouter van Twiller that his name was Thomas Hall and that he had been the hired servant of a certain George Holmes, who with thirteen other men had taken possession of Fort Nassau on the South River (the Delaware). They had come from Virginia planning to make a settlement on the river, and he had taken the opportunity to desert. For once the governor reacted swiftly and sent a boatload of soldiers to stop the invasion. It took them only a few weeks to bundle the interlopers out of Fort Nassau and transport them as prisoners to Fort Amsterdam.

It had taken the Virginians rather longer to organize this ill-fated expedition. Its moving spirit had been Thomas Young, who in September 1633 received a commission in London to set up trading posts on what he called the Charles River. In 1634 he made two or three reconnaissance trips up the Delaware, and when he returned to Virginia he told the colonists that the Dutch had deserted Fort Nassau.

Virginia was now twenty-eight years old, and going through difficult times. Its capital, Jamestown, was surrounded by malarial swamps, and its climate was as unhealthy as ever ("the English die there very fast," wrote De Vries), although the settlers were slowly becoming used to it. Politically the situation was precarious that year, after a mutiny that had almost cost the governor his post, and economically it was not much better. Several attempts to set up industry had failed, and excessive planting of tobacco had led to a greater demand for land and shipping than the colony could meet. And while Sir John Harvey was on his way to London for redress and help against the mutineers, the provisional governor, a planter called John West, agreed to the Delaware expansion scheme. Perhaps he hoped to get rid of some of his most obstreperous subjects, consisting—as the New Englanders said disdainfully—of "hot brained adventurers and reprieved prisoners."[2]

At the beginning of 1635 the expedition, led by George Holmes, left Point Comfort—to end up, after a brief stay at Fort Nassau, before Van Twiller in Fort Amsterdam. For the director there was no point in punishing them. He asked De Vries, who had just finished his second visit to New Amsterdam and was on the verge of leaving for Jamestown, to wait and in September they were hustled aboard his ship "bag and baggage." The Dutchman sailed at once and dropped them off two days later in Virginia. Thomas Hall, wisely, stayed behind in New Amsterdam.[3]

It was the only time that Virginia created real trouble for the Dutch, and trading between Virginia and New Amsterdam continued uninterrupted. For the Virginians, the Dutch ships that transported their tobacco from New Amsterdam back to Europe—in defiance of an order of 1621, which made it obligatory to send all goods from the colony direct to England—were indispensable.[4]

Much more serious than the threat to Fort Nassau was news that reached New Amsterdam in 1633: the English had encroached upon the region along the other border of New Netherland, the Fresh, or Connecticut, River. The Dutch had discovered the river in 1614, and ten years later, when the *Nieu Nederlandt* arrived, they sent two of their families and six other men to settle on its banks. These stayed for only two years, but since then an extensive trade in furs had grown up. According to Bradford, when De Rasières visited New Plymouth in 1627, "seeing us seated in a barren quarter," he invited the English to come and live at the Fresh River. "But our hands being full otherwise, we let it pass."

The Dutch suggestion was followed by an appeal from the Mohicans. Driven from the Hudson by the fierce Mohawk tribes, they had settled on the Fresh River, where they were now being overrun by Pequots. In the hope of securing strong allies, they begged the English to come and settle there too. They had to wait till 1632 when Edward Winslow, at the time the energetic governor of New Plymouth, made a trip to the river and discovered it "to be a fine place." Realizing that it would be impossible to hold the river without a trading house, he picked out a spot and it was soon occupied by a handful of English traders.[5]

The Dutch on Manhattan, noticing the sudden activities of the English on the river—and having forgotten De Rasières' offer, if it was ever made—decided to move fast. In June 1633 Van Twiller sent his commissary Jacob van Curler to the Pequot Indians who lived on the banks of the Fresh River—"in their tongue, Connettecuck"—with instructions to purchase from their chief a piece of land "one league down along the river and one third of a league in width to the high land." Van Curler was instructed to construct

CROWDING ON

a trading house at once, which was christened optimistically the House of Good Hope and fortified with two cannon.[6]

In New Plymouth the news was received with concern. The Pilgrims did not feel themselves strong enough to tackle the Dutch singlehanded, and Bradford and Winslow appealed to their new neighbor, the Puritan settlement at Massachusetts Bay. Its governor, John Winthrop, had arrived with a party of nine hundred settlers only three years earlier, and although he was interested in reports of the beaver treasure and the rich agricultural soil around the Fresh River, he felt that his people were not ready for expansion. The Pilgrims realized that they must go it alone. They built a big bark, put the frame of a house onto it, and in September 1633, under the command of Lieutenant William Holmes, they sailed defiantly upriver to the spot Winslow had selected.

When they arrived at Good Hope, the Dutch stopped them and asked where they were going. The English answered: "Up the river to trade," and Van Curler burst out: "Strike and stay or we will shoot you." But the traders showed him their commission from the governor of New Plymouth and sailed on. "The Dutch threaten us hard, yet they shoot not," remarked Bradford later triumphantly.[7]

Nine miles upriver Holmes and his men erected the prefabricated fort, built a stockade, and bought the land from the Indians —in this case the first tenants, the Mohicans.

Winthrop in Boston soon had second thoughts and sent John Oldham as a spy to the Connecticut. He returned to tell of "many very desirable places upon the same river, fit to receive many hundred inhabitants," and to urge the governor not to give away to the Dutch this property of the King of England. Winthrop dispatched the newly-built thirty-ton bark *Blessing of the Bay*— the first small product of Massachusetts' wharves—to New Amsterdam to remind Van Twiller of English rights on the Connecticut.[8]

Van Twiller wrote back a conciliatory letter on October 4, 1633, arguing that "in this parte of the world are diverse heathen lands that are emptye of inhabitants, so that a little parte or portion thereof there needs not any question." He thought it would be better to leave the "limits and parting of these quarters" to the States and the King, and he made it clear that in the meantime business would go on as before.[9]

A translation of this letter from "Gualter of Twilley" was hastily sent to the Council of New England, but this moribund institution was unable to react, and Winthrop made an appeal to his brother-in-law, the well-known Puritan lawyer Emmanuel Downing. "I understand of ill news from New England," wrote Downing in December to Secretary of State Coke, ". . . the Dutch have intruded upon the principal and best river in New England." But the Secretary had other worries, and anyway, by August 1634 the news was better. "The Dutch will now be confined to their boundes, unless they mean to fight for more," reported Downing.[10]

He had probably heard how seventy Dutch soldiers, sent from New Amsterdam by Van Twiller, "in warlike manner with colours displayed," had failed to chase away the determined Pilgrim traders. This time the failure of the Dutch troops could not be blamed on Van Twiller's incompetence. He was very eager to attack, but the company, misjudging the danger, had discouraged him from military action.[11]

Winthrop and Downing had other reasons for believing that they had got the better of the Dutch. The Pequot Indians, who had sold the land to Van Curler, came to Boston in the autumn of 1634 to appeal to the English. In the contract with Van Curler it was stipulated that the House of Good Hope should be neutral ground to which all the warring tribes "might freely and without any danger resort for the purpose of trade." Its neutrality had not been respected. The Pequots had killed not only some of their own Mohawk enemies near the fort, but also Captain Stone, the Virginian who had tried to steal a Plymouth ship from New Amsterdam a year earlier, and who had been trading with the Dutch at Good Hope. Van Curler had retaliated by executing the murderers, and the incensed Pequots sent envoys to Boston in the hope of getting the English on their side.[12]

Till then fear of the bloodthirsty river tribes had been one of the obstacles to Puritan settlement on the river. So Massachusetts jumped at this chance and before the end of 1634 a treaty was signed with the Pequots that gave Boston all the trade on the Connecticut. In the winter that followed, "the hand of God" made trading even safer in the region—an epidemic of smallpox almost wiped out the Indians. Some Dutch fur traders came back from the forests to tell the Pilgrim traders how they had spent the winter with a remote

CROWDING ON

tribe and almost starved to death in the snow and freezing cold, "for it has pleased God to visit these Indians with a great sickness, and such a mortalitie that of a 1000, 900 . . . of them dyed, and many of them did rot above ground for want of buriall."[13]

Bradford, who learned the news in New Plymouth, was less than pleased by it because his neighbors from the Bay Colony, "understanding that the Indians were swept away with the late great mortalitie," now came in swarms to the Connecticut with the blessing of the General Court of Massachusetts."[14]

Winthrop's people forged ahead relentlessly, and were soon trying to elbow their Plymouth compatriots out of the way. One of the Pilgrim traders, Jonathan Brewster, wrote angrily to New Plymouth: "The Massachusetts men are coming almost dayly some by water, and some by land, who are not yet determined where to settle, though some have a great mind to the place we are upon." The Plymouth men at first tried to be helpful, and escorted some of the Boston newcomers downriver to the Dutch settlement to see if they might be allowed to settle near the House of Good Hope. The Dutch refused, and the fate of the Plymouth post was sealed. A group from Dorchester in Massachusetts settled down around the blockhouse, determined that if they could not throw out the Pilgrims, "they should have but a smale moyety left to the house." Windsor was founded.[15]

New Plymouth protested this un-Christian behavior, reproaching Boston with having "cast a rather partial if not covetous eye upon that which is your neighbours." Massachusetts' answer was bland. "We at first judged the place so free that we might with God's good leave take and use it . . . it being the Lord's wast." Plymouth replied sharply that "if it was the Lord's wast, it was themselves that had found it so and not they." But after another group of Massachusetts invaders from Watertown arrived, followed in 1636 by the whole population of Newtown, New Plymouth gave up. "To make any forcibel resistance was far from their thoughts," commented Bradford. Instead they sold fifteen-sixteenths of their share in the Connecticut possessions.[16]

The Dutch watched with disbelief the English fighting over what they considered company territory. Their own station was slowly being engulfed by a tide of emigrants from Newtown under their pastor, Thomas Hooker, who founded what is now called Hartford. The Dutch refused to give in so easily, and kept

A SWEET AND ALIEN LAND

up the struggle for some time longer than the Plymouth Puritans. The episode at least brought them an ally in their future struggles with the English. New Plymouth, which, as the Dutch commissary later wrote, has "as much cause to complain of Windsor as we have of Hartford," never forgave Massachusetts' high-handed behavior and never wholeheartedly supported plans to usurp Dutch land.[17]

Dutch historians have attacked the Pilgrims of New Plymouth on the ground that they ought to have left New Netherland in peace after the Dutch hospitality they had enjoyed in Leiden and Amsterdam. "It can scarcely be believed that men so conscientious, that they considered themselves in duty bound not to make the least concession in any disputed point about religious rituals . . . should so little care about their Netherland neighbors of the same profession, should so little respect their anterior possession," wrote one of them. But apart from the incident on the Connecticut, New Plymouth was always a very unaggressive neighbor, and the Dutch could thank Massachusetts for the fact.[18]

While the Dutch and English colonists squabbled among themselves for possession of the Connecticut, a deal going through in London raised another threat to the Dutch occupancy of the river. It was the result of intensive in-fighting among all those in England with a stake in North America. Chief among them was the aging Sir Ferdinando Gorges, for whom the huge North American territory granted to his Council of New England in 1620 had never lost its fascination. That body had by now dwindled to a mere two members—himself and the Earl of Warwick.

During Gorges' absence in 1628 Warwick, an enthusiastic Puritan, had given away a sizable chunk of the Council's territory to the New England Company, largely Puritan in interest. At once a party of settlers under John Endicott had left and set up Salem. The following March the company was transformed by a royal charter into the Massachusetts Bay Company, and by the time Gorges returned to London, the Great Puritan Emigration was under way. To his horror, he discovered that Warwick had given away the land he had already assigned to his son Robert. Efforts by Robert to save some of it failed—he was "thrust out by the

CROWDING ON

intruders"—and not surprisingly Sir Ferdinando was bitterly hostile to these Puritans, who, as he complained to the King, with their "new laws, new conceits of matters of religion," had "surreptilliously" grabbed his land. He now formally surrendered his own patent, "with reservation of the lawful right," trusting that the King would restore some order to the chaos.[19]

Meanwhile Charles I, who had heard other complaints about the autocratic Puritans, had taken the affairs of New England into his own hands, appointing a subcommittee of the Privy Council to investigate Massachusetts. The Bay Colony settlers heard of this threat to their existence with alarm; and they were more alarmed still when in 1634 the committee was transformed into a Commission for Regulating Plantations, headed by their archenemy William Laud, now Archbishop of Canterbury and the most influential person in Charles' government. Gorges was delighted, and felt that his dreams were about to be realized when the King appointed him governor, recognizing him as the man "who made the first discovery of those coasts and understands the state of those countries." All former charters were revoked, and nobody was to be allowed to settle in New England without the permission of Sir Ferdinando.[20]

Unfortunately for Gorges, New England was three thousand miles away, the King had not a penny to spare, and he himself was without funds. The old man had never been lucky in his transatlantic plans: when he had been about to go to New England for the first time in 1632, he fell from his horse and complained of being "in soe much extreme of paine as I'm not able to move or stir." And in 1634 the ship that was being built to take him to his promised land broke as it was being launched.[21]

The Puritans had not waited for his arrival to go into action. The governor of New Plymouth, Edward Winslow, left for London in 1633 to ask the new Lords Commissioners for protection against the Dutch on the Connecticut, "where they have raised a forte and threaten to expell your petitioners thence." Boston asked him to put in a word for that colony, but after all the trouble between its people and the Plymouth men on the Connecticut, it perhaps did not count on the wholehearted support of Winslow. It was well Boston didn't expect too much. Winslow had hardly arrived in London when he was thrown into prison by Laud, on the ground that he was a dissenter from the Established Church.

A SWEET AND ALIEN LAND

It was clear that the Laud Commission meant business.[22]

But so did the Puritans in Massachusetts. Emigration to the Bay had been swelling in the last few years, and the colony itself was already showing signs of an independent spirit. The Puritan colonists were often men of considerable means and education, dogmatic and pious. They had believed before they left England that they would readily convert the Indians, as a contemporary ballad reveals:

> The native people, though yet wyld,
> Are all by nature kinde and mylde,
> And apt already (by reporte)
> To live in this religious sorte.[23]

And they had no intention of letting Laud interfere with the building of the true "City of God," free of bishops and prayer books and ceremonies, on the other side of the Atlantic.

They decided to send their own envoy and selected the twenty-nine-year-old son of their governor. John Winthrop Jr. was a man of wide-ranging interests and talents, charming, sympathetic, and persuasive. He would have been outstanding in any European capital. In New England he was unique—and the obvious choice. When he sailed in 1634 he had instructions to try to delay any activity of the Lords Commissioners, and at the same time to recruit more of the right kind of English colonists for Massachusetts.[24]

The question of delay took care of itself. Charles I had growing domestic problems, and his attention was soon deflected from the colonies. Winthrop's efforts at recruitment were also successful—but perhaps not quite in the way Boston had had in mind. While in England he married the eighteen-year-old Elizabeth Reade, a young lady to whom the Puritans could have no objection, since she was the stepdaughter of one of their staunchest supporters, the Reverend Hugh Peter.[25]

The Massachusetts officials would have been less pleased if they had heard about another courtship of their young envoy in London. A group of wealthy and influential English Puritans, of whom two (Viscount Saye and Sele, and Baron Brooke) were peers with plenty of influence at Court, wished to create their own American domain. They operated on the basis of a charter given

CROWDING ON

to Robert Rich, second Earl of Warwick, in 1632, which was as imprecise as most. It covered a slice of America from the Narragansett River down to Manhattan and was never legally confirmed.

These "men of qualitie" had been greatly taken with the charming and able Winthrop. On July 7, 1635, the day after his wedding, they asked him to plant their new colony, and he accepted. Storm clouds were gathering over England, the outlook for Puritanism seemed dark, and what these important investors seem to have had in mind was the creation of a well-founded Puritan bolt hole on the other side of the Atlantic, independent of the middle-class autocrats of Massachusetts. Winthrop was asked at once to get under construction some "convenient buildings for the receipt of Gentlemen," since "there are like to come more over next summer." He was to recruit fifty workmen in Massachusetts.[26]

In the circumstances the welcome that John Winthrop Jr. received from Boston in October 1635 was less than warm, and it was five months before the magistrates there recognized his legal title to the land. But Winthrop wasted no time. Hearing that the New Amsterdammers were planning a more extensive occupation on the Connecticut, he sent an advance party to Kievitts Hook, on Long Island Sound, in November. Arriving at the mouth of the Connecticut, the Englishmen found the usual symbol of Dutch occupation—a sign painted with the arms of the States General, which had been fixed to a tree three years earlier. Irreverently they tore it down and nailed up in its place the painting of "a ridiculous face." A party sent by Van Twiller to stop the English settlement left without being able to do anything.[27]

At the end of March 1636 the younger Winthrop himself was at last able to follow his advance party. He traveled on *Blessing of the Bay*, together with his engineer Lionel Gardiner. This Scotsman, married to a Dutch girl from Woerden, had become an expert on the construction of fortifications while in the Dutch Army. Winthrop's stepfather Hugh Peter had engaged him in Rotterdam for the Puritan investors, who sent him at an annual salary of one hundred pounds to the Connecticut River, with instructions to build a strong fort—a task he carried out with zeal and without loyalty to his former Dutch teachers. This first settlement was named Saybrook by Winthrop, in honor of his employers, and if it never grew into an important town, it was nevertheless the first

A SWEET AND ALIEN LAND

major step in the career of this Englishman, who many years later was to play a key role in the decline and fall of New Amsterdam.

To Van Twiller in the capital, it was already clear that the Fresh River could be written off by the Dutch. The English had embarked with conviction on the policy that was a few years later so well described by Sir William Boswell, English ambassador to The Hague, as "crowding the Dutch out of those places they have. . . ." The Heeren XIX in Amsterdam, however, preferred to close their eyes for the moment. Possibly they believed that the English invasion was an easy and cheap way to populate their colony and hoped that these foreigners would respect Dutch rights and leave their fur trade alone.[28]

Van Twiller knew better. In 1637 his tiny band in the House of Good Hope was surrounded by 800 English, of whom 150 were of fighting age. He warned the company that "those on the Fresh River . . . are well stocked with goods and do not let any skins go by if they are to be had." And he added that if the West India Company expected to remain the exclusive traders, "they will be defeated." It was no longer necessary to be a prophet to foresee this.[29]

A

NEW THREAT

The failure of the Heeren XIX to react to the appeals of their director general in New Netherland for support against English aggression was not entirely due to inertia. The fact was that they had by now lost all confidence in Wouter van Twiller, and even his uncle Kiliaen van Rensselaer was no longer able to save him.

It was Lubbertus van Dincklage who started the ball rolling. The schout, whom Van Twiller had so warmly welcomed in 1634, had soon fallen out with him—and strangely enough with Everardus Bogardus, the governor's archenemy, as well. After violent rows, Van Twiller sacked him and sent him home without pay. In Amsterdam a resentful Van Dincklage composed a memorial to the States General in which he attacked the maladministration of their province in North America. He related how he had been excommunicated by Dominie Borgardus, and "that consequently such procedures had been started against him, that he had been forced to hide in the wilderness, where by lack of the necessary food he had fed himself for twelve days with the grass of the fields."[1]

David de Vries had once more been a spectator of the chaos reigning in the province, and with his usual bluntness reported the facts to Amsterdam. Alcohol played a prominent part in these incidents—as on the occasion in June 1636 when De Vries took Van Twiller and Bogardus for a trip to the domain of Pavonia, where they were welcomed by Commissary Cornelis van Vorst. The object of their visit was the Bordeaux that Van Vorst had brought back from New England—"as the commander was fond of tasting good wines." Well in their cups, the three began a heated argument about a murder recently committed in Pavonia, but De Vries successfully calmed them and they parted good friends. For the fuddled Van Vorst, however, this "friendship" had a highly unpleasant sequel. When he attempted to celebrate it with a salvo from the pebble gun in front of his house, "a spark flew on the house, which was thatched with rushes, and in half an hour it was entirely consumed."[2]

In his memorial Van Dincklage—who, as Van Rensselaer wrote to his nephew, was a lawyer and therefore could "see deeper into a matter"—dwelt less on these private drunken brawls than on the amount of land that Van Twiller and some of his associates were greedily appropriating for themselves. On Long Island, for instance, the director general had helped himself to at least ten thousand acres, giving more to the company official Jacob van Curler. (This was the nucleus of New Amersfoort, now Flatlands, the first settlement on Long Island.) In 1637 Van Twiller extended his personal holdings by buying Nut Island (Governor's Island) and two smaller islands in the Hellgate.[3]

But while Van Twiller prospered privately, the affairs of the West India Company and the community in New Netherland went from bad to worse. For the Heeren XIX, the expenses were disturbing, and furs from the province no longer covered their outlay. For the New Netherlanders, the harvest from their neglected farms was no longer adequate; they survived only by buying corn from the Indians. The only way they could make any money was by smuggling and illicit dealings with the Indians—again to the detriment of the company.

By 1637 the denunciations of Van Dincklage had had their effect both on the States General and the Heeren XIX, and it was decided to recall Van Twiller. On September 6 they appointed his successor, Willem Kieft.

Uncle Kiliaen, greatly concerned for the family reputation, wrote two weeks later to his nephew, urging him to come back as soon as possible "so that you may clear yourself at least from the unbearable slanders, with which the fiscal [Van Dincklage] and his wife have besmirched your person through the whole land."[4]

A NEW THREAT

The New Amsterdammers welcomed their third director general with suspicion when on March 28, 1638, he arrived on board the company ship *Haring*. The officials dreaded a timely spring cleaning, which was certain to raise a lot of dust, and the settlers had only a faint hope that this new representative of the Heeren XIX would turn out to be any better than his predecessors. As it happened, both were right.

The appointment of Willem Kieft, who came from Amsterdam, where his grandfather had been a highly esteemed magistrate, was another aberration on the part of the Lords Directors. Nothing in his past recommended him for this important post. Significantly, perhaps, no man ever called Kieft his friend, and no one spoke in his favor. His enemies, on the other hand, were numerous. A pamphlet, *Broad Advice*, published in Antwerp by some of them, revealed that Kieft as a merchant, "having attended to his own and his masters business a long time at Rochelle, . . . neglected it" and had failed. His portrait had been fixed to a gallows to put him to shame, and he had left France "in a hurry." Later he had been employed to ransom some Christians from the Turks. "The money was entrusted to this bankrupt; and he went and released some Christians for whom the least was to be paid; but others, whose friends had contributed the most money, he let stay there."[5]

Kieft was well educated (he wrote Latin and spoke a little English) but he was certainly not intelligent. All the evidence shows him to have been an arrogant, short-tempered, and authoritarian man who would admit no opposition. It was probably precisely these qualities that recommended him to the Heeren XIX. What they wanted at this juncture was a director general who would get tough with their province, put an end to the spate of scandals that was giving it a bad name in the Netherlands, and above all, make it pay.

Kieft set about this task with a will. He began by immediately appointing a Council that gave him absolute power. It consisted of himself (with two votes) and one other man, Dr. Johannes La Montagne, to whom he gave one vote. The forty-four-year-old La Montagne, a pleasant and rather irresolute Walloon, had arrived a year previously. He was a "learned gentleman" who had studied

A SWEET AND ALIEN LAND

medicine and law at Leiden. There he had become close friends with Jesse de Forest and his family, and he was one of the signatories of the round robin of 1621 applying for permission to emigrate to Virginia. He sailed with De Forest, was with him when he died, and was almost certainly the author of an account of this voyage published as *Jesse de Forest's Journal.* By 1625, now thirty-one years of age, he was back in Leiden, where he married one of his beloved De Forest family, the seventeen-year-old Rachel. After a stay of six years in Tobago, he arrived in New Amsterdam on March 5, 1637, on board the *Van Rensselaerswyck* with Rachel and their three children.[6]

Kieft immediately selected this dignified Huguenot, who had set up a chandlery, for his Council and engaged him at a salary of thirty-five guilders a month. His other officials were a more characteristic choice. One was Cornelis van Tienhoven, a shifty and loud-mouthed *bon vivant* who had been keeping the company books ever since his arrival with Van Twiller five years earlier. The New Amsterdammers thought little of him, but the distant company was satisfied and had recommended him to Kieft as his secretary. Van Tienhoven got a considerable raise—to a monthly salary of thirty-six guilders, plus two hundred guilders a year for board. The German Ulrich Lupolt was at first kept on by Kieft as his schout, or sherrif, but a year later was replaced by Cornelis van der Huygens. The way Kieft dealt with these appointments made it obvious to the people of New Netherland that they were to have no say at all in their affairs, and soon they were complaining: "Had we been under a king, we could not be worse treated."[7]

The company's officials had no reason to be better pleased. Kieft put an end to their personal deals by issuing a proclamation forbidding them to trade for furs with the natives, or to export any article without declaring it first. To stop smuggling, he forbade sailors to remain ashore after sunset, and private communication between ship and shore became an offense. He attempted to bring order to the chaos of the company offices by ordering the clerks to clock in and out at fixed times. To discourage immoderate drinking, he withdrew the licenses from all taverns except "those who sold wine at a decent price and in moderate quantitie." And finally he warned the whole population "to abstain from fighting; from carnal intercourse with heathens, blacks or other persons; from rebellion, theft, false swearing, calumny, and all other immoralities." In short, New Netherland was to be compelled to grow from a pioneer community into a civilized province, where a court would sit in judgment every Thursday on the morals of its inhabitants.[8]

Kieft's first measures were by no means excessive. The fur traders and sailors who lived permanently or temporarily in New Amsterdam were a rough lot. Drinking and fighting were their favorite pastimes. There had been several executions for manslaughter, and a great many convictions for theft.

When Kieft arrived, the city even had its own prostitute, Griet Reyniers, wife of one of the most colorful people in the settlement, the mulatto Anthony Jansz van Salee or van Vees, nicknamed the Turk. Born in the Moroccan port of Fez that had given him his name, Anthony was the son of a Dutch buccaneer, Jan Jansen, who had become admiral to Sultan Muley Zidan. The Turk arrived at New Amsterdam in 1630 and was soon singled out for his size and muscular build by Griet, a former barmaid from Amsterdam, after her arrival in 1633. She had traveled on the *Southberg* with Van Twiller and other officials, and had not been mean with her favors to these gentlemen, but Van Salee had no objection to this, and attempted to make an honest woman of her. The marriage was fairly stormy, and excited bystanders once rushed to tell Schout Lupolt of a punch-up between the two during which Griet threatened to smash the skulls of her two children—the fruits of her profession—against a wall. She told her husband that she was fed up with being a "nobleman's whore" and that in future she would prefer a real he-man of a "Jan Hagel" or Jack Tar.

The Court of New Amsterdam attempted to prove its authority by condemning her and her husband to "eternal banishment and payment of the costs." Its ruling merely demonstrated its ineffectuality, since the couple hung on for some time, and only finally traveled as far as s'Gravesande on Long Island.[9]

All this went on in a city that must have shocked Kieft when he arrived. The streets were muddy lanes where hogs and goats roamed freely. The houses, scattered about haphazardly, were built entirely of timber, including the chimneys, and roofed with reed or straw. The public buildings constructed under Van Twiller were badly in need of repair, and the first five stone houses were in ruins. In no way did the place resemble the clean, orderly cities of the Fatherland.

The fort was in even worse shape, but that was hardly Van

Twiller's fault. Under the supervision of master builder Jacob van Stoffelsen, the company's Negro slaves had worked for three years at repairing the walls. It was finished in 1635 and had cost the penny-pinching company 4,127 guilders and 10 stuivers, a modest price for a fort about 300 feet long and 250 feet broad. The Heeren XIX for once had nothing to grumble about, but their economy turned out to be a false one. By August 1636 Van Twiller was already complaining that the fort was falling into ruin, "as it is built up of wooden pallisades, which at present are completely decayed," and he told the company that it was essential to rebuild it entirely of stone, "as the pallisades can not stand more than three or four years at the most." Van Twiller's prediction proved accurate. Stoffelsen testified later that at his arrival, "Mijnheer Kieft found Fort Amsterdam totally and wholly in a ruinous condition."[10]

Outside the capital, Kieft inspected the six bouweries. Number One had been leased by Van Twiller, who had built there a large house, an excellent barn, a boathouse, and a brewery "covered with tiles." But while this bouwery looked prosperous, the others were in a dismal state of decay. It was obvious to Kieft that New Netherland was badly in need of more farmers, and he lost no time in appealing to Amsterdam. The Lords Directors, under pressure from their shareholders and the States General, which was taking an unexpected interest in New Netherland, had come to the same conclusion. But how to induce the Dutch to go?

Already in 1633 the West India Company had tried to convince the States that it was almost impossible to find anybody interested in emigrating—"all those who want work here [in the Republic] can earn their living easily," they wrote in a memorial, "and don't feel tempted to leave their homes for an uncertain future." The Heeren XIX felt they had done all they could for the moment, and turned their attention to their other, and more important, possessions. The company had reached its zenith around this time. It had debts of eighteen million guilders, but on the other hand, it was sovereign over vast territories. In South America lay the crown of its properties, the northern part of Brazil, conquered from the Portuguese. In the West Indies it called Curaçao and other islands its own; in Africa it held the most important stations of the Gold Coast and the slave market of Angola. With so many richer and more profitable colonies, it was not surprising that it considered

New Netherland no more than a "step-child."[11]

The States initially accepted the company's indifference toward New Netherland, but, aroused by the importance that England appeared to attach to the American coast, it sent in 1637 an unusually sharp questionnaire to the Heeren XIX. "Whereas the Lords States-General," it began, "obtain unreliable information on the affairs of New Netherland; that it is retrograding more and more, to the injury of this state and its inhabitants it is demanded . . .," and there followed seven questions. In the first place the States wanted to know if the original limits of the province were still intact, and if the company was able to defend itself against intruders. If there had been intruders, by what right had they come? Another important point the questionnaire raised was that of profit or loss. Finally, the States proposed to take the government of the province into its own hands.[12]

The Lords Directors, angry and dismayed, sent on April 30, 1638, their answers—almost as short as the questions. No, they no longer had the original limits, because "the English extend now from New England into the Fresh River." There was no question of right or wrong, as "the right is that of the strongest." No, the company had not made a profit, but the possibility existed, mainly from grain. No, they had no intention of handing New Netherland over to the States, "unless they derived profit by it." They added as a softener that since they could "not people it themselves, a plan of throwing it open must be considered."[13]

Vague plans were indeed in preparation, but nothing much was being done about them, and in exasperation the States appointed a special committee, which at last came up with a solution: after sixteen years the company's monopoly would be virtually abolished. In the resolution that was adopted in September 1639, the Company's fur monopoly was ended, restrictions on trade were considerably eased, and the cultivation of the soil was thrown open to everyone, "denizens or foreigners." Free passage was now promised to any farmer and his family. Each settler would be furnished with a farm for six years, if he took with him enough laborers, four horses, four cows, sheep, swine, and farming implements. He would only have to pay a rent of one hundred guilders a year, plus eighty pounds of butter. The director general was ordered at the same time to give the immigrant as much land as he could cultivate. But a proposal to give more people the opportu-

A SWEET AND ALIEN LAND

nity to become a patroon was resisted by the Heeren XIX, who preferred to reserve this privilege to themselves.[14]

Kiliaen van Rensselaer, who had now been a patroon for ten years, was astonished by the company's lack of foresight, "for instead of the many poor beggars it now gets, it would find people of means who with their money could send all sorts of men." He wrote to Kieft on May 12, 1639: "If the Company admits no more colonies, the bounds of New Netherland will not be extended but contracted and approached upon, as is done even now by the English as well as the Swedes." In the end he got what he wanted. In July 1640 the Lords Directors gave in, and extended the patroonship to "all good inhabitants of the Netherlands" who could afford to send over fifty settlers in three years. A Dutchman who could go over with five persons would become a "master."[15]

This change in company policy had limited success: within a few years New Netherland had more than one hundred farms instead of the meager six Kieft found on his arrival. But the "rush" had its disadvantages. As Van Rensselaer had foreseen, many of the colonists came over to get rich quick through fur dealing rather than farming, and in the end the province derived little profit from these adventurers, who would always outnumber the bona fide settlers.

In his letter to Kieft of May 1639 Van Rensselaer had spoken of a Swedish encroachment on New Netherland, a threat discovered only a few days after the governor's arrival in 1638. This Swedish invasion took place with the knowledge, and the full cooperation, of one of the Heeren XIX: he was Samuel Bloemaerts, who had considerable connections in Sweden, owned a large brass factory outside Stockholm, and was Sweden's representative in Holland. The leader of the Swedish expedition was another old acquaintance of the Dutch West India Company, none other than their own former director general, Peter Minuit, who had bought Manhattan for them in 1626, and been sacked five years later. In 1634 Minuit, restless and jobless in Amsterdam, had been invited by Bloemaerts to lead the expedition.

The Swedes had been talking for years about the possibility of a colony in America. The idea had come originally from Willem

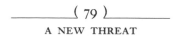

Usselinx, once the eccentric dreamer of a Dutch Eldorado in the colonies. He had left the greedy Republic in 1624, and had found the willing ear of King Gustavus Adolphus of Sweden. In 1627 a company was formed in Stockholm with the ambitious object of trading with Africa, Asia, and America. The prosperity of Holland was a powerful incentive to the Swedes, as the prospectus of the Royal Swedish General Trading Company showed. The Republic "has become so powerful by . . . voyages to the East Indies, Guinea and other distant places, that it has already been able to resist the king of Spain," it said, glancing with envy at Amsterdam, where "the inhabitants have become rich . . . as it were sleeping. And in all this time Sweden had until the present day lost or not shared in all the aforesaid profits . . . because its inhabitants were not willing to risk in anything extraordinary."[16]

The Swedes were not asked to "risk in anything" for a while, since the death of their King on a German battlefield put a stop to the plan. It was shelved until January 1, 1634, when the Swedish government under Chancellor Axel Oxenstierna—possibly full of good resolve for the New Year—asked the still active Usselinx to help raise funds for the semidefunct trading company. When Usselinx traveled to Holland in the hope of interesting Dutch capital, he found the doors and the safes locked against him. The Dutch were no longer willing to let foreigners enjoy the advantages of their trade in the western hemisphere.

Oxenstierna realized that he was betting on the wrong horse, and on his way home from a visit to France, he stopped off at Amsterdam, where he called on Sweden's commissary, Samuel Bloemaerts, to discuss the American affair. The Dutchman understood perfectly well Sweden's need for new outlets for its important copper and brass industry, and he told the Chancellor that Usselinx was by no means the right man for such an important affair, "as he had neither the respect nor the credit."[17]

Bloemaerts now took matters into his own hands and approached Peter Minuit as the very man for such an enterprise. The ex-governor grasped the opportunity with both hands and by the autumn of 1635 was in Sweden, where he composed a memorial for Oxenstierna urging that Sweden "no longer . . . abstain from making her name known in foreign countries." To capture part of the New World, he demanded a ship, twelve cannon, a crew of twenty to twenty-five, cargo for trade with the Indians estimated at ten thousand guilders, and supplies for twelve months.[18]

Long and secret negotiations followed between the Swedes on one hand, and Bloemaerts and Minuit on the other, and at the end of 1636 the Swedes decided to take the plunge at a total cost of twenty-four thousand guilders, of which half came from Bloemaerts and Minuit personally. The result was a patent that gave the Swedish-Dutch Company the exclusive right to trade for twenty years on the Delaware—an area well known to Bloemaerts, who had once possessed there the domain of Swanendael, which in 1635 he had sold back to the company for sixteen thousand guilders.[19]

A time of great activity began for Minuit. Two ships had to be equipped and manned with thirty-six men each; thousands of yards of duffel, a hundred axes, hatchets and knives, mirrors and gilded chains, rings and combs for trade with the Indians had to be bought. The first settlers destined for the colony arrived, and by the end of November the two ships *Kalmar Nyckel* ("Key of Calmar") and *Fogel Grip* ("Griffin") were ready to sail. The Swedish invasion was under way.

Van Rensselaer was at that time still an innocent contributor to the enterprise. When Minuit's ship put in at Texel to shelter from storms in December 1637, the patroon brought him several cases of merchandise and six settlers for his domain. Van Rensselaer paid him 220 guilders for their transport, asking Minuit to deliver them to New Amsterdam.[20]

Ten days later, on December 31, the Swedish ships left Holland, bound, as Minuit reported to the Dutch, for Virginia. He did indeed arrive there in March, but stayed only ten days to take on fresh water. From Jamestown an incredulous Jerome Hawley wrote to London that a ship had come with a commission from the "yong Queene of Sweden" to go to the Delaware to make a plantation and plant tobacco like the Dutch at Hudson. "All which being His Mats territorys, I humbly offer the consideration there of. . . and yf his Matie shall be pleased to think upon any course . . . for removing them."[21]

By the time the letter reached London, Minuit's fifty colonists were already entrenched on a tributary of the Delaware. He had prudently given New Amsterdam a wide berth, sailing straight to Fort Nassau on the Delaware, where he told the Dutch that he was on his way to the West Indies. A few days later Minuit "threw off his disguise," and while his colonists were busily making a small

A NEW THREAT

garden for "raising salads, pot-herbs and the like," he was deeply involved in negotiations with the Indians. Thirteen years later their sachem, Mattehoorn, told a committee in New Amsterdam that "when Minuyt came to the country with a ship, he lay before the Minquas Kill, where the Sachem then had a house and lived; that Minuyt presented him with a kettle and other trifles, requesting of him as much land as Minuyt could set a house on, and a plantation included between six trees, which he, the Sachem, sold him and Minuyt promised half the tobacco that would grow on the plantation." With regret he added that "it was never given to him."[22]

As soon as the transaction was concluded on March 29, 1638, work was begun on a fort about fifteen miles below Fort Nassau. By the time Kieft in New Amsterdam heard about the Swedish doings on the Delaware, the fort (at what is now Wilmington) had already been completed and named after the twelve-year-old Swedish Queen, Christina. New Sweden was born.

On May 6 Kieft sent off an indignant letter in which he reminded his predecessor, "who style yourself commander in the service of Her Royal Majesty of Sweden," that the river was Dutch. It had been "secured above and below by forts and sealed with our blood, which even happened during your administration of New Netherland." He threatened to uphold Dutch jurisdiction "in such manner as we shall deem most expedient."

Minuit departed, unperturbed, in the *Kalmar Nyckel* in June on his way to Florida. But he never arrived. Stopping at the island of St. Christopher in the lesser Antilles, he was invited for dinner on board the Dutch ship *Vliegende Hert* ("Flying Deer"), and during the feast the ship was driven out to sea in a sudden squall and disappeared without a trace. Later that year the *Kalmar Nyckel* arrived without Minuit at the Dutch port of Medemblik, where it was detained for a year.

It was the only retaliation the Dutch made that year against the Swedish enterprise. Kieft's menaces were hollow since he simply did not have enough troops to attack Fort Christina, which was protected by twenty-four soldiers. In the end he would not regret it. The ever-encroaching English had rediscovered the Delaware, and soon enough the Dutch governor needed the Swedes as his allies against his greedy neighbors.

DOUBTFUL NEIGHBORS

The English neighbors who in 1639 were studying with so much interest the prospect of a settlement on the Delaware—"the Amazon of North America"—were in fact already living within the technical boundaries of New Netherland, only about sixty miles from New Amsterdam. They were a group of unbending Puritans, headed by the autocratic Theophilus Eaton, and his former schoolmate, the Reverend John Davenport. Fleeing Laud's increasing threats to Nonconformists, they had come to North America and settled initially at Boston. But they were ambitious to set up a mercantile colony, and finding that there were no decent harbors left within the Bay Colony, they moved on and finally settled in 1638 at the mouth of the River Quinnipiac, a place they optimistically named New Haven.

The colony was wealthy to begin with, many of its members being London "merchants of considerable estates and dealing in the world," who had once been parishioners of the Reverend Davenport in his City church of St. Stephens. When that indefatigable traveler Captain David de Vries stopped there in 1639, he counted three hundred houses and saw a "fine church."[1]

But the expense of the transatlantic move (which had been made in style), the winter in Boston, and the finely-built houses of the neat little town had eaten into the colony's capital. It never managed to get a patent—the Dutch called it a "pretended colony"

—and its fine dreams of commercial expansion seemed doomed to disappointment. In 1639, however, they were revived by the energetic George Lamberton, one of the settlement's leading spirits. Trading to Virginia in his bark the *Cock*, he entered the Delaware to find the Dutch at Fort Nassau and the Swedes at Fort Christina fully occupied in the fur trade. Lamberton sailed jubilantly back to New Haven to report his discovery. While the merchants there happily contemplated their prospects, he sailed again to the Delaware in 1640, with an associate, Captain Turner. He had been instructed to buy land on the banks of the Delaware (still the South River to the Dutch), but to be careful not to upset the Dutch or the Swedes. When the *Cock* arrived in the river, Lamberton ignored his orders and made an attempt to buy land near the two forts within the Dutch boundaries. The Indians, for once, were surprisingly loyal to the Dutch and refused to sell.

Lamberton now received help from an unexpected quarter. The New Englanders had recently fought and won a bloody war with the Pequot Indians from the Connecticut Valley, many of whom had fled to the Delaware, and it was one of their sachems who came to the rescue of the New Haven enterprise. "He, taking notice of the English and their desire, persuaded the other sachems to deal with them," noted an impressed John Winthrop Sr. in his journal. The Indian had told his tribesmen "that howsoever they [the English] had killed his countrymen and driven them out, they were honest men and had just cause to do as they did, for the Pequots had done them wrong." The other chiefs were obviously as impressed as Winthrop, since they "let them have what land they desired."[2]

And the English desired a lot. Lamberton, watched warily by the Dutch and the Swedes, bought land on both sides of the river without any respect for Swedish rights. He even encouraged the Indians to pull up the boundary poles bearing the Swedish coat of arms and to bring them back to Governor Peter Ridder at Fort Christina. Loaded with furs and their pockets full of title deeds, Lamberton and Turner sailed to New Haven, where the elated merchants started to organize a Puritan crusade. At a session of the General Court on August 6, 1641, it was decided to found a Delaware Company "for the advancement of public good in a way of trade, so also for the settling of churches and plantations in those parts." The general approval was "expressed by holding up of

A SWEET AND ALIEN LAND

hands." New Haven had officially moved in on the South River.[3]

When Governor Kieft in New Amsterdam heard about this fresh effort to encroach on his territory, he exploded; but he had to wait till 1642 before he could take action. His opportunity came when the first vessel with twenty families on board, on their way from New Haven to the Delaware, touched at New Amsterdam. Kieft at once summoned its captain, Robert Coxwell, and ordered him in no uncertain terms "not to build or plant on the South River . . . unless he would settle under the Lords the States General . . . and become subjects to them as other inhabitants do."[4]

Coxwell had no intention of doing this, but his assurances that his settlers would respect Dutch rights pacified Kieft sufficiently and he let them go. It was a big mistake. Once arrived on the Delaware, the New Haven crusaders started to build a blockhouse in full view of a surprised and angry West India Company commissary at Fort Nassau, Jan Jansen van Ilpendam, who immediately raised the alarm. On May 15, 1642, Kieft and his one-man council adopted a resolution to expel the English "in the quietest manner possible."[5]

A week later the governor informed Van Ilpendam that the company sloops *Real* and *St. Martin* were on their way, and that, "provided with as many soldiers as can conveniently carry away," Van Ilpendam was to call on the English settlement to ask for their commission. "If they have no royal commission . . . he shall oblige them to depart immediately in peace, so that no blood may be shed." Should they refuse to go, then he was free to arrest them, bring them to New Amsterdam, and "to lay waste that place."[6]

Van Ilpendam acted accordingly. The English put up no fight, but they refused to leave and the commissary, with the help of the Swedes, had to arrest most of them, burning the storehouse and "ceising uppon their Armes and goods." George Lamberton was deported to New Amsterdam, but soon released; and the last settlers straggled wretchedly back home in 1643, passing through New Amsterdam, where Kieft generously came to their rescue with food and money.[7]

Lamberton made one more attempt on the Delaware in June 1643, but this time he was arrested by the new Swedish governor, the four-hundred-pound John Printz, who fined him for trading under the walls of Christina. The court at New Haven made noises

DOUBTFUL NEIGHBORS

asking for satisfaction from Printz, Winthrop Sr. protested from Boston, but the New Haven venture to the Delaware was temporarily at an end. This time when Lamberton stopped at New Amsterdam on his way home, he was compelled to pay stiff duties on the pelts he had collected, and the dismayed merchants of New Haven recorded a loss of one thousand pounds.[8]

The Dutch director general was by this time getting used to visitors who dropped in to claim or merely occupy parts of his territory. One of them, a Scotsman called James Farrett, arrived in 1640 as the agent of Henry, Earl of Stirling, who claimed to have received a slightly obscure charter for Long Island from the Plymouth Company. Kieft simply ignored him, and Farrett left the town further humiliated by the New Amsterdammers, who jeered and booed at him as his ship moved out of port.[9]

The visit had, however, awakened Kieft to the dangers that threatened Long Island, the "crown of the colony," and when he heard that Farrett had sold the island of Monchonock to Lionel Gardiner—who called it after himself—he hastily dispatched Secretary Van Tienhoven to the Carnarsie Indians on Long Island. Fourteen years after selling Manhattan to Peter Minuit, they now sold to the Dutch "all the hereditary rights and titles" to that part of Long Island owned by their chief, Penhawitz, which meant almost all of it.

Penhawitz honored his bargain by warning Kieft in May 1640 that "some interlopers or vagabonds have come on the lands [Kieft had] purchased from him, and have begun to build houses, cut down trees and . . . that said vagabonds have cut down the arms of their High Mightinesses there."[10]

What Kieft had dreaded had happened: the intrusion was the work of Farrett. The Scotsman had tried to persuade the inhabitants of Lynn in Massachusetts to cross to Long Island, and he had succeeded in convincing ten of them, who, led by Captain Daniel Howe, settled at Schouts Bay, or Cow Neck. It was shocking news, and after "mature deliberation" in the Council, Cornelis van Tienhoven was appointed on May 13 to clear out the intruders with the help of twenty-five soldiers.[11]

Next morning at sunrise early risers in New Amsterdam

A SWEET AND ALIEN LAND

watched Van Tienhoven march his little army out of the fort. According to his instructions, the secretary was to "endeavour to arrive unawares . . . at break of day" and surprise the English. This was not difficult. When the Dutch soldiers arrived, they discovered that the entire invasion consisted of eight English men, one woman, and a little child, living together in one house while building a second. Very much frightened, they told the Dutch that Farrett had given them permission to settle there. The Scotsman, after tearing down the arms of the States and replacing it with a fool's head, had departed for New Haven with Captain Howe, promising to come back later with their commission.

Van Tienhoven decided not to wait for Farrett's return, and marched six of the men back to New Amsterdam, ordering the other two and the woman to pull down their buildings and take themselves off. On May 19 the six, who had been locked up in the fort's prison, were found not guilty of having torn down the arms of the States (Kieft realized they had simply been misled by Farrett) and were set free, on condition that they never come back, which they readily promised. This story was somewhat distorted when it reached London. In the English version the Dutch were supposed to have put the men in "irons, threatening them to send them prisoners to Holland, unless they would promise to desert the place."[12]

They never did return; but their leader, Captain Howe, refused to give up so easily. In the autumn he arrived again on Long Island, with another grant given to him by Farrett, this time for a piece of land at the "eastermost point of Long Island, with the whole breadth from sea to sea." Together with his associates he founded there the town of Southampton, so distant from New Amsterdam that Kieft shrugged and left them in peace.[13]

Farrett made one last deal before he died that year, this time with the merchants of New Haven, who, despite their preoccupation with the Delaware, still nursed dreams of a commercial empire based on the Long Island Sound, with harbors on Long Island as well as on the mainland. They bought from him the place where in 1642 the Reverend John Young founded Southold on the north shore—again without any opposition from New Amsterdam.[14]

Another candidate for Dutch territory presented himself in New Amsterdam in 1643, claiming to be the "Earl-palatine of the province of New Albion." In England this eccentric gentleman

DOUBTFUL NEIGHBORS

was better known as Sir Edmund Plowden, who had spent considerable time in a debtors' prison. On his release, he felt it prudent to leave for the colonies, and asked Charles I for a patent for the Delaware (called the Charles River by the English). With the help of some friends, he managed to procure a grant for a piece of land stretching from Cape May along the Delaware, up north for forty leagues, then east to Sandy Hook on the Hudson River, and then back to the Cape. He successfully interested forty-four peers and speculators in the development of this new colony between the Hudson and the Delaware (now in New Jersey), and gave his company the grandiloquent title of "Albion knights for the conversion of the twenty-three Kings."[15]

By the time Sir Edmund approached Kieft in the summer of 1643, he had a sad story to relate. His first effort to take possession of his "country palatine" had already ended in disaster. He had left England that winter, and in May he had sailed from the little port of Heckemack in a bark with a crew of sixteen. The lord—an extremely disagreeable person—soon had difficulties with his crew, and they put him ashore "without food, clothes and arms" on tiny Smith's Island off the coast of Canada in Hudson's Bay, deserted apart from wolves and bears. By chance he was found four days later by a passing sloop, "half dead and black as the ground," but he recovered and proceeded to New Amsterdam. His mutinous crew, meanwhile, had sailed on up the Delaware, where they were stopped by the Swedish governor, John Printz. When one of the crew members revealed to him their mutiny against Sir Edmund, the governor arrested the captain and his men and sent them off to Virginia, where most of them were executed.[16]

Kieft considered Plowden's claim ludicrous, and Sir Edmund retired to Virginia with the generous remark that "he did not wish to have any strife with the Dutch." It took him some time to recover from this setback, but seven years later the idea of "New Albion" was revived. Sir Edmund paid a visit to his palatinate on the east bank of the Delaware, but "having lost the estate he brought over," went back to England via Boston, where he informed Winthrop that he had to go to London to raise funds so that "he could get sufficient strength to dispossess the Swedes." In England he published a *Description of New Albion*, got together some colonists, and found himself backers; but he never reached the Delaware again. The New England colonies, alerted by Win-

A SWEET AND ALIEN LAND

throp, successfully headed off this rival claimant to a territory in which so many of them had an interest.[17]

It spared the Dutch another expensive expedition.

If Kieft could give little time and attention to these adventurers, it was mainly because he had to deal with other, much more persistent and serious intruders. Convinced of their rights, the New Englanders were spreading rapidly into his territory around New Amsterdam, and the reports that he received and sent on to Holland about the Connecticut settlements were particularly disquieting.

De Vries, visiting the river in 1639, had already warned him that Hartford, on the opposite bank to the House of Good Hope, had grown into a town with a hundred houses and a church. At Kieft's request, De Vries went to see Governor John Haynes to restate the Dutch claims. Dining with him on June 9, 1639, "I told him that it was wrong to take by force Company's land, which it had bought and paid for," related the Dutchman. "He answered that the lands were lying idle . . . that it was a sin to let such rich land . . . uncultivated." And he made it very clear that the English would never budge, having by that time built Hartford, Windsor, and Springfield on the river.[18]

De Vries' plain speaking left the English unmoved. At Hartford they were becoming increasingly aggressive toward their Dutch neighbors, and in April 1640 the first serious clash between the two communities took place. The Dutch agent Gysbert van Opdyck had gone to see the English magistrate to tell him defiantly that he would be working his field, but Hopkins insisted that he had no right to do so since the field had been bought from the wrong tribe. Undeterred, the Dutch began work next morning, and were attacked by the English constable and ten men, armed "with sticks and plow staves in a hostile manner." One of the Dutch farmers, Evert Duckings, had his head split open.

The day after this onslaught the Dutch bravely went back to finish their ploughing, only to discover that the English had begun to sow their own corn in the field. Van Opdyck made a protest to Hopkins—who refused to accept it, "as it was in Dutch." The tussle over the field continued, and when Van Opdyck led his men

DOUBTFUL NEIGHBORS

out for the sowing, another battle broke out. This time the Dutch were ready, and came off best, but when they tried to harvest their crops in August, the English obstructed them so persistently that they finally had to give up and watch the crops rot.[19]

Meanwhile the English kept up a campaign of niggling persecution. A horse was taken away "upon pretence that he had eaten their grasse"; in June a cow and calf disappeared; and an English minister sank so low as to steal a load of hay from the company, which he "applyed . . . to his owne use without giveing any recompense." Winter brought a lull, but by the end of 1641 the list of complaints Van Opdyck sent to Kieft in New Amsterdam was longer than ever. April 5—Hartford people beat up some of the Dutch; May 7—"The English have spoilt the lands that our men have plowed and sowed, Cuting the strings of our Plowgh," after which they threw it in a ditch; May 27—the English put posts on the roads to the fields; June 17—Hartford sold a hog that had trespassed; July 24—another hog was locked up "out of meer hate;" July 26—hogs again driven to Hartford. It was a depressing record of petty intimidation, and things were just as bad the next year.[20]

Kieft was maddened by the English behavior, but there was very little he could do about it since their numbers and military strength were greatly superior. But at least once, goaded beyond endurance, the Council accepted a resolution to send fifty soldiers, under the command of Councillor Johannes La Montagne, "to prevent . . . such hostilities as the English have wickedly committed against our people." The expedition never left Fort Amsterdam, however, since trouble with the Indians compelled Kieft to call it off. In the end all he could do was to order a boycott of all English goods coming from the neighborhood of Hartford and the other English towns on the Connecticut.[21]

In July 1642 this measure at last provoked an English reaction. The General Court of Connecticut, founded in May 1637 with full powers of government over the region the Dutch still claimed, decided to send a delegation to New Amsterdam. "Master Weytinge" (Whiting) and Master Hill arrived in the capital of New Netherland on July 9, armed with a counterlist of grievances: the Dutch had sold guns to the Indians, helped prisoners to escape, persuaded servants to run away, and behaved badly toward the English in general. But the main object of the delegates was to get

A SWEET AND ALIEN LAND

rid of the Dutch once and for all, and to that purpose they offered to buy the House of Good Hope.[22]

Kieft refused point blank. He pointed out that "said land was Anno 1633 by us purchased from the right owners and paid for" before any Christians had been there. The best solution, suggested Kieft, was for the English to acknowledge the States and the Prince of Orange, and to pay rent, a tenth of all their products. The delegates left discouraged, promising to talk it over, and provisionally accepting the proposal. It never came to anything. The Connecticut settlements already felt much too strong to listen to their shrinking neighbor. They went on "crowding out" the Dutch, and "in the end the House of Good Hope had so little land, that the commissioner with his family cannot well live." The English had left him twelve morgens of land, and built their pallisades so close to his house that he could hardly leave or enter it.[23]

Kieft was more successful with another group of English, who in early 1640 settled on the mainland just a few miles from New Amsterdam, calling their town Greenwich. A year later they recognized his authority, taking the oath of allegiance to "Their High Mightinesses" in the Republic and the company, promising to prevent treason to this country, "and to protect and defend it."[24]

The terms under which these and other English groups were allowed to settle were very generous. Kieft not only offered them freedom of religion—a novelty for those who had lived under the strict rule of the Puritan leaders in New England—but also the liberty to appoint their own magistrates, although Kieft reserved the right to approve them. These conditions were very attractive to the English. Some "respectable gentlemen" from Massachusetts, shaken by the Civil War now breaking out in England and uncertain of their Puritan future, came to make some inquiries. But at the last moment their General Court told them severely that they were making a mistake by "strengthening the Dutch, our doubtful neighbors," and they stayed at home.[25]

Others had less hesitation, unable to hold out any longer against Puritan pressure to conform and attracted by the offer of freedom of conscience. In 1642 the Reverend John Throckmorton arrived

DOUBTFUL NEIGHBORS

with thirty-five families to settle at Vreedenland, now in Westchester county, only twenty-five miles from New Amsterdam. He was followed by the Reverend Francis Doughty, who had dared to tell the Pilgrims that "Abraham's children should have been baptised." They ejected him, and Kieft then gave him a large tract of land on Long Island, where he founded Newtown (also called Mespath).

Two ladies of independent mind also moved in. The first was the fearless Anne Hutchinson, who had thrown the whole of Boston into religious ferment by preaching grace before works. Ejected from the city in 1638, she and her disciples had first settled in Rhode Island—later described by a Dutch minister as "a place of errorists and enthusiasts;" the English called it the "latrina of New England." Fearing that Massachusetts or Plymouth would take advantage of the Civil War to clean up this "sink," Anne moved in 1642 to the place now called Pelham Neck on the river that bears her name.[26]

The other woman who preferred the freedom of New Netherland was "Lady Deborah Moody," a "nice and anciently religious woman" who, having made the mistake of declaring herself against infant baptism, was expelled from Massachusetts in 1645 and founded Gravesend on Long Island. Other groups of English settlers had meanwhile founded Hempstead (in Dutch Heemstede).[27]

In general it looked as though the autocratic Kieft was more generous to the refugees from New England than to his own Dutch settlers, but in allowing them to select their own "bodye politique and civill" he only proved himself a realist who had taken note of the greater communal spirit among the English, based on a common interest of religion and a common ownership of land. In the early days of the Great Puritan Emigration whole congregations had often uprooted themselves from England and crossed the Atlantic to settle down together and found a town. Many villages springing up like mushrooms all over New England were the developments of similar splinter groups, breaking away from the parent settlement. This cosy neighborliness was unknown to the average Dutch settler, who arrived free and independent in New Netherland. Only with the greatest difficulty could the Dutch be induced to live together in villages; they much preferred to scatter

A SWEET AND ALIEN LAND

their farms and houses over a country full of dangerous natives.[28]

The West India Company did its best to encourage a change of attitude, promising self-determination for those places where "the dwelling places of private colonists should become so numerous as to be accounted towns," and urging them to organize life "in the manner of villages, towns and hamlets, as the English are in the habit of doing, who thereby live more securely." But it was in vain. The wide open spaces of New Netherland proved irresistible to emigrants from the densely populated Republic, and by 1646 only one Dutch community in New Netherland had received its town charter. It was Breukelen (now Brooklyn), settled by a handful of Dutch on the spot where Fulton Street runs today.

Kieft's generosity to the English was thus hardly at the expense of the Dutch, and at the same time it was helping to populate New Netherland. By 1642, "having noticed the great number of English who come daily to reside here under us," he appointed in December an Englishman as extra secretary to help him in the "innumberable law suits and their consequences occurring." His eye had fallen on George Baxter, an ensign who had been Lady Deborah Moody's escort, but had preceded her to New Amsterdam. He was now offered—thanks to his "experience in law case"—a job at the yearly wage of 250 guilders.[29]

But if Kieft was happy about this steady English influence, not everyone was. Kiliaen van Rensselaer, once more showing his foresight, warned him in 1643 against too much leniency toward the English, fearing that "the arrival of so many . . . will later give trouble." He added doubtfully: "The Lord grant that it may turn out better."[30]

On September 1, 1642, at about six o'clock in the evening, the Royal Standard of King Charles I of England was raised in the town of Nottingham to which he had retreated, "summoning all the lieges to assist His Majesty." The Civil War—so long expected and so much dreaded—had begun.[31]

The Dutch government remained officially neutral, but under the influence of the House of Orange, it was cautiously pro-Royal.

DOUBTFUL NEIGHBORS

In 1642 the future Stadholder Willem II even married Charles' daughter Mary. And the rich merchants of Amsterdam showed their sympathy—and mercantile spirit—still more openly by lending huge sums of money to meet the costs of the war to Henrietta Maria, Charles I's wife, whose romanizing influence had contributed so greatly to his problems with Parliament. One Amsterdammer gave her, as an advance for a couple of English horses, the small fortune of 213,000 guilders.[32]

In the first year of the Civil War, Charles' New World colonies were the least of his preoccupations, but other English claimants continued to follow colonial affairs closely. And they were shocked by the reports from Connecticut of clashes between the English and Dutch. In July Lord Saye and Sele, who had in 1635 commissioned John Winthrop Jr. to build a colony at the mouth of the river, decided to intervene, and sent a sharply-worded memorial to the Dutch ambassador, Albert Joachimi.

The Earl of Warwick, upon whose patent Lord Saye and Sele based his claim, had already sent off an equally strongly worded protest to the States General, in which he threatened that the Dutch "within the year" would be expelled from Connecticut if the States would not arrange the matter. He called it ridiculous that the Dutch with their "small factory" should claim the entire country from Narragansett Bay to the Hudson, since it was populated by no more than five or six company settlers, as opposed to two thousand English. Moreover, he added pointedly, "they live there without rule, in a godless manner, beseeming in no wise the Gospel of Christ." He urged the States to write a letter to the Dutch at the House of Good Hope, ordering them to "comport themselves in a peaceable and friendly manner with the English."[33]

Not all the English agreed with these bullying tactics, and the Dutch could count among their friends one of the best-known pastors of New England, the Reverend Hugh Peter. This indomitable preacher had lived in Rotterdam for several years after his outspoken Nonconformism had compelled him to flee England, and he still had many friends in the Republic—he even spoke Dutch. Arriving in New England in 1634, where his stepdaughter joined him in 1635 as Mrs. John Winthrop Jr., he had the courage to speak up for the Dutch, and a few years later he suggested to

A SWEET AND ALIEN LAND

Winthrop Sr. that Boston conclude a treaty with its neighbors in New Netherland. He had offered to go himself "to speak with the Dutch Governor," but had been turned down.[34]

In 1641 Massachusetts decided to send a delegation to Europe, and the minister was included, together with Winthrop Jr. While the latter had as his mission to stave off the colony's creditors— with the fall of Archbishop Laud, the main incentive for emigration had gone and business was going badly in the colony—Peter was told to go to the Dutch Republic and attempt to settle the question of the borders between New England and New Netherland. His "power of attorney" was signed by the governor of Massachusetts, John Winthrop Sr., and that of Connecticut, John Haynes. In their proposals to the West India Company the governors suggested that since the population of the whole of New England now amounted to more than forty thousand souls, "being of the same religion"—the Dutch should be more cooperative if they wished their province to survive. The governors asked that if the company was willing to sell its claim to the Connecticut, it should name its price. And they assured the Heeren XIX that the New Englanders were "a people who covet peace in their ways," desiring "the planting of the gospel above all things."[35]

The outbreak of the Civil War delayed Peter's mission considerably. The fiery pastor, a fanatic anti-Royalist who later became Cromwell's chaplain, joined the bloodthirsty Society of Adventurers to give the Catholic Irish a beating, and it was not until 1643 that he got to The Hague. But there, too, his antipathy to Charles I got the better of him, and he traveled around the Republic fulminating so violently against the King that the English ambassador, Sir William Boswell, complained to the States.[36]

Peter's efforts in the anti-Royalist cause were crowned with success. Wherever he preached, people were so moved that they often gave him their wedding rings to add to the Parliamentary funds. His mission for New England, on the other hand, was a failure. As in England, he found the government of the Republic completely uninterested. The Civil War seemed to the Dutch sufficient guarantee of peace in America. The States instructed Joachimi to assure London, and in particular the Earl of Warwick, that New Netherland was too weak to be a threat to New England,

DOUBTFUL NEIGHBORS

telling itself confidently that England was "rent in twain . . . and therefore she was not to be dreaded."[37]

It was another miscalculation that would have to be paid for. And it was certainly not much help to Kieft in New Amsterdam.

A SWEET AND ALIEN LAND

THE

DUTCH BABEL

A place with "the arrogance of Babel" was a Frenchman's description of New Amsterdam in the 1640s. The "village" planted by Peter Minuit in 1626 and enlarged by Wouter van Twiller had become under Willem Kieft a cosmopolitan center in which, as the director general told Father Isaac Jogues, there lived men of eighteen different languages.[1]

Father Jogues, the first missionary sent by the French to the warlike Iroquois, arrived in New Amsterdam in 1643, after being rescued by the Dutch from the hands of the Mohawk Indians. Despite his religion, he was warmly welcomed as "a martyr of Jesus Christ" by Kieft and the international population of the city, which he examined with curiosity. In his *Novum Belgium* Jogues only mentions three nationalities—Irish, Portuguese, and Polish—but apart from the many Englishmen, New Amsterdam also counted among its inhabitants a number of Germans, Norwegians and Swedes, at least two Danes (Jochem Kuyter and the well-known Jonas Bronck, whose library was the largest in New Netherland and who gave the Bronx its name), Walloons and French, Italians and Spaniards.[2] The total number of citizens was not more than four or five hundred, according to the Jesuit, but the harbor was always full of ships whose crews added more life to the bustling city, while fur traders from the outward posts, Indians, and Negro slaves completed the scene.

The streets were now laid out more regularly, and many wooden houses began to give way to stone ones, roofed with slate instead of thatch and reed. Kieft's new official residence signified that the first pioneering days were over. It measured one hundred feet in length, fifty feet in width, and twenty-four feet in height, and was "quite neatly built of brick." It stood, however, in the middle of a fort that had once more fallen into ruin. Although an English visitor in 1644 called this fortification on the "Machidam" River "a castle of great use for keeping under the natives adjoyning, but likewise for their more free trading," Jogues saw it differently. Walking around this fascinating little city, dressed in the "good cloak and hat in their own style" given him by Kieft, he had two months to look around. The four bastions at the corners, originally mounted with artillery, had "crumbled away, so that one entered the Fort on all sides." The moat dug and widened during Van Twiller's reign had been filled up with earth. Workmen had started to repair the fort and face the gates and bastions with stone, but the walls remained as weak as ever, built, despite Kieft's protests, "in an economical manner by use of good clay and firm sods" at the explicit orders of the Company Board of Account in Amsterdam.[3]

The construction of a more solid building inside the fort was under way when Jogues finally left for Europe at the end of 1643. The Calvinist faithful of New Amsterdam were at last getting their own temple, after having for years congregated in the room above the horse mill, and then in the small chapel—a "mean barn" —Van Twiller had built near the East River.

It was the ever-energetic Captain David de Vries who had given the first push. During a visit in 1642 he told Kieft over dinner that "it was a scandal to us" when English visitors saw that the city had no real church, especially since the company "was deemed to be the principal means of upholding the Reformed Religion against the tyranny of Spain." In New England, he pointed out, the Puritans built their churches at once "after their dwellings." There was plenty of material at hand—fine oak wood, good mountain stone, and good lime, even better than in Holland, De Vries argued —and "the lovers of the Reformed Religion" would provide the money.

Kieft at once took him up on the suggestion, saying that he as proposer ought to contribute a hundred guilders. The quick-wit-

A SWEET AND ALIEN LAND

ted De Vries countered that the director general should set an example by being the first to give, and Kieft agreed to donate "several thousand guilders on behalf of the Company." The two men contrived to persuade the community to pay the rest.[4]

A perfect opportunity for fund raising presented itself almost immediately. Dominie Bogardus had ended his noisy bachelorhood five years earlier by marrying the rich widow Anneke Jansz, and was again anticipating a wedding, this time as the stepfather of the bride. Anneke's daughter Sarah had made an excellent match with one of the city's two doctors, Hans Kierstede from Magdeburg in Saxony. After the ceremony the punch started to flow freely and Kieft shrewdly felt that the moment had come. "After the fourth or fifth round of drinking he set about the business," it was later remembered, by telling the guests how much he would give for the construction of the church. "All then with light heads subscribed largely, competing one with another," the reporter related, adding indignantly that "although some well repented it when they recovered their senses, they were nevertheless compelled to pay."[5]

To the great annoyance of the community, the autocratic Kieft decided that this first Protestant church, called St. Nicholas after the patron of Amsterdam, should be built inside the fort. Rowdy and rather unsaintly disputes followed. The governor argued that the fort was the best place to protect the church against possible attack by the savages, but his opponents felt that it should be in the city itself, as it ought to "be owned by the congregation at whose cost it was built."[6]

As usual, Kieft brushed aside objections, and signed a contract with two English builders, John and Richard Ogden, to construct the church inside the fort, where it rose—so his opponents commented—"as suitable as a fifth wheel to a wagon." The builders, for a payment of twenty-five hundred guilders in cash or merchandise, did a good job. The church measured seventy-two feet long, fifty-two feet wide, and sixteen feet high; it was built of quarry stone and covered with oak shingles, "which by exposure to wind and rain turn blue and look like slate." It survived, somewhat altered in 1691, until it was destroyed by fire in 1741. Although the "lovers of the Reformed Religion" had paid most of the cost, Kieft made it a monument to his own glory by placing a slab in the wall with the inscription "A°D° MDCXLII W. Kieft Dr.Gr. Heeft de

Gemeente dese Tempel doen Bouwen." (Anno Domini 1642 Willem Kieft Director General, has caused the Community to build this temple.)[7]

The building of the church must have eased Kieft's conscience somewhat. Up till then he had mainly worried about less celestial constructions—like the Stadt's Herberg, the City Tavern. This was "a fine inn of stone" that could lodge the many English merchants he had formerly had to put up himself, and from whom, he confessed to De Vries, "he suffered great annoyance." The two-story tavern stood just outside the town, facing the East River, and was thirty by forty feet in dimension, with a very large and useful cellar for the company's wines. The jenever and brandy the inn-keeper served probably came from the distillery that Willem Hendricksen of Weesp had built on Staten Island in 1640 (by special permission from Kieft), while his beer came from the brewery just behind the tavern.[8]

The tavern's first host was Philip Gerritsen, originally from Haarlem, who paid three hundred guilders a year for his occupancy, but was allowed to make a profit of six stuivers a mug. Although lucrative, the job was not without its hazards. Three months after Gerritsen took over, he was in bed with a stab wound under his shoulder blade, given him by Churchwarden Jan Damen. He died soon afterward, but his wife, after marrying another Gerritsen, Adriaen, renewed the lease and was hostess until 1653, when the tavern became the City Hall.[9]*

Another very popular tavern opened around this time was Het Houte Paerd ("The Wooden Horse"), run by a lively Parisian, Philip Geraerdy. With this name he commemorated his military career in the New World, which had ended with his being sentenced "to ride the wooden horse"—a standard punishment for soldiers who had been absent from duty without leave. He had had to sit for hours on a crossbar with—significantly enough—a pitcher in one hand and a drawn sword in the other, while heavy weights hung from his feet. Not surprisingly, he resigned from service. His tavern, much frequented by the locals, stood on the corner of Marcktveldt and Brouwerstraat (now Whitehall and Stone streets).[10]

---

*The tavern stood on what is now a parking lot on the north side of Pearl Street in New York, thanks to the expansion of Manhattan well away from the riverbank.

Although settlers, traders, and sailors were welcome, one section of the province's population was not allowed in the Stadt's Herberg and the other inns of New Amsterdam. The Indians had taken a great liking to alcohol, and after furs, the traffic in liquor was to them the most important. For a long time it had been unrestricted, but in 1641 Kieft forbade the sale of alcohol to Indians. His ban was ineffectual, and had to be stiffened in 1647 by the threat of a fine of five hundred guilders for the first offense and banishment for the next. Even so, the New Amsterdammers observed that "daily drunk Indians run along the Manhatans," which forced the governor to impose corporal punishment for those who gave them "strong drinks under whatever name."[11]

Before the arrival of the Dutch, the Indians had never touched a drop of alcohol. The "journalist" Nicolaes Van Wassenaer records that the natives in New Netherland "have nothing with which they can become intoxicated," drinking "clear river water to their fill." And Adriaen van der Donck reported later that the "common drink is water from a living spring or well." The juice of grapes they drank fresh, and "drunken men they call fools," having no word for drunkenness. Thanks to the Dutch traders, they made a rapid conversion to liquor, which unfortunately had the effect of making them "insolent, troublesome and malicious."[12]

Learning of the existence of alcohol had been one step to civilization, learning the use of firearms another. "Their weapons formerly were bow and arrow, which they employed with wonderful skill," remembered Van der Donck, but soon enough they were "exceedingly fond of guns, sparing no expense for them" and becoming—as the colonists realized too late—"so skillful in the use . . . that they surpass many Christians." The company had forbidden the sale of arms, but few traders could resist the temptation to barter a gun for a pile of precious furs—a fact the New Englanders complained about constantly.[13]

Their newly acquired needs for alcohol, guns, and ammunition had given the Indians (the Dutch called them *Wilden* or "savages") a dependence on the invaders of their country. An appreciation for European cloth furthered this dependence. Without a backward

THE DUTCH BABEL

glance, the natives shed furs and feathers to wrap themselves in the red and blue duffel blankets that the traders were only too willing to exchange for their furs.

The Dutch (the Indians called them *Swannekens*, "the people from the salt sea") had much better reasons to be grateful to the Indians. The advantages of the use of tobacco are perhaps doubtful, but introduction to the Indians' cereal—maize or corn—saved many lives in New Netherland and New England. Much of the land was not good enough to grow the finer European grains, but Indian corn grew in almost every soil. The Indians had developed at least twenty different varieties, and the colonists learned willingly. Another discovery they owed to the Indians was that of maple sugar, and the savages' knowledge of medicinal herbs must have surprised even the best Dutch quack.

It was this willingness to learn, combined with the traditional tolerance of the Dutch government, that made it possible for Dutch and Indians to establish a sort of peaceful coexistence. Unlike the Puritans, who in 1637 had decimated the Pequot tribes around New London, they felt no hatred or even dislike for the savages. The Dutch had received a friendly welcome from the Indians, and in their first instructions the early colonists were specifically enjoined to treat them fairly and kindly. The punishment of troublesome natives was to be left to their own tribes, and they would also have legal protection against acts of the settlers. Court records show that up to a point the Dutch kept their word —if only to avoid the consequences of Indian anger and revenge. In 1638, for instance, the Court of New Amsterdam fined a man for assaulting an Indian, and a year later another Dutchman was ordered to restore a load of wampum to a native.[14]

Of course, not everyone obeyed the rules. In 1648 some Indians complained that a group of settlers had refused to pay them for work they had performed. In response the governor issued a special proclamation ordering all inhabitants "who owe anything to an Indian . . . to pay without dispute."[15]

But even the West India Company did not always honor its principle that settlers and savages were equal. From the beginning it refused to allow Indians to ride on horseback; and natives working at the fort received two stuivers a day against the Dutch seaman's eight—in line with the Republic's custom of considering the value of a slave only a quarter that of a free man, though few Indians were ever actually enslaved.[16]

There was often difficulty in enforcing the order to pay an Indian for the land a settler of the company bought, and to have the sale ratified. The excellent example that Minuit had given when he paid sixty guilders for Manhattan to the Canarsie tribe was not faithfully followed.

The Canarsie were but one of the many tribes that populated the country around New Amsterdam. Like their rivals, the Iroquois, they belonged to the Algonquin nation, a splendidly healthy race that according to Van Wassenaer knew no "cross-eyed, blind, crippled, lame, hunchbacked or limping men." Someone else described them as "generally well set in the limbs, slender around the waist, broad across the shoulders," with black hair, dark eyes, and yellow skin.[17]

The best authority on the Indians, especially the Mohawks of the Iroquois nation, was Johannes Megapolensis (his name was a latinization of Grootstede), who arrived at Rensselaerswyck in 1642 with his wife and four children. The minister traveled extensively in the Mohawk country surrounding Fort Orange, and even made a study of the Mohawk language. In his *Short Account of the Mohawk Indians*, published in 1644, he describes the Indians as "like us Dutchmen in body and stature." In the summer they went naked, "having only their private parts covered with a patch," and in the winter "they hang about them simply an undressed deer or bear or panther skin." Some sewed a few beaver or otter skins together, or "they bought two and a half ells of duffel" and threw it over their shoulders. "They look at themselves constantly and think they are very fine."

Stockings and shoes were made of deerskin or from plaited leaves of corn. Jewelry consisted of belts made of wampum worn around the waist, while ears were pierced for wampum rings. "The women let their hair grow very long and tie it together a little and let it hang down their backs. The men have a long lock of hair hanging down, some on one side of the head, and some on both sides. On the top of their heads they have a streak of hair from the forehead to the neck, about the breadth of three fingers, and this they shorten until it is about two or three fingers long, and it stands right on end like a cock's comb or pig's bristle; on both sides

THE DUTCH BABEL

of this cock's comb they cut all the hair short." To complete their hair-do, they smeared it with bear grease, which prevented lice. On top they sometimes wore a hat or cap "bought of the Christians." Their faces were painted red or blue, "and then they look like the devil."[18]

Even the Dutch colonists, who were none too fussy about their own cleanliness, were appalled by the Indians' lack of hygiene. "They are very foul and dirty," De Vries noted. But they had already invented the sauna, which they used once a year, "in the autumn, when it begins to grow cold." On the banks of a river they made a small oven "large enough for three or four men to lie in it. In making it they first take twigs of trees, and then cover them with clay, so that smoke cannot escape." A few big stones were heated up and put in the oven until it was hot enough, after which the stones were replaced by the natives, who had a splendid sweat until "every hair has a drop on it." To the horror of the Dutch spectators, the Indians concluded this treatment by a plunge into the icy river, "saying that it is very healthy." The colonists shivered and decided to "let its healthfulness pass."[19]

Surrounding their strongly-fortified "castles," the Indians built villages of huts, which Van Wassenaer described as "commonly circular, with a vent hole above to let the smoke out . . . and mostly made of the bark of trees." They were "very close and warm." Some were decorated inside with rough carvings of faces and images that looked menacing to the Dutch. They could, in fact, be a ferocious people. One of Megapolensis' predecessors, Johannes Michaëlius, called them "entirely savage and wild . . . uncivil and stupid as garden poles," but Adriaen van der Donck, who knew them better, described them as "high-minded enough, vigorous and quick to comprehend or learn."[20]

The fact that they were not at all eager to be converted may have blinded Michaëlius to their qualities. The Indians were convinced that God was so preoccupied with a beautiful female that he had no time for the world.* Of the Dutch God, they told the colonists: "We have never seen him, we know not who he is." And they added tellingly that if the white men knew this Almighty God and

---

*The creation of the world was caused by a pregnant woman, who fell from Heaven onto the back of a tortoise and scraped the earth together from the bottom of the water until the globe was formed. She returned to Heaven after she was delivered of the animals that live on earth.

A SWEET AND ALIEN LAND

feared him, they would be severely punished by him, since there were "so many thieves, drunkards and evildoers" among them. They themselves would escape these punishments, they reckoned, since God had never warned them against those deeds.[21]

The spiritual world of the Indians was peopled mainly by minor devils, while every soul had a good spirit to watch over it, called Manitou. He was represented by the head of a man carved on a small stick, which every Indian carried round his neck in a bag. The Indians believed strongly that there was a difference between body and soul, and that the latter was immortal and must be carefully looked after. Funerals were accordingly elaborate. The corpses were washed and painted, and placed in a grave, which was left open for several days so that the body could get used to its resting place. David de Vries was present at such a funeral, and noted with fascination that the Indians treated the corpse with the utmost care, putting it in a grave lined with boughs of trees "so that no earth can touch it." Later they covered it over with clay and formed the grave, seven or eight feet high, in the shape of a sugar loaf, building pallisades around it.[22]

Death was the mystery, but the reality was hunting, fishing, and agriculture. The last was mainly done by women, the first two by the men, who also acted as traders. By 1640 the days of "trinkets and baubles" were long since past. Payment was mainly in wampum, recognized since 1634 by the West India Company as legal tender in New Netherland.

The Indians were shrewd traders—"a craftey people," according to one New Englander, who "will cussen and cheat. . . . A suttell peple." Van Wassenaer complained that they were "very cunning in trade; yea, frequently after having sold everything, they retract the bargain"—a practice they were particularly prone to when dealing in land, which they often sold twice over. Van der Donck claimed the Indians had become more deceitful since their first contacts with the colonists.[23]

There was, according to the Dutch, "no law, no justice" among the natives. "The strongest does what he pleases and the youth are master," wrote one, and Dominie Megapolensis confirmed this. "There is no punishment here for murder and other villainies, but every one is his own avenger." All the same, he added wistfully, "there are not half so many villainies or murders committed amongst them as among Christians," and killing only took place

THE DUTCH BABEL

"in a great passion of a hand-to-hand fight."[24]

The fact that the Indians lived without laws under the weak authority of their chiefs, the sachems, sackmos, or sagamos, astonished the Dutch, as did the lack of a matrimonial bond. "A man and a woman join themselves together without any particular ceremony," reveals one Dutch report. The man simply gave the girl some wampum—which he took away again as soon as they separated. And that happened frequently. "Both men and women are utterly unchaste and shamelessly promiscuous in their intercourse," the reporter wrote disapprovingly, "which is the cause that the men change so often their wives and the women their husbands." De Rasières went into more detail, noting that the marriage ceremony was much less casual when the bride was still a virgin, in which case the prospective husband had to wait six weeks before he was allowed to sleep with her, "during which time she bewails or laments her virginity, crouching in a corner with a blanket over her head."[25]

Separation was not always a simple matter. If a woman committed adultery, the husband "thrashes her soundly." When he wished to get rid of her, he asked the sachem for help. If the sachem decided she was guilty, her hair was shaven off "in order that she may be held up before the world as a whore, which they call Poerochque." The Dutch Secretary De Rasières, who seems to have made a special study of the natives' marital life, gave an even more vivid account of how an unfaithful husband was treated: "The wife is permitted to draw off his right shoe and left stocking . . . she then tears off the lappet that covers his private parts, gives him a kick behind and drives him out of the house; and then 'Adam' scampers off."[26]

There is no record of how often this actually happened, but these strict rules certainly did not much inhibit the Indian's liberal attitude to sex. Officially there was little mixing between the Dutch and the Indians, and sleeping with an Indian woman was forbidden from the start—a rule reemphasized by Kieft in 1638. But it was impossible to stick to it in a world where white women were scarce, and Dominie Megapolensis once complained that "our Dutchmen run after the Indian girls very much."[27]

Van der Donck also admitted that the Indian girls were "well favoured and fascinating," and that several Dutchmen had been "connected with them before our women came over." His excuse

A SWEET AND ALIEN LAND

was that they were so similar to the Dutch women—"seldom very handsome and rarely very ugly"—that there would be little difference between them "if they were instructed as our women." That the Indians were no Calvinists in their sex life is proved by the name of one place in the province—Hoerekill, or Whores' Creek —on the Delaware, which derives, according to tradition, from the generous behavior of some of the Indian girls toward the colonists.[28]

In spite of their promiscuity, the Indians had a great love for their children. Dominie Megapolensis noted that the women took childbirth almost literally in their stride. "The women, when they have been delivered, go about immediately afterwards, and be it very cold, they wash themselves and the young child in the river or the snow . . . and we cannot see that they suffer any injury by it." The New Netherlander men tried to persuade their own wives to try childbirth the Indian way, finding "the way of lying-in in Holland a mere fiddle-faddle" by contrast, but to no avail.[29]

After the birth—and even when she separated from her husband—the mother kept her child, and her devotion was without question, as Dominie Michaëlius noticed when he tried to take some Indian children away from their parents in the hope of saving their souls. "They are very loth to part with them, and when they are separated from them . . . take them away stealthily or induce them to run away."[30]

But however mean or cheating or infidel the Indians might be, the Dutch were always impressed by their courage in war, their favorite occupation. "When in trouble they disregard and despise all pain and torture that can be done to them and will sing with proud contempt until death terminates their suffering," one Dutchman reported. There was obviously no pity or mercy for prisoners of war in their world. Megapolensis told with a shudder: "They first bit off the nails of the fingers of their captives and cut off some joints and sometimes even whole fingers." After this treatment the captors forced their prisoners to sing and dance stark naked until finally "they roast them dead before a slow fire for some days and then eat them up." The arms, buttocks, and trunk were given to the common people; the head and heart were reserved for the sachem.[31]

The Jesuit Father Jogues had been a victim of at least part of this treatment. He had been captured by the Mohawks, who killed one of his companions in front of his altar. The badly manhandled

THE DUTCH BABEL

Jogues (his thumbs were cut off and his nails pulled out, among other cruelties) was forced to accompany them on their warpath for months—until the Dutch at Fort Orange managed to rescue him and smuggle him onto a boat to New Amsterdam.

As a Frenchman, Jogues had no reason to expect mercy from the Mohawks. This powerful tribe had been bitter enemies to the French since 1609, when Champlain—who had founded Quebec for King Henri IV the previous year—allied the French with the Hurons. These traditional enemies of the Mohawks had bloodily defeated them at Ticonderoga, on the lake that now bears Champlain's name. The Hurons and the French were not the only enemies of the Mohawks. They were at the same time busy subduing the Mohicans, who lived around Fort Orange, and whose land they had overrun before the Dutch first came to New Amsterdam.

Apart from occasional interruptions to the fur trade, these hostilities did not inconvenience the Dutch—in fact, they profited from them since the Mohawks desperately needed guns, which the Dutch from Fort Orange sold them against orders for up to twenty beaver skins apiece. Megapolensis could still write at that time: "Although they are very cruel to their enemies, they are very friendly with us, and we have no dread of them."[32]

It was the same with the tribes around New Amsterdam, but the greed and arrogance of Director General Willem Kieft were soon to bring about a change, and the minister's words would be no more than a deeply regretted memory for the "hundred families" of New Amsterdam. As the anonymous author of *Broad Advice* commented:

> *What Kings and Princes madly say*
> *That must their suffering subjects pay.*[33]

The
First View

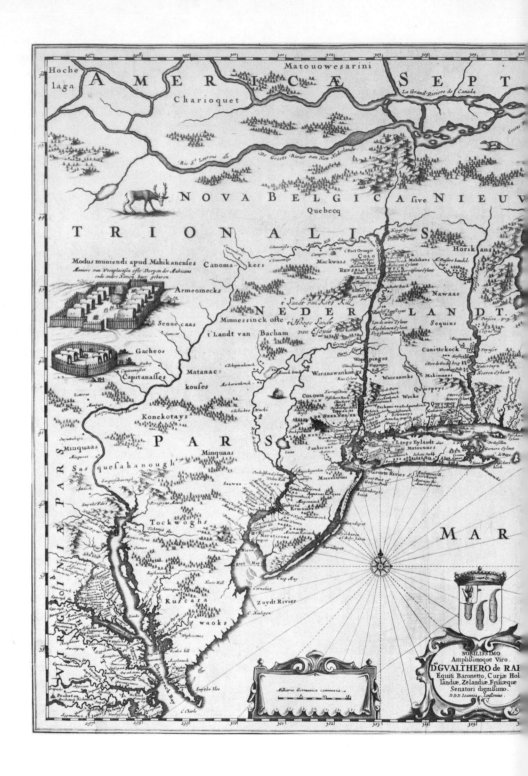

A map dating from 1647 and later used by Adriaen van der Donck in his Remonstrance.

COURTESY OF THE
NEW-YORK HISTORICAL SOCIETY,
NEW YORK CITY

The Coat of Arms of New Amsterdam,
with the crosses of Amsterdam crowned by a beaver.
MUSEUM OF THE CITY OF NEW YORK

The little hamlet of New Amsterdam, shown here, had grown
into a fair-sized town with a church, tavern, eighty houses, and a gallows.
This drawing was probably made by Augustine Heerman and sent by Peter Stuyvesant
to the company directors "to hang it up in some place or other . . ."
J. CLARENCE DAVIES COLLECTION, MUSEUM OF THE CITY OF NEW YORK

A VERY

MEAN FELLOW

"Before we weighed anchor mine eyes saw the flames at their towns, and the flight and hurry of men, women and children and the present removal of all that could for Holland." Thus the Englishman Roger Williams described the scene at New Amsterdam in March 1643. The forty-year-old Williams, founder of Rhode Island, was on his way to London to ask for a charter for his settlement of religious "errorists." He had come to the city to embark on a Dutch ship—and had arrived in the middle of Kieft's Indian War, which reached its climax that spring.[1]

Dark clouds had begun to gather at the beginning of the decade. The greater freedom to trade with the natives that the States General had given the colonists in 1639 "was soon perverted to a great abuse," stated a document, *Journal of Netherland*, prepared by Governor Kieft or one of his supporters. This new freedom had led to an increase of population in the province, but it was also "the cause of its ruin." Every settler saw in it his chance to make a quick fortune by paying court to the Indians and quarreling with any other trader, "the enemy of his gains." It was all very much at variance with the motto of the States General, *"Eendracht maakt macht"* ("Unity makes strength"), and it had disastrous consequences. The new familiarity of the Dutch with the Indians, and the special marks of attention now paid to them, "such as admitting them to the table, laying napkins before them, presenting wine," soon gave the Wilden too intimate a knowledge of the settlers' world, and it led to contempt, "the father of hate." The same happened with those Indians employed as servants.[2]

The natives had grievances against the Dutch. "As the cattle roamed usually through the woods without a herdsman, they frequently came into the corn of the Indians which was unfenced on all sides, committing great damage there." This, in turn, led to revenge on the cattle "without sparing even the horses, which were very valuable in this country."[3]

The greatest complaint of the Indians was, however, the growing difficulty they had in obtaining weapons. Only at Rensselaerswyck, surrounded by warring Mohicans and Mohawks, were arms still made available to them as the price of peace. In New Amsterdam, the strict ban on the sale of guns had been successful, and the Indians who lived on and around Manhattan—Algonquin Indians of the Haversack, Raritan, Tappan, and Wecquaesgeek tribes—were incensed by it. They grumbled and protested, and, according to the *Journal*, "it greatly augmented the hatred which stimulated them to conspire against us."[4]

The *Journal* omits mention of the fact that in 1639 Kieft, in his usual high-handed manner, had decided to tax the Indians, an act they bitterly resented. David de Vries was one of the first to realize the danger of Kieft's action when he visited his friends the Tappans on the Hudson. They told him that they were very much surprised that "the Sachem, who was now at the Fort," dared to exact a contribution of their corn. "He must be a very mean fellow to come and live in this country without being invited by them, and now wish to compel them to give him their corn for nothing." It was particularly hard on them as they had grown just enough "for their own necessities, and to barter some with us for cloth." Kieft later claimed that he had received orders from the West India Company to raise this tribute—"the seeds of war," he told the New Amsterdammers, "were first sown by the Fatherland." But it was untrue.[5]

The angry Raritan Indians near Staten Island gave a first demonstration of their fury in the spring of 1640, when they attacked a company yacht (unsuitably named the *Vrede*—or "Peace") on its rounds to collect taxes and furs. The three crew members under Master Cornel Pietersz managed "with the gracious help of God" to drive off the savages with the loss of one canoe. A few weeks

A SWEET AND ALIEN LAND

later some swine were stolen from David de Vries' new plantation, Vriesendael, on Staten Island, and the robbery—actually the doing of some company seamen—was blamed on the same Raritans.[6]

This was enough for Kieft, who once again forgot the company principle: "Tis better to rule by love and friendship than by force." On July 16, 1640, he called together his councillor, the gentle Dr. La Montagne; the company secretary, Van Tienhoven, who was increasingly attacked for his dishonesty and lechery; and Schout Cornelis van der Huygens, whose "only science" was drinking. Satisfaction, Kieft told them, was necessary. The Indians were no longer ready to listen to Dutch requests for indemnification. "They only laugh at our demands," he said, "and whereas this is a matter of great importance . . . for the respect and interest of the Honourable Company and the safety of our own lives and our cattle," a punitive expedition was demanded. The same day Van Tienhoven led out of the fort an undisciplined troop of fifty soldiers, bolstered by twenty sailors from a visiting ship, the *Neptune*. Their instructions were to confront the Indians, and if they refused to come voluntarily to an agreement, to "cut down their corn and bring as many prisoners as they can."[7]

On arrival at the Raritan River, the secretary demanded satisfaction from the tribe for the attack on the *Vrede* and the theft of the swine. The Indians obstinately refused. Van Tienhoven hesitated, but his little army was spoiling for action so the secretary took the easy way out. Well aware of what was likely to follow, he told the soldiers he would not be held responsible for any violation of their orders, and left. Before he had gone more than a quarter of a mile, the troops fell on the savages and killed several of them. The Raritan chief's brother was taken prisoner by Govert Loockermans, a clerk from New Amsterdam, who, as De Vries related, committed an "act of tyranny" by torturing the Indian "in his private parts with a piece of split wood." The Indians had killed only one of the Dutch attackers, the supercargo of the *Neptune*.[8]

After this, an uneasy calm descended on the province, which was shattered in the summer of 1641 when Manhattan was shocked by news of a cowardly and apparently unprovoked act of Indian violence. The young Wecquaesgeek Indian who, years earlier, in the days of Governor Minuit, had witnessed the murder of his uncle by three company servants, had not forgotten his vow of revenge. The boy had swallowed his pride and hidden his hatred,

A VERY MEAN FELLOW

even while working for a Dutchman. But in August 1641, a fully-grown man, he decided at last to appease the restless spirit of his uncle. As his victim he chose an old man, Claes Cornelissen Swits, better known as Rademaker (the wheelwright), the father of his former Dutch employer.

One afternoon he went to call on Rademaker, who lived in a small house at Deutels Bay (now Turtle Bay). The old man welcomed his guest with food and drink, and after the meal the Wecquaesgeek showed him some furs that he said he wanted to exchange for duffel. Rademaker went to a chest in the corner of the room, and as he stooped to get out his duffel cloth, the Indian snatched up an axe and "struck Claes Rademaker on the neck therewith, so that he fell down dead"—partly decapitated. The Indian plundered the house and ran away. "This outrage obliged the Director to demand satisfaction from the Sachem, who refused it," a later report related, "saying that he was sorry that twenty Christians had not been murdered and that this Indian had only avenged the death of his uncle."[9]

Two weeks later, on September 1, the Raritans, who had been brooding over the massacre by Van Tienhoven's soldiers, took their own bloody revenge. They attacked De Vries' plantation on Staten Island, killed four of his people, and burned down the house and tobacco sheds. An Indian who worked for him managed to escape unharmed, and brought an insolent challenge from the Raritans: "The Swannekens would now come to fight them on behalf of our men" and not on account of the swine, whose theft had been charged "upon the innocent Indians." Not surprisingly, De Vries, who from the beginning had had almost as little respect for Kieft as for Van Twiller, took an even stronger dislike to the governor. It was "through the conduct of Commander Kieft" that he had lost his infant colony.[10]

The director general's fury was now thoroughly roused against the Raritans. He invited the other tribes around New Amsterdam to join the Dutch in their counterattack, offering them ten fathoms of wampum for every head of a Raritan, and twenty fathoms for one of the Staten Island murderers. The bait worked only too well, and on November 2 the chief of the Haverstraw Indians, Pacham, walked to the governor's house with a dead hand dangling from a stick. It was, he asserted, the hand of the chief who had led the assault on Staten Island. Pocketing his reward, he told the Dutch

A SWEET AND ALIEN LAND

crowding around him that he had taken revenge for their sake "because he loved the Swannekens, who were his best friends."[11]

The pressure Kieft put on the Raritans was effective, and before the end of 1641 peace was concluded. It was a tactical triumph that left Kieft's hands free for the attack on the Wecquaesgeek tribe he had been planning since their refusal to hand over the murderer of Rademaker. The settlers, learning of Kieft's plans, grew jittery. The last thing they wanted was war, and "people began to reproach him," De Vries heard, "with being himself protected in a good fort, out of which he had not slept a single night." The settlers suspected that the governor was eager for war in order to distract attention from the failures of his government. Kieft, sensing that their mood was turning against him and needing at least a show of popular support for actions against the Indians, had already in August decided to share his responsibilities with the colonists. "Whereupon all the commonalty were called together" to delegate twelve men from among them. It was the "first dawning of popular government" on Manhattan.[12]

The Twelve—among whom were De Vries; Churchwarden Jan Damen; the overseer of the company's Negroes, Jacob van Stoffelsen; a former employee of Van Rensselaer, Maryn Adriaensen; and the farmers Abram Planck and Gerrit Dircksen—also included a fair sample of the Dutch "Babel." Among these were the wealthy Dane Jochem Pietersen Kuyter from Darmstadt, who had served as naval commander in the East Indies, and had owned a prosperous farm in New Amsterdam since 1639; and the Walloon Joris-Janes Rappelje, whose only claim to fame is that he was the father of Sarah, the first "Christian daughter" to be born in New Netherland.

Accounts of the first meeting of the Twelve at Fort Amsterdam on August 29 are confused. Kieft's supporters related in their *Journal of New Netherland* that the council "resolved at once on war"; but De Vries says that on the contrary the representatives asked for time, pointing out that the cattle "were running at pasture in the woods" and that the population was too scattered to be protected. According to them it was madness to wage a war with the Indians until they were much stronger, and De Vries reminded Kieft that the company was certainly not in favor of such an action since "no profit was to be derived from a war with the savages."[13]

But if Kieft had called a people's council, he certainly had no intention of listening to it. The men were only chosen "to serve as cloaks and cats-paws." Kieft—"who himself imagined, or certainly wished to make others believe, that he was sovereign"—insisted that before the end of the year the village of the murderer should be attacked. The Twelve argued for restraint, and in spite of Kieft's efforts to divide them, they succeeded in delaying the expedition and forced him to send delegates—"one, two and three times"—to the Wecquaesgeek tribe to ask for the murderer.[14]

But in January 1642, after the peace with the Raritans, they could no longer stop him. The Indians had stubbornly refused to take any action and the Twelve were obliged to agree that unless something were done, they would lose all authority with the Indians. On January 12 they gave their consent to a punitive expedition—but only if Kieft promised that he would personally accompany it, in order to prevent a repetition of the atrocities committed by Dutch troops against the Raritans in 1640.

Two months went by before Kieft could send his soldiers on their way. First the Indians had to be lulled into believing that the Dutch were harmless, and it wasn't until March that Kieft's spies reported the savages "lay in their dwelling-place suspecting nothing." Ensign Hendrick van Dyck left at once with eighty men, only to return next day "without having accomplished anything." The guide had lost his way in the darkness, and the ensign had lost his patience. The expedition had not, however, been in vain. "The Wecquaesgeeks, who remarked by the trail made by our people in marching that they had narrowly escaped discovery, sought for peace," reported a satisfied Kieft supporter. This peace was concluded in the course of the spring by Van Tienhoven, at the farm of Jonas Bronck, north of Manhattan. The only condition imposed on the Indians was that they should "either deliver up the murderer or inflict justice themselves." It was a promise they never kept.[15]

Contrary to his undertaking to the Twelve, Kieft had not accompanied the March expedition against the Indians. It had not been necessary for him to leave the safe walls of Fort Amsterdam, since the Twelve by then no longer existed. Kieft's first exercise

A SWEET AND ALIEN LAND

in democracy had, as far as he was concerned, not been a great success. The "cats-paws" had soon unsheathed their claws.

It had happened on January 21. Having nine days earlier at last consented to revenge against the Wecquaesgeeks, the Twelve thought the moment opportune to ask for something themselves. They handed the amazed Kieft a petition, the first of its kind, in which they demanded a drastic reorganization of local government. The colony was rapidly coming of age, and the settlers had had enough of being silenced. They were controlled by the two-man council and a court completely in the power of their dictatorial director; they were not even free to come and go without notifying him; and the "burgher-guard," they had noticed, was not up to the company's requirements. In their petition they now proposed the formation of a Council of at least five persons, while the Twelve should in certain matters have free access to the Council. There should be a rotation of Council members, elected from among the Twelve. Other demands were for freedom of movement around the country, and restrictions on the import of English cattle (which spoiled their herds) and the export of money.[16]

Kieft answered carefully. Some of the points he accepted provisionally, such as the extension of his Council and the mustering of a militia. But, unable to disguise his irritation, he told the Twelve haughtily that he was not aware of having given them "fuller powers than to give advice respecting the murder of the late Claes Swits." And on February 8 a notice was pinned up next to the gate of the fort in which Kieft thanked the Twelve for "the taken trouble." He promised to make use of their "written advice in its own time," and ordered them not to hold any further meetings, "as the same tends to a dangerous consequence and to the great injury both of our country and our authority." Kieft had restored his "sovereignty" over Christians and Indians alike.[17]

His triumph was short-lived. New incidents showed that the Indians were far from ready to settle down in peace and quiet— their dissatisfaction with the way that "very mean fellow," the Dutch sachem, had treated them was too deep-rooted. Miantonimo, the chief of the Narragansett Indians in New England, found the "Dutch" Indians thirsting for action when he came to New Netherland in the hope of stirring them into general war against their European oppressors. There was sporadic violence all

A VERY MEAN FELLOW

over the province. In one of the clashes the English servant of a Dutch farmer was killed, and the *Journal* reports that the Indians even attempted to poison Kieft and "to inchant him by their devilry."[18]

One particular occurrence in the summer of 1642 shocked the whole community. Gerrit Jansz van Vorst, a farmhand who was working in the small settlement of a certain Meyndert Meyndertsen on Staten Island, was shot at point-blank range by a drunken Hackensack Indian. David de Vries had met the savage shortly before the deed was committed. On a short stroll from Vriesendael to a neighboring farm, an Indian came up to him complaining that he had just been at Meyndertsen's, where they had sold him watered brandy and stolen his beaver coat. Drunkenly caressing De Vries' arm as a token of friendship, he told him that "he would go home and get his bow and arrows, and would kill some of the villainous Swannekens who had stolen his goods." De Vries went on and warned his neighbor not to mistreat the Indians, as "they were a very revengeful people, and resembled the Italians that way." His warning was too late. On his return to Vriesendael, the patroon learned that the Indian had carried out his threat and killed Van Vorst while the Dutchman was thatching the roof of a barn.[19]

That same day some chiefs of the Hackensack tribe came in a panic to De Vries and asked him what they should do to prevent the revenge of Kieft. They offered their usual blood money, two hundred fathoms of wampum, for the widow, but the Dutchman persuaded them to go to the fort, where Kieft curtly refused the gift of wampum and demanded the surrender of Van Vorst's murderer. "They said they could not do so as he had run away a two days' journey," but afraid that he would detain them, they promised to do their best. The chiefs did not leave before telling Kieft —in front of De Vries, who reveled in the embarrassment of the director—that the Dutch themselves were to blame for all the trouble, because they sold the young Indians brandy or wine, "making them crazy." The example the Dutch gave the natives was not much better: "they had seen our people . . . frequently intoxicated, and fight with knives." It was the end of the "audience" and nothing was ever heard of the murderer.[20]

But if for De Vries "the matter passed off," for Kieft it was a challenge to his authority that he was determined not to let pass.

A SWEET AND ALIEN LAND

He was supported by some citizens who, thoroughly aroused by Indian aggression, told him that if he would not take revenge, they should do it themselves—"be the consequences what they might." This was in fact only a small group of people, led by Van Tienhoven, who were smarting for action against the Wilden. Most of the colonists, led by De Vries, La Montagne, and the garrulous Bogardus, were in favor of punishing lawbreaking Indians—but were very much opposed to all-out war.[21]

In February 1643 Kieft and his adherents got their chance at last. The Tappan and Wesquaesgeek Indians had been attacked by ninety Mohawk warriors, who had killed seventeen of the Algonquins near Fort Orange. According to the Kieft war party, it was the "vengeance of God." About five hundred Indians "fled through deep snow" to the farms on and around Manhattan, starving and destitute. De Vries found his house invaded by them on February 22, but he refused to protect them, pointing out to the bewildered savages that the Mohawks also were the friends of the Dutch, and that he could not interfere in their wars.[22]

The Indians proceeded the next day to Pavonia, and on February 24 De Vries crossed the almost frozen Hudson to Kieft's house on the west bank to discuss the matter. It was an encounter he never forgot. Deeply shocked, he was forced to listen to a venomous outburst from the governor. Kieft no longer concealed the fact "that he had a mind to wipe the mouths of the savages." He had made thorough preparations, and he had even arranged his alibi. According to his account, some Dutchmen had handed him that same afternoon a petition asking him to make war on the Indians.[23]

This piece of chicanery had been dreamed up by Van Tienhoven, who, during a hearty dinner at the house of his stepfather-in-law, Churchwarden Jan Janse Damen, had produced a petition already written out by himself and only needing some signatures. Damen and both the other guests, Maryn Adriaensen and Abram Planck—all members of the now defunct Twelve—belonged to the militant party. What the adroit Van Tienhoven told the three men is unknown—the pro-Kieft *Journal* prudently speaks only of "a protracted discussion too long to be reported" —but in the end the inebriated diners signed. "God having now delivered the enemies evidently into our hands, we beseech you to permit us to attack them," said the petition. Kieft had his per-

A VERY MEAN FELLOW

mit for war against the Hackensacks, who had taken refuge on Manhattan and Pavonia.[24]

De Vries protested. "Such work could not be done without the approbation of the Twelve Men." Kieft merely shrugged. "He had," concluded De Vries, "with his co-murderers determined to commit the murder, deeming it a Roman deed."

The next day, Kieft invited De Vries to come with him to the large hall he had lately added to the already imposing Governor's House. There De Vries found the mercenary troops of the West India Company ready to cross the river to Pavonia. The wise and gallant Dutchman made one last effort to stop Kieft's insane expedition. Standing in front of the soldiers, he begged them to reflect. "Let this work alone; you wish to break the mouth of the Indians, but you will murder our own nation," he warned Kieft. But Kieft assured him indifferently that there was no danger.

"So was this business begun," De Vries noted down sadly, "between the 25th and 26th of February in the year 1643." The pleadings of Bogardus and La Montagne made little impression on Kieft, who dismissed them with the words: "The order is gone forth; it shall not be recalled."[25]

The governor, who had sent scouts to spy on the Indians, had decided that to surprise all the natives at once, he must split up his "army." The eighty soldiers under Van Tienhoven and Corporal Hans Steen were to go to Pavonia, the volunteers (forty-nine freemen under Maryn Adriaensen, "a man of brutal character") were to attack the Indian refugees behind Corlaers Hook on eastern Manhattan.[26]

De Vries stayed up all night, sitting in front of the fire in Kieft's kitchen in anguished suspense. At midnight he heard the first piercing cries of the Indians and ran at once to the ramparts, from where he looked across to Pavonia. "I saw nothing but firing and heard the shrieks of the savages murdered in their sleep." Heartbroken, he had just returned to the fire when an Indian and his squaw entered, looking desperately for a hiding place. He told De Vries that the Mohawk Indians from Fort Orange had surprised them and that they wanted to conceal themselves in the fort. "I told them that they must go away immediately," De Vries related later, revealing "that they who had killed their people at Pavonia, were not the Indians, but the Swannekens."[27]

At sunrise burghers and soldiers were back in the fort, where

A SWEET AND ALIEN LAND

a highly satisfied Kieft thanked them warmly, "taking them by the hand" and congratulating them. According to him, they had done "a deed of Roman valor." De Vries and his party saw it in different terms, and he later gave a heartrending account of the massacre:

> *Infants were snatched from their mothers breasts, and cut to pieces in sight of the parents, and the pieces thrown into the fire and into the water; other sucklings were bound to wooden boards, and cut and stuck or bored through, and miserably massacred, so that a heart of stone would have been softened. Some were thrown in the river, and when the fathers and mothers endeavoured to rescue them, the soldiers would not let them come ashore again, but caused both old and young to be drowned. . . . Some came to our people on the farms with their hands cut off; others had their legs hacked off and some were holding their entrails in their arms.*

Even in the morning there was no mercy for the Indians. "Those who had fled the onslaught and concealed themselves, were murdered in cold blood when they came out to beg a piece of bread, and to be permitted to warm themselves." The freemen, killing forty savages, had been no better then the soldiers, who accounted for eighty. "A disgrace to our nation, who have so generous a Governor in our Fatherland as the Prince of Orange, who has always endeavoured in his wars to spill as little blood as possible," was De Vries' disgusted comment.[28]

The Indians recovered only slowly from the shock. For a few days they still believed that they had been attacked by Mohawks, but when they realized that the massacre had been the work of Swannekens, a fierce guerrilla war began. Soon the River Indians won the support of the Canarsies on Long Island, who had initially remained neutral, but were driven to war by Dutch raiding parties. Within a few weeks the colonists were facing a closed front of eleven tribes. "All the men whom they could surprise on the farmlands they killed," reported De Vries, "but we have never heard that they permitted women or children to be killed. They burned all the houses, farms, barns, grain and destroyed everything they could get hold of."[29]

For the colonist there was no choice but to flee to the small overcrowded fort at New Amsterdam, and slowly Kieft realized the consequences of his actions. It was in that month of March 1643 that Rhode Island Governor Roger Williams visited the capital of the Dutch province on his way to England. He urged Kieft to make peace at once, before the whole country was ruined, but Kieft raised objections and demanded that the Indians come to the fort to negotiate.

When some Dutch settlers, by now exasperated and furious, threatened to ship him off to Holland, the governor gave in. He was saved from complete loss of face by three Canarsie Indians, who came on March 4 from Long Island with a white flag of peace. They invited the Dutch to send emissaries, but only De Vries and another man had the courage to leave the safety of the fort and go with them to their chief, Penhawitz.

The negotiations in the deep forests of Long Island threatened to be long. Laying down a little stick for every grievance against the Dutch, the one-eyed Indian chief embarked on a long diatribe. Seeing that he had a whole bundle in his hand, De Vries interrupted him politely and invited him to come to the fort and talk there with Kieft. To his relief, "they all rose and said that they would go with us." Arriving at the canoes, De Vries' heart sank when a young Indian told the chiefs that they were mad to trust the Swannekens, who now would keep them all in prison. The Indians wavered a moment, but Penhawitz turned to De Vries. "We will go on the faith of your word," he remarked.[30]

Kieft for once received the chiefs graciously at the fort and talked a long time, persuading them to conclude a treaty. They left with presents but without committing themselves, returning at last three weeks later to make peace. At the same time they promised to mediate between the Dutch and the River Indians.

It looked as though calm might now return, and Kieft could start to organize the reconstruction of the devastated province. The dissatisfaction of the five hundred colonists, however, was not easily appeased. Everything they owned had been razed, and the man responsible for this cataclysm had to be punished. Kieft hurriedly manned his defenses. They were only paper thin—the petition signed by the three freemen, Damen, Planck, and Adriaensen. The settlers rejected this and pointed out that since the governor had refused to allow the Twelve to meet, he was solely responsible.

One of the men who had signed the petition, Maryn Adriaensen, hearing of Kieft's apology and accusations, could not contain himself. During the war he had, in the words of Kieft, "at his request led the freemen in the attack on the Indians, and . . .

afterwards undertaken two bootless expeditions in the open field." He had also lost his own house, and he refused now to shoulder the responsibility for the whole war. As an ex-freebooter and sailor of the company, he was known as an "insolent man." He would show that he deserved his reputation.

On the afternoon of March 21 he left his house in a rage with a sword and "a loaded and cocked pistol," rushing to the house of the governor, whom he found in his bedroom. He pointed the pistol at the frightened Kieft with the words: "What devilish lies have you been telling of me?" For once La Montagne, who had followed him, overcame his usual hesitations and caught the pan of the pistol, letting the hammer snap on his thumb. With the help of some bystanders Adriaensen was overpowered and thrown into jail.[31]

It was the signal for a general explosion. Jacob Stangh, Adriaensen's servant, rapidly spread the news that his employer was in prison, and an hour later a crowd of excited New Amsterdammers, headed by Stangh, poured into the fort. When Stangh shrilly demanded the release of his employer, Kieft simply turned his back on him and walked to his front door. He had barely closed it behind him when two bullets slammed into the wall beside it. Another shot rang out at once. The fort sentry had reacted immediately, and killed the trigger-happy Stangh on the spot.

Stangh's head was stuck up on a pole as a warning to other rebels; and for a moment New Amsterdam held its breath. But that evening a noisy crowd gathered in front of the Governor's House demanding the release of Adriaensen. The door opened a few inches and four of them were let into the house by an anxious Kieft, who told them that he had decided to leave this affair "in the hands of the community," trusting that the culprit would be punished.

The crowd hurriedly chose a jury of eight men, who, as Kieft later charged, "without having been presented to the Council for confirmation," promptly pronounced sentence. Adriaensen was to be freed on payment of a fine of five hundred guilders, and on condition that he stay away from Manhattan for three months. The badly shaken Kieft now pulled himself together, and "for the sake of maintaining the respect due to justice," took matters into his own hands. He attempted to induce "some prominent men" to reinforce his Council and give Adriaensen a proper trial. But he

A VERY MEAN FELLOW

could find nobody willing to assist him, and in the end, "in order to avoid the charge of being moved by passion," he shipped Adriaensen off to Holland.[32]

A month after this incident, on April 22, 1643, there was better news at last for Kieft and his troubled province. The Canarsie Indians had succeeded in persuading the Hackensack and Tappan tribes to accompany them to New Amsterdam and negotiate an end to the war. It took only a day to come to terms, but at the end of this day Kieft once more made a mistake that was to prove fatal. As the chiefs left, the close-fisted governor handed over the traditional presents—but they were decidedly stingy.

The affronted Indians later told a distressed De Vries: "He could have made it by his presents that as long as he lived the massacre would never be spoken of; but now it might fall out that the infant upon the small board would remember it."[33]

The disastrous year of 1643 was not yet at an end.

THE ENGLISH
SAVIOR

On October 8, 1643, Captain David de Vries embarked on a vessel from Rotterdam which had arrived ten days earlier in New Amsterdam on its way to Virginia. Sickened by the cruelty that had reigned for the last years in and around New Amsterdam, and disgusted by the incompetence of the company rulers, he had decided to return to the Netherlands. Before he went on board he took his leave from Governor Kieft, and as usual he did not mince his words. "I told him that this murder which he had committed on so much innocent blood, would yet be avenged upon him." Before Kieft had been able to answer, he left, never to return to the New World.[1]

Like so many of the settlers, De Vries had lost everything he owned and lived in fear for his life—although the Indians trusted this "good chief" more than anybody else. After a winter in Virginia he finally reached his paternal city of Hoorn in June 1644, where he thanked God "that he should have brought him again to my Fatherland . . . through so many perils of savage heathens." Many colonists would have liked to follow De Vries, and several did, but having invested so much effort and money in their new country, most of them stayed in the hope that matters would soon take a turn for the better.[2]

This hope seemed slight. The summer of 1643 had been marked by incidents between the Indians and settlers, and it was obvious that the war was not over. Again it had been De Vries who in July of that year—thanks to his excellent contacts with the Indians—had warned Kieft of a new threat. An Indian chief had told him that he was having problems with the youth in his and other tribes because the Swannekens had killed their relations or friends, and the presents Kieft had given them "were not worth picking up." Typically Kieft's only reaction had been to offer the chief two hundred fathoms of wampum if he would kill the young turks. De Vries could not believe his ears. "I laughed within myself that the Indian should kill his friends for 800 guilders to gratify us," he remembered later, and he was right. The chief refused indignantly.[3]

In the meantime another chief was doing his best to incite the youths to action. Pacham, the sachem of the Haverstraw, who two years earlier had come to New Amsterdam with the hand of an Indian murderer to prove his love for the Dutch, had now changed sides and was "urging the Indians to a general massacre." The Wappingers, a tribe living fifteen miles from New Amsterdam, with whom the Dutch had never before had conflicts, were the first to rise. In August they attacked a boat coming from Fort Orange with four hundred furs and killed one of the crew. It gave them a taste for blood. Two other boats were attacked, and nine settlers, including two women, were murdered, while six Indians lost their lives.

The worst blow fell in September, when an uprising of the Indians in Connecticut spread to the Hudson, and seven different tribes, numbering fifteen hundred warriors, once more flooded New Netherland with terror and devastation. Within a few days they were occupying Pavonia, the greater part of Manhattan, and most of Long Island.[4]

The settlers, who had just begun the reconstruction of their homes and farms, fled for the second time to Fort Amsterdam, where they lived almost defenseless in hastily built straw huts under the decrepit walls. As in 1641, a desperate and beaten Kieft turned once more to the people for advice. With little hope and no enthusiasm, a board of Eight Select Men was formed, including only two members of the former Council of Twelve, Jan Jansen Damen and Jochem Kuyter. Among the other six were two Englishmen. One of them, Thomas Hall, who in 1634 had betrayed to

A SWEET AND ALIEN LAND

the Dutch the group of Virginians settling on the Delaware, was now a tobacco planter at Turtle Bay on the East River. The other was Master Isaac Allerton, one of the original *Mayflower* Pilgrims, who after some differences with the government of New Plymouth, had in 1638 come to live in New Amsterdam. The rest of the Council were Dutchmen, and one of them, Cornelis Melyn, the patroon of Staten Island, was chosen as president.

Melyn, a tanner from Amsterdam, had arrived in New Amsterdam in August 1641, after an adventurous voyage. Pirates from Dunkirk had seized his ship, imprisoning him and his family and servants. He had to pay a ransom before he could continue his crossing, and to the great annoyance of De Vries, settled as a neighbor on his Staten Island. Melyn was a forthright man who had no intention of putting up with Kieft's tactics, and who made it plain from the start that he had no time for Kieft's old collaborators. Damen, one of the three signatories of Kieft's "war permit," was at once kicked out of the Eight. When he protested vehemently that Kieft had misled him, the seven others refused to sit with him, and he was replaced by Jan Evertsen Bout, a farmer from Pavonia.[5]

On September 15 the first meeting was held. The Eight decided unanimously to attack the Algonquin River tribes, but to keep the peace with the Long Island Indians in the hope that these might help them find "some heads of the murderers." On the advice of Allerton, they made an even more sensible decision—to hire an expert in Indian warfare, the English Captain John Underhill, who together with Captain John Mason had led New England's soldiers in their three-week war with the Pequot Indians in 1637.

Like Allerton, the captain was not unfamiliar with the Dutch and their language. While the first was a tailor in Leiden, Underhill was learning the art of war from the Prince of Orange. He married a Dutch girl and in 1630 came with John Winthrop Sr. to Massachusetts, where for a salary of fifty pounds a year he trained the Boston militia. In 1638 Underhill discovered the charms of Manhattan and the Hudson Valley during a visit to his sister, Petronella, who was married to the schout of New Amsterdam, Ulrich Lupolt.[6]

In a booklet called *Newes from America* Underhill loudly sang the praises of the Dutch province, which he described as a part of New

THE ENGLISH SAVIOR

England. It was, according to him, "a place exceeding all yet named, the River affords fish in abundance . . . the only place for Beaver that we have in those parts."[7]

He would have done better to stay there rather than return to Boston, where the Puritan magistrates soon discovered a dangerous streak of heresy in the "savior" of the Pequot War. His career came to an end when he was charged with adultery with a certain Mistress Miriam Wilbore, at whom he had stared during a lecture. Underhill, tongue in cheek, had admitted "his sin," but had stated that he had not looked "with lust." Hugh Peter, the formidable pastor of Salem, asked why he had not looked at the other ladies present, and Underhill innocently answered: "Verily they are not desirable women." For Peter, this was enough proof of guilt and Underhill was excommunicated. When he demanded by which law he was condemned, Winthrop Sr. assured him that "Brother Peter" had certainly made one "against this very sin."[8]

As he had already signed a petition in support of the "errorist" Anne Hutchinson, he lost his job, and in 1639 left for Stamford, the English settlement just past Greenwich, where he stayed until Allerton appealed to him in 1643. This amusing reprobate, unacceptable to the Puritans, soon convinced the Dutch that they had made the right choice.

Unlike the Indians of the Pequot War, who had been armed only with bows and arrows, the natives of New Netherland had guns. After one look at the 50 to 60 mercenaries and the "militia" consisting of about 250 burghers, Underhill pointed out that they were completely inadequate to stem the Indian flood. Together with Allerton he convinced the Eight that help from New England was needed, and Kieft was asked to send the two Englishmen to the "pretended colony" of New Haven to ask for 150 men. For their pay they proposed a bill of exchange for twenty-five thousand guilders, while the province should be mortgaged to the English for security.[9]

On October 27, 1643, Underhill and Allerton put their request to the General Court at New Haven, presided over by the stern governor, Theophilus Eaton. The New Haven men studied the Dutch proposal seriously, and "although they were affected with a due sense of so much Christian blood . . . lately shed by the Indians" they felt they had to reject it, "nott clearly understanding the rise and the cause of the warr." They promised to reconsider their decision in the spring and in the meantime to help with food.[10]

The Dutch felt that their last hope had gone, and on November 3 the Eight sat down to compose a heartbreaking plea to their overlords, the States General, for "such assistance as your High Mightinesses will deem most proper." The situation could not have been worse.

Almost every place is abandoned. We, wretched people, must skulk, with wives and little ones that still survive, in poverty together, in and around the Fort at the Manahatas where we are not safe even for an hour; whilst the Indians daily threaten to overwhelm us with it. Very little can be planted this autumn and much less in Spring; so that it will come to pass that all of us who will yet save our lives, must of necessity perish next year of hunger and sorrow, with our wives and children. . . .

They pointed out that the garrison was no stronger than fifty to sixty soldiers, who, in any case, lacked ammunition; that Fort Amsterdam, "utterly defenceless, stands open to the enemy day and night;" and that the Indians, seven nations strong, were provided with guns, powder, and lead by private traders so that they, "poor forlorn people," were left as "a prey, with wives and children, to these cruel heathens." If help did not soon arrive, they would have no choice but to hand themselves over to the English in the east, "who would like nothing better than to possess this place."[11]

Accompanied by a petition to the Heeren XIX, this remonstrance was shipped off to The Hague. But the settlers could not wait for an answer. Winter was coming on, the Indians were growing bolder, and from their hiding places in the forests they were attacking one settlement after another. Even Stamford, Underhill's residence, had not been spared, and Anne Hutchinson, together with her family and servants, eighteen persons in all, had been massacred early in October (only her little daughter survived and was taken captive), while Lady Deborah Moody at Gravesend only escaped the same fate because of her forty-strong bodyguard.

All over the province farms went up in flames and harvests rotted in the fields, while the complaints of the settlers about their disastrously incapable governor grew louder daily. At last Kieft was goaded into action. He assembled two hundred burghers and

THE ENGLISH SAVIOR

the company's meager troop of fifty mercenaries, putting them in command of Jochem Kuyter, one of the Eight. Underhill led an English contingent of forty men, and the whole small army was put in charge of Councillor La Montagne.

In January 1644 it made its first sortie, to Staten Island. But when the men arrived, the place had been deserted by the Indians, and they came trailing back to New Amsterdam. About this time the head of Mayn Mayano, sachem of a tribe that lived between Greenwich and Stamford, was brought into New Amsterdam. Mayn had been thought loyal to the Dutch, but he had suddenly attacked some settlers with bow and arrow, killing one of them before he was shot. "It was then known and understood for the first time that he and his Indians had done us much injury," reports the *Journal*, and a punitive expedition of 120 men was at once dispatched to Greenwich. But once more the Indians had been warned, and the disheartened troops moved on to Stamford. Here they found vengeance when some of the local settlers led them to an Indian village. Twenty Indians were killed, and several prisoners taken to exchange for Dutch captives. One of these, an old man, offered to lead them to the stronghold of their most hated enemies, the Wecquaesgeek tribe.[12]

Under the command of Kieft's English secretary, Lieutenant George Baxter, sixty-five men followed their guide to the three castles the savages had built north of Manhattan, not far from the Hudson River. The forts were empty, but the soldiers were deeply impressed by their solidity, "since [they] were constructed of plank five inches thick, nine feet high and braced around with thick balk full of portholes." Thirty Indians would have been enough to defend them against two hundred soldiers—and with that in mind the soldiers burnt two, "reserving the third for a retreat."[13]

The destruction of the Wecquaesgeek forts was some comfort to the Dutch at New Amsterdam, who learned at this time that Sachem Penhawitz of the Canarsie had again turned against them, ordering his people to kill and burn wherever they could. The desperate settlers felt that the traitor must be taught a severe lesson, and La Montagne, together with Underhill, personally led an operation against the sachem. It was one of the most ruthless exercises of the war. Arriving on Long Island, the troops marched to Heemstede, where they divided their attentions with great suc-

A SWEET AND ALIEN LAND

cess between several settlements. More than 120 Canarsie Indians were killed, while the troops lost only one man.[14]

This victory was not enough for the frenzied and elated soldiers. They took four prisoners, of whom just two reached New Amsterdam. Underhill, noted in New England for his clemency toward Indians, had, under pressure from his bloodthirsty militia, ordered two of the prisoners to be tied up and drowned in the sound. Their fate was happy compared to that of the two survivors, whom the troops, "flushed with victory," dragged triumphantly through the streets of the capital, while brandishing the heads of other victims on sticks. When one of the heads fell on the ground, Van Tienhoven's French mother-in-law, Adrienne Culville, the wife of Jan Damen, was so exulted that she gave it a kick. Not everyone enjoyed the sight, or approved the massacre, and some of the other women violently "upbraided" Adrienne, whose husband and son-in-law, they felt, were responsible for the war.

But the soldiers paid no attention to this scuffle. Drunk with victory, they fell on their two prisoners with long knives, stabbing them repeatedly. One of the Indians attempted his "kinte kaeye," the traditional dance of death, but he was so much wounded that he died on the spot. At this, some Indian women began to shout out in horror: "Shame, what foul and unspeakable villainy this is," but they were compelled to look on helplessly while the other prisoner met an even worse fate.

According to the pamphlet *Broad Advice,* another less squeamish spectator was Kieft who, with typical cruelty, looked on, "rubbing his right arm and laughing out loud, such delight he had in the work," while the soldiers hacked "living slices" from the body of their victim. Even La Montagne was reported to have watched with enjoyment while the Indian was castrated and, with his testicles stuffed in his mouth, finally decapitated.[15]

But there was no time to linger over these victories. Captain Underhill had hurried back from a visit to his wife at Stamford with news that the Indians were massing near Greenwich "to celebrate some peculiar festival." He and Ensign Hendrick van Dyck (whose right arm was crippled from a shot wound received in October of the previous year) at once embarked with an army of 130 men in three yachts, sailing for Greenwich in a heavy snowstorm. Early next morning Underhill led a frightful march, clambering over stony hills covered with snow and ice, wading through

THE ENGLISH SAVIOR

two wide rivers before his frozen soldiers reached the Indian settlement at eight o'clock that night. They decided to wait till ten
before attacking the village's three streets of huts. When the Dutch
and English finally charged, the moon was at its full, and threw
"a strong light against the hill so that many winter days were not
brighter than it then was." Swords in hand, the men surrounded
the Indians, who tried to defend themselves by making two sorties.
This only resulted in the death of 180 of their warriors.

Underhill decided to cut the battle short and gave orders to set
the huts on fire, "whereupon the Indians tried every means to
escape, not succeeding in which they returned back to the flames,
preferring to perish by fire than to die by our own hands." For
once the mercenaries and the militiamen shivered with admiration
for the courage of the Indians, who perished—men, women, and
children—without uttering a cry. Some five hundred (others reported seven hundred) Wecquaesgeeks and about twenty-five
Wappingers died, and only eight escaped.

The troops from New Amsterdam tended their fifteen
wounded, one of whom was Underhill, and left next day for Stamford, where the "English received them in a very friendly manner." Two days later they were back in New Amsterdam, and "a
day of thanksgiving was proclaimed on their arrival."[16]

It took the remonstrance of the Eight Select Men five months
to reach the States General, and, as it turned out, they might have
spared themselves the trouble. The States, very much shocked by
the news from their province in America, wrote to the West India
Company on April 5, 1644, urging the Heeren XIX to send immediate help. The company's Chamber of Amsterdam, the "guardians"
of New Netherland, read the message from the States with disappointment. That same day the "guardians" wrote back that even
though they felt "in the innermost recesses of our hearts the miserable and desolate condition of the poor people there," they were
unable to support "their luckless colonists" unless the States
would give them a grant of about one million guilders.[17]

Their claim of insolvency was not exaggerated. The West India
Company, which in 1640 had been at the peak of its greatness, had

within four years collapsed under the weight of mismanagement and misfortune. A rebellion in its most precious possession, Brazil, had almost drained its resources dry. And when the remonstrance of its North American province reached the Company, the Lords Directors saw only one way out: to refer the matter to a committee. This time it was their own Rekenkamer, the Board of Account, that finally in December produced a devastating report.[18]

In the first place, the report condemned in strong terms the actions of Kieft, whose hasty proceedings against the natives with the aim "to exterminate all enemies" had resulted in the murder of many settlers and soldiers and of about one thousand Indians. It was therefore necessary to replace him, since the natives, "calling daily for Wouter, Wouter—meaning Wouter van Twiller," would never conclude a peace treaty with him. As his successor, they proposed Lubbertus van Dincklage, who had been sacked by Van Twiller and whose feud with the company about his unpaid salary was now forgotten.

At the same time, the whole system of government in the province should be revised. The director general should be assisted by a vice director and the Council expanded by two "capable members" of the community. Finally, the Board of Account advised the Heeren XIX to spend rather more than twenty thousand guilders a year on their civil servants in New Amsterdam, and to repair the fort as soon as possible.[19]

The Lords Directors found nothing in the report that pleased them, and they contented themselves for the moment with writing a long letter full of good wishes to the colony. As it was later said: "The Managers of the Company . . . had more regard for their own interest than for the welfare of the country, trusting rather to flattering than true counsels."[20]

New Amsterdam, looking more and more like a frontier town, had in the meantime received help from an unexpected quarter. The rapid decline of Dutch influence in Brazil had led to an exodus, and in May 1644 some four hundred Brazilian Dutch arrived in Curaçao, where the company's governor, Peter Stuyvesant, had no place or food for them. Remembering the plight of his colleague

THE ENGLISH SAVIOR

in New Amsterdam, he shipped 130 soldiers and 70 civilians off to the province, where they arrived at the beginning of July, on board the *Blaue Haen* ("Blue Cock").

The situation in New Netherland had improved slightly in the last few months. After the raid on the Wecquaesgeeks in February, the Indians had been quieter. John Underhill probably felt it was time to put an end to the massacres, and he had approached some of the chiefs in an effort to make peace. In April they came to the fort and solemnly signed a treaty with Kieft. But most of the Indians on and around Manhattan were still up in arms, and the troops from Brazil were most welcome.[21]

As far as Underhill and his "English auxiliaries" were concerned, the arrival of the Brazilian Dutch meant the end of the war. Kieft politely dismissed the mercenaries, delighted to be rid of an expense that had already led to a new and heated confrontation between him and his Eight Select Men. In June the governor, running out of money, had decided to tax the settlers for the first time. For once sticking to Dutch principle—that the imposition of taxes must be approved by the people—he reluctantly called the Eight to his house. He had not summoned them since the previous November. Plainly resenting this encroachment on his sovereign power, Kieft was in a vile temper and received them "with sundry biting and scoffing taunts." He listened impatiently when the Eight told him that the people were too poor to pay taxes, and when they went on to remind him that such a step ought to be decided by the Company, he exploded. Jumping up, he shouted: "I have more power here than the Company and therefore I do whatever I please. I have my commission not from the Company, but from their Lords, the States."

The startled Select Men decided to consent in principle. Kieft took this as sufficient encouragement to impose a tax of fifteen stuivers on each beaver skin, and two guilders on every tun of beer, from the brewers as well as the tapsters.[22]

Anticipating a hostile reaction, Kieft decided to convene the Eight once more before publicly announcing the taxes, but by the time they arrived, he had changed his mind once more. Indignant, Kuyter and Melyn later told how "he left us sitting in the room from 8 o'clock until noon, without asking a question." They left in anger, "as wise as we went." The settlers by this time were nearing mutiny, disgusted with the arbitrary behavior of a gover-

A SWEET AND ALIEN LAND

nor whose power, as the usually loyal La Montagne once muttered, seemed to be even greater than that of the Prince of Orange.[23]

The despised Kieft even made the welcome arrival of the *Blaue Haen* from Brazil seem bad news for the colony. He had imposed his first taxes with the promise that they would be discontinued when relief arrived; but instead he called another meeting of the Eight to raise them. His excuse was that the new troops had to be clothed—"Naked men are useless"—and armed. Shelter was easily found; he simply billeted them in the already overcrowded houses of the citizens. The new meeting of the Eight took place on July 21, and it was, as usual, stormy. The Eight refused to consider raising the duty on beer by one guilder. Undeterred, Kieft dismissed them and went ahead with the tax.[24]

For the New Amsterdammers it was bad enough to be taxed twice over on one of the rare pleasures remaining to them. But as the long hot Manhattan summer dragged by and the troops for whose upkeep they had been taxed stayed idle in the garrison, their resentment rose to fresh heights. The city split into two factions: the angry supporters of the Eight, and those who still stood behind Kieft. The latter were few in number, but the governor had his own ways of discouraging criticism. "Those who were on his side," it was reckoned, "could do nothing amiss, however bad it was," while those who were against him suffered the consequences of his order "to reckon half an offense as a whole one." Some of his unhappy citizens later reported that "the jealousy of the Director was so great that he could not bear without suspicion that impartial persons should visit his partisans."[25]

A few of his opponents, however, succeeded in getting together in the deepest secrecy. After a cry for help, written in August by Cornelis Melyn, had been smuggled out of the country to the States General, the Eight gathered around the table in October to compose a more formal complaint. Govert Loockermans was just leaving for Holland, and promised to hand it over to the Heeren XIX.

This time their letter was not so much a complaint about the situation in their country as a formal indictment of their governor; a rebellious but moving and dignified document, the first proof of the nascent "democratic temper" of the New Amsterdammers.

The Eight began by telling the Fatherland about their hopes and expectations when the *Blaue Haen* and her troops had arrived. It

THE ENGLISH SAVIOR

had given New Netherland a total force of between three hundred and four hundred men, which could easily have attacked the Indians and concluded the interminable war. "But nothing in the least has been done. In all this time, scarcely a foot has been moved on land, or an oar laid in the water." Experienced soldiers had been sent back to Holland by Kieft, who at the same time made them presents of Indian prisoners who should have been used as scouts and guides. Other Indians had been sent away as a present to the governor of Bermuda.

"Our fields lie fallow and waste: our dwellings and other buildings are burnt," they lamented; "we have left our beloved fatherland and unless the Lord our God had been our comfort, we must have perished in our misery." A record of all Kieft's misjudgments and cruelties followed, and the Eight ended with the plea:

> *This is what we have, in the sorrow of our hearts, to complain of; that one man, who has been sent out sworn and instructed by his Lords and masters, to whom he is responsible, should dispose here of our lives and property, according to his will and pleasure, in a manner so arbitrary that a king would not suffer legally to do it. . . . That a Governor may speedily be sent with a beloved peace to us.*

The only alternative was a massive exodus of all the inhabitants. It was a complaint that was to echo for a long time through New Amsterdam.[26]

The winter of 1644–1645 was hard. Provisions were scarce, the houses on Manhattan were overcrowded with refugees and soldiers, it was difficult to get hold of firewood, and trade had almost come to a standstill. The fort was as defenseless as ever, and even the church, hardly finished, already had an air of neglect. The atmosphere was tense and suspicious, and Governor Kieft could only keep order by dragging rebellious characters before his court.

The English auxiliaries dismissed by Kieft roamed the streets of the city idle and drunk, and their commanders added to the tension by outrageous behavior. John Underhill, disillusioned by his humiliating dismissal after having done so much to save the province, decided to teach the Dutch a lesson. One evening, together with Kieft's secretary, George Baxter, and the former Plymouth trader Thomas Willett, he smashed open the door of the Stadt's Herberg, where a startled Dominie Bogardus, his stepdaughter Sarah, and her husband Hans Kierstede were entertaining some other Dutch couples. With his sword Underhill swept the glasses from the table and threatened the guests. They protested weakly, but scurried away when the Englishman told the minister to clear out, "for I shall strike at random." The only revenge they could take was a formal complaint against the boisterous Englishman. He left New Amsterdam shortly after in disgust, to settle quietly—at least for the time being—into the Dutch-English community at Heemstede, the scene of his bloody triumph over the Indians.[27]

The first signs of spring had never been so welcome to the New Amsterdammers, and with the spring came new hope for peace. On April 22 some tribes came to the fort and signed a treaty. For Kieft it was an occasion to ring the church bells and salute the peace with a shot from one of the cannon, a brass six-pounder. This was an unfortunate idea, for the gunner, Jacob Roy, bungled his job and lost his right arm when the powder exploded too early.[28]

The peace of April caught on, and in May more tribes came to Kieft asking for an end to hostilities. To complete his "victory," the governor went to Fort Orange to make terms with the powerful Mohawks and Mohicans. The New Amsterdammers could not believe their eyes when they saw their governor sail away, for in seven years he had "never been farther from his kitchen and bedchamber than halfway up the Island [Manhattan]." Far away from the safety of his home, he succeeded in his mission, sealing the treaty with presents to the sachems, for which, broke or mean, he borrowed money from Adriaen van der Donck, at that time schout of Rensselaerswyck.[29]

Finally, on August 30, 1645, peace was completely restored to New Netherland. On that day all the chiefs of the surrounding tribes, five men strong, came wrapped in their red and blue duffel blankets to the fort, where they sat solemnly in front of the gate. The negotiations were quickly concluded. The Indians promised to refer future complaints to the director general and not to renew war, while the settlers would have access to their sachems. Neither party was allowed to come near the other's settlements on Manhat-

THE ENGLISH SAVIOR

tan. On these terms "a solid and durable peace" was concluded in front of the whole community, sealed by smoking the great calumet "under the blue canopy of heaven."[30]

After five years and one month Kieft's Indian War was at last over. More than sixteen hundred Indians had been killed, but thousands still surrounded New Amsterdam, and the colonist population around the fort had shrunk to no more than 250 souls—the town had dwindled into a village again. As De Vries had predicted, Kieft had murdered his own nation.

THE ISRAELITES

"And whereas there is yet among them an English girl whom they promise to conduct to the English at Stamford, which they yet engage to do, and if she is not conducted there, she shall be guided here in safety. . . . " So read the fourth point of the peace treaty that ended the war between the Dutch and the Indians. Although thousands had been killed and wounded, there was only one captive left in the hands of the savages: Susanna, the daughter of Anne Hutchinson. At the age of eight she had been dragged away by the Indians after the massacre in her mother's house near Stamford. Now two years older, the little girl returned by way of New Amsterdam to Boston, no longer able to speak English, and—like so many Dutch children later, who "taken prisoner by the Indians, on being returned to their parents, would hang around the neck of the Indians"—anxious to stay with her captors.[1]

The English in New Netherland, like the Dutch, had suffered terribly from Kieft's War. Apart from the bloodbath at Hutchinson's house and the attack on Lady Deborah Moody, the Reverend Francis Doughty with his followers was driven away from Mespath (Newtown) on Long Island to look for shelter in New Amsterdam. Heemstede, Greenwich, and Stamford had been raided by the Indians, but only a few of their English settlers had returned to the Puritan colonies in the east, possibly preferring the Indian terror to the religious persecution of Massachusetts and its neighbors. There had even been newcomers, such as the group evicted from Boston, which in the spring of 1645 founded the settlement of Vlissingen (Flushing) not far from Mespath.

The English settlers had fought loyally with the Dutch against the Indians, but little help had come from the English colonies. New Haven, having refused Kieft's first request for support, had never kept its promise to reconsider and had even tried to buy back Captain John Underhill for the sum of twenty pounds. Governor Winthrop of Massachusetts had been just as unhelpful. He criticized Underhill severely for his part in the war—"doubting the justice of the cause"—and saw his employment by the Dutch as a plot to involve the English. Loudly, and inaccurately, he claimed that it was thanks to an Englishman—the "notoriously heretickal" Roger Williams—that a temporary peace had been concluded.[2]

Fifteen years later an Englishman living in New Amsterdam, Samuel Maverick, asserted that the town would have been destroyed by the Indians "had it not been for a small partie of the English." The natives, according to him, had approached the English with the promise to kill all the Dutch and give them the land, and the refusals of the English to accept that offer "are the cheif Cause that the Dutch are growne to that height."[3]

In New England in particular there was little sympathy for the fate of the English settlers in New Netherland. When the news of the massacre at Anne Hutchinson's farm reached Boston, one inexorable pastor wrote: "God's hand is the more apparent seen herein to pick out this woeful woman to make her and those belonging to her an unheard-of heavy example. . . ." John Winthrop Sr. also saw it as a just punishment for those who "had cast off ordinances and churches and . . . their own people."[4]

Kieft's War, however, had taught the English colonies one lesson. Realizing that they too could be subjected to such troubles—the Narragansett chief Miantonimo was not the only New England Indian with plans for a rising—they came to the conclusion that unity would make them stronger. The unfortunate expedition from New Haven to the Delaware in 1642 and the constant troubles with the Dutch in Connecticut around the House of Good Hope had underlined this need for concord, especially since help from the Motherland, which was torn by civil war, could not be expected. On May 19, 1643, the United Colonies of New England were constituted at Boston: in essence, as a Dutch historian has

A SWEET AND ALIEN LAND

pointed out, it was very similar to the Union of Utrecht of 1579, the foundation of the United Provinces, "with which the Brownists, during their stay in Holland, had become acquainted."[5]

After years of confusing charters, patents, and grants, the map of New England was now drawn. In the northeast was the Maine colony of Sir Ferdinando Gorges—very Anglican and therefore not much cherished by its neighbors. Bordering it was the Puritan settlement at Massachusetts Bay, usually known as the Bay Colony, which in spite of many difficulties was, with its fifteen thousand inhabitants, the most powerful of the colonies. The Commonwealth of New Plymouth, with three thousand colonists and a less rigid government, kept to itself in the southeast, while Connecticut, its three thousand souls scattered among different towns, was still not much more than the "garden suburb" of Massachusetts. New Haven's right of existence as a separate colony was debatable, and among its twenty-five hundred inhabitants there were many who hesitated to acknowledge the government of Theophilus Eaton. The settlement, spread along the Long Island Sound, was certainly the most puritanical of the lot, very different from the fifth colony, Rhode Island.

Each of these states (whose combined populations numbered about twenty-five thousand souls) went their own way, independent of each other and almost independent of England. They had their own form of government, their different constitutions, and their singular character. Each relished its freedom, and did not intend to give it up easily, in spite of threats from London or the closer peril of Dutch and Indians. The United Colonies was therefore a very loose confederation, comprising Massachusetts, Connecticut, Plymouth, and New Haven. Rhode Island, with its unorthodox heretics, was "not to be capitulated with" and was never permitted to join.

The New England Confederation, as it was usually referred to, had little authority over its four members, and the eight commissioners—two from every colony—were strictly forbidden to interfere "with the government of any of the jurisdictions." They were allowed to talk, and made generous use of the permission, but like the members of the Dutch States General, they had to consult their own governments before decisions were taken. It was "a firme and perpetual league of friendship and amity," with the aim of "preserving and propagating the truth and liberties of the Gospel and

THE ISRAELITES

for their own mutual safety and wellfare"—and it was not much more.[6]

Director General Willem Kieft in New Amsterdam saw the formation of the confederation as a great opportunity to unburden himself, and at the same time establish better relations with his neighbors. During a lull in the Indian War he sent a sloop to Boston in July 1643 with a letter, written in Latin, for Governor Winthrop, congratulating him on the new-found unity, and asking him to intervene in the Dutch conflicts with Hartford at the Connecticut and with New Haven at the Delaware (for the Dutch still, respectively, the Fresh and the South rivers). Reports had reached the Dutch governor of the protest that Lord Saye and Sele had handed Ambassador Joachimi in London the previous year, as well as news of his threat to oust the Dutch within a year from their House of Good Hope. Kieft pointed out to Winthrop that the Honorable Lord had grossly misinterpreted the English rights. He concluded the letter by asking his English colleague "whether he should aid or desert him, so that he might know his friends from his enemies."[7]

Winthrop answered kindly that he hoped to sustain the friendship that had always existed between the people of Massachusetts and the Dutch, suggesting that the border differences ought to be settled by arbitration in Holland or England. The conflict with Hartford, said Winthrop, he found too unimportant to cause a breach between two American Protestant communities.

That the Hartford people did not agree with this viewpoint became clear in September when the first meeting of the commissioners was held in Boston. Both New Haven and Hartford protested excitedly against the treatment they had received from the Dutch, and Winthrop had to write Kieft a much sterner letter, demanding satisfaction.

To the Dutch settlers in New Netherland, the New England Puritans—the "Janikens" (Johnnies) as they called them—were a race apart. They had known a few of those Brownists when they lived in Amsterdam and Leiden, but never understood the religious fanaticism that drove so many Englishmen to the Dutch

A SWEET AND ALIEN LAND

province. They disliked, too, the rather unhealthy Puritan preoccupation with the sins of the flesh. Company Secretary Isaack de Rasières during his visit in 1628 to New Plymouth had been struck by the severe laws against fornication and adultery, and had himself been attacked because of the "barbarously" lax way the Dutch lived. David de Vries admired the sober way the New Englanders lived—"they drink only three times at a meal"—but he was much less enthusiastic about the disciplinarian measures taken against a drunkard—"they tie him to a post and whip him, as they do in Holland thieves."

De Vries had witnessed a "comical incident" when a young man who had had intercourse with his fiancee was denounced by his brother. Both he and the girl were whipped in public and forbidden to see each other for six weeks. De Vries shook his head at such repressiveness. "These people see themselves as Israelites," while the Dutch, and the Virginians, were to them nothing but Egyptians. And he could not resist telling the governor that "it would be impossible for them to keep the people so strict, seeing that they had come from so luxurious a country as England."[8]

The Puritans thought differently. That was precisely why they had come. Massachusetts, Plymouth, New Haven—and to a lesser extent, Connecticut—were all founded by religious-minded men who had fled Archbishop Laud's England to "those vast and unpeopled countries . . . frutfull & fit for habitation" in order to set up their own City of God, and worship him in their plain, severe way.[9]

The Puritanism of that age was no faith for milksops. On the contrary it was a highly muscular Christianity, ideally suited to pioneer life. The Puritans believed not merely in good works, but also in hard work. Idleness was the great sin—"a mispense of precious time"—and if hard work was crowned by material prosperity, that simply showed that God approved it. For the Puritans, there was nothing saintly about poverty.

The great majority of English emigrants in the 1620s and 1630s came from the Nonconformist stronghold of East Anglia and the Cloth Counties, which had been particularly badly hit by a general economic depression. The typical English colonist, far from being a rootless adventurer, was much more likely to be a good family man, of sound middle-class or yeoman stock, and often well educated. A farmer, artisan, or shipbuilder, he crossed the Atlantic for two motives—to find a better life for himself and his family, and to practice his faith in peace.

What was more, he came determined to stay. When Governor Eaton's discontented wife once proposed that they return to England, Eaton sternly replied: "You may, but I shall die here." He spoke for most of the colonists, whose eyes were on an American future.[10]

Unlike the Dutch, who appealed for supplies to the distant and reluctant West India Company, the English settlers had nobody but themselves to rely on. They had been obliged to set to work as soon as they landed, building houses, planting crops, fishing, hunting, and improvising a whole way of life with all possible speed before the descent of the long New England winter—harsh, violent, and "so Colde as some had their fingers frozen and in danger to be lost." The land of New England was not much more welcoming than its climate. Apart from the meadows scattered here and there along the shores and rivers, it was covered with dense forests through which roamed the gray wolves that remained a terror for most of the century.[11]

Before they left England the Puritans had spoken grandly of the benefit that the "savage and brutish" Indians would derive from their new white neighbors. They would, thought the Puritans, "learne from us to improve a parte to more use than before they could doe the whole"—but in fact the boot was on the other foot. The English, like the Dutch farther south, would have been lost without Indian help in learning to till the stubborn, glacial soil. From those ignorant brutes, they learned how to grow maize, pound it into meal, and cook it like the Indian *nasaump*—"a kind of meal pottage, unpartch'd . . . which is the Indian corne, beaten and boil'd, and eaten hot or cold with milke and butter. . . ." They copied the Indian way of using up the enormous strawberries which, as Roger Williams noted, "is the wonder of all the Fruits growing naturally in those parts . . . the Indians bruise them in a Mortar and mix them with meale and make Strawberry bread."[12]

Few of the New England settlers were paupers, and Winthrop did his best to see that they left England as well supplied as possible. "Thou must be sure to bringe no more companye, then so many as shall haue full Provision for a yeare and halfe," he wrote

A SWEET AND ALIEN LAND

back urgently to his son in England during his first year in America. And the early settlers constantly bombarded friends and relations back home with lengthy shopping lists of necessities unprocurable in Massachusetts: ". . . meale and pease, and some otemeale and Sugar . . . good store of Saltpeeter . . . the strongest welt leather shoes and stockings for Children; and hats of all Syzes . . . the coursest woollen clothe . . . store of shoemakers thread, and hobnayles, Chalk and Chalkline and a paire or 2 or more of large steel Compasses" were just a few of the items John Winthrop begged his wife to bring with her in 1631.[13]

Though life was indeed hard during the first few years, the Puritans could console themselves with the fact that they seemed to thrive on it: "there hath not died aboue 2 or 3 growne persons, and about so many Children all the last yeare, it being very rare to heare of any sick of agues or other diseases," reported Winthrop in 1634 to one of the colony's London patrons.[14]

In the New World, as in East Anglia, the English grouped themselves naturally into villages and small towns, planting their houses neatly along a High Street, each with its own garden plot. For architectural design, they simply recalled the frame and timber houses they had left behind.

The center of each new town was the church, forbiddingly plain and simple in structure, with little inside but pews and a pulpit, from which the typical New England minister delivered the long thundering sermons that were all the settlers got in the way of entertainment. By 1645 there were twenty-three churches in the Bay Colony alone; by this date New Amsterdam had hardly completed its first. Massachusetts, New Haven, and Plymouth were all virtually Bible commonwealths, in which for years the godly were the rulers. Church membership was the key to power; orthodoxy of the Puritan brand was more rigidly enforced than under all but the most despotic of European governments—and sinning was ridiculously easy.

Almost every kind of fun was not merely sinful but actually illegal. Adultery was almost too awful to contemplate, and punishable by death. Lesser sexual offenses drew down the wrath, and the prurient curiosity, of the magistrates; the early court records of Plymouth and New Haven come close to pornography in their enumeration of physical detail. In Massachusetts one could be fined five shillings for keeping that disorderly festival known as

THE ISRAELITES

tmas; dancing, singing, and card playing were frowned on; eboard and bowling were banned. Any kind of unnecessary was forbidden on Sunday—gardening, cooking, or making the beds; and Boston became famous for its baked beans, a dish that could be left cooking overnight on Saturday in the cooling fire and eaten on Sunday. The time saved by all those undone chores was to be given to God alone. It was a misdemeanor to waste the Sabbath going for a stroll or visiting friends. Massachusetts even passed sumptuary laws regulating excesses of fashion—the colony was to be kept pure of European "fantasticalnes."[15]

Many of the inhabitants chafed under the iron rule of the clergymen. Some sidestepped the rules, others simply ignored them. An anonymous letter from England to John Winthrop in 1637 revealed disapprovingly that "many in your plantacions . . . write over to us for lace, though of the smaller sorte . . . for cuttwork coifes . . . for deep stammell dyes; and some of your owne men tell us that many with you goe finely cladd. . . ."[16]

The young New Englanders, who must sometimes have been very nearly desperate, became ingenious at improvising their own festivities. The weekly lecture delivered by the minister—hardly the lightest of entertainment—became a high spot. New Haven discovered that its night watch was degenerating into a revel in the guardhouse on the green, and did its best to spoil the fun: "young and less satisfying persons shall be joyned with another more antient and trusty."[17] One Thomas Langdon was haled before the New Haven magistrates and fined a stiff twenty shillings for the dreadful crime of singing and drinking with other young men, in his own house at nighttime. "If we were in old England, we could sing and be merry," he remarked rebelliously. It was hardly surprising that so many people were lured away down the coast to the bright lights and sinful glamor of New Amsterdam.[18]

Puritan rigidity, coupled with extreme intolerance of other creeds, soon gave Massachusetts a daunting image as far away as England. One of the colony's original supporters wrote bitterly in 1637: "It doth not a little grieve my spirit what sadd things are reported dayly of your tyranny and persecution. . . ." And even Cromwell could only contemplate New England with a shudder: "poor, cold and useless."[19]

But if New England had been built on nothing more than intol-

A SWEET AND ALIEN LAND

erance and repression, it certainly would not have survived. The New England way of life had another, much warmer and more attractive side, seen at its best in the Winthrop family.

At the time the New England Confederation was formed, John Winthrop Sr. was fifty-five years old, and the doyen of the Bay Colony. He was very much the typical English country squire. A Calvinist of the first degree in Puritan East Anglia, he had no longer felt at home in a country that seemed every year to slip further away from true Reformed Protestantism. Laud the Arminian was the rising power; Puritanism was dangerously close to being outlawed. "The Lorde hath admonished, threatened, corrected and astonished us, yet we grow worse and worse," he wrote in May 1629. "He hath smitten all the other churches before our eyes, and hath made them drinke of the bitter cuppe of tribulation." All over Europe the Protestants were being driven into a corner, and Winthrop feared the worst. "I am verily perswaded God will bringe some heavy affliction upon this lande," he told his wife.[20]

Like most emigrants, Winthrop was influenced by economic considerations as well. Dutch competition and the war in Germany and the Low Countries had between them brought the cloth industry—basic to the prosperity of eastern England—almost to its knees, forcing down land prices and bringing about a general slump that hit even fairly wealthy families like the Winthrops of Groton Manor. "My means are so shortened . . . as I shall not be able to continue in this place," wrote Winthrop to a friend when he was forced to give up his Crown office in the Court of Wards and Liveries; he preferred like a good soldier to quit "with honour . . . rather than be forced." The dissolution of Parliament in 1629 was the deciding factor. Winthrop had followed closely the fortunes of John Endicott's Puritan settlement at Salem. Now he decided that it was his own turn.[21]

Other leading Puritans with the same idea, among them his brother-in-law the lawyer Emmanuel Downing, got together with several wealthy London merchants to plan a mass emigration to North America. The result was the Massachusetts Bay Company, incorporated by royal patent on March 4, 1629, whose members invited John Winthrop to be governor. Five months later he signed an agreement to transfer the company lock, stock, and barrel to

THE ISRAELITES

America and "plant" the new colony. As he had written in May: "If the Lord seeth it will be good for us, he will provide a shelter and a hidinge place for us and ours."[22]

On April 8, 1630, he sailed with part of his family, arriving in America two months later. More ships brought him between nine hundred and a thousand emigrants, and they spread over the grim and windy hills around the bay to found the little town of Boston. The first winter was very hard, and more than two hundred of the newcomers died. Some of the survivors returned to England, others moved to less barren parts of New England, and some even made it to New Netherland. Such good accounts of the Dutch colony reached London that Downing and another signatory of the Bay Agreement, John Humphrey, advised Winthrop to move with his planters to the Hudson "as it is warmer".[23]

Winthrop decided to stay in his "hidinge place" and built in a few years time a colony known at first for its agriculture and later for its shipbuilding. The earliest product of its wharfs was the thirty-ton vessel *Blessing of the Bay*, which Winthrop sent in 1633 to New Amsterdam with a letter of protest addressed to then Governor Wouter van Twiller against the Dutch "aggression" on the Connecticut.

This was his first official contact with the Dutch settlement, but it was certainly not the last, and over the years the Dutch governors increasingly turned to him, as Kieft did in 1643, when he complained bitterly about the behavior of Hartford and New Haven. Winthrop always reacted kindly and honestly, stating over and over again that he preferred to leave the border question to the King and the States General. He once went so far as to intervene mildly on behalf of the Dutch, urging Connecticut to leave a little more land to them around the House of Good Hope (it had only thirty acres left), but generally he followed the same line as the other colonies when dealing with their Dutch neighbors.[24]

Kieft never completely gave up hope of drawing Winthrop into his camp. In 1644 and 1645 he bombarded him with flattering and complimentary letters, which Winthrop answered with understanding, praising Kieft's "faithfulness to that State which have sett you in place and reposed trust in you." Nonetheless the message came through loud and clear; the Dutch had no right to the Fresh River. Winthrop made one effort to solve the problem by diplomacy, and invited Kieft or an envoy to come to the meeting

A SWEET AND ALIEN LAND

of the commissioners in September 1644 to talk matters over. But Kieft, still preoccupied with his Indian War, did not turn up, and sent no representative.[25]

Two years later the Dutchman was back with complaints. New Haven, in greater and greater financial difficulties, had bought a piece of land twenty miles east of the North River and sixty miles from the Dutch fur center at Fort Orange. A worried Adriaen van der Donck, schout at Rensselaerswyck, reported that the new trading post was established for no other purpose than to divert the fur trade of the North River or to destroy it, and Kieft reacted swiftly.[26]

On August 3, 1646, he wrote two forceful letters, one to Governor Eaton of New Haven—"the place we call Red Hill"—and the other to the Commissioners of the United Colonies. The tone of both letters was typically Kieft's—arrogant and undiplomatic, even in Latin. But his irritation was in this case forgivable, and his threat to recover the land "by such means as God affords" understandable. New Haven's new settlement was in the heart of his province.[27]

Eaton had already written to Winthrop about this new controversy, in a way that made Kieft's letter seem an example of conciliation. "A cloud merely seemes to threaten us from the west," Eaton wrote condescendingly. "We lately built a small house within our limites (if at least we have any interest in these parts and that the Dutch be not Lords of the countrye, for they write the plantation in New Netherland)." According to the Dutch, the New Haveners had already robbed them of "hundreds, nay thousands of skins," but according to Eaton, the loot had not been bigger than twenty beaver furs.[28]

When he received Kieft's letter, specially delivered by George Baxter, Eaton answered the governor in slightly politer terms. He told him that he had never heard of the North River and denied that he had set foot on any territory to which the Dutch had a title. His people had only built a small trading post on the "Paugussett River" (now Derby, Connecticut), on land bought from the Indians.

On September 9, 1646, the Commissioners of the United Colonies met, this time at New Haven, and the new confrontation with the Dutch was the main subject of discussion. The New Haven merchants were not alone in their complaints—the planters from

THE ISRAELITES

Connecticut joined eagerly in the chorus. The behavior of the Dutch commissary in the House of Good Hope, David Provost, had become insufferable, they told the meeting. Their people could hardly bear any longer the "insolencies and iniuries with a high hand lately committed." One of Hartford's special grievances was the Dutch protection of an Indian slave. She had fled from her master to the Dutch fort and Provost hit the Hartford guard who came to collect her, striking his arm with a sword with such force that the weapon broke.[29]

New Haven followed with an account of their new trading venture near the North River, and the session that day was concluded with the writing of a long epistle to Kieft. To begin with, the commissioners reminded him of Winthrop's invitation to come himself or to send an envoy to their meeting. Since he had not done so, he must take the consequences, and recent incidents proved that thorough inquiries were badly needed if peace was to be preserved. They asked him to send them a satisfactory explanation with the special messenger they dispatched in a desire "to embrace and pursue righteousness and peace."

The letter Kieft sent a week later was in no way conciliatory. In flowery Latin he rejected the complaints of Connecticut, having, he said, himself enough evidence of the way the English had treated the Dutch settlers at the House of Good Hope. He would not go into detail, but merely gave a few examples "as by the claw they may judge the talons of the lion." The Indian girl, he stated, was not a slave, but brought by her father into the fort for her education. The attack on the Hartford guard was in self-defense.

Certainly when we heare the Inhabitants of Hartford complaining about us, we seem to hear Aesops wolf complaying of the lamb, or the admonition of the young man who cried out to his mother, chiding with her neighbours: "O mother revile her, least she first takes up that practice against you." But being taught by precedent passages, we received such an answer to our protest from the inhabitants of Newhaven as we expected—the Eagle always despises the Beetle Fly.

He ended his statement by protesting the fact that the commissioners had dared come to New Haven, "within the limits of New Netherland," accusing them of being "breakers of the common

A SWEET AND ALIEN LAND

league and also infringers of the special right of the Lords, the States."[30]

The commissioners were, to put it mildly, deeply shocked by the tone and content of the letter, but felt it pointless to answer in the same terms. They stated coolly that Kieft was misinformed about the slave and many other matters, skipping over his insulting expressions and proverbs with the remark that they would leave those "to your calmer consideration." The protest against their meeting was, they told him, very much in the same vein, and had given them more reason to be offended than he was by their meeting in New Haven.[31]

It was the end of Kieft's correspondence with the United Colonies. All he could do was report the business to the Heeren XIX, who asked him in their usual careful way to inquire about the Indian rights to sell the land to New Haven and told him not to make war about it. The best thing he could do, they ingenuously suggested, was to keep an eye on his English neighbors and stop further encroachments.

What Kieft thought of this advice is not recorded. His troubles, at any rate, were almost over. After a very cold winter (the Hudson was for four months covered with thick ice), followed by a rainy spring that almost washed away Fort Orange, the New Amsterdammers received news that they were to be liberated from the dictatorship of their "little Caesar." Their petitions and protests had had their effect; the Heeren XIX had decided to recall him.

Kieft himself notified his New England neighbors of his departure for Holland in a letter to Winthrop. "We expect here at the beginning of next month the arrival of the new Director, who passed the winter at Curaçao," he wrote on April 17, 1647.[32]

What the New Englanders thought of his departure and of the man himself can best be judged from the remark the Massachusetts governor made when he heard a few months later of Kieft's unhappy end. It was the (for the Puritans always convenient) "observable hand of God" striking at the man, who had, so Winthrop wrote, "continually molested the colonies of Hartford and New Haven, and used menacings and protests against them upon all occasions."[33]

THE ISRAELITES

ANOTHER
FATHER

The island of Curaçao, the principal Caribbean possession of the West India Company, had been a great disappointment to the Dutch. They had been looking for a base for their raids on the Spanish and Portuguese in the West Indies—preferably one handsomely endowed with profitable saltpans and forests full of good timber—and Curaçao, with its safe and sheltered bays, had seemed at first a perfect choice. It was only after its conquest from the Spanish in 1634 that the company realized the island was barren, and its deep bays difficult to defend.

In 1638 the conquerors of the island, Director Johannes van Walbeeck and his military assistant, Major Pierre le Grand, were sent to Brazil, where the company was making great advances, and replaced by Jacob Pieters Tolck, a former company official from Brazil. He arrived on the island together with Petrus Stuyvesant, an ambitious and active young man in his late twenties. Stuyvesant, who had worked for the company since the beginning of the 1630s, had been appointed chief commercial officer for Curaçao and the two adjoining islands of Aruba and Bonaire, with the task of checking the cargoes of the Spanish prizes, and keeping Amsterdam informed of their contents.[1]

The young man had come a long way since the start of his life (in 1610 or 1611) in the tiny hamlet of Peperga in Friesland, where his father, Balthasar Stuyfsant, or Stuyvesant, was a minister. The

A SWEET AND ALIEN LAND

Stuyfsants were a well-to-do family with a history that went back to the thirteenth century.*

Peter's mother, Margaret Hardenstein—at the time of his birth already in her mid-thirties—came from a patrician family in Gelderland. Together with his sister Anna, who was two years younger, the boy spent his early years in the vicarage of Peperga. In 1622 his father was transferred to Berlikum, near the Friesian capital of Leeuwarden.[3]

Little is known of Peter's youth in Friesland, the only one of the seven United Provinces that had managed to resist the overpowering influence of Amsterdam. But life among these independent and proud—some would say stubborn—people, with their stern Calvinism, must have made a lasting impression on the boy. So, too, must the closeness of the sea that surrounded the low green plains, hardly secure behind their enormous dikes. On a minister's salary, the Stuyvesant way of life can hardly have been luxurious, but the province itself was prosperous, thanks to its fishery and its highly developed agriculture, which enabled it to export butter, cheese, and horses. The port of Harlingen was an active center for trade, where Friesian sailors gained the experience they used against the Spanish and in the extensive Dutch exploration of the world.[4]

The province even had its own university at Franeker, founded in 1585, and it was there that Peter was registered on January 12, 1630. He was then nearly twenty years old. His mother had died in May 1625, and two years later his father had married the widow Styntjen Pietersen from Haarlem, who would give him four more children. The dominie probably felt that the strict discipline of Franeker's Hogeschool would do his eldest son no harm. It was only a small university with several hundred students, mainly theological; but the Calvinistic severity of its founder, Sybrandus Lubbertus, seems to have had little influence on Peter, who after two or three years of study was asked to leave. As a sign of disgrace, a little sketch of a gibbet was drawn next to his name in the album of the Student Club, which he had joined in December 1629. According to later accounts, Peter had been ousted because he had "taken the daughter of his own landlord at Franeker, and was

---

*Their coat of arms showed a hare fleeing over drift sand (Stuyvesant), being chased by a hound, while a deer watched from firmer ground (of belief). The family motto was *Jovae praestat difere quam homine (nomine)*—Trust in God rather than in man (or the name).[2]

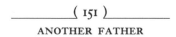

ANOTHER FATHER

caught at it." It had required the intervention of his father to get him off with suspension only, but Stuyvesant thought it wiser to remove his son away from the university and send him to Amsterdam to learn a profession.[5]

The minister must have had some contacts there, because soon enough his son found employment as a clerk in the offices of the West India Company. He had learned his lesson at Franeker and now worked so hard that in 1635, when his father wrote the company asking for a promotion for Peter "according to his merits," the young man was appointed as supercargo at Fernando Noronha, a small island 125 miles east of Brazil. He returned to Holland in 1638 to be transferred to Curaçao but not before making a will assessing his possessions as "salary, monthly pay and prize money to be earned and gained."[6]

In the first years life on Curaçao was quiet. Apart from checking the Spanish prizes, Stuyvesant had very little to do. Curaçao later became the center of the slave trade, but at this time it had little commerce, and only now and then did he have to intervene when smugglers tried to land their goods, or traders created difficulties with the normally friendly natives. The small settlement round the fort—called, as in New Netherland, Fort Amsterdam—contained only a few houses, and the rest of the island, arid and sultry, was very little developed. Among the few Dutchmen who lived there, however, was a close friend, John Farret, who had arrived at the same time as young Stuyvesant.

Curaçao had little to offer in the way of entertainment so the two bachelors had to invent their amusements. One of them was the then fashionable pastime of writing rhymes, so-called *trantveersjes*. Both of them excelled in rather crippled rhymes, which certainly show little talent, but do at least demonstrate that Stuyvesant was not the sour, humorless man some have painted him. He must have been fairly popular in the small community on the island, as his friend Farret readily admits—"it seems that you have attracted everyone by your favours," teasing him that in the end Peter's sword was "his only love."

Stuyvesant played the game adroitly and answered in the same vein:

> *Farret, my dearest friend,*
> *You know so very well,*

A SWEET AND ALIEN LAND

That my hand is not made
To write in florid Latin
Or in distinguished French.
I only want to use my hand
To write in simple Dutch
As proof of my great love
To language and to country.
You asked me as a prize
Of our true friendship
I should try
To please you with a poem,
I'll do it now for you
And follow in your way
But fear the shame,
That certainly one day
My quacking next to yours
Will land on me. [7]

Farret's recall to Holland in 1639 put an end to this lighthearted camaraderie, but Stuyvesant soon had less need of distraction, for Director Jacob Tolck departed in 1643, leaving Stuyvesant behind as acting director general. He was almost immediately confronted with a problem.

For some time the company had considered moving its West Indian headquarters to Puerto Rico. The Dutch had been there before and expected that it would not be too difficult to drive the Spanish out. For that exercise the company needed a springboard, and the eyes of the Heeren XIX had fallen on St. Martin, which was also in the hands of the Spanish.

In 1643 Stuyvesant received orders to conquer this little island. The immediate difficulty was in finding sufficient troops, but events in Brazil came to his aid. In the beginning of 1644 the *Blaue Haen*, with three hundred soldiers on board, arrived at Curaçao. They had just been defeated in a battle in the Brazilian province of Maranhão. Stuyvesant at once engaged them, scraped the last rations of food together (the harvest had failed that year), and sailed on March 16, 1644, to St. Martin. A month later he was back in Fort Amsterdam. His expedition had been a fiasco, and he himself had lost his right leg, crushed below the knee by one of the first Spanish balls and amputated by a surgeon. [8]

It had been a disastrous enterprise from the beginning. The

Maranhãoan soldiers, disheartened and mutinous after their defeat in Brazil, refused to cooperate, and discipline was nil. The thirty-four-year-old Stuyvesant had hardly any military experience, and he found it difficult to establish his authority over the rabble that formed the mercenary army of the company. "Everything went on as disorderly in that expedition as had never happened in any expedition," related the anti-Stuyvesant pamphlet *Broad Advice.*[9]

Stuyvesant gave the Heeren XIX a different account, complaining bitterly about his troops, who during a siege of twenty-eight days, had declined to budge. "It is difficult to catch hares with unwilling dogs," he later exclaimed. The fact that he had lost his leg had been, as he said modestly, "no small impediment." Now, back on Curaçao, things were not improving. Some one hundred of the Maranhãoan soldiers had run away to St. Christopher, while the rest were without food. The troubles that his colleague Willem Kieft was having with the Indians in New Amsterdam offered him an excellent opportunity to get rid of all the unruly troops. He himself, so he wrote on July 31, was in great pain and had finally fallen "into a great illness the outcome of which I commended to God."[10]

The company directors felt that Stuyvesant had done all he could, praised his enterprise as "a Roman achievement," and called him back home to recover. In September 1644 Stuyvesant, whose stump was healing very slowly, left Fort Amsterdam on the *Milkmaid* for a long and painful voyage home. Storms tossed the boat continuously, and most of the passengers suffered from scurvy. By the beginning of November—the vessel had now been more than two months on its way—conditions had become unbearable. Only two hogsheads of fresh water were left and gales made it impossible to round the dangerous coast of Ireland. On November 9, the captain decided to put into the first Irish harbor he could find, and from there Stuyvesant traveled overland to the Republic, where he arrived in December at the house of his sister Anna, now Madame Bayard, in Alphen aan de Rijn, not far from Rotterdam.

The news of his homecoming and his heroic defeat at St. Martin had already reached his friend John Farret, who welcomed him with an ode entitled "On the Off-shot Leg of the Valiant Seigneur P. Stuyvesant, of the Island of St. Martin."

A SWEET AND ALIEN LAND

What mad'ning thunder-ball comes on your leg
My dearest Stuyvesant and plunges you down yonder
That right-hand pillar, that was used to bear your body,
Was thus in one blow crushed and also amputated.

You dared too much, oh all too cruel fate
My Stuyvesant, who falls and tumbles on his post
Whereas a valiant soldier he challenges his foe
To lure him to the field, the Island of St. Martin.[11]

But for Stuyvesant, there was more serious business. The time had come for marriage, and he had been much attracted by Anna's sister-in-law, Judith Bayard. She was a demure spinster of about thirty-seven, a few years older than himself, but, as the daughter of a Huguenot vicar, she had an impeccable background. On August 13, 1645, Stuyvesant, leaning heavily on his new wooden leg (which was strengthened and decorated with a silver band), walked with Judith up the aisle of the Eglise Wallon in Breda. It was the same church in which the bride had been baptized on November 16, 1608.[12]

The Heeren XIX were greatly preoccupied that summer of 1645 with the problems of New Netherland—well publicized by Melyn's letter, and by the plea of the Eight Select Men that had been smuggled out of New Amsterdam. It was agreed that Kieft must be replaced, and the best man they could think of was the former schout Lubbertus van Dincklage, who, although not a particularly inspiring personality, was at least a sound, reliable man with considerable local knowledge. His appointment was tentatively approved, and the company began to look about for someone to send out as his assistant.

Stuyvesant arrived in Amsterdam to find the company offices on the Heerengracht buzzing with these matters, followed the discussions with the closest attention, and came to the conclusion that *he* was the very man for the job of director general. He already knew a certain amount about the colony's affairs—news had filtered down to Curaçao from time to time, by way of Dutch traders—and his experiences in Curaçao, he reckoned, would be a

ANOTHER FATHER

further qualification. The prospect of immediate employment had another charm. Idle convalescence was irksome to the energetic former governor, who, now thirty-five years old, had lost none of his ambition.

From the moment of his return he lobbied the delegates to the company's assembly in Amsterdam, and in May the Lords Directors, "being well pleased with his services at Curaçao," revoked their decision to send Van Dincklage and appointed Stuyvesant in his place. Van Dincklage would become his second man, and Ensign Hendrick van Dyck, disabled for military service because of his shattered right arm, was to become Stuyvesant's schout-fiscal (sheriff and attorney).

Stuyvesant himself got down to work at once, reading through the files on New Netherland and hammering out his own remedies for the appalling mess his predecessor had made of the province. In September he put these ideas together in a memorial which he handed the directors. It received their usual ponderous attention, and—together with the Board of Account's report—ought to have resulted in a complete rethinking of the colony's trading system. Among the ideas now being studied by the Heeren XIX was, for instance, the suggestion that in order to stimulate agriculture, the New Netherlanders should be free to trade and export their goods. There was an excellent market for grain and livestock in the West Indies. Trade within the province itself had been free since 1639, but the carrying trade—to Holland or elsewhere—was still in the hands of the monopolistic company. From now on, it was suggested, everyone should be free to load and unload in the port of New Amsterdam, which at the same time would become the port through which all ships coming from neighboring countries must pass for registration of their cargo. New Amsterdam would be the center of the colonial trade in the western hemisphere.

As usual, the Heeren XIX were not able to agree on such a revolutionary idea and the discussions went on for months. The States General, growing impatient at this continued bickering, refused to ratify Stuyvesant's commission until the company came up with a waterproof scheme for the province.

It was almost too much for the newly appointed governor, already known for his explosive temper. Trying to force matters, he traveled (a slow business in the Lowlands with the *trekschuiten,* horse-drawn barges for thirty to forty passengers) between Amsterdam, The Hague, and Middelburg, the capital of Zeeland and seat of the influential Zeeland Chamber of the company. In October 1645 he thought for a time that he had won the battle. The Zeelanders, who with the other chambers were now sharing the burden of New Netherland previously borne by Amsterdam alone, had at last promised to equip the vessel that would bring Stuyvesant, his wife, and "court" to New Amsterdam. Stuyvesant hurried on October 5 to Middelburg to thank the chamber and take his farewell. The gentlemen thanked him also and wished him a prosperous voyage, but Stuyvesant got no further than Amsterdam before he heard that the plans had again been canceled.[13]

By April 1646 Stuyvesant still did not know when he might be able to leave. "Mister Stuyvesant does not yet know when the gentlemen will have the funds," an acquaintance wrote to New Amsterdam, "and must still go patiently to meetings for five or six months." It was a fairly accurate estimate. Four months later there was a sudden flurry of activity.[14]

On July 13 the States General, in an impatient memo to the West India Company, asked the Heeren XIX what they were going to do about New Netherland and "the complaints presented heretofore to their High Mightinesses, in the name and on behalf of the inhabitants of New Netherland." The company suddenly reached agreement on the free shipping question; funds were somehow raised; and on Saturday July 28 Petrus Stuyvesant could appear at last before the Assembly to take the "proper oath" as director general of New Netherland and of the islands of Curaçao, Bonaire, and Aruba, which had been added to his responsibilities. Earlier that day the States General had given him his commission. He would receive a monthly salary of 250 guilders and a yearly bonus of 900 guilders.[15]

The tribulations and complications were not yet over. A small convoy of four ships had to be equipped, and it was Christmas Day 1646 before it was able to leave the port of Texel. Stuyvesant and his wife Judith traveled on the *Groote Gerrit* ("Great Crow"), together with Van Dincklage and his wife, Van Dyck, and a newcomer, Brian Newton, an Englishman who had worked for the company in the West Indies and was now employed as chief military officer for New Netherland. In the other ships, the *Princess*

ANOTHER FATHER

Amalia, the *Zwol,* and the *Raet,* were a detachment of soldiers, a large group of immigrants, and a number of traders with their merchandise.

Even the voyage itself was not without difficulties. Stuyvesant's fellow passengers were in a hurry to make the stormy winter crossing, but the new governor had other ideas. Since he was also responsible for Curaçao, he decided to pay it a visit before tackling all the problems of New Amsterdam. In blithe disregard of all promises and "public printed notices" he gave the captain of the *Groote Gerrit,* Ielmer Thomassen, orders to set a course to the Antilles. Van Dyck and others protested loudly, but Stuyvesant paid no attention to them. The unhappy settlers in the uncomfortable spaces between-decks, and even the more prosperous traders and merchants in their small cabins, were shattered. The journey, which normally took a miserable eight to ten weeks, was now certain to last three to four months. The traders were furious because it meant a financial loss, and the seasick settlers were, Van Dyck said, "reduced to such grief and discouragement that many of them died of broken hearts."[16]

Van Dyck's later testimony was perhaps not unbiased. The former ensign, now schout-fiscal, was to prove a great disappointment to Stuyvesant. Petty, vengeful, and worst of all a heavy drinker, he was the last man who could have worked successfully with the impatient, methodical, and abstemious governor. Clashes were inevitable and the first happened not far from the island of St. Martin, where Stuyvesant had lost his leg two years earlier. The cause was a Dutch ship, the *Liefde,* from Schiedam. Stuyvesant, sighting it near St. Christopher, hailed and boarded it to see whether the captain had company permission to trade in the West Indies, now his territory. As he suspected, the captain was an "interloper," and his ship and cargo were confiscated and taken to Curaçao.

Stuyvesant had made his decision without consulting the schout, who stormed into his cabin to protest, but was ejected with the words: "Get out, whenever I need you, I'll call you." At a meeting with the councillors later on, while Stuyvesant was discussing the fate of the prize, Van Dyck, now completely drunk, stumbled again into the governor's cabin. The irate Stuyvesant gave him orders to retire to his own cabin, slamming the door in his face. For the rest of the voyage, he completely ignored his schout, "strutting along in his sovereign mood."[17]

Arriving at Curaçao, Van Dyck made an effort at reconciliation and offered "to attend the Company's rights in discharging the ships," but Stuyvesant pushed him brusquely aside, saying: "You are no fiscal of Curaçao." He told Van Dyck not to leave the *Groote Gerrit,* and while the others were out on shore leave, the unhappy schout was confined to the ship for three long weeks.[18]

The last stretch of the journey passed more quickly, since Stuyvesant, whose wife Judith was by now pregnant, was suddenly in a hurry to take up his new duties. On May 11, 1647, almost exactly twenty-one years after Peter Minuit had arrived in the bay, the *Groote Gerrit* dropped anchor in the busy port of New Amsterdam. While the cannons of the fort used their last powder for a festive salute, Stuyvesant was rowed to the wall, where Willem Kieft and a guard of honor waited.

Along the shore most of the inhabitants of the capital had crowded together in the hope of catching a first glance of their new director general, the fourth since their city had been founded. A tall, impressive man solemnly stepped onto the pebbled quayside, the silver band on his leg glittering in the sun. He was vigorous, not unattractive, and carefully dressed, wearing the usual simple jacket, decorated with silver buttons and a flat lace collar, and dark breeches, over which was a tailored black cloth coat. The only touch of fantasy were slashed hose, fastened at the knees by a knotted scarf, and a rosette on his one shoe. It was obvious to everyone that Stuyvesant was conscious of his new importance in this small community, and some described his arrival—"which was longed for very much"—as that of a "peacock, with great state and pomp."[19]

The greeting between Kieft and his successor was formal. Kieft welcomed him with a few words and then turned to the public, thanking them for their loyalty. It "was more than reasonable," some of the bystanders thought crossly, and the solemnity of the occasion did not stop them from speaking out "roundly," but calm returned when Stuyvesant—who styled himself Lord General— began to speak. He "should be in his government," he told the colonists, "as a father over his children, for the advantages of the Privileged West India Company, the Burghers and the Country." For the first time the tension eased and there were a few scattered cheers as he walked together with Kieft into Fort Amsterdam.

ANOTHER FATHER

Not everyone felt confident. The experience of his predecessors had been unhappy, and the citizens would not soon forget that. Furthermore, in his first speech Stuyvesant had made it clear that he only intended to stay for three years, and this, together "with other haughty expressions," caused some to doubt whether he would be much "like a father."[20]

A BAD START

"Piles of ashes from burnt houses, barns etc. demonstrate the ordinary care that was bestowed on the country." This was the general verdict of the New Amsterdammers on the government of Director General Willem Kieft. When Peter Stuyvesant arrived in May 1647, almost a year and a half after the end of the disastrous Indian War, the situation was not much improved. While the Heeren XIX were bickering with the States General and among themselves, and while Stuyvesant was making his "sentimental journey" to Curaçao, Kieft had completely lost control.[1]

The settlers had of course heard of the company's plans to replace him, and the pro-Kieft faction had rapidly disintegrated. Like rats leaving a sinking ship, Secretary Cornelis van Tienhoven and Councillor Johannes La Montagne hastily tried to convince their fellow citizens that the governor alone was to blame for the war. "La Montagne said that he had protested against it, but that it was begun against his will and to his great regrets," says one report; "Secretary Cornelis van Tienhoven, also said that he had no hand in the matters" and that he had acted solely on the orders of the director general. Even among themselves they could not agree; La Montagne was heard telling people that if Van Tienhoven had not brought false reports, "the affair would never have happened."[2]

Kieft had made desperate efforts to clear himself of all blame "by cunning and numerous certificates and petitions," but there were few who would listen to him. Even Schout Cornelis van der Huygens no longer felt any loyalty to his superior and went around "at carousels or at the guard house" telling everyone that Kieft was a rascal and a thief, "drinking every day with Mr La Montagne and then shuts his room tight." The governor had called Van der Huygens before him, hoping to retrieve at least a scrap of his authority, and had blamed the schout for all the "thefts, robberies, killing of hogs and goats and other excesses," demanding that he bring some order to the chaos and collect the duties that no one ever seemed to pay. Van der Huygens had weakly protested, having, as he said, "from time to time done his best."[3]

The climax came when Dominie Everardus Bogardus, the great enemy of Wouter van Twiller, began to meddle openly in the crisis. His vicarage in the Winckelstraat had been for quite a while the center of opposition to Kieft, and the governor, who according to *Broad Advice* was not a pious man anyway, took his revenge by making his little army exercise and play the drum while service was being held in the church. The harassed dominie did not improve relations by attacking Kieft from the pulpit, attacks the governor tried to dismiss by saying that Bogardus had been drunk.

It might have been true, but Bogardus was not the man to let such remarks pass. On January 22, 1645, in a thundering sermon, the minister denounced Kieft (who for once was present) as a man whose only aim was "to rob . . . to dismiss, banish and transport." The governor stormed out and refused to return. Bogardus, in turn, refused to announce the end of the Indian War from the pulpit. On Christmas Eve he took his vendetta too far. In a rollicking sermon he told his congregation that in Africa, "owing to the intense heat, different animals copulate together, by which various monsters are generated. But he knew not," he added, "from whence, in such temperate climates as ours, such monsters of men are produced. They are the mighty ones, but it was desirable that they were the weak. . . ."[4]

Kieft, who had, of course, been absent, was soon told of this onslaught but waited until January 2, 1646, before he answered the dominie in a biting New Year's letter. "Children might know to whom you here alluded," he wrote, accusing Bogardus of keeping people away from his church by his "bad tongue." He warned him, that "inasmuch as your duty and oath imperiously demand the

A SWEET AND ALIEN LAND

maintenance of the magistracy; and whereas your conduct stirs the people to mutiny and rebellion, when they are already too much divided—causing schisms and abuses in the church and making us a scorn and a laughing stock to our neighbours . . . therefore our sacred duty imperiously requires of us to prosecute you. . . ." He expected an answer from the minister within two weeks.[5]

The answer arrived on January 8, but was found by the governor to be "full of vain subterfuge, calumny [and] insult," and more explanations were demanded. A long correspondence followed, but the two stubborn men found no common ground. When Kieft asked Dominie Johannes Megapolensis of Rensselaerswyck and the English Reverend Francis Doughty to mediate, Bogardus defiantly asserted that he would appeal to the new director general —unaware that he had still a year's wait before Stuyvesant's arrival. In any case, Kieft rejected this proposal and ordered the prosecution to go on. A last effort to reconcile the two men was made in June, and Bogardus, under pressure from friends, consented to allow Megapolensis to preach occasionally in the church in New Amsterdam so that Kieft could attend. The hatchet was provisionally buried.[6]

By now almost all the notables in New Amsterdam were against the governor, and he in turn had little friendly feelings left for them. His principal *bêtes noirs* were, of course, Cornelis Melyn, the patroon of Staten Island, and the Dane, Jochem Kuyter—the masterminds behind the petition of the Eight, which had been secretly smuggled to Amsterdam in 1644. Whenever their paths crossed, they were icily polite to each other, and both Melyn and Kuyter testified later that never "an unkind word was exchanged between us and Kieft." But the governor was just biding his time.

After General Stuyvesant's arrival in May 1647, the community soon saw that the ex-governor was rapidly gaining the confidence of his successor, and soon he had "more favor, aid and counsel than his adversaries." It could hardly have been otherwise with Stuyvesant, a man to whom authority was sacred. An attack on a director general was pure *lèse majesté*, an affront to the power of the States General, which had appointed him. Complainants against Kieft or other company officials always found the door of Stuyvesant's "comptoir" firmly closed.[7]

Melyn and Kuyter discovered this in June when they came knocking on it with their charges against Kieft. Since the ex-

A BAD START

governor was on the point of returning to the Netherlands, they felt that his mismanagement ought first to be put on record. The new director general tried to avoid becoming directly involved, and told them that the company had given him orders to make no inquiries into Kieft's affairs. Matters might have been left at that, if Kieft had not then launched a scorching attack on Melyn and Kuyter, accusing them of having forced others to sign the clandestine petition of the Eight, "cheating the good people and endeavouring with false and bitter poison to calumniate their magistrates." He demanded a prosecution by the fiscal "according to the heinousness of their crimes."[8]

This time Stuyvesant acted, ordering Melyn and Kuyter to answer the charges within forty-eight hours. The accusors had become the accused, but they saw no need to excuse themselves. Their response nevertheless was dignified and firm. They refused to let Kieft off the hook and pointed to the ruinous state of New Netherland—"piles of ashes"—as the best proof of his guilt. "Kieft has yet to prove that his Honor lawfully and of a necessity commenced the war against those Natives," they stated. They would have preferred to keep silent—"anger is not excited against the silent man"—but felt they must defend themselves as "good patriots and proprietors of New Netherland," who had put everything they owned into the province and lost it all. If they were to be sent back to Holland, as Kieft demanded, they refused to go in disgrace as "pests and seditious persons."[9]

Stuyvesant had already given orders to his schout-fiscal to indict the two men, but when he read their outrageous document, he tore the charge up—it was not severe enough. He was determined to make it plain to New Amsterdam that he would not allow the authority of his position to be undermined. "These churls may hereafter endeavour to knock me down also," he was heard to explain, "but I will manage it so now, that they will have their bellies full."[10]

The court session on July 25, 1647, at which the general played both prosecutor and judge, was brief. The charges were heavy: Melyn and Kuyter had sent to the Republic a petition "scandalously charging, defaming, criminating and accusing" Kieft; Melyn had in addition threatened the governor personally with the gallows and wheel, calling him a *duyvelskop*—devil's head. The sentences were correspondingly heavy—Melyn received the death

A SWEET AND ALIEN LAND

penalty, and Kuyter was sentenced to eternal banishment—and it was only under pressure from his councillors that Stuyvesant was induced to soften them to banishment of seven years for Melyn, and three for Kuyter, together with fines of 300 and 150 Carolus guilders, respectively.[11]

The sentences sent a shiver of apprehension through New Amsterdam. It was felt that, far from being a change for the better, Stuyvesant's reign might be "like the crowning of Rehoboam." Stuyvesant's reaction to the news that Melyn and Kuyter planned an appeal to the States General did nothing to allay these anxieties. He summoned Melyn to his office and ordered him furiously to keep his mouth shut when he arrived in Holland. "If I knew, Melyn, that you would divulge our sentence, or bring it before their High Mightinesses" he stormed, "I would by my soul take off your head or hang you to the highest tree in New Netherland."[12]

Stuyvesant's determination to stop Melyn's appeal was understandable. Legal decisions taken by the director general and his Council in New Amsterdam were binding, but the possibility of a reversal by the States General following an appeal was not excluded. To a man of Stuyvesant's authoritarian nature, this would have been an intolerable erosion of his prestige. The mere threat of an appeal, on another occasion, provoked an outburst by Stuyvesant: "I will make him a head shorter and send the pieces to Holland, and let him appeal that way."[13]

Kieft attempted to soothe him by suggesting that a distant judgment in the Republic was "nothing more than a bugbear," but Stuyvesant was unappeased. While Melyn calmly collected evidence for an appeal, the general let it be known that "even if they come back cleared and bring an order of the States, no matter what its contents, unless their High Mightinesses summon me, I should immediately send them back." The citizens of New Amsterdam, listening in horror to these outbursts, feared the worst—"What more could even a sovereign do?"[14]

Kieft left for Holland on August 16, 1647, on the *Princess*. Few of the hundreds of settlers who lined the shores of the East River as the ship sailed can have regretted the departure of the arrogant and devious dictator under whom they had suffered so and who had succeeded in leaving a thoroughly poisoned atmosphere behind him. What the voyage itself would be like was anyone's guess.

A BAD START

Traveling together on board the *Princess* with Kieft were his two greatest enemies, Melyn and Kuyter, and the man who had denounced him from the pulpit. Dominie Everardus Bogardus had been replaced after fourteen years' service by Dominie Johannes Backerus, whom Stuyvesant had discovered in Curaçao. Another passenger was Kieft's schout-fiscal, Cornelis van der Huygens, who had been sacked. In the cramped quarters of the small ship it must have been difficult for these men to avoid each other, despite the 120 soldiers and the settlers in the between-decks.

All four men carried their own documents with them: Melyn and Kuyter the affidavits they had gathered against Kieft; Bogardus his accusations; and Kieft himself, with the convictions of Melyn and Kuyter, papers in which he accused Bogardus of drunken misbehavior, and the so-called Little Book, on which the pro-Kieft *Journal of New Netherland* was almost certainly based. It contained an account of the Indian War so absurd that even Van Tienhoven, reading it before Kieft left, "flung it from the table." Its description of New Netherland had been a source of amusement to every settler, since apart from one visit to Rensselaerswyck, Kieft had never left New Amsterdam.

Most of this document was never to reach the Republic. On September 27, 1647, the captain of the *Princess* made a navigational error while entering the Bristol Channel in heavy storms, and the ship struck on the reefs near Swansea. The company later wrote to Stuyvesant that "81 souls, men, women and children were lost." Among them were Kieft, Bogardus, and Van der Huygens. "The Lord may comfort the sufferers," commented the Heeren XIX, adding, with real regret, that nothing had been saved of the cargo (worth four hundred thousand guilders) except some of the fourteen thousand beaver skins. The rest had been stolen by thousands of Welshmen, who had gathered to watch the wreck.[15]

Melyn lost his six-year-old son, but almost miraculously both he and Kuyter survived. Melyn had scrambled onto a part of the wreck that had stuck to a sandbank, and with other survivors managed to improvise a raft. With the help of a sail made from "as many shirts and other garments as were necessary," they reached Swansea safely after eighteen hours in the water. Kuyter had clung to the after-part of the ship, where a cannon stood. In the dark he thought it was a man and began to talk to it, "but receiving no answer supposed he was dead." A huge wave later washed him

A SWEET AND ALIEN LAND

onto the beach at the feet of the curious Welsh beachcombers.

For two days the two men desperately hunted for their cases of documents, recovered one, and then traveled on to Holland. They later told friends that just before the ship broke up, Kieft had come to them and said: "Friends, I have done wrong, can you forgive me?"[16]

His fate did nothing to change Dutch opinion of him. Most saw his death as a punishment from God, and felt that, as De Vries had predicted a few years earlier, "the murder he had committed on so much innocent blood" had at last been avenged.[17]

NEW BROOMS

In the beginning of 1648 the United Provinces took the most decisive step in their history. On May 15 they signed at Munster the treaty with Spain that after a sporadic war of eighty years officially and finally recognized their independence. The Spaniards could no longer continue the fight, in which the Dutch for the last few years had received the support of France.

Six months after Munster, peace returned to the whole of Europe when the Treaty of Westphalia put an end to the Thirty Years' War that for three decades had raged between Protestants and Catholics in Germany. It left Europe in turmoil, and desperately weakened. Spain was exhausted, Portugal was still grappling with its new independence, France was on the brink of civil war, and England was still submerged in it. Germany was more divided than ever; Italy, half fettered to Spain, had little voice in its own affairs; and the Scandinavian countries were busy keeping a suspicious eye on one another. Only the Dutch Republic seemed to be more strongly united, and it had unquestionably reached its zenith. The Netherlands were "courted by all nations," wrote a French diplomat, and its major poet, Joost van den Vondel, could rhyme without blushing:

> *Netherlands peace lays down the law*
> *For Kingdoms all in awe.*

Guides them to a salutary trail,
With lanterns and with trumpets hail.[1]

But while the Dutch in general enjoyed their Golden Age, and Amsterdam had begun to build the "ninth wonder of the world," its Stadt Huys (Town Hall), the West India Company was going through a serious crisis. The Peace of Munster had put an end to the privateering activities of the company, but these in any case had lost their importance since the Heeren XIX could no longer afford to keep a fleet at sea. Much more serious was the loss of the important slave market of Angola to Portugal, and in particular the trouble the Heeren XIX were having in Brazil.

The rebellion of the Portuguese inhabitants of "New Holland," which broke out in 1644, had spread rapidly, and when its popular governor, Prince Johan Maurits, disgusted with the lack of support the company had given him, returned to Holland in 1645, the Dutch were slowly pushed into the South Atlantic. Portugal openly supported the insurgents and the States decided to send a fleet to save Brazil for the company. But it was too weak a force to achieve anything.

The inevitable loss—which was sealed in 1654—of their most important possession was fatal to the Heeren XIX, whose policy in Brazil—"with the sword and not with the plough"—had in the end been their downfall, as many had predicted.[2]

In the circumstances they studied the situation in New Netherland with renewed interest, and it brought them little consolation. Devastated by the Indian War and the maladministration of Kieft, cornered by its English neighbors and invaded by the Swedes, the colony was struggling for its very existence. The company's only hope was based on Peter Stuyvesant, the new thirty-seven-year-old governor.

His first reports had been alarming. From the hands of Kieft he had received no more than a few pieces of land: the island of Manhattan, a portion of Long Island west of Oyster Bay, a short strip of mainland along the sound to Hellgate, the contested House of Good Hope at the Fresh River, the isolated outpost of Fort Nassau on the Delaware, and the decayed Fort Orange in the north. These were the remnants of a province that had once stretched from the Delaware in the south to Cape Cod in the northeast, with the River of Canada as its northern border. In these scraps of New Netherland lived about fifteen hundred people, most of them traders, some of them officials, and a handful of them "planters." The majority had settled on Manhattan to be near the safety of Fort Amsterdam's garrison of about one hundred soldiers.

The fort would probably never be able to withstand an attack. The troops were "very disorderly and without discipline," while the fortification was still the "molehill" Father Jogues had found in 1643. Stuyvesant had been deeply shocked to see cows and goats grazing on the walls, and he told the New Amsterdammers that the state of their rampart would lead to "the contempt, yea the disgrace of this province by others our neighbours, whether English, French, Swedes, even by the Indians and heathens." The Church of St. Nicholas in the fort came also "into his hands very much out of repair" and the small capital itself, with one hundred timber-built houses and streets that were little more than cowpaths, looked to his Dutch eyes like a slum.[3]

What was left of the population was, with few exceptions, a rabble "approaching to a savage state." One report stated that "a fourth part of the city of New Amsterdam consisted of grog-shops and houses where nothing is to be got but tobacco and beer." Dominie Backerus, complaining in one of his first letters to Amsterdam about the ungodliness of his 170 "souls," mentioned only seventeen public houses, but they were enough to make the citizens "very much inclined to intoxication."[4]

"It looks as if the slackness of the late Director and the neglect of duty by the preacher have been the cause of this," was the sagacious answer of the Lords Directors when Stuyvesant informed them: "We expect your Honor will redress it." The best advice they could give him was to treat the province "like a tree, which has been growing some time and has run wild. [It] must be pruned with great care and bent with a tender hand, to be brought in good shape."[5]

This must sometimes have seemed an absolutely hopeless task to the general, but he tackled it with boundless energy. Two weeks after his arrival he issued his first ordinances, probably having in mind the saying that "new brooms sweep clean." Determined to put an end to the daily drunken brawls, he forbade the serving of alcohol after the town bell struck at nine in the evening, and before two on Sunday, except to bona fide travelers and boarders. The law against selling "intoxicants" to the Indians was reemphasized, while the drawing of a knife would be fined by one hundred Carolus guilders, to be trebled if anyone was wounded.

His second set of orders was intended to put an end to the smuggling and petty trade that had ruined the company. Many private traders were in the habit of sending their furs to Europe via New England or Virginia in order to dodge the heavy duties. From now on furs would be stamped or marked, and the traders would have to produce their books if required. At the same time they were forbidden to leave the trading posts to find pelts farther inland. Stricter harbor regulations were imposed to prevent the surreptitious passage of the smugglers' ships.

Stuyvesant's third important measure was the raising of funds for the reconstruction of the province. His predecessor having already taxed beer, he picked on wine and "spirituous liquor," for which the duty would be paid by the tavernkeepers and retailers. Furs were another source of extra revenue; future exporters had to pay a duty of thirty cents per skin.

Once Stuyvesant had funds in hand, he planned to start the repair of St. Nicholas Church and the construction of a sheet piling along the shore "to prevent the abrasion by the river." On his arrival the governor had been rowed to the shore, since New Amsterdam had still no pier, and on July 4, 1647, he ordered that one be erected "for the convenience of the Merchants and Citizens." In the end a small dock was built not far from the Stadt's Herberg (somewhat pretentiously named after the well-known Schreyer's Hoeck in Amsterdam, where Dutch sailors said a tearful farewell to their wives and friends). But the vessels arriving in New Amsterdam still had to anchor in the East River, to be unloaded by boats and canoes.[6]

The capital itself also badly needed a spring cleaning. Unlike the neat prim towns of New England, New Amsterdam had grown up haphazardly, although the broad lines of Crijn Fredericks' 1625 plan were still followed. Kieft had tried desperately to create some order by specifying the allotments of land, but the burghers had their own way of interpreting the rules. Stuyvesant, walking through the streets, had been struck by the "disorderly manner, hitherto and now daily practised in building and erecting houses." No citizen saw any harm in placing his fences far into the neighboring fields or gardens or putting his pigpens and even his "pri-

NEW BROOMS

vies" in the public road. To stop all this the governor appointed three surveyors who were empowered "to condemn all improper and disorderly buildings, fences, pallisades, posts, rails, etc." To make shopping easier, he decided to build a hundred-foot-long storehouse as a salesroom, stocked "with all kinds of goods," an idea promptly killed by the company, which felt little inclined to become a shopkeeper.[7]

For the first time in many years New Amsterdam hummed with constructive activity, but the hammering and sawing sounded very unlike music in the ears of the citizens. Robbed of the freedom to drink and fight whenever they liked, deprived of the chance to make a little something on the side by fur smuggling, and obliged to pay out their money in taxes, they grumbled loudly. Stuyvesant, they said, was busy "building, laying masonry, making, breaking, repairing and the like," but it was all for the company and little for them. They were, however, given the opportunity to air their grievances when on the advice of his councillors the general decided in August to create a board of nine representatives from the community.[8]

Until then he had been assisted by a Council consisting of six members. The most important of these was, of course, Stuyvesant's second in command, Vice Director Van Dincklage, who was at that time still impressed by and even afraid of the governor. Van Dyck, the schout-fiscal, was also a member, but after his performance on the way over he had completely lost Stuyvesant's respect. He drank more and more, he was slovenly and very venal. To those two councillors Stuyvesant had added Dr. La Montagne, not much respected in the colony after his services to Kieft; his military commander, Brian Newton, who "knew neither Dutch nor law"; and Paulus Leendertsen van der Grift, who had come over with the general as his naval agent. Adriaen Keyser, the commissary of the company's merchandise, was now and then allowed into the Council, but no one was much impressed by him. He hardly ever opened his mouth, letting, as he said himself, "God's water run over God's field."[9]

Stuyvesant kept on Kieft's secretary, George Baxter, to look after English affairs and— to the great dismay of the New Amsterdammers—he retained Cornelis van Tienhoven as his secretary. In the general view of the colony, Van Tienhoven was a shifty, deceit-

A SWEET AND ALIEN LAND

ful person, "given to lying, promising everyone and when it came to perform, at home to no one." The citizens could easily have forgiven him for being a shameless lecher—he ran around "as an Indian, with a little covering and a small patch in front from lust after the prostitutes." But no one in New Netherland was ever likely to forget that by his lies and false reports, he had led Kieft into the Indian War, and "the whole country cries out against him bitterly as a villain, murderer and traitor." For Stuyvesant, however, Van Tienhoven's long experience in local affairs (he had been fourteen years in the province) more than compensated for his shady past and unsavory reputation. Even the enemies of this vulgar, "thickset," and unattractive man, whose "red and bloated" face was adorned with a wart, had to admit that he was intelligent, subtle and sharp-witted—"good gifts," they added cynically, "when they are well used." And to Stuyvesant, as to Kieft, he was always a loyal supporter.[10]

However little liked and respected this group of officials, their advice to form a Board of Nine Select Men was a positive gesture to the community. The days of the governor's dictatorship were over, and even if the power of the Nine Select Men was very limited, it was the first hesitant step toward a semblance of democracy in the province. The company's original instructions stated that the governor was to rule according to the Dutch law, to use the Dutch language, and to sustain the Dutch Reformed Church— with tolerance to other religions. For the rest, he had to make his own decisions. He could set up courts and appoint all the public officers; he had to approve all contracts and sanction all purchases from the Indians. In short, he made and was the law.

Before Stuyvesant's time there had not been a vice director, but simply a couple of commissaries (trade agents), since the company considered commerce more important than government. The governor was, however, supported by his secretary, who played a very important role in running the administration and kept the Council minutes. It was the duty of the schout-fiscal, who was both sheriff and prosecuting officer, to arrest and bring suspects to trial, present the evidence, and publish and execute the sentences decided by the governor. All these powers would be unaffected by the new Board of Nine Select Men, but the director general no longer had a completely free hand—*vox populi* had found a mouthpiece.[11]

The announcement of the formation of the Board was made in the usual pompous way—a proclamation was hung next to the gate of the fort:

> *Whereas, we desire nothing more than that the government of New Netherland, entrusted to our care, and principally New Amsterdam, our capital and residence, might continue in good order, justice, polity, population, prosperity and mutual harmony, and be provided with strong fortifications, a church, a school, trading place, harbour and similar highly necessary public edifices and improvements, for which end we are desirous of obtaining the assistance of our whole commonalty. . . . Being unwilling to vex and harass our dear vassals and subjects in any way by exactions, impositions and insufferable burdens, but rather in a more desirable manner to induce and sollicit them to assist voluntarily . . . and whereas it is difficult to cover so many heads with a single cap . . . so did We, heretofore, with the advice of our council, propose to the commonalty that the inhabitants should, without passion or envy, nominate a double number of persons from the most notable, reasonable, honest and respectable of our subjects, from whom we might select a single number of Nine Men . . . to confer with us and our council, as their Tribunes.*

There were, of course, restrictions on the Board's powers. Stuyvesant was to appoint the president; members were forbidden to hold "private conventicles" without the approval of the governor; and while they were allowed to name three of the members to join the court on Thursday, these would only act in civil cases or as arbitrators. Finally, six would every year be replaced by new members, who were not again chosen by the community, but by the Nine themselves.[12]

A feverish election campaign began. Not only was New Amsterdam to be represented, but the rest of Manhattan, Breukelen, New Amersfoort, and Pavonia would have their delegates as well. By the end of August the eighteen candidates had been selected, and on September 25 Stuyvesant nominated the Board.

Only two of its members had any experience in Kieft's Boards of Twelve and Eight, New Netherland's first English settler Thomas Hall, and Jan Damen. The rest were new to the game. They were the former cook's mate Govert Loockermans, who had once distinguished himself by torturing an Indian, but had done an excellent service in smuggling the petition of the Eight to Amsterdam; the merchant Arnoldus van Hardenbergh; the rich

A SWEET AND ALIEN LAND

farmers Michiel Jansen and Jan Evertsen Bout; the brewer Jacob Wolfertsen van Couwenhoven; the tailor Hendrick Hendricksz Kip; and a Bohemian, Augustine Heerman, the highly intelligent son of a Prague businessman, who had come to New Amsterdam in 1643 as agent for one of Amsterdam's largest commercial concerns, Gabry and Company. As Stuyvesant had stipulated, each section of the community—merchants, burghers, and farmers—was represented by three delegates.

The first meeting, held in the city's only schoolroom, made it clear at once that Stuyvesant would no longer be allowed to have things his own way. It might have been because he himself was not present—a flu epidemic had laid him low—but the Nine Select Men rejected his plea for money to repair the fort. While agreeing reluctantly with the need for repair of the church, the construction of a school, and the erection of sheet piling along the river, they considered that the fort was the company's business, explaining that "the people were poor." Stuyvesant's enemies later claimed that everyone had been afraid that "if the Director once had the Fort to rely upon, he would be more cruel and severe," but that was certainly an exaggeration. Stuyvesant did not contest their decision and avoided a head-on clash by calling up all the male adults of New Amsterdam to work on the reconstruction of the fort for twelve days a year, or pay a penalty of twenty-four guilders. It was a job that most of the New Amsterdammers knew how to avoid, and years later the fort was still in the same derelict state.[13]

Actually there was little immediate need for the fort. Shortly after his arrival Stuyvesant had met the Indian chiefs—who christened the general "The Big Sachima with the Wooden Leg"—and reconfirmed the peace of August 1645. The Heeren XIX were very pleased, especially since it looked as though the truce might "be lasting and firm," but they warned him of "the bad disposition of the said savages . . . [and] to keep always a watchful eye on them and their doing." They turned out to be right; the Indians did indeed create trouble for the director general, but not in the way the company had expected.[14]

Stuyvesant with his zeal for reform and love of regulations (he was a true Dutchman) felt it time to enforce the prohibition against selling arms and ammunition to the Indians. Under Kieft's chaotic rule, this trade, despite the regulations, had become fairly

NEW BROOMS

open and free. His successor was less inclined to close an eye, and on May 21, 1648, he suddenly arrested Corporal Gerrit Barendt, the armorer of Fort Amsterdam, who sold arms to private dealers. The frightened man at once mentioned the names of two clients, Joost Theunis de Backer and Jacob Reyntgen, who in their turn betrayed the name of the man behind the scene, Jacob Jansen Schermerhorn, a peddler who traded near Fort Orange. All were arrested and dragged into court, where in July 1648 Schermerhorn and Reyntgen were condemned to death, a sentence "which the Director was with great difficulty persuaded to withdraw." It was changed to banishment and confiscation of all their goods, and in the end only the last part was ever executed.[15]

De Backer had an unhappier fate. Although the evidence against him was very flimsy, he was kept in prison for two weeks, while his house was ransacked and he himself threatened with the rack if he did not reveal more information. Stuyvesant finally let him go, but put him on bail and for six months the man—"a reputable burgher of good life and moderate means"—struggled in vain to clear his name. Eventually, disheartened, he tried to leave the country, but was refused a passport, and fled New Amsterdam secretly in the hope of finding justice in the Netherlands.[16]

Stuyvesant had hoped by getting tough to destroy a trade "which was putting his nation in a bad odor with its neighbours," the English. But he had not yet grasped that the sale of arms was very often the only way to keep the Indians peaceful. The company, thanks to its experiences under Van Twiller and Kieft, knew better, and in the midst of his campaign against the traders, Stuyvesant received a letter from Amsterdam telling him to provide the natives with guns, powder, and lead, but "only sparingly." For the disconcerted Stuyvesant this meant a complete reversal of policy, but orders were orders. When the traders of Rensselaerswyck, pressured by aggressive Indians, begged for permission to sell before they were murdered, the governor agreed.[17]

He went even further. The amazed citizens of New Amsterdam saw themselves suddenly confronted with a governor who made frantic efforts to confiscate their arms, "paying for them according to his pleasure"—he paid, in fact, sixteen guilders for them, twice the usual price—in order to sell them to the Indians. There were still not enough, and in August a merchant, Gerrit Vastrick, was given orders to bring a load of guns back from the Netherlands.

Nine months later, at Vastrick's return, the weapons were openly unloaded, as a gaping crowd watched. "Everybody made his own comment," a bystander later related, and when the people saw that the ship was not inspected in the normal way, rumors flew that there were many more guns on board for the governor. "Had the people not been persuaded and held back, something extraordinary would have happened."[18]

Stuyvesant might have displayed his orders from the company, but he considered this beneath his dignity. He only remarked that if anyone had complained to him of neglect in the vessel's inspection he would have dealt with the matter. A few months later, when a new treaty had been signed, he defiantly presented a gun to Orantinim, the sachem of the Hackensack Indians.[19]

It was by now plain that Stuyvesant could do little to please the inhabitants of New Amsterdam. The honeymoon between the general and the citizens had been brief, if there had been one at all. Stuyvesant had shown remarkably little tact or diplomacy. He had issued a string of draconian ordinances, and was inflexible in seeing them carried out; and he seemed to have lost what little sense of humor he had once possessed. Far from being, as he had once promised, a kindly father figure to whom all might turn, he affronted the people by his bullying manner, or terrorized them by explosions of savage rage. "Whoever has opposed him has as much as the sun and moon against him," his enemies would later remark.

The Lord General did not hesitate to use "ugly words which would better suit the fish-market," and he had all the stubbornness of a Frieslander. Occasionally he made an effort and listened, chafing visibly, to complaints, or to the discussions of his Council, but sooner or later he would impatiently cut the conversation short, reach his own conclusions, and act accordingly. He lacked Kieft's refined semi-aristocratic shiftiness, but in his own forthright way he attempted to exercise the same authority as his predecessor. And in this regard, he was soon to be dealt a severe blow by the almost-forgotten Melyn and Kuyter.[20]

The two men, after their miraculous survival from the shipwreck of the *Princess*, had returned to a cool welcome in the Netherlands. The Heeren XIX, shocked by the loss of the vessel and its precious cargo, "lamented very much . . . and grieved that two bandits, rebels and mutineers had come to annoy the Company with their complaints."[21] The Lords Directors did their best to

NEW BROOMS

hush up the whole affair. "We cannot learn that anything special happened in New Netherland," wrote an Amsterdammer to his agent in Manhattan. But Melyn and Kuyter, who had already shown that they were not easily intimidated, persevered and eventually managed to obtain a hearing from the States General.[22]

On April 28, 1648, their High Mightinesses made a sensational decision and suspended the sentence Stuyvesant had imposed on the two men. Informing the company of their resolution, they added a warning: "We, moreover, granted to and allowed the petitioners liberty, pending the case in appeal, to return hence to New Netherland . . . free and unmolested to enjoy and use their property there." It was not a complete victory for the two men, but it was shattering news for the company and Stuyvesant. The affair was crowned by a letter, specially written by Stadtholder Prince Willem II, in which he urged the "Honorable, Prudent, Discreet and Dear" Peter Stuyvesant to obey the States' order.[23]

The reversal of the governor's sentence was taken very badly by the company. The Amsterdam Chamber felt it was a bitter reprimand, and did not hesitate to vent its resentment on Stuyvesant, who had given the States the occasion to humiliate the chamber so publicly. In a long letter sent off in January 1649 the chamber told its governor in New Amsterdam in no uncertain terms to keep his nose out of such complications in the future, and to leave the affairs of his predecessor severely alone—"for before your departure you must have fully understood the dissatisfaction created . . . by several acts of his administration." As for Melyn and Kuyter: "Your Honor will soon learn how dangerous it is to intervene in other people's business. . . ." The Amsterdam Chamber would not dispute the righteousness of the sentence, "but it would have been better to let the dead man [Kieft] defend it." The biggest blow was that the two men had induced the States to summon Stuyvesant "to defend this sentence either in person or by attorney."[24]

The damage was done and Stuyvesant's authority took a beating from which it never completely recovered. He did not receive the company's letter until April, but by that time he was fully informed about what had happened in The Hague. At the beginning of 1649 Melyn and Kuyter had returned in triumph, armed with the summons for the director general. And in face of that summons, not even Stuyvesant dared to fulfill his threat to make them a head shorter and send them in pieces back to Holland.

One of the worst consequences of the whole business was that it seriously undermined Stuyvesant's standing with his New England neighbors. Melyn, indiscreet as always, had made a stop at Rhode Island on his way back, "parading" the writ. Roger Williams, the governor, took care of the rest. In an excited letter to John Winthrop Jr. he reported that "Moline" had been there with "letters from the States to call home the present governor to answer many complaints both from Dutch and English against him." It was distressing enough for Stuyvesant, but it was just the beginning.[25]

THE

FREEDOM FIGHTERS

Never had St. Nicholas Church, its high roof and belltower rising over the walls of Fort Amsterdam, been so crowded as on March 8, 1649. General Stuyvesant had called a meeting of all the citizens, ostensibly to discuss "the public affairs of the country."[1]

Things turned out slightly differently. Cornelis Melyn, who had patiently waited for the best moment to deliver the States' writ to the governor, now saw his opportunity for the complete humiliation of his persecutor. He had planned his *grand coup* with some members of the Nine, and it was merchant Arnoldus van Hardenbergh who was to read the mandamus. Rumors had already spread, and the church could hardly contain the mass of curious New Netherlanders.

Stuyvesant was unaware of the plot when he stumped into the church to open the meeting, and he was taken aback when Melyn, hardly able to hide his glee, handed the document to Van Hardenbergh, who stood up and unrolled the parchment. The governor stopped him short by asking if it was necessary to read it immediately. Melyn insisted. "Then I must have the copy," snapped Stuyvesant, red with anger, and before Van Hardenbergh knew what had happened, the paper was pulled from his hands with such force that the States' seal almost fell off, "hardly hanging to a small strip." When Melyn pointed out that the copy was attached to it, the delighted audience yelled to get on with the business. The

general regained control and handed the writ back to Van Hardenbergh, who read slowly that the director general was summoned
"to appear, by the first opportunity at the Hague before their High
Mightinesses" to defend his actions against Melyn and Kuyter.[2]

It was a moment that Stuyvesant never forgot and never forgave, but when Van Hardenbergh had finished, he answered with
apparent composure: "I honour the States and their commission,
and will obey their commands." He promised to send an agent,
maintaining that his judgment against the two men had been "well
and legally pronounced." When Van Hardenbergh asked him for
this answer in writing, the general retorted that he would give it
"whenever you deliver me an authenticated copy of the Mandamus." The merchant turned to Van Tienhoven, the only person
in the colony with the right to notarize any document, but the
secretary loyally refused, saying: "You may do it yourself."[3]

It was the end of the meeting. Stuyvesant, angry and embarrassed, dismissed the delegates, who trooped off, excitedly discussing the incident. A week later Van Hardenbergh brought the copy
to the general's house. He would have done it sooner, but Melyn
had been called away to his farm on Staten Island to check a rumor
that the Indians had killed a Dutchman. Two members of the
Nine, Heerman and Van Couwenhoven, accompanied Van Hardenbergh, who again asked Stuyvesant for his answer in writing.
The governor was about to meet his Council, and refused curtly,
telling the three men: "Their High Mightinesses' award I shall
regard."[4]

In the Council that day Stuyvesant had to deal with another
rebel, who would in the long run be far more dangerous than
Melyn. He was Adriaen van der Donck, the former schout of
Rensselaerswyck, who had once come to Kieft's rescue when the
governor found himself without money to buy presents for some
Indian chiefs. The gesture had done him no harm. Kieft had given
him a plot of land in Westchester fifteen miles from New Amsterdam, where he began a colony, called Colen Donck, soon known
as the Jonker's Manor (Yonkers).

Van der Donck came from a very good family in Holland. His
mother's father, Adriaen Jansz van Bergen, had made history by
using his turfboat in 1590 to smuggle Dutch soldiers into Breda,
which was occupied by the Spanish. Adriaen van der Donck had
studied law at the world-famous University of Leiden, but gave up

his employ as advocate in the Supreme Court of Holland to go to New Netherland. Kiliaen van Rensselaer, always on the lookout for intelligent and ambitious young men to serve in his domain, engaged Van der Donck as schout. He arrived in the colony in 1641.

But life in the rough pioneer community did not much suit the young Van der Donck, who gave up his job and retired to Welysburg on Castle Island, which was leased to him by the patroon. In 1646 the farm burned down and Van der Donck, who had in the meantime married the Reverend Francis Doughty's daughter Mary, now decided to take up the grant Kieft had given him and move nearer to Manhattan.

His charm, sense of humor, and sincerity did not go unnoticed in the small community, and when Stuyvesant in December 1648 admitted new members to the Board of Nine (only three, not six, as he had promised), Van der Donck was proposed, accepted, and at once chosen secretary. The governor must have appointed him with reluctance, for in the few years of his residence near the capital, the well-spoken and brilliant young man had become the center of opposition to company rule in general, and that of Stuyvesant in particular. Now, in a new official capacity, he ventured further than words.

It was not difficult for him to gather material that would strengthen his case. The inhabitants of the province had enough opportunity to visit their neighbors in New England and had jealously observed that although New Netherland had a much better position and soil, "New England is populous, rich, prosperous, driving an immense trade and commerce with almost the entire universe; yea, is flourishing whilst New Netherland, on the contrary is a desert."[5]

One of the reasons for the higher standard of living in New England, asserted Van der Donck and others, was the fact that the English paid no duties or taxes, not even on wares bought abroad, while the Dutch charged foreign traders 30 percent. Another factor that kept many merchants away was Stuyvesant's inclination to consider every vessel that came into port and did not belong to friends "as a prize." People from Boston had told Van der Donck that "more than 25 ships would come here [New Amsterdam] every year, if the owners were not fearful of confiscation."[6]

An even more striking difference between the colonies was their way of government. The New Englanders had succeeded in achieving a form of independence from the Motherland, choosing their own governments, and the people had the power to "make a change in case of improper behavior." New Netherland, however, was still attached to the Republic—as by an umbilical cord—through the West India Company. The director general, although free in principle, had to refer everything to Amsterdam, where the Heeren XIX, ignorant of the facts and concerned only with profits, made their leisurely judgments. Every decision had to be explained and approved, a sure way to obstruct progress or growth. In the appointment of the governor the people of the province had no say at all, and it was impossible for them to have him replaced. The case of Kieft, whose removal had required endless protests and finally pressure from the States General, was a perfect example.

Up to a certain point Stuyvesant sympathized with the ideas of Van der Donck and his followers. He himself was irked by the heavy hand of the distant Heeren XIX, always ready to rap him on the knuckles for some infringement of their wishes; and he disliked having to plead company's orders when the Nine protested or asked for changes. When the Nine decided accordingly that they must take their complaints to Amsterdam, he encouraged them to proceed, only insisting that he be consulted and kept fully informed.

The irascible governor and his Nine, led by the suave young Van der Donck, were, however, soon at odds. Stuyvesant forbade them to interview citizens when drawing up their complaints—he would tell them all they needed to know. "To be expected to follow his directions in that matter was not, we thought, founded in reason," commented Van der Donck scornfully, and he and his followers began canvassing from house to house. Stuyvesant was sure that their findings would be violently critical of both the company and himself, and at Council meetings he urged them to show him their material. But they refused point blank, and the general's initial sympathy was soon replaced by furious resentment. "Although these persons," according to Van der Donck, "had been good and dear friends with him always, and he, shortly before, had regarded them as the most honorable, able, intelligent and pious men of the country, yet as soon as they did not follow

THE FREEDOM FIGHTERS

the General's wishes, they were . . . rascals, liars, rebels, usurpers and spendthrifts, in a word, hanging was almost too good for them."[7]

The Nine went stubbornly ahead with their work. In February Van der Donck opened an office to receive the citizens' complaints. Stuyvesant soon heard of this and bided his time, till a day when Van der Donck was out of town. He himself broke into the room and left with a rough draft of the journal that the young lawyer was composing. He read it the same evening, and the next day when Van der Donck returned he was arrested and put in jail.

A few days later, on March 4, Stuyvesant called the Great Council—the normal Council plus the militia officers—and in a fiery speech accused his prisoner of *crimen laesae majestatis*. No one protested except Vice Director Van Dincklage, who at last summoned all his courage to resist the general. During the trial of Melyn and Kuyter he had supported the governor, but recently he had made it clear that he had been misled and had acted out of fear of Stuyvesant. At the Council meeting he dared to speak out openly. He reproached the governor with having acted without consulting him, and demanded Van der Donck's release on bail. Stuyvesant could not believe his ears. Fortunately for him, he had, at least for the present, the support of the other thirteen councillors. Van der Donck was released from jail, but was sentenced to house arrest until a commission of two had made a study of his journal.[8]

The lawyer told the two commissioners that his document was written in a hurry—"in consequence of him having had much to do and not having read over again most of it"—and that much had to be changed. But Stuyvesant was unrelenting and called the draft a "libel which was worth no answer," while insisting nonetheless on punishing the writer as an example to others. And on March 15, the day on which three of the Nine handed him the copy of Melyn's damaging mandamus, the governor had at least the pleasure of one small victory: the Council released Van der Donck, but not before they had decided to expel him from the Nine because he had "grossly slandered not only some superior and inferior officers, but also their High Mightinesses themselves. . . ." Only Van Dincklage refused to sign the resolution. The same day the general issued a proclamation stating that no testimony or other act was valid unless written by his secretary, Van Tienhoven.[9]

Stuyvesant believed he had quelled the rebellion, but he misunderstood the mood of his country and underestimated the persistence of Van der Donck. Within a few days he could in justice repeat what Melyn and Kuyter had once remarked:

Whenever we lay one enemy low,
On the morrow another returns the blow.[10]

Although Van der Donck and his journal were now the center of attention in New Amsterdam, Cornelis Melyn refused to disappear from the limelight. He wanted redress of his grievances, but it did not look as if Stuyvesant was going to oblige him. On the contrary, the general continued to persecute the patroon of Staten Island and his family, as Jacobus Loper, Melyn's son-in-law, realized when he asked permission to trade in the Delaware near New Sweden. The governor refused and told the Council that the company had expressly warned against Melyn, who "will do everything to create trouble and mischief for us on the side towards the Swedish Colony." The councillors asked: "Shall the sins of the father then be visited on the son?" But Stuyvesant was adamant. "It cannot be otherwise this time; he shall not go." This was enough for Van Dincklage. Together with La Montagne, he signed an affidavit, which Melyn pocketed along with many others to be used in his case.[11]

Melyn had by now realized that the only way for him to obtain justice was to go back to the Netherlands, but before he left, he composed a strong protest at the actions of the director general, again demanding that he appear at The Hague, and asking that copies of all documents relevant to his case be handed over. If that were refused, he formally objected to their being used later in Holland. This "irreverent protest" was taken to the Governor's House on August 1 by Van Hardenbergh and Van der Donck (who had probably helped draft it), and since the governor was out, it was given to his wife Judith. The general was very angry with his wife for having accepted the document, and with Melyn for not having gone through the usual channels. But that was his only reaction. He refused even to reply to the "mutineer," who had booked a cabin on the first vessel to Holland.

By now Stuyvesant felt that it was high time to present his own version of the affair, and on August 10 he wrote to the States a lengthy and virulent attack on Melyn, dwelling on his outrageous

THE FREEDOM FIGHTERS

behavior. He complained that Melyn had lowered both his and the company's credit in the eyes of their English neighbors, by spreading stories that the company was bankrupt and that Stuyvesant himself was about to be shipped back to prison in Holland—and this at a time when the English were "not very friendly to us and our Nation here on account of old boundary requisitions and claims." Melyn had even spread word that the company had asked for seven hundred soldiers for New Amsterdam so that the New Netherlanders could make war on their neighbors.[12]

After his arrival in New Amsterdam, Stuyvesant continued, Melyn's behavior had been just as reprehensible—the church episode was only one of many. He had told everyone prepared to listen that the company had not a single penny, that "your High Mightinesses had spoken very contemptuously of the Board of Directors, as being unfit and unworthy to govern your High Mightinesses' possessions," etc., etc. This had all led to great unrest in the province, which now obliged Stuyvesant to stay there in spite of the summons to appear in The Hague. "We should willingly obey your H.M.'s intentions," the governor wrote regretfully, but thanks to their attitude in the Melyn case, he had more important matters to attend to, and would send instead his secretary, Cornelis van Tienhoven.[13]

Van Tienhoven was not to enjoy a peaceful voyage. When he sailed from New Amsterdam on August 15, Melyn was also on board, as was Van der Donck, who was accompanied by two of the Nine, Jacob van Couwenhoven and Jan Evertsen Bout. Their commissions had been recklessly signed by Van Dincklage after Stuyvesant had angrily refused.

Yet another critic of the general joined them for the voyage to Europe—Johannes Cornelis Backerus, the dominie who had reluctantly been persuaded by the general to leave Curaçao for New Netherland. He had been unable to avoid being drawn into the conflict that divided the province, and while he admired the general as a man of principle and religion, he could not approve of the way he administered the country. The dominie had willingly become the "bellman" of the rebels, reading out notices of their meetings from the pulpit every Sunday, until Stuyvesant furiously reminded him that he was in the service of the company and forbidden to read notices not signed by himself or Van Tienhoven.

The unhappy dominie lacked the battling spirit of his fiery predecessor, Bogardus, and on July 6 Stuyvesant and his Council gave him permission to return to Holland.[14] It must have been a fast, if not very relaxed, voyage, because on October 13, 1649, the States General reported the receipt of the *Remonstrance of New Netherland,* delivered to them by Van der Donck, Van Couwenhoven, and Bout.

The document was in fact made up of three parts. On July 26 the Nine, including the dismissed Van der Donck plus two old hands, Jan Damen and Thomas Hall, had signed a *Petition* to the States General, to which was added a hefty folder, containing *Additional Observations.* Two days later the same group had approved the official *Remonstrance of New Netherland to the States General of the United Netherlands.* These were all lucidly, sometimes angrily, written documents, which explained to the States in plain terms that its province in America was in ruins, thanks to the mismanagement of the company and its representatives there, and that there was but one way out of the chaos: direct control from their High Mightinesses.[15]

The *Petition* was short and exact. On one sheet of paper it told the Dutch in eight points why New Netherland's condition was so "very poor and most low": unsuitable government; scanty privileges and exemptions; onerous duties, imposts, exactions and such like; long continued war; the loss of the *Princess* (with all the maps and botanical specimens); a superabundance of "Scots and Chinese" (the Dutch expression for petty traders and peddlers); great death in general; and lastly "the insufferable arrogance of the natives or Indians arising from our small numbers."

The petitioners explained that they had waited in vain for assistance from the company:

> *We, therefore, unable to delay any longer, being reduced to the lowest ebb, have determined to fly for refuge to your High Mightinesses, our gracious Sovereigns and the Father of this Province, most humbly craving and beseeching you to look with eyes of compassion on this your Province, and that your High Mightinesses would be pleased to order and redress matters so that dangers may be removed, troubles put an end to, and population and prosperity promoted, as your High Mightinesses in your illustrious wisdom shall consider best. . . .*

THE FREEDOM FIGHTERS

The Nine did not resort to protest alone. They handed to the States a series of proposals that would, they claimed, transform the situation immediately. Among these were: exemption from duties and taxes until the country had become more prosperous and populated; freedom to trade in the products of New Netherland; encouragement for the fishery; more farmers; settlement of the boundaries of the province with New England. By far the most important demand was that, in view "of the harsh proceedings and want of means" of the company, the States themselves should take over the ownership and control of the province and grant it, as in New England, "suitable burgher government . . . somewhat resembling the laudable government of our Fatherland."

The *Additional Observations* were much more explicit—ninety-one pages of angry and outspoken complaints by many of the colonists, all of which came down to the same point: the government of the province was "bad and intolerable." The name of the company "alone terrifies the inhabitants"; the director generals "comport themselves as sovereign tyrants"; their management consists "mainly in arrests, imprisonments, banishments, confiscations, harsh prosecutions, blows, scoldings, and reckoning half faults for whole ones." Here, too, solutions were offered. "Were your High Mightinesses to order that all vessels proceeding and trading to those northern parts of America should first touch at the Manhattans . . . and bring with them as many persons as may seasonably apply and they can conveniently carry at suitable fixed rates, many *liefhebbers* [amateurs] would no doubt emigrate in a short time. . . ." The "observers" thought that a crossing should cost no more than thirty to thirty-two guilders for those in the between-decks, and thirty-eight to forty guilders for a cabin.

To alleviate their heavy financial burdens, the colonists went even further than the *Petition*, not only demanding exemption from taxes, but also the lifting of the duty on tobacco, as it would encourage the farmers to turn more forests into fields. They also asked for the freedom to "export, sell, and barter grain, timber and all other wares and merchandise, the produce of this country, every where and every way." For their protection against the Indians and the English, a settlement of the border question was not enough, they would need "a company or two" of soldiers. If the fort was not repaired and no troops were sent, the petitioners believed that the English would annex New Netherland within a few years.

The most interesting of these documents was the *Remonstrance —Vertoogh van Nieu-Neder-Land, whegens de Ghelegentheydt, Vruchtba-erheydt, en Soberen Staet dessels—*the scathing indictment of West India Company policy that was the work of Van der Donck himself. It began with a description of the province, a historical summary of the Dutch rights, and of events since its discovery in 1609 by "Hendrick Hutson," then launched into a bitter denunciation of Kieft, Stuyvesant, and the company. Like the other two papers, it had been signed by the eleven men in New Amsterdam, but Van Cortland—a friend of Kieft—had added "under protest; obliged to sign as to the Heer Kieft's administration."

The company, so Van der Donck stated, had never made a profit out of New Netherland, but that was entirely thanks to its own shortsightedness. Had it concentrated more on agriculture than on trade, the province would now be flourishing and self-supporting. It had indeed spent plenty of money—but on the wrong things, such as the building of the *Nieu Nederlandt* in Peter Minuit's time and the erection of three expensive mills for brick-making, lime-burning, and salt-making, "which through bad management and calculation have all gone to nought. Had the same money been used on bringing people and cattle," the company might be rich. As it was, its assets in the province, worth only seventy thousand guilders, consisted of warehouses, workshops, etc.; apart from the church there was not even any public property. The fort was neglected, without a single functioning cannon.

The directors had all been as bad as the company, wrote Van der Donck. They had protected their privileges by cruel and petty means and were interested only in profit. Kieft's administration had been disastrous, Stuyvesant's not much better. He was dictatorial, calling himself "Mijn Heer Generael" (My Lord General), a term that had never been heard before; he taxed the people heavily and used only a small part of the money for the public good; and he bullied his Council and the Board of Nine. Worst of all, however, was the secretary, Van Tienhoven, who had been primarily responsible for the Indian War. He was deceitful and treacherous and ought to leave the country at once if it were to become a place fit to live in.

THE FREEDOM FIGHTERS

Van der Donck ended his *Vertoogh* with the call to liberate New Netherland from the company's chains: "In our opinion this country will never flourish under the government of the Honourable Company, but will pass away and come to an end of itself." Before all else, however, the province must have good governors, "godly, honorable, and intelligent rulers," since "a covetous chief makes poor subjects." If those and other conditions were fulfilled, the young lawyer predicted, New Netherland would prosper and "everyone would be allured hither by the pleasantness, situation, salubrity and fruitfulness of the country."

The Heeren XIX were definitely not pleased by the activities of the three men. On February 16, 1650, they wrote Stuyvesant a plaintive letter about these "silly people" come from his parts, "who had been badly misled by a few seditious persons," such as Melyn and Van der Donck. "These men seem to leave nothing untried to upset every kind of government, pretending that they suffered under too heavy a yoke."

The men had obviously found a willing and understanding audience in the Republic, thanks to the respected support of Dominie Backerus, who had made "common cause" with the rebels, and of former Governor Wouter van Twiller, who had not forgotten his humiliating recall. The petitioners had found still more dangerous allies in their fight for freedom—the Portuguese.[16]

At the beginning of 1650 the Seven Provinces might have been prospering, but they were anything but united. Since the Treaty of Munster in 1648 Stadtholder Willem II had been intriguing to renew the treaty with France and continue the war against Spain with the hope of dividing the Southern Netherlands, still occupied by the Spanish, between his country and the French. Willem's main opponent was Amsterdam, whose merchants wished to make their profits in peace and quiet, while keeping the increasingly land-hungry French at a safe distance on the other side of the southern *barrière,* the Spanish Netherlands. The West India Company was accordingly odd man out in Amsterdam. Having lost almost all its properties in Africa and Brazil to the Spanish and Portuguese, it sided with the Prince in the hope of retaining at least a small piece of its precious colony in South America. In

A SWEET AND ALIEN LAND

response, the Portuguese minister to The Hague received ample funds from Lisbon to subsidize any enemy of the company. One of his weapons was the publication of pamphlets, printed secretly in Holland, but seemingly coming from Antwerp.

In 1649, about the time that Van der Donck, Melyn, and the others arrived in the Republic, a pamphlet appeared called *Breeden Raedt* ("Broad Advice," or "Broad Council"), a venomous broadsheet that at once became a best-seller. It was composed, in rather rude and illiterate Dutch, in the traditional form of a dialogue, between passengers on a *trekschuit,* one of the barges drawn by horses that commuted between the cities and villages of the watery Lowlands. The writers were generally anonymous, and many people tried to guess the meaning of the initials I.A.G.W.C. under the title. The last three could have been a poor joke about the West India Company (in Dutch, the Geoctroyeerde Westindische Companie), while the first two are said to have stood for Ionker Adriaen, the lawyer Van der Donck. But the style of the pamphlet has little in common with Van der Donck's writings, and the whole document seems more likely the work of Melyn, since it included revelations that only he could have known, such as the "death scene" with Kieft.

In *Broad Advice* the conversation was between nine men of different nationalities, of whom the main characters were Captain Bouwen Krynsen and the Portuguese soldier Alfonso. There was also Charles, a Swedish student; Domingo, a Spanish barber; the French merchant Etienne; a Neapolitan called Faust; Govert, an impoverished English nobleman; Hans Christoffer, a Dutch gentleman; Judas van Schooner, a boatswain; and finally Konrad Popolski, who could only be a Pole. The subject of their dialogue was, of course, the West India Company, which was heavily attacked by Alfonso for its role in Brazil. From there the talk drifted off to New Netherland, recently visited by Captain Krynsen, who was thus well informed about it. The other passengers listened with horror to his vivid stories about the Indian War, when Kieft had run wild with his mercenary soldiers. "A certain skipper, named Isaac Abrahamsen, having saved a little boy in a sailboat and hidden him under a sail, in order to present him to one Cornelis Melyn," had told Krynsen how "eighteen German tigers" who heard the hungry child crying "dragged him from under the sail . . . cut him in two and threw the pieces overboard." The all-

THE FREEDOM FIGHTERS

knowing seaman then turned to the subject of Stuyvesant, who according to him "has so many particular qualities, of which no one is serviceable in a desirable republic, that he is not fit to rule over Turkish slaves in the galleys, much less over free Christians." When the boatswain asked: "Does he curse and storm and rage, as he used to do, striking and beating," Krynsen accused the governor of hypocrisy in religious matters, "puffed-up pride," avarice—in matters of confiscation he had "as much discretion as a wolf for a lamb"—and partiality. And the worst was "there are no hopes for the better."

Van Tienhoven received even more contemptuous treatment. He was lustful to the point that "like an Indian" he ran after the squaws. His wife was "reputed to be a whore," and he himself was like a serpent. "Those whom he stings he laughs at, and while he flatters he bites."

It was too much for the listeners on the barge—Alfonso complained: "Skipper, you have talked almost all of us to sleep with your bad news"—but Dutch readers lapped it up, and for the first time in its history New Netherland was in the general news. Till then, no one had heard of Stuyvesant, Melyn, and Van der Donck; now everybody talked about them. As the company reproached Stuyvesant in a letter of February 16, 1650: "Formerly New Netherland was never spoken of and now heaven and earth seem to be stirred up by it."[17]

A SWEET AND ALIEN LAND

Dutch
Pioneers

*David de Vries, whose journal gives a
damning impression of the first Dutch governors.*

Everardus Bogardus, one of the Dutch dominies who were better known for their hotheadedness than for their piety.
COURTESY OF THE LONG ISLAND HISTORICAL SOCIETY, BROOKLYN, N.Y.

*Augustine Heerman, the "Bohemian" diplomat of the colony,
who eventually preferred the more civilized life in Maryland.*
COURTESY OF THE NEW-YORK HISTORICAL SOCIETY, NEW YORK CITY

Cornelis Steenwyck,
one of the wealthiest men in New Netherland,
and at various times
Burgomaster of New Amsterdam.
COURTESY OF THE
NEW-YORK HISTORICAL SOCIETY,
NEW YORK CITY

THE DUKE
OF MUSCOVY

All the publicity given to New Amsterdam by the *Remonstrance* and *Broad Advice* had its effect. The States General and the Dutch public openly sided against the West India Company, and Cornelis van Tienhoven, sent to Holland by Stuyvesant to present his case, fought a lonely battle. He composed his own *Answer to the Remonstrance* while in the Republic—a cool, clever analysis of events in New Netherland, and a peremptory defense of company and governor that won little sympathy for either.

Refusing to descend to detail, Van Tienhoven dismissed many telling points in the *Petition* of Van der Donck and his associates with a curt " 'tis not these people's business." They were rebels, plain and simple. Everybody who came to the province knew that he had to accept the sovereignty of the States General, the company, and "obey the Director and Council . . . as a good subject is bound to do." The chief reason for the protest of the eleven men, furthermore, was the fact that the company was their creditor, as they had been obliged to borrow heavily during the Indian War. "This debt, amounting to 30,000 guilders, rendered many who were disinclined to pay, insolent and ill-disposed," the secretary accused.[1]

But long before Van Tienhoven could publish this rancorous defense, the States General had taken action against the company. It looked like victory for the three delegates from New Amsterdam. A provisional order published on May 25, 1650, ruled that all Dutch citizens might in future go freely to New Netherland, and the captains of ships should be ordered to take as many freemen as they could accommodate. On arrival, the freemen were to be given parcels of land and enjoy exemption from tithes on their fruit and crops; they were to be allowed to hunt and fish freely, and to sail and trade "along the entire coast from Florida to New-foundland" on condition that they pay a 5 percent duty in New Amsterdam. The States order called for a sweeping reorganization of the government of the province, the appointment of a school-master and more dominies, and the establishment of a municipal government in New Amsterdam. It might also be desirable to replace the martial Stuyvesant by someone "conversant with mat-ters of agriculture and the nature of soils": Stuyvesant's recall would have the advantage of allowing him to answer in person the charges of Melyn and others.[2]

There was, however, one great disappointment for the "free-dom fighters": the States, although strongly critical of the "per-verse administration" of the Amsterdam Chamber, refused to take the province under its own wing. As the provisional order stated: "The West India Company shall appoint and keep there a Direc-tor, competent councillors, officers and other ministers of Justice for the protection of the good and the punishment of the wicked."[3]

But for Van Couwenhoven and Bout, this reorganization was quite good enough, and armed with the order, the elated delegates sailed for New Amsterdam in the *Valkenier* ("Falconer"), leaving Van der Donck behind to continue the fight. On their return to New Amsterdam on June 28, they at once delivered the States' documents to Stuyvesant and his Council. But they soon learned that it was one thing to have reforms decreed in Europe, and another matter altogether to have them carried out in America.

The general had been privately warned by the company in April of the impending decisions, and was instructed to "act with the cunning of a fox." Stuyvesant, as always the loyal servant of the Lords Directors, did as he was told, and simply ignored Van Couwenhoven and Bout. Weeks went by, none of the reforms specified were carried out, and the hopes raised by the triumphant return of the two delegates soon subsided. Much distressed, they complained to the States: "The melancholy condition of this country remains unchanged and even has become worse . . . the Commonalty lives in fear and anguish."[4]

Since the delegates' departure for Europe the previous year, New Netherland had lived through a hard winter—so cold "that the ink freezes in the pen," as Anneke Melyn had written to her husband in Holland in December 1649. There had been shortages of every necessity—"the poor people have scarcely anything to eat, for no supplies of bread, butter, beef and pork can now be had" —made worse by the necessity of provisioning the company ships that called at New Amsterdam. As an added grievance, at a time when prices were particularly high, the Indians seemed to have plenty of wampum, and were buying up all the bread. In November the governor had forbidden the bakers to sell white bread to the natives, but the order had proved almost impossible to enforce. He had also forbidden the use of wheat for making beer or cakes, and had begged the company to send over ten thousand guilders' worth of small coins to replace the wampum. But the Heeren XIX, in their usual detached way, had simply replied: "In our present financial situation it cannot be done."[5]

Since New Netherland was still chronically short of farmers, these scarcities were not much eased by the coming of spring, and after the governor had given short shift to the States' order, the laments of the province grew loud again.

Adriaen van der Donck, who had expected only to settle a few details before returning to New Amsterdam, rose to the occasion magnificently. While the Heeren XIX fought tooth and nail to hang onto their property, and Stuyvesant defied instructions to return to Holland, Van der Donck became the ambassador of the disheartened New Netherlanders. Letter after letter reached him with the worst news possible. The governor had "with a view to insult and affront the Selectmen" removed the benches in their church pew; he had kept the arms destined for the burgher guard and sold them to Indians; and he had refused to call up the militia, dismissing them with the words: "I shall do so when I please."[6]

The only good news Van der Donck could send in return was that Van Tienhoven, on the point of returning to America in July 1650, had been stopped by the States after a complaint from Van der Donck himself. The States had already sent a notary public—Dirck van Schelluyne—to New Amsterdam with the two delegates, armed with a special commission to curb Van

THE DUKE OF MUSCOVY

Tienhoven's powers when he came back, and now they ordered that searching inquiries should be made into Van Tienhoven's responsibility for the Indian War and his maladministration. New Amsterdam heaved a sigh of relief at the news, but it was only a brief respite.[7]

The general, meanwhile, seemed bent on destroying the last traces of popular government in his province. He paid little or no regard to the Nine Select Men, who bore the anger of a community "ready to hang and burn them." The unfortunate Nine attempted to continue their duty in the hope that the provisional order from the States would soon be confirmed. But the governor had other ideas. When they came to see him in January to initiate the advised procedure by which six of them should be replaced, Stuyvesant told the startled men that he was planning to sue them for their involvement with the *Remonstrance.* "We finding ourselves overpowered and out of office, dare not meet together without getting into difficulty," they informed Van der Donck. " 'Twill not be in our power after this to watch over the public interest."[8]

One man had the courage to act. Vice Director Van Dincklage had been the general's *bête noire* ever since he had dared to stand up to him. Stuyvesant had refused even to sit at the Council table with this "fomentor of sedition and a vagabond," as he contemptuously described him. Now, together with Schout-Fiscaal Van Dyck, Van Dincklage composed in February a long protest against the actions of the general. But he paid dearly for it. Stuyvesant told the Council that he would no longer have him in court, and when the vice director bravely stayed put, he summoned the guard and had Van Dincklage forcibly dragged to the guardhouse, where he was confined for several days. Even after his release, "he was not suffered to go unmolested," an indignant Van der Donck read.[9]

Van Dincklage himself wrote despairingly: "To describe the state of this government to one well acquainted and conversant with it is a work of superogation; 'tis to wash a blackamoor. Our great Muscovy Duke goes on as usual, with something of the wolf; the older he gets the more inclined he is to bite. He proceeds no longer by words or writings, but by arrests and stripes."[10]

It was the end of a stormy career for Van Dincklage. He retired from official life to Staten Island and found there a refuge in the house of the man whom in 1648, still loyal to the general, he had helped to prosecute—Cornelis Melyn.

The patroon of Staten Island, having once again brought his case to the attention of the States, returned to New Amsterdam in December 1650. He had made a good impression in the Republic, and the company had been obliged to ask Stuyvesant for more convincing evidence against him, since the material brought over by Van Tienhoven was "rather shaky." They told the general that "a good case needs good help," but it is not recorded whether that was available.[11]

In any case, the whole business had dragged on much too long. Melyn left matters in the hands of his advocate and returned to the province. The former tanner had not wasted his time in the Lowlands: he had recruited the support of an influential Gelderland nobleman. Jonkheer Hendrick van der Capellen van Ryssel, one of the deputies in the States General, had met Melyn when he was a member of the government committee charged with the inquest on New Netherland. With some others, the jonkheer bought the ship *Nieu Nederlandts Fortuyn* ("Fortune of New Netherland"), with which he sent Melyn and twenty colonists back to Staten Island. There, Melyn's new ally Van Dincklage had obtained a new domain for the jonkheer.

It had been a long voyage, and when water and food were running out, the ship put into Rhode Island, giving Stuyvesant a wonderful pretext to harass his enemy. When the *Fortuyn* arrived in New Amsterdam, he chained up the ship with its cargo, claiming that Melyn, in breach of all the rules, had broken bulk in New England. It was an act that led to a long legal struggle, as Jonkheer Van der Capellen had no intention of letting Stuyvesant impound his ship, and an irritated company was forced to rebuke its governor.

The *Fortuyn* controversy was yet another reason for resentment against the man whom Stuyvesant considered his evil genius, and he contrived to dig up other charges. He found evidence that Melyn had traded in New England; willing witnesses also told him that the patroon had sailed secretly to Staten Island, where he had landed "a number of kegs with powder and blocks of lead . . . also a chest of muskets." Considering the relationship between Stuyve-

THE DUKE OF MUSCOVY

sant and the patroon, this last accusation was not improbable—at least, Melyn thought it sensible not to appear in court when he was summoned. Instead he fortified himself on Staten Island with a little army of 118 Raritan Indians, "each armed with a musket." Witnesses told the Court of Holland in February 1652 that the patroon had insinuated to the Indians that Stuyvesant, "as soon as he had built a wall around Fort Amsterdam," would come and kill them, and bribed them to murder the director instead. Whether this was true or not, the general from then on was accompanied by an ostentatious bodyguard of four halberdiers.[12]

It was an impossible situation, and the Heeren XIX complained bitterly to the States about Melyn, "the principal actor in these strifes and quarrels, who notwithstanding the protests of the Lord Directors was . . . allowed to return." But Melyn felt safe in his fortified and protected manor on Staten Island, establishing with the help of Van Dincklage his own government there.[13]

Another principal actor in the *Remonstrance* drama, one much more to the taste of the company and Stuyvesant, had in the meantime returned to New Amsterdam. Van der Donck had been finally unable to keep Van Tienhoven in Holland any longer, and the secretary had set sail on May 5, 1651. He did not travel alone. In his company was a young woman, Elisabeth Jansen Croon van Hoogvelt, the daughter of a basketmaker, in whose arms he had found relaxation while preparing his and Stuyvesant's defense. He had met the young girl in Amsterdam, where the couple stayed at an inn on the Overtoom. Conveniently forgetting his wife and three children in New Amsterdam, Van Tienhoven presented himself there to the keeper Elisabeth Jans as a "suitor and a single unmarried person." The innkeeper, suitably shocked when she later heard that Van Tienhoven was married, told a notary that the couple had shown "each other great love and friendship such as is the custom between sweethearts." The secretary had told her that he was going to marry the girl when he got back to New Amsterdam.

He had been unable to leave in July 1650, as he had planned, and when he was about to embark in April of the following year, Van der Donck, still hot on his heels, again drew the attention of the States to his plans and Van Tienhoven was at last called to The Hague to answer questions about his role in the Indian War. He took Elisabeth (nicknamed Liesbeth) with him, but "their contin-

A SWEET AND ALIEN LAND

ual dalliance" had no chance to flower in peace. They took lodgings in the Three Little Doves, where Van Tienhoven told a sympathetic landlord, the undertaker Arien Bock, that if anybody ever inquired about him and the girl, he should say that "he had run away with the woman, against the will of the parents, but that he intended to marry her on the first opportunity."

Not feeling very secure, the couple soon moved to the boarding-house of Margaret van Eeda. She, too, had not suspected Van Tienhoven, whom she described as "a likely person, of ruddy face, corpulent body and having a little wen on the side of his cheek," nor the young woman, toward whom, so she told a notary in The Hague, "he evinced great friendship and love, calling her always Dearest, conversing as man and wife." She gave them permission to sleep in one bed, treating them "as honest folk, whom she placed at her table along with other decent and honest folk." Had she known Van Tienhoven was a married man, she said later, "she would not have received them."

She began to doubt her earlier judgment when Van Tienhoven one day had asked her for a second room, in case some friends came to see him. She advised him to move to the Universal Friend, opposite the Begijnenstraat, but there the schouts of The Hague —possibly tipped off by Van der Donck—caught up with the furtive couple. The secretary, much put out, came a few days later to visit a friend and told him that he had been "obliged to pay the two sheriffs as a fine the sum of 82 Rix dollars, in two several divisions and above that had provided them with some oysters." Liesbeth poured her heart out to Margaret van Eeda, wondering if the schouts had "any business to interfere with free people."[14]

It was obvious that Holland's Calvinistic air no longer agreed with the libertine Van Tienhoven. He did not wait for the end of the States' inquest and, in spite of a prohibition to leave, smuggled Liesbeth on board the ship *Waterhont* ("Waterhound") and sailed away. But their arrival at New Amsterdam in the summer of 1651 was a shock for the girl, "an honest man's daughter." In the city waited Van Tienhoven's wife, Rachel, and his three children, Lucas, Johannes, and Janneken. The betrayed Liesbeth took her case to Schout-Fiscaal Van Dyck, accusing the secretary of having "debauched" her, but she got nowhere in the labyrinth of bureaucracy that suddenly swallowed up her former lover. He was much

THE DUKE OF MUSCOVY

too important to Stuyvesant to be allowed to be pestered by such an adventure.[15]

The Heeren XIX felt similarly indulgent toward the harried Van Tienhoven and had done everything they could to get him out of the hands of "some evil minded disturbers of the public peace." They had also promoted him to be receiver general of the company's domains and revenues. While Liesbeth nursed her broken heart (which must have mended by the summer of 1653, when she married company official Jacob van Curler), Van Tienhoven settled down again to his usual corrupt and shifty manipulations.[16]

One of the first problems he tackled for Stuyvesant was Van Dyck. The schout, never a favorite of the governor's, had little support in the community. He constantly neglected his duties and was so incompetent that one day a murderer escaped through the chimney after he and the schout had been drinking (Van Dyck had fallen asleep). The Nine described him significantly as a "man, whose head is troubled and has a screw loose, especially when, as often happens, he has been drinking."[17]

Stuyvesant only permitted Van Dyck to copy legal papers and to look after the hogs that destroyed the sodden walls of the fort, "a duty a negro could well afford." When Van Dyck protested, he was put into confinement and beaten with the general's "rattan." In 1651 he had had the courage to sign the long protest that Van Dincklage had written against the governor, but while the vice director had lost his job, Stuyvesant apparently did not find Van Dyck important enough to punish. But he could no longer be overlooked when Van Tienhoven laid his hands on a silly lampoon in which an anonymous writer revealed that Van Dyck, in front of witnesses, had "berated and cursed" the general as a "rogue and tyrant, with many other slanderous defamations, which cut me to the heart."[18]

Stuyvesant called his rapidly thinning Council together and told them that "although we have a different opinion of ourselves . . . yet so much insults and calumnies have been uttered repeatedly behind our back and in our presence that we cannot bear it any longer." The Council agreed and Van Dyck was suspended from his office. He at once wrote a long defense in which he accused Stuyvesant of neglecting the fort, misappropriating funds, and considering himself "a God appointed of God," but the company once more rose to the defense of the general. The directors told

A SWEET AND ALIEN LAND

Van Dyck that they had protected him for a long time "out of respect for [his] friends," but that his disorderly life and dissolute conversations" and the fact that he did "ordinarily pass [his] time in drunkenness" had persuaded them that the general had "not put him into any inconvenience without great cause." Van Dyck was succeeded—as was to be expected—as schout-fiscaal by the equally bibulous Van Tienhoven.[19]

The New Amsterdammers had by now given up all hope of ever being relieved of the governor and his bullies. They did not know that just as Stuyvesant was removing Van Dyck, Van der Donck seemed to have at last won his battle. On April 27, 1652, the States came to a final decision about New Netherland. Their provisional order had been fought with diligence and stubbornness by the company, and finally with some measure of success. The Chamber of Amsterdam was to keep complete control over the province, but immigration was to be stimulated, duties on tobacco were to be removed, and New Amsterdam—now a town of eight hundred inhabitants—was to be given a municipal government. Most important, the recall of Stuyvesant was confirmed, so that he could "give their High Mightinesses a circumstantial and pertinent information and true and actual condition of the country." The Heeren XIX were furious and immediately dispatched a letter to Stuyvesant in which they told him "not to proceed on your voyage hither with too much haste but wait until you have further advice from us."[20]

They need not have worried. Three weeks later, on May 16, the States revoked the order. War had broken out between the Republic and England; it had saved the general. His "military mind," the States now thought, might be more useful than that of a man who knew about "agriculture and the nature of soil"—not to mention the nature of his subjects.[21]

Having done everything he could do, Van der Donck felt that it was high time to return to New Amsterdam. Heerman and others had kept him well informed about the situation in the country, reporting, too, that his own private estate of Colen Donck was "going all to ruin." Nevertheless, he had lost nothing of his enthusiasm for the province, and even talked his parents and his brother into returning with him. When, however, he began to look for a vessel that could take him and his family back to New Amsterdam, he discovered what it meant to have drawn down the

THE DUKE OF MUSCOVY

wrath of the Heeren XIX. No ship was allowed to take him as a passenger, and Van der Donck was forced to stay behind, alone, branded by the company as the "most notorious ringleader [of the] lawless and mutinous rabble." Even the safe conduct the States had given him could do nothing for the haunted lawyer.[22]

Wearily, he petitioned the States General. While waiting for the answer, he continued his law studies at Leiden, taking a Doctor of Law degree, and busied himself with his life work, the *Beschryvinge van Nieu Nederlant* ("Description of New Netherland"), an excellent source for the history of the province, partially based on the *Remonstrance,* for which the States gave him a copyright in May 1653.

Six months later, after two and a half years of absence, Van der Donck finally came home to Colen Donck. It had cost him an abject petition to the company, in which he promised not to accept any office in New Netherland, and to live "quietly and peaceably in his private character as common inhabitant, submitting to the orders and commands of the Company or their Directors." The Heeren XIX graciously felt that Van der Donck had been sufficiently punished for his "mutiny," but could not resist a final piece of pettiness. His request to be allowed to practice as attorney and counsellor in their colony was rejected, as they "could not see what advantage his pleading before a court would have."[23]

A second request, that he be allowed to examine documents in the secretary's office for the completion of his *Beschryvinge,* was halfheartedly granted; but the Amsterdam gentlemen, writing to Stuyvesant, warned the director general to be careful that "the Company's own weapon may not be used against us and we be drawn into new troubles and quarrels." The Lords Directors obviously knew their servant better than they sometimes pretended to, and Stuyvesant knew them better still. He never gave Van der Donck the opportunity even of entering the secretary's office, and the lawyer completed his book without the help of official papers.[24]

In the year that it was published, 1655, Van der Donck, still only thirty-five years old, died on his domain. For five years he had devoted his whole life and energy to the struggle for New Netherland's freedom. The fact that it was a lost cause must have broken his heart. The Duke of Muscovy was now king.

A SWEET AND ALIEN LAND

TROUBLE

IN THE NORTH

Fort Orange, about 125 miles north of New Amsterdam, was New Netherland's furthest outpost. In the 1650s it was still much the same as it had been in 1643 when the Jesuit missionary Father Isaac Jogues described it as "a miserable little fort . . . built of logs, with four or five pieces of Breteuil cannon, and as many pedereros." Standing on the western bank of the Hudson, it was no more than a stockaded quadrangular enclosure with four small bastions on the corners. If Fort Amsterdam was a "molehill," Fort Orange was an anthill.[1]

In 1648 Governor Peter Stuyvesant, on a visit to the fort (in contrast to his predecessor Kieft, the general traveled his province readily and extensively), had been horrified by its condition. The place was surrounded by warring Mohawks and Mohicans, and although the inhabitants bought their peace by providing both parties with guns, powder, and lead, the possibility of a surprise attack could never be ruled out. Stuyvesant gave permission to build more houses in the fort on the condition that their rear walls replace the stockade and be built of bricks. This was probably not carried out, since the fort continued to decay because of the spring freshets that annually flooded it, rotting the wooden palisades.[2]

Few officials actually lived inside Fort Orange, and after the West India Company gave up its fur monopoly in 1639, it had gradually withdrawn its representatives and soldiers. Now the private traders flocked to this rich fur center, where they built their own little frame houses around the fort, in their spare time growing vegetables and tobacco on small plots just outside the walls.

The little trader village called Beversfuyck (Beaver Trap) was not the only one in the region. Kiliaen van Rensselaer's domain, bought in 1630, was prospering and had its own little town, Greenbush, on the opposite bank of the river. There Dominie Johannes Megapolensis had watched since 1642 over his flock of about 120 souls. As the number of independent traders increased, the original hamlet of thirty wooden houses had grown considerably. The principal house was still that of the patroon's agent, while the pastor held his services in one of the warehouses, which had been provided with a pulpit and pews. Most of the inhabitants, however, lived isolated on their farms, which were scattered over the immense hilly colony, that extended for about twenty-one hundred square miles.[3]

In spite of the warring Indians surrounding Greenbush, life was at first tranquil in the tiny settlement, but soon serious clashes between the patroon's representatives and those of the company (supported by the free traders) rocked the community to its foundations. Inevitably the chief bone of contention was the fur trade, to which the question of "first rights" added more complications. Although Van Rensselaer was a great advocate of colonization and had sent out several farmers to his domain, he had a keen eye for the loads of pelts that were carried to the fort. When the company abolished its monopoly, he had charged his commis, Arent van Curler, to build up another fur monopoly—this time for the patroon.

The first clash came in 1644, under Governor Kieft. Van Rensselaer, anxious to protect his newly acquired fur trade, had ordered Van Curler to build a fort, Rensselaers Stein, at Beeren or Barren Island, three miles south of Fort Orange. He hoped in this way to counter the private traders who came to "debauch" the Indians with spirits, and got away with the pick of the pelts. As commander of the fort, he installed there Sergeant Nicholaes Coorn with a small number of men. Van Tienhoven protested in March, but Coorn answered calmly that the patroon's charter gave him the right to "enlarge, strengthen and fortify" his domain, and that the fort was only meant to keep out "interlopers." As the company

A SWEET AND ALIEN LAND

skippers who still traded at Fort Orange were in no way affected by the presence of Van Rensselaer's fort, the matter was shelved.[4]

In the summer, however, shots destroyed the peace. Govert Loockermans, the former cook's mate who was making his fortune in the north as a private trader, refused to stop at Rensselaers Stein to pay the toll of five guilders imposed by Van Curler on every ship that passed. He also refused to lower his flag in honor of the patroon. Coorn had hailed Loockermans with the word "strike" when his yacht *Good Hope* appeared near the fort, but Loockermans, defiantly taking up the orange, white, and blue flag of the Dutch Stadtholder in one hand, shouted back: "I strike for no man save the Prince of Orange and the Lords to whom I am subject." Coorn at once fired a cannonball through the mainsail. The second shot missed, but a bullet, fired by an excited Indian, passed through the Prince's flag a foot above the head of Loockermans, who was still valiantly brandishing it.[5]

The merchant sailed on, shouting furiously at Coorn: "Fire, you dogs, may the Devil take you." He laid a complaint against him in New Amsterdam, and on October 8, 1644, the sergeant was ordered to pay damages and to show within ten months the patroon's commission for the building of the fort.[6]

Nature now intervened in the affair. At the end of 1643 Van Rensselaer, who had never set eyes on his domain, died in Amsterdam at the age of forty-eight, leaving a widow and nine children. Since the eldest, Johannes, was eighteen and still a minor, two guardians were appointed. One was former Governor Wouter van Twiller, the nephew of Van Rensselaer. As one of his first acts he ordered the evacuation of Rensselaers Stein to prevent further clashes with the authorities in New Amsterdam.

The situation might have remained calm if Van Twiller had not appointed an old friend to be resident director of Rensselaerswyck. Brandt Aertsz van Slechtenhorst was, like Van Twiller, born in Nijkerk, but had not made so distinguished a career as his friend and protector. When he was taken on in 1646 in his late fifties, he was no more than under-schout of Amersfoort. The new post, which gave him a yearly income of nine hundred guilders, a rent-free house, and four acres of land, was an impressive promotion, which Van Slechtenhorst—already known in Amersfoort for his conceited and cantankerous character—could hardly digest. To-

TROUBLE IN THE NORTH

gether with the presidency of Rensselaerswyck's court, and absolute control over all the land, forests, and farms, it made him almost equal in power to the governor in New Amsterdam.

Van Slechtenhorst arrived at Greenbush on March 22, 1648, a year after Stuyvesant set foot in New Netherland. The two men, similar in so many respects, were bound to clash. From the start, the new director ruled his domain brutally, persecuting everyone whom he thought was giving insufficient due to the rights of the "infant patroon," as he always called Johannes van Rensselaer. His ultimate aim was to elbow both the company agents and the private traders out of the fur trade. In no time at all he revived the old question of the ownership of the land under and around Fort Orange, converting the dispute into a major conflict.

Van Rensselaer had bought this land from the Indians, but had preferred not to make it an issue with the company, whose fort was protecting his farmers. In any case, the redoubt had been almost completely deserted by the soldiers, and only Commissary Carel van Brugge, with a handful of men, kept an eye on the activities of the traders. The company from its side could claim—and sometimes did—that it had arrived first, since Fort Nassau had been built in 1615. Van Slechtenhorst brushed that argument aside.

One month after his arrival (he was already hated by traders and farmers alike) he demonstrated his intention to do whatever he thought proper without any consideration for the property, or the susceptibilities, of the company. One of Van Twiller's orders had been to take over Beversfuyck (known as the Fuyck) and bring it closer to the walls of the fort. To their alarm, the inhabitants of the old fortification heard in April that Van Slechtenhorst had put up their land, including their kitchen gardens, for sale. It was the same "squeezing" tactics that the English had applied around the House of Good Hope on the Connecticut.

Stuyvesant did not like this nagging at all, but waited for the right moment to intervene. It came on the first Wednesday of May 1648. The governor had declared a day of fasting and prayer and had sent the ordinance off to Rensselaerswyck, where such orders from New Amsterdam were traditionally obeyed. Van Slechtenhorst, however, felt this was an invasion of his patroon's sovereign rights and refused to follow Stuyvesant's instruction. The general found Van Slechtenhorst's position unacceptable, and in July he sailed up the Hudson to confront his new opponent.[7]

It was not a friendly meeting. The two stubborn and authoritarian men faced each other with immense dislike. Although formalities were observed (the cannons of Rensselaerswyck shot off twenty pounds of powder), the tone of the conversation was decidedly uncivil from the start. Stuyvesant told Van Slechtenhorst without ceremony that he must keep his house "a cannon shot" away from the fort, since it infringed the rights of the company and endangered military security. He insisted also that the new director of the domain obey the laws and ordinances of the Heeren XIX and the governor. Van Slechtenhorst, dragging his "infant patroon" constantly into the conversation, had his own arguments and ended with a heated: "Your complaints are unjust. I have more reason to complain on behalf of my patroon, against you."[8]

The discussion having reached this deadlock, Stuyvesant gave orders to strengthen the fort and traveled back to New Amsterdam, where on July 23 he put his protest on paper and posted it off to Van Slechtenhorst, signed "your affectionate friend and governor." Van Slechtenhorst could hardly dredge up the courtesy to send an answer, but when he did, it contained a string of complaints. The inhabitants of the fort were cutting his best trees; they were trading freely in the domain, and now General Stuyvesant was preventing the "infant patroon" from improving his own ground. From this time on, he threatened, he would demand indemnity for losses due to the actions of the governor. To demonstrate his independence, Van Slechtenhorst forbade Commissary Van Brugge to cut any trees or quarry any stones for the repair of the fort.[9]

Stuyvesant realized that he would get nowhere with words, so on September 10, having learned from Van Brugge that Van Slechtenhorst was now building within a "pistol shot" from Fort Orange, the Council in New Amsterdam dispatched six soldiers to the north to pull down the offensive constructions and to arrest Van Slechtenhorst if he resisted.[10]

The soldiers came and went, managing only to upset Van Slechtenhorst and the Mohawks by their behavior, insulting the director—so he said—"when walking in the public street . . . and abusing God's holy name." Van Brugge made one more effort to persuade Van Slechtenhorst to pull down the offending house, but his only reaction was another letter of protest to Stuyvesant in which he compared him with "Cousin Gysbert, who, as we read

TROUBLE IN THE NORTH

in Aesop's Fables, stood at a cascade on a high hill and drank, and then complained of a sheep who stood in the stream below, to have spoiled the water." In other words, the governor was creating a problem where none existed. "Tis wonderful that the General should take such needless trouble about the Patroon's colony and worry himself about his buildings, whilst his honour tolerates a number of streets full of building within thirty paces of Fort Manhatan."[11]

The worst thing, he said, was that the Indians treated him better than his Christian brothers. When they had heard that the conflict was about a few acres of land, they offered him plenty of it "in the Mohawks country." They had been very upset, wrote Van Slechtenhorst pompously, by the rude manners of the soldiers of "Wooden Leg," and he had only with the greatest difficulty averted a clash, which would have led to "the ruin not only of the colony, but of the Manhattans and of the Christians within this land, who are all at the mercy of the savages."[12]

Stuyvesant, unimpressed by Van Slechtenhorst's troubles with the Mohawks, sent him a much more peremptory summons to come to court on April 4, 1649. After repeating his orders to Van Brugge to strengthen the fort and destroy all houses within a pistol shot of it, Stuyvesant informed the Heeren XIX of the new conflict. They, in turn, took up the matter with Van Twiller in Amsterdam, who was unrepentant and insisted that Fort Orange stood upon the patroon's land. The gentlemen were deeply shocked and complained to Stuyvesant about the former governor, "that ungrateful individual who had sucked his wealth from the breasts of the Company whom he now abuses." In the name of the young patroon, Van Twiller then lodged a complaint with the States General, which passed it on to a committee in December 1649, after which the usual silence fell.[13]

In New Netherland as well, nothing was heard of Fort Orange for some time. Van Slechtenhorst did not appear in court on April 4, and went on extending the domain by buying the Catskill and Claverack. The directors warned Stuyvesant in the beginning of 1650 that Van Twiller intended to stop the free navigation of the North River and advised the governor to resist any interference

A SWEET AND ALIEN LAND

"forcibly but cautiously." If Van Slechtenhorst planted guns near the river, then "you are to remove and store them." But Van Twiller took no action, and Stuyvesant became preoccupied with his struggle with the citizens of New Amsterdam.[14]

Adriaen van der Donck finally was the man responsible for more forceful action on the part of the company. He had been the schout of Rensselaerswyck between 1641 and 1646, and although he had left the domain on bad terms with its proprietor, he found, arriving in the Republic in 1649, a staunch supporter in Van Twiller. The former governor never missed a chance to obstruct his old enemies in the company, and the Heeren XIX, in retaliation, began to encourage Stuyvesant to take a more implacable attitude toward Rensselaerswyck.[15]

Van Slechtenhorst realized as much when he arrived in New Amsterdam in April 1651. He had come to protest the governor's demand for a subsidy and Stuyvesant's refusal to let him take possession of the Catskill, but he found himself at once under arrest. For four long months he was detained in the city until a kindhearted skipper smuggled him back to his colony.[16]

The director of Rensselaerswyck, deeply insulted by the treatment he had received in New Amsterdam, now pushed ahead in total disregard of company rights. He again forbade the company to cut wood in the domain, and intensified the building of houses around the fort. Stuyvesant reacted by declaring the orders of Van Slechtenhorst void, and published on January 2, 1652, a proclamation in which he attacked the "impertinent, unbearable and unchristianlike tyranny" of the so-called director, who forced the soldiers in the fort "to carry their fuel begged from him on their shoulders in slavish trouble and dependence through thick and thin ice and snow for the amusement of this overbearing commander." On March 6 he followed this proclamation with an ordinance forbidding the construction of houses within six hundred paces (three thousand feet) of the fort.[17]

Tension had built up in the north, and on New Year's night it erupted. Some drunken soldiers, saluting 1652 with a few volleys of their matchlocks, directed their shots at the patroon's headquarters, and its thatched roof went up in flames. Next day Van Slechtenhorst's son, Gerrit, came to ask for satisfaction, but the soldiers attacked him and "beat him black and blue," dragging him through the muddy streets of the fort.[18]

TROUBLE IN THE NORTH

One of the bystanders was the new commis of the company, Johannes Dyckman, a former clerk in Amsterdam, who had arrived with Van Tienhoven on the *Waterhont*. He was to stay at Fort Orange until he was declared deranged in 1655, but in 1652 the first signs of his mental disorder were already obvious. He shouted with joy while Van Slechtenhorst's son was assaulted, encouraging his soldiers with the words: "Let him have it now and let the Devil take him."[19]

Philip Schuyler, a brother-in-law of Gerrit, tried to intervene, but Dyckman threatened to "run him through" with his sword. The Van Slechtenhorsts were seething with rage and planned revenge, but Dyckman declared he was going to build a gallows for them all and loaded the fort's guns with grapeshot, planning to level the patroon's house. He was restrained on this occasion, but some weeks later he came storming into Van Slechtenhorst's office to hand him Stuyvesant's proclamations concerning the building limits around the fort. Van Slechtenhorst refused to publish them, so Dyckman, accompanied by three armed soldiers, posted himself on the stoop of the house to read them to the astonished burghers. The director rushed forward and pulled the documents from Dyckman's hand with such force that Stuyvesant's seal fell off. The governor in New Amsterdam must at least have had some understanding of that gesture.[20]

In the end it was Jan Baptist van Rensselaer, the second son of Kiliaen, who had arrived in the domain the year before, who calmed the shouting crowd with the good-natured words: "Go home, good friends. 'Tis only the wind of a cannon ball fired six hundred paces off."[21]

When Stuyvesant received a report on the whole affair, he felt it was time to pay another visit to the uproarious community. He arrived in March. There is no record of these negotiations between the two headstrong men, but the visit convinced the governor that he would lose the battle around Fort Orange if he did not take drastic steps. Returning to New Amsterdam, he declared on April 8 that the fort and the surrounding village, the Fuyck, from now on would be known as Beverwyck, and would have its own court.[22]

Stuyvesant had at that time subdued all his opponents in New Amsterdam. Melyn and Van Dincklage were sheltering on Staten Island, the Nine Select Men were suspended, notary Dirck van

A SWEET AND ALIEN LAND

Schelluyne was forbidden to practice, Van der Donck was still in Holland, and Schout-Fiscaal Hendrick van Dyck had been dismissed. It was the best moment to get rid of his last adversary, Van Slechtenhorst.

Not unexpectedly the director of Rensselaerswyck refused to recognize the new village that swallowed up the whole hamlet of the patroon, including his house and all the warehouses. He resisted violently, but in vain, when a group of soldiers hauled down the flag of the patroon. He, in turn, pulled down the company's placards that Dyckman stuck against the wall of the patroon's office.

The end of his struggle came on April 18. Nine soldiers burst into his house and dragged him away to the fort, leaving "his furs, his clothes and his meat . . . hanging to the doorpost." The following day he was shipped off to New Amsterdam, according to his own memorial, "to be tormented, in his sickness and old age, with unheard of and insufferable prosecutions, by those serving a Christian government."[23]

So unpopular had the old tyrant made himself that even his patroon did not come to his rescue. Jan Baptist van Rensselaer succeeded him as director, and Van Slechtenhorst—now almost sixty-five years old—stayed for eighteen months in confinement. The Van Rensselaers, of course, made a formal protest to the company at the establishment of Beverwyck, but after that the controversy petered out. The battle in the north had been won by Stuyvesant. Beverwyck (which would develop into Albany) was an undeniable fact—and relations between New Amsterdam and "the colony within the colony" were completely transformed under Jan Baptist and his brother Jeremias. They made it obvious to Stuyvesant that their support for Van Slechtenhorst was only pro forma. The governor in New Amsterdam had eradicated his last opponent in the province.[24]

LOSING
GROUND

"The English, fully aware that our country is better than theirs, endeavour to push us out of it and to seize it for themselves, which they will easily effect." This was the alarming warning the New Netherlanders gave the Dutch government in 1650. They begged the States to believe them when they said that "there will not be another opportunity or season to remedy New Netherland for the English will annex it."[1]

While General Stuyvesant was grappling with his rebellious subjects, his English neighbors had not been sitting still. The governor must often have felt very isolated, and ironically only the English in his province gave him a little consolation during the whole period. At the urging of his secretary, George Baxter, the English inhabitants of s'Gravesande and Heemstede on Long Island wrote an address to the West India Company in Holland in 1650, praising the general's enlightened dictatorship—"the power of electing a Governor among ourselves . . . would be our ruin and destruction by reason of our factions." They criticized Van der Donck and his partisans as the malignant creators of "manifold strifes . . . paying no manner of respect to the government, but trampling it under foot."[2]

The loyalty of the English to the company was probably due to the freedom they were allowed in the management of their own local affairs, but it was misplaced. As early as 1648 the Heeren XIX had told Stuyvesant to sweep away these "mild measures" as it was a "dangerous precedent"; and within a few years the English villages would feel the iron fist of "Strongheaded Peter."[3]

Relations between Stuyvesant and his New England neighbors soured after a long series of incidents, disputes and embittered correspondence. Not even the start had been promising, for the governor, who had had a quasi-honeymoon with the New Amsterdammers, had none at all with the New Englanders. He had made anxious advances in 1647, understanding only too well that New Netherland, with its fifteen hundred inhabitants, was no match for the United Colonies with their twenty-five thousand subjects. A month after his arrival he wrote to Governor John Winthrop Sr. of Massachusetts, who always struck the Dutch as a most upright and sympathetic man.

In a long letter he flattered the Englishman, telling him how much he had heard of him from his predecessor Kieft, assuring him that he was as much "a friend of peace" as Kieft, "readie at all tymes and all occasions to make good." He felt obliged to remind the aged governor that all the land between the Connecticut and the Delaware was "undubitably" Dutch, but proposed appeasingly "that yourselfe with other indifferent men . . . may be pleased to appoint the tyme and place where and when your selfe and they will be pleased to give me a meeting."[4]

Winthrop, now nearing his sixtieth year, had lost his much-loved wife Margaret that month, and falling ill soon afterward, was not able to give an official reply to Stuyvesant until August, although "the Crazines of my head and feeblenes of my hand denies me libertie to write as I doe desire." As with Kieft, he expressed personal warmth, but official coolness. The request of the general for a meeting had been referred to the Commissioners of the United Colonies, as, Winthrop told the Dutchman, "in duty I was bound." He consoled Stuyvesant with the assurance that "they do readily embrace your friendlie motion . . . to give you a meeting in tyme and place convenient."[5]

The governor in New Amsterdam already knew how the commissioners had reacted to his proposal. In a letter dated June 17 they had given the newcomer the briefest welcome possible, congratulating him on his "enterance to the government at Manatoes," and repeating mention of the old conflicts. There was in the first place the selling of arms to the Indians at "forte Aura-

LOSING GROUND

nie" and on Long Island, which "is very unsafe both for yourselves and us." In the second place there were the high duties that the Dutch demanded "not onely of your owne people, but of the English," while the New England harbors were open and free without "any such hassards." They asked him curtly to let them know what sort of excises he wanted, and in what case he would impose fines or confiscate. Stuyvesant's answer came in more direct form than they had expected, putting an abrupt end to this cool exchange of diplomatic courtesies.[6]

Secretary Van Tienhoven, during a visit to New Haven in September 1647, had discovered a Dutch ship in the little port. It was the *Sint Beninjo,* with a cargo that was the property of two Dutch gentlemen, Willem Westerhuyzen and Samuel Goedenhuyzen, both on board. They asked Van Tienhoven for a license and told him they were going on to Virginia, obviously not planning to pay the obligatory duties in New Amsterdam.

Van Tienhoven reported this to Stuyvesant on his return to the capital, and the governor exploded. As always, the soldier in Stuyvesant was stronger than the diplomat, and he immediately made plans to capture the *Beninjo,* despite its ten guns and crew of twenty-seven. Luck was with him. Just two weeks earlier the company had sold one of its ships, the *Zwoll,* to Samuel Goodyear, the deputy governor of New Haven. Under the pretext of bringing the ship safely to its new owner, Stuyvesant put a few soldiers on board the *Zwoll* on October 10 with orders to cut the *Beninjo* from its anchors and bring it to New Amsterdam.

Stuyvesant had chosen the right day: a Sunday. While the Puritans of New Haven sat through a long service, the *Zwoll* crept into the port, and the Dutch soldiers boarded the *Beninjo* without incident. By the time the alarm was raised and the angry New Haveners had come pouring out of the church, the sails of the *Beninjo* were just visible on the horizon. In Manhattan Stuyvesant confiscated ship and cargo. Two days later he sent Governor Eaton a violent protest, demanding that all ships passing through New Haven pay duty in New Amsterdam, since the colony was, after all, situated in New Netherland.[7]

The seizure of this ship from their port was a great injury to the Puritans, and Stuyvesant's attack on their sovereignty only added insult. On October 18 the irascible Eaton answered in biting terms the letter Stuyvesant had written, in "Low Dutch, whereof I un-

A SWEET AND ALIEN LAND

derstand little." He first rejected Stuyvesant's claim on New Haven, since the English had their patent from "King James of famous memory," and then went on to fulminate against the intrusion in his port, warning the Dutch governor that his people were "resolved by all just meanes, to assist & vindicate theyre right, in Newhavens lands & harbour, & their jurisdiction of both, that themselves & posteritie be not (through theyre neglect) inthralled & brought under a forreigne government."[8]

Stuyvesant had savored his triumph and felt that he could now afford to be slightly more conciliatory. He sent a second letter "more milde in phraze," in which nevertheless he repeated his claim to the ground on which New Haven was built. Embarrassingly, he had to ask Eaton in the same letter for the return of three Dutch servants who had run away and for the extradition of the two merchants, Westerhuyzen and Goedenhuyzen. On November 11 the General Court of New Haven rejected this last request, as it would give the impression that the New Haveners were subordinated to New Amsterdam, but the court's final decision proved how shocked New Haven had been by Stuyvesant's act of "piracy." It was unanimously resolved to "make some slight workes and plant some gunns for the townes present defence."[9]

The correspondence between the two governors, sometimes angry, sometimes dignified, continued to the end of the year, when an irritated Stuyvesant broke it off. In December he explained to Deputy Governor Samuel Goodyear of New Haven that he could no longer bear Eaton's pedantic sermons, "ripping up . . . all my faults, as if I were a schoolboy, and not one of like degree with himself."[10]

There was still one retort he could make to Eaton's refusal to return the fugitives and extradite the two merchants. Before the end of 1647 Stuyvesant proclaimed that from now on "any person, noble or ignoble, freeman or slave, debtor or creditor, yea to the lowest prisoner included," who ran away from New Haven would find refuge and freedom in New Netherland.[11]

The Dutch were by no means pleased with this grand gesture of their governor, which would turn their province into a "receptacle" for criminals, tramps, and other unwanted characters. Stuyvesant had to soothe them, first by assuring them that the rule did not apply to the subjects of Massachusetts and Virginia, and subsequently by countermanding the whole order. He now simply

LOSING GROUND

offered pardon to the three fugitives in New Haven. It was a master stroke. The three had recently been arrested in the English colony for drunkenness, and had been freed on a bail of one thousand guilders, paid by Westerhuyzen. Thanks to the pardon, Stuyvesant retrieved his runaways, and at the same time duped the Dutch merchant out of his money.[12]

General Stuyvesant continued to pin his hopes for a reconciliation on his colleague in Massachusetts. During the whole of 1648 he kept Winthrop informed of events, telling in April how "trulie grived" he was that his intentions of "mutuall amitie and goodwill' had not been accepted. He was deeply shocked, he said, by "scandalous reports" that he had tried to raise the Mohawks against New England, and he assured Winthrop that such a thing "being soe farre from the rules and principles of Christianitie and charitie," it was out of the question for him "soe much as to have a thought thereof."[13]

In other letters he repeated his offer to talk matters over in person, and Winthrop agreed to set up a conference in September, together with Eaton, at Hartford. Stuyvesant wrote a relieved report to Amsterdam, since the Heeren XIX had pestered him constantly with requests to arrange a border settlement.[14]

News of the coming talks at Hartford cheered the Heeren XIX considerably. Thanks to the delays of transatlantic communications, they only heard of the plans in January 1649, and the Lords Directors wrote back approvingly, giving Stuyvesant at the same time the latest news from Europe—King Charles was detained at Windsor and "kept prisoner by the army under General Fairfax and his Lieutenant Cromwell," the city of London was occupied, and "the Prince of Wales and the Duke of York have taken refuge here."[15]

Stuyvesant and the Heeren XIX rejoiced too early. The Commissioners of the United Colonies were by no means in favor of the Hartford conference, and made this known to the Dutch governor after their meeting of September 1648. In a long letter they touched on the many differences between the parties, reasserted the rights of New Haven, and demanded the return of the *Beninjo* to Westerhuyzen, who by this time had settled in New Haven. Stuyvesant, ordered by the company to be more careful —"the English nation is too strong for us"—paid no attention to the first part of the commissioners' letter, but the rest of their document was more difficult to ignore. Impatient at his lack of reaction to their complaints of arms dealing with the Indians, and their request for more information about the duties to be paid by English traders in New Amsterdam, the United Colonies now took the drastic step of boycotting Dutch merchants. "The traders within the duch plantacions, or under the duch governor whither merchants or mariners may expect noe more Liberty within any of the harbours belonging to the English Colonyes," they wrote forbiddingly.[16]

The commissioners ended their letter by offering Stuyvesant as a sop a less formal meeting in June 1649 at Boston. But in a year much can happen, and in June, instead of sitting around the table with the commissioners, Stuyvesant was engaged in another angry correspondence with them. Rumors had reached New Amsterdam that New Haven—looking, as always, for ways to expand—had dusted off its old plans to establish a settlement at the Delaware among the Dutch and the Swedes. The general reacted with an immediate protest. The answer came by return messenger from Eaton: "Our right there is well known [not only to the English] to the Dutch, and Swedes and Indians." But for the moment the Delaware plan was shelved.[17]

In March of that year Stuyvesant had lost the only New Englander on whose friendship he thought he could rely. John Winthrop Sr. had died in Boston at the age of sixty-one. The Dutch governor was deeply shocked by "the sad loss of one whose wisdom and integrity might have done so much in composing matters between us." He wrote at once to Winthrop's successor, the ponderous and self-important John Endicott, to congratulate him on his promotion, reminding him of the "passages of loving and mutual correspondence between your predecessor (of worthy memory) and myself," in the hope that the new governor would "imitate so fair a pattern."[18]

Hoping to attract another Winthrop to his camp, Stuyvesant now made advances to John Jr. He did not know that the engaging younger Winthrop, living in New London at the mouth of the Pequot River, was being courted simultaneously by the New Haven traders. They wanted him as their governor at the Delaware—"what is a body without a head, what is a people without a guide, governor," a certain Edward Elmer wrote him in August of that year—but Winthrop had other ideas.[19]

LOSING GROUND

A few months earlier, in a conversation with a friend, he had dropped a hint that he was thinking of moving to New Netherland. The Puritan atmosphere of New England had never suited the worldly and intelligent Winthrop, who had little of his father's religious fervor. In addition, the governor of Rhode Island, Roger Williams, had informed him in March that Charles I and "many great Lords and Parliament men are beheaded." Although Winthrop had never been a supporter of the King (who lost his head on January 30), he feared that a Puritan Republic of England might tighten its grip on the colonies in America. New Netherland, in that case, seemed an attractive alternative.[20]

The hint was passed on to George Baxter, Stuyvesant's English secretary, who undoubtedly delighted the governor with this good news, and was told to offer Winthrop the most generous terms. Summing up all the advantages enjoyed by the English in the Dutch province, Baxter concluded that "if you please to come in your owne person before winter I doubt not but you will have such satisfaction to your Content, that you will be incouraged to settle downe amongst us." Unfortunately, Winthrop ultimately saw a more promising future in New England, and that year, cutting his ties with Massachusetts, he officially became a freeman of Connecticut, Stuyvesant's greatest enemy.[21]

Hard on the heels of this disappointment came another blow. The June meeting with the representatives of the United Colonies had first been postponed till September, but it was now canceled altogether. The commissioners were incensed by Stuyvesant's unwillingness to give them any satisfaction in the matters they had previously raised, and refused to sit at the same table with him.[22]

A deflated General Stuyvesant added their letter to his reports to Amsterdam, but the Heeren XIX, now anxious to have the border question out of the way, were almost as indignant as the commissioners at Stuyvesant's lack of diplomacy, as demonstrated in the case of the *Beninjo*. "If in consequence of such acts we should have trouble with the English," they told him reprovingly in April 1650, "the deputies of their High: Might: would be very much displeased." Van der Donck, among others now remonstrating in The Hague, had been stirring things up and had asserted that "you may be with your precise proceedings, the cause of an eventual rupture with the English."[23]

The States of Holland had sent an envoy to England to bring up the border question, but he found London in so much confusion that there was little hope of a quick settlement—the more so since Stadtholder Willem II, giving hospitality to his exiled brother-in-law, King Charles II, had little mind for "entering into correspondence with the present government." And in July 1650 the Lords Directors urged Stuyvesant again "to keep up all possible good correspondence with our neighbours."[24]

When General Stuyvesant left for Hartford on September 17, 1650, for the first international conference in America's history, his "great state" was not exactly compatible with his political and diplomatic strength. Harassed by the West India Company, in deep trouble with his subjects in New Amsterdam, and hotly resented by the New Englanders, he nonetheless showed strength and vigor when, four days later, he stumped along on his wooden leg to the courthouse in Hartford. The Commissioners of the United Colonies had at last agreed to a meeting, and welcomed him with honor and politeness. They felt, however, that it was necessary to put the obstinate Dutchman in his place before the talks started, and found a neat opportunity in the first letter Stuyvesant addressed to them.

Writing it on his company barge in the Connecticut River, he had headed it from "Hartford, New Netherland, 23 September." The commissioners at once reproached him with ill will and a readiness to "cast a barr" before they had even started. Stuyvesant replied soothingly that the letter was a copy of one that he had composed with his Council at New Amsterdam, heading this second one as coming from "Connecticot." The English were satisfied and invited him to come and sit down.[25]

In his first letter the general had listed the subjects he thought should be discussed. Among his six points were, of course, the "usurpacon and possessing the land upon the River Conecticot or the Fresh River," and the encroachment of New Haven on Dutch territory, which made it necessary that "either a generall or provisionall lymett may be settled betwixt us." Further points were the detaining of fugitives and the repeal of the "act of prohebition of trade for our Nation with the

LOSING GROUND

native Americans in these partes."[26]

The commissioners, presided over by Edward Hopkins, the governor of Connecticut, answered in firm tones, rejecting every claim of the Dutch to that part of America, and especially to the Connecticut. They pointed out that the boycott of Dutch traders was only the consequence of the continued Dutch arms traffic with the Indians. They then presented a long list of minor grievances, which Stuyvesant thought too unimportant to be considered. For him, the establishment of a borderline was the most urgent question, and realizing that by bickering over all sorts of details they would achieve nothing, he proposed to appoint a Committee of Four to sort things out. He had taken his secretary, George Baxter, and the former Plymouth merchant Thomas Willett with him to Hartford and—still not very fluent in English—the general was relieved to leave the negotiations to them. To represent their side, the commissioners appointed the pious Simon Bradstreet of Massachusetts and Thomas Prince of Plymouth.[27]

"While these four men closeted themselves, Stuyvesant was treated like a "Prince" and entertained "with great pomp." He must have admired Hartford. Though still not much more than a small village (it only counted two hundred householders), it was pleasantly situated on the green banks of the Connecticut. The courthouse and the pretty little church were surrounded by enormous lawns, and behind the houses rose high woodlands. From the little pier where his barge was moored, the governor had, however, a less pleasant sight: the decaying remnants of the House of Good Hope, encircled by the fields in which the English farmers now worked undisturbed.[28]

By September 28 the Committee of Four had reached agreement, and Baxter and Willett came to see the governor. Reading the document, he blanched and told his delegates desperately: "I have been betrayed." A more malicious source revealed that he had begun to shout so loud that the English outside, thinking he had gone mad, "were disposed to go and fetch people to tie him." But Stuyvesant's common sense obviously prevailed and he agreed to the terms.[29]

From now on, the border on the mainland would be a line drawn inland from the sea between Greenwich, which remained Dutch, and Stamford. On Long Island the Dutch would lose considerably, as the border was to be drawn from Oyster Bay due

A SWEET AND ALIEN LAND

south to the Atlantic Ocean. West of this the island would be Dutch, east of it, English. With their lion's share of the island, the English at last got their hands on the precious wampum banks along the bay. Hartford was recognized, but the Dutch would keep the House of Good Hope as a "Manor" (which they evacuated soon afterward), while the question of the Delaware was referred to Europe for consideration by the authorities there. Both the Dutch and the English promised not to build within ten miles of the proposed new boundary.[30]

Stuyvesant's acceptance of these terms showed that, despite his arbitrary character, he was a realist at heart. From the beginning he had seen the strength of the New England colonies, and although protesting constantly and not always diplomatically against any intrusion on Dutch rights, he knew all too well that it was impossible to eject the English from what they now occupied. In the Treaty of Hartford he gave away some of the original parts of New Netherland, but he surrendered no land that was still inhabited by the Dutch.

The fact that he had persuaded the English to settle for a borderline despite their insistence on their rights to the whole of that part of America was in itself an achievement. He did not know that behind the scenes he had been aided by two of the four New England colonies. Neither Massachusetts nor New Plymouth was eager for a border conflict with the Dutch—Massachusetts for commercial considerations, and New Plymouth out of friendliness. The united front that the commissioners presented was, as so often, a facade. John Endicott of Massachusetts had sent his two delegates with specific instructions to do their "utmost endeavour to make up an Agreement betweene them [the Dutch] and Newhaven & Conecticott, least if a warre or broiles arise betweene them wee be chardged and encoragged in it."[31]

Stuyvesant had tried to achieve more. He had proposed a treaty of unity and friendship with the English colonies "against the offensive insolence and arrogance of the [Indian] Barbarians and Natives," and the commissioners had accepted. They even agreed to his proposition that in view of the difference in strength between both parties, the English contribution in men for any punitive strike should be double New Netherland's. But in reporting to the company the governor was obliged to add: "They replied that they then ought to have a double vote in declaring the lawfulness of the defence or offence." Since the States might regard that as "disreputable," the conclusion of the treaty was for the moment postponed.[32]

With these achievements in his pocket—plus a few minor concessions such as a promise to exchange fugitives—Stuyvesant returned on October 11 to New Amsterdam, arriving late at night.

At first he was given a guarded welcome by his Council, who were all eager to hear the results of the Hartford talks; but when he abruptly dismissed them, saying "nothing special had passed or occurred," they were bitterly resentful. And since the governor saw no need to give the New Amsterdammers the slightest hint of what had passed, he added fresh fuel to the resentment and hostility already so strong against him in the province.[33]

Stuyvesant's reluctance to discuss the Hartford agreement with any of his Dutch subjects—or with the company—was due to more than just his usual high-handedness. He had done what no previous director general had ever considered—he had formally signed away huge areas of New Netherland to the English. It was an act unlikely to be approved by the burghers, and even less so by the distant company. It was therefore hardly surprising that he was in no hurry to send off a copy of the treaty to the States, who had to badger him for it repeatedly over the next few years.[34]

The United Colonies never sent the Treaty of Hartford to England for ratification, and the document itself disappeared. New Haven, in any case, had not the slightest intention of sticking to it and made that clear in 1651, only one year after the conference.

Since the sovereignty over the Fresh River had been left undecided at Hartford, the old Delaware Company of New Haven thought the moment opportune to renew its claims and settle a colony there. At a court meeting on December 17, 1650, Governor Eaton gave his blessing to an expedition of about fifty settlers. They had the courtesy to write a letter to Stuyvesant, who reacted with amazing kindness, promising to "improve their just interest in the Delaware in planting and trading as they should see cause." But by the time they arrived at New Amsterdam in March 1651, the mood had changed. Constant Dutch criticisms of the Treaty of

A SWEET AND ALIEN LAND

Hartford had forced the general to make a show of his determination to stop further English encroachments, and he imprisoned the leader of the Delaware expedition, Lieutenant Seely. Only when Seely promised to return to New Haven, did the governor let him and the settlers go, threatening to send them next time to the Netherlands.[35]

New Haven sent an indignant letter to Stuyvesant in which it lamented his sudden change of face and his threat of "force of armed and Martiall opposition even to bloodshed." In September the commissioners, gathering again at Hartford, followed this up with a stiff protest against "Dutch encroachment" on the Delaware. But the support of the other colonies stopped at that point. The commissioners told New Haven that they would come to its help if the Dutch opposed the expedition—but added that the New Haveners must foot the bill themselves. It was too heavy for the moment, and the colony decided to wait for better times.[36]

The diplomatic wheels of Europe had been slowly revolving all this time. The Dutch Republic had recognized Cromwell's "Commonwealth and Free State" and emissaries had been exchanged. With the first of them, the West India Company had sent proposals to London to settle the border dispute and solve trade problems in North America, but the English had not reacted. In February 1652 the States, on behalf of the Heeren XIX, made another effort. In an extensive program of thirty-six articles to be discussed with the English Council of State were two points concerning New Netherland. One was a request for free trade with the West Indies and Virginia; and the other was the determination of a "just, certain and immovable" boundary between New Netherland and New England.

The response of the Council was insulting. It rejected the request for free trade out of hand, thereby demonstrating that despite the change of regime the proprietary English attitude toward America had in no way altered. And the councillors went on to declare that they knew nothing of "any plantation of the Netherlanders there, save a small number up in Hudsons River."[37]

The Heeren XIX were still unaware of the English decision when they notified Stuyvesant on April 4, 1652, of the talks in London, but they held out little hope—"the relations between England and this country are by no means pleasant." Relations were in fact so bad that they thought it advisable to send the governor some soldiers and ammunition, with an order to repair Fort Amsterdam, if necessary.[38]

One and a half months later the long-awaited confrontation began. Holland's famous admiral, Maarten Harpertsz Tromp, meeting an English fleet in the Channel, took too long to lower his flag in salute. Admiral Robert Blake fired on him, and when the Dutchman retaliated, a sea battle followed. In a letter written on August 6 and sent by the vessel *Anna,* the West India Company informed Stuyvesant of the "undesired rupture with the English." It promised him more troops and, although hoping that the Treaty of Hartford would protect New Netherland, it advised him to "arm all freemen, soldiers and sailors," since it was never possible to trust the English with their "sinister machinations."[39]

A SWEET AND ALIEN LAND

TOTAL WAR

The Anglo-Dutch War, officially declared on July 8, 1652, was one the Dutch Republic had tried desperately to avoid. Peace was essential for trade, the basis of existence for the small Republic. "Above all things war and chiefly by sea, is most prejudicial, and peace very beneficial," wrote a Dutchman in the 1660s. What was true then was no less true in 1652. War with England was especially dangerous, since the English fleet could easily attack Dutch shipping from their ports along the east coast and the Channel.[1]

The States General had seriously reprimanded Admiral Maarten Harpertsz Tromp after the sea battle at Folkestone. Raadspensionary Adriaen Pauw himself, the highest authority in the Republic, had gone to London to apologize and to add weight to a Dutch embassy that had already been in England for months. But even Pauw's excuses made no impression on the English, who were obviously spoiling for a fight. At the end of June the States recalled the Dutch envoys and Tromp was ordered to do as much damage to the English as possible. Pauw warned, however, with foresight: "The English are about to attack a mountain of gold, but we are about to attack a mountain of iron."[2]

The war had been almost inevitable from the moment of Charles I's beheading. The Dutch had tried to remain neutral during the Civil War, relieved that their greatest rivals on the oceans were preoccupied with internal strife. At the request of

Stadtholder Willem II, they had sent an ambassador in 1649 to plead for the life of his father-in-law the King, but Cromwell's Parliament had declined to discuss the matter. After expressing appropriate horror at the execution, the States thought it best to address Charles II simply as King, dropping "of Great Britain and Ireland" in order not to annoy the new regime.[3]

Reasoning that the "legality of war is decided by the victory," the Dutch sent a commissary to England in the hope of establishing a tentative relationship with the Commonwealth. The English received him with suspicion: Charles II was still in the Republic, equipping an invasion fleet with his brother-in-law's money; in addition, an English envoy, sent by Parliament to The Hague the year before, had been murdered and the culprits remained unpunished.

But in November 1650 Stadtholder Willem II suddenly died at the age of twenty-four, eight days before his wife, Mary Stuart, gave birth to a son. The "great Convention" of the States' deputies, held in January 1651, decided under pressure from republican Amsterdam not to give this newborn baby the title his forefathers had borne.[4]

To underline its newly found independence of the Orange family—and the Stuarts—the convention recognized Cromwell's England as "free and sovereign," and Albert Joachimi, now an aged man, returned to London to take up his old duties as ambassador. In response, Cromwell made an even more impressive gesture of goodwill. Two English diplomats, Oliver St. John and Walter Strickland, were sent over as special envoys from Cromwell with a suite of 250 persons, and made on March 17, 1651, a splendid entrance into The Hague. But the Dutch had not forgotten King Charles I, and the welcome of the Orangist crowd was decidedly aggressive. To shouts of "Regicides" and "Executioners," the two Englishmen were driven with increasing speed through the streets, finally locking themselves up in their lodgings.

They stayed till the end of July, and left empty-handed. In theory Cromwell felt a special sympathy for Holland, a Protestant Republic like his, but in practice he had one ambition: to stimulate England's economic growth. Before he could achieve this, it was necessary to smash the hegemony of the small republic across the North Sea. Holland was master of the herring fishing, it monopolized the carrying trade, and it controlled almost the whole colo-

A SWEET AND ALIEN LAND

nial trade. The choice was between war and close cooperation, and Cromwell preferred the latter. Hardly a week after his arrival, St. John offered the surprised States a "more strict and intimate alliance and union" in the form of a confederation of the two states for the mutual defense of their interests. The confederation was to be based on a community of religion, political liberty, and trade.[5]

The Dutch wanted nothing to do with such a confederation, for, as they saw it, they had just shaken off the yoke of the warmongering Orange family. The merchants of Amsterdam now wished to run their own affairs. St. John and Strickland were highly annoyed and departed to London, but sometime later they returned with a watered-down version: an offensive and defensive alliance. The Dutch digested it very slowly, and then came up with their answer. Although they did not reject the prospect of an alliance, they were more interested in freedom for fishing, trade, and navigation. This response was almost an insult to the English, and certainly not what Cromwell wanted. On June 20 the ambassadors left for London.[6]

The Dutch response did nothing to improve Anglo-Dutch relations. English jealousy of Holland's prosperity, and anger at her insolence, was still as great as under James I, when the first confrontations had taken place. An anonymous J.R., in a widely read pamphlet, *The Trades Increase,* had attacked the Dutch at that time as the "now Sea Herrs," accusing them of robbing the English merchants of their trade. Others had spoken with disdain of the "plump Hollanders" whose "chiefest, principal and only rich treasure" was the fish in his Majesty's seas. A few Englishmen were less prejudiced and admitted that "the Art and Industry of their People [the Dutch] will wear out ours." Thomas Mun, a London merchant, in his book *England's Treasure by Fforaign Trade* had roundly told his countrymen that they lost all they had to the Dutch because they were "not only vicious and excessive, wasteful of the means we have, but also improvident and careless." He told them that the Dutch were getting richer, while "we are besotting ourselves with pipa and pot [tobacco and liquor], in a beastly manner."[7]

But if fishing, the carrying trade, and the general power of Amsterdam needled the English, the Dutch monopoly in the East Indies was actively hurtful. The English had been there before any

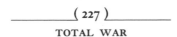

Dutchman. As early as 1577 Drake had sailed to the East Indies, and the first English trading vessels were sent in 1591. The Dutch had been hard on their heels. In 1594 a fleet left Amsterdam, to return three years later loaded with spices. The usual rush began, and within five years the Republic counted ten companies, all competing for the lucrative spice trade to the East Indies. As a result, prices soared, and Raadspensionary Johan van Oldenbarneveldt's remedy was to found the East India Company, with a monopoly of the spice trade and the obligation to build trading posts and fortifications in the East.

The English had been less fortunate. Their first fleet was lost at sea, as was the second, which sailed in 1596. But the return of the Dutch fleet in 1597 gave a fresh fillip to the English efforts. "Divers merchants, induced by the successe of the viage performed by the Duch Naton, and being informed that the Duchemen prepared for a new viage, were stirred with noe lesse affecon to advaunce the trade of their native country," a few petitioners told Queen Elizabeth I, who gave these patriotic merchants a patent for fifteen years. This time it was a success, and from 1602 onward the English possessed at the Indonesian island of Bantam their first "factory."[8]

While the Dutch East India Company was in its infancy, difficulties with the English were only minor. The foundations of the company in the East were still very shaky. But the situation changed dramatically with the appointment in 1614 of the aggressive Jan Pietersz Coen as director general of the East Indies, with headquarters in Java. He saw only one obstacle to an undisputed Dutch supremacy in the eastern trade—the English, "that unbearable nation." To his great fury, the Dutch government did not agree with him and concluded in 1619 a commercial treaty with England that would give that country one-third of the spice trade. Coen told the East India Company that it was "pressing a snake against its bossom," and he was right. Cooperation with the English was like "marriage with a difficult woman," the company soon complained.[9]

The Dutch had to wait for a divorce until 1627, when the English at last retreated to Bantam from Batavia, a settlement built by Coen on the ruins of Olim Jacatra (Djakarta). But in the meantime, the atmosphere, already tense, had been thoroughly poisoned by an incident that was to haunt Anglo-Dutch relations for at least

A SWEET AND ALIEN LAND

fifty years. While the impetuous Coen was reinforcing the company's power in the Indian Ocean by occupying one island after another, a conspiracy was discovered on Amboina. Although occupied by the Dutch, the island had an English trading station, and the Dutch governor reported that these English, together with some Japanese, planned to attack the company fort, Victoria. He arrested the English agent, Towerson, put him on the rack, and subsequently executed twenty of the plotters, among whom were ten Englishmen.[10]

The English accused the Dutch of fabricating the Amboina plot to give themselves a pretext for closing down the English trading station. Their fury at this massacre was aggravated by the fact that they were rapidly losing ground in India and the Spice Islands. As one Englishman wrote in 1640: "The insolent Dutch domineere in all places, stiling themselves allready Kings of the Indian Seas." By 1650 the Dutch were undisputed victors, with the English clinging to one small island, Pulu Run.[11]

Since negotiations at The Hague in 1651 had shown that there was no possibility of recovering a fair share of this trade by peaceful agreement, Cromwell now resolved to take it by other means. His Parliament had passed in 1650 an act forbidding foreign vessels to trade in the English colonies, and on August 5, 1651, the Council of State proposed the first Navigation Act. The new regime did not yet feel quite strong enough to brave the animosity the act would provoke in Holland, for Charles II was leading the Scots in revolt against Cromwell. But after his decisive defeat at Worcester on September 3, the moment was ripe. On October 9, 1651, the act became law. From then on, it was forbidden to import foreign goods and products into English ports save in English ships or in those of the countries from which the goods came. At the same time foreigners were forbidden to fish the English coastal waters.[12]

It was a dire blow to the Dutch, and they immediately dispatched their retired Raadspensionary Jacob Cats to London to protest. Sir Jacob met no sympathy. Thomas Mun in his *Fforaign Trade* had compared the Republic to a bird with rich borrowed feathers, but, so he added, "if every Fowl should take his feather, this bird would rest neer naked." That was exactly what the English proposed to do. They were willing to revoke the act, they told Cats, if the Republic would pay arrears of dues for the fishing

TOTAL WAR

around England, surrender the Spice Islands, and punish the murderers of Amboina. It was a direct invitation to war, and in February 1652 the States gave orders to equip fifty men-of-war, followed a few weeks later by orders for a further hundred.[13]

The negotiations dragged on a few months longer, but they were doomed by the time Tromp and Blake ended their skirmish at sea in May. The English were more than ready to let their pent-up anger fly.

In the many conflicts between England and the United Provinces the question of both nations' possessions in America had been an irritant, but only a minor one. The English always behaved as though New Netherland were just a Dutch plantation on their Hudson River, while The Hague had always reacted cautiously to the protests of James I and Charles I against the Dutch intrusion on their American coast. Despite the growing importance of New Amsterdam in Dutch political and economic life, the States felt it would be unwise to add another item to the long English list of grievances. Jacob Cats' embassy was instructed to discuss the Hartford agreement, but it was only one point among many others. However, when war broke out in 1652, North America suddenly took on a new interest in Dutch eyes. Their colony, argued the West India Company, would make an excellent springboard for attacks on the English in America and the West Indies.

The Heeren XIX composed a secret memo to the States in which they proposed that "for this purpose . . . five or six ordinary but well manned frigates could be employed, the expenses whereof could doubtless be easily defrayed out of the property taken as prizes." They warned the States at the same time to keep the plan a profound secret in case the government decided to take no action, as "the English in those parts, being very strong, must not be troubled."[14]

For the moment the Dutch government decided to wait, advising the Lords Directors in September to garrison the fort at New Amsterdam because it had received information that "New Netherland is in great danger and imminently exposed to invasion." It added that the company must take good care "that no persons be employed either in the political government or Militia, except those whose fidelity and affection for this State may be fully relied on."[15]

News of the war took months to reach New Netherland. The first letter, sent by the company together with a "goodly supply of war material" on the ship *Anna,* fell into the hands of the English, and a second one, dispatched on December 13, arrived only in March 1653. Rumors had reached Manhattan that New England was making war preparations, but it was not clear if these were defensive or aggressive. General Stuyvesant had nevertheless thought it wise to call his Council together, and on March 13, after the company's letter had confirmed the bad news, they took the first measures for the defense of New Amsterdam. The militia of the city was to keep constant guard, and Fort Amsterdam was to be completed and strengthened. Since the fort could no longer contain all the inhabitants of the town, the Council decided to "inclose the greater part of the city with upright palisades and a small rampart." The path along this wall, which stretched from the East River to the North, was soon named Wall Street.[16]

The Council was also concerned with a new local development: the installation of the burgomasters and schepens of New Amsterdam. The forming of a City Council, long overdue for a capital approaching one thousand citizens, had been one of the few tangible results of the Remonstrance of 1650. In February 1652 the company had given Stuyvesant instructions to install two burgomasters and five schepens (aldermen). He had postponed the move till February 2, 1653, Candlemas, when he issued the usual proclamation and appointed Arendt van Hattem and Martin Cregier burgomasters for one year. The Heeren XIX had only reluctantly ordered the nomination of a City Council—meant "to stop the general talk and gabble"—and Stuyvesant had therefore not felt obliged to follow their directive to hold elections for magistrates. He made his own choice.[17]

The schepens—in view of the war, all Dutchmen—were Allard Anthony, Max van Gheel, Jacob van Couwenhoven's younger brother Pieter, Willem Beeckman, and Paulus van der Grift. Jacob Kip became Council secretary at a salary of 250 guilders a year. With the installation of the City Council came the formation of a City Court. It was to sit every Monday morning from nine o'clock onward "for the hearing and determining differences and disputes between parties as far as it may be practicable." Both Council and Court were to meet in the Stadt's Herberg or City Tavern.[18]

The composition of the oldest American city council proved that Stuyvesant, for all his bullying ways, was not always a resentful man: Van der Grift was reputedly the only man to whom Stuyvesant listened, while Martin Cregier, the owner of the most popular tavern in the city and a rich merchant, had been an outspoken opponent of the general. Stuyvesant, however, made it very clear that he was not willing to let control slip out of his hands, and he appointed as sheriff of the city the detested Cornelis van Tienhoven.

The first session of the municipal council on Monday, February 20, dealt with current business and the first court cases. But news of the war at once overshadowed everyday problems and burgomasters and schepens were soon deeply involved in the question of defense. The fort was in better shape, since Stuyvesant had had the outside faced with sods and firewood, but the hogs were still rooting around, and the ring of palisades was only half completed. The wall from the East River to the North River, with a ditch five feet deep and twelve feet wide, still had to be constructed and funds were short. At the inaugural meeting of the City Council on March 13 it was decided to raise six thousand guilders from the community. Knowing that this would take a long time, the Council began by soliciting a loan from the forty-three richest burghers, who within a few days put up almost all the funds.[19]

To save as much money as possible, the company soldiers were put to work on the fort, while the citizens, "burghers, merchants, farmers or sailors and skippers" were employed in building the wall. Enthusiasm for the task was conspicuously lacking, and Stuyvesant had to pile on the pressure. In May he forbade all ships to leave port or its inhabitants to leave the capital for two weeks so that the wall would be constructed "in the best and speediest manner." Around July, when it was finished, the "good inhabitants of this city with their wives, children and property" seemed relatively safe behind the twelve-foot wall. It was built of palisades, sharpened at the top, and supported by posts. On the inside it was reinforced by a sloping breastwork of earth, while the whole construction was set off in the front by planks. At the East River end —the corner of Wall Street and Pearl Street—the fence was protected by a blockhouse with a gate, the Waterpoort. Another gate

A SWEET AND ALIEN LAND

was built at the Heerenweg (Broadway), called the Landtpoort. When the whole fortification was ready, the cost had risen to seven thousand guilders.[20]

By that time the almost inevitable clash between Stuyvesant and the City Council had taken place. It was, of course, about money. In April the governor had called a meeting of all the "principal burghers and inhabitants" of New Amsterdam to discuss the raising of funds to finish the defense works and repay the loan. The magistrates present proposed that the governor surrender the beer and wine excises to the city; but Stuyvesant rejected the idea indignantly. The meeting was adjourned and from that moment onward accusations and recriminations flew between the Governor's House and City Hall. Each party accused the other of noncooperation and ill will. Stuyvesant was adamant about the excises, which he claimed were needed to pay the company's soldiers in the fort. The citizens were equally stubborn in their refusal to pay for the repair of the fort so long as they did not have their own source of income. The general proposed to cash in the debts of many New Amsterdammers with the company, but the City Council reported that the debtors "were indisposed towards satisfaction" and that it had no power to compel them. In a meeting of August 2 the City Council decided to pay nothing more toward the works until the governor gave in.[21]

The West India Company in Amsterdam, keeping in touch with its colony with some difficulty, on account of the war, warily followed the dispute. While agreeing with his efforts to make the community pay for its own defense, the company told Stuyvesant it would not support him openly "during these dangerous and troubled times." It advised him to convince the citizens "by all possible and gentle means," but not to use force. Once more the company left its governor in the lurch, and he realized he was fighting a losing battle.[22]

The Dutch in the Fatherland had by this time come to the same conclusion about their war with the English. Only one year after it started, their opponents had the upper hand. Tromp had been killed in battle, and the younger admirals were no match for seasoned hands like Robert Blake and Sir George Ayscue. Foreign ambassadors in The Hague reported news of Dutch defeats to their capitals, where their dispatches were read with a certain glee. The Republic had not many friends left, and it looked as if it was in for

TOTAL WAR

a humiliating beating. "Never before has this nation found itself in so great and perilous a plight," wrote a French diplomat to Paris in July 1653. "Let them now feel the consequence of the bad company it has been keeping."[23]

If the States had ever thought seriously about using New Netherland as a base of attack, it had certainly forgotten the idea by 1653. It needed all its forces to prevent a total defeat on home ground.

TURNCOATS

While the Dutch were losing their war in Europe, Governor Peter Stuyvesant was doing all he could to keep the peace with his English neighbors in America. When he received news of a possible war between England and Holland, he immediately dispatched a messenger to the most important English colony, Massachusetts. "For myne owne parte I doe not only desire but shall unfailingly indeavour that all love, friendschip and neighbourlie Compliance maye be duly observed betwixt us," the general assured Governor John Endicott. He offered to come to the next meeting of the commissioners of the United Colonies at Plymouth to make a treaty, in particular against the Indians, who "would be glad to see us at variance heere in these partes that thereby they maight have occasion and opportunitie to worke mischief to either."[1]

Endicott did not answer, and on March 6, 1653, when Stuyvesant had received confirmation of the "sad rupture" between the two nations, he wrote again to the governor of Massachusetts proposing "loving newtrallitye" and "not to participat in our Countries differences." At last came a reply. Endicott wrote in terms of outrage on behalf of the commissioners, accusing his Dutch colleague of selling and even giving "great store of pouder, bulletts, gunnes and other Amunition" to the Indians—in particular, to Ninigret, the sachem of the Niantic tribe, and to the Narragansetts —with the clear intention "to arme them against the English."[2]

The first rumors about this Dutch "conspiracy" had come from Captain John Underhill, the former English "savior" of the Indian War, now sheriff in Flushing on Long Island. He was promptly arrested after publicly accusing Schout-Fiscaal Cornelis Van Tienhoven of inciting an Indian rebellion. Stuyvesant indignantly denied these charges, but his own references to the Indians in his letter to the Massachusetts governor may have been read as a veiled threat, and it was hardly surprising that the New Englanders suspected the Dutch. A letter from the West India Company, which had recently fallen into the hands of the English, advised the Dutch governor "to make use of the Indians, who as we learn do not like the English." When the chief of a Mohican tribe also revealed to Connecticut the details of a Dutch plot, New England was ready to believe the worst.[3]

On April 19, 1653, an emergency meeting of the commissioners was called at Boston to study "the best way and meanes tending to the preservation of the common safety of the English." Indignantly the commissioners discussed the insufferable behavior of the Dutch, and one of them, who had just received a letter from a friend in New Amsterdam, reported the Dutch there were boasting that they "shortly [will] have an East India Breakfast." It all smacked of the Amboina massacre of 1623—a reflection that a few months later inspired a best-seller in England. This was a violently written pamphlet entitled *The Second Part of the Amboyne Tragedy; or a Faithful Account of a Bloody, Treacherous, and Cruel Plot of the Dutch in America, Purporting the Total Ruin and Murder of all English Colonists in New England.* The anonymous writer informed his horrified English readers that the impious New Netherlanders planned to make "an assault on the English on Sunday, when the English would be together in their Meeting houses, and murder and burn all which they could effect. To succeed in this their Devilish project, they supplied the Indian Wig-Wams with arms and ammunition which they received from Holland—that Fountain of Treacherie."[4]

The writer claimed that his sources were "the Various Letters Lately Written from New England," which had obviously dealt with the commissioners' meeting in April. At that session worse news about the plot had come in. An Indian squaw, "found trusty to the English," had heard that "the Dutch and Indians generally were confederated against the English treacherously to cut them

A SWEET AND ALIEN LAND

off. The time of execution to be upon the day of election of the Magistrates in the severall colonies, because then it is apprehended the plantations will be left naked."[5]

In high excitement the commissioners resolved to send delegates to the Indians—and to Sachem Ninigret in particular—to collect first-hand evidence of Dutch perfidy. Endicott drafted a letter to be handed to the sachem, in which he claimed to have heard that "the Dutch governor hath stured up youre selfe and severall other sachems by perswasions and gifts" to fight against the New Englanders. Ninigret was flattered by the attentions paid him by the governor of Massachusetts, and admitted that he had indeed been to New Amsterdam "to take physicke." But Stuyvesant, who was to have given him at least twenty guns and a box of ammunition, had done nothing of the kind. "It was wintertime," Ninigret told the delegates plaintively, "and I stood a great part of the winter day knocking at the Governor's door and he would neither open it nor suffer others to open it to let me in." He had never received such treatment from his friends the English.[6]

This might have been reassuring, but it was hardly what the English wanted to hear. They dismissed their key witness with the disgusted comment that "the Indians know not God, but worship and walk after the Prince of Power of the Air, serving their lusts and hating one another." They composed a long manifesto to Stuyvesant in which they detailed once more all the old grievances, and added a more specific accusation: that the Indians "seem to have drunke deep of an intoxicating cup at or from the Mannatoes, against the English." Ninigret, they claimed, was the chief criminal, having entered into a league with the Dutch governor to exchange wampum for guns and entice other sachems with as much strong drink as they would like.[7]

Stuyvesant protested in letters to Endicott and Eaton, even offering to come to Boston to clear himself, but New Haven and Connecticut absolutely refused to believe their *bête noire*. Massachusetts and New Plymouth were more willing to accept Dutch innocence, and mildly suggested that further inquiries ought to be made before any action was taken.

On May 13 a commission of three men arrived in New Amsterdam. It consisted of the New Haven magistrate Francis Newman and two soldiers from Boston, Captain John Leverett and Lieutenant William David. They were coldly received by Stuyvesant, who

TURNCOATS

had read with mounting fury the accusations against himself and Van Tienhoven. And when they invited him to accompany them to New England, where they would produce their witnesses, he exploded with rage—he would not be put on trial in this manner. When the delegates then proposed the more neutral ground of Flushing or Hempstead, the Anglo-Dutch villages on Long Island, Stuyvesant agreed. He went on to suggest that the witnesses be examined not only by the English commission, but also by three of his own representatives, and he put forward the names of Councillors La Montagne and Provost, and Govert Loockermans, "who all understand English and Indian speeches." The English objected violently to Loockermans, whom they suspected of arms deals with the Indians, and it soon became clear that Stuyvesant's proposals for a judicial inquiry were not at all what they had in mind. What they wanted was to see Stuyvesant in the dock, abjectly promising them satisfaction "for the severall hostile and Injurius affronts that hath been put upon them in former and latter times."[8]

The Dutch governor, barely keeping his temper, broke up the meeting. Later he sent the three commissioners a four-point program to prove his goodwill. Again he proposed the "Continuance of all neighbourly friendshipp" and of trade and commerce and a treaty defensive and offensive . . . to prevent all differences and false reports, riseing from the Indians." This document was handed over to the three delegates on May 15, and a few hours later they stealthily departed. They left a letter for Stuyvesant that accused him of being two-faced, of giving them evasive answers, while they had expected satisfaction for their grievances.[9]

The Dutch governor, knowing that the United Colonies had decided to form an army of five hundred men, was anxious to find out whether the delegates' hard line reflected the general feeling in Massachusetts. He sent the "Bohemian" Augustine Heerman to Boston with a letter in which he expressed his astonishment at the "sudden departure" of the delegates, without "coming to any conclusion about those weighty affaires." Resorting to a previously successful tactic, he complained bitterly about the attitude of Connecticut and New Haven. New Haven, he protested, had gone so far as to say that the three commissioners had been put under arrest in New Amsterdam, whereas, on the contrary, they had been "civilly used and entertained," put up in Martin Cregier's own house. As for all the English references to Amboina, the place "is unknown to us, neither hath there been any of us there."[10]

The three commissioners had left, "cloaking their suddaine departure under pretence of the day of election" at Boston. They had found time, all the same, to drop in on Long Island, where they visited Flushing and Hempstead in the hope of digging up more conclusive evidence against Stuyvesant. But they were unsuccessful, and returning to Boston, found that Massachusetts was now opposed to taking any action on the basis of such a flimsy case.[11]

In desperation New Haven now decided to go ahead on its own. Economically, the affairs of the "pretended" colony had gone from bad to worse, and more and more its merchants saw war as their only hope of salvation. One of its founders, the Reverend William Hooke, had complained in a letter to Cromwell that "if the Dutch are not removed . . . we and our posterity . . . are confined and straitened, the sea lying before us and a rocky rude desert, unfitt for culture and destitute of commodity, behind our back." In October New Haven officially petitioned Cromwell to send help to remove or at least control the Dutch so that the English colonies "may bee freed from injurious affronts and securied against the dangers and mischievous effects which daily grow upon them by [Dutch] plotting with the Indians."[12]

The only immediate effect of the commissioners' visit to New Netherland was a small and brief rising. It was organized by the adventurous John Underhill, who, in spite of his accusations against Van Tienhoven, had been set free without trial. Returning to Flushing, where for years he had sung the praise of Dutch tolerance, he turned against his former friends and "raised the Parliament's colours." In a challenging manifesto he listed thirteen points that proved how "iniquitous" the Dutch governor was. These ranged from imposing a chimney tax to beating "an old gentleman" with his cane. Underhill's "vindication," sent to the "Worthy Commonalty of the Manhattans," ended with a rousing appeal to the inhabitants of Flushing and Hempstead—"all honest hearts that seek the glory of God and their own peace and prosperity"—to throw off the tyrannical yoke of the Dutch. "Accept and submit ye then to the Parliament of England, and beware of becoming traitors to one another, for the sake of your own quiet and welfare."[13]

The English on Long Island listened and left it at that. Under-

TURNCOATS

hill had been a little too hasty, and he thought it safer to disappear before he was again arrested. He emerged in Rhode Island, the outcast among the English colonies, where he so impressed the authorities that they gave him a commission against the Dutch—which was, in fact, a license for pure piracy. Underhill began to amass some soldiers and seamen "to seize all Dutch vessels or ships" that would pass or come into the harbors, and to liberate the English on Long Island, who were still "subjected to the cruell tyrannie of the Dutch."

New Amsterdam heard about the gathering of the troops and the burgomasters temporarily forbade the citizens to leave the city or use their yachts. Underhill, however, had other plans. Since Fort Amsterdam was too strong for him, he occupied the completely deserted Dutch trading post on the Connecticut, the House of Good Hope. He sold the crumbling outpost, with the few acres of land around it, a month later for twenty pounds to a merchant of Rhode Island. And in October, having learned a lesson from the Indians, he sold it again. That both buyers were unhappy with this arrangement is understandable, and Hartford in the end put a stop to their quarrels by confiscating the "Manor" in 1654.[14]

Underhill was not the only Englishman who, after years of happily taking orders from the Dutch, began to feel that loyalty to his own country—certainly if it was more profitable—ought to have the first claim. Another was Thomas Baxter, who had lived for years in New Amsterdam and had been contracted to build the palisade around the capital. He also left for Rhode Island, by then not so much a refuge for heretics as a nest for privateers. His activities were so energetic that Stuyvesant in September equipped two vessels with a hundred men on board to "lye in the road . . . the opening of Fairfield Harbour." He asked the New England colonies for their help (Baxter, not at all choosy, had captured a few English vessels as well), but the English refused and instead ordered "that all Dutch shipps and other smaller vessels be at their perill prohibited coming into any harbour belonging to any of the Confederated Colonies."[15]

More drastic action by the Dutch was urgently required. The towns on Long Island were suffering badly from the piratical raids, and, under pressure, Stuyvesant called a convention of representatives from the Council, New Amsterdam, and the English

A SWEET AND ALIEN LAND

towns on Long Island. On November 25, 1653, the delegates met in City Hall. Gravesend was represented by George Baxter, the English secretary to the governor. The chief point under discussion was, of course, the protection of New Netherland, and, as usual, the crucial financing was lacking. Stuyvesant had at last been persuaded to give New Amsterdam the excise on beer and wine, but that was hardly enough to pay the ministers and schoolmasters, as the governor had requested. The English towns declared at once that they would refuse to pay the company since it did not protect them, and threatened to form their own defensive union.

The New Amsterdammers, however, had thought of another way out: in spite of former unsatisfactory experience, they proposed to send a remonstrance to the Heeren XIX. In order to learn the opinion of the other communities, another meeting would be called for December 10. Stuyvesant worried over this move from municipal self-government to provincial rebellion, but felt he should not intervene. Yet he could not resist putting the record straight, and in a long statement accused the English inhabitants of "vilifying the supreme authority of the Director-General" and of the "false, forged and base calumny" that the company did not protect them. It was all their own fault if they were robbed, because they lived so far away from the villages that even if the company had "hundreds of soldiers it would nevertheless be impossible to protect these separate settlers against robbers and thieves." He had not forgotten the Remonstrance (and rows) of 1650, but he gave permission to the delegates—"reluctantly because of previous experience"—to compose "in the presence of deputies of the High Council" a remonstrance to the company in the Republic.[16]

On December 10 the delegates to the first provincial assembly or Landtag arrived at New Amsterdam in their yachts, barges, and canoes, or on horseback. They were a small group—ten Dutchmen and nine Englishmen—but they represented eight communities that were rapidly growing in importance. New Amsterdam was represented by Martin Cregier, now also commanding officer of the burgher guard, and his co-burgomaster Arendt van Hattem. There were delegates from the Dutch villages of Breukelen, Amersfoort, and Midwout, as well as English from the towns that only a short while before had been called s'Gravesande, Vlissin-

TURNCOATS

gen, Mespath, and Heemstede. Thanks to the influx of the English these were now generally known as Gravesend, Flushing, Newtown, and Hempstead.

The influence of the English had been noticeable from the start. The experience in running local affairs acquired during their stay in New England more than made up for the fact that they were in the minority in New Netherland itself. Their self-appointed leader was George Baxter, who three years earlier had been loudly praising the "enlightened dictatorship" of Stuyvesant, but who now, like so many of the English, had turned against him. The company had written just a few months earlier to Stuyvesant, who had proposed the admittance of more English farmers, to be careful "that we may not nourish serpents in our bosom, who finally might devour our hearts." The governor now realized that for once the Heeren XIX had been right.[17]

On December 11 he was presented with a document that once again was a direct attack on his government and that of the company. The *Humble Remonstrance and Petition of the Colonies and Villages in this New Netherland Province*, written by the intelligent and well-informed Baxter, was a long statement of dissatisfaction, beginning with a brilliant defense of the right of the people to protest.

While acknowledging "a paternal government which God and Nature have established in the world for the maintenance and preservation of peace," the people in New Netherland were oppressed like a "conquered [and] a subjugated population," although they had come with the consent of the Lord Patroons, had bought land with their own money, and had transformed it "with immense labour and trouble from a wilderness of woods . . . into a few small villages, with several bouweries." Baxter and the others—in contrast to the Remonstrance of 1650—objected especially to the fact that officers and magistrates were appointed without the consent of the people, and that orders and proclamations were issued by the authority of the director alone or of "one or two of his favourite Sycophants." They stated that "our consent or that of our representatives is necessarily required in the enactment of such laws and orders."[18]

Stuyvesant could not believe his eyes, and asked angrily who had written this piece of insubordination. The delegates told him it was the work of Baxter, and he exploded, asking them if there

A SWEET AND ALIEN LAND

was "no head among the Netherlands people . . . clever or capable enough to draw up a request." He pushed the remonstrance aside, telling them it was so badly and obscurely translated that he could not read it. When they insisted, he asked for copies for all his councillors.[19]

The petitioners listened unmoved to these sarcastic remarks. The same evening Stuyvesant sat down irritably to answer them, repeating with a sneer that "the cleverness of Burgomasters and Schepens may be inferred . . . when a stranger or Englishman must prescribe, what they should remonstrate and demand." He first denied that the petition represented the views of the whole population, since several communities—Fort Orange and the villages at the South River, for instance—had not been present. He then tried to divide the parties by pointing out that the English villages enjoyed more privileges than the Dutch and that the meeting had been organized by the English, "who were not inclined to do anything against their own nation."[20]

That the law was strict in New Netherland was not surprising, he went on, considering the "disorders, bad will and disposition of many of the subjects. . . . Bad morals produce good laws, says the proverb," he reminded the delegates, and rejected their request to independently select their own magistrates. In that case, "everyone would want a magistrate of his own stamp, for instance a thief would choose a thief and a dishonest man, a drunkard, a smuggler etc. their likes, in order to commit felonies and frauds with so much more freedom."[21]

Finally he dismissed the whole gathering, wondering that the burgomasters of New Amsterdam "should at this precarious time join in a plot with a nation, which they and everybody else suspect and which only a short time ago they called untrustworthy." From now on every sort of Landtag would be forbidden, and Stuyvesant declared this so-called General Assembly illegal, as it had not been convened "by order or with consent of the Director-General and Council." On December 16 he sent letters to all the villages, ordering them not to send any more delegates to meetings organized by the magistrates of New Amsterdam, "because it can only be to your disadvantage and injury."[22]

But it was not so easy to suppress the emerging spirit of self-determination. Appealing to the "right of nature" (the English could not, in view of the current war, point to the example of the

TURNCOATS

neighboring colonies), four of the original petitioners—Cregier, Van der Grift, Baxter and Lubbertsen—wrote a series of "Short Notes." In these they stubbornly asked for a greater say in the colony's affairs, describing the provinces as having "bitter foes without and suspected neighbours round about," and "discontented citizens and a government by no means as ample as the present conjuncture of affairs particularly demands."

As if this were not enough, the burgomasters and schepens also presented their demands. In a motion to the Heeren XIX, they asked for a wider brief, as was the case in Amsterdam. They wanted to get rid of Van Tienhoven as schout and have their own man, and they asked for more money, guns, and the possession of the Stadt Huys, which was till then lent by the company.[23]

The petitioners got short shrift from Stuyvesant, who by way of reply sacked Baxter and ordered court messenger Claes van Elslandt to retrieve all the secretary's papers. Then, in the hope of pacifying the magistrates of New Amsterdam, he gave them "for the sake of peace and harmony" a salary of 350 guilders a year. The schepens would receive 250 guilders. He evaded their request to appoint their successors by renominating Cregier and Van Hattem. And, as another tiny concession, he gave them permission to levy a small or burghers' excise on liquor bought for private consumption.[24]

The petition to Amsterdam fared better: To the amazement of the New Amsterdammers, the Lords Directors reluctantly agreed that they might have their own schout (they could get rid of the detestable Van Tienhoven at last); they would be given a seal authorizing them to execute deeds of conveyance of houses, etc.; and in future they could call the Stadt Huys their own.[25]

The Heeren XIX reserved their full fury for Stuyvesant. They had read both the motion of New Amsterdam and the remonstrance with anger and irritation, and by return vessel a letter arrived in which the governor was castigated for his "easy-going" ways. It was unforgivable that he had allowed such goings-on. "We think," they stated, "that you should have proceeded rigorously against the ringleaders of this work and not have meddled with it so far, as to answer protests by counter-protests and then let it pass without further notice." By this time Stuyvesant was becoming immune to the constant nagging of his distant directors. In any case, it was impossible for him to follow their instruction "to mete out due punishment for what has passed." If he did, he would be without any magistrates.[26]

Having dealt with these domestic problems, Stuyvesant had time to consider the threat from the English pirates. On February 9, 1654, he summoned his Council and the burgomasters and schepens of New Amsterdam to consider the prevention of the English incursions. Lately they had plundered two farmers, one of them the Dane Jochem Kuyter; they had stolen a ship; led off ten horses from Amersfoort; and even captured four Negroes. They had threatened many other Dutch and English inhabitants on Long Island, and had extorted protection money.[27]

The worst of the lot, Thomas Baxter, had been arrested by the merchants of New Haven, who were no longer able to pretend that he was only damaging the Dutch. Many others, however, were still at large, and the Dutch agreed to equip a vessel with a crew of thirty men to patrol the sound. This step was followed on April 8 by the decision to send a large expedition against the privateers.[28]

Before he gave permission to sail, Stuyvesant—still doing his best to keep a semblance of good relations with his English neighbors—sent Burgomaster Cregier and Schout-Fiscaal Van Tienhoven to reassure Governor Eaton of New Haven that the excursion was not directed against him, but "for the protection of the commerce on the rivers and waters between us and our neighbours." But the Dutch fleet never sailed.

On May 30 General Stuyvesant called all his magistrates and councillors together and informed them gravely that ten days earlier six ships had arrived at Boston—including "four men-of-war of the Parliament." Their mission was not yet clear, but it would be wise to prepare the province's defenses. "We cannot and shall not know their tenor and correct meaning," he warned, "until the blow is struck and then it will be too late."[29]

TURNCOATS

DANGER

FROM ABROAD

At the end of 1653 the war between England and the United Provinces had virtually come to a standstill. After several sea battles, devastating to the Dutch, the fleets were back in their ports, and in the Republic more and more were clamoring for peace. Trade and commerce were suffering badly and in formerly prosperous Amsterdam a great number of businesses had closed. "Some reported that at that time at least 3000 houses stood empty," wrote Jan Wagenaar. "But others spoke only about 1400 to 1500." The Dutch had a new leader, Raadspensionary Johan de Witt, a highly intelligent descendant of one of Holland's most important regent families. Only twenty-eight years old when he was nominated in March 1652, he was a staunch republican, who, in line with the prevailing sentiment in Amsterdam, was determined to keep the Orange family (now represented by a three-year-old Prince) out of power. For all these reasons a peace with Cromwell was essential.[1]

Talks had started while the battles were still raging. Cromwell, as always less anti-Dutch than his merchants, once more proposed a revolutionary program. This time it was not a confederation, but a complete division of the world. "Between us we can subdue the whole world under our two nations," the Lord Protector told a courtier, Sir Cornelius Vermuyden. Dispassionately, he revealed a plan that would give the Republic a monopoly in the East Indies

—with some compensation for his own East India Company—and would make the English lords of the Americas, north and south. The Dutch could keep what was left to them in Brazil, but for the next seven years must help the English seize the West Indies from Spain. Trade in Europe and Africa was to be free.[2]

"It was a worthy Calvinistic counterpart of the Pope's division of the world between Spain and Portugal of 1493," one modern historian has commented. But it ignored the facts. The Dutch were anxious to stay as neutral as possible—a condition of their trade—and were most unwilling to join the English camp against France and Spain. Even if they could "buy off" the Act of Navigation by accepting Cromwell's plan, they felt little enthusiasm for turning the Americas into an English preserve in exchange for recognition of their present monopoly of the East Indies.[3]

But both sides now longed for peace. The condition of the Republic was desperate and the Commonwealth, in spite of its victories at sea, was having a hard time as well. "There is [in England] a great scarcity of money," wrote the West India Company to Peter Stuyvesant in November 1653, "so that Parliament is very busy to find means; the people are getting tired of it and are slow in giving it." The first peace overtures from both countries did not prevent them from blackening each other as much as possible, and one pamphlet in particular made a deep impression on the English, who had a long memory. It was the relation of Stuyvesant's conspiracy with the Indians against New England. "Upon hearing the rumors from New England they have magnified these false reports," the Heeren XIX told their governor, "and have forged and published in London the most shameless and lying libel, which the devil in hell could not have produced, under the title 'The Second Amboyna Tragedy or truthful Account etc.' We have caused a translation to be made of it." This was sent to New Netherland, with the warning to Stuyvesant "to proceed with great caution, for we cannot expect the least good from that nation at present."[4]

The pamphlet did indeed have disastrous consequences. Cromwell, greatly annoyed by the refusal of the Dutch to hand over the Americas, used the pamphlet—together with New Haven's urgent request for help against New Amsterdam—as a pretext

DANGER FROM ABROAD

for equipping four warships with two hundred men apiece to take by force what he could not get by peaceful suggestion. On February 27, 1654, the expedition sailed from London under the command of Major Robert Sedgwick from Massachusetts and Captain John Leverett, who had visited New Amsterdam the previous May to investigate Stuyvesant. With them they carried a letter from the Lord Protector to the four New England colonies, urging them to help the expedition "undertaken for vindicating the English right and extirpating the Dutch." No cruelty should be committed against the Dutch, who were to be encouraged to remain under English government.[5]

Storms drove the ships apart, making the voyage much longer than usual, and it was only at the end of May that the fleet finally reassembled at Charlestown, not far from Boston. As soon as Sedgwick and Leverett were reunited, they called the Commissioners of the United Colonies together and displayed Cromwell's instructions. New Haven and Connecticut were delighted: it looked as though they would achieve their dearest ambition at last, and Governor Eaton jubilantly told his General Court that the "designe against the Dutch is likely to go on." He offered immediately to raise 150 men, while Connecticut promised 500.[6]

As usual, Massachusetts and Plymouth showed a distinct lack of enthusiasm. Governor John Endicott objected again at the colony's being officially involved in a war with the Dutch, but in the end he reluctantly gave Sedgwick and Leverett permission to raise five hundred volunteers. New Plymouth hesitantly offered fifty men, but in the end sent only Thomas Willett, who four years earlier had signed the Treaty of Hartford for Stuyvesant.

More loyal than Willett was Isaac Allerton, the Plymouth merchant who during Kieft's Indian War had had the brilliant idea of engaging John Underhill for the Dutch. He reported the arrival of an English fleet at Boston to Stuyvesant, who at once summoned his Council, the magistrates of New Amsterdam, and the representatives of the villages of Breukelen, Amersfoort, and Midwout.[7]

The meeting on May 30 took place in City Hall, and it was obvious that morale was very low. Little support was expected from the villages, which had previously refused to help fight the privateers. The burgher guard was in good shape, thanks to Commander Cregier's efforts, but it was only a small force. The English

A SWEET AND ALIEN LAND

villages on Long Island would almost certainly desert the Dutch on the spot. Stuyvesant nevertheless gave orders to check the fortifications, to enlist more paid soldiers, to distribute weapons, and to detain in port the company's ship *Coninck Salomon* ("King Solomon"), already freighted with commerce for Holland. He could well use both the cargo and the sixteen hundred pounds of ammunition that were on board.[8]

Three days later the mood among the population was much more confident. Stuyvesant's decisiveness and energy for once impressed the New Netherlanders, who in a wave of patriotism agreed to raise an army of sixty to seventy men, and even to pay taxes on their property and cattle. As the money was needed at once, a loan was secured from the richest citizens, and Stuyvesant offered his own possessions in the province and abroad as security. The English villages were to be left out of the whole enterprise, so "that we may not ourselves drag the Trojan horse within our walls."[9]

This initial enthusiasm soon subsided, and on June 3 an impatient governor tried to rouse the citizens who, as he told them, were "lulled to sleep by an idle rumor of peace." He urged them to begin repair of the fortifications, and at last the day laborers were put to work. On the same day, new and even more threatening rumors reached New Amsterdam. "The English are recruiting soldiers and pay 25 to 30 guilders a month. The plan is that three large ships will enter the Bay and offer surrender conditions to the Fort," reported the general to the burgomasters of New Amsterdam. He had realized by this time that preparations had started too late, and that the whole city was indefensible. He therefore ordered that all the cannon be moved inside the fort so they could not be turned against the city by the enemy.[10]

In the meantime the English on Long Island had been busy. Hastily they sent letters to Boston offering their cooperation, proposing to capture the *Coninck Salomon* in New Amsterdam and sail her to Virginia. The English citizens of New Amsterdam, for their part, made a great show of packing up their belongings in the hope of demoralizing the Dutch, and attempted to stir up "to mutiny the otherwise well disposed." The situation looked hopeless.[11]

DANGER FROM ABROAD

On April 5, 1654, the first Anglo-Dutch War came to an end in Europe. The English had been victorious, and in two years had taken at least seventeen hundred prizes. Grass was growing in the streets of Amsterdam, and the Republic, which had not known beggars for decades, was now flooded with them. Amsterdam had even halted the building of its pride and glory, the Stadt Huys, and rebellious crowds were calling for the four-year-old Prince of Orange as the "Savior of the Fatherland." De Witt felt that only a peace could stop them from having their way.

The conditions of the Peace of Westminster were humiliating for the once arrogant Republic. The Dutch had to pay enormous damages to the English East and West India Companies; they had to recognize the right of the English to trade in the Orient; they were forced to punish the murderers of Amboina and pay the families of the victims £ 3,615 in damages; and in the future they would have to salute the English flag in the seas around the Commonwealth. As a special gesture to Cromwell, the Dutch excluded the young Prince of Orange, William III, from the office of Stadtholder—a step not at all regretted by De Witt—and removed their protection from his uncles, the exiled Stuarts.[12]

In spite of an urgent request by the West India Company, there was no mention in the treaty of the border question between New Netherland and New England. The only point that could possibly be related to the situation in America was the first clause in the treaty, which stated that there would be a "true, firm and inviolable Peace . . . betwixt the Republic of England and the States General . . . and the Lands, Countries Cities and Towns under the Dominion of each, without distinction of Places."[13]

The West India Company was disappointed, but hoped that the matter could be dealt with later, and the directors wrote Stuyvesant an ecstatic letter announcing the end of the war. They had heard about the threat of invasion, but were sure that "meanwhile the ships of Parliament, stationed on that coast . . . shall already . . . have received different orders from their superiors in England."

The good news arrived in New Amsterdam on July 16, 1654, and Stuyvesant immediately informed the burgomasters and schepens of New Amsterdam. Hurriedly they ordered Claes van Elslandt to announce it from the steps of City Hall, where the citizens, called

A SWEET AND ALIEN LAND

together by "the usual preliminary ringing of the Bell," welcomed the news with relief and shouts of joy.[14]

Stuyvesant proclaimed a day of thanksgiving, on which he himself confirmed the good news: "Praise the Lord . . . he hath secured your gates, and blessed your possessions with peace, even here, where the threatened torch of war was lighted; where the waves reached our lips, and subsided only through the power of the Almighty."[15]

Many New Englanders received the news with less enthusiasm. The invasion fleet was still lying at Boston when, at the end of June, a ship from London sailed into port with a copy of the Treaty of Westminster. Massachusetts and New Plymouth had dragged their feet and—although "making a greate noise of greater preparations of raising forces"—their troops were still not ready. Connecticut and New Haven had been considering going it alone, but the peace now made that impossible. New Netherland could thank Massachusetts for the fact that it survived this war.

The United Colonies would have had no great difficulty in invading the small pallisaded city of New Amsterdam, but the lack of unity in the confederation had been New Netherland's salvation. Six years later an Englishman would write, with some justification, that just as religious intolerance in New England had been one of the first causes of New Netherland's population, Boston and Plymouth were responsible for "it ever keeping since."[16]

For a few weeks the general mood in New Amsterdam was elated. The letter that brought Stuyvesant news of the peace had also given New Amsterdam the freedom to appoint its own schout and have its own seal. The Heeren XIX asked Stuyvesant at the same time to put an end to all the quarrels in their province, and the governor decided to act accordingly. On July 21 he invited the burgomasters and schepens to a dinner to toast the end of the war, and in a moving speech he offered to bury all differences and "to think no more of all that had been passed heretofore and to live in all friendship." A remorseful City Council agreed, and on August 12 the citizens celebrated the double peace with a huge bonfire and as much drink as they pleased, for which the magistrates footed the bill of fifty-eight guilders.[17]

Five months later the burgomasters and schepens had occasion to return the hospitality of the governor. On Wednesday December 16, 1654, they offered him a civic banquet in their City Hall, which turned into a "gay repast" marked by a historic moment. Stuyvesant, at the end of the meal, handed over to them the new city seal that the company had sent him. At the same time, they received their coat of arms.*

It was a gracious farewell present from the governor, who was on the point of leaving for a long voyage to the other part of his territory, the Antilles. Now that the war was over and quiet restored, Stuyvesant felt it necessary to see how things were in the West Indies. Curaçao was not the only object of his travel. The British islands, in particular Barbados, were even more important since the Navigation Act seriously threatened Dutch trade there. On December 12 the governor chartered the *Pereboom* ("Peartree") and commissioned former naval agent Paulus van der Grift to command the *Dolfyn* ("Dolphin"), while Pieter Lucassen was captain on the third ship, *Abrams Offrande* ("Abraham's Offering"). On Christmas Eve the small fleet left the East River.[19]

Curaçao was the first stop. The little island where Stuyvesant had lived from 1638 to 1644, was as barren and dry as ever, but it had now become the center of the slave trade in the West Indies, and of great importance to the West India Company.

Stuyvesant himself had little to do with this trade. New Netherland was not much interested in the blacks from Africa, in spite of the company's encouragement to use them. The first ten slaves in the province had arrived in 1626, seven years after John Rolfe, the English husband of Pocahontas, had reported from Virginia that a "Dutch Man of Warre . . . sold us twenty negars." Over the years more had been brought to the province, but since the Dutch found them useless as either agricultural laborers or domestic servants, all were sold "for Pork and Peas," and "most of them just dropped through the fingers."[20]

In 1648 the States had reproached the company that "the Slave Trade hath long lain dormant to the great damage of the Company," and argued that New Netherland would have been more extensively cultivated if the settlers had used Negroes. The company had opened up the trade to Africa in 1652 so that the colonists

---

*A composition of argent per pale; three crosses saltire; crest a beaver proper surmounted by a mantle on which was a shield argent bearing the letters G.W.C. Under the base of the arms: *Sigillum Amstelodamensis in Novo Belgio;* the whole environed by a wreath of laurel. The three crosses were the arms of old Amsterdam, the G.W.C. stood for the West India Company.[18]

A SWEET AND ALIEN LAND

could import their slaves directly, and had promised to supply the patroons with "as many blacks as it possibly can." But in that same year Schout-Fiscaal Hendrick van Dyck had told the Heeren XIX that "no requests for Negroes has been presented."[21]

Not till 1655, just before Stuyvesant left New Amsterdam for Curaçao, did the first cargo of slaves arrive directly from Africa. The Amsterdam Chamber of the company had given two Dutch traders permission in November 1654 to go with their ship the *Witte Paert* ("White Horse") to Africa and trade there for slaves, which they could take to New Netherland "in consideration of the promotion of population and agriculture."[22]

But when the *Witte Paert*, coming direct from "the Bight of Guinea," moored before Manhattan, no rush had followed, and it looked as if the precious cargo would disappear to New England without any profit to the company. To prevent that, the governor slapped an export duty of 10 percent on the slaves and most of them were sold in New Netherland.

Not everybody was very happy with his bargain. Hardly a month after the arrival of the slave trader a certain Nicolaes Boot appeared in court in New Amsterdam, complaining that the female slave he had bought at a "publick auction" for 230 guilders had died the following day. The slave had seemed odd, shouting all the way to her new owner's home. "She could not well hold her feet," a witness told the court, and "her eyes standing fixed in her head," she had asked for "More, more." A passerby had explained that she was drunk, but the surgeon who was later called had told Boot she was dying, which indeed happened at nine o'clock.[23]

A slave imported to New Netherland could in general expect good treatment. The first ten slaves had been manumitted by Governor Kieft in 1644, after eighteen years of service. They had received some land, for which they had to pay yearly twenty-two and a half bushels of corn, wheat, peas, and beans and one fat hog. Their children, however, were obliged to serve the company as slaves. Some of the colonists objected to this rule, as the children of freemen could not be enslaved, but since these children numbered only three, the protests were soon forgotten.

Stuyvesant himself, who found them not "fit to learn a trade," used the Negroes mostly for work on the fort, or hired them out for a "quantity of beef and pork" to the highest bidder. He once gave three female slaves their freedom on condition that one of

DANGER FROM ABROAD

them come weekly to do housework for his wife Judith—good servants were almost impossible to find in the New World.[24]

But if New Netherland was not interested in the Negroes, New England and the West Indies were. The Calvinistic Dutch had conquered fairly rapidly their moral objections to the trade in human beings. The huge profits to be made stilled their pangs of conscience, and a lucrative triangular trade developed: merchandise was taken from the Republic to Guinea, where it was exchanged for slaves to be shipped to Brazil and Curaçao; the ships finally returned to Holland loaded with sugar and wood. The conquest of a series of Portuguese trading posts, such as Elmina and Luanda in Angola, gave the Dutch a complete monopoly of the slave trade. Between the years 1636 and 1645 more than twenty-three thousand slaves went to Brazil alone, where the Negro bought in Africa for forty to fifty guilders yielded ten times more.[25]

The English, French, and Spanish in the New World fought over the precious labor force. Like the Virginians, they had discovered very early that it "proved quite practicable to teach the savage African the one task which was required of him . . . that of tending the sugar or tobacco crops." The Civil War in England had interrupted the flow of servants to the colonies, Indian slaves were rare, and the Dutch traders were very ready to help the planters with easy credit if they would buy their slaves. They sometimes brought them over in shiploads of six hundred to seven hundred men, women, and children, stark naked during the whole voyage. The Dutch traders, with great foresight, even created their own market in the West Indies by stimulating the planters to concentrate on tobacco, sugar, and cotton, for which Negro labor was indispensable.[26]

One of the main centers of Dutch attention was Barbados. There they invested so much money and helped the colonists in so many ways, that the governor of the island, Lord Willoughby of Parham, declared its independence in 1650 rather than obey the Parliamentary act that forbade the colonies to trade with the Dutch. He had not forgotten that in 1638, when the price of tobacco fell drastically, the English merchants had left the island in the lurch and it was only thanks to Dutch money that Barbados had been saved. Lord Willoughby was severely admonished from London—"You'll do well to cherish your oune Countremen by giving

A SWEET AND ALIEN LAND

them all just advantage of Trade before strangers," was one message. The colony's answer came in a booklet, *A Declaration Set Forth*, published by the English bookseller Samuel Brown in The Hague on behalf of Barbados: "We do declare that we will never be so ungrateful to the Dutch for former helps as to deny them or any other nation the freedom of our ports."[27]

If the disobedient colony and the other British possessions in the West Indies were not willing to listen to reason, the alternative was force. London had already sent over Sir George Ayscue in 1651, who surprised thirteen Dutch vessels. Now that the war was over, it was felt that tough measures were needed. This time Admiral William Penn was sent to stop the colonies from rebelling and the Dutch from "interloping." In 1654 and 1655 he succeeded in seizing twenty Dutch merchantmen.

One of the captured ships was the *Pereboom*, with Stuyvesant on board. He had sailed into the port of Barbados in January after his visit to Curaçao, hoping to convince the English there to restore trade with the Dutch, and in particular to deal directly with New Amsterdam. He was to be bitterly disappointed. Admiral Penn had just conquered Jamaica from the Spanish and, very conscious of the English position in the West Indies, refused Stuyvesant even the smallest concession. Edward Winslow from New England was with Penn and he reported gloatingly to London: "This man's business was to settle a fair trade betweene the Netherlands and this place; but we spoiled the sport."[28]

The three Dutch ships were put under arrest out of fear, as Winslow wrote, "of him for the discovering our raw and defective forces." And not till the end of June was Stuyvesant allowed to leave. He returned to New Amsterdam on July 11, 1655. His journey had been a complete waste of time. There had been nothing to do in Curaçao—which was operating perfectly normally—and nothing to be done in the British West Indies—which were completely under the thumb of Parliament. Only some Spanish colonies had been willing to talk of trade. In fact, rumors had reached New England and New Netherland that the Governor had been slain by the Spanish, "but where, in what manner, when or why, is not made clear."[29]

During his absence New Amsterdam had struggled on with its usual problems. New Haven was once more showing signs of restless activity, and in November 1654 rumors reached Manhattan

DANGER FROM ABROAD

that at a town meeting in the English colony the question of settlement on the Delaware had once more been broached. The English, the Dutch learned gloomily, were so enthusiastic that they proposed having their governor spend "one year in one part and the next yeare in another." Since one of the sponsors of this new plan was Eaton's son Samuel, the Dutch took it very seriously. Nothing had yet come of the new settlement, but two other incidents had reminded the Dutch that, even if the war was at an end, New England had not forgotten its small neighbor.[30]

The first was caused by former Secretary George Baxter, now living in Connecticut. When he heard of the governor's absence in the West Indies, he crossed the frozen East River in January to return to Gravesend. There he told the Long Islanders that after its success in Acadia, Cromwell's fleet was again on its way to subdue New Netherland. The Council sent Van Tienhoven to calm the Dutch population, but when he arrived at Gravesend, he found the English flag waving over the village. George Baxter and James Hubbard had a few days earlier published a declaration, in which "as free-born British subjects" they claimed "the laws of our nation and Republic of England." Baxter and Hubbard were arrested on the spot and imprisoned for the rest of the year. Baxter later escaped to New England, but what was left of his Dutch property was confiscated.[31]

The other incident had taken place much nearer to New Amsterdam. In April an Englishman from Fairfield, Thomas Pell, was reported to have bought a tract of land north of the capital near Greenwich, called Vreedenland. Claes van Elslandt was sent with the city trumpeter to object, but when he arrived, he was stopped by four armed men. They tried to prevent him from jumping off his boat, but Van Elslandt answered: "I am cold," and simply sprang ashore. He later told the Council that he was placed under guard "and warned not to advance a foot further, until he who had the command came to us with a pistol, holding the barrel forward in his hand, accompanied by 8 to 10 armed men more." Van Elslandt kept his head, and read the protest, but the commander told him: "I cannot understand Dutch . . . if you send it in English then I shall answer. . . ." He repeated the rumors Baxter had spread, and assured Van Elslandt that when the English ships arrived, the problem would solve itself. "Whereupon we took our departure," reported the messenger.[32]

On his return from the West Indies, these incidents were reported to Stuyvesant, but for the moment he had no time for the English intruders. On his desk he found waiting a letter from the company in which he was ordered to tackle a much larger group of invaders—the settlers of New Sweden on the Delaware.[33]

EXIT
NUEVA SUECIA

Nueva Suecia, the Swedish colony on the Delaware founded in 1638 by the former Dutch Governor Peter Minuit, had survived its first harassed years to develop into a sizable settlement. By 1654 it counted four hundred inhabitants, and its three forts watched over a busy fur trade. The colony's relationship with the Dutch—who never officially gave up their claim to the South River—had had its ups and downs, but when the Swedes in 1654 captured the Dutch fort Casimir, the end of the uneasy peace was in sight. In November of that year the West India Company wrote instructing Stuyvesant to take revenge for this hostile act, "not only by restoring matters to their former condition, but also by driving the Swedes at the same time from the river."[1]

When the letter had reached New Amsterdam Stuyvesant was cruising in the Caribbean, and nothing could be done during the months he was detained in Barbados—to the great irritation of the Heeren XIX. Sweden was at war with Poland, and such an opportune moment might not soon come again. "We hoped that the expedition against them [the Swedes] had already been made," they wrote crossly to the Council on April 16, 1655, all the more angry because Stuyvesant had left for Curaçao without informing them of his plans. Despite his absence, "we have nevertheless decided not only to take up the project again, but also to carry it out with so much more assurance of success." They had chartered from the city of Amsterdam, they wrote, "one of their four largest and best ships, the *Waegh* ["Balance"], armed with 36 pieces, which is now being made ready for sea and will sail here with about 200 men in 12 or 14 days." The Council must act as soon as the ship arrived, because in spite of the war with Poland, "great preparations are being made in Sweden to assist their countrymen on the South River."[2]

The first troubles on the South River had started in the autumn of 1642 with the arrival of the new Swedish governor, John Printz. Up to that time, the Dutch and Swedes had got on amicably enough, even combining forces to throw out a party of English intruders at the Schuylkill, a river entering the Delaware opposite Fort Nassau. But the new governor, a massive four-hundred-pound figure who was immediately nicknamed "Big Tub," soon made it clear that he meant to champion Swedish rights. Printz was already fifty years old at that time, with an adventurous and controversial career behind him. He had been a soldier under the belligerent King Gustavus Adolphus, in whose army he had climbed to the rank of lieutenant colonel. Twice he was taken prisoner, and in 1640 he was the commander of Fort Chemnitz, which according to some sources he surrendered "shamefully," and according to others, only after an heroic defense. In any case, he was arrested when he returned to Sweden, put on trial, and deprived of his commission.

Printz was not the sort of man to take this lying down, and succeeded in proving his innocence, after which he was knighted in July 1642. His appointment as governor of New Sweden a month later, at a salary of twelve hundred specidalers, was perhaps less a promotion than a sign that not everybody was convinced of the excitable and impetuous colonel's heroism. New Sweden, where Printz and his wife Maria van Linnestau arrived with their six children in November 1642, was hardly the Swedes' idea of paradise.[3]

From the start the colony had had great difficulty in attracting settlers. Sweden itself was thinly populated and its citizens had plenty of land. The only ones willing to go were traders, but the young Queen Christina, inspired by her old chancellor, Axel Oxenstierna, wanted more than furs and in 1642 gave orders to reorganize the Royal Swedish General Trading Company. From now on poachers, deserters, debtors, and adulterers could be condemned

EXIT NUEVA SUECIA

to go to New Sweden for a couple of years to concentrate on the growing of corn and other agricultural products. The culture of tobacco was frowned upon by the sixteen-year-old Queen, who even considered stopping trade in this "unnecessary commodity" as it "in great measure brings great injury and poverty on many," but who decided to tax it heavily instead.[4]

Printz' nomination was part of the new strategy, and he sailed with express instructions to keep an eye on the Dutch at Fort Nassau. He was to be polite and tactful, but firm, and if ever the company tried to push him out, he was instructed to "repel force by force," since the Queen's subjects there "have in a just and regular manner purchased of the proper owners and possessors of the country that district of which they have taken possession."[5]

The new governor ignored from the outset one point in his instructions—"not to make inroads" on the Dutch. In March 1643 he started to build a new fort at Hog Creek, as Fort Christina was too far from the river. This fort, Elfsborg, was situated on a little island off the east shore. He worked fast, and David de Vries, visiting New Sweden in the autumn of 1643 on his way home to Amsterdam, reported that Printz had completed a third fort on Tinicum Island. Christened Fort New Gotheburg, it completely dominated the Delaware with its four copper cannons.[6]

The Dutch did not like this at all, but Kieft thought it better to keep relations cordial. His *laissez-faire* policy paid off, first when the Swedes helped the Dutch to destroy the Lamberton expedition in 1642, and then again when in 1644 a group of merchants in Boston received from Governor John Winthrop Sr. a patent to trade on the Delaware. In June their pinnace, loaded with merchandise, sailed up as far as the Swedish and Dutch forts, where both commanders agreed that Commander William Aspinall must not be allowed to proceed. They told him so in the friendliest possible manner, and the expedition sailed back down the Delaware—but not until the Dutch had entertained the English at a dinner so splendid that Winthrop later blamed the failure of the trip on the drunkenness of its leader.[7]

This spirit of easygoing neighborliness disappeared when Jan Jansen van Ilpendam, the Dutch commissary of Fort Nassau, was recalled to face charges of fraud and replaced by Andries Hudde. The new Dutch commissary, an educated man who had earlier been surveyor of New Amsterdam, was shocked to realize how

A SWEET AND ALIEN LAND

strongly entrenched the Swedish were, and reported at once to Kieft that Printz "held the river locked for himself."

Soon he had his first clash with the arrogant Swedish governor, who was claiming supreme authority over the whole region, hindering the Dutch in trading and farming. When a group of New Amsterdammers, after buying a plot of land from the Indians in 1654, erected the traditional arms of the company, Printz had it torn down. Hudde composed a dignified protest, but when it was handed to Printz, he simply flung it on the floor. The luckless messenger asked for a reply, but was kicked out without much ado, and Printz would have shot him if some bystanders had not prevented it.[8]

The Dutch decided to let the insult pass for the moment, trusting that the reign of this Swedish tyrant would soon be ended for he was scheduled to be recalled in 1646. But the Swedish government was unable to find a suitable successor, so he stayed on.

Stuyvesant's arrival brought fresh heart to the Dutch on the Delaware. Unlike Kieft, he took an active interest in the outposts of his province, and after a visit to Fort Orange in the first months of his appointment, he went to Fort Nassau in May 1648. Stuyvesant wrote to Hudde on April 27 that "if it pleases God to continue us in the present health," he would leave Manhattan on May 10 or 11 to travel overland to the Delaware with thirty soldiers.[9]

This show of Dutch strength was overdue. Printz had been busy again, fortifying the Swedish position by building a trading post at the mouth of the Schuylkill, the "high road" of the fur traders. On April 24 an Indian had come to Hudde to ask why he did not join them on the Schuylkill in an effort to halt the Swedish takeover. The Dutchman followed his advice and three days later began to erect a trading post, which he called Beversreede, near the spot where the Swedes had destroyed a previous Dutch outpost. Sachem Mattehoorn himself raised the flag of the Prince of Orange, related Hudde, "and ordered me to fire three shots in token of possession."[10]

The sun had hardly set that evening when the Swedish commissary, Hendrick Huygens, a nephew of Minuit, marched up to the half-finished Beversreede with eight men to ask for Hudde's com-

EXIT NUEVA SUECIA

mission. The Indians at once rallied to the Dutchman's defense, and accused Huygens of robbing them of their land. "Minuit, now about 11 years ago, had purchased no more than a small piece of land . . . to plant some tobacco on it," they told him. The Swedes had never paid them what they had promised, while the Dutch, the sachem insisted, were at least honest. In all the thirty years they had been there, they had never taken any land for nothing.[11]

Huygens retired discomfited, and Hudde finished the house, building—wisely, as it turned out—a solid palisade around it as protection against eventual attack. The next day a much more determined Swede, the lieutenant of Fort Elfsborg, Moens Klingh, came to visit the Dutch, this time with twenty-four men, fully armed "with loaded guns and lighted matches." He was less patient than Huygens, and after the Dutch refused again to go, he ordered his men to lay down their arms. Before the astonished eyes of the Dutch, they drew axes and "cut down the trees standing around and near the house," even destroying the few fruit trees Hudde himself had just planted.[12]

News of this outrage spurred General Stuyvesant. His planned departure on May 10 had been delayed, so to shorten the trip he left by barge on May 24. But contrary winds prevented the barge from leaving the East River, and after returning that evening to Manhattan, Stuyvesant canceled his whole trip "for secret reasons." Instead he sent Vice Director Lubbertus van Dincklage and Councillor Johannes La Montagne, who extracted from the Indian sachems a confirmation of the sale they had made fifteen years earlier to company commissary Arent Corsen, paying them at last the rest of the goods Corsen had promised them in 1633.[13]

This paper assault did nothing to deter Printz in his efforts to monopolize the fur trail, down which the Indians annually carried thirty to forty thousand beaver pelts to the Delaware trading stations. In September 1648 Alexander Boyer, the deputy commissary at Beversreede, alarmed New Amsterdam with a letter advising "your Honor agreeable to my humble bounden duty" that the Swedish governor had erected right in front of the Dutch fort a house "about thirty to thirty five feet length and about twenty feet wide." The rear gable of this house came within twelve feet of the gate of the fort, so that it completely cut off Beversreede from the waterside. By the end of the year the Swedes had pulled down the palisades around Beversreede too, and planted Indian corn on the

A SWEET AND ALIEN LAND

land around the fort, "so that we have not near the fort as much land that we can make a little garden in the spring," complained Cornelis van Tienhoven's brother Adriaen, the clerk of the court on the South River.[14]

But with their handful of soldiers, the Dutch could do little against the Swedes, and Stuyvesant had enough troubles in rebellious New Amsterdam. It was 1651 before he could spare time to worry about the Delaware, and then it was at the instigation of the company. The Heeren XIX wrote that they intended to ask Queen Christina for a settlement of the boundaries at the South River. In the meantime the governor was to maintain the rights of the company "with such discretion and circumspection that complaints, disputes and breaches of friendship with our allies be avoided."[15]

It was a typically ambiguous brief, and since the Swedish governor's behavior was becoming more and more obnoxious, Stuyvesant decided to interpret it as encouragement for a show of force. In spite of ill health, he left New Amsterdam on June 25, 1651, with a fleet of eleven ships and 120 soldiers. Sailing up the Delaware a few days later, he did his best to impress the Swedes "with drumming and cannonades."[16]

He seemed at least to have impressed the Indians, who on June 29 came to Fort Nassau—according to English sources a wretched little trading post surrounded by four or five houses—to sell the Dutch governor more land, this time below the Swedish Fort Christina. For a price of twelve duffel coats, twelve kettles, twelve axes, twelve adzes, twenty-four knives, twelve bars of lead, and four guns, the Indians were quite willing to do business with the Dutch, and when Printz called them to his house the next day, they refused indignantly to have any dealings with him.[17]

Powerless, Printz had to watch while Stuyvesant's fleet sailed to the newly-bought spot four miles below Christina and began to build not far from Fort Elfsborg, at a place the Swedes called Myggenborg because of its multitude of mosquitoes. Printz could do little more than send an official protest. By August 1 the fort was completed. It looked much more impressive than Nassau (now demolished), with twenty pieces of ordnance on its sturdy wooden walls. Before departing at the end of July, Stuyvesant named the fort Casimir (today New Castle), and left two warships behind to protect it.[18]

(263)

EXIT NUEVA SUECIA

As might be expected, the company was furious. Stuyvesant had not informed it of this expedition, which might spoil its chances for an agreement with the Swedish Queen. But Stuyvesant could at least report his aggression had worked to some purpose. From now on he was the lord of the river, forcing both Swedes and English to pay toll.[19]

Printz complained bitterly to Stockholm. The governorship had been difficult enough for him. Oxenstierna was now an old man, who from his place of retirement, Tidön, still tried to run the Swedish company. For the last five years Printz had not received any merchandise to trade with the Indians, and the Swedes had to buy their goods from the Dutch. Now he had to sit and watch while fifty Dutch families settled around Fort Casimir. His letter had some effect and the Crown Council, in the presence of Queen Christina herself, decided on March 18, 1652, to ask the Dutch for a settlement and to send a ship with provisions.[20]

Its voyage was constantly delayed, and in October 1653 the sixty-year-old Printz, fallen ill, could bear it no longer and returned to Sweden, taking twenty-five disillusioned colonists with him. The affairs of New Sweden he left in the hands of his son-in-law, Johan Papegoia, but on December 12 of that year the Queen appointed Johan Rysingh as the new governor. Apart from a salary of twelve hundred specidalers, the bachelor Rysingh received the grant "to him and his wife and their legitimate heirs as much land in New Sweden as they shall be able to cultivate with 20 or 30 peasants."[21]

Rysingh, a man of thirty-four, was an expert on trade and commerce who had spent some time in the Dutch Republic and was at the time of the appointment secretary of Sweden's Commercial College. He was younger, cleverer, and more polished than his predecessor, and although he had no military experience, he soon demonstrated that he was every bit as insistent as Printz on Swedish claims in America.[22]

Arriving on May 20, 1654, on the *Örn* ("Eagle") with 350 colonists, Rysingh found that he had come just in time. There were only sixteen families left in the colony, and they had become so desperate that they had approached Stuyvesant, asking to be placed under his jurisdiction. The arrival of the new governor with his large party of settlers gave them fresh courage, and a few days later they were even more heartened by an astonishing feat.

A SWEET AND ALIEN LAND

Seeing the desolate situation at the Swedish forts, Rysingh looked a little lower down the river, where a prosperous Fort Casimir was shining in the sunlight. When Adriaen van Tienhoven, the clerk of Casimir's court, came to welcome him, Rysingh promptly asked for the surrender of the fort. Van Tienhoven hurried back to Casimir to warn its commander, Gerrit Bicker, closely followed by twenty Swedish soldiers under the command of Lieutenant Sven Schüte.

"I welcomed them as friends," Bicker wrote defensively to Stuyvesant a week later, "judging that if they wished to attempt something, they would at least give notice." But these niceties were not observed by Schüte, who "at the point of the sword" ordered Bicker to surrender the fort. The commander hesitated and suggested that they talk about it first, but two Dutch mediators, who went to see Rysingh on board the *Örn*, came back with the message that if they did not surrender at once, "we should soon see his bullets." The luckless Bicker had no choice but to yield. The Swedes occupied the bastions of the fort and drove out the few Dutch soldiers. Bicker told Stuyvesant plaintively that he had to beg the Swedes "not to be turned out naked with wife and children." But despite such harshness, he returned a few days later and with other Dutch people took an oath of fidelity to the new Swedish governor.[23]

The story Adriaen van Tienhoven later told when he fled to New Amsterdam was a little different from Bicker's. When the *Örn* was approaching, Van Tienhoven had asked Bicker to put the fort in a state of defense. Bicker had replied: "What should I do? There is no powder," while Bicker's wife had remarked that it was a waste to give powder to the soldiers, " 'tis better to barter it for Beavers." When the Swedes had landed on Sunday morning at eleven o'clock, Bicker had received them warmly, even giving them precedence on entering. While the Swedish soldiers climbed the ramparts, Van Tienhoven had asked for Rysingh's commission. The Swede had laughed and told him that he was taking Casimir on orders from the Queen. Her Majesty had permission from the States General and the Dutch West India Company, which had told the Swedish ambassador in The Hague: "If our people are in your way there, drive them off." Tapping Van Tienhoven on his chest, Rysingh had dismissed him with the words: "Go tell your governor that." The abject Bicker had even ordered

EXIT NUEVA SUECIA

one of his sons to haul down the Prince's flag.[24]

Rysingh at least had the courtesy to inform General Stuyvesant of his safe arrival and the "voluntary surrender" of Fort Casimir —which he rechristened Fort Trefaldighet, since it was taken on Trinity Sunday. But chance gave the Dutch governor an opportunity to retaliate when in September the Swedish merchant ship *Gyllene Hay* ("Golden Shark") sailed into the Hudson by mistake. It was at once seized and the Swedish factor Hendrick van Elswyck was sent to Rysingh with an invitation from Stuyvesant to come to New Amsterdam and negotiate with him. The general warned Rysingh that until he had received satisfaction for the capture of Fort Casimir, the Swedish vessel would be detained. Rysingh refused the invitation and the cargo was sold. The *Hay* itself was sent to Holland to be fitted out by the West India Company for trade with Curaçao.[25]

Stuyvesant's preparations for his own trip to Curaçao in 1654 prevented any further dealings with Rysingh. During Stuyvesant's absence the latter had his hands full with a threat from the other side, the English. News of the Delaware expedition of Samuel Eaton of New Haven reached New Amsterdam only in November, but Rysingh had already learned of it in July. He received that month a letter from the New Haven Court, expressing its wish for "a neighbourly correspondence with them [the Swedes] both in trading and in planting." Rysingh wrote back to decline, but New Haven went ahead, stimulated by the drive of Eaton, who in November had persuaded fifty settlers to follow him. In April 1655 Vice Governor Samuel Goodyear traveled to New Amsterdam to discuss some details of the expedition with the Swedish factor Van Elswyck, but the talks gave him little joy. The Swede pointed out that their respective governments in Europe must decide New Haven's rights, and an angry Goodyear returned to New Haven to report the failure of his mission and cancel the expedition.[26]

This vague threat dealt with, Nueva Suecia had to prepare itself for a much more substantial menace. In August the first reports of a pending Dutch attack reached the colony. Rysingh at once dispatched spies to New Amsterdam, who returned with news that Stuyvesant was busily equipping a fleet of four large ships and a few smaller vessels, and collecting at least eight hundred men. The number of troops reported was exaggerated. Johannes Bogaert, a company clerk who sailed with the expedition and sent an account of it to company director Hans Bontemantel in Amsterdam, mentioned only 317 soldiers and an unspecified number of seamen. Rysingh gave a total of six hundred Dutchmen.[27]

Even so, the fleet was indeed impressive by New World standards. The *Waegh* had arrived from Holland with thirty-six cannon and two hundred soldiers on board. Stuyvesant added two yachts, the *Hollantse Tuyn* ("Holland's Garden") and the *Princess Royal,* and the flyboat the *Liefde* ("Love"). The two yachts he had taken to the West Indies, *Abrams Offrande* and *Dolfyn,* had been released by the English at Barbados in time to reinforce the enterprise, while a seized French privateer, *l'Esperance,* was commissioned to join as the *Hoop* ("Hope").

On Sunday, September 5, 1655, after the church service, the fleet sailed, but contrary winds made it a slow trip and it was not until the 10th that Stuyvesant reached the Delaware. The next day he sailed "close under the guns of Fort Casimir," where, reported Bogaert, he "anchored about a cannon-shot distance from it. The troops were landed immediately and General Stuyvesant despatched Lt. Dirck Smit with a drummer and a white flag to the commandant, called Swen Schoeten [Sven Schüte] to summon the fort." In the meantime the Dutch took what was left of Fort Elfsborg. Rysingh, who had given Schüte men and ammunition with the order to defend Casimir, heard to his fury that the commander "not only suffered the Dutch ships to pass without remonstrance or firing a gun," but surrendered the fort by "a dishonorable capitulation . . . not in the fort or any indifferent place, but on board a Dutch ship."

Schüte had indeed come on board the ship *Waegh,* to ask for consultations. He had, however, given up all idea of defense when Stuyvesant had a battery erected "about a man's height above the bushes" around Casimir. He handed the fort over on the condition that he could march out with twelve men "fully accoutred, with the flag of the crown." He forgot to stipulate his destination, and the Dutch governor shipped him with his soldiers off to Manhattan.

A detachment of nine men, hastily sent down by Rysingh from Christina, found there was very little they could do. After a skir-

EXIT NUEVA SUECIA

mish with some Dutch soldiers, they tried to flee, but only two escaped to report the loss of the fort. Rysingh dispatched Factor Van Elswyck with a drummer to Stuyvesant to dissuade him from further hostilities, but the drummer was lacking a drum and the two men were arrested as spies. Stuyvesant told Van Elswyck that he claimed the whole river. Rysingh later reported that he had collected all his people for the defense of Fort Christina, laboring "with all our might by night and by day, in strengthening the ramparts," and that on September 15 the Dutch fleet appeared opposite his fort.

"We formed ourselves into three divisions," Bogaert told Bontemantel in Amsterdam. The one under Stuyvesant dug in north of Christina, three hundred feet from its walls, with four cannon, of which one was an eighteen-pounder. The company of Frederick de Koningh, the captain of the *Waegh*, constructed at the south side a battery with three guns; while northwest of the fort the third company, under the command of Councillor Nicasius de Sille, completed the encircling with two twelve-pounders.

Stuyvesant's headquarters were in a deserted house near the fort, and it was there that he settled down to wait. The Swedes—only thirty men strong—looked incredulously from Christina at the Dutch, "not yet believing that they would, in contempt with public peace and without any cause known, commence hostilities." A letter from Stuyvesant sent by an Indian soon robbed them of that illusion. "He arrogantly claimed the whole river, and required me and all the Swedes either to evacuate the country, or to remain there under Dutch protection, threatening with the consequences in case of refusal," Rysingh's report related. The Swede called a council of war, which determined to defend the fort, although it was in a weak position, dominated by the surrounding heights, and their powder stocks were desperately low.

Stuyvesant, good company servant that he was, had no intention of wasting money by firing unnecessary shots. He simply sat there. Soon his soldiers grew bored with the picnic and, with a little encouragement from the general, started to roam around. "The Dutch now began to encroach upon us more and more every day," the Swedish governor complained. "They killed our cattle, goats, swine and poultry, broke open houses, pillaged the people . . . and higher up the river they plundered many and stripped them to the skin." Even ex-Governor Printz's daughter, Armegot Papegoia,

A SWEET AND ALIEN LAND

did not escape assault and robbery. When Rysingh received another summons from Stuyvesant, he decided to go and meet the Dutchman, who had erected a large and beautiful tent between the Dutch works and the Swedish fort. Long discussions about the Queen's rights took place, but "all this produced no impression upon them," Rysingh reported later, so he went back to encourage his men "to a manly defence."

The Swedish community, however, had had enough. "Our few and hastily collected people were getting worn out, partly sick and partly ill disposed, and some had deserted," and a dejected Rysingh went back to the tent on September 24 to sign the capitulation. After a siege of ten days, without the loss of one man or even a drop of blood (apart from that of livestock), Stuyvesant had carried out his orders from the West India Company. On the morning of the 25th the few Swedes left Fort Christina, marching out "with their arms, colours flying, matches lighted, drums beating and fifes playing."

The Dutch at once took possession, hauled down the Swedish flag, and hoisted their own. Those Swedes who wanted to stay swore an oath to the States, but Rysingh, whom Stuyvesant offered to retain as keeper of the key of the fort, refused and told the Dutch governor he wanted to return to Europe. The general gave his permission and stipulated in a secret clause of the capitulation agreement that Rysingh could land in England or France. He also advanced him three hundred Flemish pounds, which Rysingh was to pay back within six months, leaving as a security the possessions of the Royal Swedish General Trading Company.[28]

Rysingh took his defeat badly. When he arrived in New Amsterdam in October, Stuyvesant offered him the accommodation and table of his own residence "and humble circumstances," but the Swede indignantly refused. An irritated governor quartered him "in one of the most principal houses in the City," but Rysingh, "in a passionate manner," told the people there that he "would come to ravage and plunder this place." His hosts found him so provoking that "for the sake of rest they left their own lodgings during the time."[29]

With a great sigh of relief Stuyvesant saw the departure of Rysingh on board the *Waegh* on October 26. Landing at the end of December at Plymouth, the former governor was able to give the first news of the loss of New Sweden. The Dutch ambassador in

EXIT NUEVA SUECIA

London, Nieuwpoort, at once informed the States General, and on January 13, 1656, the company itself received confirmation. It was a victorious moment for the Heeren XIX, but as usual they qualified their compliments for their director. According to the Lords Directors, he had made a great mistake in asking for a formal surrender of Fort Christina. They wrote to him in April 1656 that "our reason for it is specially, that what is written and given in copy can be preserved for a long time and appears occasionally at the most awkward moment, while on the other side the spoken word or the deed is forgotten in the course of time."[30]

They were right in a way. Over the next few years the Swedes repeatedly complained about Dutch aggression in New Netherland. But the Swedish flag never rose again over American soil.

THE PEACH WAR

The last days of the siege of Fort Christina had been sheer agony for General Stuyvesant. On September 17, 1655, a letter arrived from New Amsterdam with disastrous news. On the morning of the 15th, while Stuyvesant was beginning his siege of the Swedish fort, hundreds of Indians had swarmed over Manhattan, killing and burning. About nine hundred natives were now gathered at the end of the island, preparing for an attack on New Amsterdam itself. Stuyvesant's wife Judith and his two sons were safe, reported Schout Van Tienhoven, and "as the citizens are unwilling to guard other houses far from Manhattan, we have, with her advice, hired ten Frenchmen to protect your Honors Bouwery." The schout urged Stuyvesant to come back as soon as possible, "for to lie in the Fort night and day with the citizens, has its difficulties, as they cannot be commanded as soldiers."[1]

Stuyvesant had sent a messenger back with the assurance that "if we had the wings of an eagle, we should have disdained our victories and flown away from our obvious gains, to help and console our oppressed friends and subjects by our humble word and deed." Unluckily, the winds were not favorable, and "we must have patience." He asked them to encourage "my sorrowing wife, children and sisters and my sad grieving subjects," hoping "not only that the City of Amsterdam may be secured somewhat under God's blessing, the burghers encouraged and the murderers checked, but also that your Honors may have got some courage and an opportunity to assist the remaining bouweries outside."[2]

In his letter Van Tienhoven had mentioned the possibility that the Swedes had bribed the savages to make the assault. Stuyvesant had his doubts about that, but he abruptly concluded the talks with Rysingh, leaving on September 28 with the capitulation of Fort Christina in his pocket. Sailing past Staten Island on his way to New Amsterdam, he gained a first impression of the disaster that had struck his province. Every house was a smoking ruin. The city itself was in a state of panic, with citizens and refugees from the farms crammed into the little fort, whose wooden palisades had disappeared into the fireplaces of the burghers during the extraordinarily cold winter of 1654–1655. Nobody was in the mood to give a victorious welcome to the conqueror of New Sweden.[3]

Stuyvesant's dealings with the Indians had been completely different from those of Kieft. After the conclusion of peace in 1645, the natives had been continually restless and aggressive, murdering fourteen settlers, among them the well-known Danish farmer Jochem Kuyter. The governor had refrained from taking revenge, and instead demanded in each case the surrender of the culprits, who never appeared. But there must have been more tension among the Hudson tribes than anybody had guessed, because a single incident in the month of September 1655 was sufficient to rouse the greatest part of New Netherland's Indians to attack.

This incident took place shortly after Stuyvesant had left for New Sweden. The Mohicans, Esopus, and Hackensack Indians thought the moment opportune to tackle their traditional enemies, the Canarsie tribes on Long Island. In sixty-four canoes they came down the Hudson, about nineteen hundred strong. They moored at the north side of Manhattan and in the evening some landed to get food. Not all of them intended to buy it, and a few started to plunder the orchards behind the houses along the Heerenweg (Broadway). One of these orchards was the property of Hendrick van Dyck, the dismissed schout-fiscaal who had once made a name as a soldier in Kieft's Indian War. Seeing his favorite foes in his garden, he stormed out of the house with his gun and shot an Indian woman who was picking some peaches.[4]

The news spread rapidly through the fleet of canoes, and on Wednesday morning, September 15, hundreds of Indians woke up the citizens of New Amsterdam, entering their houses under the

A SWEET AND ALIEN LAND

pretext of searching for other Indians. "During the day [they] offered and committed in many houses and to many citizens insults," Stuyvesant later wrote to the company. At the end of the day, his councillors had managed to assemble their sachems, who promised "with many and great good words" that the natives would depart to Nut Island (Governor's Island). Their authority was obviously not great, and when night fell, the restless Indians were still on the shores along the North River, looking for revenge. Van Dyck, in whose peach orchard the trouble had started, was their first victim. He received an arrow in his side, but was not mortally wounded. When Paulus van der Grift, a commanding and influential man, came with his wife to negotiate with the Indians, their only reaction was to threaten him with axes.[5]

It seemed more sensible to go and see the chiefs again, but when a group of burghers, led by Van Tienhoven, approached the canoes, "the savages," according to one account, "rushed on our people and killed Jan de Visser, whereupon the Netherlanders returned the fire, driving the enemies into their canoe." Another account was different. Van Tienhoven, hearing about the attack on Van Dyck, had called the citizens together with the cry: "Murder the savages who kill the Dutch," after which a rather disorganized group of settlers assaulted the Indians, who fled. From the middle of the river they fired a few parting shots, killing one more Dutchman and wounding others. For the rest of the night the citizens watched helplessly from the banks of the North River the ominous sight of burning farms on Staten Island.[6]

The rampage lasted for three days. The inhabitants of Manhattan, Long Island, and the village of Esopus on the Hudson fled to Fort Amsterdam, but not before the Indians had killed at least forty of them. "More than a hundred, mostly women and children, were captured, 28 bouweries destroyed and 600 head of cattle killed or taken away," was the sad reckoning of Stuyvesant. The total damage came to about 200,000 guilders.[7]

One of the Indians' prisoners was Cornelis Melyn, Stuyvesant's archenemy, whose colony on Staten Island, consisting of about forty houses, went up in flames. He, his wife, and two sons, and all his servants were kept prisoners for weeks. Melyn in the end escaped to New Haven, where he ransomed his family and settled down as a "free colonist." Melyn's neighbor on Staten Island, Lubbertus van Dincklage, the former vice director, died around

THE PEACH WAR

that time, almost certainly killed by the Wilden.[8]

Stuyvesant at his return acted with the greatest vigor. He sent troops to Long Island; borrowed six thousand guilders to pay for the strengthening of the city wall; and held all ships back in port, ordering passengers and crews to help in the defense of the capital. One of his first priorities was to retrieve the captured women and children from the Indians, and things began to look promising when on October 13 some sachems made it known they wanted to negotiate an end to the "Peach War," undertaking to release the prisoners within forty-eight hours.[9]

Days of heartbreaking tension followed. New Amsterdammers crowded the shores of the East River in the hope of seeing their lost relatives returned, but the Indians did not keep their promise. Stuyvesant had to send more envoys to Staten Island, at the same time issuing an ordinance to forbid "crowding and unseemly clamor" on the river banks. At last the savages freed fourteen captives, in exchange for powder and lead. More requests for "contraband" followed, and Stuyvesant gave it eagerly and with results. At the end of October seventy of the hundred captives were back in New Amsterdam. The Indians, who had found their prisoners a burden, but knew how to extract a high price for them, kept the others and released them slowly over the next two years.[10]

The sudden and violent attack by the Indians not only did enormous damage in the province, it also destroyed the confidence of the settlers in the future of their country. Governor Stuyvesant, sensing their mood, decided to ask the States General for help, and composed for the first time his own remonstrance. Reporting the disaster on October 31, he warned the Dutch government that the country "had gone backward so much, that it will not be in the same flourishing state for several years as it was six weeks ago." Worst of all, he wrote, the inhabitants now feared "to be again surprised so unexpectedly. . . . It makes them and many other circumspect and timid to go again in the open country . . . hence we have only to expect in consequence of the failure of cultivation and harvests, poverty, want, famine and a final ruin of the country." His question was what to do. "We are very much disinclined, to enter without your Noble Worships' knowledge, advice and assistance into an open war."[11]

The citizens of the capital optimistically added their own re-

A SWEET AND ALIEN LAND

quest: three thousand to four thousand "good soldiers, one-half with matchlock, the other half with flintlocks . . . who after having helped us to attain our end, are willing to settle in the country." They asked further for a supply, "to the value of 30 to 40,000 guilders of needed commodities for clothing and feeding the military."[12]

By the time these requests reached Holland, the worst of the crisis in Manhattan was over. The recriminations now began. In spite of his absence during the massacre, Stuyvesant had a strong conviction that it was not the Indians alone who were to blame. Van Tienhoven had been one of the first to attack the Indians after they had wounded Van Dyck, and had not tried to disperse them peacefully. As in the past, however, Stuyvesant stayed his hand and spoke only in general terms of some "hot-headed individuals" who had acted without tact and circumspection. The inhabitants of New Amsterdam refused to be satisfied with this forbearing attitude toward their most detested enemy, and protested strongly. They found a champion in a man who had only arrived in the colony two years earlier—Nicasius de Sille.

De Sille came from a prominent family in the Republic. His grandfather, whose namesake he was, had been pensionary of Amsterdam and was reputedly responsible for drafting the Treaty of Utrecht, which had created the Republic of the seven United Provinces in 1579. His father Laurens was for a while burgomaster of Arnhem, where on September 23, 1610, Nicasius was born. He studied law and became an advocate at the Court of Holland, not neglecting his military duty. When, after the Remonstrance of 1650 and the near recall of Stuyvesant in 1652, the Heeren XIX looked around for an "expert and able statesman" to be Stuyvesant's first councillor (and possibly his successor), their eyes fell on the forty-two-year-old De Sille, a widower with five children.[13]

In 1653 Stuyvesant received the news from Holland that "in consideration of the weakness in numbers of your Council in these troubled times, we have resolved to increase the number by another firm and experienced Councillor, and as among others Nicasius Sille had presented himself for the office, experienced both in law and war . . . we have engaged him. . . . ." The new councillor—with a monthly income of one hundred guilders—sailed on August 23, 1653, with his two sons, three daughters, and a maid to look after them.[14]

THE PEACH WAR

It was a hazardous crossing. The Anglo-Dutch War was still raging, and the little vessel had to prepare itself three times for battle. It escaped unharmed and on Saturday afternoon, November 3, "we anchored before Fort Amsterdam," De Sille wrote to his friend, company director Hans Bontemantel. "We fired five shots with cannon and those of the fort replied with three." The New Amsterdammers, who were expecting their new councillor, had gathered in the streets, and the soldiers were under arms. Van Tienhoven came to the shore and took De Sille to Stuyvesant's home, where, in the absence of the governor, the schout entertained him and the children. "The 11th the Honorable General and his wife came home and entertained me also. In the afternoon he convened the council wherein I was made to occupy the first seat, next to his honor."[15]

This favorable treatment did not last very long. The general made no effort to hide his jealousy of the intelligent and charming newcomer, who soon realized that his commission was not in the least respected by Stuyvesant or Van Tienhoven. The two men cast three votes each in the Council, while De Sille and the only other councillor—still La Montagne—had only two apiece. When De Sille once protested, so he wrote to Bontemantel, the general sneered at him and Van Tienhoven "scornfully laughed."[16]

During Stuyvesant's absence in the West Indies, he had left the running of the province in the hands of his schout-fiscaal. On his departure for the expedition against New Sweden, he had taken De Sille with him so as not to let him out of sight. It was, then, with all the more anger that De Sille, on his return from the Delaware, saw the desolate situation in and around the capital. He wrote an indignant letter to Bontemantel, at that time burgomaster of Amsterdam, in which he complained about the insolent behavior of the Indians "threatening us, while lying around New Amsterdam."[17]

But his most serious criticism was of General Stuyvesant. "Nobody praised him as he refuses to make an inquest and protects the schout-fiscaal," he reported. "The community wants to go back to Holland, and many merchants leave with this ship as there is no order here." He advised Bontemantel to replace Stuyvesant with a governor "who is not selfish." De Sille's letter arrived in Amsterdam at the same moment as one from Stuyvesant, in which the governor attacked De Sille and La Montagne as "men without experience, in whom I have no confidence." He denied that Van Tienhoven had been solely responsible for the Indian massacre, but he went too far in his protection of his most loyal employee.[18]

The odious schout himself made no bones about his eagerness to have a go at the savages. Waiting for support from Holland (it arrived much later in the form of a troop of fifty soldiers), Stuyvesant decided to ask his three-man Council what it thought about a total war with the Indians, since the savages still refused to give up the rest of their prisoners. He sent the councillors a questionnaire on November 10, and a fortnight later received their answers. De Sille and La Montagne were of the opinion that a war without the help of soldiers would be suicidal. Van Tienhoven, on the contrary, was adamant that the settlers should go to war as soon as possible, preferably between December and March. In the meantime, "we must dissemble, though it be unpleasant, and if possible not spare some small presents, in order to bring the savages to a truce, without making an absolute compact."[19]

Fortunately Stuyvesant did not listen to his devious fiscaal, and when at about the same time a group of Long Island Indians came to make peace and to ally themselves with the Dutch against the River Indians, the director general grasped the opportunity with both hands. He told the River Indians that they were not allowed to stay overnight in the villages and towns, and that they would lose their weapons if they ever carried them into New Amsterdam.[20]

To protect the inhabitants of New Netherland, he made a renewed effort to get them together in villages "like our neighbours in New England," something the company had been attempting since 1645, when it had advised its officials "to do all in their power to induce the Colonists to establish themselves at some of the most suitable places, with a certain number of inhabitants . . . whereby they will dwell in greater security." Stuyvesant now turned the request into a command, since "sorrowful experiences has made manifest, from time to time, that in consequence of the dwelling of the outside people apart . . . many and divers murders of men, slaying and destruction of cattle and burning of houses have been committed." On January 18, 1656, he ordered the settlers "to combine together . . . before the approaching Spring." Any who refused to obey would be fined twenty-five guilders. He pro-

THE PEACH WAR

mised that a blockhouse would be built in every hamlet.[21]

The Peach War—which, in fact, never was a war—was by that time over. The River Indians were still on Staten Island, but showing no signs of aggression, and most of the prisoners were home. For Stuyvesant, the time had come for a day of fasting and prayer. He had stated in November that the Indian assault was undoubtedly a punishment from God for all the "common, private and public sins, as drunkenness, profanation of the Lord's Sabath and Name, swearing in public and in private, done even by children in the streets." Now that the most serious threat was over, he told the citizens to come to church on March 1 and do penance. The text for the sermon was: "Ah, how hath the Lord covered us with a cloud in his anger, and cast down from Heaven to Earth the beauty of the land; the Lord hath swallowed up all our Habitations and has not pitied. He hath thrown down our stronghold in his wrath."[22]

For the citizens, this must have been a bit much. Having been driven by their schout into a calamitous clash with the Indians, they felt little inclined to accept any blame. And they received justice when the reply to De Sille's complaints against Van Tienhoven came in May. The councillor's argument had been supported by Cornelis van Ruyven, who in 1653 had taken over from Van Tienhoven as secretary and soon discovered a series of malversations, which he referred to Amsterdam.[23]

This was at last more than enough for the Heeren XIX, who wrote in a stern letter to Stuyvesant that "on account of manyfold complaints made to us," Cornelis van Tienhoven was to be dismissed from company service. The governor made a last effort to protect his faithful assistant, but the company told him impatiently that its decision was "not prompted by light and unimportant reasons." It ordered the governor not to defend Van Tienhoven anymore, "as we are confident that the charges are true. Whoever considers his last transactions with the savages, will find that with clouded brains filled with liquor, he was a prime cause of this dreadful massacre."[24]

Stuyvesant still hesitated, especially because, as a final humiliation, the company had provisionally appointed De Sille to succeed Van Tienhoven as schout, but the burgomasters and schepens of New Amsterdam gave the general no choice. On May 30 they told him they were "certainly informed that the Honble

A SWEET AND ALIEN LAND

Cornelis van Tienhoven is dismissed by the Lords Patroons," wondering when his replacement would be appointed. On June 26 Schout-Fiscaal De Sille took his seat in the City Court, between the two burgomasters.[25]

A few months later Van Tienhoven was faced with a court of inquiry, but he preferred to disappear, and on November 18, 1656, his hat and cane were found floating in the river. Nobody could believe that the loud-mouthed and lustful official had taken his own life, but after a while De Sille asked for permission to seize and seal Van Tienhoven's property. In the official annals of New Netherland, its most hated man had "absconded," the last—and only rightful—victim of the Peach War.[26]

PASTORAL
PROBLEMS

"We have had an Indian here with us for about two years. He can read and write Dutch very well. We have instructed him in the fundamental principles of our religion, and . . . he can repeat the Commandments." So wrote New Amsterdam's two ministers, Johannes Megapolensis and Samuel Drisius, to the Classis, the Committee of dominies in Amsterdam, in August 1657. It sounded very hopeful, but the two pastors went on to destroy at once every illusion. "He took to drinking brandy, he pawned the Bible, and turned into a regular beast, doing more harm than good among the Indians."[1]

They were not the first Dutch dominies to complain about the natives' uncooperativeness. Johannes Michaëlius had already reported in 1628 that the Indians "serve nobody but the Devil." He wondered how these people could be "best led to the true knowledge of God and of the Mediator Christ," and thought that the only solution was to begin with the children: "They ought in youth to be separated from their parents; yea, from their whole nation." Unfortunately, the parents were so fond of their children that they would not let them go, or at once stole them back. In a word, it was hopeless. And it would remain hopeless throughout the whole history of New Netherland.[2]

The Indians were not interested in the God of the Dutch, and for the Dutch the question of saving souls was never so important as it was for the English, the French, or the Spanish. In their first instructions the West India Company had encouraged the colonists to try to convert the Indians through education and good example, and the first company chronicler, De Laet, still believed in 1624 that "with mild and proper treatment and especially by intercourse with Christians" the Indians might be converted, "particularly if a sober and discreet population were brought over and good order preserved."[3]

But neither happened. The Dutch, as always, were more intent on trade and the spreading of the gospel of commercialism than on the spiritual welfare of their customers and suppliers. The first settlers were a rough lot. The dominies and comforters of the sick had their hands full with them, and hardly ever left the settlements to confront the savage heathens.

This is not to say that all the clergy were indifferent toward the religious improvement of the natives. Megapolensis, a generous and warmhearted man, was deeply disappointed by his failure to make the natives see the Light, but he saw no way to accomplish it. He expressed his frustration once in a conversation with the Jesuit Father Simon le Moyne, who told him that he had lived twenty years among the Indians. Megapolensis asked him bitterly "whether he had taught the Indians anything more than to make the sign of the cross," and the father had judged it better to avoid a discussion about this obviously touchy subject.[4]

The attitude of the Dutch in the matter of conversion was understandable. Their Republic in Europe was known for its religious tolerance, which was even proclaimed in the Treaty of Utrecht of 1579, the cornerstone of the United Provinces. While the state recognized officially only the Calvinistic Reformed Church, different Protestant sects had great freedom, Roman Catholics were winked at, and Jews from all over Europe found a safe asylum in Amsterdam. It was to be expected that this broadmindedness would be reflected in New Amsterdam, even if there it was mainly for the sake of peace, prosperity, and material progress.

The West India Company made it very clear in the regulations of 1638 how it wished religious life in its American province to be run. "Religion shall be taught and practised there according to the Confession and formularies of union here publicly accepted, with which everyone shall be satisfied and content, without, however, it being inferred from this that any person shall hereby in any wise

PASTORAL PROBLEMS

be constrained or aggrieved in his conscience. . . ." But this declaration of freedom of religion did not stop the Heeren XIX from keeping a very strict watch over the appointments of ministers, comforters of the sick, and schoolmasters.[5]

The first choice of clergymen for the colony was relegated to a commission of the Classis of Amsterdam, the Deputati ad res Indicas, but the selection had to be approved by the company. It was an unhappy situation. The Heeren XIX, who in 1638 had stated that "each householder and inhabitant shall bear such tax and public charge as shall hereafter be considered proper for the maintenance of clergyman," forgot that the community in New Netherland was still pioneering and poor. During their dealings with candidates they were constantly offering considerable salaries, which the ministers, unfamiliar with the situation in the colony, eagerly accepted. Once on the spot, they were abandoned to the generosity of the poor and small congregations.[6]

Michaëlius had been the first to realize that the company's promise of some land was "void and useless," adding: "For their Honors well knew that there are no horses, cows, or labourers to be obtained here for money." The files of the Amsterdam Classis and the West India Company are filled with letters from destitute ministers and schoolmasters begging for their wages, and even after their return to the Republic they very often had to fight hard for their well-earned arrears of income.[7]

It was, in fact, amazing that the company succeeded in finding pastors who were willing to herd for so long the faraway, unruly flock. These were not always of the highest standard, but most were dedicated and enthusiastic men who played an important role in the community life of New Amsterdam and the villages of New Netherland.

The first pastor was Johannes Michaëlius, who in 1628 succeeded Jan Huygens, the comforter of the sick. A brother-in-law of Governor Peter Minuit, Huygens (who was later joined by Bastiaen Jansz Krol) had, like all "comforters," very limited powers. He was allowed to "console"—"which is an Instruction in the Faith and the way of Salvation to Prepare Believers to Die Willingly"—and to read each Sunday "a few texts of Scripture with the commentaries." He was probably not capable of doing much more, as most of the comforters were uneducated, indeed often almost illiterate.[8]

A SWEET AND ALIEN LAND

But if Huygens had been a not too effective temporary solution, the term of office of Michaëlius was hardly more successful. Born in 1581, the son of a minister at Hoorn, he had studied in Leiden and had come under the influence of the stern reformist Adrianus Smoutius, famous in Amsterdam for his fiery and punishing sermons in which no tolerant Dutchman was spared. Michaëlius made this energetic agitator his example, and from his pulpit in the horse mill next to Fort Amsterdam his tongue lashed colonists and their officials without mercy. Soon enough he was involved in the conflicts that raged around Governor Peter Minuit.

There was little to distract his attention, except his three children. His wife had died shortly after arrival in New Amsterdam, and Michaëlius wrote Smoutius: "I find myself by the loss of my good and helpful partner very much hindered and distressed—for my two little daughters are yet very small; maid servants are not to be had, at least none whom they can advise me to take; and the Angola slave women are thievish, lazy and useless trash." He got little help from his parishioners. They had initially received him with "both love and respect," but these sentiments had cooled under his incessant ranting. When he became involved in the struggle at the top, and violently attacked Minuit in particular, the Classis decided it was time to recall him. He left the same time as Minuit, reported extensively about his "divers encounters with the commander" to the Classis, was kindly thanked, but was never allowed by the company to return.[9]

His successor, Everardus Bogardus, was of similar character. More than twenty-five years younger than Michaëlius and still a bachelor when he arrived with Governor Wouter van Twiller in 1633, he too adopted the role of castigator of company officials. Both Van Twiller and his successor, Willem Kieft, were his special enemies, and like Michaëlius, he did not hesitate to use the pulpit to tell the fascinated congregation of their shortcomings. Van Twiller was only "a child of the Devil," but Kieft was worse. He was intelligent enough—after the experience of his predecessor— to collect from the start a record of all the incidents the pastor caused, and on January 2, 1646, he produced an impressive list.[10]

The pastor had always been a healthy drinker, and it had been noted: September 25, 1639—"being thoroughly drunk, you grossly abused the Director; March 1643—after the conviction of Maryn Adriaensen, who had tried to kill Kieft, "you fulminated for about

PASTORAL PROBLEMS

14 days and desecrated even the pulpit by your passion"; 1644—
Laurens Cornelissen, convicted perjurer and thief "found immediately a patron in you, because he bespattered the Director with lies and you were daily making good cheer with him"; Summer 1644 —"You came drunk into the pulpit in the afternoon; also on the Friday before Christmas of the same year." Kieft once reprimanded the pastor when he arrived drunk for a supper at the fiscaal's house, and Bogardus hit back from the pulpit, asking "what else are the greatest in the land but vessels of wrath and fountains of evil."[11]

This was the start of a long feud that was with the greatest difficulty patched up only after one and a half years, thanks to the mediation of other dominies. But Bogardus' vicarage remained the center of resistance to the pompous and short-tempered director general. The violently anti-Kieft pamphlet *Broad Advice*, of course, found excuses for the bad image of the pastor. "Everhardus Bogardus, many times in his sermons freely expressed himself against the horrible murders, covetousness, and other gross excesses. The Director reported falsely of the minister that he was drunk in the pulpit. . . ."[12]

What the company thought of this firebrand is not known, but the Classis told him that if he wished to return, they "shall not fail to defend the honour of a minister, our honoured colleague." It was not necessary. Bogardus, who traveled back in 1647 with Kieft on the *Princess*, perished with the governor and all his panoply off the coast of Wales.[13]

One more fighting minister was to climb into the pulpit—which during Bogardus' time had moved from the little wooden church near the East River to the stone Church of St. Nicholas in the fort —before moderation took over. This was Dominie Johannes Cornelis Backerus, a not very bright or well-educated man, who in 1640 was rejected by the Classis as comforter of the sick since he could not sing, "having a natural defect." A year later he applied again, but now it was the company that wanted nothing to do with him, since it had decided "not to take any more idiots as ministers in their service." Backerus succeeded in changing the directors' minds, and was sent in 1643 to Curaçao for a salary of one hundred guilders a month, two hundred guilders board a year, and free firewood. When, on his way to New Amsterdam in 1647, Peter Stuyvesant made a detour and stopped at the is-

A SWEET AND ALIEN LAND

land, Backerus' term of office had just come to an end and the governor offered him a trip to Manhattan, from whence he could take a boat to Holland.[14]

Arriving in New Netherland, they learned that Bogardus had received his letter of recall, and Stuyvesant persuaded the reluctant Backerus to stay until a permanent successor was chosen. The newcomer was appalled by the state of affairs in the province, and asked immediately for "pastors without fear for punishing the sinners." Schoolmasters, too, were badly needed, since the children for lack of a decent school were running wild. "Their parents are so depraved, that they are now ashamed to learn anything good."[15]

Probably moved by compassion for his flock of 170 souls, he joined the rebels against the company regime, and like his two predecessors made his church hall a center for their meetings. He supported so openly the composer of the Remonstrance of 1650 that Stuyvesant personally had to call him to order. After Backerus returned to the Republic in 1649, his continuing help to the petitioners aroused the wrath of the company, and it was impossible for him to get a new appointment. In the end he left for the East Indies.[16]

New Amsterdam was now without a minister, but not for long. Stuyvesant, who had taken a liking to Johannes Megapolensis, the calm and distinguished pastor of Rensselaerswyck, saw his opportunity when the dominie ended his employment in the north and came to New Amsterdam to sail back to Holland. His wife and four children were already on their way when the governor approached him. The forty-six-year-old Megapolensis was understandably reluctant—after seven years in New Netherland he wanted a change. But Stuyvesant went ahead in his usual forceful way, and on August 2, 1649, a resolution was adopted by the Council, which stated that "the extreme needs of the church work imperatively demands, that at least one clergyman remain in this province . . . were it only for administering Baptism to the children who are commonly presented here every Sunday at the Manhatans for baptism alone sometimes one, sometimes two, yea even 3 and 4 together." The Council therefore had decided not to accept the excuses of Megapolensis and to retain him "with flattering force and as it were against his wishes." Megapolensis reluctantly recalled his family.[17]

PASTORAL PROBLEMS

The pastor was the first of New Amsterdam's preachers who did not meddle in the many confrontations between authority and citizenry. He kept strictly to his ecclesiastical work, relieved to be freed from the task Kiliaen van Rensselaer had given him when he left in 1642 for the patroon's domain—that of keeping an eye on the young men who ran Rensselaerswyck, and who, according to the Dutch merchant, "do not think at all of my interests."[18]

He had earned very little. Van Rensselaer paid him only one thousand guilders the first three years, and twelve hundred the last three, but in spite of financial problems, Megapolensis had patiently spread the gospel and made a thorough study of the Mohawk Indians around the trading post at Fort Orange, collecting a vocabulary of their language. The Indians had not been very helpful, he complained: "One tells me the word in the indicative; one in the first, another in the second person; one in the present, another in the preterit. So I stand sometimes and do not know how to put it down." Still, his *Short Account,* sent to Holland in 1644, did not portray the natives as scathingly as had the reports of his predecessor Michaëlius.[19]

For the sake of the simple-minded colonists, Megapolensis wrote during his stay at the northern border a shortened catechism, the *Schriftelicke Examinatien ofte Confessie* ("Written Examination or Confession"), which his wife Machteld took with her to Amsterdam in 1649. She showed the book to the Classis and the West India Company, which published it for use in New Netherland and Brazil.

At Rensselaerswyck the Calvinistic pastor also demonstrated his generosity toward his Roman Catholic "competitors" for the souls of the Indians. When Father Isaac Jogues, after a year of imprisonment and torture by the Mohawks, came into the neighborhood of Rensselaerswyck in 1645, Megapolensis played an important part in his rescue. His tolerance toward him and later Jesuit visitors was the more astonishing as Megapolensis, born in Cologne, had been a Catholic himself until the age of twenty-three. He did not lack prejudice against "Popery," but he certainly did not have the fanaticism of so many converts. In 1645 he saved another Jesuit priest, Father Bressani, from the Indians, and later he graciously played host to Father Simon le Moyne. This priest, however, went a bit too far when he sent the minister three booklets he had written about the Pope, heretics, and the Council. In the accompa-

A SWEET AND ALIEN LAND

nying letter he told Megapolensis that "Christ hanging on the Cross was still ready to receive him." The dominie composed a convincing reply, ending it nevertheless with the kind words: "Thine and Yours, with affection of heart even to the Altars."[20]

In 1649 this kindhearted and mild-mannered man, with his wife Machteld and his four children (Hillegont, twenty-one; Dirrick, nineteen; Jan, seventeen; and Samuel, fifteen), settled into the bustling and rebellious community of New Amsterdam, which was growing so rapidly that in 1652 a second clergyman was engaged. He was the fifty-year-old Samuel Drisius (Dries), considered a discovery by the Classis and the company. He had been a minister in London, but had come back to Holland "on account of the perturbances in England." On February 26, 1652, he had presented himself to the Classis of Amsterdam to ask for employment in New Netherland. Since the West India Company was looking for a dominie who could preach in both English and Dutch, the Classis gave him a trial, which was, according to the reports, "not only sufficient, but to the great satisfaction of the brethren." It told the company that "His Reverence is considered a very desirable person to serve the Church of God in New Netherland."[21]

The Heeren XIX wrote enthusiastically to Stuyvesant, who had asked for assistance for the "old gentleman, ds. Megapolensis." "He has the reputation of being a very pious man and possessed of great gifts, is able to preach in both languages, English and Dutch, and if necessary even in French." Almost more important was that "he is said to be of a very peaceful disposition and agreeable conversation." They had allowed him a salary of 100 guilders a month and 250 guilders for board, and since he was still a bachelor, they thought that he could live with the La Montagne family.[22]

Drisius did not disappoint them. In fact, he proved to have great diplomatic talents. Stuyvesant sent him in December 1653 as an envoy to Virginia's governor, Richard Bennet, to work out a continuation of the "correspondence, peace and commerce between them" in spite of the Anglo-Dutch War. Drisius did not succeed in completing an agreement, but Virginia at least kept out of the hostilities that New England organized in 1654.[23]

Megapolensis and Drisius got on very well, sharing their task equally. The latter took over duties in the villages around New Amsterdam, preached for the English in Flushing and Hempstead,

PASTORAL PROBLEMS

and visited the Huguenots on Staten Island every two weeks. The last was a very rich group, now growing so rapidly that in 1656 the public documents in the province were not only drawn up in English and Dutch, but in French as well.[24]

In 1654 Drisius was relieved of one part of his heavy burden when Dominie Johannes Theodorus Polhemius (Polheim) joined the clerical fraternity in New Netherland. The fifty-six-year-old pastor, born in the Palatinate, had a stormy past. Having twice fled from his home country, which was tormented by religious persecution, he had asked the West India Company in 1635 to send him to the West Indies. That year he arrived in Brazil, from whence he, his wife Catharina, and his four children were again driven away, this time by the Portuguese, who in 1654 reconquered the whole of Brazil from the Dutch.[25]

Polhemius arrived in the summer of that year at Manhattan on board the *St. Charles*, penniless and without his family, whom he had sent straight to the Netherlands in the hope of collecting his arrears of salary from the company. The congregations of Midwout, Amersfoort, and Breukelen had for some time urgently requested their own dominie, and Stuyvesant asked Polhemius to take on the job. The adventurous minister accepted at once, but even for him it must have been a thankless task. The company was slow in paying, and the pious in the province were not much better.

While his wife in Holland struggled to keep her head above water, Polhemius had to live on credit. When at last in 1656 Catharina—the Classis called her a "very worthy matron [who] always conducted herself modestly and piously"—came over with the children, his debt amounted to nine hundred guilders and his vicarage was still unfinished. Stuyvesant had once shipped over "110 green planks," but they disappeared, and the dominie complained to the governor that his "house remains open as it was and I with my wife and children must live and sleep on the bare ground and in the cold."[26]

Catharina Polhemius had not been able to raise much cash for her husband. The company had refused to give her the money she demanded, and had paid only for her crossing to New Netherland. The villagers decided, therefore, to pass the hat around and collected six hundred guilders. But it was for one time only, and at the end of December 1656 Stuyvesant intervened and obliged Breu-

A SWEET AND ALIEN LAND

kelen to pay a yearly stipend of three hundred guilders. Amersfoort owed the same sum, and Midwout four hundred guilders. Breukelen opposed the decision violently. "Every two weeks he comes here only for a quarter of an hour on Sunday afternoon," they wrote to the governor, adding that he "gives us only a prayer instead of a sermon, from which we learn and understand little." But Stuyvesant was adamant and brought the congregation into court, where they received a fine and a sermon they understood very well. By 1658 most of the problems in the Long Island congregations seemed to have been solved. Polhemius could even tell his two fellow dominies in New Amsterdam that at last a little church had been built.[27]

After the first years the thin sapling of Dutch Calvinism in New Netherland, shaken by the vengeful hands of the pioneering pastors, had taken root under the caring hands of the last three ministers and was now a tree, ready to withstand the storms that threatened it from without.

HERETIC
CONFUSION

On the French privateer, *St. Charles*, which brought Dominie Polhemius to New Amsterdam, were other and less welcome immigrants—twenty-three Jews. Like the minister, they had been driven from Brazil by the Portuguese victors, and the Dutch ship carrying them back to the Netherlands was halted by a Spanish freebooter. This, in turn, was captured by the *St. Charles*, whose master dropped off his miserable passengers in September 1654 in the nearest port, New Amsterdam. They were received with hostility in the capital where, just a month before, the first Jewish traders had arrived from Holland.[1]

The refugees—"healthy but poor"—turned to one of those first Jews, the Amsterdammer Jacob Barsimon, who was known to have arrived with some money. They had promised the French captain, Jacques de la Mothe, to pay twenty-five hundred guilders for their transport, but most of them had nothing left. Barsimon, pitiless, said "he would not lend them a single stuiver," and it was the kindhearted Megapolensis who came to their rescue. He wrote to Amsterdam that they had come several times to his house, "weeping and bemoaning their misery," and although he was not at all happy with their coming, he spent "several hundred guilders for their support."[2]

The church was not rich enough to solve the problem of their passage money, and on September 7 Master De la Mothe requested the City Court to sell "whatever furniture and other property" the Jews had on board to pay their debts. One of the Jews appeared in court and told the magistrates that about nine hundred guilders had been paid and that the rest would follow. The court gave him twenty-four hours, but he failed to appear and on September 10 De la Mothe received permission to sell the goods within four days.[3]

The sale was not a great success—it raised nothing like twenty-five hundred guilders—and on September 16 the greatest debtors disappeared into the cell under City Hall "until they shall have made satisfaction." They must have found money quickly, since on October 5 only one debtor—for a sum of 106 guilders—reappeared in court, Asser Levy. He protested that he was not bound to pay any more, as he had offered payment before the auction, on condition that his goods should not be sold. The court was unrelenting.[4]

The newcomers began to look around for accommodations, with the obvious intention of settling down. The Dutch watched in horror (in spite of the company's instructions, New Amsterdam was never as tolerant as Amsterdam), and General Stuyvesant at once wrote a violent letter to the Lords Directors asking them to recall the Brazilian Jews, and to stop their emigration from the Republic, as nobody could trust these people "with their usual usury and deceitful business towards the Christians."[5]

The governor's protest was supported by Megapolensis, who for all his kindness felt that New Amsterdam was rapidly turning into a religious Babel. "We have here Papists, Mennonites and Lutherans among the Dutch," he wrote in March 1655 to the Classis, "also many Puritans or Independents and many atheists and various other servants of Baäl . . . it would create a still greater confusion, if the obstinate and immovable Jews came to settle here." He had heard that more would come from the Republic and Brazil, and that they had plans to build a synagogue. "This causes among the congregation here a great deal of complaint and murmuring," the pastor reported. "These people have no other God than the Mammon of unrighteousness and no other aim than to get possession of Christian property."[6]

Both governor and dominie knocked at the wrong door. The company in Amsterdam had no intention of recalling the Jews, seeing their immigration as a valuable contribution to the population of New Amsterdam. It was typically the attitude of Amsterdam, where the Jews had received permission to establish their first congregation in 1605. There they were not forced to live in ghettos as they were in the rest of Europe or to wear a distinguishing sign, and their customs were respected. The Jews in Amsterdam formed a community, which was not loved but was at least left in peace. Many of them amassed great wealth, and the Sephardic Jews in particular, who had fled to Holland from Portugal and Spain, made an important contribution to Dutch intellectual life and the commercial supremacy of Amsterdam.

The West India Company, struggling to stay afloat, needed Jewish money badly and would at no cost insult at least 4 percent of their investors by boycotting any Jewish trader who might wish to go to New Netherland. They had been free to go to Brazil. To call them back now "would be unreasonable and unfair, especially because of the considerable loss, sustained by the Jews in the taking of Brazil," the Heeren XIX piously wrote to Stuyvesant, adding more honestly: "and also of the large amount of capital which they have invested in shares of this Company." The letter was sent on April 26, 1655, and on its receipt Stuyvesant had to hastily revoke a resolution, handed over to the burgomasters of New Amsterdam by Van Tienhoven on March 1, in which the Jews were ordered "to depart forthwith."[7]

Permission to stay did not mean that Stuyvesant considered them normal burghers. The company had instructed him to give the Jews "the same privileges, as they have here [in Amsterdam] . . . only as far as civil and political rights are concerned, without giving the said Jews a claim to the privileges of exercising their religion in a synagogue." But the general thought even that too generous.[8]

From the start he obstructed the Jews in every way possible. When two of them leased houses in December 1655, he tried to stop them, and at the same time forbade them to trade on the Delaware and at Fort Orange. On November 29 the Jews petitioned him not to restrict their activities, but Stuyvesant rejected the request "for weighty reasons." A new petition followed in March 1656, in which the Jews reminded the governor of the rights the company had granted them. They told him they were "willing and ready . . . to contribute according to their means," if they were allowed to enjoy the same liberties as the other citizens. Stuyvesant turned

A SWEET AND ALIEN LAND

to Amsterdam for advice, and on June 14 the Lords Directors made it clear that the Jews were indeed free to trade and purchase real estate. They were highly displeased with the general and told him reprovingly: "We wish . . . that you had obeyed our orders, which you must always execute punctually and with more respect."[9]

A number of restrictions were upheld. No Jews could be employed in any public service, nor were they allowed to have "open retail shops." They could exercise their religion only "within their houses." Stuyvesant added to this list of company instructions one of his own: he refused the Jews the right to join the militia of the city, in view of the "disgust and unwillingness of the trainbands to be fellow soldiers with the aforesaid nation." Instead they were to pay an exemption tax of sixty-five stuivers a month.[10]

The Jews were not resentful, and they were more generous than the governor. When in the aftermath of the Indian massacre of 1655 the burgomasters asked for a contribution for the strengthening of the city wall, five Jews gave five hundred guilders between them, one-twelfth of the total. This might have influenced Stuyvesant's decision shortly afterward to grant them a concession he had refused a year earlier—they were now allowed to have their own burial place outside the city (at what is now Chatham Square in Chinatown), a mile from the wall.[11]

But an underlying resentment of the Jews remained, and when in 1658 a Portuguese Jew, David de Ferrera, involved in a confusing transaction with beavers, uttered "hasty words in Hebrew" to the schout, he was sentenced to a public scourging at the stake, banishment from the province, a fine, and confiscation of all his goods. It took the intervention of a friend, Joseph d'Acosta, an important shareholder of the West India Company, and an appeal to Stuyvesant, to reduce the punishment to a fine of twenty guilders.[12]

Less fortunate than De Ferrera was a twenty-three-year-old Englishman, Robert Hodgson, who arrived in New Netherland on August 6, 1657, with the intention of showing the Dutch the emptiness of their religion. Hodgson was a member of the Society of Friends, or Quakers, and had together with eleven other fanatical adherents of this new sect crossed the Atlantic on a small ship, the *Woodhouse,* looking for the Mount Ararat on which they might land

HERETIC CONFUSION

their ark. Their first stop in this search was Manhattan, where the Dutch gazed in astonishment at the strange ship "having no flag flying from the topmast, nor from any other place." It failed to fire the customary shots and the leader, Robert Fowler, received the schout on board without "honour and respect."[13]

Peter Stuyvesant, who came to the quayside to have a look at the bizarre intruder, was startled to see before him a somberly dressed man who kept "his hat firm on his head, as if a goat." With relief he heard that they were on their way to New England and Rhode Island, and his welcome was "moderate both in words and actions."[14]

Relief soon changed to outrage. The *Woodhouse* did sail the next day, but, reported Megapolensis, it left "several behind them here, who laboured to create excitement and tumult among the people —particularly two women, the one about twenty, and the other about twenty-eight." The two young women, Dorothy Waugh and Mary Weatherhead, had begun, in the words of the dominie, "to quake and go into a frenzy, for the day of judgment was ahead. Our people not knowing what was the matter, ran to and fro, while one cried 'Fire' and another something else." The schout finally led them both to jail, where they "continued to cry out and pray according to their manner," until they were hastily shipped off.[15]

One of the group, Robert Hodgson, fled to Long Island, where for two months he succeeded in spreading his gospel, bringing "several under his influence." In Hempstead, however, he was arrested and taken to New Amsterdam. The court, "in order to repress the evil in the beginning," sentenced him "to work at the wheelbarrow for two years with the Negroes." Hodgson refused and when the New England merchant Thomas Willett warned the general of the dangers of this new sect—"men of perfidious opinions"—Stuyvesant listened. Hodgson was sentenced to be whipped on the back in public.[16]

The Quaker was not only young and fanatical, but tough as well, and he refused to give in. "After two or three days he was whipped in private on his bare back, with threats that the whipping would be repeated again after two or three days," revealed Megapolensis. But Stuyvesant's sister, Anna Bayard, intervened and under her influence the governor stopped the punishment and left Hodgson quietly in his cell. According to Megapolensis' story,

A SWEET AND ALIEN LAND

Stuyvesant had also received an anonymous letter in English proposing: "My Lord Director, whether it is not best to send him to Rhode Island, as his labour is hardly worth the cost."[17]

Hodgson was hardly on his way to Rhode Island when his place was taken by other Quakers, who concentrated their attention on Long Island. The Flushingers willingly gave shelter to the "heretical and abominable sect." They even had the impertinence to protest a Council order of February 1656 that forbade all conventicles and meetings except "the usual and authorised ones, where God's reformed and ordained word is preached . . . conform to the Synod of Dort."[18]

It was not the first time that Flushing had rebelled against such an order. In November 1656 the inhabitants had flocked together to listen to "one William Wickendam, while the latter . . . had neither by ecclesiastical or secular authorities been called." The self-appointed preacher was sentenced to a fine of one hundred Flemish pounds and banishment, but when Stuyvesant heard that he was a poor cobbler with a wife and several children, he remitted the fine and let him go "on condition that if he is caught here again, he must pay it." The governor was much less lenient with Schout William Hallett, who had allowed the meetings to go on, and forced him to pay a fine of fifty pounds before exiling him.[19]

Hallett's successor, Tobias Feake, was almost as bad. It was under his guidance that the Flushingers harbored the Quakers and wrote a remonstrance in 1658, in which they refused to persecute them, "for out of Christ God is Consuming fire and it is a fearful thinge to fall into the handes of the liveing God," they wrote, adding: "wee desire therefore in this case not to judge least wee be judged, neither to Condem least wee been Condemed but rather let every man stand and fall on his own." They pointed out to the governor that this attitude made them in fact "true subjects both of Church and State," as it was according to "the Pattent and Charter of our Towne given unto us in the name of the States Generall." But Stuyvesant was not impressed and Feake was arrested when he came to New Amsterdam to deliver the document. He was later dismissed as schout and banished.[20]

The trouble with the pertinacious Quakers was by no means over, and Stuyvesant judged it necessary to organize a day of prayer in order to ward off the "Spirit of Error" which scattered "its injurious poison amongst us." But the fasting and praying of

_____ (295) _____

HERETIC CONFUSION

January 21, 1659, against the "unheard of abominable Heresy called Quakers" was a very softhearted measure compared to those taken in New England. The Puritans of Massachusetts boasted that by the autumn of 1659 over forty Quakers had been whipped, sixty-four imprisoned, more than forty banished, one branded, three had had their ears cut off, and four had been put to death. One victim was so brutally tortured that "his Flesh was beaten Black, and as into Gelly, and under his Arms the bruised Flesh and Blood hung down, clodded as it were in bags."[21]

Stuyvesant in the end found the only reasonable solution: banishment. In 1663 he sent the leader of the Friends, John Bowne, to Holland. There he found a kind ear with the Heeren XIX, who again adopted the pragmatic view that population was more important than religion. "Although we heartily desire, that these and other sectarians remained away from there, yet as they do not," they wrote to Stuyvesant, "we doubt very much, whether we can proceed against them rigorously without diminishing the population and stopping immigration. . . . You may therefore, shut your eyes."[22]

This order of leniency came too late for Dominie Johannes Ernestus Goetwater, the Lutheran pastor who arrived in New Amsterdam on the *Meulen* ("Mill") in July 1657, a few days before the first Quakers.

There was a considerable number of Lutherans in New Amsterdam, and until 1653 they had gone meekly to St. Nicholas Church. On October 4 of that year they petitioned Stuyvesant for their own minister, but the governor—"good of religion"—told the worried Megapolensis and Drisius that "he would prefer to lose office than to permit this." The two clergymen advised the Classis not to grant the request, as New Netherland "threatened to become a receptacle of heresies." The Classis agreed.[23]

The Lutherans remained restless. They had two objections against the Reformed Church, both having to do with the baptism of children. According to a recently introduced formulary, parents were asked at the christening if they acknowledged "the dogma taught in the Christian Church there according to the Synod of Dort"—the cornerstone of the Reformed Church—and there was

A SWEET AND ALIEN LAND

a rule that both parents had to be present at the baptism. Stuyvesant and the two dominies refused to change these procedures, and when the Lutherans started their own meetings, some of them were thrown in jail.[24]

The Heeren XIX were again displeased with the high-handed action of their intolerant governor, who threatened with his persecutions their precious population. "We would have been better pleased, if you had not . . . committed them to prison, for it has always been our intention to treat them quietly and leniently," they wrote to him on June 14, 1656. One month later it leaked out in New Amsterdam that the West India Company had given freedom of worship to the obstinate Lutherans. This was denied by the company, which, in fact, had only given them permission to have "free religious exercises in their houses." Only a year later, however, the Lords Directors confirmed Johannes Goetwater as the first Lutheran pastor in New Amsterdam, in accordance with the treaty made after the conquest of New Sweden, which stipulated that a Lutheran pastor should be allowed to stay in the province.[25]

The Classis protested that this was a precedent "which would in the future damage the Truth," and sent a hasty warning to Megapolensis, who went into action the moment Goetwater arrived. Together with Drisius, he composed a lengthy petition to the governor, the burgomasters, and the schepens of New Amsterdam, begging them to get rid of this "snake in our bosom." As a result Goetwater was summoned before the Council and ordered by "Gen. Stiebzandt" to abstain from all clerical activities until his commission arrived.[26]

Megapolensis was far from satisfied with this maneuver and begged Stuyvesant to exile Goetwater for "the prosperity of our church." But the general hesitated, and by the time he finally agreed in October, the pastor had already gone into hiding. Anxiously Megapolensis told the Classis that "his bedding and books were two days ago removed, and that he has left our jurisdiction." He knew that the Lutherans at Fort Orange had collected beaver skins to the value of eight hundred guilders for Goetwater, who was now able to stay in hiding for some time, paying "Laurens the Norman" six guilders board a day. But eventually he became ill and was obliged to give himself up, and in the spring of 1659 he sailed disheartened back to the Netherlands.[27]

HERETIC CONFUSION

The Heeren XIX, with their customary flexibility in matters of conscience, had in the meantime found a solution to the problem, which satisfied the Lutherans completely. In letters written in May and June of 1658 they advised Stuyvesant to go back to the old formulary of baptism, and also to omit the words "present here in church" so that Lutheran parents could from now on stay away if they wanted to.[28]

One sadly neglected group of believers in the province was the Roman Catholics. Both Father Isaac Jogues and Simon le Moyne had visited some of them. "Entering a house quite near the fort he saw two images on the mantlepiece, one of the blessed Virgin, the other of our blessed Louys de Gonzage," wrote Father Buteux about Jogues' visit to New Amsterdam in 1643. The Jesuit was told by the master of the house that his wife was a Catholic from Portugal.[29]

Father Le Moyne, fifteen years later, met more of his co-religionists, who under the suspicious eyes of Dominie Megapolensis flocked around him during the eight days he spent in the capital. "He . . . liberally dispenses his indulgences," reported the dominie telling "the Papists (in the hearing of one of our people who understood French) that they need not go to Rome." With this message, the Catholics in New Amsterdam had to be content, as no other visit by a Roman Catholic priest is recorded.[30]

The English Protestants were not much better off. Flushing had been left without a pastor since 1655, when Reverend Francis Doughty had gone to Virginia. Discouraged by lack of support from the congregation, Doughty left the field open to "troublesome fellows" like the cobbler William Wickendam and the Quakers. At Newtown an Independent preacher—"of the same way of thinking," noted Megapolensis happily—took care of the souls, but he died on October 13, 1653, "of a pestilential disease," leaving a wife and eight children.

The Dutch ministers in New Amsterdam accepted the Independents but preferred the Presbyterians, and Presbyterianism had for a long time a pastor in New Netherland, Richard Denton at Hempstead. He was, Megapolensis assured the Classis, "a pious, godly and learned man, who is in agreement with our church in

A SWEET AND ALIEN LAND

anything," and he was respected by Presbyterians and Independents alike. But Denton, "complaining of lack of salary," returned in 1657 to England, where a legacy of four hundred pounds awaited him.[31]

Places like Gravesend and Oostdorp never had a minister, and Megapolensis and Drisius both informed the Classis that they were "in great want of English ministers." If the company did not take care, "errorists and fanatics may find opportunity to gain strength, and New Netherland might become as bad as Rhode Island."[32]

The Classis did nothing about the problem, and the Heeren XIX contented themselves with telling Stuyvesant that the only solution for the shortage of ministers was to use "the least offensive and most tolerant means, so that people of other persuasions may not be deterred from the public Reformed Church, but in time be induced to listen and finally gained over to it."[33]

If not the most satisfactory advice, it was at least cheap.

THE FAILURE
OF AMSTERDAM

The souls of the English population in New Netherland were a cause of great concern to the dominies of New Amsterdam, but they were much more worried about the spiritual welfare of the Swedish subjects of the West India Company at the Delaware. After New Sweden's capture by Governor Stuyvesant in 1655, the two hundred Swedes living in and around Fort Christina had been left in the care of their Lutheran pastor, Lars Lokenius. He was, in the words of Dominie Megapolensis, "a man of impious and scandalous habits, a wild, drunken, unmannerly clown, more inclined to look in the wine-can than into the Bible." Worse still, when "the sap is in the wood his hands itch and he wants to fight whomsoever he meets."[1]

In the spring of 1657 one incident particularly startled and amused the mixed community of Swedes and Dutch on the South River. The minister had been "tippling" with the local smith, "and while yet over their brandy they came to fisticuffs, and beat each other's head black and blue; yea, that the smith tore all the clothing from the preacher's body, so that this godly minister escaped in primitive nakedness."[2]

These scandalous goings-on were reported to the two embarrassed clergymen by Jean Paul Jacquet, who straight from Brazil had been appointed vice director of the newly-conquered colony in 1655. Andries Hudde, the commissary at Fort Casimir, became

A SWEET AND ALIEN LAND

his schout and secretary. The two men ran the affairs of the trading station, keeping a wary eye on the subdued Swedes, who were unexpectedly reinforced by the arrival of 130 colonists on board the *Mercurius* in March 1656.[3]

The newcomers were deeply disappointed that the colony had changed hands while they were at sea. Governor Stuyvesant at once sent orders to Jacquet not to let them land, but the stubborn Swedes sailed on and settled a few miles from Casimir. The captain of a Dutch warship, still cruising in the river after the conquest, was instructed to arrest them, and returned to Manhattan with the *Mercurius* in tow. A short skirmish about duties followed, but after the Swedes had paid 750 guilders, they were allowed to return to their native country.[4]

The nominal fee that the Swedes had paid for their trespass was small consolation to the West India Company, which was still smarting over the cost (about twenty-five thousand guilders) of Stuyvesant's conquest. But the city of Amsterdam came to the company's rescue. Much interested in the timber along the heavily-forested South River, which could make Amsterdam independent of the Baltic for the many masts the port needed, the city magistrates approached the Heeren XIX. In the middle of 1656 Stuyvesant heard that they were negotiating with "their Noble Worships the Lords Burgomasters of this city in regards to the establishment of some colonies there, which negotiations we think, will soon be brought to an end." The deal was concluded not long afterward and Fort Casimir, with all the land from Christina Kill to the mouth of the Delaware, changed hands for the sum of 700,000 guilders. Fort Christina remained the property of the West India Company.[5]

Amsterdam tackled the organization of its new possession with great enthusiasm, appointing six directors, who at once drew up grandiose plans for the development and populating of what they called New Amstel. A small town would be the first priority, protected by a wall and a moat. The land inside was to be divided into streets, a market, and lots for houses. In the center would be built a "public building suitable for Divine service," a school, and a vicarage. The whole should be governed by three burgomasters and five to seven schepens, "to be chosen by the Burghers, from the honestest and fittest."[6]

To attract settlers, the most favorable conditions were offered.

THE FAILURE OF AMSTERDAM

"Every farmer shall have in free, fast and durable property as many morgens, as well of plough-land as of meadow, as he and his family can improve." The colonists would not be taxed for ten years, they could cut as much wood as they needed for their houses or ships, they were allowed to hunt and fish wherever they liked, and they would be able to buy all the necessities of life in a warehouse amply stocked by Amsterdam.[7]

The publicity campaign was carried out in great style, and on December 19 the West India Company told Stuyvesant that the effect was evident "in the thronging of people." Six days later the first three ships with 160 new colonists left Texel.[8]

That Amsterdam had been serious in promising a well-stocked warehouse was proved by the long list of goods that went over with the expedition. Among other items, the cargo included two hundred pairs of Iceland stockings, forty pairs of Persian blue stockings, fifty men's hats, one hundred pairs dyed wool hose for women, and one hundred neckcloths. For the inner man, there were sixteen barrels of beef, nine of pork; four tierces of Spanish wine, four of brandy, and six of French wine; hundreds of bags of groats, dried peas, and beans; eight tons of salt; 250 pounds of cheese; codfish; and even two schepels of mustard. The 150 soldiers who had been promised to New Amstel (under the command of Captain Martin Cregier and his lieutenant, Alexander d'Hinoyosa), would be equipped with seventy-five muskets, seventy-five firelocks, and seventy-five swords, plus all their gear, and seventy straw beds. The whole bill came to the impressive total of 24,850 guilders.[9]

Although the venture appeared promising, the first voyage might have been seen as a bad omen. It was described in a letter that Jacob Alrich, leader of the expedition and the first director of New Amstel, wrote later from New Amsterdam. Three days after departure the three ships, the *Prins Maurits* with 128 souls on board, the *Geldersche Blom* ("Gelderland Flower") with 11, and the *Beer* ("Bear") with 33, were separated by a heavy winter storm, which seriously damaged the *Maurits*. The sails were blown out of their bolts, the cannon rolled from the carriages, and seven members of the crew, who tried to repair the damage, were almost swept overboard. The ship was obviously not very seaworthy, and its master had to take a southerly, less stormy route, reaching the coast of America on February 17, 1657.[10]

Neither the captain nor any of the senior officers had ever been to New Netherland before, and in pitch darkness they went hopelessly off course. The ship entered shallow waters and ran aground. "We were not a moment certain whether we should leave there alive or perish," Alrich wrote. But daylight came after a night of "the greatest anxiety and fear" and the travelers discovered that they had landed "about a gunshot from the shore . . . between the shoals and the strand." Some of them boarded a leaky boat and rowed "in severe, bitter and freezing weather with drifting ice" through the dangerous breakers to the shore. They arrived at a barren piece of land "on which neither bush nor grass nor any firewood [was] to be found," and had to wait three days in the biting cold before some Indians appeared and told them they had landed on a foreland of Long Island, called Secoutagh (near present-day Islip).[11]

Alrich managed to persuade the Indians to carry a letter to Stuyvesant, asking for help for the desperate new colonists. They were all safe, but the *Maurits* was slowly breaking up, stranded "in a situation as if it were upon its burial ground." The general immediately sent a small sloop with a rescue party and two days later came himself to watch the salvage operation. They and the passengers succeeded in saving most of the cargo before the vessel was battered to pieces.[12]

In New Amsterdam Alrich had to charter another ship, the *Vergulde Bever* ("Gilded Beaver"), and sell part of the settlers' commodities, such as duffel and linen, to pay the rental fee of three thousand guilders. On April 13 he could at last announce that "the ship is ready to sail with us to the South River. God grant that we may arrive there speedily and in safety."[13]

It was another two weeks before the disheartened colonists reached New Amstel, but what they discovered there was some consolation after all their hardships. "I find the land here right good and well timbered," wrote schoolmaster Evert Pietersen in August. It was exactly what mast-hungry Amsterdam wished to hear. "I have been full 5 or 6 hours in the interior in the woods and found fine oak and hickory trees." The land was also very fertile, so that one to two thousand farmers could reap an "excellent crop."[14]

Alrich set to work with energy and determination. Wharves were laid out, land allocated, the winter grain was soon in the

THE FAILURE OF AMSTERDAM

ground, and Pietersen opened a school for twenty-five children. Even more encouraging was the arrival of the *Waegh* with more immigrants. With them traveled the first clergyman, Everardus Welius, still a young man, but "very laudable and promising in his way of life, his studies and his intercourse."[15]

The second expedition was not as easy to launch. When the directors of the new colony had asked for a loan of thirty-six thousand guilders to finance it, the burgomasters of Amsterdam had been astonished and irritated. New Amstel had cost them seventy-seven thousand guilders—twenty-five thousand for the first voyage, two smaller loans of six thousand and ten thousand guilders, and now thirty-six thousand for the second expedition. They felt it was time to take a closer look at the whole business, as "it was not the Council's intention to foster said Colony by excessive and endless expenditure."[16]

To the directors of New Amstel, the burgomasters sounded unpleasantly like the Heeren XIX, and they hastened to calm their backers. They told the City Fathers that no expedition in future would cost more than sixteen thousand guilders, "not doubting but the good fruits of the planting this colonie would manifest themselves in a short time, sooner or later." The magistrates studied these reassurances and, after some hesitation, voted the money in the hope of receiving "from time to time . . . more probable tokens of a good result."[17]

They waited in vain. All the news that reached them from their "pride and glory" was gloomy and depressing. Almost no crossing of the shiploads of immigrants took less than three months, and these were made dreadful by storms and high mortality at sea. The colony itself was plagued with epidemics of "a general feverlike disease," which spared no one and were caused, it was thought, by the miasmas from the low soggy soil with its rotting vegetation. Alrich himself almost died in July 1658, and in October he reported that "almost all people here . . . but a few old ones have died . . . rather many young children, who could not endure it." The harvest rotted away in the heavy autumn rains; "a worm has appeared in vast quantities," it was reported, "and seriously injured the crops and gardens." The morale of the colonists sank.[18]

House building for the projected town went ahead very slowly, and the former Fort Casimir—"in a great state of decay"—had to serve for storage, although the river had washed away part of it.

A SWEET AND ALIEN LAND

Alrich's own house was uncomfortably damp—"the greater part whereof still so leaky, that it is with the greatest difficulty anything can be kept dry." He had started to build a new guardhouse and a bakery, but wrote in October 1658 that half of it was still unroofed "for want of tiles."[19]

Provisions were quickly running out. Amsterdam had ordered Alrich to buy most of his supplies from Manhattan, but there were scarcities there too, and he begged Holland urgently to provide the colony, for at least its first year, "with whatever is not produced as yet in this country." The nine hundred skepels of grain that had been sown had yielded only six hundred; there was no butter; the price of peas was exorbitant; and cheese was beyond price. A winter that fell early and lasted long, with continuous dreary rains, stopped "all the labours of house and farm . . . for many months," and Alrich had to turn to Stuyvesant in New Amsterdam, begging him in January 1659 to "provide us somewhat with grain, peas and bacon as quickly as possible. . . ."[20]

Stuyvesant did what he could, but New Amstel's neighbor, the Company's colony Fort Christina on the Delaware, was not much better off. Around the former Swedish fort a small village had grown up, Altona. Jean Paul Jacquet had run its affairs until April 1657, when Governor Stuyvesant had been forced to dismiss him for incompetence and dishonesty. Since then, things had got out of hand. Schout Andries Hudde was no match for the many fur traders, and smuggling had become almost more frequent than regular trade, damaging the company's revenue from customs. The general had taken a look himself in May 1658 and had been flabbergasted.[21]

To bring some order, he appointed in June 1658 a new vice director. Willem Beeckman, one of the capital's first schepens and its most respected burgher, arrived in the village at the end of October, with a salary of fifty guilders per month and two hundred guilders a year for board.[22]

His neighbors at New Amstel were now in their third year and matters were no better. The year 1659 began badly for Alrich personally: his wife died of the fever in January. The rains never seemed to stop, and a desperate director wrote to Amsterdam in August that the year had been so wet and unseasonable that there was hardly grain enough for the people and the cattle—"add to which a multitude of new cases of sickness." Over one hundred

THE FAILURE OF AMSTERDAM

persons had died, and many cattle had been lost as well. The wretched settlers were so discouraged that scores of them begged to leave for Manhattan. They scraped their last money together and, according to one report, "offered it to Alrich and besought him with clasped hands to accept it in payment for their debts." But he refused, reminding them that they were bound for four years.[23]

There was only one way out—flight to the neighboring colonies of Virginia and Maryland. "About 50 persons, among them many families, removed within a fortnight," Stuyvesant was told, but Alrich made light of it, describing the people who had left as servants or deserting soldiers.[24]

The stories that these fugitives spread among the English had an unexpected result: they aroused the special interest of Maryland, the colony of the Roman Catholic Cecilius Calvert, second Baron of Baltimore. As the son and heir of George Calvert—who had just before his death in 1632 received a patent for a stretch of land from the River Potomac to present-day Philadelphia on the Delaware—he had sent over the first colonists in 1634. They were violently opposed by neighboring Virginia, which considered the charter for Baltimore an intrusion on its territory. This resentment was all the stronger since the Baron intended to make his colony a Catholic one. To promote immigration, he had, however, to promise religious tolerance, and in the end he was forced to restrain the zealous Jesuit priests in his domain, since their fanatical proselytizing did more harm than good.

In the years of Cromwell's Puritan Commonwealth, it often looked as though Baltimore would lose his patent. Protestants, crowding in, were rapidly gaining power, while the Virginians from their side did everything to encourage them. Baltimore, complaining to Cromwell, won and kept his colony, where in 1657 he appointed his strong man, Josias Fendall, as governor. With peace and quiet restored, Fendall was instructed by Baltimore to subdue the foreign plantations in his territory—in other words, to annex New Amstel and Altona, which lay on the Maryland side of the Delaware. The dissatisfaction that reigned in these colonies made the moment opportune in Fendall's eyes.

Alrich heard the first rumors in May of 1659 and asked New Amsterdam for troops, as he had only ten to fifteen men. But he decided not to wait for their reply and took the initiative by dis-

A SWEET AND ALIEN LAND

patching a messenger to Maryland in July to demand Dutch fugitives, in the hope of getting to know more about Fendall's plans.[25]

The news was bad. Colonel Nathaniel Utie, the president of Maryland's Council, had told the Dutch envoy that he had a commission to proceed to the Delaware. It had been sent by "Lord Balthus Moore." The news created great commotion on the Delaware, and Alrich wrote Amsterdam that everyone "is trying to remove or escape," using it as an excuse not to pay their debts.[26]

The dreaded Marylanders finally appeared on Saturday, September 9, 1659. "In the evening Col. Nathaniel Utie with his suite, altogether seven men, arrived at New Amstel," reported Beeckman from Altona. Nobody tried to stop him, and he walked around for two days before he asked for an interview. Alrich granted it hastily, pressing Beeckman to be present, and at the meeting Utie "first delivered a letter to Mr. Alrich and upon our request a copy of his instructions." Sharply he told the two Dutchmen that they were under Lord Baltimore's jurisdiction and he ordered them either to leave or to subject themselves. He wished for a direct answer, "else he would be obliged to use other means, of which bloodshed he should consider himself not guilty." He ended his threatening message by explaining that Maryland held the upper hand, "for your people are mostly run away and those, whom you have yet, will not assist you."[27]

With a great show of military correctness, Utie retired, leaving the two confused and agitated officials to settle on a plan of action. Beeckman proposed to arrest the Englishmen, but Alrich feared that "it would cause a revolt among the citizens, who were already much irritated against them." Instead, a protest was composed in which they rejected Baltimore's claim and declared themselves astonished by "these proceedings and treatment on the part of Christian brethren and neighbours," with whom they wanted nothing but friendship. The whole thing was in any case a breach of the Peace of Westminster, whereby "they were all ordered and commanded not to inflict, the one or the other, any hostility. . . ."[28]

Playing for time, they added that the colonel might as well leave, since they were unable to come to a decision without the permission of their directors. On September 11 Utie marched off, giving them three weeks' breathing time. Beeckman and Alrich sent off

THE FAILURE OF AMSTERDAM

messenger after messenger to New Amsterdam, but none of them got through for days. The Indians were at war and killed four of them, while another came back after eight days, unable to break through. In New Amstel there were no more than fifteen soldiers, half of them sick. From the other side of the border came information that Utie was gathering five hundred soldiers, who could be on the Delaware within one and a half days.[29]

At last, on September 23, one of the couriers reached the capital. Governor Stuyvesant at once wrote a castigating letter in reply. He did not understand how Alrich and Beeckman could have allowed Utie "to sow his seditious and mutinous seed among the community there for 4 or 5 days. . . . Forsooth, it shows of bad reflection and discouragement . . . he rather deserved to be arrested as a spy and sent hither." Fortunately the general did not limit himself to these severe words: he added that his secretary, Cornelis van Ruyven, and Burgomaster Martin Cregier were on their way with sixty soldiers.[30]

Stuyvesant was very angry with Alrich, and complained bitterly about his "shortsightedness" in a letter to Amsterdam. It would cost him a lot of trouble to redress the situation; military arguments would not be enough "to remedy what passed and to correct the blunders"; he would have to send an embassy to Maryland as well.[31]

Augustine Heerman, the Bohemian businessman, and Underschout Resolved Waldron left on Tuesday, September 30, for Maryland, with a strong protest against Utie's proceedings and Baltimore's claim. The journey was hazardous and tense. Their small boat was leaky, almost sank, and had to be repaired with some old rags. Well knowing that Utie would try to stop their mission at all costs, they sailed stealthily past his residency on Bear's Island in Cheassepeake Bay. In near-panic they listened to the shots and military music that came over the water from the island, spotting about fifty men, who looked ready for instant action. Heerman and Waldron halted at St. Mary's, a little coastal town, where from the house of their Dutch host, Simon Overzee, they asked for an audience with Governor Fendall, who was residing at Patuxent. They also sent a protest, in which they pointed out that the Dutch had been at the Delaware since 1623 and that there had been no objection to their presence from Virginia and Maryland until Colonel Utie arrived in September with threats to

A SWEET AND ALIEN LAND

take New Amstel "by force of arms, fire and sword."[32]

A week later they had a chance to go into greater detail. Philip Calvert, Lord Baltimore's half-brother and Fendall's secretary, sent them an invitation to come to Patuxent, where on the afternoon of October 6 Fendall and his Council, including Utie, welcomed the two Dutch envoys. After dinner Heerman and Waldron discovered that the Marylanders were not exactly well informed about the affair. They were under the impression that New Amstel was only a colony of Amsterdam and had nothing to do with the rest of New Netherland. Heerman protested and delivered a long speech, in which he went back to the days when the Netherlands were still under the rule of the Spanish, who, as the first discoverers of the New World, had given the Dutch in 1648 all the rights to such countries as had been conquered by them. This included New Netherland, of which New Amstel was a part.[33]

Utie was not impressed and angrily told his colleagues "not to take notice at all of this matter . . . and that if again commanded, he would act in a like manner." Heerman answered boldly that in that case he would be arrested "as a disturber of the public peace." This was too much for the choleric colonel, who demanded angrily whether he had to listen to these threats from people who had come uninvited. "Had he met us or have known of our coming, he would have detained us there and then," Heerman reported.[34]

The meeting broke up in confusion, but later in the day the two Dutch envoys heard that next morning they would be allowed to examine Lord Baltimore's patent as proof that he was the rightful owner of the Delaware. The rest of the evening was spent "in private conversation" over a glass of wine. Both Heerman and Waldron got on very well with most of their neighbors, and found that the majority favored "an intimate correspondence and confederation for reciprocal trade and intercourse." Even Fendall told Heerman that "he would prefer to continue in peace and quietness than to live in hostility and war."

Next day the Marylanders had reason to regret showing their guests Baltimore's patent. Heerman at once pointed out that it gave the Baron specifically "a tract of country in America which was neither cultivated nor planted but only inhabited, as yet, by barbarous Indians." It was obvious to him that it had not been the King's intention to bother the Dutch. Nonsense, retorted Fendall, the King had granted the patent "with full knowledge of the case."

THE FAILURE OF AMSTERDAM

Impatiently he asked Heerman to show them the patent of New Netherland. "We answered that we did not have it to show them, indeed our purpose in coming had been to prepare a way for a future meeting of deputies of both sides."

When the two Dutchmen were preparing to take their leave the following morning, Fendall handed them a protest at the Dutch intrusion on the Delaware, addressed to Governor Stuyvesant, and the debate started all over again. Heerman asked the governor if the Dutch would have to keep their army at New Amstel, and received the reply "that we must please ourselves in this matter, as they for their part would act as they thought best . . . and in this manner terminated our meeting."

After breakfast the next day, Sunday, October 9, they could at last go. It was "a friendly leave," and Philip Calvert in particular went out of his way to reassure the Dutch envoys that nothing would happen until Lord Baltimore's instructions had been received. Back in St. Mary's, Heerman wrote out his report, with which Waldron returned to New Amsterdam, while he himself traveled on to find out if the Virginians were still as pro-Dutch as ever.

Philip Calvert had clearly been impressed by the suave and able Heerman, and when the Bohemian, who was an expert mapmaker, as well as a successful businessman, dropped in at Patuxent again on his way home from Virginia, Calvert asked him to draw a detailed map of Maryland and Virginia. Heerman later received in payment a tract of land at the head of Patuxent Bay, where he built a stately manor, Nova Bohemia.

The reports that Calvert sent his half-brother in England must have been discouraging, since Lord Baltimore now abandoned military action in favor of diplomacy. In 1660 he sent a representative, Captain James Neale, to Holland to demand the ceding of the Delaware "in love and friendship," but the Heeren XIX declared themselves "surprised" at such a request and curtly rejected it.[35]

Later that year it looked for a moment as though the threat might be renewed. Fendall, after leading a rebellion against Lord Baltimore, was deposed as governor and replaced by Philip Calvert. Stuyvesant reported to the company that this "violent Papist" had received a confirmation from London of the Baron's patent and that Baltimore, not at all satisfied with the company's reaction in early 1660, "has now more hope to attain his aim and intention."[36]

In all this time not much had changed at the Delaware. Amsterdam, heartily sick of the mere name New Amstel, had tried in 1659 to sell the colony back to the West India Company, which understandably refused. In growing dismay the Amsterdammers read Alrich's desperate dispatches. He complained of "the superabundance of lazy, idle and all-devouring men . . . who are only good to eat and drink," of the diseases that went on tormenting the community, of the lack of provisions, and so forth, so that "this Colonie like a tender plant, has been crushed and downtrodden."[37]

At the end of 1659 the military commander of New Amstel, Lieutenant d'Hinoyosa, added more gloom. " 'Tis too late, the little ham is all eaten, the store is empty," he wrote. Alrich and he were by now bitter opponents. The director, ill for three months, was completely defeated and saw no future for New Amstel. He waited passively for ships with provisions to calm his restless colonists, while d'Hinoyosa wanted to fight on—"the Regents of Amsterdam should not allow to stop so noble a work," he urged in his letter.[38]

But he was alone. Dominie Welius, who had been a forceful peacemaker in the colony, died in December of the fever, after only eighteen months in New Amstel. And an eyewitness reported that the condition of the settlers was so abysmal that the colony could hardly be saved. The final blow seemed to come when the exhausted Alrich died on December 30, 1659, and d'Hinoyosa, "somewhat sharply and harshly," took his place. The settlers protested violently, but the lieutenant stayed on, and with some success. In September 1660 skipper Jacob Jansen Huys, the captain of Amsterdam's trading galliot *New Amstel,* wrote the directors in Amsterdam that not all hope was lost for their possession. "Were there a tolerably healthy population and a reasonable harvest, and a parcel of good farmers, it would still prosper, and the people who still remain there would again begin to pluck up fresh courage."[39]

It was not exactly the sort of news that the Amsterdam city fathers had anticipated when they had bought their colony four years earlier.

THE FAILURE OF AMSTERDAM

CLASH

WITH BOSTON

Of the three great rivers that had once been the arteries of New Netherland, the Fresh or Connecticut River was completely lost to the Dutch by the end of the 1650s; the South or Delaware River was under constant threat; and only the North or Hudson River seemed safe from English expansion. In 1659, however, the New Englanders proved that even this important trade route, along which tens of thousands of pelts yearly descended to New Amsterdam, had not escaped their attention. And surprisingly, the initiative for this assault on the heart of the Dutch province came from Massachusetts, the English colony that together with Plymouth had in the past been their most reasonable neighbor in the northeast.

Since the end of the Anglo-Dutch War in 1654, relations between the small Dutch province and the ever-growing New England colonies had been cool, but calm. The West India Company had expressed to Stuyvesant in 1656 the hope that "the undisturbed peace with England . . . will easily appease the ruffled mind of the English in the North," and for once the company seemed to be right. The Heeren XIX thought the moment had come for a settlement of the provincial boundaries, and they urged the States General to put the Hartford Treaty before the English. The States had obeyed, but without result. Cromwell was by now as much obsessed by the thought of a totally English America as the Stuart monarchs had been.[1]

Stuyvesant received proof of this in 1657 in the form of a letter addressed to the English subjects on Long Island, stirring them up to rebel against the government in New Amsterdam. Cromwell's letter "to the English well affectet in Habitaing, on Long Islant, in America" was never read by them. The magistrates of Gravesend sent it on unopened to Stuyvesant, who—himself afraid to break the seal of the Lord Protector—forwarded it to Amsterdam.[2]

The message from London was in any case well known, thanks to a pamphlet that had appeared in 1656 in London, called *A brief Narration of the English Rights to the Northern Parts of America*. It ignored completely the Treaty of Westminster, which had promised peace between England and the Republic and in "the lands under the Dominion of each;" and stated the old argument that the Dutch were intruders. James I had only granted Staten Island to the Netherlands as a "watering-place," the document claimed, and the Dutch had recognized English rights even there by initially calling their province Virginia. It was thus obvious that any Englishman living in New Netherland who subjected himself to the rule of Stuyvesant was betraying English rights.[3]

This propaganda had not discouraged Stuyvesant from getting in touch with the commissioners of the New England Federation to propose new talks, but their reaction had been chilly. They stated frankly, if undiplomatically, that "wee take noe pleasure in any contests with you." No new approaches for a meeting were made from either side, and contacts were rare and formal.

For Stuyvesant the response was more than enough, and he went out of his way to avoid any possibility of a new clash. When in October 1656 Solomon La Chair, notary and innkeeper, described the English in public as "a deceitful people," he was condemned to be tied to the stake and whipped, half his property was confiscated and he himself was imprisoned, because his remark was "directly contrary to the articles of peace entered into between both nations." La Chair apologized by declaring that he had spoken only about a certain Englishman and that he had "no idea of alluding to the whole English nation," upon which his punishment was reduced to a few weeks of house arrest.[4]

CLASH WITH BOSTON

In June 1659 this almost idyllic situation came to an abrupt end when Johannes La Montagne, since 1656 vice director at Beverwyck, was visited by some very distinguished gentlemen from Boston. He welcomed them with all honors, saluting them with the cannon of Fort Orange, and entertaining them with "a treat and a feast," that cost him 132.40 guilders.

But after their departure he had worrying news for Stuyvesant. The New Englanders had been looking for land, telling him that Massachusetts' charter gave it the right to all the territory north of the 42nd parallel. This meant, in effect, that Fort Orange lay within the jurisdiction of Boston, and that the border of New Netherland ran no further than eighty miles north of New Amsterdam. Massachusetts did not intend to occupy all the land, but the gentlemen, eager for a part of the fur trade, planned to build a trading post on the Hudson. They had picked a lovely spot near the mouth of Wappinger Creek, near present-day Poughkeepsie.

Quite apart from the fact that this spot was well below the 42nd parallel, the Boston settlement on the Hudson would be able to intercept Dutch fur traders and easily grab the monopoly. The company had just warned the governor once again to be on his guard against his neighbors "on account of their haughtiness and obstinate inclination to quarrel and to arrogate to themselves all authority." And Stuyvesant, realizing that "many hounds are the hare's death," knew the danger all too well. The English had played the same game at the Connecticut.[5]

The only way to stop the English strategy "to crawl along in time and finally obtain their end," the governor told the Heeren XIX, was to populate the land with twenty or thirty families. He hoped that the company would send him as soon as possible "some homeless Polish, Lithuanian, Prussian, Jutlandish or Flemish farmers." He himself, just recovering from a serious illness, would go in the autumn "to view the land and buy it from the savages."[6]

This letter, written on September 4, 1659, had hardly been posted when an astonishing communication from the commissioners of the United Colonies reached New Amsterdam. "We presume you have heard from your people of ffort of Orania that some of our English have bin lately in those partes," the commissioners wrote. They had come, they told Stuyvesant, to look for a place to settle within the bounds of Massachusetts, "without entrenchment of the Dutch rights." Foreseeing some difficulties for a

A SWEET AND ALIEN LAND

plantation so far from New England, they now requested free passage up the Hudson, as that "would very much accommodate them in their designe."[7]

The demands were even more serious than Stuyvesant had expected: an English trading post at the Wappinger Kill, free passage, and possibly even settlements around and above Fort Orange. In a hurry he dispatched the commissioners' letter to Amsterdam, asking for immediate help. At the same time, he rejected the request of the New Englanders in a firm letter, telling them that he had no idea what they were talking about, as he had never heard of a river called Hudson. If they meant the North River, then their demand for free passage was very unreasonable, "in regard that your Worships about 12 or 13 yeares time have forbidden, charged and hindred our Nation of any passage and Trade to and with the Indians Dwelling within your Bonds." And the Hartford Treaty had made it very clear that "the whole English nation" should not approach the North River nearer than ten miles.[8]

The answer, this time from the General Court of Massachusetts, was delivered to Stuyvesant by two delegates from Boston, Major William Hawthorne and John Richards, who came to New Amsterdam "to lett you understand our cleare & honest Intentions in the business."

In its long missive the Court explained that on the basis of Massachusetts' patent it was entitled to "some part of Hudsons River—a name," they added sharply, "well-knowne to the English before the arrivall of any Dutch in those parts." Till then Massachusetts had not bothered about the Dutch intrusion on their territory, "by reason of our remoteness," but being now "Increased & wanting Convenient places to settle or people, wee conceive no reason can be Imagined why wee should not Improve & make use of our just rights." It would be ridiculous, the Bostonians stated, for the Dutch not to allow free passage up the Hudson, since they "cannot be ignorant that the Rhine, the Elb with many other rivers passe through the Territories of divers Princes, yet afford passage to all in Amity." The Court denied finally that the "Contract made at Hartford" was binding for Massachusetts, whose commissioners at that time had only been arbitrators between New Netherland and Connecticut and New Haven.[9]

The two envoys from Boston hung on in New Amsterdam for

CLASH WITH BOSTON

some weeks, but could not succeed in convincing Stuyvesant. He told them "it would cost him his head" if he should permit them to sail up the Hudson. He offered to refer the whole matter to England and Holland, but Hawthorne and Richards refused, knowing, they told him, that he had a commission from the West India Company and the States General to negotiate himself. An exasperated Stuyvesant, remembering constantly that the power of New England "overbalances ours tenfold," tried to keep them talking and in the end "they parted placidly," promising that they would be back toward the end of the summer for a definitive answer.

Passing in February 1660 through New Haven on their way back to Boston the two envoys had talks with the Reverend John Davenport, who wrote in concern to John Winthrop Jr. in Hartford that "if the business proceeds as Major Hawthorne thinks it will, all the Colonies are likely to be engaged in a war with the Dutch."[10]

Stuyvesant waited till April 20 before sending a formal answer to Boston. He had not yet received a reply from the West India Company to his request for help—it had only been dispatched in March, and it contained the imaginative advice that he should chase away any "unlawful usurper"—but he knew about Massachusetts' aggressive plans and felt that he could wait no longer.

He began by telling Boston that the New Englanders might indeed have a patent from Charles I for the northern part of New Netherland, but that they had forgotten to mention the date of their charter. "English and Dutch histories teach us," he remarked cynically, that this King succeeded his father in 1625, while the Dutch had built their first fort on the North River, near Fort Orange, in 1615, taking "really and effectually" possession of the river in 1623. "Your Honors," the governor continued, "will unquestionably approve the general rule accepted by all Christian nations: qui prior in possessione, prior est in jure."[11]

In talking of the Elbe and the Rhine, the Court in Boston had made one great mistake—"Your Honors would have solved yourselves the question, if you had substituted the River Thames in the place of the aforesaid," for on that river the English had never allowed other nations free passage. He assured them that he would never prevent any Indian from trading with anyone, "but we do not allow it upon our streams and rivers." He would do everything

A SWEET AND ALIEN LAND

possible "to maintain, protect and guard" the rights of the West India Company upon the South and North River. Even the threats, "which are so much more suspicious, as you cut them short by an emphatic Etc.," would not deter him, and he signed his letter, "Your Honors' affectionate friend and neighbour, Peter Stuyvesant."[12]

The governor had thrown his hat in the ring, but he knew very well that he would never be able to put up a fight, and the next day he appealed again to the Lords Directors to send "in good time such assistance in troops, ammunition and goods, as your Honors may think we need in the dangerous situation of the country."[13]

A sudden change in England came to the rescue of New Netherland. On September 3, 1658, Oliver Cromwell died, leaving the Commonwealth in the hands of his inept and irresolute son Richard. The younger Cromwell's rule lasted only eight months. He resigned on April 22, 1659, and the army, which had ruled the country for ten years, was unable to provide another able and authoritative leader. On January 2, 1660, General Monck, a Royalist at heart, came marching down from Scotland to put an end to all uncertainty, and five months later Charles II, who had again become a welcome guest in Holland, crossed from the port of Scheveningen to take possession of his throne.

Stuyvesant, of course, heard about the changes in England, but he warned the company in April, just before Charles' return, "not to put any hope in the weakness of the English government in Europe, and its disposition to meddle in affairs here." He knew how independent the New Englanders had become, and he suspected they might seize the chance of "the present monstrous conditions of the English government" to make their attack, trusting that London would be too preoccupied to intervene.[14]

For the moment he was wrong. The colonies, on hearing of the Restoration, decided to abstain from aggression. This was reason enough for the company to tell its governor that it no longer gave "credit to the common report and belief that the English neighbours were still bent upon making a settlement on the North River." It was sending troops and ammunition, but it was sure he would never need them. England was now ruled by Charles II and, the Heeren XIX wrote happily, "better things may be expected from his honesty and righteousness, than from the former unlawful government." Feted and lionized at vast

CLASH WITH BOSTON

cost by the repentant Dutch government, Charles had uttered a few gracious words at his departure. They were taken at face value by the Heeren XIX, who were now convinced—so they told Stuyvesant—that the New Englanders would find no support "for their unjust usurpation, especially as the King shows himself very friendly to our government."[15]

Though Stuyvesant's relations with Boston remained tense that summer, he received at least some reassurance from the other side of the province. There had always been great sympathy as well as a brisk trade between New Netherland and Virginia, and the Dutch governor now felt the time had come to seal their relations with a treaty. Augustine Heerman's visit to Jamestown in October 1659 had been a success, and in February 1660 Stuyvesant sent his brother-in-law, Captain Nicholas Varleth, and Captain Brian Newton, his loyal English adjutant.

Governor Samuel Mathews, one of the pioneers of the Crown colony, had died and been replaced by Sir William Berkeley, the respected and progressive former governor who had been dismissed by Cromwell in 1652. Berkeley had always been pro-Dutch, since the Dutch merchants frequently came to the rescue of Virginians in times of need, in contrast to the neglectful English. Even after the introduction of the Navigation Act, the shipping of tobacco by Dutch vessels had gone on, and after New Amsterdam abolished the duties on tobacco in 1653, Dutchmen were always warmly received.

The same welcome awaited Varleth and Newton and their talks with the governor went smoothly. Both parties agreed that free trade between them was essential, and Varleth and Newton returned to New Amsterdam with a treaty that was soon ratified.[16]

Berkeley, however, had one great disappointment for his Dutch colleague, who had asked him to procure an acknowledgment of the Dutch title to New Netherland. The governor's answer was extremely apologetic but negative—"for I am but a servant of the Assembly; neither do they arrogate any Power to themselves, farther than the miserable Distractions of England force them to." Stuyvesant ought to wait until things had quieted down in En-

A SWEET AND ALIEN LAND

gland, and the King could decide, but in the meantime, Berkeley assured him: "I shall labour all I can to get you a satisfactory answer."[17]

It never came. A few months later London reminded Virginia that the laws passed during the Protectorate for the regulation of trade and navigation were still in force, and the Virginians must annul their treaty with the Dutch. For Stuyvesant, it was a warning before the storm.

CLASH WITH BOSTON

THE

ESOPUS WAR

Nicholas Varleth and Brian Newton had talked of more than politics and trade with Governor Berkeley during their embassy to Virginia in the spring of 1660. Stuyvesant had instructed them to raise some troops—preferably "as many Scots as possible"—and talk the Virginians into an offensive and defensive league against the Indians. Their neighbors, in view of the uncertain situation in England, had temporarily refused both requests.[1]

Just two weeks before the two men left for Jamestown—on February 12—Stuyvesant, his Council, and the two burgomasters of New Amsterdam had decided to declare a war against the Esopus Indians, who had been very active for the last two years. The general had tried every possible means to avoid such a war, despite a series of incidents that, since the Peach War in 1655, had cost the lives of about twenty settlers. The West India Company did not agree with his pacific attitude and in May 1658 urged him to take strong action, telling him "that we are by no means willing that these commotions, robberies and violent proceedings of the barbarous tribes should be submitted any longer." The general had, however, remained cautious, knowing all too well that his forces were too weak to tackle the Wilden once and for all.[2]

New incidents in 1658 almost put an end to his patience. They happened at Esopus, a small settlement of about eighty farmers halfway between New Amsterdam and Beverwyck. In the words of Dominie Megapolensis, it was "an exceedingly good country," with rich cornfields rolling over the gentle hills toward the green banks of the Hudson. The settlers, who had fled to the capital during the massacre of 1655, had by 1657 returned and were "doing very well." Ignoring Stuyvesant's instruction to organize themselves within a village, protected by a wall and a blockhouse, the colonists had rebuilt their scattered farms and lived in them again, tilling their fields and trading with the unruly and savage Esopus tribe. The exchange of furs for brandy had led to some skirmishes —one farmer, Jacob Adriaensen, had lost his child during an attack and had his eye knocked out.[3]

These isolated incidents gave way to more concerted action at the beginning of May. Stuyvesant learned the alarming news a few days later. "Great trouble has arisen here through the fearful intoxication of the cruel barbarians," wrote Thomas Chambers, the unofficial leader of the colony. "I myself with Pieter Dircksen and Hendrick Cornelissen came today to the tennis-court* and saw that the savages had a ancre of brandy lying under a tree. . . . According to all appearances they got madly intoxicated and about dusk fired and killed Herman Jacobsen." Later in the night they had again attacked the farm of Adriaensen and set fire to it. Immediate help was needed so that the place—"which if well peopled could feed the whole of New Netherland"—could be saved.[4]

Stuyvesant hesitated, hoping that the settlers would be able to organize their own defense, but two weeks later Chambers again appealed to him. "They use great violence every day, which we are not capable to retaliate, and derisively they say, that if they kill a Christian or more they can pay for it in wampum." The young Indians were particularly insolent, refusing to listen to their sachems, and the settlers were obliged to stay in their houses, "as the savages would immediately attack us." Chambers asked for fifty to sixty men, pointing out to the governor that "it is useless to cover the well, after the calf had been drowned."[5]

On May 28 the Council decided that the general himself should go, taking fifty men with him, and next day he boarded Govert Loockermans' packetboat, *Stede Amsterdam* ("City of Amsterdam"), which went regularly to Fort Orange. Arriving at Esopus, Stuyve-

*The predecessor of modern lawn tennis, court tennis spread in the thirteenth century from France to England, and then abroad. It was played on roughly constructed open courts, at first with the hand, and later with a racket.

THE ESOPUS WAR

sant found the frightened settlers waiting eagerly, but he had little patience with them. He told them sternly that it was impossible to protect them while they stayed on their own farms instead of building a village. They protested they had no money to build new houses and palisades, and that anyway they could not spare the time until the harvest was gathered in. The governor insisted, and promised that he would stay on with his soldiers until the settlement was finished. If they did not agree, he would return forthwith, leaving them to the savages. The threat worked, and a few days later the whole population was busy sawing, cutting, digging, and building, while guards kept a careful eye on the Indians who came to look at all this activity.[6]

News of Stuyvesant's decisive action reached the sachems of the Esopus tribe quickly, and on the second day of his stay the arrival of twelve chiefs was announced. Leaving his headquarters, Stuyvesant found them sitting under a tree, intimidated. He greeted the sachems kindly and listened while one of them, gathering all his courage, started to complain about the treatment the Dutch had given the tribe during the time of Willem Kieft. Patiently the general answered that all these things were of the past. Then, suddenly changing tactics, he burst out: "Your overbearing insolence at Esopus is known. . . . We have not had a foot of land without paying for it. . . . Why then have you committed this murder? Why have you burned our houses, killed our cattle and continue to threaten our people?"[7]

The sachems remained silent; "bowing down, they let their heads fall, and looked on the ground." At last one of them got up and told Stuyvesant in a shaking voice that they were not able to control their youngsters after "the Swannekens" sold them "strong water." Stuyvesant, erect and impressive, turned now to the young men, who almost ran away when he started to shout at them. "If any of your young savages desire to fight, let them now step forth. I will place man against man," the governor told them, then corrected himself: "Nay, I will place 20 against 30 or 40 of your hotheads." Stamping with his wooden leg, he burst out: "If this is not stopped, I shall be compelled to retaliate on old and young, on women and children."[8]

It was enough for the moment, and calming down again, he asked the elder to sell him all the land around Esopus, and then leave for the interior. "It is no good to live near the Swannekens,

A SWEET AND ALIEN LAND

whose cattle might eat your maize and therefore cause more disturbances." The sachems promised to consider the matter and left. Next day they were back, shame-faced. Stuyvesant wrote that evening in his journal that they begged him not to tell others that their young men had not dared accept his challenge to fight. They told him then "that they had agreed to give me the land, which I desired to buy . . . to grease my feet, because I had made such a long journey to come and see them." At the same time the chiefs promised "to put away all their evil intentions and that in the future none of them would do any harm to the Dutch, but that they would go hand in hand and arm in arm with them." It looked as if everything was settled, and when three weeks later the colonists had finished their little fortress, the governor sailed back to New Amsterdam, leaving twenty-four soldiers behind.[9]

In October he was back. The Indians had not kept their word. They had not moved to the interior; they were again pestering the colonists; and they had refused to hand over the land they had promised. They even forced the farmers to plough their maize fields, threatening to set the Dutch village on fire if they refused. This time Stuyvesant was peremptory. He called the sachems together and told them that he wanted the land and several hundred wampum belts as damage. The Indians tried to stall, telling him that most of the sachems were hunting and could not be reached for consultation. They offered him a few beavers as compensation, and promised a rich fur trade if he left them in peace. But the general was not to be distracted by beavers—he wanted peace, and dryly he asked them what they intended to do with the land. "It belongs to the chiefs who are not here today," was the answer and, scurrying away, they promised to come back next morning.[10]

No Indian appeared that day and Stuyvesant, impatient to get back to the capital, sent a soldier into the forest, who returned complaining that the sachems had laughed at him and told him they had no intention of giving any satisfaction. There was little the governor could do. Outraged but helpless, he returned to New Amsterdam on October 19, leaving behind fifty soldiers under Ensign Dirck Smit."[11]

THE ESOPUS WAR

The trouble at Esopus was viewed with concern from Beverwyck and Rensselaerswyck. Jeremias van Rensselaer, the twenty-six-year-old son of the first patroon, who in 1656 had succeeded his brother Jan Baptist as director of the domain, wrote in June 1658 to his mother in Amsterdam that the situation looked very bad. "If war is started there, our colony will hardly remain exempt, for the places are but 13 or 14 miles apart. . . ." However, that winter the situation remained calm. It was bitterly cold in the north, so cold that "several people had their hands and feet frozen," while Jeremias himself, racing his sleigh on the frozen river, collided with another sleigh "so that I severely hurt my left hand." The following spring it simply rained every day, and farmers and Indians alike were obliged to stay at home. Even during the summer of 1659 the Esopus Indians kept quiet, and the only unrest was around Beverwyck.[12]

War had started up again between the Mohawks and their archenemies, the Hurons, who were supported by the French. The settlers and traders at Beverwyck wondered how far it would affect them, and on September 6 they got their answer. A delegation of Mohawks appeared out of the dense forest and walked to La Montagne's house in the fort. They had come to settle a few things.

"The Dutch say we are brothers and joined together," they told the vice director. That was all very well, but it only worked when they brought pelts; for the rest, they were forgotten, and had to fight their lonely struggle with the Hurons and their powerful allies, the French. Worse still, the Dutch sold liquor to the Mohawk warriors, who when they were drunk could no longer fight. "We ask that no more brandy shall be sold to our people, that the liquor kegs should be plugged up," they said, adding that everyone who brought strong water into their country would be punished. Handing over gifts, they demanded at the same time the help of thirty men to build their forts, powder and lead for their guns, and if possible fifty to sixty soldiers to assist them against their enemy.[13]

La Montagne assured them that "the brotherhood between the Dutch and the Mohawks should always be maintained," but explained that he could give no definitive answer to their request until "Wooden Leg" appeared. He sent a messenger to New Amsterdam, who returned with a letter from Stuyvesant. The governor was too ill to come himself, but he gave his vice director orders to secure an alliance with the powerful Mohawks.

On September 24, an imposing group of twenty-five Dutchmen on horseback, among them Jeremias van Rensselaer and Arent van Curler, left Beverwyck for a journey of forty miles to the first of the three castles of the Mohawks, Caughnawagah. What they found could not have failed to impress them. Compared to the little decayed molehill that was called Fort Orange, this fort was huge. Surrounded by thick palisades, and only accessible through two gates, it stood at the border of a creek, dominating the countryside. Inside the fortification stood solid houses, their flat roofs covered with bark. The tidy streets were bustling with children playing naked in the dust; proud women dressed in colorful gowns, decorated with wampum; and fierce-looking warriors, their faces painted red, white, and blue, their bodies swathed in the red or blue duffel blankets they had bought from the traders.

The Dutch delegation was received with great solemnity. The council fire was burning and only after the great calumet had been smoked did one of the colonists stand up. "Brothers, we have come here to renew our old friendship and brotherhood," he began. He apologized that they had come without cloth, "but we could not get the men to carry it," and he excused the absence of the Great Sachem from New Amsterdam, "but he has fallen very sick." He assured the Mohawks that everything they said was with the authority of the governor, "all the other chiefs and of all the Dutch and their children."

Handing over seven boxes of wampum, the speaker reminded the Indians of the sixteen years of peace that had reigned between them and the colonists, and expressed his certainty that in the future, too, it would be "as if we had lain under one heart." There was one snag. The Mohawks had asked them not to sell brandy, but this was difficult. "Our chiefs [in New Amsterdam] are very angry because the Dutch sell brandy to your people," he assured them, "and always forbid it." But only a few days ago twenty to thirty kegs had been smuggled into Beverwyck by the Indians to be filled, and the only way to prevent that was to take those kegs away from them. If the sachems did not do it, the Dutch authorities would act, "but then if we do so, our brothers must not be angry with us."

The speech was ended by the presentation of powder, lead, and knives to the Indians. To compensate for the fact that he could not fulfill their request to help with the construction of their fort—the hills were too steep for the horses and the Dutch were all too ill —he gave them fifteen axes.

The Mohawks accepted the presents gratefully, passing the calumet again and chatting excitedly, while admiring the gifts. But the festive mood was spoiled when a breathless Negro stormed into Caughnawagah. He was the slave of La Montagne, sent to warn his representatives to be careful on the road back. The Indians had again attacked the village of Esopus and killed several settlers. Unrest was spreading rapidly.

The Dutch at once reported the news to the Mohawk chiefs, "who listened with great astonishment" and promised the delegates that this would strengthen the friendship they felt for them. If now the Esopus or other River Indians should come with presents and ask for assistance to fight against the Dutch, they would kick them and say: "You beasts, you pigs, get away from here, we will have nothing to do with you."[14]

Reassured, the Dutch left next morning, reaching Beverwyck the same evening. They had to wait for four days before more detailed news from Esopus reached them: on September 29 La Montagne received a letter from Ensign Dirck Smit in which he related the whole drama.

It had begun on the night of September 20 when eight Indians, who had been "breaking off corn-ears" for Thomas Chambers, were given brandy as a reward. They soon became drunk, and when their supply was finished, persuaded a soldier to sell them another bottle. "Making a terrible noise," they spent the evening under the bushes outside Esopus, where the worried inhabitants sat listening to the din. Some of the Indians stayed sober enough to realize the danger—the summer had been tense and full of little incidents—and tried to get their friends back to their wigwams. One of them made special efforts to break up the merry party, telling them "he felt some sensation in his body as if they all should be killed." He was jeered at, and the singing and shouting went on.[15]

Ensign Smit, who had just that day received orders from Stuyvesant to return to the capital with eighteen of his soldiers, commanded Sergeant Andries Lourissen to take eight men on a scouting party. On his return, Lourissen reported seeing a crowd of drunken Indians, fast asleep. Jacob Jansen Stoll, a farmer whose horse had been killed by the Indians a year earlier, had already undressed to go to bed when the noise started. Followed by other inhabitants, he hurried in his underpants to the guardhouse, where he heard Lourissen's report. It seemed the ideal opportunity to teach the insolent Indians a lesson, and he offered to go with some other men to investigate. Later he wrote to Stuyvesant that when they arrived near the bushes, "the savages, perceiving us, fired immediately. We replied and one savage, who had helped himself freely to brandy, was killed."[16]

It had not been as straightforward as that. Other witnesses told Smit later that, in contradiction to any orders he had given, the settlers had attacked the drunken Indians in their sleep. One of the party was shot, another knocked on his head with an axe. Most of them escaped, and one was taken prisoner. Stoll told Smit defiantly: "We wanted to slap their mouths, for the dogs have vexed us long enough."[17]

From within the village soldiers and citizens watched next day in helpless fury while the Indians, taking revenge for the attack on their friends, rampaged through the fields destroying the harvest, setting barns and haystacks on fire with burning arrows, and killing livestock. Without reinforcement from the capital nothing could be done against the five hundred to six hundred savages, who were armed with guns and bows and arrows. A petition to Stuyvesant was hastily composed and a group of eighteen men, guarded by Sergeant Lourissen and eight soldiers, went to the shore to send off the letter by barge. On the way back, past the tennis court, they were surprised by a large group of Indians, to whom they surrendered themselves without a shot. Only seven of the settlers reached the safety of the village.

The fate of the prisoners in the Indians' Fort Wildmeet was terrible. Foiled in their attack on Esopus by its heavy defenses, the Indians turned in fury on their captives. One settler escaped and told how eight of the Dutch, among them Jacob Jansen Stoll, were tied to the stake, tortured and finally burnt alive.[18]

Word of the attack on the village soon reached the capital, and spread rapidly over Manhattan and Long Island. It created the usual atmosphere of panic. Farmers left their fields and Fort Amsterdam became once again a haven for frightened settlers. Stuyvesant, still a victim of the fever, pulled himself together and left his

THE ESOPUS WAR

bed. Riding on horseback through New Amsterdam and the villages on Long Island, he did his best to calm the citizens, and although he succeeded in that, he could not persuade them to join in a fight against the "barbarious Wilden." He called the burgomasters and the magistrates of the other communities together and told them that he himself would go to Esopus to raise the siege, and that he needed a strong army. They proposed to enlist volunteers to go with him, attracting them by "good prizes," but the general, fearing an undisciplined band of looters and riffraff, refused. After three days of recruiting, his force was still only thirty-six men strong, including four of his own servants.[19]

Again he summoned the burgomasters, instructing them to call up the three companies of the burgher militia. Next morning the troops marched into the fort, where the governor inspected them from the steps of St. Nicholas Church. Still weak from illness, he addressed them nonetheless in rousing terms, appealing to their sense of duty and honor. But it made no impression and only twenty-four volunteers stepped forward. Stuyvesant then ordered the officers of the three companies to draw lots to determine which one would accompany him. Striding angrily away, he told them to be ready by the following Sunday.[20]

That Sunday, October 6, 1659, an army consisting of about 150 men and almost as many loyal Indians, embarked "after the second sermon," arriving four days later in pouring rain at Esopus, where the siege had just been lifted thirty-six hours earlier. The Indians, realizing that the villagers would never surrender, had retired into Fort Wildmeet. The siege had cost the life of one Dutchman, and six had been wounded.

For the next few days the rain continued, making it impossible to pursue the savages, and Stuyvesant decided to return to Manhattan. Much relieved by the lack of action, the volunteers and soldiers marched from the village to the riverbank to embark. While the troops were boarding, one of the guards shot a dog that had tried to bite him. The burghers, not very warlike anyway, thought that the Indians were attacking, and to Stuyvesant's shame, some of them became so panicky that they "threw themselves into the water before they had seen an enemy." Shamefaced, and to the jeers of their more courageous friends, they crawled on board, leaving the governor muttering about "the unsuitability of the citizens as protectors and upholders of the country."

A SWEET AND ALIEN LAND

The Mohawks came to the help of the Dutch, and thanks to their mediation Ensign Smit was able to report to the governor on November 1 that a peace had been concluded with the Esopus Indians, and that two of the prisoners had been returned. Stuyvesant advised him not to rely too much on a treaty, and wrote to the company for more troops. It was the only way to keep the colonists from leaving the country. The Heeren XIX thought it would be cheaper to employ their old allies, the Mohawks, but the governor did not agree. They are, he wrote, "a vain-glorious, proud and bold tribe," already too arrogant after their victories over the Hurons and the French. To depend on them would make the Dutch "contemptible in the eyes of the other tribes," while the Mohawks themselves would become more demanding. "It was therefore safer to stand on our own feet as long as possible."[21]

He went up to Esopus once more to see to the release of the last prisoners and to conclude a more permanent treaty, but he waited in vain for the Indians to appear and left again on December 3. It seemed quiet had returned, and on December 28 La Montagne received reassuring news from Esopus—"apart from some friendly trading with the savages, there is nothing of note to record."[22]

General Stuyvesant was not deluded by the calm that had suddenly descended on the village, and he used the winter to organize sufficient defense so that he would be able to restore what he called the "almost ruined Batavian reputation."

It was a tense winter. Massachusetts and Maryland were both very active, brandishing their claims to Dutch land, and there was always the possibility that the Esopus Indians would seek English help in their efforts to exterminate the Dutch north of Manhattan. Events never went that far, but the Indians certainly hoped for support from New England. As one of their chiefs later remarked to some Englishmen, the Esopus—like their predecessors in Kieft's Indian War—never understood why in 1660 the New Englanders had not used the opportunity "to have rooted oute the Dutch & to bee revenged for wrongs done them and setling the govermt and lands upon themselves."[23]

The Esopus Indians remained isolated in their fight, and when spring arrived they were faced with considerable force. Stuyvesant, who had two hundred mercenaries from the West India Company at his disposal (of whom about a hundred were in Fort Amsterdam), had with great difficulty enlisted another hundred soldiers from among the population. He had also convinced his Council and the burgomasters of New Amsterdam that only a total war could end the constant threat of the Wilden. On February 12, 1660, "after many debates pro and contra it was decided by a plurality of votes" that he should have his way.[24]

Stuyvesant at once dispatched a long "missive" to Vice Director Beck in Curaçao, asking him for clever and strong Negroes to work at the fort and to help them in the war against the Indians, "either to pursue them when they run away or else to carry the soldiers baggage." He also wanted some horses, "strong stallions or geldings," and three or four mares with saddles and bridles. Finally he would like to borrow some money—"12 to 1500 pieces of eight."[25]

Before starting the war, Stuyvesant wished to secure the peace on and around Manhattan, and on March 6 spectators in front of City Hall watched in amazement the arrival of one martially attired Indian sachem after another. Almost all the southern tribes were represented, together with the Provincial Council and the magistrates in New Amsterdam, and a new treaty of peace was solemnly signed, stating that "no war shall be commenced for any private action."[26]

On March 15, 1660, Stuyvesant embarked on the yacht *Haen* ("Cock") to go to Esopus, and a few days later Secretary Cornelis van Ruyven received a letter from him. The wind had been contrary and he had not been able to reach the village before the evening of March 18. "We fired immediately a shot and received an answer from the fort," Stuyvesant told him. "To my great astonishment and not less anxiety no men came out of it." He quickly learned the cause. Ensign Smit had left the day before with forty men for an expedition against the Indians. He returned a day later, reporting success. He had found their Fort Wildmeet, which was defended by sixty savages. They had fled without resistance, but Smit had been able to capture and kill four.[27]

Stuyvesant, not completely happy with this partial victory, traveled on to Fort Orange to assess that outpost's strength. Finding the situation satisfactory, he declared war on March 25. In a proclamation all citizens were warned not to travel alone on roads, streams, and rivers, while skippers were to sail down the North River only in convoys of three or more ships.[28]

Smit went immediately into action, and while Stuyvesant returned to New Amsterdam, he chased and harried the Indians wherever he could with his army of "73 good soldiers." It was not long before tentative peace feelers were again put out by the harassed Indians, but Stuyvesant—as he made clear in a letter to Amsterdam—was not yet willing, now that he had hope "of a favourable final result," to make peace, "in order to give a sharp lesson to others." To make the lesson even harsher he ordered on May 25 that eleven of the Esopus prisoners, all the ringleaders, should be shipped off to Curaçao or Bonaire "to work for the Company."[29]*

Smit, in the meantime, had scourged almost the whole region around Esopus. Proudly he related an incident that took place during the conquest of a village. The inhabitants had fled before the troops, leaving the "oldest and best of their chiefs," Preummaker, behind. The old man received the soldiers undaunted and with raised gun, but without much effort a soldier pulled it out of his hands. There followed a short discussion about his fate, and it was quickly decided. "As it was a considerable distance to carry him we struck him down with his own axe," Smit wrote laconically.[30]

The Indians, lost without their leaders, made it known in June through the Haverstraw and Hackensack tribes that they were at last ready for peace. For the sixth time in three years Stuyvesant traveled to Esopus, this time with the two burgomasters of New Amsterdam. He arrived on Sunday, July 11, but in spite of all promises no Esopus sachem turned up. Messengers were sent, but the response was evasive, and on July 14 Stuyvesant summoned the River tribe mediators and told them that, as the Esopus Indians were "obviously trifling not only with him but with all the other tribes as well," he would go home before the end of the day.

It worked miracles. The same evening four sachems appeared in the village, and on July 26, 1660, back in the capital, the governor could report to the company that "after many debates finally the

*Stuyvesant's brother-in-law, Nicholas Varleth, took charge of the transport, at a fare of thirty silver guilders a head.

THE ESOPUS WAR

peace had been concluded." All former acts were forgiven and forgotten; the country for two or three miles on either side of the Esopus Kill was given to the settlers as reparation for damages; the Indians were not allowed to come armed into the village, nor to drink there; and for the murdered Dutch prisoners the Indians would give five hundred skepels of Indian corn.[31]

Most of the prisoners were exchanged, except for the eleven Indians who were on their way to Curaçao and a young Dutchman, the son of the Esopus farmer, Evert Pels. One of the group that had been captured near the tennis court in September 1659, he had been adopted by the Indians and had even taken an Indian wife, "who became pregnant, and [was] unwilling to part with him or he with her."[32]

A SWEET AND ALIEN LAND

The
Stuyvesants

*The mansion of Peter Stuyvesant at the south side of
what is now known as Pearl Street, near the foot of Whitehall Street.*
COURTESY OF THE NEW-YORK HISTORICAL SOCIETY, NEW YORK CITY

The only known portrait of Peter Stuyvesant,
probably painted by the Franco-Dutch artist
Hendrick Couturier, who came to New Amsterdam in 1650.
COURTESY OF THE NEW-YORK HISTORICAL SOCIETY, NEW YORK CITY

*Peter Stuyvesant's signature on one of
the last documents to be drawn up before
New Amsterdam was captured by the English in 1664.*
MUSEUM OF THE CITY OF NEW YORK

Stuyvesant's sister Anna with her husband,
Samuel Bayard, in front of the
Bayard homestead in Alphen aan de Rijn, Holland.

Nicholas Willem Stuyvesant,
the youngest son of the governor,
at the age of seventeen.

HERE

TO STAY

"I am and remain still very sick and weak, having neither inclination nor appetite for anything to eat," Peter Stuyvesant wrote on September 4, 1659, to the West India Company in Amsterdam. It was one of the rare personal asides the Dutchman ever made to his employers. He had been ill for four weeks, suffering from the "hot fevers" that swept through the colony, "whereof many died." As the governor told the Heeren XIX: "I did not think, that I would be able to address your Honors once more."[1]

The general was now approaching fifty, and he had been running the affairs of New Netherland for twelve exhausting years. He was still as active, energetic, and impatient as ever, but experience had taught him a little more consideration and diplomacy. Slowly and very reluctantly he had given in to the demands of the proud and self-assured Dutch settlers for more control over their own affairs; and while keeping an authoritative eye on the whole province, he allowed himself more time for his family and his own pleasures.

His marriage to the Huguenot vicar's daughter Judith Bayard must have been a happy one. No scandal ever reached the ears of eager enemies, and the governor during his many travels often ended his letters with a request to give his love to his wife and the children.

Judith—of whom no portrait exists—kept herself completely in the background, like any ordinary Dutch housewife. She was a gracious hostess who sometimes traveled with the governor to the outposts of the province; but she was mainly occupied with her two sons, Balthasar Lazarus and Nicholas Willem. The two boys, who were twelve and eleven years old in 1659, had both been born in New Amsterdam and christened in St. Nicholas Church. They had their own tutor and lived a sheltered life on their father's bouwery, just outside the city.

This farm, bought by Stuyvesant from the company in 1651 for sixty-four hundred guilders, was the first of the six started by Peter Minuit in 1625. It was the general's pride and joy. A large staff, among them forty slaves, looked after its 550 acres of orchards, meadows, cornfields, and woods, interspersed with running creeks and a few ponds. The property, extended by purchase from private owners, stretched at one time from present-day Fifth Street to Seventeenth Street, and from the East River up to Fourth Avenue. It was dominated by a large Dutch farmhouse, surrounded by a flower garden and sloping lawns, with a fine view of the river. Wouter van Twiller in his time had built a barn, a boathouse, and a brewery, and since then both Kieft and Stuyvesant had added to the property. After the Indian massacre of 1655, the general invited some farmers to settle in the neighborhood, and a little hamlet had grown up near his house.[2]

The New Amsterdammers were free to walk through the domain, and they used this opportunity frequently. By 1660 it had become "a place of relaxation and pleasure," and the attraction became even greater when in that year Stuyvesant built his own chapel on the spot where St. Mark's-in-the-Bouwerie now stands. He asked Dominie Henricus Selyns to come—"at his expense"— to preach the evening service, and Selyns had welcomed this opportunity to earn an extra 250 guilders a year. The twenty-four-year-old dominie from an old Amsterdam family had come to New Netherland in the summer of 1660 and was installed as Breukelen's first parson. He was highly intelligent and a poet, and Stuyvesant undoubtedly enjoyed his sermons.[3]

The governor, almost absolute in his power over the colony, was head of the state church as well, and often used his influence as deacon and chairman of the consistory. His efforts to keep the exercise of religion uniform—he opposed the settlement of Jews,

A SWEET AND ALIEN LAND

Lutherans, and Quakers—were in vain, however, and made in a manner that the more tolerant Fatherland could not accept. The Dutch settlers found the situation difficult enough, but the English —who had often fled to New Netherland to get away from the religious fanaticism of Puritan New England—were his most important opponents. Over the years, under the pressure of the company, he lost his battle with them, to the advantage of the Dutch as well.

Rigid as he was in religious matters, Stuyvesant was certainly no prude. When in 1663 the daughter of Dominie Gideon Schaets at Fort Orange gave birth to an illegitimate child and called it Benoni (child of suffering), he proposed instead that it should be called Barrabas (bastard). His own half-sister Margriet, who came in 1656 to New Amsterdam as the wife of Jacobus Backer, was after Backer's death involved with a rich bachelor, by whom she had a child without the blessing of the Church. When the bachelor died, she married another man, with the consent of the governor.[4]

Margriet was not the only Stuyvesant who had followed the general to New Amsterdam. Anna Stuyvesant, his younger sister, who had married Judith's brother Samuel, had been widowed and in 1654 left Holland with her three sons for the colony. There she met her second husband, Captain Nicholas Varleth, a merchant and shipowner. They married in 1658, and although Anna, like her sister-in-law, stayed out of politics, her husband played an important role in the small diplomatic world of New Netherland. In 1660 he was sent as an envoy to Virginia, and in the same year he organized for his brother-in-law the transport of the captured Esopus Indians to Curaçao. Later, as an acquaintance of Governor John Winthrop Jr. of Connecticut, the captain would repeatedly try to mediate in border problems.[5]

The Varleth family—Nicholas' father Caspar had settled in 1651 in New Amsterdam, but soon retired to Hartford—was one of the most colorful in the little capital. Nicholas' sister Jenny had married the "Bohemian" Augustine Heerman, with whom she left in 1661 for his new estate, Nova Bohemia in Maryland. The family seems to have quarreled with Stuyvesant shortly after, because the merchant, "a lover of the country" who became a gentleman-farmer, was arrested when he returned sometime later to New Amsterdam. Family tradition tells that he feigned insanity, and

HERE TO STAY

asked for his favorite horse to keep him company in prison. He then leapt on horseback through a window, rode off, and swam across the Hudson to freedom.[6]

Another Varleth sister was Judith, who later married Nicholas Bayard, the son of Stuyvesant's sister Anna. Living in 1662 with her father in Hartford, she was faced with charges of witchcraft, then fairly common in New England but unknown in New Netherland. Nicholas Varleth had to intervene and asked the help of his brother-in-law. Stuyvesant at once wrote a long letter to Winthrop in Hartford, telling him: "Wee realy beleeve and out of her knowne education, Lyfe Conversation & profession off faith we deare assure, that Shee is innocent of such a horrible Crimen and therefore I doubt not he [Varleth] will now as formerly fynde your Honn'rs favour & ayde for the Innocent." This intervention was successful, and Judith was acquitted.[7]

The Varleths lived in New Amsterdam next to the townhouse that Stuyvesant had built on Op't Water, the Strand of the East River, on the corner of present-day Whitehall and State streets. It was a typical Dutch stone house with a gabled facade and a double staircase leading up to the stoop in front of the impressive door. The governor had it constructed in the mid-1650s, on a lot that had been the property of a certain Jan Pietersen, who had sold it to Thomas Baxter. This rich merchant had turned privateer during the Anglo-Dutch War and was—in Stuyvesant's words—"a bankrupt and fugitive from this Province in consequence of great indebteness." The governor had initially simply seized the plot and spent a fortune on making it ready for building, having it "fenced, damned, and raised up, at great cost and labour, out of the water and swamp." He had used about nine thousand loads of sand to make it high enough, and in 1658 "an expensive and handsome building" was ready. To secure it for the future "in case of his dismissal from office or death," he asked the burgomasters and schepens that year for a patent to this lot. The request was approved on February 14.[8]

The Great House, as it was known in Stuyvesant's days (it later became Whitehall), replaced the Governor's House in the fort, which from then on served as an office. The new mansion was most imposing, surrounded at the back and sides by lawns and a formal Dutch flower and vegetable garden. The front overlooked the market, while a flight of stairs at the side went down to the river, where the governor's personal barge was moored. Stuyvesant was never rich—he had begun his career in New Netherland on a yearly income of thirty-nine hundred guilders and no raise has been recorded—but the interior of his house was opulent, full of solid, gleaming Dutch furniture, silver, and Delft china, while, following Dutch fashion, paintings covered the walls.

One of these paintings was the general's portrait, almost certainly painted by Hendrick Couturier de Jonge (the Younger), a linen draper from Leiden, who arrived in the province around 1650. The portrait shows no great talent, but certainly conveys the impression Stuyvesant made on people—that of a stern, cool, and proud man, reserved and well aware of his own importance. The inclusion of a cuirass demonstrates that he was still a military man at heart, even if diplomacy was taking the greater part of his time, and his little black cap suggests that he had no time for fancy new periwigs, the first of which were now being worn in New England.[9]

He had little time for merry socializing either. His journeys, which he greatly enjoyed, took him away often. Without any hesitation he embarked on the company's yachts to go to Esopus, Fort Orange, or the Delaware, and when the Anglo-Dutch War was over, he was anxious to set out on the long journey to Curaçao and Barbados. He frequently visited Long Island, and was the first Dutch governor ever to set foot in New England, when he went to Hartford in 1650.

At home, at the Great House, he held court, receiving envoys from neighboring colonies, captains of the company's ships, West India Company officials, and the magistrates of New Amsterdam. But if it was a "court," it was one where simplicity was the rule. The governor himself traveled on foot in the town, almost always surrounded by four halberdiers, a relic of the stormy days of 1650. Sometimes he took his carriage, for which Jeremias van Rensselaer had supplied him two horses "as nearly of the same colour and markings as they can be obtained."[10]

Only on the bouwery could Stuyvesant relax and receive the few friends he had made, like Cornelis van Werckhoven, the rich gentleman-farmer from Long Island; Paulus van der Grift, the opulent merchant; and the Varleths with their children. His rhyming days were certainly over, but he must have spent a lot of time reading, for his letters were laced with many quotations from the

HERE TO STAY

classics. He was careful about the style of these missives, telling an official once "that a word in season is like a silver apple in the golden peel."[11]

In one respect at least this stubborn product of Calvinistic Friesland had changed completely during his years in the province. He had arrived there the dedicated representative of the Heeren XIX in Amsterdam, prepared to stay three years in this unruly colony, expecting to change it within that short period from a crude pioneering settlement into a civilized extension of the Netherlands. His first aim had been to satisfy the West India Company, providing the profit it wanted. The period of three years had lengthened to twelve, and Stuyvesant's point of view had undergone a radical change. He had become the loyal and often inspiring leader of the settlers in their constant struggle for survival against Indian warriors and English usurpers.

He remained what he had always been, the faithful servant of the West India Company, but it was undeniable that distance was beginning to tell and that he, like the colonists, felt that the long arm of the Lords Directors was too often gripping them in a stranglehold. They often treated him like a disobedient schoolboy, and the question of money in particular led to constant conflicts.

The company in 1660 was poorer than ever before. Its shares, once quoted at 206 percent of their original value, had dropped to 28 percent in 1650, and were sinking to 11 percent in 1661. In 1654 it had lost Brazil for good, and although it still had footholds in the West Indies and Africa, the company's most important slave market, Angola, had been recaptured by the Portuguese. At home, in Amsterdam, its poverty reached the point of humiliation when in August 1654 the Heeren XIX had to sell their imposing headquarters on the corner of the Heerengracht and Haarlemmerdijk. They left it in 1656 because they could no longer even afford to pay the rent. Fortunately the Heeren XIX had possessed since 1641 an impressive warehouse on the Rapenburg, overlooking Amsterdams' port, and they now installed their offices there.[12]

The sale of New Amstel on the Delaware to Amsterdam for 700,000 guilders in 1656 had been only small relief. The debts of the company ran to three million guilders, of which "twelve ton of gold," discounting the money collected through duties and taxes, had been spent on New Netherland. It was perhaps understandable that the directors grumbled and protested constantly at any request for help, but as the Remonstrance of 1650 had remarked: "Had the Honourable West India Company, in the beginning, sought population instead of running to great expense for unnecessary things . . . the account of New Netherland would not have been so large as it is now." Their penny-pinching shortsightedness had cost them dear, and Stuyvesant felt that the settlers, most of them hard-working and responsible people, ought not to suffer for it.[13]

With growing irritation he read the arrogant and peremptory letters from Amsterdam: reproaching him for keeping the gentlemen there "entirely ignorant and blindfolded in regard to the expense and revenues of the Company"; telling him of their "displeasure" that he could not persuade the community—constantly ravaged by wars with the Indians—"to raise subsidies"; scolding him when he bought a ship for trade with Curaçao and drew eight hundred guilders on them (they sent the draft back unpaid); and blaming him for misunderstanding their orders when they led to trouble. When he raised a loan without waiting for the permission that would take at least four months to reach him, they were furious because he should have imposed a tax instead and used his "proper authority, as all competent rulers would do." When he introduced a duty without consulting them, the Heeren XIX were just as angry because he was upsetting their "promises," and they told him haughtily: "You may remonstrate to us and then we shall adopt such measures for the future, as we deem necessary. . . ." Appeals for troops and ammunition were hurriedly passed on to the States General, and any petitions from the New Netherlanders, which Stuyvesant had by now learned to send on without comment, were impatiently brushed aside. The Heeren XIX were not to be moved by cries for help like the one that arrived in September 1658, when New Netherland was again threatened by an Indian war and the colonists complained: "We shall be reduced to poverty and die in the fullness of our day, beholding the misery and calamity of our wives, children and friends."[14]

For the Lords Directors, only one thing counted, and they made it clear in almost every message to the governor: "Economy must always be to you a matter of the greatest importance, so that the company, to whom the Province has cost so much may at last reap some benefit."[15]

Stuyvesant must have laughed sometimes, and shrugged his

HERE TO STAY

shoulders at others, but he was often desperate. His letters over the years became more defiant and aggressive, and sometimes he could not resist a touch of irony. In September 1659 he thanked the Heeren XIX profusely for their "zeal and inclination to make this country prosperous." They had at their own expense just sent over a ship full of "free people," for which he was very grateful. The only trouble, he explained, was that on arrival, they all turned out to be "persons unaccustomed to labour, who quickly became a charge of the poormasters." The company could save its money by selecting people more carefully. He ended his letter with the hope that his advice "shall not be misinterpreted."[16]

To the New Netherlanders, their governor had not changed much. He was still, as one modern historian has remarked, "an autocrat by conviction, an enemy on principle to all theories of popular rights, a tyrant by military habit, opinionated and stubborn." He was certainly no warmhearted father figure. On the other hand, he was no longer the calculating slave of the company.[17]

The welfare of the province had by 1660 become more important to him than the pockets of the Lords Directors. And when in that year he held his first church service in his own chapel forty yards from his farmhouse, it was clear to everyone that he was there to stay.

A

BRAVE PLACE

The New Amsterdam of 1660 was very different from the town Peter Stuyvesant had found when he arrived thirteen years earlier. The capital then had been a cosmopolitan hamlet of about one hundred houses, built in a disorderly straggle along muddy roads and grouped around a fort that the governor called a disgrace even to "the Indians and heathens." By 1660 it was a town. Jacob Jansen Huys, the master of Amsterdam's trading vessel *Nieu Amstel,* wrote his employers on September 30, 1660: "This place, the Manhattans, is quite rich of people, and there are at present, full over 350 houses, so that it begins to be a brave place."[1]

City surveyor Jacques Cortelyou counted exactly 342 houses, in which lived 1,500 citizens, 350 men, the rest women and children. He made a map, which Stuyvesant sent proudly to Amsterdam on October 6, writing that "in case you should be inclined to have it engraved and published, we thought it advisable to send you also a small sketch of the City, drawn in perspective by Sieur Augustin Heerman three or four years ago; or perhaps you will hang it up in someplace or the other there."

The Heeren XIX were pleased to receive the map, but could not resist pointing out that "according to our opinion too great spaces are as yet without buildings." They thought that the city might be easier to defend if the houses were built closer together, but added politely: "We leave this to your consideration and care."[2]

Englishmen looked with some envy at the thriving and busy town, lying so strategically between the Hudson and the East River, "the whirlpoole which the Dutch call the Hellgat." One admirer was the former merchant from Massachusetts, Samuel Maverick. He, like many English, preferred the less rigid atmosphere of New Netherland, and had moved there in 1650. Ten years later he composed a report for the government in London in which he sang the praises of the capital: "very delightsome & convenient for scituation especiallie for trade haveing two maine streames or rivers running by, with an excellent harbour; the end of the sd Rivers or Streames is"—very important to roving English eyes— "the ordinary passage from & to New England and Virginia."[3]

Another, unknown Englishman added to his praise in 1661 with a *Description of the Towne of Mannadens* in which he also gave a fair share of attention to the port on the east side, where "all ships usually ly at anchor, to lade and unlade goods, secure from hurt of any wind or weather." He was particularly struck by the canal that the Dutch, true to their traditions, had dug in the years 1657– 1659 on the site of today's Broad Street. Named the Heerengracht, after one of the main waterways in Amsterdam, it was crossed by two large and three small bridges. The Heerengracht was "keyed on both sides with timber" and was dry at low tide, but "at high water boats come into it, passing under the two bridges and go as far as the three small bridges," where they were unloaded.[4]

The main port in the East River, improved by Stuyvesant in 1646 with the little dock near City Hall, had been extended again with a "hooft," or pier. Work on this had begun in April 1659 and four months later the first ships could anchor. It was soon too small, and had to be enlarged in November 1660. For the use of it the skippers paid eight stuivers per last.[5]*

There was never a quiet moment on the seashore. The governor, whose urge to confiscate trespassing ships had initially kept many traders away, had had to relax the rules, and vessels from all over the world came to the city, which was fast becoming the trading center of the East Coast. Most of the ships were, of course, Dutch, but the number of English traders was increasing every year, and French privateers and Spanish galleons frequently stopped by. From New England came beef, sheep, wheat, flour, fish, butter,

*A last is the equivalent of two tons.

A SWEET AND ALIEN LAND

cider apples, iron, and tar; from Virginia tobacco, ox hides, pork, and fruit. In exchange the Dutch sent "Holland and other linnen, canvass, tape, thrid, cordage, brasse, Hading cloth, stuffs, stockings, spices, fruit, all sort of iron work, wine, Brandy, Anis, salt and all usefull manufactures."[6]

The beaver trade was still the most important, and otter and musk skins, timberwood and corn, were other profitable export articles. In 1656 Fort Orange alone sent thirty-five thousand pelts down to New Amsterdam, and in October 1660 Stuyvesant mentioned that in the first month of the year about thirty thousand skins had been received, giving him sixteen thousand guilders in export duties. And that was a bad year, he explained to the company. Before the Indian massacre of 1655 and the Esopus War of the last years, he had collected respectively twenty-two thousand guilders in 1654 and twenty-eight thousand in 1655.[7]

The governor, although realizing very well that colonization was of great importance, knew that New Amsterdam could only survive through trade and commerce. He looked everywhere for new contacts. His visit to Barbados had been in vain, but the possibilities for trade with Curaçao were great. The company sent him a ship especially for this purpose, the Swedish vessel *Mercurius*, confiscated in 1656 and converted into the *Diemen*. But on its first trip, loaded with salt from Curaçao, it ran aground and disappeared without trace.[8]

The same fate swallowed up the *Jean Baptiste*, a ship that was to have opened up a new prospect of trade with Canada, at the invitation of the Canadian deputy viceroy, d'Ailleboust, through the mediation of Father Simon le Moyne. The Jesuit priest, grateful for his warm reception at Fort Orange and New Amsterdam in 1657, had approached the deputy viceroy with a proposal from Stuyvesant to give the Dutch free entry into Canadian ports. D'Ailleboust had consented "under the condition that they submit to the same customs as French vessels, forbidding trade with the savages and the public exercise on land of their religion."[9]

Le Moyne had enthusiastically transmitted the message to "my dear friends of the Manhattans," inviting them "to draw your furrows through the sea to our Quebec." The priest did not preach to deaf ears. Calvinistic Dutch merchants always felt that trade had nothing to do with religion. Jean de Pré, a twenty-nine-year-old Flemish trader, loaded his *Jean Baptiste* with tobacco and sugar in

A BRAVE PLACE

New Amsterdam and sailed away on July 2, 1658—only to be wrecked on the shores of Anticosti, leaving his widow with huge debts.[10]

It was discouraging, but the traders of New Amsterdam were not to be deterred. The West India Company, in spite of certain concessions for the inland trade and shipping to the Fatherland, still kept the foreign trade very much in its own hands. In 1659 Stuyvesant approached the Heeren XIX with a request from New Amsterdam's businessmen that they be given the liberty to trade abroad themselves. The answer of the Lords Directors was typical. "We find this a matter of importance and especially benefitting your people, but of doubtful advantage for the Company," they wrote back, "for a wide door will thereby be opened to further defraudation and the Company's revenues here in this country considerably reduced."[11]

For once, however, they decided to be generous. The foreign trade was opened "under the express condition, that the ships, sailing thence for French, Spanish, Italian ports, the Caribean Islands and elsewhere . . . shall be bound to return either to this City of Amsterdam or the place of your residence in New Netherland," in order to pay their duties. The fur trade was excluded from this liberality and Stuyvesant was sternly advised to watch it closely so "that the good will and intention of the Company for the welfare of the community may not lead to its suffering. . . ."[12]

In the same letter the company warned the Governor to keep an eye on smugglers. The cause of this ever-increasing practice was the high duty of 10 percent the merchants had to pay on all goods entering New Amsterdam. Since the English ports were free, nothing was easier than to unload a cargo into boats in New Haven, and then cross the sound to Long Island. From there, the cargo was carried by night over the East River to Manhattan. Kieft and Stuyvesant did all they could to stop the smugglers (one of the reasons for the construction of the city wall in 1658), but they had little trouble getting through the gates.[13]

In 1659 the company came up with a few ideas of its own. An arrested smuggler was to be fined four times the value of his goods. To discourage sailors from making a little on the side, a guard was to be posted on board every ship while it was in harbor. "Promise the soldier a share of discovered smuggled goods," the ever practical Heeren XIX suggested. "The method has worked well in Holland." They also instructed the general to look for "reliable men as supercargoes." All these measures were widely publicized so "that everybody may be warned to live up to them without being in a position to plead ignorance."[14]

Another irritant to officials and merchants was the great number of petty traders—"Scots and Chinese," as they were called—who came to New Amsterdam to make a quick deal, and then disappeared with the best wares without paying taxes. Stuyvesant had tried in 1654 to put a stop to this nuisance by ordering that only residents of four years' standing and "in actual possession of a decent house and farm" could do business. The company had lifted this restriction the next year with the reproving—and hypocritical —remark that "the growth of a community, yet in its infancy, must be rather promoted by encouraging unlimited privileges." The directors told Stuyvesant that to compel individuals to settle somewhere was "disgusting, indeed horrible." For them it was sufficient that a trader keep "open store," so that "interlopers and pedlars" would be checked.[15]

This was no help, and in 1657, under pressure from the aggrieved merchants of New Amsterdam, the city fathers petitioned for the introduction of the Burgher-recht, a system of municipal privilege that had existed in the United Provinces for centuries. Following the plan that was adopted by Amsterdam in 1652, the governor and his Council proposed a dual form: the Groote (great) and the Kleyne (small) Burgher-recht. The first was for members of the government, magistrates, clergy, and officers. The second was for all persons born in the city, and all who had lived there for at least a year and six weeks. Others, on approval of the magistrates, could buy it for twenty guilders. The Groote Burgher-recht was, after strict scrutiny, available for fifty guilders.

It seemed a certain way to stop unwanted intruders, since from February 13, 1657—the date the ordinance was published—only burghers could trade or exercise professions or handicrafts in the capital. Great Burghers were also exempt from arrest upon the order of an inferior court and were the only people who could hold important offices. Every burgher would lose his rights if he failed "to keep fire and light" (a residence) within the walls around the city.[16]

The introduction of the Burgher Right was a success from the

A BRAVE PLACE

start. At once two hundred citizens enrolled as Small Burghers and over the years their number grew rapidly. The system of Great Burghers was less successful. In the young province there were hardly any class barriers, and although twenty persons claimed the rank at first—among them Stuyvesant himself, Megapolensis, and Rachel van Tienhoven, the widow of the secretary—no one later wished to climb a social ladder that was only one step high.

The citizens could find a much better use for the fifty guilders needed to buy their Great Burgher right. Life in New Amsterdam was very expensive, they bitterly complained. The duty of 10 percent on all imported goods (and 16 percent on those coming from New England) was for them an unbearable burden. At the same time the "official currency," the seawan or wampum, was devaluing so rapidly that Stuyvesant had to intervene.

In 1650 he had for the first time tried to fix its value, at the rate of six white or three black beads for one stuiver, asking the company at the same time for small coins to replace the shells. The West India Company refused because it was "beyond our means," and the chaotic situation had gone on, aggravated by the New England traders, who had now obtained the monopoly through their possession of the eastern half of Long Island and its wampum banks. They came to New Netherland able to pay 25 percent more wampum for their goods than the Dutch, "whereby this place is so overstocked," explained the citizens in 1658 in a petition, "that it is held in no esteem, and bakers, brewers, traders, labourers and others are so particular, that much difficulty is experienced in managing with it."[17]

Stuyvesant had already asked the company for advice, and it suggested that he reduce the value of wampum from six to eight per stuiver, a measure the governor introduced in October 1658. It made no difference, since from now on the trader simply had to give more for his beaver skins, while no baker or butcher obeyed the order against raising prices. In 1659 Stuyvesant had to devalue the beads again, now to sixteen white or eight black for a stuiver, and the effect was disastrous.

"The poor farmer, laborer and public officer, being unable to obtain beaver"—together with silver, the only stable currency—"and being paid in seawan, are almost reduced to the necessity of living on alms," the community lamented. Proposals from Stuyvesant to establish a provincial mint were rejected by the company

A SWEET AND ALIEN LAND

since it saw no way to keep the money from circulating outside the colony, and in the end Stuyvesant simply raised the value of whatever currency there was by 20 percent. In 1663 these moves at last paid off. The price of wampum fell from sixteen to eight per stuiver, and some degree of financial stability returned.[18]

Newcomers to New Amsterdam, sailing into the beautiful bay, were at first sight unaware of these difficulties in the province. For most of them, it was enough simply to have arrived. They stared in amazement at the green slopes of Long Island on the right and the pine-covered Hudson banks on the left. Ahead was the lively town of New Amsterdam, with its houses on the waterfront dominated by the steeple of St. Nicholas Church, its oak shingles polished by rain and wind. The arrival of a ship—certainly of one bringing new settlers—was still an event in the small community, which had very often been warned of its coming by other, faster vessels. The citizens crowded together near the Stadt Huys, and while cannon boomed the usual welcome, watched, fascinated, while the schout-fiscaal went on board to check the cargo before anybody was allowed to disembark.

The first pioneers had been impressed by the beauty of the island, where no house had yet been built; the colonists of the 1650's and 1660's must have been astounded by the overwhelmingly Dutch character of the town that had grown up there in thirty-five years. "Most of the houses are built in the old way," wrote a visitor, "with the gable end toward the street; the gable end of brick & all the other wall of planks. . . . The streetdoors are generally in the middle of the houses and"—just as in any Dutch town or village —"on both sides are seats, on which during fair weather, the people spent almost the whole day. . . ." A later witness described some of the houses as being "very stately and high. The Bricks . . . are of divers Coullers and laid in checkers, being glazed, look very agreable." The interiors were "neat to admiration."[19]

No longer were the streets lined with "privies." The governor, who on arrival had been shocked by the sight of those smelly cubicles "with an opening to the street, so that hogs may consume the filth and wallow in it," had in August 1658 ordered them to be removed, if necessary by force, as "they not only create a great

A BRAVE PLACE

stench and therefore great inconvenience to the passers by, but also makes the streets foul and unfit for use."[20]

Some of the streets were now paved, very often at the initiative of the inhabitants themselves. The first had been the Brouwerstraat (Stone Street), where Burgomaster Oloff Stevensen van Cortland lived with his seven children. He and his neighbors had petitioned the City Council in 1654 that "for our own accommodation and the public good, ornament and welfare of this city" they wished to pave the street with "round stone." But it was not until January 1658 that the order was given to start the work.[21]

There was some question as to who was going to pay for the paving, and the same happened when the Heerengracht had to be skirted. But in the end the problems were solved with the help of the governor, who gave a thousand guilders out of the company's chest.[22]

The gracht had at once—as in old Amsterdam—become the community's dustbin, and in February 1657 the city, in the hope of making an end of this nuisance, opened five places where rubbish could be brought, one on the Strand, one near City Hall, and others on the riverbank around the gallows. Those who dumped their filth in the street would be fined up to six guilders.

The ordinance obviously did not do much good, since another order was issued before the end of the year. "It having been found, that some burghers . . . throw into the just commenced graft all their filth, as ashes, dead animals etc to the great inconvenience by bad odors of the people working there," the magistrates had decided to raise the fine to twenty-five guilders. The canal remained, however, a running sore in the heart of the town, and in 1662 the burgomasters had a lock built to keep it full of water so "that especially the great and unbearable stench may be suppressed, which arises daily when the water runs out."[23]

Another reason for keeping the Heerengracht full was the possibility of fire. Many of the chimneys in New Amsterdam were still made of wood and only lightly plastered, despite a series of ordinances instructing the citizens to build them of stone. The risk of fire was increased because, as Stuyvesant said in 1657, "for want of stone or brick many wooden house are built . . . the one adjoyning the other." He gave orders that year for fire buckets, ladders, and hooks to be provided at the corners of every street and in public houses. To pay for them, one beaver or eight guilders in wampum

A SWEET AND ALIEN LAND

had to be collected from every house. The burgomasters called four shoemakers to City Hall for an estimate in August 1658, and two of them got the order after quoting a price of six guilders each for 150 buckets. These were delivered and hung at strategic points in January 1659, stamped with the city's arms.[24]

At the same time a rattle watch was introduced to look for fires and guard against Indian invasion. Nine men were taken on, of whom four had to patrol the capital every night, for a wage of twenty-four stuivers, candles to light the way, and wood to warm them. Discipline under Captain Lodewyck Pos was, however, completely lacking. He himself was once involved in a drunken brawl in the Blue Dove, and was humiliatingly robbed of his sword. His men obstinately refused to call the hours before daylight, as they "do not want to be ridiculed by other people."[25]

The days of improvisation were nonetheless over. The burgomasters were now firmly established and had in 1658 received permission to propose a double number of their possible successors to the governor, who then made his choice. One burgomaster was always in City Hall, where he was occupied with all the financial and executive business of the city. Together with the schepens, the burgomasters controlled all the properties of the capital, kept the seal, were able to impose special taxes, and commanded the burgher militia. The city now also had a grain measurer, a weight controller, and a measurer of apples; there were twelve sworn butchers and inspectors of bread; and for the expectant mother, there was a midwife, Hillegond Joris, with a yearly salary of one hundred guilders.[26]

For the sick, a small hospital was opened in 1656 behind the five stone company houses, the oldest buildings in town, then used as warehouses. In the hospital Dr. Jacobus Varevanger and his colleague Hans Kierstede practiced with the help of a "matron." There was also an orphan court and, in the good tradition of the homeland, an almshouse took care of the aged and the poor.

New Amsterdam even had its official post office. In the early days letters were normally sent by friends "whom God may bless," but in 1660 it was possible to deliver letters for the Republic at the office of the provincial secretary. It remained safer, however, to make three copies, which were mailed via Virginia, Curaçao, and England.[27]

Funerals also became more strictly regulated. The burial

A BRAVE PLACE

grounds were just off the Heerenstraat (Broadway) next to the company gardens, and court messenger Claes van Elslandt Sr. was in charge. He had to ring the bell to announce the funeral, "also to preserve the pall, collect the hire thereof, for the church as well as the fee for ringing the bell," and, of course, keep a record of all who had died. He seems not to have been a great success. His son was summoned by the magistrates and instructed to tell his father to behave—"to walk decently before the corpse and to demand and receive pay only for his services, without asking for more." A month later, on March 4, 1661, Elslandt himself was called to court, since people complained that he did not behave well "as a grave-digger and when inviting people to a burial." The burgomasters gave him one more chance "because of his age and long residence," but in May 1662 he was removed from his delicate office.[28]

New Amsterdam was always a busy city, but it became particularly crowded in the months of May and November, when its aspect changed from that of a port town to that of a cattle market. From far and near farmers and traders arrived with their cows, sheep, and pigs to settle for a month in the marketplace on the Strand, in front of Stuyvesant's Great House.

Other markets were held every Saturday. Until 1656 the farmers, coming with their wares to the city, had simply sat down on the Strand in the hope that the citizens would turn up. "They must often remain there . . . a long time to their great damage, because the community . . . do not know that anything has been brought for sale," Stuyvesant had explained, "which is not only an inconvenience for the burghers, but also a great loss for the industrious countrymen." In 1659 the burgomasters completed the market, which had a "shamble" covered with tiles for the meat, while the half-yearly cattle market moved from Pearl Street to the Heerenstraat near the churchyard.[29]

The rural aspect of the capital was, however, only superficial. With the sea wind blowing through the streets, the smell of drying fish, pelts, and tar, the many masts in the harbor, which could be seen from almost every corner, and the great number of sailors swaying through the town, New Amsterdam was first of all a port.

A SWEET AND ALIEN LAND

LAW

AND DISORDER

On Monday mornings New Amsterdammers knew that justice
would be done—or at least so they hoped. The bell in the little
turret on the roof of the Stadt Huys chimed at nine o'clock, and
on the stoop, town crier Stoffel Michielsen announced the cases
that were called for judgment by burgomasters, schepens, and
schout. Defendants, plaintiffs, witnesses, and curious spectators
shuffled into the courtroom, which was decorated with the orange,
white, and pale blue flag of the West India Company and the
tricolor of the States General. Behind the judge's bench they saw
the window made by glassmaker Evert Duycking in 1659, engraved
with the arms of New Amsterdam—the three crosses of the
mother city in the Republic, crowned with a beaver. The same
arms were repeated on the twelve cushions made by the poet Jacob
Steendam, for the seats of the magistrates.[1]

On the bench itself was a little box with the seal that the company had sent in 1653 as the symbol of New Amsterdam's status as
a city. Beside it were the legal books, called *Ordinances and Code of
Procedure before the Courts of the City of Amsterdam,* which had been
shipped over from Holland for the guidance of the new judges in
the province. While the crowd chatted and studied the comings
and goings, court secretary Johannes Nevius and messengers Pieter Schaefbanck and Claes van Elslandt Sr. (after 1660 replaced by
his son) sat down behind a table covered with green baize. Then,

announced by bailiff Matthew de Vos, the burgomasters and schepens would sweep in, followed by Pieter Tonneman, the city's own schout, who was at last appointed in 1660.

Silence fell and after a prayer by one of the dominies, the session would start. Many of the cases were ordinary questions of property, debt, and arbitration. If there were complications, the magistrates could invite some "respectable citizens" to sit with them in judgment, and although there was a right of appeal to the governor and the Council, few people ever made use of it.[2]

But, as elsewhere, life in New Amsterdam was not only a question of trade, money, and property. This was at once demonstrated by the case that opened the court's very first proceedings on February 10, 1653. It was proof as well that in the capital, as in any society, the lives of those at the top were a favorite target of gossip. The case involved Allard Anthony, a rather unpopular schepen who was sitting as one of the judges.

Joost Goderis, an employee at the weighing house, dragged into court six citizens who had taunted him with his wife's infidelity. One of them had told him: "Joost Goderis ought to wear horns, like the cattle in the woods"; another had revealed that Allard Anthony had "had your wife down on her back." Goderis had given one of them, Isaack Bedloo, a slap in the face, after which Bedloo had drawn a knife and cut the "cuckold" in the neck. The case went on for weeks, but nothing was done and Goderis, who continued to be the victim of constant harassment, became more and more distracted and in the end lost both his wife and his job.[3]

Another respectable notable whose name was sullied was Willem Beeckman, the vice director of Altona. His wife, it was said, had been seen with a sailor in the bushes. The seaman was brought into court, together with the wife of Geurt Coerten, who had spread the rumors. He related that he had only received "such a kiss from her [Mrs. Beeckman] that I could scarcely compose myself." It had been the price for his silence, since—still according to the scandalmongers—he had caught her with another man, the rich storekeeper Cornelis Steenwyck. Mrs. Coerten told her neighbors that the sailor had also received some wampum, but "that he regretted he had not taken the gold ring from her finger." In court she vehemently denied the charge of slander, pleading for "forgiveness if she had repeated one word to the injury of Mme Beeckman."[4]

A SWEET AND ALIEN LAND

Hilletje Jans was another gossip who appeared in court after spreading a story about the wife of Christiaen Anthony, who had been "in the bush with the supercargo of the *Beer* ["Bear"] . . . unbecoming to a honest woman." Mrs. Anthony—no relation to the schepen—was a strange character anyway. She had once visited a public house "clad in man's clothes, having a pair of whiskers painted black" and had asked for a pint of beer.[5]

It was not unusual for a sailor to meet a bored housewife willing to grace him with her favors; but if he was not so lucky, New Amsterdam, like any other port, had its prostitutes. Cornelis van Tienhoven, with the eye of an expert, had already identified them in 1654. He told the City Court "that not long since very indecent and disgraceful things had been perpetrated . . . by certain women."[6]

The first and most famous prostitute of Manhattan, Griet Reyniers, the wife of Anthony the "Turk," had long since retired and now lived in Gravesend on Long Island, where she had brought up her four daughters to be respectable young ladies and married them off into good families. But others had taken her place, and the city had a reputation that even reached the Netherlands. Jeremias van Rensselaer received a motherly warning from Amsterdam to "shun the company of light [women] of whom New Netherland is full."

Stuyvesant tried to clean up the place in 1657 and reported in August to the company that he had ordered "some light women" to pack their cases, but it is improbable that he succeeded.[7]

If the girls were deported, it was without appearing in court, as no case is recorded, unlike the "voluntary" exile of the wife of a certain Hendrick Janzen Sluyter. After a fight with another woman she had "in presence of respectable company, with their wives, hoisted her petticoats up to her back and showed them her arse." This "being an offence not tolerated in a well ordered province," she was called before the judges. She told them that she had raised her petticoat "at her husband and not at the people," and her embarrassed husband apologized for her, offering the magistrates to ship his obnoxious wife off to Holland, a solution that was accepted.[8]

A few years earlier the court had had another petticoat case, with a happier ending. It concerned Mme. Annetje Bogardus, the widow of the drowned pastor. She was accused of exhibitionism, having displayed her ankle in public. A friend came to her help, testifying that Annetje "passing the blacksmith shop . . . placed her hand on her side and drew up her petticoat a little, in order not to soil it, as the road was muddy."[9]

Stuyvesant, a puritan at heart and a disciplinarian by profession, tried by all possible means to force his bawdy citizens to live according to Christian rules. Days of fasting and prayer were announced by plackets that sounded like the Old Testament, urging the people to turn "away from our crying and God-irritating sins . . . our drunkenness, feasting, voluptuousness, adultery, deception and other heinous sins, which prevail among us to our shame before Christian neighbours and barbarous natives." If they would not change their ways, his subjects could "only expect, that like others we shall perish and that not the tower of Shiloa but the wrath of God will fall upon us from Heaven and envelop us in flames for our greater punishment."[10]

Those sermons had as little effect as the more secular regulations for the closing times of the taverns, or Stuyvesant's efforts to stop street fights. After having discovered that the citizens would sooner pay the statutory fine of "one pound Flemish in wampum" than be cheated of a good fight, he instituted, on December 25, 1657, penalties of twenty-five guilders "for a simple blow with the fist," and if blood flowed, four times as much.[11]

One source of constant unrest was, of course, the many taverns, inns, and taprooms in New Amsterdam. The most famous was still the Wooden Horse, now run by Marie, the widow of Philip Geraerdy, but the most popular was the Blue Dove on Paerelstraat (Pearl Street). Run by carpenter Claes Jansen de Ruyter, it was a special favorite of the rattle guards. Opposite was the taproom of ship chandler Michiel Taden, while Captain Lodewyck Pos kept a small tavern in his house near the mill on Beaver's Path. The wife of Solomon La Chair, the notary, kept herself occupied by serving wine, like the daughters of Captain Martin Cregier, who in 1659 opened a tavern on the Heerenstraat (Broadway).

When Stuyvesant asked the burgomasters in 1657 to reduce this chaos to some order, they summoned all the owners of taverns, taprooms, and grog shops, and twenty-one had appeared. The City Court had thereupon ordered the tapsters to take out a license every three months, for which they had to pay six guilders each time. But if the court hoped to discourage any of them, it was disappointed. All twenty-one agreed to pay, "provided that they may afterwards sell their wine and beer and that no price be fixed thereon, inasmuch there is considerable trust and bad pay, and no one can serve for nothing." The court yielded halfway. The price of beer remained fixed—twelve stuivers the half-gallon—but the price of wine was decontrolled.[12]

In the same year Stuyvesant had reemphasized the rule that no taverns could be kept open during the sermons on Sunday. In the evening they had to close their doors after the ringing of the bell. He also reminded the tapsters not to sell to the Indians. These orders were part of another effort by the governor to "purify" his province, and to establish the Sabbath as a day of piety and prayer. From October 30 onward, "all persons performing, on the Lord's day, by us called Sunday, any ordinary work such as ploughing, sowing, mowing, building, woodcutting, working in iron or tin, hunting, fishing, etc.," would be liable to a fine of one pound Flemish. The fine would be doubled for people who were caught in "games, drunkenness, frequenting taverns or grog-shops, dancing, card-playing, backgammon, tennis, ball-playing, bowling, rolling nine pins, racing with boats, cars or wagons."[13]

But the Dutch were not to be dragooned like Puritan New England; they simply went ahead and did what they thought fit. A splendid example was the long-standing controversy that reached a climax in 1654 when Stuyvesant made it an offense "to ride the goose on the feast of Bacchus at Shrove-tide." It was a cruel and "pagan" sport, the governor rightly felt, involving a live goose, hung on a cord between two poles at a height of three meters from the ground. The object of the competitors was to ride under the goose on horseback, at full speed, and try to pull or cut off its head, which had been rubbed with soap. It was a popular sport in the Netherlands, and the burgomasters of New Amsterdam saw no reason to obey the general's order.[14]

Without informing the aldermen, a furious Stuyvesant summoned the goose riders before the Provincial Council, where they behaved so insolently—"threatening, cursing, deriding and laughing at the chief magistracy"—that he sent them straight to prison. The city fathers felt "aggrieved in their quality," and it led to one of their many clashes with the governor, who replied haughtily that the establishment of City Court "does in no way infringe upon or diminish the power and authority of the Director-General

LAW AND DISORDER

. . . especially if they are for the glory of God, the welfare of the inhabitants or the prevention of sin."[15]

It was, however, a hopeless struggle, and after one more effort in 1655 to stop the citizens from celebrating "New Years Day and May Day [with] the firing of guns, the planting of Maypoles and the intemperate drinking," Stuyvesant gave up and issued no more such ordinances.[16]

On one question, however, he insisted till the bitter end: the regulations for marriage. As in the Republic, a couple was able to marry after their marriage banns had been thrice proclaimed, but more and more it happened that the marriage was then put off. In January 1658 he put an end to this practice by commanding that "all persons, who have been published shall, after three proclamations have been made and no lawful impediments intervening, solemnize their marriage at least within a month after the first publication." No single man and woman should live together as a married couple, he stated, under pain of forfeiting one hundred guilders.[17]

He was equally strict about adultery, and punishment was harsh, as Ytie Jansen found out. This young Dutch woman had lived with an Englishman, Jan Parcel, at the request of her husband, who himself preferred a certain Geesje Jansen. Despite these mitigating circumstances the court sentenced her to be whipped and banished. When Ytie and Jan—"two sorrowful sinners"—appeared two weeks later in court to ask for permission to marry, the magistrates were unrelenting and gave them three months to pack, telling them to "separate from each other at once."[18]

It is almost certain that Ytie never had to undergo the whipping. In New Netherland—unlike New England—this sentence seldom got further than a symbolic flogging in the case of women, which meant that the offender was led to the stake, partly stripped, and given two rods on her hands, after which she was untied and banished. One spectacular example of this leniency was Lysbeth Antonissen, a young slave belonging to Martin Cregier, who had set her master's house on fire. She confessed and was sentenced "to be conveyed to the place of execution, to be chained to a stake, strangled and then burnt." Almost at once the Provincial Council revoked the sentence, and directed that all the preparations for strangling and burning should be made, but that the girl at the last moment should be pardoned and given back to her master.[19]

The treatment for men was considerably less generous. Pieter, the city's hangman, a burly Negro, was an expert in whipping and went to work with dedication in spite of the fact that his payment was constantly in arrears. When a male adulterer was caught, Pieter had to take him to the stake, tie a rope around his neck, and flog him. Sometimes the punishment was completed by cutting off the right ear and banishing the criminal for fifty years. Theft was punished by scourging with rods, and branding on the cheeks was a frequently used penalty for hardened criminals. For sailors, the punishment very often consisted of being dropped from the yard arm, and running the gauntlet. The use of the rack to force a confession is recorded only a few times, and only once in the case of a woman.[20]

The death penalty was hardly ever executed during Stuyvesant's government, or before. One of the most sensational cases was that of the West India Company Negro, Manuel Gerritsen. He was one of a group of nine who had confessed to the murder of another slave, Manuel the Giant, and was chosen by lot to be hanged as an example. But the gallows on the Strand was not built for his size, the cord broke, and the Negro fell to the ground, "whereupon all the bystanders called out, Mercy. Which was accordingly granted."[21]

Jan Quisthout van der Linde, a soldier from Brussels, was less fortunate. He committed in 1660 a "crime condemned of God as an abomination" together with Hendrick Harmsen, an orphan from Amsterdam. On June 17 he was condemned "to be taken to the place of execution and there stripped of his arms, his sword to be broken at his feet and he then to be tied in a sack and cast into the river and drowned till dead." The crowd, which as always came to the place of execution, waited this time in vain for the town crier to come panting up with a written remission of the penalty, and the citizens themselves for once took no initiative in asking for mercy. The orphan was "privately whipped" and sent away.[22]

There was more clemency for the only suicide that was registered. The tapster Hendrick Jansen Smit, who appeared in court on May 27, 1664, was accused of serving after hours in his tavern in Bridge Street. He was condemned to a fine of sixteen guilders, but did not pay. When Schout Tonneman on July 16 went to ask him for the money, he discovered that Smit had hanged himself

LAW AND DISORDER

"on the branch of a tree at the Kalckhoeck." The schout demanded that the court confiscate his goods, and that the corpse should be "drawn on a hurdle as an example and terror to others, and brought to the place where it was found hanging and there shoved under the earth; further that a stake, pole or post shall be set in token of an accursed deed."[23]

Eight of Smit's neighbors, hearing this, signed a petition for mercy and the magistrates decided that "whereas Smit has been an old Burgher here, of whom no bad behaviour was ever heard," he should have a decent burial "at the corner of the churchyard in the evening after the ringing of the nine o'clock bell." Peter Stuyvesant, who was asked for his advice, approved.[24]

It was an act of the humanity that generally characterized the attitude of the Dutch to orphans, the old, the poor, and even prisoners. The damp, dark prison in the old fort was rarely used; most of the prisoners were kept in cells under City Hall, where jailer Anthony Baeck and later Pieter Schaefbanck kept an eye on them. Their charges were allowed to sit in the large prison chamber with "candle and light," and in 1658 Schaefbanck got permission to "lay in beer for the prisoners, also wine and liquors, free of excise, likewise fire and light gratis." The only condition was that this not lead to "any parties directly or indirectly."[25]

HOMAGE IN VERSE

I'm a grandchild of the Gods
Who on th'Amstel have abodes
Whence their orders forth are sent,
Swift for aid and punishment.
I, of Amsterdam, was born,
Earley of her breasts forlorn;
From her care so quickly weaned
Oft have I my fate bemoaned.

This was the *Klacht van Nieuw-Amsterdam*, the "Complaint of New Amsterdam," that the local poet Jacob Steendam sent in 1659 to the United Provinces. It was addressed to the "mother" of the small capital at the Hudson, to the richest and most powerful city in the world—Amsterdam. Only too well aware that the Heeren XIX considered their offspring more like a "step-child," Steendam turned to the town that had given its name to the new settlement.

Life in the province was hard and difficult that year. The Indians were again on the warpath and the settlers were frightened:

From the moment I was born
Indian neighbours made me mourn,
They pursued me night and day
While my mother stayed away.

The English as well were pushing harder at the borders, while creating unrest inside the province:

> Fraught with danger, for the Swine
> Trample down these crops of mine;
> Up-root, too, my choicest land;
> Still and dumb, the while I stand.

It was a sad fate for a city, of which Steendam said:

> From my youth up left alone
> Naught save hardship have I known
> Dangers have beset my way
> From the first I saw the day

Over the years little had changed:

> When I thus began to grow
> No more care did they bestow
> Yet my breasts are full and neat
> And my hips are firmly set.

What this young maiden needed:

> Is for men to till my land;
> So I'll not in silence stand
>
> I'll my mother's kitchen furnish
> With my knicknacks, with my surplus
> With tobacco, furs and grain;
> So that Prussia she'll disdain.[1]

In this allegorical way Steendam tried to attract attention to the land he had loved from the moment of his arrival in 1650. The thirty-five-year-old poet had not come to New Amsterdam merely to become the city's first versemaker. He was a successful business-man who had served the West India Company in Guinea since 1641. He had enjoyed his years in Africa's Gold Coast, but was happy to return in 1649 to Amsterdam, the town he called:

> A good example of the everlasting realm,
> Where we do hope to live through all eternity
> In constant, highest joy, and in true happiness, Amen.[2]

A SWEET AND ALIEN LAND

His "eternity" in Amsterdam was very short. After marrying Sarah de Rosschou and publishing some earlier poems under the title *Distelvinck* ("Thistle Finch"), he left for New Netherland, where he settled as a farmer at Mespath on Long Island, buying property also in New Amsterdam. Soon he concentrated mainly on commerce, and rhyming.

Steendam was a strong-willed man with an independent mind, who signed his poems "Steendam—Noch Vaster" (Stone dam—still firmer). He ran his business with a touch of bohemianism and had regular brushes with the law. In 1655 he appeared for the first time in court, accused of having erected a house—at 61 Stone Street —"wholly out of line of the street." The court appointed two members to go and have a look, and in spite of Steendam's defense that "he could build on his lot as he pleased," the court decided that he had to "regulate the building."[3]

His wife Sarah was clearly in charge of collecting the rent from their divers properties. She had already been in court in November 1654, complaining about a tenant who had "departed from this city" without paying her the ten guilders he owed. Two years later she was back, together with her husband. On March 6, 1656, the couple had a case against notary public and innkeeper Solomon La Chair, who had refused to pay the rent. La Chair admitted that he had lived in their house, but told the magistrates that "it was not delivered tight, nor in good order," and the case was referred to two arbitrators.[4]

The case on March 20 was more serious. Sarah, arriving at the house of tenant Aryan Woutersen, had been received with a stream of abuse. The wife of the house, Catalyntie, had called her "swine, cheat, etc.," but Sarah, having a ready tongue, told Catalyntie that she was a "whore and a slut." Aryan, just coming home, took the side of his insulted wife and struck Sarah on her head, "knocked her against a barrel and shoved her out of doors," to the amusement of "a great mob in the streets." The court gave Woutersen just the order to pay his rent within two weeks.[5]

A year later Steendam was less kindly treated by the judges in New Haven, where he had some possessions as well. He was called into court by a certain Edward Perkins, who complained that the poet's hogs had destroyed his field of peas. Steendam apologized and told the court that he "had agreed with men to make it [the fence] new, and hath paid them all or part of it, but they neglected and did not performe according to promise. . . ." He was neverthe-less sentenced to pay Perkins "six bushells of peas and the charges of the Court," with the advice to "seeke remedy from those who were to doe his fenc and did it not."[6]

Aiming at bigger things, the enterprising Steendam applied on May 3, 1660, together with some other Dutch merchants, for "leave to trade for slaves along the west coast of Africa." This was granted. It was the second effort by private traders in New Neth-erland to get a share in a business that was still very much in company hands. Governor Peter Stuyvesant was constantly in touch with his vice director, Beck, in Curaçao, the center of the slave trade. In 1659 Beck sent him five Negroes, "all dry and well conditioned and marked with annexed mark," but the governor complained that they were too expensive for the colonists in New Amsterdam—150 guilders each. Another group of twenty arrived in 1660. They were cheaper, but now the governor complained that most of them were old and sick. Furious, he told Beck to give preference to "the Christians and those of the Honble Company" before selling the good ones to "Spaniards and unbelieving Jews." He wished "stout and strong fellows, fit for immediate employ-ment." In 1661 he at last got what he wanted: forty "sound slaves" for a reasonable price. He gave three of them as a present to the magistrates of New Amsterdam and successfully auctioned off the rest against payment in "beavers, beef, pork, wheat or peas."[7]

There was clearly room here for private enterprise, but Steen-dam's initiative never got off the ground, and in July 1660 he sold his house on Pearl Street and returned to Holland. He could not forget New Netherland, and two years after the *Complaint* was published, he gave free reign to his nostalgic memories in *T Lof van Nieu-Nederlandt* ("The Praise of New Netherland") in the hope of encouraging emigration:

> For me, it is a nobler theme I sing
> New Netherland springs forth my heroine;
> Where Amstel's folk did erst their people bring,
> And still they nourish.
> Who'ver to you a judgment fair applies,
> And knowing, comprehends your qualities,
> Will justify the man who, to the skies,
> Extols your glories.

A SWEET AND ALIEN LAND

It was his intention, as he stated in a foreword, to show the Dutch "the excellent qualities which it possesses in the purity of the air, the fertility of the soil, production of the cattle, abundance of game and fish, with its advantages for navigation and commerce" and he did not lack for words:

> It is the land where milk and honey flow;
> Where plants distilling perfume grow;
> Where Aaron's rod with budding blossoms blow;
>   A very Eden.

> The elk, the hind, and hart which, fleeing, bound
> Far in the wood, entangled here are found;
> And when at last they feel the fatal wound
>   Die hard and crying.

It had nothing in common with the cloudy, soggy, and windy Republic. The winds in New Netherland were the breezes of health:

> From damp, and mist, they set it free;
> From smells of pools, they give it liberty:
> The struggling stenches made to mount on high,
>   And be at peace here.[8]

In short, it was "the noblest spot on earth." And the poem with its 288 affectionate lines, was an excellent piece of public relations, the first romantic homage to Dutch America.

With the departure of Steendam, New Netherland was still left with two poets, company official Nicasius de Sille and Dominie Henricus Selyns. The poetic triumvirate had been brief—Selyns arrived just before Steendam left, and it is not very probable that New Amsterdam ever possessed a Poet's Corner.

Nicasius De Sille, fifty years old in 1660, had made his peace with General Stuyvesant, and his influence had grown consistently. After the dismissal of Cornelis van Tienhoven in 1656, De Sille had for four years been the schout-fiscaal for both province and capital.

Stuyvesant had even taken a liking to his contemporary, admitting freely that his first assistant was "better versed in offensive and defensive siege operations . . . than your humble servant."[9]

The intelligent and witty De Sille had fallen in love with New Netherland, and he had kept the promise he made in 1654: "I shall not try to leave it as long as I live." He had discovered a favorite corner of Long Island, where he founded New Utrecht. He was the first schout of the little hamlet, where he built his mansion, a house forty-two feet long, topped with a roof of red tiles and surrounded with a high stockade. Dividing his time between his duties as councillor, fiscaal, and churchwarden in New Amsterdam and that of "lord of the manor" and schout at New Utrecht, he still found time to write a *Description of the Founding or Beginning of New Utrecht* from 1657 till 1660.[10]

It was a great day for his infant settlement when in February 1660 General Stuyvesant came to visit. De Sille presented the village with the Prince's flag, while one of the citizens prepared a dinner "in as good a stile as the place could afford." Stuyvesant stayed only very briefly, advising them to surround the village with "good heavy palisades" as protection against the Indians. To prove he was serious, he sent them some Negroes to help in building the stockade.[11]

The affairs of New Utrecht helped to distract De Sille from his matrimonial difficulties. Arriving in New Netherland as a widower with five children, he had met Catherina Cregier, the eldest daughter of Captain Martin Cregier. The first meeting might have taken place in the tavern that the young girl ran for her father, a fact that was to influence their married life from the start. Catherina had acquired a taste for alcohol and in 1659 De Sille asked for a divorce "on account of her unbecoming and careless life, both by her wasting of property without his knowledge, as by her public habitual drunkenness."[12]

It was an embarrassing situation for the councillor, whose official papers were once freely handed out by his intoxicated wife. The court hesitated and referred the matter to Peter Stuyvesant. De Sille told him "that his wife being drunk on last Sunday eight days," he had to appoint some person to watch her. The governor tried to patch up the marriage, especially since De Sille's son Laurens and his daughter Walburga had married a sister and a brother of their stepmother Catherina, but although the

A SWEET AND ALIEN LAND

councillor withdrew his request for divorce, the couple remained estranged.[13]

De Sille retired more and more often to his country estate, where he revealed that under the dignified cloak of the councillor and the stern harness of the soldier, there beat the heart of a poet. Almost all his poems were dedicated to the place he loved so much and which he considered his creation, New Utrecht:

> *I now am satisfied by th'honor of my name,*
> *By grain and orchard fruit, by horses and by kine,*
> *By plants and by a race of men—all growth of mine.*

Pained by the unhappy relationship with his wife, he had an intense sympathy with the difficulties of the settlers, consoling them that:

> *He comforts who in pain and sorrow are;*
> *His pow'r is inexpressible and grand.*
> *Oh God, stretch out to us Thy helping hand,*
> *And keep Thy children in Thy tender care.*[14]

If the brisk businessman Steendam might not have understood the melancholy elegies of De Sille, New Netherland's third poet, Dominie Henricus Selyns, certainly did. After a youth in Amsterdam in a family circle that spoon-fed him culture and religion, he had been attracted by the romantic heroism of Dutch pioneering and had eagerly accepted the offer from Breukelen to come as their dominie for the yearly salary of twelve hundred guilders. Arriving as a twenty-four-year-old youngster with a load of "small psalm and prayer books for the instruction of the congregation," he discovered that the tiny village just outside New Amsterdam had overreached itself and could hardly pay more than three hundred guilders. The offer from Stuyvesant of an extra 250 guilders for Sunday night service in the governor's chapel was a great help. And the congregation in Breukelen—which flocked to the barn that took the place of a church to hear his heartening sermons—gratefully made up the rest in beavers and grain, build-

HOMAGE IN VERSE

ing a spacious vicarage for him at the same time.[15]

Selyns was a great success and was able to report in 1664 that his flock had increased fourfold. He was conscientious as well, and worried deeply about the lot of the Negro slaves. Some of them asked him to baptize their children, but he refused, explaining to the Classis that he had done so "partly on account of the worldly and perverse aims on the part of the said negroes." According to him, they wanted nothing else "than to deliver their children from bodily slavery, without striving for piety and Christian virtues." Finding this point of view too harsh on reflection, he had taken to catechizing the slaves. "This has borne but little fruit among the elder people, who have no faculty of comprehension; but there is some hope for the youth."[16]

His life was lonely in spite of the increasing numbers of his parishioners. Contacts with his co-poet De Sille were rare, and there was hardly any communication with his confreres. He had arrived on the *Vergulde Bever* ("Gilded Beaver") together with Dominie Hermanus Blom, but the thirty-two-year-old Blom had traveled on to Esopus. Dominie Polhemius, who had come to Breukelen when Selyns was installed, was busy enough with his own rowdy congregations at Midwout and Amersfoort and now, in his middle sixties, felt that he had "to hold himself in constant preparation for the grave," instead of organizing a "form of a Classis, after the manner of the Fatherland." Drisius and Megapolensis were also much older than Selyns, and were anyway too busy with their growing congregation of New Amsterdam.[17]

The only consolations Selyns found were thinking of the girl he had left behind in Utrecht, Machtelt Specht, and writing poetry. It was inevitable that the one influenced the other and he expressed his wish to be reunited with her:

> *Should someone seek the stuff, wherewith to squander praise,*
> *To edge the tongue, to view a sweet and alien land,*
> *Recline thee here; this is a school to train the mind,*
> *Uproot whate'er is bad, keep what is good, Then know*
> *Ywis, that good is always good and bears salvation:*
> *So come, embrace the here and now, for they are good.*[18]

Just before he had left the Republic he had written of his love in much more lighthearted and less emotional terms. The *Birthday*

Garland for Machtelt's twentieth birthday was an ode to the maidens of Utrecht:

> *See the nymphs of Utrecht flying,*
> *See them tripping o'er the street,*
> *See them little chaplets buying*
> *Chaplets for adorning meet.*

It was, of course, to make garlands for

> *The sweetest creature of the town;*
> *Who for evil no ill breathing,*
> *Evil sees with horrors frown*
> *Who, when with her pet she's playing*
> *Image is of modesty,*
> *Who all wantoneers betraying*
> *Leads a life of purity.*[19]

Machtelt, after two years of hesitation, could no longer resist the poetic advances of the dominie. She arrived in time to be married on July 27, 1662, in St. Nicholas Church in New Amsterdam.

One and a half years later another wedding inspired Selyns to grasp the quill, this time to compose an epithalamium. It was in honor of his friend Dominie Aegidius Luyck, who had arrived in New Netherland in 1662. He had hardly set foot on land before he had fallen in love with a certain Judith van Isendooren. According to Selyn's poetic fantasy, called the *Bridal Torch*, it had been the fault of Cupido, who from the walls of New Amsterdam, had used his bow and arrows:

> *While Judith stands beneath, Luyck looks from the*
>   *embrasure,*
> *And ere they see or think, he shoots Luyck in the*
>   *breast,*
> *Nor does one shaft suffice his cov'nant-making*
>   *pleasure.*
> *"Where did he shoot? Where was't he shot?" inquire*
>   *the folks.*
> *Luyck speaks not, for he feels something his heart*
>   *is boring.*
> *As all look up at Luyck, so Judith upwards looks.*
> *He shoots a second time and pierces Isendooren.*[20]

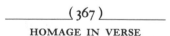

HOMAGE IN VERSE

The result of this happy shooting party was a marriage just before Christmas 1663. But for Selyns it was almost the end of his stay in New Netherland. On June 9, 1664, he wrote to the Classis in Amsterdam that, since his parents were getting older and "most anxious for my return," he wanted to leave Breukelen. He sailed in August, accompanied by a letter in which Dominie Drisius regretfully wrote: "We could have wished, that Domine Selyns had longer continued with us, both on account of his diligence and success in preaching and catechizing, and of his humble and edifying life. By this he has attracted a great many people, and even some Negroes, so that many are sorry for his departure."[21]

As with Steendam—who had left Amsterdam for the East Indies, where he died in 1672—Selyns' departure from New Amsterdam did not mean an end to his poetic career. He returned to New Netherland in 1682 (where he died in 1701), and was so prolific "sending poems to all persons in all places and on all occasions" —that the Reverend Cotton Mather, the well-known pastor of Boston, called him "upon this, as well as upon greater accounts . . . a David under the flocks of our Lord in the Wilderness."[22]

The arrival of Dominie Aegidius Luyck in 1662 was the beginning of a new period in the education of young New Amsterdammers. General Stuyvesant, who always maintained that "nothing is of greater importance than the early instruction of youth," had invited him to come to the province to teach his two sons, Balthasar and Nicholas, by now fifteen and fourteen years old. Luyck was still a theological student, "a youth, but very modest, a good reader, and well versed in languages." The Stuyvesant boys made such good progress under him that the governor decided to give their friends' sons the opportunity to extend their knowledge, and within a few months Luyck was instructing twenty young students.[23]

In contrast with the Fatherland, New Netherland had had a constant struggle with the question of education. Initially the dominies had taken care of the most eager youngsters, but soon there were too many of them, and in 1633 Adam Roelantsen had arrived to take up the challenging job of teaching New Amsterdam's rebellious youth, acting at the same time as reader and

A SWEET AND ALIEN LAND

sexton in the church. His private life, however, was not exactly the best example (he was once caught with a young girl), and in 1642 he was replaced by Jan Stevensz, who stayed for only four years, leaving the children "running wild" again.

It was Dominie Backerus, who arrived with Stuyvesant in 1647, who decided that something must be done about the intolerable situation. He asked Amsterdam at once for schoolteachers. But Amsterdam did not react and in the end the governor asked the surgeon Pieter van der Linde to act as schoolmaster. He was clearly not very satisfactory and in 1650 the New Amsterdammers complained in their Remonstrance: "The school is kept very irregularly, one and another keeping it according to his pleasure and as long as he thinks proper." They asked for a public school "provided with at least two good masters, so that first of all in so wild a country, where there are so many loose people, the youth will be well taught and brought up."[24]

The community got at least partially what it wanted: when New Amsterdam in 1653 received its city rights, the city magistrates undertook to pay the schoolmasters and ministers, but Willem Vestiensz, who had arrived in 1650, often had to beg them for payment and in 1655 he complained bitterly to the Provincial Council. They made it clear to him "that he had fulfilled his duties only so-and-so and that he did little enough for his salary," Dominie Megapolensis wrote to Amsterdam. "Therefore when he asked for an increase last year, he received the answer that if the service did not suit him, he might ask for his discharge." Vestiensz did.[25]

His successor was Harmen van Hoboken, like Stevensz unlicensed and without a classroom. For a while he used his own house for classes, but when his wife was expecting her fifth baby it became too much and he asked the burgomasters and schepens if he could have the use of a room in City Hall. They apologized as the "rooms are required for other purposes," but added that "in order that the youth, who are here quite numerous may have the means of instruction" he might hire a proper house, for which they gave him a hundred guilders a year.[26]

The situation outside New Amsterdam was even worse. "As far as we know, not one of all these places, Dutch or English, has a schoolmaster," reported Megapolensis in 1657 to the Classis, "except the Manhattans, Beverwyck and now also Fort Casimir."

Some of the parents gave their children a little vague instruction, but the results were far from satisfactory and the minister predicted pessimistically: "We can expect nothing else than young men of foolish and undisciplined minds."[27]

It would be some years before any real change occurred, but in 1661 a second school was at last opened on Manhattan. Van Hoboken was moved to Stuyvesant's bouwery to teach the young blacks there, while the New Amsterdam school was taken over by Evert Pietersen, who had been until then the schoolmaster of Amsterdam's colony on the Delaware, New Amstel. Pietersen had survived the many epidemics that had ravaged the settlement, but it had been a hard struggle to keep his pupils at work. "I have no paper nor pen for the use of the children," he had once complained. The colonists, even the adults, were eager enough to learn and came to his classroom in the winter, when they could no longer work the soil, "but I have nothing from which to teach them."[28]

At the end of his term of service in 1660 Pietersen returned to Holland, but when, a year later, Stuyvesant begged him to return and work in the capital, he accepted. For the first time New Amsterdam had a qualified and able teacher, and the City Fathers felt that some rules were not overdue. In November 1662 they composed their town's first school program:

> In the first place he [the schoolmaster] shall take care that the children in his charge come at the specified time to school, and well at eight o'clock and in the afternoon at one;
> In the second place he will keep a good discipline;
> In the third place he shall teach the children and pupils the prayers, the Ten Commandments, the baptism, the Lord's Supper and the questions and answers from the Catechism;
> In the fourth place he shall, before the class ends, sing some verses from a psalm.

The rest of the program was left to the teacher, but his income was stipulated with more care. He could charge every pupil who "learned to spell the a.b.c. and to read" thirty stuivers per term, those who learned to read and write fifty stuivers per term, and those whom he taught arithmetic sixty stuivers. He was not allowed to take more.[29]

A SWEET AND ALIEN LAND

New Amsterdam also came to have quite a few private schools. The best was that of David Provost, a successful merchant who had been commissioner at the House of Good Hope and later a member of the Provincial Council and notary public. Another was the school of Jacobus van Curler, Provost's predecessor at Good Hope, who had moved first to Gravesend, where Lady Moody was the undisputed boss of the predominantly English population. He left in 1657 for New Amsterdam after the English had made it very obvious that they no longer appreciated the presence of Dutchmen in their community. In 1658 Van Curler opened a private school in New Amsterdam, but only a few weeks later Schout-Fiscaal De Sille ordered him to close it since he had no license. The parents protested loudly. They had been very satisfied with Van Curler, who taught their children "in reading, writing and cyphering, which was much more than any other person" had done. But even the support of the city magistrates could not change Stuyvesant's mind. He felt that Van Curler had done wrong in not asking his permission, and the school remained closed.[30]

With the appointment of Pietersen there was at last order in the lower echelons of New Amsterdam's school system. Higher up, unrest persisted. Stuyvesant had mentioned the need for a Latin School in 1651, and the West India Company had agreed. The Heeren XIX suggested Councillor Johannes La Montagne, doctor and lawyer, as its teacher for a yearly salary of 200 to 250 guilders, recommending that the school be kept in City Hall. La Montagne was probably not too enthusiastic because no school was opened, and in September 1658 the magistrates of New Amsterdam took a new initiative and petitioned the governor for a Latin School. The nearest grammar school was in Boston, they told him, and they were sure that the establishment of an "academy" would enhance their city as "a place of great splendour."[31]

The request could not have been better timed. The company directors had already asked Stuyvesant in May of that year what he thought of Dominie Drisius's proposal to open a Latin School. They were in favor of it as long as it was "kept up with the least expense to the Company." Stuyvesant now passed the petition of the burgomasters and schepens on to Amsterdam, where the Heeren reacted with amazing speed and on April 10, 1659, engaged Alexander Carolus Curtius, previously a professor in Lithuania, for, they informed the governor, "a yearly salary of 500 guilders,

HOMAGE IN VERSE

board money included; we give him also a present of 100 guilders in merchandise to be used by him upon his arrival there." Stuyvesant was to give Curtius a piece of land "convenient for a garden or orchard," and he was also to be allowed to hold private classes.[32]

On July 29 Stuyvesant reported the schoolmaster's arrival, and the hope "that the community shall reap the desired fruits through their children to which God may give his blessing." The start of the Latin School in Broad Street had seemed indeed promising, and Stuyvesant reported of Curtius: "As to his services and diligence, we must truly testify that his industry is astonishing and the progress of the young people remarkable."[33]

But Curtius soon began to complain about his salary. The first time he knocked on their door, the magistrates, still full of goodwill, gave him a raise of two hundred guilders, and for just this once an extra fifty guilders. Curtius was not satisfied for long. He explained that he had only a few pupils, each paying but six guilders per quarter, and he could not possibly live on their fees. Besides, the establishment of the school entailed great expenses. The burgomasters and schepens disagreed with him, so Curtius, without their permission, charged every boy a beaver extra.[34]

The magistrates summoned him on February 25, 1661. After lecturing him for imposing higher charges, they added that he should keep a better discipline, as some parents had complained that the boys "fight among themselves and tear the clothes from each others bodies, which he should prevent or punish." Curtius answered that the beavers were a present from the parents, and that it was impossible to keep discipline, because "his hand were bound as some people do not wish to have their children punished."[35]

In July he was back in the courtroom, again to ask for more money. He proposed to raise the city subsidy of two hundred guilders to six hundred, on the condition that he would no longer by paid by the students. The irritated magistrates referred the matter to Stuyvesant, who had had enough of the grasping schoolteacher and closed the school. Curtius, angry and hurt, sailed back to Europe.[36]

A year later the school was reopened, under the guidance of Aegidius Luyck, who was and remained such a success that

A SWEET AND ALIEN LAND

Stuyvesant, praising him in the beginning for his "piety, talents, and diligence in instructing children," gave him a salary of one thousand guilders a year and never again had to interfere in school affairs.[37]

HOMAGE IN VERSE

RECONNAISSANCE

[Only] six weeks sayle from Holland [was a country] under the best clymate in the whole world [where] seed may be thrown into the ground, except six weekes, and the yere long; there are five sorts of grape wch are very good and grow heere naturally . . . : heere groweith tobacco very good, it naturally abounds, . . . furrs of all sorts may bee had of the natives very reasonable . . . ; marvellous plenty in all kinds of food, excellent veneson, elkes very great and large . . . ; the sea and rivers abounding with excellent fat and wholesome fish wch are heere in great plenty. . . .

This paradise overflowing with milk and honey was New Nether-land, and with this glowing description the West India Company advertised it in 1661 in England, in the hope of attracting "all Christian people of tender conscience."[1]

It seemed to the Dutch the right moment to find more settlers for their still critically underpopulated colony. England in partic-ular looked a promising ground for recruitment. The Restoration of Charles II in 1660 would inevitably lead to another exodus of Puritans, whose days of glory under Cromwell were decidedly over, and whose support for the regime of the Lord Protector had not endeared them to the new King.

The States General had taken the initiative for the publicity campaign. On February 14, 1661, it published an act, which prom-ised "full liberty to erect a colony in the West Indies between New

England and Virginea in America, now within the jurisdiction of Peter Stivazent, the States Generall's Governor for the West India Company." What it had in mind was the populating of the rich stretch of land between New Amsterdam and the South River, the Delaware, still almost unexplored and only inhabited by warring Indian tribes.[2]

The advertisement was perhaps not completely truthful. It told prospective candidates that the natives were "naturally a mild people, very capable," who were virtually waiting "to be drawne out of their blind ignorance to the saving light by Jesus Christ." But the concessions the West India Company offered were very favorable: "fifteen leagues of land in breadth along the seaside, and as farr in depth in the continent as any plantation hath . . . the free property of the said colony"; no taxes for twenty years and no customs on furs that were exported; together with "full liberty to live in the fear of God." It was a far cry from the mean conditions under which the first Dutch colonists had been allowed to settle.[3]

Stuyvesant might have doubted that advertising the advantages of his province in England was the right answer to his problems. He had enough trouble with the English already present in New Netherland, and even more with the New Englanders, who wanted to see the borders between them and the Dutch province disappear. Massachusetts, Connecticut, New Haven, and Maryland all had claims still outstanding, and even if the Restoration had temporarily silenced them, he was very much anticipating future threats.

In all his letters to Amsterdam in the years from 1659 onward, the boundary question cropped up constantly, and he insisted on an official settlement of the borders with London. "You have declared formerly and also declare now your title . . . but if more powerful and stronger neighbours maintain the same and besides exhibit a royal patent, expressly describing the limits," he wrote on June 25, 1660, "while we cannot do it in your name, will they be satisfied by our bare assertion?" He knew what the reaction would be—"they would only laugh."[4]

The Heeren XIX, far away in Amsterdam, thought they knew better. Over and over again, they repeated that the good King Charles II would never support the New Englanders "in their unjustified claims, much less encourage them to usurpation, as the

RECONNAISSANCE

preceeding government had undoubtedly done." And they seemed to be right, at least for a while, because on December 9 Stuyvesant reported with relief: "It is at present very quiet regarding the English claims at the South and North as they are apparently diverted from their intentions by the changes in England."[5]

The new royal government, according to the Dutch governor, had been received by the New Englanders with "less commotion" than he had expected. "As a rule they are now as good Royalists, as they formerly were Cromwellian or Parliamentarians," he wrote the company in October 1660. "We are told that the three Colonies of New Plymouth, Hartford and New Haven have proclaimed the King and do all business in the King's name which they never did in the old King's time." Only Massachusetts was more obstinate and "remains faithful to its old principle of a free state, depending only upon God."[6]

The news of Charles' accession had in fact not been welcome at all in New England. While Virginia and Maryland—having been as anti-Cromwell as possible—acknowledged Charles II at once, the colonies northeast of New Netherland, with the exception of Rhode Island, hesitated. New Plymouth proclaimed the King only in June 1661. Connecticut had in March done no more than petition Charles II "for his favour, & for the continuance & confirmation of such privileges & liberties as are necessary for the comfortable settlement of this colony"—without even proclaiming him King.[7]

Massachusetts in particular did everything in its power to sidestep official acknowledgment, fearing that "the reformation gained by so much war and blood should be given up again to Papists and heretics." There were no public celebrations and not long after Charles had taken his place on his throne, Captain John Leverett warned Boston from London that the King was much displeased with this attitude. The General Court in Boston reacted, like Hartford, by composing a petition in which the colonists begged the King for the "continuance of those privileges and liberties which they have hitherto enjoyed." At the same time, Governor John Endicott gave Leverett instructions to "intreat gentlemen of worth in Parliament or near the King to favour the cause."[8]

For the moment the colonies felt they had gone far enough to gratify Charles II. This became obvious when the King demanded that they arrest the regicides Edward Whalley and William Goffe.

This duo, who had directly participated in the execution of Charles I, had after the Restoration fled to New England, where they arrived in July 1660. They settled down in Massachusetts, but after news had come that they were not to be pardoned by Charles II, they fled to New Haven, the staunchest opponent of the King. In May 1661 a royal order arrived in Boston for the arrest and deportation of the two regicides, and Endicott sent a missive to all the colonies—and even to Peter Stuyvesant in New Amsterdam— repeating the command from the King. All the colonies, and Stuyvesant as well, promised to do their best to obey the order, but the two men were not found, a fact that Charles never forgot.[9]

For the irritated King this was fresh evidence that the royal writ did not run in these rebellious colonies, a situation he had no intention of allowing to continue. To bring his subjects in the New World to heel, he appointed in December 1660 a "Counsil for Foraigne Plantacon." It was the first step toward a consistent colonial policy, designed by Lord Clarendon, his fifty-two-year-old Lord Chancellor.

Clarendon, born Edward Hyde, the third son of minor East Anglian gentry, had gone far. A hard worker, he had been discovered by Archbishop Laud, who pushed his protégé "in many Occasions." Hyde was a snob and a born climber, as well as an ardent Church of England man and Royalist. He had loyally accompanied Charles II into exile. As one of the King's most trusted if irritating councillors, he had married his daughter Anne to the Duke of York, and he returned with Charles in 1660, more powerful and influential than ever. "This minister," the Venetian ambassador Geronimo Giavarino wrote in 1661, "possesses all the King's esteem and respect and at present seems the sole director of affairs."[10]

Despite the fact that, as the same ambassador wrote, "he applies himself exclusively to the country's internal affairs," Clarendon showed great interest in the colonies in America, if only with the aim of creating a market for English products, a stimulus to English shipping, and a cheap provider of those goods that England itself could not produce. The New England colonies had in that sense not been a success. The enormous forests did not supply enough masts to meet the competition of the Baltic, and colonial industries such as agriculture and fishing, far from being a source of cheap supply to the mother country, were actually in competition with her.[11]

Reemphasizing Cromwell's Navigation Acts was not sufficient to redress the situation, and with the founding of the Council for Foreign Plantations, together with a Council for Trade, London intended to go much further. The forty-five members under the presidency of the Lord Chancellor were instructed to bring the many remote colonies—"in so many ways considerable to our Crown"—under uniform inspection. They were to write the divers governors to ask for "an exact account of their affairs, of the nature and constitution of their laws and government, the number of men, fortification, etc." The Council's task was also to "apply what is good and practicable to the English plantations; to call experienced merchants, planters, seamen, etc. to their assistance" to see that those "willing to be transported thither may be encouraged," and to send over vagrants and others "who remain there noxious and unprofitable." Of course, ministers were also to be dispatched, with "instructions for the regulating and reforming the debaucheries of planters and natives."[12]

The Council turned out to be a cumbersome body. Its procedures were complicated and its membership large, so its efficiency was within a few months reduced to nil. For New England, this defective royal bureaucracy was only an advantage, and the Dutch may have thought that it would be the same for them. Shortly after the Restoration the States General had followed up its hospitable reception of Charles II in The Hague (which had cost more than two million guilders) by sending an embassy to London in November 1660. Among the many points for discussion was the question of the boundaries of New Netherland.

The West India Company, which had asked the States to approach the "Most Illustrious King" in the hope that both nations in America "may live as good neighbours in good correspondence," was optimistic about the result. The Heeren XIX wrote to Stuyvesant on December 24, 1660, that the States ambassadors had already had several audiences with Charles II and "we must now wait the result in patience." They were certainly ambitious: not satisfied with the borders established by the Hartford Treaty of 1650, they desired as well "redress for the usurpation of our lands and trespass upon our jurisdiction at the Fresh River [Connecticut] and upon Long Island." They were sure that their requests would be "treated in their good cause with more fairness and justice by the present King."[13]

A SWEET AND ALIEN LAND

Their hopes were soon shattered. Rumors of a possible marriage between Charles II and the Portuguese princess Catherine of Braganza, which would bring England closer to Portugal, the arch-enemy of the Republic, revived all the old tensions, and Stuyvesant in New Amsterdam followed events from afar with increasing concern.

He first learned of the deteriorating situation from Schepen and Vice Director Willem Beeckman, who had received at New Amstel a letter from his brother in The Hague, and who on August 7, 1661, reported at once to the governor that "very likely new quarrels would break out between our country and England. The King is said to have a firm alliance with Portugal and is about to marry the Infanta. . . ." In his next letter to the West India Company, on September 24, Stuyvesant expressed regret about the "imminent rupture," which had already led to reports of "new attempts to invade and take Long Island."[14]

These attempts were the work of Henry, fourth Earl of Stirling, the grandson of the earl whose agents had in the past pestered both Kieft and Stuyvesant. Immediately after the restoration, he had petitioned the King for his rightful inheritance of a part of New England and the whole of Long Island. In his petition he stated that his ancestors had "at great cost planted many places of that Island; but of late divers Dutch have intruded." His request was referred to the Council for Foreign Plantations and in the end was denied. But the reports of his action had created confusion and fear among the New Netherlanders, who, according to Stuyvesant in July 1661, "do not hesitate to say and affirm, that the present King has already confirmed the grant."[15]

The West India Company made faint efforts to calm the panic, telling Stuyvesant that "little or no credit can be given to such scattered reports," which it considered "to be only ruses to make our people uneasy." The directors added that the rumors should never be "communicated to our inhabitants," hardly a realistic suggestion for the governor of a province full of rebellious Englishmen.[16]

Long Island in particular was prone to believe the slightest bit of information from London. Part of the island was completely under the control of Connecticut and New Haven, while the Dutch half was almost equally divided between five English towns —Newtown, Hempstead, Flushing, Jamaica, and Gravesend—and

RECONNAISSANCE

five Dutch towns—New Amersfoort, Midwout, New Utrecht, Breukelen, and Boswyck—whose inhabitants formed only a third of the island's total population. The area seemed ripe for a takeover, and while Stirling's petition was still pending, a second contender suddenly appeared in court in London.

He was Captain John Scott, a twenty-nine-year-old adventurer with a questionable and intriguing past. Much maligned as "unscrupulous," he was more honest and gallant than is often suggested, but he made little effort to improve his image.

Scott was the son of an officer who had lost his life for the honor of Charles I. The boy decided in 1642, at the age of ten, to join the King's cause and was caught while "cutting bridles and girts of the then parliament's horses." Under the "perfidious" care of the well-known Puritan lawyer Emmanuel Downing, he was deported to New England in 1643, where he lived at Salem in a Quaker center. Five years later he ran away, but was caught. Finally, in 1652 he was at last freed. As for any penniless twenty-year-old of that time, the sea and its opportunities beckoned, and he left for Tortuga, where he joined the bucaneers.[17]

After having made a fortune in plunder, he returned in 1654 to North America to make the most of the advantages that the Anglo-Dutch War offered the English around Long Island Sound. Together with his friend John Young, the son of Southold's pastor, he patrolled the coast to prevent Indian interference in the war, but he could not resist a little privateering. This brought him into conflict with the Dutch in the spring of that year, and he appeared in court in New Amsterdam. He was released and settled near Southampton, where he bought—with the help of Deborah Rayon, the wealthy girl he married in 1658—"near one third of the Island" from the Indians and became his town's attorney.[18]

The forceful and personable captain, remembering the resolution he had made as a youth "to make America the scene of the greatest actions in my life," saw his opportunity at the Restoration of Charles II. He had always remained a staunch Royalist, even rejecting Cromwell's offer to revoke his banishment, and in 1660 he embarked from New Amsterdam on the *Eyckenboom* ("Oaktree") to seek in London investiture as the governor of Long Island. With the help of friends he managed to be presented to the King, who was taken by his intelligence and pleasant manners and

A SWEET AND ALIEN LAND

promised to study his request, referring it to the Council for Foreign Plantations.[19]

Scott was clever, and rapidly perceived that the increasing animosity between the English and the Dutch would certainly have its influence in America, and that Long Island in particular, with its heterogeneous administration by New Amsterdam, New Haven, and Hartford, was ripe for an English takeover. With enthusiasm he began to intrigue against the West India Company, accusing it of smuggling and of carrying on a contraband tobacco trade with Virginia. The English listened eagerly, and the effects of Scott's activities were soon evident in New Amsterdam, where the English merchant Thomas Willett showed Stuyvesant letters from friends in London and Boston in which an impending invasion with three frigates was announced.[20]

This had certainly been Scott's ambition, but the arrival in London of another Englishman in September 1661 killed his high hopes. John Winthrop Jr., the governor of Connecticut, came with different designs on the Dutch province, which in the end would be much more effective that Scott's dreams.

Winthrop's voyage had been ordered in May, when the General Court of Connecticut assembled at Hartford, at last ready to acknowledge the King, if only for the practical reason that Connecticut needed a royal charter. For that purpose a flowery petition was prepared by Winthrop himself, in which Charles was begged to look favorably upon this colony, "a little branch of your mighty empire," and grant it a charter that stretched from the Connecticut to the "Delliway River," proposed borders that not only swallowed New Netherland but New Haven as well. Winthrop himself was asked to go as envoy to London to plead the case, with five hundred pounds in his pocket for the costs.[21]

Before his departure he had one awkward question to resolve. New Haven was as much in need of a patent as Connecticut, but the small colony at the mouth of the Quinnipiac River had no money to finance a delegation to London. Governor William Leete had approached Winthrop, asking him to speak for the New Haven colonists in London, but Winthrop, bearing in mind his own colony's designs on New Haven's territory, had answered him evasively. Thus he felt it would be awkward for him to make his departure from New Haven.

RECONNAISSANCE

He had no such scruples about New Netherland—also included in Connecticut's proposed charter—and accordingly wrote Stuyvesant on June 21, that, "having information of a good ship that is shortly to sayle from New Netherland," he wished to come to New Amsterdam to embark there for Europe. "I might thereby have opertunity to waite upon your Honor, having hitherto been disappointed of the happiness of such a visit."[22]

Stuyvesant went out of his way to please Winthrop, and the welcome he gave him on July 8 was very impressive. When Winthrop's barge arrived in the Hudson, no less than twenty-seven pounds of shot were used for the salute. Stuyvesant, waiting on the quayside, told him at once that not one ship but three were waiting: the *Trouw* ("Faith"), the *Arent* ("Eagle"), and the *Hoop* ("Hope"). He thought the *Trouw* was perhaps the most suitable for Winthrop's passage, since it was the largest, and the master, Captain Bestevaer, "speackes very good English."[23]

Bestevaer, however, had a few slight problems to solve before Winthrop could sail. To Stuyvesant's embarrassment, the captain refused to pay wharfage, and his papers were confiscated. He had to appear in court, where he offered to pay a third of the fee, with the remainder to be paid by those who had received the freight, but his proposal was not accepted and the session was adjourned until the next day.[24]

While the case was being fought out, the two governors had time to get to know each other. Stuyvesant had always kept up a friendly correspondence with Winthrop Jr., as he had with his father in the 1640s, but he must have realized now that they had little in common. The English governor at fifty-five was only five years older than his Dutch colleague, but in the company of this urbane and cultivated man of the world, Stuyvesant looked like a provincial notable. Winthrop had only been governor for the last four years, but he had traveled a great deal, and had dabbled in a variety of business enterprises—not always successfully, though Stuyvesant probably did not know this. The Dutchman was a blunt military man with a strong puritanical streak, the Englishman an accomplished diplomat with a wide-ranging curiosity about medicine, chemistry, and mathematics, and a degree of religious tolerance unusual in New England. It says much for Winthrop's engaging personality that Stuyvesant liked him immediately despite all these differences. Over the next few years they

A SWEET AND ALIEN LAND

kept in touch, and it was very often to the sympathetic Winthrop that Stuyvesant first turned—as he had before to Winthrop's father —when there were difficulties with New England.

The delay in port also gave Winthrop the opportunity to see New Amsterdam. Walking through the capital, constantly surrounded by a guard of honor, he must have liked the look of the bustling city, whose busy port was such a contrast to the rural quiet of his own colony's capital. And he was certainly impressed by the fort.

In connection with Connecticut's plans for the Dutch province, a spot of reconnaissance by him and his companion, Reverend Samuel Stone, was not out of place, and when they left, they almost certainly carried the *Description of the Towne of Mannadens* with them. In this report, which was published in September 1661 in London, much attention was given to the fort—"foursquare, 100 yards on each side, at each corner flanked out 26 yards. In the midst of the East and Westside is a gate opposite each other; the walls are built with lime and stone, and within filled with Earth to a considerable breadth of planting guns, whereon are mounted 16 guns." It was an excellent assessment of Fort Amsterdam's strength, with only one important error: the gates faced north and south.

The visitors from New England discovered further that the city possessed another point of defense, a small bulwark in front of City Hall in the form of a half-moon of stone "where are mounted 3 smal bras guns, tho it be large enough to mount 8 guns on it." The city wall seemed quite solid, and indiscreet Dutchmen told the English that thcy planned to build two "halfe moons more" between City Hall and the wall.[25]

Winthrop missed meeting the most reliable source of information about New Amsterdam, Samuel Maverick. This former Massachusetts businessman, who had lived since 1650 in New Amsterdam, had left the city just before the Restoration. He too had given a short description of the fort—"Considerable . . . of some 30 pieces of ordinary brasse, Canon, demi Culverin & others"—and in London became Clarendon's main advisor on matters concerning New Netherland and New England. Deserting his former Dutch hosts, Maverick insisted constantly on "his Maiesties titell to that great, and most considerable tract of land usurped by the Dutch."[26]

Maverick was just as insistent on a reorganization of New England. He had come to America in 1623 to help to found Sir Ferdinando Gorges' Anglican principality, and then had moved to Massachusetts after its failure. After a while, however, he had left the oppressive atmosphere of the English colony for New Amsterdam. Maverick kept in touch with his friends in Boston, who often complained of their autocratic leaders, and he hoped now that the Restoration would not only mean the fall of New Netherland, but also the end of the restrictive religious policy of the New England authorities. He was the first to point out to Clarendon that Connecticut had no charter, and advised him to take the affairs of New England into his own hands. Maverick admitted that the New Englanders were "great and Considerable people," but then added: "the sooner reduced the better." The best way to deal with them was to appoint a "generall Governor" over the whole of the colonies.[27]

Maverick's activities and his growing influence on Clarendon were by no means unknown to Winthrop, who was therefore all the more anxious to reach London. He had to wait for the result of the Bestevaer case, but was finally able to sail on July 13. General Stuyvesant again gave him all possible honors, personally conducting him on board the *Trouw*, and inspecting with him an honor guard of fifty-eight soldiers. The guns of the fort belched their salute while the vessel sailed slowly out of the East River.[28]

The first—and the last—state visit of an English governor had come to an end. The Dutch had given an impressive demonstration of their hospitality and their sense of occasion, and Peter Stuyvesant must have congratulated himself. What he discussed with Winthrop is not known, but the Dutch governor certainly had no inkling that his charming guest carried with him plans for the eradication of his "noxious neighbour." Winthrop, noncommittal as always, had left with diplomatic "words & promises."[29]

ANNEXATION
ON PAPER

John Winthrop's Atlantic crossing was unpleasant and long. Storms frequently assailed the small fleet of three ships, and the governor suffered badly from seasickness. He managed all the same to keep a "Journal of My Voyage"—perhaps to distract his thoughts. Quite soon his ship the *Trouw* lost sight of the other vessels, and the *Haerlemse Saterdaghse Courant* of Saturday September 17, 1661, reported only the arrival of the *Arent* on Monday the 12th, with the news that the *Trouw* and the *Hoop* had been sighted near the English coast. "In the *Trouw* comes mr. Winthrop, governor of Connecticut, together with the Rev. mr. Stone, on a mission to his Majesty of England." The *Trouw* arrived late that Monday night at Texel, and by the time the paper appeared, Winthrop was already in Amsterdam.[1]

It was not his first visit to the Republic. Nearly twenty years earlier he had taken advantage of a mission to London on behalf of Massachusetts to pay a quick visit to Europe, and Amsterdam in particular. In the Dutch capital he was able to indulge his curiosity about current European advances in medical and scientific thinking, buy the latest books, and meet distinguished scientists like the German alchemists Abraham and Johann Kuffler, Petraeus, and the well-known pharmacist Johann Glauber.[2]

But there was no time now for these private pleasures, and he went on almost immediately to The Hague, where he arrived on

September 22, to be entertained by his cousin Sir George Downing, the English ambassador in the Republic.

Downing, in 1661 only thirty-eight years old, had already succeeded in making himself the most hated man in the Netherlands, on top of being heartily disliked by most of the English politicians. Even his employer Lord Clarendon found him thoroughly antipathetic, and while admitting his expert knowledge of Dutch affairs, called him a "Man of a proud and insolent Spirit, who would add to any imperious Command of his, somewhat of the bitterness of his own spirit." Diarist Samuel Pepys, who had worked for him, was much sharper, calling the ambassador "a perfidious rogue"; while the Scottish pastor Dr. Gilbert Burnett, a refugee in The Hague, described Downing as "a crafty fawning man, who was ready to turn to any side that was uppermost."[3]

In spite of their common background, and the fact that Downing's mother Lucy was his aunt, Winthrop too disliked his selfish and arrogant cousin. Both had been born in England, and both had early in life departed for Massachusetts, Downing when he was only thirteen. His father Emmanuel had settled at Salem, where he became representative to the General Court in Boston. George was one of the first nine students to enter the newly-founded Harvard College at Cambridge, where he obtained in 1642 the degree of Bachelor of Arts. Being "strongly inclined to travill," the twenty-two-year-old graduate left in 1645 for a voyage to the West Indies, to preach to seamen at Barbados and Nevis. In 1646 he arrived in England, where he joined the Scottish regiment of John Oakey as a preacher. He was befriended by the kind "regicide," whom he betrayed after the Restoration by forcing the Dutch to hand him over to London. Oakey on the scaffold forgave the man "who formerly was my Chaplain, but did pursue me to the very death," but the English Puritans never forgot such treachery.[4]

Joined to this streak of heartless opportunism was a first-class brain, and Downing—"a very able scholar, and ready of wit and fluent utterance," as uncle John Winthrop Sr. remarked—was soon picked out by Cromwell, who in 1649 made him his Reconnaissance patrol leader at the age of twenty-six. But a career in the army held little interest for the ambitious young man, and in 1654, after having married a "very beautiful lady of a very noble extraction," Frances Howard, the sister of the Earl of Carlisle, he directed his attention to diplomacy and politics. His first commis-

A SWEET AND ALIEN LAND

sion was to France, where he represented Cromwell at the court of Louis XIV, and in December 1657 he was sent to The Hague as English ambassador, the most important post in the diplomatic world.[5]

Cromwell recommended him in the warmest possible terms, telling the States General that Downing was "a person of eminent quality, and after a long trial of his fidelity, probity and diligence in several and various negotiations, well approved and valued by us." But the Dutch soon thought otherwise. In particular, his success in making life difficult for the exiled Charles II, in Holland on a visit to his widowed sister Mary and her son William III, upset the "Orangists," and Downing only just escaped an attempt to assassinate him.

The Dutch Raadspensionary Johan de Witt had other reasons to dislike the zealous diplomat, who constantly pestered him with protests about incidents at sea between Dutch and English ships —in 1658 he received no less than ten memorials in six months.[6]

In March 1660 Downing realized that the wind in England was changing and, flexible as always, promptly switched sides. He asked his brother-in-law, Charles Howard, to convey a message to Charles II, "alleging to be engaged in a contrary party by his father, who was banished into New England." He explained contritely that in the colony he "had sucked in principles that since his reason had made him see were erroneous." Howard was so successful that when the King passed through Holland on his way back to London, he not only received Downing, but knighted him as well.[7]

Charles was shrewd enough to perceive that this man "of restless brain" was extremely knowledgeable in the affairs of England's most important competitor, the Republic, and would serve him better alive than dead. Thus he decided to forgive Downing, whom he "hated exceedingly." The States were understandably unhappy, and complained bitterly "that his Majesty would depute a Person to have his Authority, who had never used any other Dialect to persuade them to do any Thing He proposed, but Threats. . . ."[8]

Its members were relieved when Downing left early in 1661 to take up his seat in the House of Commons, where he bored his fellow MPs with long-winded speeches—"which naturally they don't like"—but where he was almost more dangerous to the

ANNEXATION ON PAPER

Dutch than in The Hague. "He took all Opportunities to inveigh against the Usurpation in Trade," wrote Clarendon later.[9]

Even before the Restoration, Downing—"wiser in trade than any of the merchants"—had pointed out loopholes in the Navigation Act of 1651, and put forward proposals to amend it in the hope, as he once wrote to Clarendon, that if England had as many ships and commerce as the Dutch Republic, it would be "good night Amsterdam." In 1661 he was appointed president of Charles' new Council for Trade, and given the opportunity to enforce his ideas. Downing felt that Cromwell's act was too indiscriminate in prohibiting all import through foreign vessels. He proposed that only specified goods be imported by English ships, or those belonging to the exporting countries themselves. On other goods high duties should be paid. The colonies could only import goods carried in English vessels, while those ships that violated the law would be seized.[10]

It was a device of masterly simplicity designed to cripple the Dutch carrying trade. Downing followed it up in 1663 with the Staple Act, which obliged the English colonists to buy from England almost all the European goods they needed. Downing could hardly be called a successful ambassador—he was impetuous, often created needless friction, and was a bad judge of men—but he was undeniably a brilliant economist, and the historian Charles Wilson has rightly written: "If mercantilist practice in England had a father, George Downing must have the title."[11]

Such ideas did nothing to make him popular with the States General, which with disgust and concern saw him return in May 1661. Downing complained to Clarendon on June 6 that "none from the aforesaid States came that afternoon to compliment my arrival, according to what I knew to be due to the character I beare," but on June 8 he was received in audience. He made a small effort to ingratiate himself with his hosts by assuring them that "as to their trade and commerce the world is large, there is trade enough for both," adding warningly that "it is good for both that the Realms and Kingdomes of the King my master and the United Provinces do remain in a very good and cleare understanding."[12]

When Winthrop met his cousin in September 1661 they certainly discussed the business of New Netherland, a country that Downing, as a good New Englander, always pretended to the Dutch did not exist, but whose port, New Amsterdam, played an important

A SWEET AND ALIEN LAND

role in the colonies' evasion of England's Navigation Act. Winthrop, however, did not stay for long, and after one day in The Hague embarked on September 23 for London.

Winthrop found the politicians in the English capital as much preoccupied with the Republic as the Dutch had been with England. Even before Downing was sent back to The Hague, the English and the Dutch had begun to negotiate a treaty of friendship. Clarendon was very much in favor of it and had reminded the militant Downing in August 1661 of "the streights and necessities we are in for money, the emptinesse of all our stores and magazines." He was well aware of the "old animosity and rancour" against the Dutch among English merchants, who were clamoring for war, but thought it wiser to replenish first the empty chests and stores. "In the mean time, I think we should anger as few as possible."[13]

The Dutch had signed that month a treaty of peace with Portugal, ending the long war between these two countries that had been fought mainly in the East Indies. The Dutch gave Brazil, which they had effectually lost in 1654, to the Portuguese for eight million guilders, but kept all the possessions the Dutch East India Company had conquered in the East Indies. It was a slap in the face for the English, who had been negotiating with the Portuguese for their support in the East in exchange for English help against Spain. The projected marriage between the Infanta and Charles II was part of the package, but the Dutch had been too fast. "The arrangement made between Holland and Portugal also serves to increase suspicion," reported Giavarino, the Venetian ambassador in London. It excluded the English from the trade in the Far East, and Downing fumed with rage. He had protested against it and, wrote the Venetian, "he is at present considering how he can put things straight."[14]

Charles for the moment had to be satisfied with a watered-down agreement with Lisbon and the dowry of his bride-to-be—Bombay and Tangier. The latter did not seem much, but a courtier assured him that "it was a Place of that Importance, that if it were in the hands of the Hollanders, they would quickly make a Mole," so that they would "ride securely in all Weather; and they would keep the place against all the world and give the Law to all Trade of the Mediterranean." The argument impressed the King sufficiently to draw him away from the side of the sparkling Barbara Palmer,

ANNEXATION ON PAPER

Lady Castlemaine, long enough to welcome the plain, dowdy Catherine of Braganza, whom he married in May.[15]

Negotiations about the Anglo-Dutch treaty of friendship dragged on for months, and possibly only Giavarino was still fascinated by them. Week after week he patiently reported to Venice that the Dutch were thinking of giving it a rest ("it is the general opinion that they will not come back"), that they then decided again to stay for further negotiations, that the English, impressed by rumours of a Franco-Dutch treaty, had insisted on resuming the talks, but put them off again when they "discovered that the Most Christian [Louis XIV] had not decided anything." In May the breaking point seemed to have come, and he reported: "The merchants desire this beyond expression . . . seeing that the Dutch are cleverly drawing to themselves a great part of the trade. . . ."[16]

In June even Clarendon turned against the Dutch. His son-in-law, the Duke of York, as president of the recently created Royal Company of Adventurers had sent three ships under Commander Sir Robert Holmes to West Africa "to stabilize" the trade there, which was, of course, mainly in Dutch hands. Holmes was received in Africa with Dutch cannonballs, and the news had got back to London. The Lord Chancellor, speaking to Parliament in June, could not contain himself and burst out against the Dutch with their "insatiable appetite."[17]

All of London was equally indignant, and in the coffeehouses and taverns there was talk of war. But, as Pepys noted in his diary, the English had "no money, no credit and no stores," while the now confirmed Dutch treaty with France "makes them fearful." Downing tried to stir up the war party by assuring the English that it was time to strike. "Let me tell you," he wrote in August, Raadspensionary Johan de Witt feared only one thing: a war. "He remembers the last . . . and there is terror upon the people, and particularly upon the seamen, . . . they can presse no man in this country."[18]

But the moment had not yet arrived, and on September 22, 1662, Giavarino wrote to Venice: "The negotiations are at last concluded. . . . The contents of this agreement are not of the consequence imagined, as they only confirm and continue the ancient friendship and the adjustment between the two nations." All the

A SWEET AND ALIEN LAND

agreement did, in fact, was to smooth over a few long-standing grievances on both sides. The Dutch agreed to lower the flag to English ships and to give them back their foothold in the East Indies, Pulu Run; the English allowed the Dutch to fish around the British Isles outside a zone of ten leagues, and dropped all actions for damage done their ships in the Indies. The accord was signed on September 4, but without great enthusiasm. "In the general opinion the peace will not last long," was Giavarino's comment.[19]

John Winthrop could hardly have chosen a better moment to put forward his claim to New Netherland. In this atmosphere of increasing animosity, the prospect of settling the borders of the Dutch province seemed remote to the States General, the more so since Clarendon and the Stuart Court agreed about one thing: the existence of the Dutch enclave made the execution of their new Navigation Act in America practically impossible. They were eager to have New Netherland integrated into one of their colonies.

Winthrop went slowly and carefully to work. He had his enemies and competitors in London: John Scott, whose request for a patent for Long Island was still pending, and Samuel Maverick, who was agitating for a complete subordination of Puritan New England to the King. But Winthrop had his friends as well, including Lord Saye and Sele, one of the owners of the old Warwick Charter of 1632, the shaky basis upon which seventeen years earlier Winthrop Jr. had become Connecticut's first governor. The nobleman, too old to leave his country estate, sent his recommendations to the Lord Chamberlain, the Earl of Manchester. The governor's other supporters were the son of Lord Brooke, another patentee, and, more important, Benjamin Worsley, who together with Winthrop's cousin Downing had been the mastermind of the Navigation Act of 1660 and who had the ear of Clarendon.

Nonetheless, Winthrop needed patience—and money. Since the Restoration, life in London had become extremely expensive. Charles had been saddled with a debt of three million pounds, left behind by Cromwell, and its effects were felt all around. Giavarino complained bitterly: "Prices have risen exorbitantly and . . . there is no sign of any approaching amendment." Very often he was faced with court officials who wanted to have their palms greased

ANNEXATION ON PAPER

before doing a thing, and it is certain that Winthrop was in the same situation. He had taken very modest lodgings, but he had great difficulty in cashing his letter of credit for five hundred pounds, given to him by the Court of Hartford. It was even more difficult to find the extra money he needed for the regular and irregular expenses—an estimated six hundred pounds—that he had to meet before the charter was at last granted on May 10, 1662.[20]

His persistence was handsomely rewarded. It was a complete victory for Connecticut, that from now on stretched from the "Norrogancett Bay" to the Delaware and clear across the continent to the Pacific Ocean. At one stroke New Haven, Rhode Island, and New Netherland were wiped off the map. The colony itself became a corporate government, with a governor and a company formed by the freemen, which meant that the internal organization would not change.[21]

Winthrop was, however, almost at once disappointed in his expectations of returning home. New England's outsider, Rhode Island, had sent its own agents to ask for a charter—John Clarke and Stuyvesant's former English secretary, George Baxter. The two men had no intention of standing idly by while their colony was annexed by Connecticut, and they put up a brisk fight that kept Winthrop in London until the spring of 1663. Then at last it was decided to shift Connecticut's eastern border from the Narragansett Bay to the Pawcatuck River, leaving Rhode Island intact.

Not waiting for this decision, Winthrop had dispatched the new charter triumphantly to Hartford, where it was shown to the Commissioners of the United Colonies at their session in September 1662. Massachusetts and New Plymouth acknowledged the document immediately, but New Haven's representatives could not believe their eyes. While Winthrop had been in London, Governor Leete had urged him in his letters to ask for a charter for the small colony, and he had always answered kindly, but without revealing his plans. According to the New Haveners, Winthrop had even told friends before he left that they would always be free to decide for or against integration, so they felt understandably cheated when they saw the charter. Adding insult to injury, the General Court at Hartford invited

A SWEET AND ALIEN LAND

them to send representatives to the next session on October 9, called to celebrate the unification of the two colonies.

New Haven was not so easily talked into giving up its freedom, and over the coming years the fragile unity between the English colonies would be shattered completely.

ANNEXATION ON PAPER

TWICE
TRICKED

The news of Connecticut's new charter, which reached New Amsterdam in September 1662, was received with incredulity. Stuyvesant had had great confidence in Winthrop, who, as he had heard in the summer, had quashed Captain John Scott's evil plan for Long Island. Much relieved, he had written on July 15 to the West India Company that the request made by Scott "to the prejudice of this province" had been "postponed and finally been denied" after Winthrop's arrival in London, and that he was waiting for "more exact and correct information about this matter, when Mr. Winthrop, who is daily expected in his government, shall have returned."[1]

The Englishman's arrival was much later than Stuyvesant anticipated, but he did not have to wait until then to learn the bad news. The General Court at Hartford had instructed Captain John Young, the pastor's son from Southold, to annex all of Long Island, the Dutch part included. Young went into action at once and visited four of the five English towns under Stuyvesant's government—Gravesend, Newtown, Hempstead, and Flushing. He left behind letters in which he told the English that "whereas it hath pleased his Majesty to involve Long Island within Connecticut Patten: by virtue whereof the General Assembly at Hartford have ordered me to give notice to every Town upon Long Island, that they are under the Jurisdiction of Connecticut." He concluded with the order to "forbeare from taking any Oath that may be Imposed upon them by any other Prince or State whatsoever."[2]

William Lawrence, one of the magistrates of Flushing, was the first to alert Stuyvesant, sending him a copy of Young's letter with the news that the General Court in Hartford planned to take no action "till Mr. Winthrop come from England." The governor read Young's missive with rising anger, and dispatched Under-Schout Resolved Waldron to Long Island to collect the original documents, at the same time summoning to New Amsterdam the magistrates of Hempstead—the only ones who had not informed him of Young's visit. They duly appeared and reported that Young had only stayed a few hours, telling them what was in the letter. They had replied "that if he had anything to say concerning jurisdiction, he should address himself to the Director General and Council of New Netherland."[3]

It looked for the moment as if the towns would remain loyal to the Dutch government, but Stuyvesant decided to protest to Hartford immediately: "I cannot omit to acquaint you . . . that one John Younge, whether uppon your orders (as he pretends) I doubt, had undertaken as by his seditious Letters may appear to divert and revoake the English towns in this province . . . off their Oath and due obedience unto us their Lawful Gouvernour," he wrote to the Hartford Court, still hopeful that it was all a mistake. He pointed out that Young's activities were in breach of the Hartford Treaty of 1650, and insisted again on leaving the whole matter of the boundaries to "our Superiors in Europe." He had little faith in the good will of the Hartford authorities, but his confidence in Winthrop was still unshaken, and he proposed to wait till his "desyred arrival" before taking any other action, "confydinge & trusting more in the words and promises of the honourable Gouvernor Winthrop, as he did depart from hence."[4]

Hartford's answer was as might be expected. It was, according to the General Court, undeniably Connecticut's right to occupy what belonged to it. "We know no New Netherland unless you can show us a Royal Patent for it from his Majesty," was the Court's comment. If Stuyvesant was not willing to give in voluntarily, bloodshed would be the consequence.

Much distressed, the governor informed the Heeren XIX of Hartford's new aggression. Sending them on January 8, 1663, a copy of the Connecticut patent, "which a good friend has procured

TWICE TRICKED

for us," he asked Amsterdam to put it beside the claims of Massachusetts. "You will find and learn that not a foot of land is left there to you, because Boston claims Fort Orange and the land thereabout from ocean to ocean and Hartford the remainder as far as Maryland and Virginia. You may easily imagine, how much all this discourages your people here."⁵

The West India Company was still optimistic and wrote consolingly about the treaty of friendship that had been concluded between England and the Republic in September 1662. "Therefore such attacks from the English are not to be expected henceforth." All hope, however, of reaching a border settlement with London had been given up. It must be effected in America and—with the same misplaced trust in Winthrop as Stuyvesant—the Lords Directors thought that the return of the governor "will undoubtedly offer you a good opportunity" to come to an agreement. "He has always shown himself a friend of our nation," they told Stuyvesant. He would have liked to come to Amsterdam "we are told, and confer with the Company," but the fear of raising suspicion in England and America had prevented him. Winthrop's technique in avoiding confrontations was improving.⁶

Stuyvesant, who was by now becoming skeptical of Winthrop's friendship for the Dutch, wrote back that "we rejoiced to learn from your letters the settlement of the difficulties between the Crown of England and our government," but it only diminished his fears "somewhat," as Hartford was still pushing its claims. He was made almost desperate by the lack of insight of the gentlemen in Amsterdam, who had shifted the responsibility for the borders back to him, and he tried again to explain that it was "impossible to obtain a favourable settlement . . . here from people, actuated by such a haughty and insatiable spirit," and furthermore supported by a new patent "so ample and unlimited in regard to your territory."⁷

Connecticut's greedy charter had, in the meantime, given Stuyvesant some unexpected allies in his struggle against Hartford. They came from New Haven. The patent dispute between Connecticut and this small neighboring colony had gone on for months, and some of New Haven's less Puritan towns, relieved to be free of the strictest "Israelites," had capitulated. There was, however, a hard core that resisted violently, and some of them,

A SWEET AND ALIEN LAND

preferring to lead their own way of life in a tolerant foreign province rather than struggle under their own godless compatriots, were once more looking longingly toward the Delaware.

Already in 1661, after the publication of the company's advertisement for people of "tender conscience," Mathew Gilbert, deputy governor of New Haven and leader of the "elder faction," had approached Stuyvesant. The Restoration had raised fears of the King's revenge, which were bolstered by the first rumors of Connecticut's ambitious plans. Should a "merger" happen, he told the Dutch governor, the people of New Haven would like to start a New Canaan under Dutch rule. In November 1661 Gilbert formed a committee, under the presidency of Robert Treat, which traveled to New Amsterdam to discuss with Stuyvesant the "planting under his rule for the enlargement of the Kingdom of Christ Jesus." The committee was sweeping in its demands, asking Stuyvesant, who entertained them "courteously," for the establishment and protection of their church, which, "according to Scripture," was allowed to suppress "heresies, schisms and false worship." They also asked for their own courts and laws without appeal to other authorities, and for the right to vote on prospective settlers.[8]

The governor had no objections, except to the establishment of courts based on the laws of New Haven. He insisted on the right of appeal to the Provincial Council and on his own right to appoint the magistrates, but nonetheless he decided to ask the company for advice. It came in the spring of 1663, and it was as pragmatic as the Heeren XIX could be. Eager for more population—"of such importance to our nation there"—they thought that in such cases as "adultery, fornication and similar offenses, which they punish according to the law and word of God," Stuyvesant should give in to their demand, "although the laws of our Fatherland close our eyes to them." If it was a case "of ordinary proceedings and where the testimony makes it dubious and uncertain," the laws of the Republic were to stand.[9]

Stuyvesant at once sent a letter to Robert Treat to tell him that he and his people were welcome, but for the moment the urgency of the Puritans' situation had disappeared. Captain John Scott had made a short appearance at New Haven in November 1662 to assure the colonists that they should not take the Connecticut

TWICE TRICKED

patent too seriously, since matters were still very much in the air. He sailed back to London with a commission to defend the case of New Haven.

If the Puritans had lost interest in the South River, the Catholics, in the person of Maryland's owner, Lord Baltimore, had not. Persisting in his claim to what he considered his border river, he had obtained a new charter from the King after the Restoration, and now seemed more inclined than ever to occupy the Dutch colonies on the Delaware.

His diplomatic approaches to the company in 1660 and 1661 had been rebuffed, and this time he tried different tactics. On November 11, 1662, a worried citizen of New Amstel, Willems, reported mysterious happenings in the colony to the company's vice director at Altona, Willem Beeckman. In the middle of the night Lieutenant Alexander d'Hinoyosa, director of Amsterdam's colony, had left in a sloop, together with his schout, Gerrit van Sweeringen. The only thing Willems had been able to discover was that D'Hinoyosa had received a letter from the governor of Maryland, Baltimore's half-brother Philip Calvert, inviting him to visit Nova Bohemia, where Calvert was staying as the guest of Augustine Heerman. Without informing his Council, d'Hinoyosa had obeyed the order. "I have thought, it would not be unadvisable, to communicate it to your Honour," Willems wrote, "for who knows what it means; perhaps it is the result of much strange talking together in the valley."[10]

He advised Beeckman to be on his guard and to inform the "old Patroon at the Manhatans." Lieutenant D'Hinoyosa returned after one night, but refused to reveal to Beeckman what had been discussed. "Only I heard the other day," Beeckman reported to Stuyvesant on November 24, "that his Honour had been informed by Governor Calvert, the Manhatans would in a short time be summoned by those of New England to surrender." This was hardly news to Stuyvesant, who was in the middle of his confrontation with Hartford about the Connecticut charter.[11]

The company officials had no reason at all to trust Amsterdam's representatives at the Delaware. From the moment that his predecessor, Jacob Alrich, in a touching deathbed scene, had handed over to him the government of New Amstel, D'Hinoyosa had been obnoxious to both the company's officials and his own subjects. The settlers had complained to Stuyvesant, but Amsterdam had

A SWEET AND ALIEN LAND

nonetheless appointed D'Hinoyosa director on August 28, 1660. At the same time, it had accepted a plan for a wholesale reorganization of the colony. It pruned the number of its civil servants; shipped off about thirty farmhands; gave the local court more power; and promised more land to prospective settlers.[12]

D'Hinoyosa's new responsibilities had gone to his head, and by the middle of 1661 Beeckman was reporting continuous clashes with him. The lieutenant obviously considered himself the equal of the vice director of the company's colony, and even demanded that passing vessels should lower their flags when passing New Amstel. Beeckman insisted that the river before New Amstel was under the West India Company's jurisdiction, and on May 15, 1662, he summoned D'Hinoyosa to appear in court at Altona. New Amstel's director refused the summons and was overheard ranting in a tavern that he would invite the English, Portuguese, Swedes, or Danes to come and settle here, for "What the devil did he care whom he served? He should have his revenge." Taking a drop of wine on his finger, he threatened: "If I could drown or poison them [in New Amsterdam] with this, I should not use a spoonful."[13] With these menacing words in mind, Stuyvesant and Beeckman followed with understandable suspicion the movements of the rebellious director.

Amsterdam—and D'Hinoyosa—however, had different plans for the colony. The increasing interest of the English in New Netherland had made the Dutch more and more aware of the value of their colony in America, and the merchants in Amsterdam decided to give New Amstel a last chance. In April 1662 a group of twenty-five Mennonites (a religious sect that believed in a society based on the expectation of Christ's second coming and in total religious freedom for every Christian) applied for emigration to New Amstel. On the 25th the City Council gave them permission, helping each family with a loan of a hundred guilders and free passage.[14]

The instigator of the plan was a kindhearted and idealistic citizen from Zierickzee in Zeeland, Pieter Cornelisz Plockhoy, who had come up with a revolutionary scheme for colonization. He had tried it out on Cromwell, whom he had approached in 1658, but the death of the Lord Protector put an end to his hopes and he returned to the Republic, where in 1661 he published a pamphlet entitled *Short and clear plan serving as a mutual contract to lighten*

TWICE TRICKED

the labor anxiety and trouble of all kinds of handicraftsmen by the establishment of a community or colony on the South River in New Netherland. . . .[15]

The little booklet with the long title numbered sixteen pages, in which Plockhoy told his future "republicans" that the first principle of "this society was an equality, to which aim every man—not older than 24, unless married, and not a servant—who wished to join this community has to promise on his manly loyalty or truth that he will never strive to a special governing power, nor will accept that anybody in this community shall make an effort to obtain this." To prevent confusion, the settlers had, however, to elect a sort of leader—a man of about forty years of age.

The little state would be "free-thinking" as well, and would have no dominie, "to prevent endless haggling and squabbling." There were to be no church services for this community of "agriculturists, seafaring persons, all kinds of necessary trades people and masters of good arts and sciences," only weekly meetings on Sunday, where the Bible would be read and psalms sung. Everyone was free to have his own meeting places and teachers, "this being a matter, that does not concern the community in general." But the state would not be as free-thinking as all that. "Those in communion with the Roman See, Usurious Jews, English stiff-necked Quakers, Puritans . . . and obstinate modern pretenders to revelation," would be excluded.

Jacob Steendam, just back from New Netherland, gave the scheme his full support and reached for his pen to write a glowing introduction to Plockhoy's brochure:

> *New Netherland's the flower, the noblest of all land,*
> *With richest blessings crowned, where milk and honey flow;*
> *By the most High of All, with doubly lib'ral hands.*[16]

Plockhoy's plan sounded very unrealistic and Steendam's praise perhaps a bit too romantic, but the City Fathers of Amsterdam were sufficiently liberal—and eager for colonists—to give permission to go ahead.

The general must have shivered when he received news of this bunch of "errorists," but by the time they left Holland a great change had occurred at the Delaware. After the Swedes and the English, it was now Amsterdam that nibbled at a large slice of

A SWEET AND ALIEN LAND

Stuyvesant's territory, but this time with the consent of the company. Realizing that the existence of two colonies with different authorities would remain a cause for conflicts, the city and the company had begun negotiations about an amalgamation of New Amstel and Altona.

The city's directors for New Amstel at once composed a lengthy memo, in which they urged the magistrates of the city not to give up their interests and to save the colony on the South River from ruin. They assured them that "if it were peopled, no one can embarrass us, it being beyond contradiction the finest country in the world; where every thing can be produced that is grown in France or the Baltic, and which can in course of time be as great as both these kingdoms together." It should not be too difficult to find the right sort of settlers, as warring Sweden, Denmark, Poland, and Germany had all been "ruined within two years by hard times," while the dragonnades of Louis XIV in the Vaudois had already sent the Waldensians as refugees to the Republic. Optimistically, the directors were convinced that a settlement would pay dividends within two years "were the matter taken seriously in hand," and, so they stated, "the City will . . . never again be applied to for money for this purpose, but on the contrary . . . repay it in a few years."[17]

This argument, together with the yearly Indian delivery of about ten thousand furs, convinced Amsterdam to accept on February 7, 1663, all responsibility. D'Hinoyosa, in Amsterdam for a short visit, returned in August 1663 as director of the whole of the Delaware, bringing one hundred new settlers and the promise of three hundred more to follow.[18]

Stuyvesant heard the news in October, when he was ordered to hand over the territory to those "who shall thereto be authorised by the City of Amsterdam." The governor was also instructed to carry off "the ammunition of war, the ordnance and everything belonging to it and further all the Company's property," plus the money for the poor. In a second letter the Heeren XIX explained that surrendering the South River to Amsterdam was the best way to protect it "against the invasion and intrusion by the English neighbours on the South."[19]

Governor Stuyvesant had discovered how right they were, just two months earlier, when Governor Calvert of Maryland had visited New Amstel. Schout Van Sweeringen, in the absence of

D'Hinoyosa, had received him with great hospitality, even sending a vessel to fetch the governor. A surprised Vice Director Beeckman in Altona had watched while several Indians chiefs gathered on August 12 in Amsterdam's colony to pay their tribute. Only then did he discover what his difficult Dutch neighbor had been up to these last years. Bursting with indignation, he wrote Stuyvesant that "without giving us information," the high-handed D'Hinoyosa had, together with the Marylanders, concluded a treaty of peace and friendship with the Indians two years earlier. A proud and gleeful Van Sweeringen told Beeckman that they had tried also to settle the border question, and that Calvert had promised him to write to the "old Lord Baltimore."[20]

It had been a great step forward, and even Stuyvesant had to admit that D'Hinoyosa had played a clever game with the Marylanders, achieving more than the general himself had with his opponents from Connecticut. On December 22, 1663, D'Hinoyosa was able to come without fear to New Amsterdam, where the Delaware was solemnly handed over to him.[21]

A SWEET AND ALIEN LAND

WAR
AT WILTWYCK

"The Heaven began with beautiful phenomena, the Earth followed with furious upheavings," Father Hierosme Lallement wrote from Quebec at the beginning of 1663. With amazement and some consternation, French, English, and Dutch settlers watched in January an enormous meteor—"a large globe of flame"—that seemed to come "out of the bosom of the moon . . . which made the night quite as light as day." What was even more curious was the apparition of three suns, twice in the same month.[1]

Consternation soon changed to panic when in February the earth began to tremble. In Quebec "the walls of the houses sway to and fro, the stone walls shaking as if they were loose; the roofs bend first on one side and then on the other," reported Father Lallement, "the bells ring often themselves . . . everyone rushes out, the cattle run wild; children cry in the streets." The earthquakes lasted till August, slowly diminishing in violence, and they extended to New England, Acadia, and the northern part of New Netherland. Jeremias van Rensselaer wrote later in the year from Beverwyck: "Last winter we had an earthquake here, which further inland was very severe."[2]

It had been an extraordinary winter for the inhabitants of the area around Beverwyck. At first it looked as if the cold would never come, but in the beginning of January it suddenly started to freeze. "It then froze for fourteen days in succession as hard as within the memory of Christianity it has ever done," wrote Jeremias to Burgomaster Oloff Stevensen van Cortlandt of New Amsterdam, whose daughter Maria he had married in June. "With the sleigh one could use the river everywhere, without danger."[3]

The cold winter was followed by a rainy spring, and in the summer "the water was so high . . . that it ran all over the islands and caused much damage." Most of the grain harvest was washed away by a freshet. An epidemic of smallpox raged through the colony at the same time and in one week twelve citizens of Beverwyck died, while at least a thousand Indians succumbed.[4]

Everything conspired to make 1663 a disastrous year for New Netherland. It was more than ever in danger of English invasion, ravaged by nature, and threatened by the Indians. "Here they constantly speak of nothing but war," Jeremias reported in August. The Mohawks had forced General Stuyvesant to come to Beverwyck in the summer of 1662 to rescue a group of English prisoners they had taken on the Kennebec. Captain Thomas Breeden, the governor of Nova Scotia, had traveled with him, but the Mohawks refused to give up their captives until the Dutch governor had pacified them with some presents. Hardly a month later the startled citizens of Beverwyck had received some other victims of the savages, three Frenchmen, the only survivors among the seventeen inhabitants of a post near Montreal that had been attacked by the Mohawks. The Indians had nourished the three (who had hardly been alive) and sent them on to New Amsterdam.[5]

Throughout the winter and summer of 1663 the Indians around Beverwyck remained restless, but the expected war started fifty miles further south. After three years of peace the Indians around Esopus (now called Wiltwyck) renewed their attacks on the colonists in June 1663. A year earlier Stuyvesant had warned the West India Company of coming conflicts, begging the Heeren XIX not to reduce the troops in New Netherland, as they planned, but to let him keep the 125 men, "as we have been warned that the Esopus savages are planning an attack." It had not come that year, but now the governor's worst fears became reality.[6]

He was preparing for another trip up the Hudson to renew the peace treaty with the Esopus Indians when the news of their attack on Wiltwyck reached him. The tribe had not forgotten the Indian

A SWEET AND ALIEN LAND

captives he had sent to Curaçao in 1660 and were out for revenge. Captain Thomas Chambers, the schout of Wiltwyck, had on June 5 notified the sachems of the governor's imminent arrival, but two days later, at eleven o'clock in the morning, a group of Indians walked into the village, pretending to come for trade. A quarter of an hour later a messenger on horseback stormed into Wiltwyck to warn the citizens: other Indians had attacked the new village just a few miles away. They had chosen the right moment, reported Chambers later to Stuyvesant, "for the village was almost bared of men, who were pursuing their necessary occupations in the fields."[7]

Within a few minutes the new settlement had been set on fire, while some of the inhabitants were murdered and others taken prisoner. The Indians in Wiltwyck, hearing the news, also went on the rampage and ran around shooting and setting fire to the houses. Chambers, wounded in the first onslaught, managed to get some of the men together, and at twelve o'clock the Wilden were driven out, leaving a trail of death and destruction behind.

Dominie Hermanus Blom risked his own life trying to console the victims. He was heartbroken. "There the burnt, the killed bodies, the hurt were lying," he wrote the Classis in Amsterdam. "The agony of the many and the wailing and moaning was unbearable to hear. . . . We had to look on how God's herd was taken away as prisoners of the heathen and how death snatched away the children from their cradles, the young men on the streets. The dead bodies of men lay here and there like dung heaps on the field and the burnt and roasted corpses like sheaves behind the mower."[8]

The Indians, ruthless and spiteful, had spared nobody and the list of victims that the magistrates of Wiltwyck sent to New Amsterdam was terrible to read. "Lichten Dirreck's wife burnt, with her lost fruit. . . . Mattys Capito's wife killed and burnt in the house; Jan Albertsen's wife, big with child, killed in the front of her house; Jan Albert's little girl murdered with her mother; Willem Hap's child burnt alive in the house; Marten Harmensen found dead and stripped naked behind the wagon."

Dominie Blom added to this shattering document his own story: "The burnt bodies were most frightful to behold. A woman lay burnt with her child at her side, as if she were just delivered. . . . Other women lay burnt also in their houses and one corpse with her fruit still in her womb was most cruelly butchered, with her husband and another child."[9]

His confrere in Breukelen, Dominie Henricus Selyns, was moved to tears and commemorated the massacre in a few verses:

> *Alas! House after house, with Indian monsters posted,*
> *Child upon child burnt up, and man on man laid cold*
> *Barn upon barn consumed, and pregnant women roasted. . . .*[10]

More than twenty colonists had been killed, forty-five had been made captives, and twenty-five were missing. The new village was entirely destroyed except for a barn, one haystack, and a little stack of reed. Wiltwyck was only saved from burning down completely by a change of wind. "We doubt not your Honor's utmost pity shall be extended to us and we will speedily be succored by soldiers, with ammunition and clothing," Wiltwyck's magistrates begged the governor, "for the inhabitants have mostly been robbed of it and are almost naked. . . ."[11]

They had assembled sixty-nine men, rebuilt the palisades around the village, and organized a guard. And on June 16 they received reinforcements when forty-two soldiers under Sergeant Christiaen Niessen succeeded in reaching Wiltwyck. The troops had been attacked by the Indians, "but owing to the courage and leadership of the Sergeant," they had defeated their assailants, wrote Wiltwyck's magistrates in relief to Stuyvesant. The party lost only one man, "having six wounded."[12]

The massacre once more created an atmosphere of panic in New Amsterdam, where the citizens feared a general uprising of the Indians. Stuyvesant sent Councillor Johannes de Decker to Fort Orange to ask for volunteers, but he came back alone. Jeremias Van Rensselaer and Vice Director Johannes La Montagne later explained to the indignant Stuyvesant that "surrounded as we are by the savages we are first obliged to take care of ourselves and not get otherwise involved." The fear of the settlers in the Mohawk country was even greater than in the capital, "for no one can distinguish friend from foe," and the colonists fled to Van Rensselaer's little fortress, Crailo.[13]

It was left to Stuyvesant to raise all the necessary troops. On June 25, 1663, a proclamation was issued asking for volunteers. The Council had decided to wage war with the Indians "until the same

A SWEET AND ALIEN LAND

shall be destroyed with the help of God or all those, who will send one of their farmhands or servants, able to carry arms." The conditions were advantageous—"free plundering and all the barbarians that are captured; exemption from tithes for six years"; and proper treatment "by the surgeon with good remedies" if wounded, plus generous compensation for the loss of a limb, varying from eight hundred guilders for the right arm or both legs, to four hundred for the left hand.[14]

Enthusiasm was as usual almost nil. The general himself visited several places, but could not inspire the colonists to enlist. The army that arrived at Wiltwyck was mainly composed of eighty company mercenaries and thirty English soldiers under Sergeant Nicholas Stilwell, accompanied by forty Long Island Indians. It was not a very impressive force, but the troops were under the command of New Netherland's best warrior, Martin Cregier, the experienced commander of the burgher militia in New Amsterdam. He was assisted by Pieter van Couwenhoven, another captain of the burgher guard, now in charge of the Indians.

Captain Lieutenant Cregier, at that time about forty-five years old, had, like so many excellent soldiers, served his military apprenticeship in the Dutch armies of Stadtholder Frederick Hendrick, Prince of Orange. He was a pleasant, intelligent, and able personality, a born leader. Apart from his tavern, he ran a prosperous shipping business. Official appointments had been heaped on him since his arrival around 1643—firewarden, orphanmaster, militia commander—and ten years later he became the first burgomaster of New Amsterdam, a function he would frequently fulfill and which he had relinquished upon taking command of the vital campaign at Esopus. It was to become the crown of his career.

The operation began with a stroke of luck. Rachel La Montagne, daughter of the vice director of Fort Orange, and now wife of Gysbert van Imborgh, had been one of the Indians' prisoners. She returned to Wiltwyck on July 4, having escaped with the help of some Mohawks. Rachel was an observant young woman who gave Cregier all the information he needed. The Indians had, she revealed, a fort about thirty miles from Wiltwyck. "The road to it was good enough for a wagon to use, with only one or two bad hills. . . . There are three or four little creeks on the road, but they are almost dry and quite easily crossed," she told him. The Indian fort was at the foot of a hill, but it had a good view over the surroundings and was protected by a barricade of palisades. Inside were the houses, where the men slept, while the women and children slept outside the fort.[15]

It took some time before the first expedition was organized, but on July 26 Cregier left in search of the enemy at the head of a force of 121 soldiers, 41 volunteers, 41 Indians, 7 Negroes, 2 cannon, and 2 wagons. The army was well provisioned: each man had one pound of powder and a pound of ball, two pounds of bread and pork, and half a Dutch cheese. They marched out of Wiltwyck at four o'clock in the afternoon, and halted only when the darkness of the forests made it impossible to move the cannon and wagons any farther. After daybreak the march continued over a terrain not nearly as easy as Rachel—who accompanied Cregier as his guide —had reported. The ground was covered with rocks and the little creeks had turned into torrents, over which bridges had to be built. The "bad hills" were mountains so steep that the soldiers had to dismantle the wagons to cross them. And when they reached the Indian fort, it turned out to be empty.[16]

The fortress itself was very impressive, defended by three rows of palisades, while the houses were solid blockhuts, each surrounded by a stockade. The army spent the night there, but after the soldiers searched in vain for the tribe, it was decided to destroy the fort and the harvest in the fields. They returned to Wiltwyck on August 1 at nine o'clock in the evening, without Indians, but with "a considerable quantity of plunder."[17]

The whole month of August was spent in idling. Day in day out, the rains poured down "in such torrents" that the fields were completely flooded. The bridge over the nearby creek was swept away, as were the palisades around the village. Cregier sent orders to the schout to repair the fortifications, but he demurred: "It cannot be done at present, inasmuch as the grain in the field is almost ruined and it is necessary to draw it home as soon as possible with the aid of all hands." Even Stuyvesant's troubleshooter, Willem Beeckman, who had recently arrived from Altona to take up the post of schout in Wiltwyck, could not force the farmers to leave their precious harvest.[18]

Discipline in the motley army was breaking down rapidly. The soldiers, bored with being locked up in the mill where they were quartered, started to drink heavily and Cregier had to order the

A SWEET AND ALIEN LAND

citizens of Wiltwyck not to give them credit and the soldiers not "to sell, pawn and pledge their necessities." Others left their posts to help the farmers in the fields "or on some other pretence," for which offense they were fined forty stuivers. The stealing of some-one else's gun or powder was punished corporally. But it was difficult to prevent mutiny, and a certain Jan Hendricksen was a particular troublemaker. He refused to listen to Cregier, who wrote in his journal that he had given Hendricksen three slaps with his sword after the soldier had told him that he only took orders from Long Peter in New Amsterdam, "whom they, for-sooth, called their cornet." Hendricksen had after the slaps "put himself in a posture against me, but I being close up to his body, he could not act as he wished."[19]

Hendricksen was the cause of another scene ten days later, when he and a friend started to shoot at some passing Indians. Cregier stormed out of his headquarters and asked them "what they were doing with their guns." They answered imperti-nently: "We will shoot the Indians." But when Cregier told them to stop, Hendricksen shrugged and answered: "We will do it though you stand by." Cregier threatened to send them back to New Amsterdam. "They then retorted," he wrote later, "I might do what I pleased, they would shoot the savages to the ground, even though they should hang for it." Hendricksen and his friend did not hang, but were imprisoned until both of them promised to behave better.[20]

With a sigh of relief, Cregier saw the clouds breaking at the end of August, and, having heard that the Indians had built another fort, he began at once to organize a second expedition. The soldiers were eager for action, but this time the villagers were less coopera-tive. They refused to give up their horses, which Cregier badly needed for the transport of goods and the return of wounded. "One said, let those furnis horses, who commenced the war." Another said: "I'll give 'en the Devil, if they want anything they will have to take it by force," and a third wanted first some secu-rity. But on September 3 the captain lieutenant had 8 horses, and with an army of 125 men he marched out of Wiltwyck, with a Wappinger Indian as his guide.[21]

The dry spell was brief, and camping on the first night on the banks of a creek, the army was almost washed away by a fresh downpour. Next morning the waters in the creek were so high that it was impossible to ford it, and six men had to go back ten miles to Wiltwyck for ropes and axes to build a makeshift bridge. But after a march of one and a half days, Cregier discovered in the forest the new Indian fortification, still under construction. It was smaller than the first fort, but already strong, with a wooden wall fifteen feet high and two towers, built from trunks "the size of a man's body." Cregier commented that "Christians could not have done it better."[22]

The Indians had chosen an excellent point for their defense. The fort stood on a slightly elevated part of the country overlooking the fields, and when an advance party tried stealthily to approach it, it was discovered by a woman, who warned the others with "a terrible cry." The Indians ran into their houses to get their weapons, but the Dutch army, appearing out of the forest, was too fast for them and most of the natives fled without their arms. They were pursued up to a creek at the end of the fields, which the Indians crossed under heavy firing. The few who had got hold of their guns turned on the other bank and started to shoot at the soldiers who, led by Cregier himself, waded through the river and killed most of the enemy.[23]

In the eyes of the Dutch the expedition was a great success. They had lost three men, but had killed at least thirty Indians, among whom were Chief Papoquanaehem and three children. Fourteen Indians had been taken prisoner, one an old man who, when he refused to budge, was given his last meal. Better still, the Dutch recovered twenty-two of the prisoners from Wiltwyck and found booty "sufficient to load a shallop."[24]

The good news reached New Amsterdam on September 10, and a jubilant Stuyvesant told Cregier "to thank God the Almighty from the bottom of our hearts and pray that his Divine kindness may bless our further exploits."[25]

Still one more expedition was needed before the stubborn Esopus Indians gave up. They were by now virtually annihilated and what was left of the tribe—about thirty men, fifteen women, and some children—roamed through the forests, plaguing the farmers around Wiltwyck.

On Monday, October 1, Cregier and his army (102 men strong plus 46 Indians) were on their way again in the pouring rain. Soaked to the skin, they reached the fort that they had attacked a month before and that was still deserted. Cregier was horrified by

A SWEET AND ALIEN LAND

what he saw: five large pits "into which they had cast their dead. The wolves had rooted up and devoured some of them. Lower down on the Kill were four other pits full of dead Indians and we found further on, three Indians with a squaw and a Child that lay unburied and almost wholly devoured by the ravens and the wolves."[26]

There was little they could do. "We pulled up the Indian Fort and threw the palisades one on the other in sundry heaps and set them on fire, together with the wigwams which stood around the fort." This took them two days, and on October 4 at ten in the morning they returned to Wiltwyck.[27]

The destruction of their harvest meant the end of independent existence for the Esopus Indians. They fled to the Wappinger tribe, and for a while it looked as if they would succeed in persuading them to join their struggle with the Dutch. Secretary Cornelis van Ruyven in New Amsterdam received on October 14 reports that the tribes were making a plan to "come down, 500 or 600 men strong, to destroy first all the Dutch plantation, over the River, at Hoboken . . . and then the Manhattan Island . . . and that it should be done in a few days." A letter from Cregier confirmed the bad news, and the Council and the burgomasters organized an emergency meeting to study the situation.[28]

They decided to send twenty soldiers to New Haarlem, the town at the upper end of Manhattan which had been founded in 1659, and to place two yachts with soldiers in the North River. The attack never came, and on December 10 Oratamy, chief of the Hackensack tribe, appeared in the Council Chamber in New Amsterdam with an offer of peace from the Esopus and Wappinger Indians. "To promote it the Sachems had promised to come down here with the five captive Christians, who are still in their hands, within eight days."[29]

Nineteen days later a shamefaced Oratamy was back, together with Matteno, the chief of the Staten Island tribes. The Esopus chiefs had let him down, he admitted. Their chief, Seweckenamo, was anxious for peace, but he could not assemble the five prisoners. "The Esopus savages are obliged to make their living by the chase, as they have no corn and everyone with his prisoner is scattered here and there," Oratamy reported. He asked for an armistice of two months, so that they could collect the captives and then make peace. Matteno was much sharper about Seweckenamo and his tribe, telling the Dutch that he was ashamed "to speak any more for them." He did not wish to live "amidst such animosities [and] if no peace was made, he would remove to the South and live there."[30]

Oratamy tried to calm Matteno, assuring the Dutch "that the heart of Seweckenamo is good," but swore that if he did not come with his prisoners in two months' time, Oratamy would "help us with all his people to defeat the Esopus and take our prisoners by force." Stuyvesant and his councillors, De Sille, Van der Grift, and Van Cortlandt, hesitated and retired to discuss the offer, which was finally accepted for only one reason—the English. These, the Council minutes stated, "do not only threaten to bring this province under England's Majesty, but have already debauched for that purpose the majority of the English inhabitants of the English villages on Long Island." And Cregier had recently discovered a new menace to be added to this one: a group of twenty Englishmen had gone to the Newesingh Indians near Rensselaerswyck to buy land west of the Hudson. To prevent this new invasion, Stuyvesant had decided to erect a blockhouse and garrison it with forty men, and "this would be impossible, if the whole garrison were left at Esopus," the governor explained. "For this and other reasons we are compelled (notwithstanding that for many reasons it may be thought necessary to follow up during this winter our advantages over the Esopus savages) to agree . . . to an armistice."[31]

On January 1, 1664, Captain Lieutenant Cregier at Wiltwyck received an order to return to New Amsterdam with thirty soldiers. He embarked at once, and on January 3 he closed his journal with the note: "Having weighed anchor again drifted down anew with the ebb to the end of Manhatans Island, where we made sail about eight o'clock in the morning, the wind being westerly, and arrived about twelve o'clock at the Manhatans." His Esopus campaign had come to an end.[32]

DESPERATE
DIPLOMACY

In the middle of the Indian war at Wiltwyck one of Governor Stuyvesant's most persistent irritants, the English village of Westchester, began making trouble for him again. On July 20, 1663, a commissioner from Connecticut, Captain John Talcott, arrived in the village with a band of eighteen men. He dismissed the magistrates chosen and appointed by the Dutch, absolved the inhabitants from their oath to the States General, and took over in the name of Connecticut. It was the deepest penetration of the English into New Netherland. Westchester was, Stuyvesant wrote the West India Company, "hardly one half of a league from Helle Gatt or Manhattans Island and not a league from the North River."[1]

That Westchester was stirring again was no surprise to the general. From its foundation in 1654 by Thomas Pell, a former Gentleman of the Bedchamber to Charles I, the little place had created problems. The English settlers had unashamedly declared themselves for Cromwell's Commonwealth, occupied land that the Indians had already sold to the Dutch, and sided with the savages during the Peach War of 1655. Stuyvesant had made a feeble effort in 1654 to get rid of the English, but in 1656 his patience finally ran out and he sent a little army to arrest the intruders or force them to take the oath of allegiance. When the soldiers came back, they had twenty-three prisoners locked up in the vessel *Waegh* ("Balance"). These were threatened with deportation to Holland.[2]

This tactic had worked; on March 16 one of the prisoners, Thomas Wheeler, had sent a petition to Stuyvesant, stating that "whereas it doth appeare that you make claim to the place where we are, to be the writ of the hye and myghtie States of the Netherlands, wee whose names are underwritten are willing to submit ourselves. . . ." The Dutch governor released most of the settlers and gave them permission to return to the place he had optimistically named Vreedland (Land of Peace), a title that was later changed to the more realistic Oostdorp (Eastdorp).[3]

The inhabitants' new loyalty was only superficial. While the Dutch saw the village as east of Manhattan, they considered it west of New England, and significantly rechristened it Westchester. They never forgave Stuyvesant for his invasion and complained later in a letter to the Commissioners of the United Colonies that twenty-three of them had been committed prisoners "into the Hould of a Vessell, where they continued in restraint from all friends for the space of thirteene dayes, fed with rotten provisions crawling with wormes, whereby some of them remained diseased to this day, after which they were carried away in Chaines and layed in their Dungeon at Manhattoes."[4]

When in October 1662 a letter arrived from Hartford in which it was announced that they were now under the jurisdiction of Connecticut, the citizens of Westchester received it with joy—and did not inform Stuyvesant. The winter went by without any reaction from the director general. In March 1663 it was time for Westchester to change its magistrates and to send the annual nomination to New Amsterdam for approval by the governor. Resolved Waldron, the under-schout of the capital, came to Westchester but could get no satisfaction. The inhabitants insisted that they were under the dominion of Connecticut and only began to hesitate when Waldron—"a mongrel English and Dutch man"—showed them a letter from some Hartford commissioners to Stuyvesant, in which they expressed the desire that they and "the Governor of the Manhatens might enjoy as formerly and live in peace with each other."[5]

Richard Mills, a Connecticut delegate, dashed off a letter to Hartford, begging the commissioners there to make an end to "our miserable condition." He would like to know if they had indeed retracted their claim to Westchester, "so we may rather run, then lie in their stinking prison until we rot, as we are threatened."

A SWEET AND ALIEN LAND

Hartford failed to respond, and Mills did indeed disappear for a few weeks into the dreaded prison. Westchester then decided to do penance and begged Stuyvesant for forgiveness. Mills was freed in June, after promising not to meddle again in Dutch affairs. He died soon afterward.[6]

It was only a month later that Captain John Talcott appeared to "conquer" Westchester for Connecticut. Stuyvesant, with most of his soldiers at Wiltwyck, could only look on helplessly. His sole weapon was his quill, and he knew that its sharpness did not impress the men at Hartford. There was, however, one person who might be willing to listen to him: Governor Winthrop, who had at last returned from London in June 1663. Nicholas Varleth was just leaving to do business in Hartford, and once again Stuyvesant asked his brother-in-law to speak with Winthrop, still—he hoped—"a friend of our nation."

The response to his complaint about Westchester—and about John Young's activities on Long Island—was disappointing. Winthrop answered evasively that he was not in a position to act since the General Court, which had taken over his responsibilities during his absence, had not yet reinstated him. He was, however, sure that the question would come up during the next meeting of the Commissioners of the United Colonies at Boston in September. In the meantime he hoped that they would live peacefully together. "I shall not be wanting," he promised, "if opportunity be offered any time, to help forward such means as may conduce to those ends. . . ."[7]

In his letter Winthrop had made a vague suggestion that the Dutch send a representative to the next meeting of the General Court at Hartford in October, but Stuyvesant found the question urgent enough to act sooner, and to act himself. The Heeren XIX in their last letters had admitted complete defeat in the matter of border talks with London and urged him again to reach a settlement in America. On September 11 he left New Amsterdam for Boston.[8]

It took Stuyvesant eight days to reach the capital of Massachusetts. The inveterate English traveler John Josselyn, who was visiting his brother Henry in Boston, met the general's ship when it

DESPERATE DIPLOMACY

sailed into the bay and reported that the Dutch governor "was received and entertained . . . with great solemnity." The authorities of Massachusetts indeed did their best, and an impressed Stuyvesant gained an idea of his opponents' strength when he saw the guard of honor that waited on the quayside: "four companies of citizens and a hundred cavalrymen."[9]

Boston in 1663 was a far larger city than New Amsterdam, with five thousand to six thousand citizens. It stretched over a four-mile-long peninsula, overlooking a bay "large enough for the anchorage of five hundred sail of ships." On the two hills that flanked the city, the Dutch governor at once noticed fortifications: one "with some Artillery mounted, commanding any ship as she sails into the Harbour," the other with a "very strong battery, built of whole Timber and fill'd with earth." The mountain that rose up behind Boston and dominated the town was also part of the defense—"furnished with a Beacon and great guns."[10]

Below these fortresses he saw a pleasant, busy city. Along the seabank most of the houses were constructed, "with great industry and cost," on stilts, some of them of wood, but most of stone. The harbor itself was "filled with ships and other vessels" that made it obvious to him that Boston was now the commercial center of the English colonies. From there most of the goods coming from England and elsewhere were redistributed. Cotton, tobacco, sugar, indigo, wine, fruit, and salt were brought in from the West Indies, Virginia, and Newfoundland, as well as from England, France, Spain, Portugal, and Holland. The cargoes were exported again by the energetic Puritan businessmen of Boston, together with their own produce such as fish, grain, and beef. The Navigation Act had not been able to stop the growth of this hardworking town, which had survived the difficulties of the 1640s and 1650s and which was unwilling to accept the restrictions of a government so far away in London.

Waiting for his first meeting with the commissioners, Stuyvesant did what Winthrop had done two years earlier in New Amsterdam. He walked around to do some sightseeing, admiring the houses of "Brick, Stone, Lime handsomely contrived." The many large streets, "paved with pebblestone," were lined with "many fair shops," and, like John Josselyn, he must have admired the house that a Mr. Gibbs was building on the shore, "a stately edifice, which it is thought will stand him in little less that £.3000 before it be fully finished." It was convincing proof of Boston's prosperity.

While New Amsterdam still had to make do with one church, Boston counted three "fair meeting-houses . . . which hardly suffice to receive the inhabitants and strangers that come in from all parts." But most ostentatious was the Town Hall—"a very Substantiall and Comely building"—which had been in use since 1658. Sixty-six feet in length and thirty-six feet in breadth, it rose on a colonnade of twenty-one pillars ten feet high, jutting out three feet over the street. It was crowned on three sides with gables and on one side with a "walk fourteen feet wide protected with turned banisters." On the first floor was the Chamber, "where the Merchants may confer," while on the second floor "they keep their Monethly Courts."

It was in this building that on September 20 Stuyvesant appeared before the eight Commissioners of the United Colonies. Among them were John Winthrop and, as a painful reminder to the Dutchman of the Westchester occupation, Captain John Talcott. To the two men from Hartford, the sight of the Dutch governor was thoroughly disagreeable. Connecticut still had its troubles with New Haven, and they had hoped the meeting would concentrate on solving that dispute. Now they were first confronted with New Netherland.

"After a due and honourable reception coming to the business," Stuyvesant went straight to the point, complaining that Connecticut had broken the Hartford Treaty of 1650, and asking the commissioners if they considered that agreement still valid. It was an embarrassing situation for the New Englanders, who tried to get out of it by leaving the two men from Hartford to do the talking, since "the matter of complaint appeering to bee more emediately." Winthrop and Talcott shifted and grumbled, but found a way out. They had received no notice of Stuyvesant's coming, they stated, and the "question being of great concernment there may be occation of the presence of some persons principally concerned in the place." They "humbly craved a Respet" until the next meeting of the commissioners, the following year at Hartford.[11]

But it was now impossible to avoid the second point Stuyvesant had tackled, the recognition of the Hartford Treaty by the other commissioners. Once again the unity between the English colonies proved fragile, and without listening to the protests of Winthrop,

DESPERATE DIPLOMACY

the others, led by Governor Simon Bradstreet of Massachusetts, assured the Dutchman that the agreement was "binding according to their true intent and meaning and that they will not countenance the violation thereof," adding, however, "Saveing theire allegence and Duty to his Majesty our Royall Sovereign."[12]

The session was suspended for the day, and Stuyvesant and his delegation retired to consider the answers. The next day's session opened with a violent protest by the Dutchman, through his interpreter Captain Thomas Willett, that in the document he was addressed as the "Lord Generall of the Dutch Plantations in America" instead of Director General of New Netherland. He did not dwell long on that point but went on at once to make clear his displeasure with the answer the commissioners had given him about the Hartford Treaty, saying that it was drawn "conditionally and not so categorically as wee had expected." He was, however, willing to acquiesce for the moment. But he was not willing to accept the request from Winthrop for delay in the question of Westchester—it was "as cleare as the Sun that shines att noone day to bee but frivolous." He had a better proposal: an impartial commission to go into the matter, and in the meantime Westchester would be handed back to the Dutch. It was, stated Stuyvesant in his memo, the only way "for the Prevension of further Distempers yea blood-sheed itselfe."[13]

The uncomfortable commissioners did not know what to answer and left it at that for the day. Next morning they were confronted with another missive from their stubborn Dutch guest. He told them that he had come to settle the "lymetts," but admitted that it now seemed impossible. He was therefore going back to New Amsterdam and would refer the matter to "both superiors." In the hope of getting at least something out of his voyage, he asked "whether there may not be between the nations heer such Correspondencye and trafficke with the goods and grouth of this poore Countrye as in Europe" and a "Naighbourly Confederacy and union" against the Indians.[14]

The answer that came from the commissioners on September 23 gave Stuyvesant little joy. It began disagreeably by telling him that they did not accept "youer honors superlative title." They were in favor of mutual trade, and were "not consciensious to ourselves of any neglect," but they were also bound by the English laws. The proposal to refer the border question back to Europe was unac-

A SWEET AND ALIEN LAND

ceptable: "It would have little tendency to the end proposed," and if they had acted according to their charters, the Hartford Treaty would not have existed. Even Stuyvesant's proposal for joint action against the Indians was given a lukewarm reception and termed "a matter of great labour and difficultie." They promised, however, to "present youer honors motion to our respective generall courts," under the circumstances, the best way to kill it off.[15]

Before the Dutch governor sailed from Boston, the son of Edward Winslow, Josiah, who represented New Plymouth at the meeting, made one last effort to come to a solution. Possibly remembering the hospitality the Dutch had given his father in Leiden, he offered to mediate, but it was to no avail. "After several negotiations and conferences, mutually honorable and friendly entertainment, they separated without coming to any final conclusions," Stuyvesant reported to the company after his return to New Amsterdam at the beginning of October.[16]

While he was still in Boston, an express letter from his Council in New Amsterdam had given Stuyvesant news of dangerous trouble on Long Island. Captain John Talcott had sent the Scotsman James Christy with a letter to the miller of Newtown, Captain John Coe. In this letter the Connecticut commissioner told Coe that the moment had come to rise, since "we understand that Steversone [Stuyvesant] is bound for Bostone." Talcott promised him to do "what may be for your enlargement" while he himself was in Boston.[17]

Coe acted at once and sent Christy to Gravesend, Flushing, Hempstead, and Jamaica to tell the people there that they were now under the government of Hartford. Christy got no farther than Gravesend, where Lieutenant Nicholas Stilwell—recalled from the war at Wiltwyck—was schout. Stilwell hardly allowed him time to read the message to the assembled villagers before he arrested him on the spot. On September 25 he took his prisoner to New Amsterdam, but when he returned alone next day to Gravesend, it was obvious that something was brewing.[18]

"About 9 o'clock a young man had come to his house," he reported later, and proposed to drink the health of a certain girl. While the toast was going round, the young man had left with the words: "Go on, I shall return immediately," but he had hardly gone when another young man hurried in to tell Stilwell that there

DESPERATE DIPLOMACY

was a party of men near his house. The schout left through a back door and watched from a hiding place as about a hundred men broke into his house, "saying, they would have Stilwell alive or dead, because he had caused James Christy's arrest."[19]

Stilwell fled to the house of his son-in-law, who went to see what had happened. "Returning he said that they had made themselves at home in his house, drunk two tankers of brandy . . . lighted candles everywhere and opened all doors but they had not taken any goods." Stilwell thought it wise to leave for New Amsterdam, where he roused the Council. The rescue party, which had been organized by Coe, returned the next day to their villages.[20]

In an attempt to calm the situation Councillors De Sille, Van Cortlandt, and Van der Grift dispatched a letter to the English villages, warning them against "diverse persons driven with a spirit of mutiny ayming at nothing but to fish in troubled waters." They were, of course, certain that the inhabitants would not give any "consentment to such troublesome spirits," and asked them to arrest those men at once. The citizens of Gravesend were not so easily calmed, and in an indignant letter protested Stilwell's behavior. He had "threatened in a violent manner . . . caused violence to bee used to the messenger and had caused a greate Hubbub and furie in our towne." They promised the Council "subjection and obedience," but refused to allow that "greatest disturber of our peace" back in town.[21]

The councillors nodded understandingly, but told Gravesend that it was more a "wordy quarrel, than a matter of great importance." Stilwell, they wrote, had admitted to having been upset, but what he had said was "in the heat of passion." The arrest of Christy had been right, and they had now "no doubt and trust, that you will not fail always to protect the person and property of our said lieutenant Stilwell against all invasions and violences."[22]

When Stuyvesant returned empty-handed from Boston, the storm at Gravesend had been weathered, but another was about to break. Letters from Newtown informed the governor that "a party of mutineers had again taken up arms and was stirring there, to reduce that and other villages on Long Island for the Colony of Hartford." He commissioned his secretary, Cornelis van Ruyven, to go there, together with Thomas Willett and another Englishman, John Laurence, to find out who were the ringleaders, and on whose order they acted.[23]

The answer was obvious, and a week later a delegation of three was on its way to Connecticut to protest. Again Van Ruyven and Laurence were included, but instead of Willett a much more impressive personage was sent, Burgomaster Van Cortlandt of New Amsterdam. The envoys left by sloop on October 15, "with the rising of the sun," and arrived two days later at New Haven, looking for horses for the rest of the journey. A young man from Hartford offered at first to hire his horse to them, but hesitated at the last minute, explaining as Van Ruyven recorded in his journal, that "his folks at Hartford would find fault with him for assisting us." Their hosts in New Haven, who had no kind feelings toward Hartford, were furious and told the young man to give up his horse, "which he at last, though reluctantly, did."[24]

On Thursday, October 18, they arrived at four o'clock in Hartford, where the General Court was in session. The three men were immediately given an audience, and handed over their protests and proposals, but, noted Van Ruyven, "no other answer was made than that they would examine the letters." The Dutchmen, who spent the night at the house of Marshal Jonathan Gilbert, paid a visit next morning to Winthrop, who was, to the Dutch, still the most amenable Englishman in Hartford. They asked him what had been said in the Court after they had left their letters but, noncommittal as usual, Winthrop replied that he did not know "as he left the meeting a little while after us, being indisposed."

On leaving, they met Gilbert, who told them that a committee of three had been appointed to deal with them, and after dinner with the governor and the Court in Town Hall, the talks would start. The three members of the Hartford Committee were Matthew Allyn, his son John, and the omnipresent John Talcott, all active opponents of New Netherland who made no bones of their only wish: to destroy the Dutch province.

The afternoon and the following morning were taken up with long and sometimes violent discussion about the rights and wrongs of Hartford, but it came back again and again to the obstinate refusal of the two Allyns and Talcott to leave Westchester and Long Island alone. Allyn Sr. stated their position very clearly in a "long harangue." He was, he told the angry Dutchmen, "well assured that the English towns would no longer remain under the Dutch government, and in case we should compel them, that they were resolved to band together and to risk life and property in

DESPERATE DIPLOMACY

their defense." Van Cortlandt answered with dignity that "it should not now nor ever be allowed."

When asked how they viewed the treaty made in this same town in 1650, the New Englanders answered: "Absolutely as a nullity and of no force, as His Majesty had now settled the limits for them." Even if the other English colonies recognized the treaty, as they had in Boston a month earlier, the Hartford men would not obey, "saying that they had, in that respect, nothing to do with the other colonies."

The weekend interrupted the discussions. Winthrop graciously invited the Dutchmen for dinner on Saturday and again to supper on Sunday. The three went to church in the morning and saw, to their annoyance, the "deputies" of their own towns, Westchester, Newtown, and Jamaica, who, as they had discovered earlier, had "free access to the principal men." After supper in Winthrop's residence the question of the new charter naturally came up, and the governor assured them "frankly" that it had never been the intention of the English "to claim any right to New Netherland, but that it only comprehended a tract of land in New England." This was music to the ears of the delegates, and they asked Winthrop hurriedly for "such a declaration in writing." He declined, "saying that it was sufficiently plain from the patent itself." Van Ruyven explained that "a different construction was put on it by others," but the governor was not to be moved, and "we took leave."

The following Monday was spent in waiting, and only on Tuesday did the Hartford Committee reconvene. The Dutch at once tackled the New Englanders with Winthrop's remark, but the three simply shrugged—"the governor is but one man." For them the patent extended from the Massachusetts line westward to the sea. Almost desperate, the delegates from New Netherland asked them where in that case their own country was: "They answered without hesitation: They knew of no New Netherland."

The proceedings were interrupted for dinner, again at Town Hall, and in the afternoon the worn-out and shattered Dutch envoys were at last confronted with Hartford's demands. They were to give up Westchester and all the land between that town and Stanford; the towns on Long Island would be left alone if the Dutch "wil forbeare to exercise any Coercive Power." Any differences would be put before an impartial body, while those magis-

A SWEET AND ALIEN LAND

trates from Hartford who were now in power on Long Island should be kept "until there be an Issue off these differences."

The Dutch answered that "they were wholly unreasonable. . . . We desired that they should desist from their pretensions to the towns on Long Island." To "obviate further mischief," the three men made an offer to the English. They sacrificed Westchester until the border question was definitely solved, but Long Island was to remain under Governor Stuyvesant. With the Hartford Committee's promise to answer them the next day, the meeting ended.

That evening the three deflated Dutchmen went to see Winthrop to take their leave. When they complained that "nothing more was done on our reasonable proposals," Winthrop politely answered that "he wished something had been fixed upon," but that he could do little, as "it was so concluded upon in the Assembly." Coming to their lodgings, they found a letter from the committee, offering a final insult. It was addressed to the "Right Honnorable Peter Stuyvesant dr. generael at the manados." The envoys protested and told the secretary who brought it that the title ought to be Director General of New Netherland. "He answered, that it was at our option to receive it or not." The three men left immediately.

After a journey on horseback and by sloop they were in New Amsterdam on October 26. Stuyvesant was waiting impatiently. He was appalled by their report and wrote a depressed letter to Amsterdam. "Your Honors will be able to see . . . what efforts have been made agreeable to your Honor's letters, to conclude in this country a settlement." He now foresaw "bloodshed, and with bloodshed—which they seem only to wish—loss of all we possess."[25]

Winthrop did make one small effort to restrain his greedy subjects, and proposed to send "some fitt persons . . . to know the true state and condition of those plantations towards the dutch . . . and to have power to treat with the dutch Generall concerning them," but his was a voice crying in the wilderness. Shortly after, Hartford received Westchester as a member of its corporation, while the villages of Long Island demonstrated that they had no intention of sticking to the agreement.[26]

By the beginning of November the first news reached New Amsterdam of an army of three hundred Englishmen that was

DESPERATE DIPLOMACY

preparing to take over the English villages. It was gathering near Jamaica. Stuyvesant, ill in bed, dispatched Nicasius de Sille with a letter to all the villages, ordering them "to oppose such mutinous illegal acts." In a long letter to Winthrop he complained bitterly that "sum inquiet troublesome and seditious spirits" under the command of Captain John Coe had threatened both Dutch and English on the island "to fyre and to sword iff they would not Ilde [yield] to their unlawful and irregular actings." They had deposed and replaced the magistrates, "which doeing beinge absolutely contrary unto your Honors proposals." He concluded with expressions of hope that Winthrop would "use and endeavour all meanes to suppress such persons."[27]

But even Stuyvesant's confidence in the "friendship" of Winthrop had by now failed, and if the further decay of New Netherland was to be prevented, reinforcements from Holland were urgently needed. His financial resources were running out. The war at Wiltwyck had cost a fortune, and the troubles at Long Island, together with the embassies to Boston and Hartford, had exhausted the treasury. He had already "pawned" four brass cannon in the fort to storekeeper Cornelis Steenwyck, as security for a loan of twelve thousand guilders, but much more was needed. For the first time a Provincial Assembly (de Gemeene Landts Vergaderinghe) was called with the approval of the governor.[28]

On November 1, 1663, the delegates from Breukelen, New Amersfoort, Midwout, New Utrecht, Boswyck, Bergen, and New Haarlem met with the burgomasters and schepens of the capital in City Hall. The English towns stayed away (they did not even answer the invitation). The Dutch towns, maturing fast in the face of the English and Indian threats, decided to send a delegation to the Fatherland to impress upon the West India Company the sad state of the province. Stuyvesant agreed wholeheartedly, and on November 10 a petition was sent off, carried by Jeremias van Rensselaer and former Schepen Johannes Pietersz van Brugh.[29]

It was a long cry of despair. The company, the petition said, had without a proper patent attracted settlers to the province, placing its people "on slippery ice" by giving them land it did not possess. If the Heeren XIX did not act rapidly, the inhabitants would be forced to leave and become "outcasts with their families." "The total loss of this Province is infallibly to be expected and anticipated . . . or at least it will be so cramped and clipped, that it

A SWEET AND ALIEN LAND

will ressemble only a useless trunk, shorn of its limbs. . . ."[30]

Stuyvesant sent an accompanying letter in which he gave the West India Company the practical advice to send as soon as possible a patent, marked with the Great Seal of the States General, "at which the English commonly gapes as at an idol." He would show it to the respective towns, giving the company time to work out a lasting arrangement with England. The steps he proposed seemed sufficient to cope with the situation on Long Island, but they were hopelessly inadequate—and far too late—for the new dangers that were emerging.[31]

PRESIDENT
SCOTT

Departing early in 1663 with his new charter for Connecticut, John Winthrop Jr. left behind in London a redoubtable opponent to his claims on Long Island. When Captain John Scott returned to England, after a fleeting visit to New Haven and Long Island, he found the atmosphere in the English capital greatly changed. Lord Clarendon, the Lord Chancellor, was in poor health and his power was declining rapidly. His careful policy of peaceful coexistence with the Dutch Republic—until the treasure chest was full enough to strike—was detested equally by merchants and Court. Headed by the King's brother, James, Duke of York, and faithfully assisted by the rabidly anti-Dutch Secretary of State Henry Bennet, an important faction was intriguing for war against the Netherlands. From The Hague, Downing did his utmost to encourage them. "Talking onely would doe no good, nor obtaine any satisfaction for what is past," he wrote in November, advising London to do "some thing that was reall and did bite."[1]

The Dutch West India Company was James' personal *bête noire*. His Royal Company of Adventurers, since 1663 called the Royal African Company, and made more respectable by the directorship of Queen Catherine and Queen Mother Henrietta Maria, was constantly harassed by the Dutch on the coast of Africa, and the chance of royal profits thereby greatly reduced. It was high time to teach the Heeren XIX a lesson and, as Downing assured him, "he might expect a good issue" if he would try "something in revenge against the West India Company." In October 1663 he sent Sir Robert Holmes with two warships to the coast of Guinea to capture the Dutch forts there.[2]

For John Scott, this was an excellent moment to come forward again with his plans for Long Island. His first contacts with the Court had not been forgotten, and Scott, a smooth talker, did not lack friends. One of them was Sir Joseph Williamson, the shrewd confidential secretary of Henry Bennet. Other useful contacts were Samuel Maverick, still hovering around the Council for Foreign Plantations, and George Baxter, the representative of Rhode Island and by now the resentful enemy of his former employers, the Dutch. The three together made enough impression to be called before the Council, where Scott complained convincingly about the Dutch, who "have of late yeares unjustly intruded upon and possessed themselves of certaine places on the maineland of New England and some Islands adjacent, as in perticuler on the Manhatoes and Long Island."[3]

The possession of those regions was not only unjust, the three men pointed out, because it was "without giveing obedience to his Matie," but also because "the good intencion of the late Act of Navigation is in great part frustrated by their practices." The Council in some concern therefore asked Scott, Maverick, and Baxter to draw up "a briefe narrative of and touching these perticulers," and to report about the title the King had to the region, the strength of the Dutch and their trade, and lastly "of the meanes to make them acknowledge and submit to His Mats governmt, or by force to compell them therunto or expulse them."[4]

In October 1663 Scott sailed back to America, armed with this commission, and with the knowledge that the Duke of York was eager to reduce New Netherland. Wisely, he kept his mouth shut at Hartford, where he succeeded in charming Winthrop with the latest gossip from London while omitting any mention of the Duke's plans and his previous commission from New Haven. The governor had never had a great liking for this young adventurer, but his sudden zeal and his suggestion that he could bring the Long Island towns under Hartford changed Winthrop's opinion, and in December the Hartford General Court appointed Scott its commissioner at Setauket, the Long Island town where he had his manor. At the same time, the captain was invested with magisterial

PRESIDENT SCOTT

powers over the whole island and took the oath—before Winthrop himself—"to the faithful discharge of his place."[5]

Scott reported triumphantly on December 14 to Sir Joseph Williamson in London that the "Gentlemen of Connecticut, . . . themselves a people jealouse of his Majesties concernes," were going to take care of the English on Long Island, so long "having been inslaved by the Dutch, their cruell and rapatious neighbours." A few days later he was back in Setauket, together with two other well-known antagonists of the Dutch, the captains John Talcott and John Young.[6]

On the island itself unrest was increasing by the day. Some of the towns were in favor of annexation by Connecticut, but complained that they received no help; others feared the Puritan regime of Hartford and wished to become independent. The return of their famous captain raised hopes that at last something would be settled, and on December 13 Scott received at his manor an urgent appeal from Hempstead. "In the behalf of sum hundreds of English heer planted on the west end of Long Island wee address ourselves unto you," it began, "the business is that wee ware put uppon proclaiming the King by Capt. John Young who came with a trumpet to Heemstede and sounded in our eares that Conecticot would do great things for us, which hath put us to greate trouble, and extreamly divided us." They asked Scott to come and sort things out, as "the Dutch threaten us; our neighbours abuse us and nothing comes from Conecticot but if so bees and doubtinghs."[7]

Before the end of the month Scott arrived with 170 men on horse and foot at Hempstead, where at last he threw off his mask. Telling the citizens that the King had promised the island to his brother, the Duke of York, he advised them to manage their own affairs until the Duke gave them further instructions. Riding from town to town, Scott issued his proclamations, sacked magistrates, and invited new ones to join his "Combination," which would run the island, independently of Connecticut—and, of course, of New Netherland.

It was the solution most of the inhabitants of the English towns had waited for, and on January 4, 1664, they elected John Scott as president—the first America had ever known—"until his Royal Highness the Duke of York or his Majesty should establish a government among them." Without any qualms Scott resigned his

A SWEET AND ALIEN LAND

commission from Hartford, absolved himself from the oath he had taken before Winthrop, and "proclaimed the majesty of our dreaded sovereign Charles II."[8]

Now the Dutch villages on the island were approached. Followed by his 170 men, "President" Scott proceeded first to Breukelen, where his reception was icy. Undiscouraged, he at once sent off a letter to Governor Stuyvesant, in which he assured him that he had not come "with any hostile view, unless his Majesty's good subjects, whose liberty is more dear to me than my life, should be deprived of their just right, which God and nature have conferred on them."[9]

The news of Scott's progress over the island had been received in New Amsterdam, as in Hartford, with fury and dismay, and when Scott's letter arrived, the General refused to accept it. The Englishman had addressed it to "Petrus Stuyvesant," and the indignant general told the messenger that "There was no other Peter Stuyvesant here than the Director-General of New Netherland; if Capt. Schot meant him, then his honor must be acknowledged in that quality."

The messenger told Stuyvesant " 'twas better to open the letter; that Capt. Scott, although he had at present with him a numerous troop of horse and foot, came only in friendship." With the English flair for compromise, he offered to open the letter himself and to read it, a solution that was accepted. The missive was an invitation to the governor to come the next day to Midwout, but Stuyvesant had other ideas and at once sent his secretary, Van Ruyven, with Van Cortlandt, Cregier, and Laurence, to Scott's headquarters at Breukelen to demand that the captain come to New Amsterdam.[10]

An irritated "President" Scott refused to follow the four solemn Dutchmen to the capital. He insisted that Stuyvesant should come to him, threatening that if he brought troops with him he would "run a sword through his body." Creigier's young son, who had accompanied the delegation, stood listening to this outburst in astonishment, and Scott, still fuming, ordered him to take off his cap to the English flag, which was waving over the village. The boy refused and the Englishman gave him a ringing slap on his ear. One of the bystanders jeered that he ought to strike grown-ups and not children, a remark that almost cost him his life as four of Scott's soldiers fell upon him. Swaying with his axe, the Dutch-

PRESIDENT SCOTT

man fled between the houses, pursued by the shouting soldiers, who threatened to set the whole village on fire if he did not give himself up. Scott himself restored discipline by calling them back, and, turning again to the Dutch embassy, offered to wait at the Breukelen ferry head for the general.

His offer was declined and Scott, unperturbed, went on with his presidential progress. Midwout and New Amersfoort were his next stops, and in both towns, after hoisting the English flag, he made the same speech. From now on the inhabitants were under Charles II, he proclaimed, who would give them more freedom than they had ever known. No longer should they pay taxes to Governor Stuyvesant nor obey him, and if they refused to listen, they knew what to expect. The Dutch listened indeed, but were not impressed. Some of them told Scott that he ought to settle these matters with Stuyvesant. The Englishman answered that he intended to go to New Amsterdam, but only to proclaim the King under the walls of the city.[11]

The Dutch general's hands were itching, but it was impossible for him to do anything. Most of his troops were still at Wiltwyck, where the two months' truce with the Esopus Indians was nearing its end. Humiliated and frustrated, he had to follow Scott's impertinent activities helplessly from Fort Amsterdam. The five Dutch villages on Long Island, confused and afraid, waited in vain for help, and when some Englishmen drove them from their lands under the protest of new grants, they sent a petition, which Stuyvesant read with increasing anger. If no troops were sent, they wrote, "we roundly declare that we cannot longer dwell and sit down on an uncertainty, but shall be obliged to our heart's grief to seek, by submitting to another government, better protection as well against such vagabonds as against barbarians."[12]

It was a hard blow for Stuyvesant. The loss of the Dutch towns would mean a victory for Scott, the total domination of Long Island Sound by the English, and death by strangulation for New Amsterdam. In a hurry he called the City Fathers together. Scott had left the Dutch part of Long Island, but had promised—or threatened—to come back in March to show his commission, and the governor wanted to know if he should then be opposed with force.

The magistrates gave him a lengthy answer that rang with bit-

A SWEET AND ALIEN LAND

terness against the company and its officials. It was impossible to do anything, because high taxes and duties had been the cause of the departure of many Dutch from the province, they began. "Many houses stand empty and unoccupied, whereby the Burghery is so enfeebled and impoverished, that many are unable to earn their living, much less to undertake military expeditions." If only the Heeren XIX had used the money they had received in duties "for the benefit of the country" and had sent a few hundred "brave discharged soldiers," the trouble would never have started. Since this was not the case, they felt that the citizens were only bound to defend "this place within its walls." The rest of the country was the responsibility of the company, which should not be too much afraid of the English soldiers, "as the greater part is a ragged troop."[13]

They promised, however, to take the greatest possible care in the defense of the capital, "adorned with so many noble buildings at the expense of the good and faithful inhabitants, principally Netherlanders, that it nearly excels any other place in North America," adding the hint that "were it duly fortified it would instil fear into any envious neighbours."

The City Fathers refused to go into the question of whether New Netherland "be the King of England's soil or their High Mightinesses," but for the sake of defending their own "properties, freedoms and privileges," they promised to devote all their revenues to defense, and to raise more funds. On condition that the capital would enlist 200 men and maintain 160 soldiers, Stuyvesant now surrendered the excise on the tavernkeepers to the magistrates, who with this as security had no difficulty in raising a loan of 27, 500 guilders from the "poor" burghers, a sum that included a thousand guilders from the governor.

The day approached when Scott was due to summon the Dutch towns on Long Island to yield, and Stuyvesant still hesitated over his course of action. Public opinion was deeply divided. Some "denounced his non-resistance and abstinence from hostility as a disgraceful and contemptible cowardice," while others were in favor of negotiation. Stuyvesant unburdened his heart in a long letter to the company, written on the last day of February, and signed "your faithful, forsaken and almost hopeless servant." He saw no other way of dealing with Scott—"President, as he styles

PRESIDENT SCOTT

himself"—than to compromise, he told the Lords Directors, as "their intolerable menaces have no other object than to get our blood. . . ."[14]

Stuyvesant had heard of the great interest the Duke of York took in the Dutch province when Scott himself had given a Dutch delegation in mid-February the advice "to come to an agreement with the Duke of York, inasmuch as he knew, for certain, that his Majesty had granted that Island to His Royal Highness." What was more, the Duke's appetite had been whetted by hearing that "said Island could produce yearly several thousand pounds sterling."[15]

The Dutch delegation that Stuyvesant mentioned had been led by Burgomaster Van Cortlandt. He had met Scott in the company of that English soldier of fortune, well known to the Dutch, John Underhill. Still under the illusion that Scott was operating on behalf of Connecticut, Van Cortlandt had provisionally agreed that the English towns on Long Island would remain under the King of England for the next twelve months. In the meantime His Majesty and the States would try to determine all their differences, and Scott would leave the Dutch towns alone.[16]

Stuyvesant did not like Van Cortlandt's compromise at all, but, realist that he was, it took him only a week to swallow his pride. On March 3, escorted by ten soldiers, he traveled to Hempstead, where the English towns were holding an assembly under "President" Scott. It was the right occasion for the solemn signing of the agreement.

The Dutch governor must have studied in dismay the ever-shrinking map of his province. The Connecticut River was lost, Westchester had been taken by Hartford, and half of Long Island was now under Scott. Even the Delaware was no longer his responsibility, but that of Amsterdam. New Netherland was collapsing around him like a house of cards.

For Scott it was a glorious moment. He was sure that the Duke of York would send some ships to establish English authority. If only he could entrench himself firmly against any claims from Connecticut, he was convinced that "were the Dutch reduced to the authority of the King of England he would be allowed to control the region beyond the East River."[17]

His days of glory were, however, short. The captain might have forgotten his Connecticut commission, but Hartford had not. Pos-

A SWEET AND ALIEN LAND

sibly even more enraged than the Dutch, the authorities of Connecticut followed Scott's progress through their recently "conquered" towns, and indignantly read reports of his impertinent behavior. What Stuyvesant had not been strong enough to do, Connecticut now prepared to do for him. The General Court at Hartford resolved to arrest the traitor, and at a session in March drew up a list of accusations, containing crimes as various as defaming the King, receiving bribes, profaning the Lord's Day and "acting treacherously" to Connecticut.[18]

When Scott visited New Haven on March 21, a surprise waited for him in the person of Marshal Jonathan Gilbert from Hartford, with a warrant for his arrest. But the authorities of the little port town, still fighting Connecticut's demand for its adherence to the Hartford jurisdiction, refused to allow him to be captured, and Scott left unhindered for Long Island. Another marshal from Hartford, Nathan Seeley, had more luck the next day. Dispatched with a group of Indians to Scott's manor at Setauket, he found the "president" at home. He again showed him the warrant, but Scott challenged him: "Take me if you dare. I will see if the proudest among you will dare lay hands on me." After a violent struggle, Seeley's Indians overpowered the captain and carried him proudly off to Hartford, where Scott disappeared into the jail, laden with "a long iron chaine."[19]

From all sides protests streamed in. A petition from Flushing testified that Scott had worked with the consent of the people and that "in their silence, the very stones might justly rise to proclaim his innocence." Even the three other New England colonies sent delegates to interfere, and Governor Thomas Prence of Plymouth wrote to Winthrop on behalf of Scott, "a gentleman well deserving of the country, and one that his Majesty hath been very pleased to employ in his service." Scott himself addressed "an humbell petition" to the General Court, explaining that "having run himself into a labrinth of misery by the evil advice of bad instruments," he now begged for mercy "which shall be deemed by your poor suppliant a signal kindness never to be forgot."[20]

An embarrassed Winthrop resolved to absent himself, leaving the dirty business to the Court. On May 24, Scott appeared at last before his judges to face no less than ten charges, one of them relating to the "Sunk Squaw," an Indian Queen whom he was supposed to have robbed of a piece of land. The verdict was easy

PRESIDENT SCOTT

to predict—he was found guilty on all charges. The sentence was heavy: a fine of £250, confinement to prison during the Court's pleasure, and degradation from his Long Island magistracy. He was stripped of all his political and judicial rights, and finally he was to be banished.[21]

Scott had no intention of rotting away during the Court's pleasure in his cell on the third floor of the prison, and when in July his wife Deborah visited him, she hid under her wide gown not only the baby she was expecting, but also a long rope. That evening Scott lowered himself to the ground and escaped unhindered to Long Island. This time Winthrop left him alone, but Scott's colorful presidency had definitely come to an end.

MAD

FOR WAR

When Jeremias van Rensselaer arrived in Amsterdam in January 1664 with the protest from New Netherland against the English intrusion, news of Scott's escapades on Long Island had not yet reached the Dutch. The revelations in the document Van Rensselaer carried with him, and Stuyvesant's request for a seal in order to impress the greedy New Englanders, startled the West India Company sufficiently. Shocked by the "unreasonable and unjustifiable proceedings of the English," the furious Heeren XIX turned at once to the States General.[1]

"On the 21st of this month the West India Company has presented a great memorial," reported the writer Abraham de Wicquefort to King Frederick III of Denmark. "They complain of the violences the English of New England have committed to their colony, New Belgium. . . . Those from the colony of Hartford are the cause of the trouble, they threaten to drive the Dutch out with fire and blood." The company now asked the States to make a boundary settlement with Charles II, to beg the King to return the occupied settlements, and finally, if these moves failed, to give permission for the Dutch to oppose the English by force. But little happened—"all what is done now, is to protest with Downing," reported Wicquefort.[2]

Sir George Downing had indeed been summoned by Raadspensionary Johan de Witt, who expostulated against the English, "incroaching (as is pretended here) upon the Dutch in New Netherland," Downing reported to Clarendon. "I replied, that I had heard much of it at London, and that our people doe say that they heare are the incroachers." He advised the Lord Chancellor not to answer directly, but to wait three or four months, and then promise that the King would make inquiries. "That answere will serve for a yeare longer, which is their way of treating others."[3]

De Witt's intervention was not so much for the sake of the Heeren XIX, for whom he had no love at all, but for the sake of the province itself. For some time now De Witt had been increasingly irritated and disturbed by the ineptitude of the West India Company, which was constantly coming cap in hand to ask for loans, but seemed nonetheless to be perpetually losing its assets abroad to the English or the Portuguese. What he planned was a drastic reorganization of the company, with particular emphasis on New Netherland, which would at last receive almost complete autonomy.

Certain pamphlets published around this time made no secret of De Witt's plans. One was called *A Short Account of New Netherland's Situation . . . and Peculiar Fitness for Population*, another *Netherland Glorified by a Restoration of Commerce*. In both tracts the company came under heavy fire for its blunders in New Netherland. Only the government could now redress the situation, with the help of the cities, which would lend the necessary money.[4]

This sudden interest came rather late, but De Witt was convinced that he could still save New Netherland, so excellently situated for breaking the hated Navigation Act. The situation was important enough to be made an issue with the English, and Alviso Sagredo, the Venetian Ambassador in Paris, reported: "There is at present a most disagreeable not to say perilous dispute between the Dutch and the English over the differences which have arisen in North America, called New Belgium because it there borders New England." According to him the English would not be content with words alone, "unless the Dutch make up their minds to give way and yield a great deal there."[5]

The Dutch had no intention of doing so, but Downing was unimpressed by their resolve. He dispatched another company pamphlet about the dispute to London with the message: "If his Maty thinke fitt to leave that matter to me, I shall deale well enough with them and repay them in their own manner."[6]

A SWEET AND ALIEN LAND

London left it all too willingly to the ambassador, who, as the government knew very well, was expert at antagonizing the detested Dutch. At Court and in the coffeehouses in London where the merchants gathered, his activities were followed with delight. Anti-Dutch feeling in England had now reached the level of general hysteria, and Samuel Pepys, who as clerk at the Admiralty was well informed about the deplorable state of the English fleet, wrote anxiously of the tough talk about the need for war. One day it was a friend who told him of "the good effects in some kind of a Dutch warr and conquest," another day it was the King's Brewer who declared that "all the Court are mad for a Dutch war."[7]

The emerging leader of the war faction was the King's brother, James, Duke of York, who, having decided "to give himself up to business" and prove that he was "a Noble Prince," wished nothing better than to humiliate the proud merchants of the Dutch Republic. The semipiratical expedition that Sir Robert Holmes had undertaken for the Duke's Royal African Company had been successful. Holmes had captured the Dutch trading station, Cabo Corso, on the Gold Coast—an important center for the lucrative slave trade—and James was greatly encouraged by this coup. He was convinced that the "Dutch are not in so good a condition as heretofore," and that a "barefaced war" against them would lead to a victory for England. Like the city, reported Pepys, the Duke believed "that the trade of the world is too little for us two, therefore one must down."[8]

The diarist learned of these sentiments at first hand when in April he met the Duke himself, strolling through Whitehall. "He called me to him and discoursed a great deal," Pepys noted, "and after he had gone, twice or thrice staid and called me again to him, the whole length of the house; and at last talked of the Dutch; and I perceive [he does] much wish that the Parliament will find reason to fall out with them." Three days later he was back with the Duke for discussions on the condition of the fleet, "in order to a Dutch warr, for that I perceive the Duke hath a mind it shall come to."[9]

Apart from his patriotic and genuine concern for the betterment of English trade and economy, James had other, more personal reasons for wishing a war with the Republic. Now thirty years old, the stubborn and rather dull-witted Duke found life at Court tedious, and war—together with a succession of rather plain

MAD FOR WAR

mistresses—was his great interest, "having been, even from child-hood, in the command of armies and in his nature inclined to the most difficult and dangerous enterprises." As Lord High Admiral of England, a good brisk war offered him the best opportunity to establish his own position at Court and in the country.

The Dutch seemed to him the perfect objects for such an enter-prise, and not simply because they were his country's most danger-ous commercial competitors. He had an intense personal dislike for the solemn, conceited Dutch statesmen who, during Crom-well's Protectorate, had frequently chased his brother and himself away from the court of their sister Mary in The Hague. He also strongly resented the refusal of the Republican regents to ac-knowledge his young nephew William III, who had been deprived of his hereditary title of Stadtholder of the United Provinces.[10]

James' feelings about them were well known to the Dutch, and they soon added another grievance to the long list the King's brother was drawing up. He became the favorite butt of the many anti-English lampoons and pamphlets, at which the Dutch ex-celled. King Charles II himself was not spared, and shocked for-eign ambassadors reported to their capitals that his English Maj-esty was portrayed with his pockets turned inside out, "indicating the scantiness of the royal treasure."

This was nothing compared to the abusive caricatures of James, and Downing was kept busy protesting them. Lampoons had been pasted on walls with the permission of the burgomasters of the towns, and on February 15 he told London indignantly: "I caused another one of those papers to be taken downe from a place neer one of the entries into the Court," in The Hague. He had com-plained to De Witt, but "they make so slight of the matter. . . ." It was not a "fitting way" to treat "any that weares a swored, much less for Princes," he fumed.[11]

With all this in mind, the Duke began to press for war, giving orders, as president of the Council for Trade, to collect all the complaints any company or merchant had against the Dutch. His efforts were followed with great interest by the King, who hoped "by getting underhand the merchants to bring in their com-plaints," Pepys wrote, "to make them in honour begin a warr, which he cannot declare first, for feare they should not second him with money." The States heard about the Duke's activities with

A SWEET AND ALIEN LAND

anxiety, and Downing wrote happily to Clarendon: "They begin now to take the allarme att the great talkes in England of warr with this country, especially because of Parliament now comeing to sitt, and that complaints will be made against them."[12]

De Witt had tried once again in February to persuade the English to sign a treaty "for the regulating trade within and without Europe," but Downing had warned Clarendon not to walk into this trap, as the Dutch "will certainly thereby become what they do desire to be, viz, the common carriers of the world." But the mere suggestion had made it clear to him that the Republic had no desire for war, and he reiterated this just before Parliament assembled in April. "I assure you, those that govern here have neither designe nor desire to fall out with his Matie. On the contrary, it is the thing in the world they dread the most."[13]

Pepys saw Downing's letter when, on his way to Parliament, he met Secretary of State Sir William Coventry, who, as one of the directors of the Council for Trade, revealed to him that all the complaints against the Dutch had been gathered in and that they now "were resolved to report highly the wrongs they have done us." Pepys added with a sigh that "God knows, it is only our owne negligence and laziness that hath done us the wrong."

Parliament saw it otherwise and listened with mounting anger to the litanies of complaints from the great trading companies—which had been obstructed in their commerce; had been attacked by the natives, who were stirred up by the Dutch; had lost their ships and seen their factories destroyed, while the obnoxious Dutch called themselves "Lords of the Southern Seas."[14]

Their claim for damages was considerable—£700,000, and the debate lasted two weeks. In the end Parliament asked the King "to take some speedy and effectual means for the redress thereof and for the prevention of the like in the future." Pepys wrote on April 30: "All the newes now is what will become of the Dutch business, whether warr or peace." But the King still hesitated, deciding to wait a little longer. "The King and Parliament have appointed commissioners to make report," Sagredo told Venice.[15]

The King's temperate reaction to Parliament's war cries gave De Witt hope that the tension would now ease. When in May he received Charles' demand for satisfaction for all the complaints, he went out of his way to placate him, referring the most thorny questions to the mediation of France. An unhappy James had to look on while his more pacific brother spoiled his chances for glory.

Fortunately for the Duke, he still had his interests in America, which activated his private war against New Netherland. Captain John Scott had acted prematurely in taking over Long Island, but James was going to make sure that its annexation by Connecticut would be short-lived.

For Peter Stuyvesant, the arrest of Scott, with whom he had just made a year's truce, had solved nothing. Governor Winthrop felt that the time for kind dissimulation was over, and on March 29, 1664, made it clear to his Dutch colleague that the "Combination" of the five English towns on Long Island was by charter right indisputedly under the control of Hartford. At the same time, the harassed Stuyvesant received word of renewed efforts by the people of Westchester to buy from the Indians the land between their village and the Hudson, including the old plantation of Adriaen van der Donck.[16]

The savages who told him this had come with even more dangerous news. The truce with the Esopus Indians was over, and the dispersed tribe had not been sitting still. According to Stuyvesant's informants, it had joined forces with the English at Westchester. The English would take Long Island and Manhattan, and if the Dutch did not surrender voluntarily, the Indians would help the English kill them. The Indians were so eager for the massacre that they had even promised the English all the land on the Esopus.

The transaction had occurred at the beginning of March, just before Stuyvesant had concluded his treaty with Scott, which changed everything. When the Indians came to the English shortly after to discuss the last details, they were told: "It cannot be done at present, our Sachem has made an agreement with Stuyvesant for a year." The Esopus and their allies, the Wappingers, protested, but to no avail and they left angrily, muttering: "It is better to make peace with the Dutch, the English are only fooling us." The plot with Westchester sounded almost too fantastic to be true, and Stuyvesant immediately sent Lieutenant Pieter van Couwenhoven to the Indians to find out more. The envoy came back with the sworn statements of at least ten Indians as proof of the plot.[17]

This added another dreadful dimension to a situation that was slowly becoming unbearable for the governor and the people in the province. In addition to the English and Indian threat, they now received information of another: a Swedish fleet of two ships with forty guns and two hundred soldiers was on its way to reconquer the Delaware. "If we are to be surprised on the South River by the Swede," lamented Stuyvesant on February 28, "troubled on Long Island by malignant neighbours and English vassals and on the other side by barbarous Indians; between three stools one falls to the ground, as the proverb has it."[18]

He had still heard nothing from the company and the States General about the petition or the request for help he had dispatched in November 1663, and something had to be done. He agreed at once when the burgomasters and Schepens of New Amsterdam approached him on March 18 with a request to summon again a General Assembly to discuss "this highly imperious necessity."[19]

The meeting started on April 10 and was attended by two representatives from each of the twelve towns. It began badly, with a heated discussion about the chairmanship. New Amsterdam claimed it for the capital, while Jeremias van Rensselaer, just back from his mission to Holland, insisted it belonged to the oldest settlement, Rensselaerswyck. His right was conceded, but "under protest."

The second point of discussion was the defense of the country against the Indians and the "malignant English," and it almost led to a clash between Stuyvesant and the townsmen. Rather impertinently, the representatives turned to the governor and asked for protection. If he could not give it, to whom should they address themselves?[20]

The governor, somewhat older and wiser than in 1653, when he had impatiently dismissed the first General Assembly, told the meeting that the West India Company had sent two hundred soldiers, but that now the New Netherlanders themselves must contribute by, for instance, ordering every sixth man to take up arms. To pay for the defense, he proposed a tax on cattle and mills, since the company was short of funds, having by now spent at least 1.2

MAD FOR WAR

million guilders on the province. For him, he explained patiently, the problem was whether the inhabitants wanted to force the English to relinquish the country they had taken over, and whether the delegates wished to continue the war against the Indians, now that the truce was ended.[21]

The delegates were obviously shocked by the responsibilities the governor had suddenly heaped on their shoulders, and they scattered like frightened birds, adjourning the meeting for a week. When they reassembled, Stuyvesant had some good news for them. The charter that the States General had given the company in January had at last arrived, with the Great Seal attached. It stated categorically that the colony had been established "in conformity with our sincere intention," and still included—somewhat optimistically—the Fresh River, now called the Connecticut, and "other places in New Netherland, situated even more easterly, even unto Cape Cod." The Treaty of Hartford of 1650 was only provisionally accepted by the company.[22]

The delegates and Stuyvesant must have smiled bitterly at this trophy, but the document was at least a sign that they had not been completely forgotten. Letters from the States to the English villages on Long Island, in which it insisted on obedience to the governor and promised the posting of sixty soldiers, encouraged these feelings. With more enthusiasm than the week before, the discussion now resumed.

First the English threat was tackled. The company had ordered them to drive out the invaders from Long Island, but the delegates were more realistic. "The English rebels were as six to one" and could expect the aid of Hartford, they answered. It was therefore better to leave them alone for the time being, in the hope that the letter from the States would make an impression.

As for the Esopus Indians, the Assembly advised the governor to conclude a peace treaty with them before English plotters could do more harm. Stuyvesant agreed and wrote to the West India Company, which wanted them exterminated, that "they are so tired out and dispersed" that it would be better to come to a peaceful solution. The war had, anyhow, cost eighty thousand guilders in the last year, while the revenue from the province was no more than thirty thousand. It was the best argument he could find for a treaty with the Indians.[23]

The peace treaty with the Indians was concluded on May 16. On

A SWEET AND ALIEN LAND

that day eleven chiefs, led by Seweckenamo of the Esopus tribe, came to Fort Amsterdam to conclude, as the sachem told Stuyvesant, "a peace as firm and compact as his arms," and under the salvo of the cannon, the treaty was signed. According to the terms, everything that had happened was forgiven and forgotten, the Indians were to leave the land around Wiltwyck to the colonists (including the two forts that Cregier had destroyed), and no native was in the future allowed to visit the village, with or without arms.[24]

The dealings with the English towns on Long Island were less satisfactory. Stuyvesant sent Under-schout Waldron and court messenger Claes van Elslandt with copies of the States' letter to Gravesend, Hempstead, Flushing, Jamaica, and Newtown, urging them to turn their backs on Connecticut. But on June 10 the governor wrote: "They had no effect whatever upon the English, at least not on their intruding Magistrates and the followers of the latter." As the bearers reported, they hardly condescended to receive, much less to read the letters, but sent them immediately to Hartford, without having opened them, as if they wanted to say: "You may get your answer from there."

The impression the letters made in Hartford was not much greater. Thomas Willett, "and other well-affected Englishmen," told the general that the General Court believed "that they had been fabricated and forged by the Company in Holland or by your own servants here; they say, the States General have nothing to do with this province, they knew it belonged to the King."[25]

Stuyvesant made one more desperate effort to save Long Island. Winthrop, now openly in possession of the English towns, paid a visit to them at the beginning of June 1664. He deposed the magistrates Scott had given them, appointed others, and promised the citizens protection against the Dutch. Stuyvesant heard about his tour and hurriedly left the capital with several notables in the hope of meeting him before he could return to Hartford.

The governor of Connecticut, highly satisfied, had just left Hempstead when his Dutch colleague caught up with him. A discussion followed, but it "was all in vain, as if [he] talked against a wall," wrote Stuyvesant to Amsterdam. He had pointed out that the Dutch had held possession of the island for forty years, twenty years before the English came, but Winthrop was unshakable in his declaration: "It is the King's land, they are mostly the King's

MAD FOR WAR

born subjects and it shall be and remain as it is without further discussion."[26]

Defeated, Stuyvesant returned to New Amsterdam with the last vestiges of his belief in the goodwill of Winthrop totally destroyed. "You may easily see, how unfounded your supposition is, that . . . it does not appear the rebels will receive support from elsewhere [and that] Governor Winthrop will not approve of them," he wrote to the company on August 4.[27]

Changing
Hands

*James, Duke of York, who
received New Amsterdam as a gift from his
brother, Charles II, and gave the city its name, New York.*

Johan de Witt, the Dutch Raadspensionary,
who like most of the Dutch
realized the importance of New Amsterdam too late.

John Winthrop, Jr.,
Connecticut's governor.
COURTESY OF THE
FOGG ART MUSEUM,
HARVARD UNIVERSITY
PORTRAIT COLLECTION

John Winthrop, Sr., founder of
Massachusetts Bay, and one of the first
to encroach on New Netherland's territory.
COURTESY OF THE FOGG ART MUSEUM,
HARVARD UNIVERSITY PORTRAIT COLLECTION

Cornelis Evertsen,
whose reconquest of
New Netherland in 1673 was
very little appreciated by the Dutch.
IES LAMAIN, MIDDELBURG

A last view of New Amsterdam.
MUSEUM OF THE CITY OF NEW YORK

New York's City Hall in 1679, as shown in a later drawing.

THE STADTHUYS OF NEW YORK IN 1679.
Corner of Pearl St and Coentija Slip.

THE DUKE'S
INVASION

Samuel Maverick, the former merchant from Massachusetts and New Amsterdam, had not forgotten the English government's commission, given to John Scott, George Baxter, and himself, to investigate the state of New Netherland. He returned to New England and in 1663 the Council for Foreign Plantation received his first report. From that moment on, the normally kindhearted and tolerant Maverick never relaxed his pressure on England to assert "the rightful claims of the King of England" on this small Dutch province. A complete publicity campaign was organized in London to prepare the English for the "take-over." Booklets and pamphlets appeared in which the writers went back to the days of Henry Hudson, "an English gentleman," who had discovered the "Manadaes," but sold it to the Dutch "without authority from his Sovereign." The "monsters and bold usurpers" had been very ungrateful and had "put him to sea in a small boat after they had got what they could of him."[1]

Maverick claimed that he had met some Indians at the Hudson who still remembered very well "that it was an English flag they first saw in the sd river and that an Englishman was the first that traded with them and that for certaine kettles, Hatchets, Knives and other trading ware they gave the sd Englishman that land, where the Dutch fort and Cittie now standeth." His reports were followed up by a stream of nagging letters to Lord Clarendon, in which he described how the Dutch "incroach and increase," how the English had to put up with their "bad neighbourhood," and how much profit—"yearly above one hundred thousand beaver skins"—the English could derive from the colony.[2]

The last argument weighed heavily in London, but it was not only greed that encouraged the English government. The Navigation Act of 1661, followed by the Staple Act of 1663, made it obligatory for the colonies to send all their most important goods direct to England, while London was the sole source of supply for the European goods they needed. With the Dutch enclave in the heart of English America, this provision was almost impossible to enforce, and in December 1663 the Council for Foreign Plantations remarked with fury that the English colonies "both by land and water carry and convey great quantities of tobacco to the Dutch, whose plantacons are contiguous." His Majesty was in that manner defrauded of at least ten thousand pounds a year, a sum his treasury could ill afford to lose.[3]

In January 1664 three members of the Plantation Council—one of them Sir John Berkeley, the brother of Virginia's pro-Dutch governor, Sir William—met to study England's grievances against the Dutch province. Before them was the *Brief Narrative*, written by Maverick and his colleagues, together with a number of the merchant's letters, in which he warned them that "the Dutch governor hath sent for a supply of men and ammunition," and that Holland was preparing three ships "for the strengtheninge the New Netherlands." England had to act rapidly. And before the end of the month the subcommittee advised the King that he should immediately send ships and soldiers to reduce the Dutch.[4]

The King had never felt any great affection for his younger brother. In character the two men were poles apart. The cynical and easygoing Charles, who enjoyed nothing more than being King—and wished to remain so—had little patience with James because of his complete lack of humor and ponderous sincerity. But he was very much aware of his brother's devotion and loyalty to him—unaccountable though he might often have found it—and he appreciated the efforts the Duke was making to reorganize the navy and bring order to the American colonies. These considerations made it almost inevitable that Charles should decide to present his brother with a generous slice of America.

In 1662 Lord Clarendon had already purchased the charter for Long Island from Lord Stirling (for which he never paid), and this was made into the nucleus of the new province. On February 29, 1664, the famous Duke's Charter was presented to the Royal Secretariat, where it was ratified with amazing speed and published on March 12. The charter covered, among other areas, all the territory of New Netherland, including Long Island. New Haven and part of Connecticut were swallowed up as well, and the blow must have been as severe for Winthrop as for Stuyvesant.[5]

The fact that the Dutch province was not yet conquered was inconvenient, but easy to rectify, and in the greatest secrecy preparations were started for a small expedition that would confirm the Duke's possession of his property. Money was a slight problem, but on the same day that the Duke's Charter was presented, a sum of four thousand pounds was allocated by Parliament, and an additional two thousand pounds was easily found when needed for extra "stores of war." On April 25, the administrative problems having been dealt with, the formation of a small fleet got under way.[6]

Maverick in his letters to Clarendon had insisted not only on the reduction of New Netherland, but also on the subordination of New England. The Puritan colonies were so used to having their own way that a touch of majestical correction would do them no harm. He eagerly reported the divisions among the English settlers, which were so deep that those opposed to the autocratic governments of Boston and Hartford would welcome a Royal Commission with open arms. The others could easily be subdued by "debarringe them from trade a few monethes." After that, disputes would be unlikely, if New England received "libertie of Conscience in some reasonable large measure, and be as little burdened by taxes or otherwise as may be." To do exactly that London had already appointed a Commission of Four in 1663 to send to New England. This group now decided to combine the task of calling the New Englanders to heel with that of conquering New Netherland.[7]

Maverick was one of the commissioners; the others were Colonel Richard Nicolls, Colonel George Cartwright, and Sir Robert Carr. Not all were considered a suitable choice: Bennet's secretary, Sir Joseph Williamson, had a great disdain for Cartwright and Carr, the first an incompetent officer, the second a "weake" and till then unknown country gentleman. But Maverick's inclusion was inevitable, and generally approved. He had the advantage of knowing the field; his dedication to the American cause was well known; and even if he was highly prejudiced against the Puritans and the Dutch, he was also intelligent and humane.[8]

The fourth commissioner was perhaps the most outstanding. The forty-year-old Colonel Nicolls, the fourth son of a minor Bedford barrister, was a close friend of the Duke of York, whom he had followed into exile and whose Groom of the Bedchamber he later became. The Duke trusted this moderate, intelligent man, and the military command of the whole expedition was placed in his hands.[9]

In May the four royal commissioners embarked at Portsmouth. Their fleet was anything but impressive—most of the vessels were fourth-raters, and only the flagship *Guinea*, with its thirty guns, could be considered a ship-of-war. The others were the *Elias*, with about thirty-five guns; the *Martin*, with fourteen; and the merchant vessel *William and Nicholas*, with ten guns. Their departure, however much shrouded in secrecy, did not go unnoticed by the Dutch, and the West India Company at once sounded the alarm to the States. "Having for a long time observed the jealousy which the English nation hath entertained of the trade and commerce of this country," the Heeren XIX told the States, they have "now not hesitated to advance their projects by open force. . . . On 25 May last four ships sailed from Portsmouth with 300 soldiers to take possession of New Netherland, or at least of Long Island."[10]

Wicquefort reported to Copenhagen that the company had asked for battleships, but that the States had refused in order to prevent another "brouillerie" between the Republic and England. Downing had received the same impression of caution when he was summoned by Raadspensionary De Witt. "He told me they had a great allarme about a new business, viz, that the English should be now about sending to take New Netherland," he wrote on May 6 to Clarendon. "I replyed that I knew of no such country but only in the mapps. That indeed, if their people were to be believed, all the world were New Netherland." De Witt had not pressed the point. The Dutch statesman had preferred to trust the letters from his ambassador in London, Van Gogh, who reported that Charles had again told him "that he had no desire to damage the understanding he had with the States."[11]

The royal word was believed, and the company was sufficiently reassured to tell Stuyvesant that the King had sent commissioners to New England to "install the Episcopal government as in Old England." Naively optimistic, the Heeren XIX even began to see possible advantages for New Netherland emerging from this commission. The English colonists who had fled to America to escape the tyranny of bishops would not be at all happy about the new state of affairs. Certainly the English in New Netherland "will not give us henceforth so much trouble, but prefer to live free under us at peace with their consciences, than to risk getting rid of our authority and then falling again under a government from which they had formerly fled."[12]

Obviously, none of the company's spies had been able to lay hands on the actual commission given to Nicolls and the others on April 23. The document began with directions for the Puritan colonies themselves, but then made no bones about the main aim of the expedition—the reduction of the Dutch at "Long Island or any where within the limits of our owne dominions to an entire obedience to our own government . . . now vested by our grant and Commission in our Brother the Duke of York."[13]

The instructions sounded oddly reminiscent in tone of one of the Dutch pamphlets against which Charles had so frequently protested. The Dutch province was described as "a constant receptacle and sanctuary for all discontented mutinous and seditious persons, who flying from our justice as malefactors, or who run from their master to avoid paying their debts, or who have any other wicked designe as soon as they shall grow to any strength or power." Stuyvesant would hardly have recognized his own clipped country in the King's description: it had as its "business to oppress their neighbour and to engrosse the whole trade themselves." Even the old specter of Amboina was resurrected, with a shudder at its "inhuman proceedings . . . and therefore 'tis high time to put them out of a capacitie of doeing the same mischeife here and reduceing them to the same rules and obedience with our owne subjects there."

The commissioners were allowed to reveal these plans as soon as possible to the governors of New England, in the expectation that, as the King wrote in a special message to Boston, "you will joyn and assist them vigorously in recovering our right in those places now possessed by the Dutch." He added that, after submis-

THE DUKE'S INVASION

sion to his government, the settlers in New Netherland were to be "treated as neighbours and fellow subjects and enjoy quietly what they are possest of by their honest industry."

The Atlantic crossing of the small squadron under Colonel Richard Nicolls had been highly unpleasant, and it was impossible to stick to the agreed rendezvous at Gardiner's Island at the tip of Long Island.

Maverick, arriving north of Boston on the *Martin* on July 20, wrote to Coventry in London: "Its almost ten weekes since wee came out of Portsmouth Road; For the first fifteene or sixteene dayes, wee had as good wind & weather, as could be desired; ever since which time, wee have not only met crosse winds, but very bad weather; Yet all our ships kept company till the 13th day of this month, when by reason of very great Foggs we lost company of the *Guiney* and since the 16th day wee have not seen the *Elyas.*"[14]

Nicolls anchored on July 22 with the *Guinea* and the *Elias* at Nantasket near Masachusetts Bay. He soon discovered that the officials in Boston were not impressed by the King's orders. They had known about the expedition as early as May, when the General Court had passed a vote for a supply of provisions for the fleet. But when Nicolls asked them for troops, the Council was less cooperative. It was almost impossible to raise any soldiers, the councillors told the colonel, because it was harvesttime.

On July 27, Nicolls made a formal request that "the government of Boston would pass an Act to furnish them with armed Men, who should begin their March on the Manhattans, on the 20th of August ensuing, and promised, that if they could get other Assistance, they would give them an account of it." The reaction was negative. Governor and Council, understanding too well that occupation of New Netherland by the Duke of York would only encourage their enemies, dragged their feet, and Nicolls was told that they would communicate his proposal to the General Court.[15]

Winthrop's reaction was different. He had first heard of the coming invasion on June 18, while still traveling on Long Island, relishing the beauties of this wild wooded island that had just been added to his colony. The news came by letter from Captain John Underhill, who announced that a fleet was on its way to "settle government and reduce the Dutch." The implications for Connecticut were not immediately clear, but soon enough he must have discovered that the Duke's Charter annulled in great part the patent he had obtained with so much difficulty in 1662. There was little he could do, and, flexible as always, he decided to wait and see.[16]

Nicolls wrote to Winthrop on July 29 "from Anchor neare Nantascot Island," informing him that he had been sent by the King "to doe him some service neare yore government & as soone wee have fitted ourselves & enquired after our Associates (for our long voyage and ill weather have put us into some disorder) wee shall make haste to you and wee give you notice that you may be ready to assist us." In spite of the veiled language, Winthrop understood perfectly well what was meant, and he prepared himself for action.[17]

Rumors of a planned invasion by the English had been rife in New Amsterdam since July 8. On that day Stuyvesant had received a letter from the English merchant Thomas Willett, still loyal to his Dutch friends, in which he informed him that a fleet under "Nicles" was on its way to Boston. Stuyvesant immediately called the burgomasters of the city to his office and told them the news, which had been confirmed "by reports of persons worthy of belief."[18]

The question now was what to do. According to the information the governor had received, the fleet had at least 40 to 50 guns, 300 soldiers, and 150 seamen on board—a considerable force. The stock of powder and lead in the Dutch fort was very low, two thousand pounds at the most; the city wall on the north side was still a wooden fence with old and rotten palisades; and along the banks of the river the capital was wide open. Fort Amsterdam itself, with its twenty-four pieces of artillery, was not a very commanding bulwark. Stuyvesant described it later as situated "in an untenable place . . . for the purpose of resisting any attack of the Barbarians rather than an assault of European arms." The hills on the north side commanded it completely, so that "people walking on that

THE DUKE'S INVASION

high ground can see the soles of the feet of those on the esplanade and bastions."[19]

But even with these meager resources, the governor was convinced that the capital must be defended by all possible means, and the burgomasters agreed, reporting to Stuyvesant that "it is necessary to bring this place forthwith into posture of defence." Messages were sent to Beverwyck for money, and to the Delaware for ammunition. The emergency, however, suddenly receded. Thomas Willett, for Stuyvesant a most trusted source, began to fear that he might be compromised by his loyalty to the Dutch and now reported that it was all a mistake. The English fleet had come simply to settle the borders of New England; the troops had landed and the frigates had been sent away.[20]

It seems doubtful that Stuyvesant entirely believed him. The governor had just received a letter from the company, in which the Heeren XIX told him reassuringly that they had heard the English fleet was only sent "to consolidate the existing English provinces," and he had written back on August 4: "I feel that their real design is rather upon Long Island and your other possessions here." He also knew by now of the charter that gave the province to the Duke of York, and he was sure that "for that purpose the frigates have been so well provided with ammunition and soldiers." But he was resigned—"only time will tell what their real intentions are." He assured the company, however, that "we continue to reinforce our defenses and be on our guard."[21]

In the circumstances, it is difficult to understand why Stuyvesant decided to leave the capital for Fort Orange on August 6. He went with the permission of the Council, which informed the company on August 17 that he had gone to make peace between the warring Indians in the north. The threat of that war may have seemed more immediate than the possibility of an English invasion. And Stuyvesant, a man who hated to delegate, must have felt confident that with his considerable personal authority and experience in dealing with the sachems, he could quickly secure his situation in the rear, before turning back to deal with the English. And in any case, he expected to be gone for no more than a few days.[22]

A "dangerous and pernicious war" in the north raged between the Mohawks and the Northern or Onakouques Indians. As early as May the Dutch had tried to arrange a peace between them, but,

A SWEET AND ALIEN LAND

wrote Jeremias van Rensselaer, "when the ambassadors of the Maquas with the peace [offerings] on their backs came into the fort of the Northern Indians, they were murdered there." The Mohicans had also sided against the Mohawks, and overran the country around Fort Orange, killing cattle and setting fire to the house of Abraham Staets. "Jantie who lived there with his wife and a boy was found burned in the house."[23]

The warring Indians, aware of the increasing tensions between New Netherland and New England, came on July 12 to Fort Orange with a startling story. "The English," the Mohawks reported to company director Gerrit van Slechtenhorst, "have told and directed the Onakouques to fight or kill the Dutch and Mohawks and the English have threatened: if you do not do as we tell you, we shall kill you."[24]

Van Slechtenhorst had at once informed Stuyvesant, who reacted cautiously. He asked Thomas Willett to report the story to Winthrop, but the governor had already heard it from John Pynchon, a rich trader from Springfield, who had written indignantly to him about the slanderous activities of the Mohawks. "My pore advice is that some way be thought on spedily to certifie the dutch of the falsehood of all such reports . . . I never heard anything that way from any of our People."[25]

Winthrop had followed this advice and wrote in the beginning of August to Willett, thanking him for the "loving and friendly intimation" by Governor Stuyvesant "of those evill intentions of the Mohake Indians agt the English." He stated emphatically that his people "doe disclaime and abhorr any such plotts, or contremets with Indians." And, having done with this business, he left with his son Fitz-John for Long Island to wait for the English fleet, now on its way to New Amsterdam.[26]

Stuyvesant had been very skeptical about the Indian accusations, and wrote, just before he departed for Fort Orange, to the company that he was inclined to believe that "it is a fabrication of the Mohawks to engage us as allies in this war." All the same, he found it advisable to go and see if he could reestablish the peace, adding that "if the boundaries are once settled between us and our neighbours then the daily quarrels, bickerings and jealousies and claimes shall be avoided . . . [and] these pernicious wars between the Mohawks and the Northern savages" would soon be settled.[27]

The border question was decided faster than Stuyvesant had expected, and certainly not as he would have wished. Nicolls, sailing the long way around Long Island to avoid Hellgate—that "violent stream," with its islands of rocks, "which the Current sets so violently upon that it threatens present shipwreck"—arrived on August 26 with the *Guinea* in the little Nayack Bay between Coney Island and New Utrecht, now known as Gravesend Bay.

Winthrop received a message from his representative on Long Island, Samuel Willys, that "the men upon the Iland from 16 to 60 yeares of age [were] warned to attend the designe against the Manatoes who are to meet at Gravesend upon next Monday." It was a signal for the governor to travel at once to Gravesend, together with his son, to meet Nicolls. In his company was Thomas Willett, who had at last openly broken his ties with the Dutch and who joined the expedition as the representative of New Plymouth.[28]

The governor of Connecticut was present when Nicolls came ashore in Gravesend to proclaim the Duke's authority over the island, and he must have swallowed hard. Nonetheless he declared without a blush that until now Connecticut, not having a legal claim to Long Island, had only occupied the place "to serve the King's interest as the nearest English jurisdiction." Before he made this statement, however, he showed for once that the trust Stuyvesant had placed in him in the past had not been wholly misplaced. At his insistence, Nicolls undertook in an official letter to proclaim to New Amsterdam that "if the Manhadoes be delivered up to his Majesty, I shall not hinder, but any people from the Netherlands may freely come and plant there." Winthrop even obtained permission to convey the message to his Dutch colleague.[29]

THE FALL
OF THE CITY

On Monday, August 25, 1664, Peter Stuyvesant returned to New Amsterdam after an absence of three weeks. He had fallen ill at Fort Orange and had been forced to stay much longer than he had intended. An express letter from his Council, warning him of the approaching English fleet, forced him to hurry back to the capital. Still feeling unwell, he began to organize the defense of the city. Over the weekend, the burgomasters had put their own slaves and twenty-five employees of the company at work on the city wall, and now that the sails of the *Guinea* were visible off Long Island, the burghers themselves set to work with "shovel, spade or wheelbarrow."[1]

When on August 26 Nicolls set foot on Gravesend, the guard in New Amsterdam was already organized, and every man provided with one pound of powder and one and a half pounds of lead. Now that it looked as though provisions from the outside would be scarce, the brewers were ordered not to malt any grain for eight days, and only to brew lowgrade beer. The governor himself offered all possible assistance to the City Council, which pointed out to him that if the city was lost, the company's fort was "not tenable or very little so." He at once sent the city all it required—six cannon in addition to the fourteen it had, one thousand pounds of powder, six hundred pounds of lead, and finally a "corporal's guard" of soldiers.[2]

At Gravesend the enemy was rapidly gathering strength. The *Guinea* had been joined by the other vessels, and four hundred soldiers disembarked to march to the ferry at Breukelen, opposite New Amsterdam. Nicolls ordered a blockade of the capital, and took over the small clapboard blockhouse on Staten Island, which the inhabitants had erected the previous year against the Indians. He issued proclamations to the different villages and towns on Long Island, in which he promised that those who submitted to the King of England would remain undisturbed. When Stuyvesant sent a request to the Dutch towns on the island asking the citizens to come and defend the capital, the reaction was negative. "It is impossible for us to comply with it, as we ourselves are living here on the Flatland without any protection and must leave wife and children seated here in fear and trembling, which our hearts would fail to do," was the answer from Midwout.[3]

Stuyvesant then turned to Fort Orange, commanding the soldiers there to come to the capital as fast as possible. "If that is lost, the whole country is lost," he wrote, warning the sergeant to be careful and send an Indian ahead "to find out, whether any strange vessels are in his way." If there were, he was to land immediately and come through the woods. Furs should be kept at Beverwyck so they would not fall into the hands of the enemy.[4]

It was now Friday, August 29, and time to find out what the English, still hidden in Nayack Bay, were up to. At the request of the City Fathers, the governor sent a delegation of four men to Nicolls, among them the old dominie Megapolensis and his son Samuel. Arriving at Gravesend, normally a quiet rural village of three hundred inhabitants, they gazed in horror at the massed force of soldiers and volunteers from New England crowding through the muddy streets. Even the indomitable Captain John Scott had made a comeback. Nicolls received the Dutch graciously and read with interest the letter in which Stuyvesant asked him "with the utmost respect and civility . . . the intent and meaning of the approach."[5]

The Englishman's answer came the next day, but Stuyvesant sent it back, as it was unsigned. On September 1 an English delegation appeared at Fort Amsterdam with a signed letter. The message was short and clear: "His Majesty of Great Britain, whose Right and Title to these Parts of America is unquestionable . . . hath commanded me, in his Name, to require a Surrender of all

A SWEET AND ALIEN LAND

such Forts, Towns or places of Strength, which are now possessed by the Dutch, under your Commands. . . ." The English commander asked for unconditional surrender, promising that "his Majesty being tender of the effusion of Christian blood, doth by these Presents confirm and secure to every Man his Estate, Life and Liberty, who shall readily submit to his Government." Those who decided on resistance "must expect all the Miseries of War."[6]

As if to emphasize his sincerity, Nicolls now commanded his fleet to leave the safety of Nayack Bay, and sail up the Hudson, where the four vessels dropped anchor near Governor's Island, sealing off the Narrows. Inside the fort, Stuyvesant, his councillors, and the city magistrates were that day constantly in conference. Work on the city's defenses was still far from finished, and the fort itself looked flimsy, with walls only three feet thick and eight feet high. To make effective use of it, the Dutch would first have to tear down some of the wooden houses crowded up against the walls—and it was no mystery how the burghers would react to that. Even then, there was great danger of fire in the fortification itself, for the roof of the church was made of oak shingles, and the barracks were also built of wood. A last stand in the fort in case of an attack from within the city would be suicidal. Scaling the walls would be no problem—a few ladders from the neighboring houses were all that was needed—while one or two mines placed in the cellars under the walls would do the rest.[7]

The citizens' situation was just as perilous. The small fort was hopelessly inadequate to shelter the city's twelve hundred women and children; and food and water were both scarce. There was no well or cistern within the walls, and the fort had been hurriedly provided with twenty-four water barrels, confiscated from ships in the port. And in a city already straitened for food (two ships loaded with the previous year's harvest had been sent by the governor to Holland and Curaçao), the arrival ten days earlier of the *Gideon* with 290 slaves on board "at such an unseasonable moment" had not made things easier. The new crop was harvested, but not threshed, and even Stuyvesant's own Negroes, threshing away on his bouwery, could not deliver enough to feed a besieged city.[8]

But in spite of all these deficiencies, Stuyvesant was convinced that he could not accept the demand for surrender. The burgomasters urged him to show them Nicolls' conditions, but he refused, fearing that the easy English terms might undermine the morale

THE FALL OF THE CITY

of the citizens, who watched the activities of the English fleet with anxiety. From the shore, they could see that sloops and barges were being stopped, and when one of them tried to get away with a number of the city's Negroes on board, the burghers tensely followed the chase. Some of the slaves fled into the woods.

Isaack de Forest, a prominent burgher, was less fortunate. Approaching New Amsterdam after a trip to Virginia, he was taken prisoner after an English soldier fired "some grape" at him, but he was later released to create even more panic by telling the New Amsterdammers, who crowded around for information, that there were at least eight hundred soldiers on board the English ships.[9]

It was certainly an exaggerated estimate, but the English army of about four hundred men, strengthened by two hundred men from Massachusetts, had grown rapidly after Nicolls gave Captain John Coe permission to "beat the drum" in the Long Island villages to raise as many men as "they can for his Highness." In the city the burghers listened with increasing fear to stories of the enthusiasm of the English from Long Island—"our most bitter enemies"—who, eager for plunder, flocked to the ferry at Breukelen to join Nicolls' troops.

The Dutch had no more than 150 soldiers, while at the most 250 citizens were able to use arms. Only six hundred pounds of powder turned out to be good enough to use, and the gunner of the fort did nothing to improve morale by telling Aegidius Luyck, the head of the Latin School, that if the governor gave orders to shoot, his stock of powder would be of no use. "If I begin in the forenoon, 'twill all be consumed in the afternoon."[10]

The burgomasters and schepens knew this all too well and decided to prepare only for a surprise attack, trying in the meantime to "obtain good terms and conditions." Stuyvesant felt that the mood of the city was rapidly turning against him, and he complained that evening in a letter to the company (which never reached its destination) about the "popular murmurs and disaffections." He was hardly surprised that the English citizens of New Amsterdam—with the exception of Thomas Hall—had deserted him, but it was a bitter blow when John Laurence, the Englishman who had served him so loyally during all the talks with New England and Long Island, now came to him, asking to be considered a neutral.

The governor had taken one day to consider Nicolls' request to

A SWEET AND ALIEN LAND

surrender, but on Tuesday, September 2, he sent another delegation to the *Guinea* to make a formal protest. He rejected the claims of the King of England, having shown Nicolls' delegation the day before the charter of the States General, and reminded them of the long possession of the various forts—"Fort Orange about 48 or 50 years, the Manhattans about 41 or 42 years, the South River 40 years and the Fresh Water River about 36 years"—as proof of Dutch rights. If the King "were well informed of these Passages, he would be too judicious to grant such an Order, principally in a Time when there is so straight a Friendship and Confederacy between our said Lords and Superiors, to trouble us in the demanding and Summons of the Places and Fortresses, which were put in our Hands. . . ." He told Nicolls defiantly that he was obliged "to repel and take Revenge of all Threatenings, unjust attempts, or any Force whatsoever, that shall be committeed." Finally he proposed that no move should be made until further orders came from Europe.[11]

Nicolls' answer was even shorter than his first letter. "It did not concern him," he told the Dutch delegation. "He must and should take the place." Refusing from now on any "parleys," he gave Stuyvesant forty-eight hours to surrender.[12]

A tense Wednesday dragged by. The English squad, riding in the bay, was reinforced by an English merchant ship. The bakers in New Amsterdam, summoned to City Hall, reported that there were only 975 skepels (bushels) of grain left. And a trickle of citizens began to leave the capital, among them Mme. Van Ruyven, the wife of Stuyvesant's secretary. Only the 150 soldiers in the fort appeared to support the general in his wish to oppose the enemy, and riots broke out between them and some of the less warlike citizens. More and more of the burghers stayed away from their guard posts. The wife of a rich merchant was overheard telling people not to trust a single soldier. "The rascals will fight as they have nothing to lose thereby, and we have our property."[13]

On Thursday morning the guards on the shore saw a little rowing boat with a white flag coming from the *Guinea* toward the public wharf. On board were the six commissioners of Massachusetts, Connecticut, and Plymouth, among them John Winthrop. Under escort, the six men were taken to the nearest tavern, while Stuyvesant was alerted. "I went with the Council and two Burgomasters to greet them," the governor later reported. "After some compliments, they declared that they had come to offer us and all the inhabitants in the King's name fair conditions, and in case these were not accepted, to excuse themselves for any mischief that may follow." Discussions followed—"too long to repeat"— but Stuyvesant was adamant and refused to give in.[14]

The commissioners rowed away to the *Guinea*, but before he embarked, Winthrop turned to his old acquaintance to hand him a sealed letter. The general, with his entourage, walked back to the Council Chamber in the fort, and there, opening Winthrop's personal letter, read it aloud. It contained the offer for free trade that Winthrop had obtained from Nicolls, but his "friendly advertisement" boiled down to one thing—a "serious advice . . . to your selfe and all your people, as my loving Neighbours & friends . . . that you would speedily accept his Majesty's gratious tender which I understand hath been declared & resigne your selves under the obedience of his sacred Majesty, that you may avoid effusion of blood & all the good people of your nation may enjoy all the happiness tendered." If they would not do this, the New England colonies "are obliged & ready to attend his Majesties service."[15]

Burgomasters Van der Grift and Steenwyck, having listened, took their leave to go to City Hall, but returned almost at once to ask for a copy of the letter. Stuyvesant, clearly worried that the contents would reach the population of the city, refused this request and the two men left, "disgusted and dissatisfied." An infuriated Stuyvesant, still with the letter in his hands, took no time to reflect and tore it to shreds.[16]

It was the desperate gesture of a man who knew that he was alone. The forty-eight hours of respite were running out fast, and there was almost nothing the general could do. This became clear to all the citizens when in the afternoon two vessels detached themselves from the English fleet and sailed slowly up the North River in the direction of the capital. Stuyvesant at once took command, and leaving Nicasius de Sille with fifty men in the fort, marched into the streets of New Amsterdam with a hundred soldiers to post them on all strategic corners, "in order, if the English would attempt to land here or there, to hinder them as much as possible." The two ships, however, steered slightly to the left and it looked as if they were going to bypass the fort.[17]

With amazing speed, the one-legged governor stumped back to the fort and climbed up to the bastion, where a gunner stood ready

A SWEET AND ALIEN LAND

with a lighted match. The frightened citizens looked up at the silent general, who seemed about to order the gunner to fire on the ships, when suddenly Dominie Megapolensis and his son Samuel left the anxious crowd. They went up to Stuyvesant and, taking him gently by the arms, led him away.[18]

The governor knew that the end of his lonely battle was in sight, but he decided to make a last stand. The two vessels had dropped anchor north of the city, within the distance of a cannon shot, and the New Amsterdammers, seeing their city threatened from both sides, gathered before the City Hall. Despite Stuyvesant's refusal to make public the letters from Nicolls and Winthrop, they knew perfectly well what they contained. The English proclamations to Long Island had also been read in the capital, and the citizens shouted now to see the official documents. The burgomasters, foiled in their efforts to persuade the general to show them the letters, had given orders to stop work on the city wall in retaliation, and when Stuyvesant heard this, he stamped angrily to the City Hall to ask the magistrates to resume the work, personally urging the burghers to go back to their spades and wheelbarrows.[19]

He was confronted by a shouting mob, and the unhappy governor had to swallow a stream of insults. "All agreed in this: that they required a view and copy of the letter; that it was impossible to defend the place; . . . that no relief was to be hoped for . . . and that to resist so many [Englishmen] was nothing less than to gape before an oven," he wrote later. Fearing a mutiny, Stuyvesant went back to the fort, where he reported the scene to his councillors. "It was resolved to bring together as well as possible, the pieces of the torn letter."[20]

It took Nicasius de Sille some time to solve the jigsaw, but when the letter was glued together, Stuyvesant's English clerk, his nephew Nicholas Bayard, was entrusted with its translation, which was delivered the same afternoon to the burgomasters. That night the magistrates and some prominent citizens conferred, and the next morning, Friday, September 5, a petition was handed to the governor, begging him to surrender the city.

"We your sorrowful community and subjects, beg to represent, with all humility, that we can not conscientiously foresee that anything else is to be expected for this fort and city of Manhattans (as your Honour must be convinced) than misery, sorrow, confla-

THE FALL OF THE CITY

gration, the dishonor of women, murder of children in their cradles, and, in a word, the absolute ruin and destruction of about fifteen hundred innocent souls, only two hundred and fifty of whom are capable of bearing arms, unless you will be pleased to adjust matters according to the conjuncture of the time." There was only one "adjustment" possible, the petitioners stated—"not to reject the conditions of so generous a foe, but to be pleased to meet him in the speediest, best and most reputable manner. Otherwise (which God forbid) are we obliged, before God and world, to protest against and call down on your Honour the vengeance of Heaven for all the innocent blood which shall be shed in consequence of your Honour's obstinacy."[21]

It was a forceful document, signed by ninety-three of the most important inhabitants of the capital: former burgomasters, like Martin Cregier and Van Cortlandt; Schout Tonneman; merchants like De Forest and Beeckman; tavernkeepers and traders. Even his family had deserted the general. One of the names was that of his brother-in-law, Nicholas Varleth, and even more painful for him to see was the eighth signature, that of his seventeen-year-old son Balthasar.

There was no option left to him, and Stuyvesant, who a day earlier had still declared that he would "rather be carried out of here" than surrender, now appointed a commission to discuss terms with Nicolls. He offered them his bouwery as a meeting place.[22]

On Saturday, September 6, the two parties met at eight o'clock in the morning. Neither Stuyvesant nor Nicolls was present, but the negotiators chosen by both sides were persons of consequence. The Dutch sent Councillor Johannes de Decker, Nicholas Varleth, Dominie Megapolensis, the two burgomasters of New Amsterdam, Van der Grift and Steenwyck, and Schepen Cousseau. From the English side, two of the royal commissioners, Carr and Cartwright, came in the company of four New Englanders, John Winthrop, John Pynchon of Springfield, Thomas Clarke of Boston, and Samuel Willys of Hartford.

The twelve men had little difficulty in hammering out the basis of a treaty, containing twenty-three articles. The Dutch delegates, anyway, had little choice. Looking from the windows of Stuyvesant's farmhouse, they could see the English ships riding on the North River, a sure sign of their defeat. They were certainly

A SWEET AND ALIEN LAND

not happy with the treaty, but Nicolls, as he had promised, was generous. No private Dutch interest, either in person or property, was to be molested; and the Dutch would enjoy liberty of conscience and free trade with Holland.

The only hitch came when the cost of the transport for the Dutch soldiers was discussed. The Dutch insisted that the English should pay for it, as it was unjust to the company first to rob them of their province, and then to charge them for the fare of their defeated army. But the English refused pointblank, and in the end four of the Dutch delegation offered to pay for it out of their own pockets. The English commissioners then made a friendly gesture in return, proposing that every soldier who wished to stay in New Netherland would receive fifty acres of land for farming.

To one point the English gave in—the agreement was to be conditional. "If at any time hereafter," the truce stated, "the King of Great Britain and the States of the Netherlands do agree that this place and country be redelivered into the hands of the said States, whensoever His Majesty will send his Commands to redeliver it, it shall immediately be done."[23]

As satisfied as possible under the circumstances, the Dutch delegation returned to New Amsterdam to report to the governor, while the English were rowed back to the *Guinea*. Stuyvesant agreed to the conditions, and on Sunday morning the bells of City Hall rang to call the citizens of New Amsterdam to listen to the terms of their surrender. They were relieved that it had been concluded without any bloodshed and were glad to hear that the city would not be occupied by the troops from New England, which were waiting at Breukelen "with desire to pillage the place." Instead, Nicolls had promised to send in his own troops.[24]

Fifty-five years after Hudson discovered Manhattan, thirty-nine years after Peter Minuit bought it from the Indians, and eleven years after New Amsterdam had become a city, Director General Peter Stuyvesant signed on Monday morning, September 8, 1664, the documents that surrendered New Netherland to the English. Two hours later the general led his 150 Dutch soldiers out of Fort Amsterdam to the *Gideon*, lying in the East River, "with their arms, Drums beating, and Colours flying." Their place was taken by 168 soldiers sent by Nicolls, and when Stuyvesant returned from the embarkation and the final inspec-

THE FALL OF THE CITY

tion of his troops, the fort had already been rechristened Fort James in honor of its new proprietor, the Duke of York, and Nicolls was proclaimed governor.

It was a highly satisfactory moment for the English, and Winthrop wrote at once to Clarendon: "I saw the towne upon the Manatos Iland reduced to the obedience of our Soveraigne Lord the King whereby ther is way made for the inlargement of his Maties dominions by filling that vacant wildernesse in tyme with plantations of his Maties subjects."[25]

The burgomasters of the city, who for the moment remained in office, reported the surrender a few days later to the West India Company in Amsterdam. "We, your Honours loyal, sorrowful and desolate subjects cannot neglect nor keep from relating the event, which thro' God's pleasure thus unexpectedly happened to us in consequence of your Honours neglect and forgetfulness. . . ." The city had changed hands and "how that will result, time shall tell." Their sad testament ended with the words: "Meanwhile since we have no longer to depend on your Honours promises of protection, we with all the poor, sorrowing and abandoned Commonalty here must fly for refuge to the Almighty God, not doubting but He will stand by us in this sorely afflicting conjuncture and no more depart from us. . . . Done in Jorck, heretofore named Amsterdam in New Netherland."[26]

THE BIRTH
OF NEW YORK

News of the surrender of New Amsterdam took six weeks to reach the Dutch Republic. On October 24, 1664, the West India Company informed the States General that the Duke's fleet, instead of "consolidating" New England, had conquered the "whole of New Netherland province," and "also immediately called the same by the name of York."[1]

The news merely confirmed the first rumors. On September 19 Van Gogh, the Dutch ambassador in London, had received a visit from skipper Claes Bret, coming from "The Manhattes," who had heard there that the English under "one Capt. Schot" had taken Long Island, and that "as soon as the fleet, which they were expecting from England, should have arrived, they intended to attack and, if possible, to master the City of Amsterdam and other places there." The Dutch skipper's information had not been entirely accurate—he went on to relate that General Stuyvesant had prepared the city for the defense, "being able . . . to enroll a good number of people from the inhabitants thereabout, to the number of two thousand men."[2]

In London, where the victory in America was known around October 10, people at Court and in the city were rubbing their hands with glee. Samuel Pepys heard "that the King did joy mightily at it," asking one of his courtiers in mock concern: "How shall I do to answer this to the Embassador when he comes?" To his sister Henrietta in Paris Charles wrote proudly: "You will have heard of our taking New Amsterdam, which just lies by New England. 'Tis a place of great importance. It did belong to England heretofore, but the Dutch, by degrees, drove our people away and built a very good town, but we have got the better of it and 'tis now called New York."[3]

Colonel Nicolls had not stopped at the conquest of the capital. He had sent Commissioner George Cartwright to Fort Orange, whose population had been warned by a message from Councillor Johannes de Decker. De Decker was at once banished by Nicolls for this effort to "alienate the minds of His Majesty's Dutch subjects from that happy reconcilement without bloodshed." The fort surrendered, however, without a fight, and Cartwright, after rechristening Beverwyck Albany, at once concluded a treaty of friendship with the Mohawks and the Senecas to secure the fur trade for the English.[4]

Sir Robert Carr, who was sent to the Delaware with the *Guinea* and the *William and Nicholas* to reduce New Amstel, had a more difficult task. The conditions he was authorized to offer the Dutch and Swedish colonists were generous enough, including complete "liberty of conscience." Should there be any resistance, Carr was to ask the English neighbors—Virginia and Maryland—for help, although if Lord Baltimore seized on this chance to put forward any claim on the territory, Carr was to set it aside firmly with the excuse "that you only keep possession till his Majesty is informed and satisfyed otherwise." Above all, Carr's instructions insisted, he was to "protect the inhabitants from injuries as well as violence of the soldiers."

But Director Alexander d'Hinoyosa with his fifty soldiers, had not the slightest intention of surrendering without resistance. When Carr arrived at Fort Casimir, he was received by "three volleys," and fighting broke out. It was only a brief struggle, and casualties were slight—three Dutch soldiers killed and fifteen injured—but in the heat of the moment Carr forgot his instructions. The rest of the Dutch soldiers were promptly put into irons and shipped off to Virginia to be sold as slaves, and Sir Robert did nothing to restrain his excited soldiers when they began to plunder the fort and the Mennonite farms. He himself led the way by appropriating the farm of d'Hinoyosa, and distributing other estates to his brother John and some of his officers.[5]

When Nicolls in New York heard about all this, he was furious and wrote to London that he was going to the Delaware himself "to dispose thereof to his Matyes service and not to private uses."[6]

On October 1, the last treaties were signed, and New Netherland passed officially into English control, exchanging—in the words of a modern historian—"the control of a moribund trading company for that of a dictator of royal blood." The New Netherlanders did not yet know just what the new regime might mean for them, but the magistrates of New York wrote hopefully a few days later to their new overlord: "It has pleased God to bring us under your Royal Highness' obedience wherein we promise to conduct ourselves as good subjects are bound to, deeming ourselves fortunate that His Highness has provided us with so gentle, wise and intelligent a gentleman as governor as the Hon. Col. Nicolls, confident and assured that under the wings of this valiant gentleman we shall bloom and grow like the cedar on Lebanon. . . . Praying then his Royal Highness to be pleased to take our interests and the welfare of this country into serious consideration. . . . Done at New York in Manhattans Island 1664."[7]

But if the Dutch in New York accepted their new masters easily, the Heeren XIX and the States General were certainly not ready to bow to English aggression. As Admiral Michiel de Ruyter had already embarked with twelve warships to restore Dutch suzerainty along the vital Gold Coast, Raadspensionary Johan de Witt determined in the case of New Netherland to attempt a diplomatic solution.

After the company had communicated the loss of its province to the States—complaining in a lengthy remonstrance about the "intolerable violences committed against said Company by those of the English nation"—the Dutch government on October 31 gave Ambassador Van Gogh in London orders "to expostulate, strongly and seriously, with his Majesty on the matter." At the same time, it was decided to tackle Sir George Downing in The Hague.

The English ambassador had already been briefed by Clarendon, who wrote on October 28 that the Dutch "have no reason to imagine that his Maty will ever . . . deliver any places back to them, especially those which in truth doe of right belong to him." But when De Witt strolled across to the English ambassador's residence one afternoon early in November to discuss the matter, he

THE BIRTH OF NEW YORK

made no demand for restitution. Although De Witt produced "a billet" about the English action, he struck Downing as amazingly lukewarm about the whole invasion. And when Downing asserted in his usual insolent way "that it was not true and that it could not be," De Witt gave the impression of believing him. Downing reported triumphantly to Clarendon "that that difficulty might be surmounted."[8]

His relief was premature. A few days later he was summoned by De Witt, who told him bluntly that the King had taken New Netherland "by force, without so much as saying a word to us." Downing retorted unabashed that "as for New Netherland . . . his Matie did not looke upon himself as obliged to give them any account of what he did in relation thereunto, for that he did not look upon them as att all interested therein; no more than he should thinke himself obliged to lett them know his mind, or to have their consent, in case he should thinke fitt to proceed against any Dutch that live in the Fenns in England." De Witt stuck to his guns. Before dismissing Downing, he repeated firmly: "As to New Netherland, that it must be restored."[9]

The Dutch ambassador in London found himself up against the same brazen disregard of history when he protested to the English King during an audience. Charles blandly asserted that "said country was a dependancy under his authority, being situated there among other his lands, and therefore had been occupied and settled before this by the English." The English had only permitted the Dutch nation "at the outset to settle there, without any authority having been thereby conferred on the Dutch West India Company or any other person."

Van Gogh rehearsed once more the Dutch case from first possession; he denied that it was possible for the English to take New Netherland away from the Dutch with "even a shadow of right in the world"; and he begged Charles to study the facts of the case. But the royal patience was running out. Charles cut short his protests with the statement that he was having "a written vindication made of and respecting all, as it has been already commenced." He was clearly anxious to end the audience. Van Gogh, grimly persistent, warned him finally that the English action in America "could have no other effect than to produce a widening of the breach between the nations." Charles shrugged, and fell back on the classic defense of the aggressor. He denied that he had

A SWEET AND ALIEN LAND

begun that "business." It was all the fault of the Dutch, he burst out. He had always shown himself "a lover of peace," but he had to maintain and defend the rights of his subjects.[10]

The English soon dropped even this pretense. Sagredo, the Venetian resident in Paris, who had excellent sources in both London and The Hague, reported to the Doge soon afterward that "the King of England now admits that he gave orders" to take New Netherland. The Dutch had published an official demand for the restitution of their American province, Sagredo wrote, and handed copies to all the foreign ambassadors.[11]

Shortly after, news reached London that De Ruyter's mission to the Guinea coast had been triumphantly successful. He had completely routed Holmes' English raiders. Along with this news came a spate of rumors of terrible atrocities committed by the Dutch on the Guinea coast. Pepys heard from a "Swede or Hamburger" that the Dutch had tied the English—men, women and children—back to back, and thrown them into the sea. The Swede was "whipt round the 'Change'," and confessed it was a lie; but in the current mood of anti-Dutch hysteria, people remembered Amboina with a shudder and even Pepys feared that "there was something of truth in it."[12]

The clamor for war against the "butterboxes" grew by the day. "I never saw so great an appetite to a war as in both this town and country," Charles wrote to his sister in France, adding piously, and probably for the benefit of Louis XIV, her brother-in-law: "All this shall not govern me, for I will look merely what is just and best for the honour and good of England." But the news from the Guinea coast made it clear where England's honor and good lay. And when Downing reported to Charles that the Dutch had prepared a fleet to follow De Ruyter to Africa, the King at last gave orders that the English fleet, under command of his famous cousin Prince Rupert, should sail as well.[13]

The news was particularly welcome to the Duke of York. "Less phlegmatic in general than his royal brother appears to be," as Sagredo noted, he had made no secret of his eagerness for war. After learning Charles' order, he had buttonholed the astonished Dutch ambassador in a corridor one day and poured out a long, threatening tirade. The Dutch might think that the English were "in jest," he assured Van Gogh, but "the Prince [Rupert] which goes in this fleete to Guinny will soon tell them that we are in earnest." James himself could hardly wait for the day when he would take command of the fleet "here at home," and he warned Van Gogh that Dutch hopes of a division among the English on the question of war were unfounded. They would stick together as they had done under Cromwell, who "notwithstanding the *meschants* in his time, which were the Cavaliers, did never find them to interrupt him in his foraigne businesses." James ended this characteristic outburst with the threat that "he did not doubt but to live to see the Dutch as fearful of provoking the English, under the government of a King, as he remembers them to have been under that of a Coquin."[14]

James himself plunged energetically into the preparation of the English fleet, appearing daily to inspect progress on the Thames and to confer with Pepys. But after this initial flourish of Anglo-Dutch hostilities, a lull set in. As a French diplomat at Whitehall reported, "one cannot agree about the time and the way to start."[15]

The fact was that for all De Witt's tough talking, the Dutch were desperately anxious to avoid a war. As Downing had so often pointed out, they remembered only too well their defeat in the first Anglo-Dutch War ten years earlier, and they knew that war could only cripple their trade. This time they were better prepared, but they were demoralized by a fearful epidemic of the plague that had killed twenty thousand people in Amsterdam alone. In December De Witt made a last desperate attempt to achieve an honorable peace and offered the English a new treaty. According to its proposed terms, the two countries would either restore everything they had conquered from the other, or would keep everything, and hostilities would only be allowed outside Europe. But London refused this offer of a straight swap of assets, and the Dutch began warily to make ready their main fleet, which had already been berthed for winter.

Lest they should remain in any doubt about English resolution, Downing fired another broadside at them on December 20 on the subject of New Netherland. He began by stating that it was nonsense for the Dutch to speak of "a surprise or anything of that nature, it being notoriously knowne that the spott of land lyes within the limmits and is part of the possession of his [the King's] subiects." The few Dutch that had settled there "have lived there meerly upon connivance and sufferance, and not as having any

A SWEET AND ALIEN LAND

right there unto." The English had only allowed them to stay "provided they would demean themselves peaceably and quietly, but that the said Dutch not contenting themselves therwith, did still endeavour to encroach further and further upon the English." Nor were the Dutch to imagine that the case of New Netherland was covered by the treaty of friendship between England and Holland. In that treaty, Downing asserted, it was only stipulated that "matters of piracies, robberies and violence" should be redressed by each party. It did not concern "the rights and inheritance of lands."[16]

The States answered on February 9, 1665, and the tone of its *Observations*—a report composed by a special commission—made it clear that the Dutch were rapidly losing patience with the obnoxious ambassador. The commission compared the accusation of Dutch encroachment on New England to the story of the wolf accusing the lamb "of having muddied the water, although she had drank at the lower end of the stream; the Wolf complaining that he was constrained to drink muddy water, was therefore, a mere pretext for tearing and devouring the poor Lamb." The commission pointed again to the fact that the Dutch had been in possession of the land for more than fifty years, and noted that if the King believed he had any right to it, "he ought to have spoken of it and reserved it at the time of the conclusion of the Treaty."[17]

For all the bellicose talk of his brother and his ambassador, Charles II had his own little difficulty to overcome before he could declare war on the Dutch—the fact that he could not afford to foot the bills. But early in 1665, Downing, with his excellent intelligence system, had got wind of highly secret orders sent to De Ruyter in December. After finishing his task on the Guinea coast, the Dutch admiral and his fleet were to sail to Barbados, New Netherland, Terreneuf, or other islands, to "do damage and destroy as much as possible." The ambassador dashed off an excited letter to Clarendon, almost every word underlined: *This intelligence I have* from one of *my old and constant friends in the States G'rall. . . . No Admiralty knows* any thing *hereof,* but only De Wilda, *Secretary of the Admiralty of Amsterdam;* and he is to take care *that victualls,* and all *things necessary, be sent him* [De Ruyter]."[18]

By January news of De Ruyter's transatlantic mission had spread all over the Republic, and Downing was able to add a significant detail. In a letter of the 20th he wrote: "They begin generally to discourse and speake of a second order sent to De Ruyter." Not only was he to take English ships in the Caribbean Sea and land "in some places to make waste and burne," but he also had definite orders to retake New Netherland.[19]

It was one item too many on the long charge sheet the English were drawing up against their trade rivals. In February Parliament voted 2.5 million pounds for a war against the Dutch, for which highly popular cause the city of London spontaneously added its own generous contribution. And on March 4, 1665, Charles II declared war. In his proclamation he maintained that the Dutch had been the first aggressors, and had refused to make good the damages that had been inflicted upon the English by the East and West India Companies. They had even aggravated these injuries by sending De Ruyter to the coast of Guinea. From now on, English ships were allowed to "conquer and take all ships, vessels or goods belonging to the States General or their subjects."[20]

RETURN

OF A PATRIOT

New York, which Governor Richard Nicolls called the "best of all his Majesty's towns in America," was adapting itself rapidly to its new situation; and certainly its new master had done his best to make the transition as painless as possible. The Dutch magistrates had all been kept on, and when Schout-Fiscaal Pieter Tonneman left in November, Nicolls allowed another Dutchman, Allard Anthony, to be appointed his successor.[1]

The only friction in the first months arose when on October 14 Nicolls requested that every Dutch New Yorker swear allegiance as "a true subject to the King of Great Britain." He appeared personally in City Hall, and noticing that ex-Governor Stuyvesant was absent, sent orders to fetch him. In the presence of his predecessor the English governor then read out the oath, according to which the Dutch would obey the Duke of York and his governors. At once the meeting broke up in chaos. Many of the Dutch suspected that the oath was designed to evade the terms of the honorable surrender that had been given them as Dutch subjects; and it was suggested that the words "Conformable to the Articles concluded on the Surrender of this Place" should be added. Not everybody agreed, and "divers words occurred over and hither thereupon." Nicolls put an end to the arguments by walking angrily out of the Council Room.[2]

A few days later he summoned Burgomasters Van der Grift and

Steenwyck, and handed them a sharply worded letter. "Whereas there is a false and Iniurious assertion cast upon the Oath of Obedience to his Matie, his Royall Highnesse the duke of Jorck and Governor and officers appointed by his Matie's Authoritie and that some people have maliciously sought to distract the minds of the Inhabitants of NewJorcke by suggesting that the Artycles of peace so late and solemnly made signed and sealed were intended by that Oath to be made Null and of no offect," he now assured them that the articles of surrender would not be "broken or [were] intended to be broken by any words or expressions on the same Oath." Those who said otherwise would be prosecuted as "disturbers of the peace."[3]

At a meeting of some prominent New York citizens two days later it was resolved that the oath could be sworn without any danger, provided that Nicolls "shall seal his given writing." And soon after every Dutchman who wished to remain in New Netherland took the oath, Peter Stuyvesant among them.[4]

The former governor had retired to his bouwery and had made no plans for returning to the Republic. When New Amsterdam fell into the hands of the English, he had been living there for eighteen years and it was home to him. His two sons had been born there, and had never even seen the Fatherland. His sister and half-sister had joined him in the New World, and he himself at the age of fifty-four (exactly half those years had been spent in foreign service) felt little nostalgia for the country of his birth.

In February 1665, however, a ship appeared in the port of New York with a message from the West India Company ordering Stuyvesant's return to the Republic. The Heeren XIX needed a scapegoat for the loss of their now-cherished province, and Stuyvesant was the obvious choice.

The old general prepared his case with care, collecting the necessary documents and statements and arranging his personal affairs so that his wife Judith should have no worries while he was away. In the last weeks before his departure in April he appeared twice in City Hall. On the first occasion he attended a court case to settle a debt of 180 guilders someone owed to him. The second time he came on a more delicate errand. He told the burgomasters, schepens, and schout (since March 1 these were called mayors, aldermen, and sheriff) that he was about to leave New York, and that he wished them "every luck and happiness." He must have

A SWEET AND ALIEN LAND

hesitated a moment before he went on to request that "they accord him a certificate of his comportment, which may avail him or his children today or tomorrow."[5]

The thoughts of those present must have gone back to all the angry quarrels and differences of the past; to Stuyvesant's high-handed attempts to thwart the city's growing yearning for independence; to the many honest and useful men who had been victimized or banished by him in the early years. But city and governor had come to a better understanding. From being a loyal and ruthless servant of the company, Stuyvesant had developed into the dedicated leader of the province he now loved as his own country. And without any hesitation the City Fathers wrote down the reference he had asked for:

We the undersigned schout, burgomasters and schepens of the City of New Yorck on the Island of Manhattan, formerly named New Amsterdam, certify and declare, at the request of the Hon. Peter Stuyvesant, late Director-General of New Netherland and who now on the change by the English is to return to Patria, that his Honor had during eighteen years administration conducted and demeaned himself not only as Director-General according to the best of our knowledge ought to do, on all occurring circumstances, for the interest of the West India Company, but besides as an honest proprietor and patriot of the province and a supporter of the reformed religion.[6]

A few days later Stuyvesant sailed away, with his youngest son Nicholas, on board *Het Gekruyste Hart* ("The Crossed Heart"). The voyage was certain to be lengthy—the Anglo-Dutch War was then raging—and sure to lead to a confrontation that would be painful.

Stuyvesant had a clear conscience, and an excellent case. Mainly through his efforts and persistence, the colony had grown from two thousand souls in 1647 to around ten thousand by the time of the English invasion. The capital had become a thriving and prosperous center of trade, and the country itself, at last at peace with the Indians, had become a "white man's land."

That the West India Company had lost the province to the English was not, he knew very well, his fault. He had begged them to settle the boundaries, he had made humiliating journeys to Hartford and Boston to try and do it himself, he had asked them for reinforcements. Their only response had been facile suggestions that "the impertinent usurpations of the neighbours should be resisted." When the invasion was already under way, they had still closed their eyes and left it to him to defend the city with 150 soldiers and a handful of disheartened and resentful citizens. It had been an impossible task and no man could have done more. But Stuyvesant knew his employers of old, and feared the worst.

On October 16, 1665, the company informed the States General that the late director general of New Netherland had arrived "to make a report to you, High and Mighty, of his administration," and that he was ready "as soon as you . . . will be pleased to grant him a favourable audience."[7]

Peter Stuyvesant had prepared a concise and dignified statement in his own defense, in which the West India Company was criticized by implication rather than directly. While still in New York, he told the States: "I was informed, verbally and in writing, that the unfortunate loss and reduction of New Netherland were, in consequence of ignorance of the facts, spoken of and judged in this country variously by many, and by most people not consistent with the truth, according to the appetite and leaning of each." He therefore, "sustained by the tranquillity of an upright and loyal heart, was moved to abandon all, even his most beloved wife, to inform you, Illustrious, High and Mighty, of the true state of the case that you, when so informed, may decide according to your profound wisdom."[8]

"I dare not interrupt your Illustrious High Mightinesses' most important business with a lengthy narrative of the poor condition in which I found New Netherland on my assuming its government," he went on, describing in a few terse words the trouble with the neighboring English and the wars with the "cruel barbarians" that had forced many people to flee the province. He then touched on his lack of support from the company, adding pointedly that only the Honorable Directors were able to judge "by what unpropitious circumstances" assistance had been so long delayed.

When the fleet under Nicolls appeared, he told the States, he had been forced to come to terms with the English because of "powder and provisions failing and no relief or reinforcement being expected." In addition to this, he had had to cope with "a general discontent and unwillingness to assist in defending the place" among the New Netherlanders, who had been demoralized by the latest encroachments on Long Island and Westchester from Hartford, and by the recent Esopus War.

He had warned the company often enough, Stuyvesant stated, and he had sent them not only his own letters, but "the entire communalty's grievances, remonstrances and humble petitions of redress." The Lords Directors had not even replied, and the principal citizens had told him: "If the Honble Company gives themselves so little concern about the safety of the country and its inhabitants as not to be willing to send a ship of war to its succor in such pressing necessity, nor even a letter of advice as to what we may depend on and what succor we have to expect, we are utterly powerless and therefore not bound to defend the city, to imperil our lives, property, wives and children . . . and to lose all after two or three days' resistance."

The burghers had given him a hard time, Stuyvesant assured the States, with "disrespectful speeches and treatment." They had been frightened of the English troops "on account of the threats of plundering heard from some of the soldiers," who were said to be eager "to find an opportunity to pepper the devilish Chinese, who have made us smart so much." How well justified this fear was had been demonstrated at the Delaware, where the Dutch and Swedes had been "invaded, stripped, utterly plundered and many of them sold as slaves to Virginia."

He could add "many more reasons and circumstances" for the surrender of the city, but "fearing that your patience, Illustrious, High and Mighty, will be exhausted," he ended his statement with the hope that they would "judge therefrom that this loss could not be avoided by human means, nor be imputed to me, your Illustrious High Mightinesses' humble servant." He added a heartfelt plea: that they send him back to the New World "as quickly as your more important occupations will possibly allow."

The States General may well have been sufficiently convinced by Stuyvesant's reasoning to dismiss the whole matter. They were perfectly aware of the shortcomings of the Heeren XIX, and in any case, the war with England demanded all their attention. But the West India Company was out for blood. The Heeren XIX had no intention of letting their former governor off the hook, and they prepared a vicious counterattack. But they set about it in their usual leisurely manner, and it was not until the following spring, in April 1666, that their answer finally came.

Stuyvesant read it with fury and disbelief. All the evidence that had been collected, the Heeren XIX airily stated, was "amply sufficient to convict the aforesaid Stuyvesant of neglect." There had been enough powder and lead to fight, and it had been up to him to encourage the people to hold the fort until the fleet under De Ruyter had come to relieve them. In particular, the director general's trip to Fort Orange just before the arrival of the English fleet had been an example of his gross misjudgment.[9]

It was more than Stuyvesant could bear and worse than he had expected, but Secretary Cornelis Van Ruyven in New York, to whom he sent an angry account of these transactions, was not surprised. "It is nothing new for good servants to be paid in such wages," he wrote back consolingly during the summer. "I cannot myself imagine on what pretext the loss of the country can be laid to your charge."[10]

Stuyvesant now decided that he need spare no longer his ungrateful and devious employers. And going through his files, he composed a long and carefully documented remonstrance that left out nothing: the letters he had sent to the company asking for help; the directors' indifference; the lack of money to build proper fortifications; and their greed for furs and duties. One by one he demolished their arguments. There was, for instance, the letter he had received before he left for Fort Orange, in which the directors assured him that the fleet under Nicolls had nothing to do with New Netherland. And he dismissed their argument about De Ruyter's relief mission as requiring "little or no answer." He had not even known that De Ruyter had been sent to Guinea, much less "that he was to return along the coast."[11]

But the States General, up to its eyes in a European war, had no time to spare for these recriminations. It heard with equal indifference Stuyvesant's defense in October 1666 and the company's shrill counterattack that came in the spring of 1667, when the directors not only repeated their former accusations but flung in a charge of cowardice for good measure. Peace negotiations with England had by this time got under way, and the business of New Netherland had dwindled into irrelevance. The Dutch had already resigned themselves to its loss, in exchange for peace in the much more profitable East Indies, and English recognition of their rights in Surinam. On July 31 the Peace of Breda was signed, by which each party was left with the "places, cities and forts which during

A SWEET AND ALIEN LAND

the war had been taken." New Netherland formally passed into history. And Stuyvesant was free to return at last to the New World.[12]

The three years Stuyvesant was compelled to spend in Holland had been momentous ones for Europe, and he was able to follow events closely. Like most wars, the Anglo-Dutch War of 1665–1667 was proving equally ruinous for both sides. Three great sea battles in 1665 and 1666 had emptied both Dutch and English treasuries. And the year 1666 inflicted a triple blow on the English. In January Louis XIV announced that in fulfillment of his treaty obligations to the United Provinces, he was entering the war. He was followed by Denmark. By the spring of 1666 it was already clear that frantic quarantine measures had not saved England from the great plague that had devastated Amsterdam the previous year—by that summer twenty-six thousand people were dead. And in September of this disastrous year the Great Fire of London finally brought England to her knees. That winter Charles II sent out the first peace feelers.

With things going so badly for England, the Dutch were in no hurry to conclude a peace, hoping that the longer the war went on, the better the final terms would be. But in May 1667 they were rudely awakened from this dream. Their ally Louis XIV coolly advanced with a large army into the Spanish Netherlands, which separated the United Provinces from France, and claiming them as the rightful dowry of his Spanish wife, Maria Theresa, pulled down the *barrière* so precious to the Dutch.

The English perked up at this unexpected turn of events; De Witt's policy, based on the French alliance, collapsed; and peace became a matter of pressing urgency. When the English, too poor to pay their navy, had it laid up in June, the Dutch seized on this chance to force their hand. On June 19 a fleet of seventeen Dutch ships sailed impudently up the Medway, cut the chain laid across the Thames at Chatham, burnt several ships at their moorings, and carried off the pride of the English fleet, the *Royal Charles*. Panic seized London. A month later, July 31, 1667, the peace was signed.[13]

These events, which shook Europe, raised scarcely an echo in the New World. There had been one alarm in 1665, when De Ruyter's fleet was half expected to loom over the horizon. In July Winthrop "sent out directions to all the townes by the sea side to be in order and rediness to defend themselves." But the Dutch admiral, feeling he could do more good in the North Sea, had simply raided Terreneuf in Newfoundland and left the rest of North America undisturbed.[14]

The New World turned back to its own affairs, and Stuyvesant, coming home after an absence of three years, was amazed to find how little New York had changed. Indeed, his successor Sir Richard Nicolls, who was about to be replaced, was grappling with problems that were only too familiar to the ex-governor—a shortage of cash and arguments about boundaries. The towns of Long Island were forever clamoring to be restored to Connecticut. Always restive, they were now protesting against their "usurpation" by the Duke of York, and chafing under his heavy taxes.

Fortunately, Nicolls was on excellent personal terms with Governor Winthrop, but they both had to exercise the utmost tact in sorting out these matters. And Nicolls was doubtless delighted to hand over his office, soon after Stuyvesant's return, to Sir Francis Lovelace, an old Cavalier with two years' colonial experience in Virginia.

For the old Dutchman, the problems of government were becoming increasingly remote. His wife and his children, his friends and his farming now absorbed his interest. He gave up his dignified townhouse on the Strand to the new governors, who christened this typically Dutch mansion Whitehall, after the English Royal Palace, and made it their official residence.

The last four years of Stuyvesant's life were spent peacefully in the country, at his bouwery, where he died in February 1672. He was buried in the chapel he had had built there. His widow Judith later handed over the building to the Reformed Dutch Church with the proviso that "the vault or tomb which was built by my deceased husband in said church shall be preserved," and that "if the church decay or be demolished, then from the materials a cover shall be made to the said vault."[15]

The chapel did indeed fall into decay, and in 1799 it was replaced by St. Marks-in-the-Bouwerie, where a plaque set into the wall states, not wholly accurately:

In this vault lies buried Petrus Stuyvesant, late Captain General and Governor in Chief of Amsterdam in New Netherland now called New York and the Dutch West India Island, died in A.D. 1671/2, aged 80 years.

More moving was the epitaph composed by Dominie Henricus Selyns in Holland:

Stir not the sand too much, for here lies Stuyvesant,
Who once commanded all that was New Netherland,
And much against his will delivered it to foes.
If grief and sorrow any hearts do smite, his heart
Did die a thousand deaths, so lethal was the smart.
His first years were too sweet; his last, too full of woes.[16]

EPILOGUE

On a hot August day in 1673 New Yorkers crowded to the banks of the East River to watch an astonishing sight: a squadron of eight warships sailing in close formation up the bay, with the red, white, and blue flag of the United Provinces fluttering from their masts. The ships dropped anchor before Staten Island, while the citizens —English and Dutch—buzzed with alarm or delighted speculation. One thing was clear. The squadron was there for no friendly purpose; since April 1672 England and the Republic had again been at war.

The arrival of the Dutch invasion force—one and a half years after Stuyvesant's death—was more the result of luck than of careful planning. The United Provinces were in no condition to mount ambitious operations overseas. Attacked simultaneously by England and France, their seven provinces reduced to four, half the country around Amsterdam still struggling back to normal after the floods that had followed the defensive opening of the dikes, the Dutch were fighting for survival under their youthful leader, William III of Orange. On land, their condition was desperate.

But at sea, they were still free, and they were formidable. The Dutch fleet under the invincible Michiel Adriaensz de Ruyter had licked the combined English and French fleets at Sole Bay in May 1672, just before the French armies fell on the Republic. This victory in that Rampjaar (Disaster Year) gave the Admiralty of Zeeland—second most important of the provinces—the encouragement to strike a telling blow at the English. In December, it dispatched a small squadron of four men-of-war for a punitive expedition along the American coast, under the command of the brilliant Admiral Cornelis Evertsen the Younger. His targets were St. Helena, Bermuda, and, if possible, New Netherland, now New York. His instructions were "to capture and ruin everything there that shall be possible." New York must have seemed a particularly appropriate target, since it was the personal property of England's former High Admiral, the Duke of York.[1]

Cruising near Martinique in May 1673, Evertsen had the luck to run into another small Dutch squadron—four warships from the Admiralty of Amsterdam, under Jacob Binckes. Between them, they were able to muster a force of six hundred soldiers. The two admirals at once decided to join up and carry out Evertsen's instructions.

They reached New York on Tuesday, August 8, and after their sensational appearance in the Hudson, the two admirals must have wondered what to do next. There was no sign of activity from the fort and none from the harbor, no small boat scurrying out toward them bearing a white flag, and not a single gunshot.

Once more they were lucky. On the evening of their arrival, some Dutch farmers plucked up the courage to row out to the Dutch fleet. They told Evertsen that Governor Lovelace was absent, there was hardly a soldier in the place, and all the fort's heavy guns were trained in the wrong direction. They were enthusiastic about the arrival of the Dutch force, and "complained much about the harshness of the English government." It was all too good to be true: an unpopular regime, a defenseless capital, and a friendly populace waiting to greet them with open arms. Immediately Evertsen called a council of war on his flagship the *Swaenenburgh* ("Swan Castle"), and it was resolved to take the fort the next day. Meanwhile a letter was sent off to the "pious inhabitants" of the capital, urging them to surrender.[2]

In the absence of Governor Francis Lovelace, Captain John Manning was in command of the city's defenses. They were, he knew only too well, virtually nonexistent, as a later report made clear. "Their was neither Bedd, Spade, Hanspike or other material. . . ." Many of those heavy guns pointing in the wrong direction

_____ (483) _____

could not even be trained around: "the platformes and carriages [of the forty guns on the four bastions] were alsoe Badd, either the carriages broake or they could not bring them to pass againe. . . ." Worst of all, there were only seventy to eighty soldiers in the garrison.[3]

Manning did his utmost. He gave orders that the fort be got ready for defense, and had "Provisions, beare, liquors and such necessaryes" brought in. At dawn the next morning he paraded his troops, who "very cherefully" made themselves "as ready for a brush as wee were able." Manning even sent out letters to the towns on Long Island asking for volunteers, though he knew perfectly well what the response was likely to be. Only a dozen Englishmen turned up, while all the Dutch remained neutral.[4]

Under the circumstances, Manning fell back on the only hope left—he played for time. On Wednesday morning at ten, he sent out envoys—the governor's brother, Thomas Lovelace, Captain John Carr, and John Sharpe—to the Dutch ships, in a small boat flying a white flag. Halfway to the fleet, their boat passed a Dutch sloop dashing to the city, also flying a white flag. On arrival at the *Swaenenburgh*, the envoys and the admirals politely exchanged civilities, which were cut short when the English bluntly asked what the Dutch were doing there. Evertsen proudly replied that he had come to retake the city and the country for the States General and the Prince of Orange. Thomas Lovelace asked to see his commission, but Evertsen gestured to one of the ship's great guns, and gave the classic reply: "It's stuck in its mouth."[5]

The Dutch trumpeter Evertsen had sent over in the sloop to New York had in the meantime reached the city, where he asked Manning for its surrender. The captain avoided a direct answer, but entertained his visitor generously, keeping him "two or three houres, treating him with meete, drinck, wine & such accomodations, thinking that they would not weigh anchor to approach the fort till they had received an answere." He thought wrong. Tired of waiting for his trumpeter, and "both wind and tyde being fayre," Evertsen decided to up anchor and sail toward the shore. As soon as the English noticed this, the trumpeter was sent quickly back with a letter from Manning insisting that he be allowed to confer with his own envoys before deciding whether to surrender. While Evertsen considered this request, the English begged him not to use violence, and he finally promised to wait half an hour, pointedly setting his hourglass to mark the time.[6]

The Dutch ships were already within cannonshot of the fort when a freak current spun them broadside, "and had those of the fort shot on us, they could have made great damage," reported Evertsen later. Those of the fort, luckily for the Dutch, were much too alarmed, and thought the turning of the ships was a cunning maneuver. Within half an hour Sharpe was back on board the *Swaenenburgh* with another temporizing message from Manning. He asked for an extra day in which to discuss the matter with the mayor and aldermen.[7]

But Evertsen refused to play Manning's game any longer. He sent Sharpe back demanding that the English deliver the fort within half an hour or face the consequences, turning his hourglass again to show that he meant business. Then he gave orders for the six hundred soldiers to be embarked in sloops, ready for action.

A tense thirty minutes passed without a sign from Manning. Then, after a warning shot, the Dutch guns opened fire. For an hour they banged away at the fort, while the six hundred marines, under the command of Captain Antony Colve, were landed on Manhattan, just behind the governor's garden, at Trinity Church. They marched down Broadway toward the fort, silently watched by the English, but welcomed with "all the demonstrations of joy" that the Dutch citizens could make.[8]

Manning had attempted to reply to the Dutch gunfire, but the rusting guns of the fort collapsed one after another, and when the Dutch troops stopped at the gates, suddenly the King's flag was lowered to be replaced by a flag of truce. Colve sent to ask Manning if he was ready to surrender. Still nobody appeared, and Colve released Carr, whom he had been keeping prisoner, to tell Manning that he had a quarter of an hour left. Carr promptly disappeared—to turn up months later at the Delaware. But the English commander got the message.

The gate opened, and John Sharpe appeared. He still wanted to discuss the terms of surrender, but Colve told him that it was too late. The English soldiers must be marched out as prisoners of war. Manning obeyed, and New York was on August 9, 1673, retaken by the Dutch with the loss of one English soldier, and two or three Dutch wounded. That same day it was christened New Orange.[9]

———— (485) ————

EPILOGUE

In the evening Evertsen received a note from the English governor asking if he might come to see him. Lovelace had been away in Connecticut for a few days as the guest of Governor Winthrop, and on the day the Dutch fleet arrived at Manhattan, he was just leaving Hartford. Not till he reached New Haven did he learn the news, and he at once sent off a hurried report to Winthrop. The Dutch soldiers, he wrote angrily, "have breakfasted on all my sheep and cattle on Staten Island." He had decided to go to Long Island to raise an army of volunteers to repel the invaders. Other reports were reaching Hartford by this time, some wildly inaccurate. Winthrop wrote to his son Fitz-John that "the Dutch had landed 3000 men upon Manhatas Iland."[10]

Lovelace obviously found little response on Long Island and on Saturday, August 12, the disheartened English governor arrived in New Orange. He found that his house and that of Manning had been plundered by the Dutch, but serious damage had been prevented by strict orders from Colve that no citizen be molested— orders he had emphasized by having one soldier shot for looting.

Lovelace was given no chance to protest the invasion. The luckless man had barely arrived when he was unceremoniously thrown into jail for debt, at the request of some Dutch citizens, and told that he would not be allowed to leave the country till he had paid up. His brother Thomas and Captain Manning were hustled aboard one of the Dutch ships and later transported miles up the coast to be put ashore in Newfoundland.[11]

Having disposed of the city's former authorities, Evertsen appointed Antony Colve as governor *pro tem*. He sent another detachment of soldiers up the Hudson to recapture Fort Albany, and changed its name to Fort Nassau, and one-time Beverwyck, called Albany by the English, was rechristened Willemstad. Evertsen then turned to Long Island and summoned all its towns to submit immediately—a demand that the five Dutch towns and Gravesend obeyed with alacrity.[12]

The news of Evertsen's conquest created consternation in Hartford. Winthrop still hoped to secure a foothold for Connecticut at the eastern end of Long Island, and at the time of the Dutch invasion, the future of this area had been under discussion. If the Dutch could make themselves masters of the whole island now,

A SWEET AND ALIEN LAND

however temporarily, it would simply be handed wholesale back to Charles II, who would turn it over once more to his brother, the Duke of York. The Dutch must be stopped at once.

On Thursday, August 17, Winthrop called the Hartford Assembly into emergency session. The anxious deputies appointed a Grand Committee with summary powers to recruit men and requisition animals, ships, and other means of transport. At the same time, two deputies were sent posthaste to New York. They arrived on Wednesday, August 23, and were at once received by Evertsen and Colve, to whom they handed an indignant letter from Hartford. The conquest of New York itself was hardly touched upon —"the cheife trust of those parts did reside in other hands." But Hartford protested in the strongest terms Evertsen's demand for submission "of the people his Majesties subjects seated on Long Island eastward of Oyster Bay."[13]

The three envoys received their answer next day. Drafted by Stuyvesant's nephew, Nicholas Bayard—newly appointed as English secretary to New Orange—it was uncompromising. Long Island, Evertsen pointed out, had formerly belonged to the Dutch, and it would therefore revert to Dutch rule now. All its inhabitants would be required to take an oath of loyalty, and if they refused, they would be compelled to obey.

The Hartford delegates took this answer back to the Commissioners of the United Colonies, who were meeting at Hartford in the beginning of September, and who at first were unanimous in their fury and resentment. An attack on one member would be considered as an attack on all. But Massachusetts soon had second thoughts. Why should it waste good public money pulling Winthrop's chestnuts out of the fire? While the first English towns on Long Island, Huntington and Brookhaven, were surrendering to the Dutch, Massachusett's General Court decided that any joint operation was "not expedient at this season." Plymouth was equally lukewarm, and only the outcast, Rhode Island, offered help, in the hope of being "accepted" at last by her grand neighbor Connecticut.[14]

Under the circumstances, Evertsen and Binckes felt they could safely return to Europe, leaving only two ships—the largest being the twenty-four-gun *Surinam*—and 130 men to safeguard their conquest. But the sight of the Dutch sails disappearing toward the Atlantic emboldened some of the Long Island villages, which at

EPILOGUE

once protested against the oath they were required to swear, to be "true and faithfull to the High and Mighty Lords the States General of the United Provinces and his serene Highness the Lord Prince of Orange . . . provided that wee shall not be forced in armes against our own nation if they be sent by authority of his Majesty of England." They sent news of their stand to Hartford, and much encouraged, the General Assembly there drafted, on October 30, a new protest to the Dutch governor.[15]

"It being not the maner of Christian or civill nations to disturbe the poore people in cottages and open villages," it began, "we cannot but wonder to heere that some of yours . . . having been lately down towards the easterne end of Long Island and have urged his Matie's subjects there to take an oath contrary to their due allegiance. . . ." In the same letter Winthrop threatened an attack on Colve's "headquarters" if he did not leave the Long Islanders alone. Immediately after, he sent a small force of fifty men—commanded by his son Fitz-John as the "Sarjt. Major" and by Deputy Samuel Willys—to Long Island.[16]

The Dutch and the men from Hartford finally confronted each other at Southold, but with sharp words only, since the Dutch were unarmed. Colve protested at this interference, but neither party made a further move—the Dutch because they were uncomfortably aware of their exposed position, and Winthrop because he was still hoping for assistance from the other New England colonies.

New Orange, meanwhile, was struggling to adjust to this astonishing turnabout in its destiny. In its few years of English rule New York had grown and prospered. A visitor had described it in 1670 as "built most of Brick and Stone and covered with red and black tile, and the Land being high, it gives at a distance a pleasing Aspect." But Colve must have felt quite at home: there were five thousand solid Dutch burghers in the city and, with its canals, paved streets and tall brick houses, it had a distinctively Dutch look about it. John Josselyn, visiting at about this time, was deeply impressed by its prosperity, evident in the houses "built with Dutch Brick alla-moderna, the meanest house therein being valued at one hundred pounds."[17]

Before his departure, Evertsen had appointed Colve governor general and composed a council of war to assist him, choosing one of the city's richest Dutch burghers, Cornelis Steenwyck, as first

A SWEET AND ALIEN LAND

councillor. He had released the city magistrates from their oath to Charles II, and reinstated the old Dutch system of burgomasters —three this time—schepens, and schout.

Colve's first priority, understandably, was the defense of the city. In October, at his orders, the houses huddled close to the walls of the fort were at last pulled down, and the walls strengthened from the inside. To pay for all this, he decided to tax the 133 richest citizens—those worth more than one thousand guilders "wampum value"—borrowing the money in advance from 65 of them.*

These measures did nothing to make Colve popular, and he seems not to have been a very likable man anyway, "of resolute spirit and passionate." The English were bound to resent him, but he was far from popular even with the Dutch; the tolerance and generosity with which Sir Richard Nicolls had stamped the English administration of New York now paid dividends. Matthias Nicolls, the English secretary of New York (and no relation to Sir Richard), who had fled to Connecticut, wrote that when Colve's "violent" government was over, it "will not be lamented by friend or foe." Even the Dutch reproached Colve, according to this Englishman, "not to have dealt our countrymen with equall Civility as they received from us during the English government." A highly prejudiced John Sharpe was particularly incensed by the methods Colve used to persuade the English citizens to take the new oath of allegiance: "hard imposures and molestations, [which] cannot but draw tears from all tenderhearted Christians."[18]

So bitter, indeed, were the English refugees in their denunciations of the Colve regime that Winthrop began to hope they might succeed where he had failed, and rouse Massachusetts to action. Certainly the Bay Colony's attitude of cautious nonintervention was infuriating to those New Yorkers who had found refuge there. Angrily they petitioned the Boston General Court in November to reconquer their town, "for the service of his Majesty, the welfare of this people and for the glory of our English nation."[19]

There the matter might have rested. But it was the Dutch themselves who finally roused the spirit of Massachusetts. A Dutch ship, the *Expectation,* was shipwrecked at about this time off Nantucket. Some English sailors managed to salvage the abandoned vessel and brought it into Boston harbor. Colve at once protested

*Cornelis Steenwyck, with a capital of fifty thousand guilders, was only the second richest.

EPILOGUE

and demanded that it be handed over, but to no avail, and soon afterward the Dutch retaliated by seizing four trading ketches from Massachusetts. Boston woke up with a start. In a fiery message it declared to Colve that it intended "to endeavour a full reparation by force of arms," and in December the Court resolved "that two of our best ships be forthwith fitted, furnished with all respects for the present designe against the common enemy, and two hundred soldiers to be transported in them for the defence of our Navigation, and to Joyne with our Confederates as matters may present."[20]

After all this brave talk, Boston's war effort in the end boiled down to the fitting out of one large vessel and a small ketch, although an army of 560 "foote souldiers" and two troops of horse were planned. New Plymouth hesitantly followed Boston's example, and recruited one hundred men.[21]

On learning of these measures, Colve at once redoubled his own efforts to strengthen New Orange's defenses: 180 great cannon were installed in the fort, and a powerful militia was recruited among the burghers, in addition to the solid garrison of 120 Dutch marines. Exaggerated accounts of Dutch strength circulated in New England. "They have 800 men in the garrison," it was reported, "and [the Dutch] say . . . they will be with us quickly, for now the flame is kindled they must follow it." But for all his guns and soldiers, Colve was an uneasy man. He was still waiting for definite news and instructions from Europe, where, as he knew very well, the fate of New Orange would ultimately be decided. To prevent his beleaguered city from being demoralized by rumors, he forbade all communication with New England.[22]

It was weeks before the Old World caught up with events. Cornelis Evertsen had sent off a long account of his exploit to the States of Zeeland, but the ship on which it was sent, the *St. Joseph*, was attacked by the English, and its captain panicked and threw the report overboard. On arriving in Zeeland, this dull man was able to report only the bare facts, and even when he was cross-questioned by Caspar Fagel, the Raadspensionary of the United Provinces, who was understandably avid for all the details, the captain turned out to be "of so little curiosity, that he had no

A SWEET AND ALIEN LAND

particulars to report." Another long report, this time sent off by the burgomasters, had no better luck. They entrusted it to Cornelis van Ruyven, who was leaving for Europe, but his ship was the ill-fated *Expectation*, which was shipwrecked off Nantucket.[23]

In the end it was London, not Amsterdam, that first learned in any detail of the dazzling Dutch coup in America. The news came at the beginning of November 1673, and the merged Council for Trade and Plantations met at once to consider the situation. It concluded that "shipps cannot be conveniently be sent thither, till after Christmas," but that they must certainly be sent in January, and the English colonies were warned to have their troops in readiness. But where these ships were to be found was a mystery: there was no money left to equip them. England had achieved nothing in the last Anglo-Dutch War for all the millions it had cost her, and national sentiment was by this time entirely against the King and with the Dutch. Even those who had been shrillest in their outcry against the "butterboxes" were now denouncing England's nominal ally, Louis XIV, as a popish tyrant and were loud in their sympathy for the heroic Protestant Dutch. Under the circumstances, Charles II was ready to call it a day, and when the Dutch made overtures for peace in December, they were not rejected.[24]

The Dutch offered to restore all conquered lands, and when Binckes, at about this time, returned to his country with details of the capture of New York, the Dutch hastened to include the restitution of New Netherland in their peace package, "in order to manifest to your Majesty the special esteem which we entertain to your friendship." Pending a definite decision about the fate of the reconquered Dutch province, the States General formally placed it under the control of the Admiralty of Amsterdam, whose secretary Joris Andringa was appointed its nominal governor. Significantly, the now virtually defunct West India Company was not even consulted in these transactions.[25]

It was plain from the speed with which the province was offered to England that the Dutch never entertained the slightest idea of hanging onto New Netherland, now that luck had tossed it back into their hands. They were far more anxious to secure English recognition of their rights to Surinam. When Charles II, himself playing for time in the hope of getting more generous terms, told Parliament that he doubted Dutch sincerity—their peace over-

EPILOGUE

tures had been made "solely to gain time"—the States General protested angrily, reminding him of the first Dutch offer and insisting that it demonstrated "sufficiently to what degree we wish to deserve your Majesty's affection since we offer to restore to you so considerable a conquest as New Netherland, without the hope of receiving anything in exchange for it."[26]

This time Parliament insisted that Charles II accept the Dutch terms, and penniless as he was, he had no choice. On February 19, 1674, the Peace of Westminster was signed, in which it was stated that "all lands, islands, towns, ports, castles and fortresses" taken by one party from the other should be restored.[27]

There was another long pause before news of this settlement filtered back to New Orange. The States General had already signed away the Dutch slice of America for the second and last time when it received at last a euphoric account of Evertsen's exploits, sent off by the burgomasters early in the New Year. With wry smiles, their High Mightinesses must have read of the "happy conquest" of the three towns and thirty villages in New Netherland after nine years of English occupation. The burgomasters pointed to the great advantages of the recapture: New Orange could easily become a haven for those in the Republic who wished to flee from the invading French; the province could be the "granary" of the Dutch, "having last year exported 25,000 schepels of grain"; and it would be a useful watchtower from which to "keep an eye on the King of England's actions here."[28]

At almost the same moment that the Peace of Westminster ended the Anglo-Dutch War in Europe, the last Anglo-Dutch battle in American history was taking place. Fitz-John Winthrop with his fifty men had settled at Southold on Long Island to uphold the Connecticut claim. At the end of February a Dutch squadron of four vessels arrived in front of the town with guns trained. A Dutch messenger was sent to ask for its surrender, Fitz-John refused, and a short gun battle followed. Despite their greater force, however, the Dutch retired, never to return.

Rumors about the peace reached New Netherland by the spring. John Sharpe confirmed them in May after hearing, during a visit to New England, that New York had been restored to the English. One of the first to hear Sharpe's news was Isaac Melyn, son of the redoubtable Cornelis, who was so enraged by the States General's betrayal that he called the burghers together, and for a

A SWEET AND ALIEN LAND

time it looked as though a mutiny might follow. The Dutch, in "such a distracted rage and passion," threatened to set the city on fire and cut the governor's throat. But Colve, who must have known by this time that the end was in sight, acted coolly and decisively to restore calm. Sharpe and Melyn were arrested, the one charged with fomenting "mutiny and disturbance," the other with uttering "very seditious and mutinous language."[29]

On July 11 there was no denying the rumors any longer. Colve at last received a copy of the treaty. Among the Dutch, as Jeremias van Rensselaer wrote, the news caused "no little emotion," but he probably spoke for them all when he added philosophically: "Well, if it has to be, we commend the matter to God, who knows what is best for us." There was nothing left for Colve to do but tidy up the last traces of the Dutch occupation. Confiscated English property was restored, the four trading ketches were returned to Massachusetts, and Colve settled down to await his English successor.[30]

On November 1 the new governor, Major Edmund Andros, disembarked at Manhattan. He brought with him a reassuring message from Charles II to the anxious citizens: "all inhabitants there should enjoy all there rights and privileges of which they were in the enjoyment before the war." Colve asked for eight days in which to wind up his administrative and personal affairs, and on November 10 he embarked with his soldiers in a Dutch frigate, leaving Andros his coach and three horses.[31]

In the brief Court Records of New Orange a final entry was made: "On the 10th November, Anno 1674, the Province of New Netherland is surrendered by Governor Colve to Governor Major Edmund Andros in behalf of his Majesty of Great Britain."[32]

Thus unobtrusively, almost casually, the Dutch relinquished their North American territory—the fertile plains, the thousands of acres of virgin forests, the flourishing port, and the best and most strategically sited harbor on the eastern seaboard.

Had they no notion of the value of this fantastic prize they now tossed into the lap of the English? It seems not. To the Heeren XIX of the West India Company, New Netherland had been an expensive mistake; to the regents an embarrassment; to Johan de Witt, a useful pawn in the European chess game. Almost to the end of the existence of New Netherland, the Dutch remained curiously blind to the potential and importance of their North American colony, and callously indifferent to its fate.

It is easy to understand how the Heeren XIX, with their record of blind self-seeking, came to miss the point so badly. They had established a trading settlement; they had no idea of founding a colony. And this board of well-fed and complacent Amsterdam businessmen was simply incapable of grasping the implications, human or political, of their financial adventure.

It is harder to find excuses for the Dutch government. The West India Company's disastrous mismanagement of New Netherland had been common knowledge in the Republic for years. Yet appeal after appeal from the desperate Dutch colony fell on deaf ears at The Hague. By the time Johan de Witt developed a colonial conscience for them, it was already too late.

When on November 10, 1674, the Dutch flag in New Amsterdam was lowered to make place for that of the English, it marked much more than the end of the hesitant Dutch involvement in the New World. The changing of the guard in what was to remain New York was the clearest sign of the steadily growing power of the English nation. The Dutch Golden Age was drawing to a close.

NOTES

Key to Abbreviations Used in Notes

Bowier Mss.—A. J. F. van Laer, ed., *Van Rensselaer Bowier Manuscripts.*

Cal. Hist. Mss.—E. B. O'Callaghan, *Calendar of Historical Manuscripts in the Office of the Secretary of State of New York*

Clarendon Papers—Earl of Clarendon, Clarendon Papers, 1660–1667, 19–22

Conn. Col. Rec.—J. H. Trumbull, ed., *The Public Records of the Colony of Connecticut, 1638–1678*

Corr. JVR—A. J. F. van Laer, ed., *Correspondence of Jeremias van Rensselaer, 1651–1674*

CSP Col.—*Calendar of State Papers—Colonial Series, 1574–1660*

CSP Dom—*Calendar of State Papers—Domestic 1664–1665*

CSP Venetian—*Calendar of State Papers and Manuscripts Relating to the English Affairs*

DCH—John Romeyn Brodhead and E. B. O'Callaghan, eds., *Documents Relative to the Colonial History of the State of New York*

Doc. N.H.—Nathaniel Bouton, ed., *Documents and Records Relating to the Province of New Hampshire, 1623–1686*

Eccl. Rec. N.Y.—E. T. Corwin, ed., *Ecclesiastical Records, State of New York, 1621–1800*

Hist. Gen.—Historisch Genootschap, *Bijdragen en Mededelingen van Historisch Genootschap*

Mass. Arch.—Massachusetts Archives

MOC—B. Fernow, ed., *Minutes of the Orphan Masters Court of New Amsterdam, 1655–1663*

New Haven Col. Rec.—Charles J. Hoadley, ed., *Records of the Colony and Plantation of New Haven*

New Netherland Papers—*New Netherland Papers*, Brevoort Collection and Moore New York Papers, New York Public Library

NNN—J. Franklin Jameson, ed., *Narratives of New Netherland, 1609–1664*

NYHS—New York Historical Society Collections

Plymouth Col. Rec.— N. B. Shurtleff, ed., *Records of the Colony of New Plymouth in New England, 1620–1692*
RNA—Berthold Fernow, ed., *The Records of New Amsterdam*
Stokes—I. N. Phelps Stokes, ed., *The Iconography of Manhattan Island, 1489–1909.* Vols IV, VI
Winthrop Letters—John Winthrop, *Winthrop Letters*, Mass. Hist. Soc. Coll.
Winthrop Papers—John Winthrop, *Winthrop Papers*, Mass. Hist. Soc. Coll.

Chapter 1 The Best Buy

1. New York Historical Society Collections, I: 37 (hereafter cited as NYHS).
2. Alg. Rijksarchief (Gen. States-Archives, The Hague) St. General 3185, folio 451 verso.
3. F. C. Wieder, *De Stichting van New York in 1625*, 35.
4. Schuyler van Rensselaer, *History of the City of New York in the 17th Century*, I: 49.
5. J. Franklin Jameson, ed., *Narratives of New Netherland, 1609–1664*, 6, 7 (hereafter cited as NNN).
6. *Ibid.*, 7; NYHS, 2nd ser., I: ii, 45.
7. NNN, 7, 18.
8. *Ibid.*, 19, 22, 27.
9. *Ibid.*, 7, 28.
10. *Ibid.*, 9.
11. *Ibid.*, 38.
12. John Fiske, *The Dutch and Quaker Colonies in America*, 106.
13. NYHS, I: 10.
14. NNN, 39; Simon Hart, *The Prehistory of the New Netherland Company*, 52.
15. J. E. Elias, *Het Voorspel van den Eersten Engelsche Oorlog*, II: 118.
16. NNN, 7.
17. Historische Genootschap, *Bijdragen en Mededelingen van Historische Genootschap*, Nieuwe Serie XXXVII: 334, 367 (hereafter cited as Hist. Gen.).
18. John Romeyn Brodhead and E. B. O'Callaghan, eds., *Documents Relative to the Colonial History of the State of New York*, 1: 362, 465 (hereafter cited as DCH).
19. Elias, *Voorspel*, II: 122.

Chapter 2 Settling Down

1. NNN, 75.
2. *Ibid.*
3. *Ibid.*
4. Nicolaes van Wassenaer, "The Description and First Settlement of New Netherland," in *Collectanea Adamantea*, XXVII, 2: app. I, 43, 44.
5. *Ibid.*, app. II, 46, 47.
6. NNN, 77.

7. NYHS, 2nd ser., I: v, 220, 221.

8. *Ibid.*, 222.

9. A. J. F. van Laer, ed., *Van Rensselaer Bowier Manuscripts, Being the Letters of Kiliaen van Rensselaer, 1630–1643,* 152 (hereafter cited as Bowier Mss.).

10. I.N. Phelps Stokes, ed., *The Iconography of Manhattan Island, 1489–1909,* IV: 53, 54 (hereafter cited as Stokes).

11. NNN, 82, 83.

12. DCH, IV: 132.

13. NYHS, I: 368.

14. F. C. Wieder, *De Stichting van New York in 1625,* 14.

15. *Ibid.*, Illustr. I

16. NNN, 83, 86.

17. Wieder, *De Stichting van New York,* 60, 62, 73, 74.

18. *Ibid.*, 47; NNN, 83, 84.

19. A. Eekhof, *Jonas Michaëlius,* 57; NNN, 122, 123.

20. NNN, 105, 131.

21. Stokes, IV, 72.

22. Bowier Mss., 169.

23. J. E. Elias, *Voorspel* II: 185.

24. Schuyler van Rensselaer, *History of the City of New York in the 17th Century,* I: 101, 102; Nathaniel Bouton, ed., *Documents and Records Relating to the Province of New Hampshire, 1623–1686,* I: 50 (hereafter cited as Doc. N.H.).

25. NYHS, I: 40.

26. Stokes, IV: 945.

Chapter 3   Never So Good

1. Michiel Adriaensz de Ruyter, *Journaal 1664–1665,* LXII: 7.

2. L. van Aitzema, *Saken van Staet en Oorlog,* II: 484.

3. Hist. Gen., Nieuwe Serie XXXVII: 408.

4. *Ibid.*, 421.

5. *Ibid.*

6. *Ibid.*, 405.

7. W. P. C. Knuttel, *Catalogus van de pamflettenverzameling, berustende in de Koninklijke Bibliotheek,* 3735, 67.

8. Hist. Gen., XXXVII: 416.

9. Pieter de la Court, *Interest van Holland ofte Gronden van Hollands Welvaren,* 38.

10. Violet Barbour, *Capitalism in Amsterdam in the 17th Century,* 13.

11. J. E. Elias, *Voorspel* I: 100–102.

12. Jan Wagenaar, *Vaderlandsche Historie,* XI: 264, 265; H. Brugmans, *Geschiedenis van Amsterdams "Bloeitijd," 1621–1696,* III: 26.

13. Dixon Ryan Fox, *Yankees and Yorkers,* 40.

14. *Beschrijvende Catalogus der Scheepsmodellen en Scheepsbouwkundige teekeningen, 1600–1900* (Amsterdam: Nederlandsch Historisch Scheepvaart Museum, 1943).

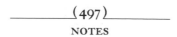

15. DCH, XIV: 134, 116; A. Eekhof, *De Hervormde Kerk in Noord-Amerika*, II: 95.

16. John Winthrop, *Winthrop Papers*, Mass. Hist. Soc., II: 247 (hereafter cited as Winthrop Papers).

17. NNN, 68.

18. Winthrop Papers, II: 303, 304.

19. John Josselyn, *An Account of Two Voyages to New England*, 13, 14.

20. Winthrop Papers, II: 259.

21. Jacob Steendam, *Noch Vaster: A Memoir of the First Poet in New Netherland;* NNN, 131.

22. NNN, 168, 169.

23. NYHS, 2nd ser., I: v, 179, 180; NNN, 168.

24. Henry C. Murphy, *Anthology of New Netherland*, 191, 193.

25. NNN, 147, 176n.

26. *Ibid.*, 161, 162.

27. Bowier Mss., 233.

28. DCH, XIV: 195, 388; *New Netherland Papers*, Brevoort Collection and Moore New York Papers, New York Public Library (hereafter cited as New Netherland Papers).

29. Th. Morton, *New English Canaan*, 68.

30. John Underhill, *The History of the Pequot War*, Mass. Hist. Soc. Coll. 3rd series, VI, 13; NNN 223.

Chapter 4 First Rights

1. NYHS, I: 45.

2. *Ibid.*, 46.

3. *Ibid.*, 50.

4. *Ibid.*, 52.

5. *Ibid.*, 56.

6. *Ibid.*, 51; E. B. O'Callaghan, *History of New Netherland*, II: 344.

7. NYHS, I: 59.

8. *Ibid.*, I: 60; *Calendar of State Papers—Colonial Series, 1574–1660*, VI: 154 (hereafter cited as CSP Col.).

9. J. E. Elias, *Het Voorspel van den Eersten Engelsche Oorlog*, I: 61, 62.

10. Charles H. Wilson, *Profit and War*, 3.

11. George Edmundson, *Anglo-Dutch Rivalry during the First Half of the Seventeenth Century*, 19, 32, 33.

12. *Ibid.*, 51, 52.

13. *Ibid.*, 78.

14. Stokes IV, 45.

15. Sir Ferdinando Gorges, "A Brief Narration," in *America Painted to the Life*, 31.

16. CSP Col., I: 26; DCH, III: 6, 7.

17. DCH, III: 7–8.

18. *Ibid.*, 8.

19. CSP Col., I: 18.

20. O'Callaghan, *History of New Netherland*, II: 343.

21. Hakluyt, cited in John Romeyn Brodhead, *History of the State of New York*, I: 172.

22. DCH, III: 16.

23. Charles M. Andrews, *The Colonial Period in American History*, I: 320.

24. Comte D'Estrades, *Lettres, Mémoires et Négociations de Monsieur le Comte d'Estrades*, III: 340.

25. Andrews, *The Colonial Period in American History*, I: 323.

26. CSP Col., II: 50.

27. Brodhead, *History of the State of New York*, I: 121.

28. William Bradford, *History of Plimoth Plantation*, 22; Brodhead, *History of the State of New York*, I: 121.

29. Brodhead, *History of the State of New York*, I: 121.

30. O'Callaghan, *History of New Netherland*, I: 84.

31. DCH, III: 9.

32. *Ibid.*, 8.

Chapter 5 A Pilgrimage

1. William Bradford, *History of Plimoth Plantation*, 196.

2. Jan Wagenaar, *Vaderlandsche Historie*, XI: 26.

3. NYHS, 2nd ser., I, 361, 2.

4. *Ibid.*, I: 361.

5. *Ibid.*, 362.

6. *Ibid.*, 362, 363.

7. *Ibid.*, 363.

8. Bradford, *History of Plimoth Plantation*, 116, 121.

9. NNN, III, 112.

10. NYHS, 2nd ser., I: 364, 365.

11. NNN, 176.

12. *Ibid.*, 110.

13. NYHS, 2nd ser., I: 365.

14. DCH, III: 38.

15. *Ibid.*, 366, 367; E. B. O'Callaghan, *History of New Netherland*, I: 128.

16. Bowier Mss., 169, 170.

17. CSP Col., VI: 156.

18. *Ibid.*, 154.

Chapter 6 Drunken Fools

1. Stokes, IV: 945.
2. A. Eekhof, *Bastiaen Jansz Krol*, 25–30.
3. *Ibid.*, app. 21–22, xxiii.
4. Bowier Mss., 137–153.
5. J. S. C. Jessurun, *Kiliaen van Rensselaer, 1623–1636*, 22–26.
6. Bowier Mss., 154.
7. *Ibid.*, 158–161.
8. E. B. O'Callaghan, *History of New Netherland*, I: 124.
9. Schuyler van Rensselaer, *History of the City of New York in the 17th Century*, I: 95.
10. Bowier Mss., 217.
11. NNN, 313, 314.
12. O'Callaghan, *History of New Netherland*, I: 137.
13. Eekhof, *Krol*, 25–30.
14. NNN, 186.
15. N. de Roever in "Oud Holland," jaargang VIII, app. G. 272, 273.
16. NNN, 187, 188.
17. Eekhof, *Krol*, app. 32, xxv, xxxi.
18. *Ibid.*, app. 31, xxix.
19. DCH, I: 72–81.
20. Eekhof, *Krol*, app. 32, xxix.
21. DCH, I: 72–81.
22. *Ibid.*
23. *Ibid.*
24. Eekhof, *Krol*, app. 32, xxix.
25. NNN, 189–192.
26. William Bradford, *History of Plimoth Plantation*, 386, 387.
27. Bowier Mss., 267–269.
28. DCH, XIV: 69–71.
29. Bowier Mss., 267.
30. DCH, XIV: 16.
31. W. C. Menkman, *De West-Indische Compagnie*, 113.
32. Bowier Mss., 267.

Chapter 7 Crowding On

1. David Pietersz de Vries, *Korte Historiael ende Journaels . . .* , III: 168, 169.
2. Charles M. Andrews, *The Colonial Period in American History*, I: 462.
3. NNN, 195.

4. CSP Col., VI: 171.

5. William Bradford, *History of Plimoth Plantation,* 370–374.

6. DCH, II: 139.

7. Bradford, *History of Plimoth Plantation,* 374.

8. Winthrop cited in Charles M. Andrews, *The Colonial Period in American History.* I: 6g.

9. DCH, III: 18, 19; CSP Col., VI: 171.

10. Emmanuel Downing to Secretary of State Coke, cited in George L. Beer, *The Origins of the British Colonial System, 1578–1668,* 23, 24.

11. Bradford, *History of Plimoth Plantation,* 374.

12. DCH, II: 139.

13. Bradford, *History of Plimoth Plantation,* 387.

14. *Ibid.,* 402.

15. *Ibid.,* 402, 403.

16. Ronald D. Cohen, "The Hartford Treaty of 1650," 321; Bradford, *History of Plimoth Plantation,* 405–407.

17. Bradford, *History of Plimoth Plantation,* 280.

18. NYHS, I: 98.

19. CSP Col., VIII: 204, 205.

20. *Ibid.,* II: 256, 257.

21. E. B. O'Callaghan, *History of New Netherland,* I: app. D, 416.

22. Bradford, *History of Plimoth Plantation,* 390, 391.

23. CSP Col., VIII: 180.

24. Winthrop Papers, III: 198.

25. *Ibid.,* 198.

26. *Ibid.,* 212.

27. NNN, 309.

28. J. H. Trumbull, ed., *The Public Records of the Colony of Connecticut, 1638–1678,* I: 565, 566 (hereafter cited as Conn. Col. Rec.).

29. Stokes, IV: 84.

Chapter 8 A New Threat

1. A. Eekhof, *De Hervormde Kerk in Noord-Amerika,* I: 57.

2. NNN, 197, 198.

3. E. B. O'Callaghan, *History of New Netherland,* I: 172, 174.

4. Bowier Mss., 352.

5. *Broad Advice,* 139; NNN, 202.

6. DCH, XIV: 8; Bowier Mss., 382.

7. O'Callaghan, *History of New Netherland,* I: 394.

8. *Ibid.,* 183, 184.

9. A. Eekhof, *De Hervormde Kerk,* I: 140; M. J. Hershkowitz, "The Troublesome Turk," 299–311.

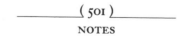

10. O'Callaghan, *History of New Netherland*, I: 171; Stokes, IV: 84; Berthold Fernow, ed., *The Records of New Amsterdam*, I: 96 (hereafter cited as RNA).

11. Hist. Gen., XXI: 355.

12. NYHS, I: 106.

13. *Ibid.*, 107.

14. O'Callaghan, *History of New Netherland*, I: 200, 206.

15. Bowier Mss., 428, 429.

16. DCH, XII: 3.

17. J. E. Elias, *Het Voorspel van den Eersten Engelsche Oorlog*, II: 202.

18. Amandus Johnson, *The Swedish Settlements on the Delaware*, I: 87–97.

19. Violet Barbour, *Capitalism in Amsterdam in the 17th Century*, 136.

20. DCH, III: 20.

21. *Ibid.*, I: 598.

22. *Ibid.*, XII: 19.

Chapter 9 Doubtful Neighbors

1. Rev. William Hubbard, *General History of New England*, 318; NNN, 203.

2. John Winthrop cited in Amandus Johnson, *The Swedish Settlements on the Delaware*, I; 208–210.

3. Charles J. Hoadley, ed., *Records of the Colony and Plantation of New Haven*, I: 56, 57 (hereafter cited as New Haven Col. Rec.)

4. Amandus Johnson, *The Swedish Settlements on the Delaware*, I: 213.

5. N. B. Shurtleff, ed., *Records of the Colony of New Plymouth in New England, 1620–1692*, Acts, II: 13 (hereafter cited as Plymouth Col. Rec.); DCH, XII: 23.

6. DCH, XII: 23, 24.

7. NYHS, II: 4; NYHS, 2nd ser., II: 4; XIV: 413.

8. Plymouth Col. Record. Acts I, 13; NYHS, II, 4.

9. E. B. O'Callaghan, *History of New Netherland*, I: 215; Schuyler van Rensselaer, *History of the City of New York in the 17th Century*, I: 165.

10. DCH, XIV: 28.

11. *Ibid.*, 28.

12. *Ibid.*, 28–31; NYHS, II: 4;

13. CSP Col., 154.

14. C. M. Andrews, *The Colonial Period in American History*, II, 163–165.

15. O'Callaghan, *History of New Netherland*, I, 282.

16. A. Johnson, *The Swedish Settlements on the Delaware*, I, 381, 382.

17. O'Callaghan, *History of New Netherland*, I, 282; DCH, XII, 51.

18. NNN, 203, 204.

19. NYHS, I, 272; O'Callaghan, *History of New Netherland*, I, 213.

20. NYHS, I, 273–276.

21. DCH, XIV, 35.

22. Ibid., 40.
23. Ibid., 41; NYHS, 278.
24. O'Callaghan, *History of New Netherland*, I, 252; DCH, XIV, 24.
25. John Winthrop, *The History of New England*, II, 34.
26. Van Rensselaer, *History of New York*, I: 182–184.
27. NNN, 400.
28. DCH, I: 632; *American Historical Review*, 6: 10–12; Dixon Ryan Fox, *Yankees and Yorkers*, 66–70; A. C. Flick (ed.) *History of the State of New York*, I, 284.
29. DCH, XIV: 41.
30. Van Rensselaer, *History of New York*, I: 184.
31. Stokes, IV, 96.
32. Jan Wagenaar, *Vaderlandsche Historie*, XI: 328.
33. NYHS, I: 128, 130.
34. Winthrop Papers, IV: 113.
35. DCH, II: 150.
36. NYHS, I: 567.
37. L. van Aitzema, *Saken van Staet en Oorlog*, II: 392.

Chapter 10 The Dutch Babel

1. NNN, 253, 259.
2. Dingman Versteeg, ed., *The New Netherland Register*, 130–132.
3. William Castell, *A Short Discoverie of the Coasts and Continents of America*, 23; NNN, 259; DCH, I: 152, 153
4. NNN, 212.
5. *Ibid.*, 326.
6. *Ibid.*, 325, 326; NYHS, 2nd ser., I: xii, 382.
7. NYHS, 2nd ser., I: 383.
8. NNN, 212; Stokes, IV: 93.
9. Stokes, IV: 95.
10. RNA, II: 49.
11. *Ibid.*, I: 3, 9, 10.
12. NYHS, 2nd ser. I:v 192; NNN, 69.
13. NNN, 303.
14. A. W. Trelease, *Indian Affairs in Colonial New York in the 17th Century*, 65.
15. RNA, I: 11.
16. F. C. Wieder, *De Stichting van New York in 1625*, 30.
17. NNN, 72, 300.
18. *Ibid.*, 173.
19. *Ibid.*, 218.
20. *Ibid.*, 70, 176, 302, 126, 300.
21. NYHS, 2nd ser. I:v 213, 214.

22. NNN, 223.

23. Winthrop Papers, III: 17; NNN, 72.

24. NNN, 271, 179.

25. *Ibid.*, 302, 107.

26. *Ibid.*, 108.

27. *Ibid.*, 174.

28. NYHS, 2nd ser., I:v 191.

29. NNN, 174.

30. *Ibid.*, 128.

31. *Ibid.*, 175

32. *Ibid.*

33. *Broad Advice*, 150.

Chapter 11 A Very Mean Fellow

1. William Rogers, cited in James G. Wilson, *The Memorial History of the City of New York*, I, 205.

2. NNN, 273.

3. *Ibid.*

4. *Ibid.*, 274.

5. *Ibid.*, 322.

6. *Ibid.*, 208; DCH, XIII: 7.

7. DCH, XIII: 7, I: 410.

8. NNN, 208; DCH, I: 410–414.

9. NNN, 213, 275.

10. *Ibid.*, 211.

11. *Ibid.*

12. *Ibid.*, 275, 214; Schuyler van Rensselaer, *History of the City of New York in the 17th Century*, I: 178.

13. NNN, 275, 214.

14. *Ibid.*, 333; NYHS, 2nd ser., I: 277, 278.

15. DCH, I: 410–414; NNN, 213, 275.

16. NYHS, I: 201, 203.

17. *Ibid.*, 203.

18. NNN, 276.

19. *Ibid.*, 215.

20. *Ibid.*, 216.

21. *Ibid.*, 276.

22. *Ibid.*, 277, 225.

23. *Ibid.*, 226.

24. *Ibid.*, 277; NYHS, I: 410–414.

25. NNN, 226, 227; E. B. O'Callaghan, *History of New Netherland*, I: 267.

26. NYHS, I: 410–414.

27. NNN, 227.

28. *Broad Advice,* 148, 149; NNN, 228.

29. NYHS, I: 410–414; NNN, 229.

30. NNN, 230–232.

31. O'Callaghan, *History of New Netherland,* I: 272.

32. DCH, XIII: 12, 13; NNN, 278; NYHS, I: 410–414.

33. NNN, 232.

Chapter 12   The English Savior

1. NNN, 234.

2. *Ibid.*

3. *Ibid.,* 232.

4. *Ibid.,* 279.

5. NYHS, I: 410–414.

6. Winthrop Papers, II: 324, 325.

7. *Ibid.,* 4th ser., VI: 18.

8. Schuyler van Rensselaer, *History of the City of New York in the 17th Century,* I: 216, 217.

9. NNN, 280.

10. New Haven Col. Rec., I: 116.

11. NYHS, I: 139, 140.

12. NNN, 281.

13. *Ibid.*

14. *Ibid.,* 282.

15. *Broad Advice,* 151–153; NYHS, I: 410–414.

16. NNN, 282–284.

17. NYHS, I: 141, 142.

18. P. J. Blok, *Geschiedenis van het Nederlandsche Volk,* 349–352; J. E. Elias, *Het Voorspel van den Eersten Engelsche Oorlog,* II: 123–126.

19. NYHS, I: 245, 246.

20. NNN, 321.

21. NYHS, I: 209–213.

22. *Ibid.*

23. *Ibid.,* 206.

24. E. B. O'Callaghan, *History of New Netherland,* I: 310.

25. NNN, 328.

26. NYHS, I: 209–213.

27. Van Rensselaer, *History of New York,* I: 234, 235.

28. Stokes, IV: 104.

29. NYHS, I: 209–213; O'Callaghan, *History of New Netherland,* I: 356.

30. NYHS, 2nd ser., I: 275, 276.

1. NYHS, 2nd ser., I: 276; *Broad Advice*, 153.

2. Schuyler van Rensselaer, *History of the City of New York in the 17th Century*, I: 229.

3. NYHS, II: 2.

4. Van Rensselaer, *History of New York*, I: 228, 229.

5. NYHS, 2nd ser., I: iv, 100.

6. Ronald D. Cohen, "The New England Colonies and the Dutch Recapture of New York, 1673–1674," 57; R. B. Nye and J. E. Morpurgo, "The Birth of the U.S.A.," 131; Dixon Ryan Fox, *Yankees and Yorkers*, 78.

7. E. B. O'Callaghan, *History of New Netherland*, I: 280.

8. NNN, 204.

9. William Bradford, *History of Plimoth Plantation*, 32–33.

10. Charles H. Levermore, *The Republic of New Haven*, 30.

11. Winthrop Papers, II: 271; Bradford, *History of Plimoth Plantation*, 95.

12. Winthrop Papers, II: 141

13. *Ibid.*, II: 305, III: 21.

14. *Ibid.*, III: 166, 167.

15. C. M. Andrews, *The Colonial Period in American History*, II: 180, 181; Thomas J. Wertenbaker, *The First Americans, 1606–1690*, 262–281.

16. Winthrop Papers, III: 402, 403.

17. Levermore, *The Republic of New Haven*, 51–56.

18. *Ibid.*, 101.

19. James T. Adams, *The Founding of New England*, 256–261.

20. Winthrop Papers, II: 91, 92.

21. *Ibid.*, 126, 91, 92.

22. *Ibid.*

23. *Ibid.*, 333, 334.

24. Winthrop Papers IV, 488.

25. Ibid.

26. NNN, 305.

27. Plymouth Col. Rec., IX: 61, 62.

28. Winthrop Papers, V: 95, 96.

29. NYHS, I: 189.

30. *Ibid.*, 196.

31. *Ibid.*, 199.

32. Winthrop Papers, V: 148.

33. Van Rensselaer, *History of New York*, I: 272.

Chapter 14 Another Father

1. W. R. Menkman, *De West-Indische Compagnie*, 105, 106; J. H. P. Kemperink, "Pieter Stuyvesant: Waar en wanneer werd hij geboren?", 56–59; *New York Historical Society Bulletin* 10: 3–12; Martha Eerdmans, *Peter Stuyvesant; Nieuw Nederlandsch Biografisch Woordenboek*, VIII: 1191.

2. Alg. Rijksarchief (Gen. States-Archives) Div. Zwolle, Inventory no. 107.

3. M. Eerdmans, *Peter Stuyvesant.*

4. P. J. Blok, *Geschiedenis van het Nederlandsche Volk*, IV: 30, 31.

5. Alg. Rijksarchief (Gen. States-Archives) Div. Leeuwarden, *Registration in Matriculation Book for the years 1586–1685 of Franeker Hoge-School;* Blok, *Geschiedenis van het Nederlandsche Volk*, IV: 38.

6. *Broad Advice*, 160; *New York Historical Society Quarterly Bulletin* 10: 3–12.

7. W. J. van Balen, *Holland aan de Hudson, een verhaal van Nieuw Nederland*, 125, 126.

8. J. E. Elias, *Het Voorspel van den Eersten Engelsche Oorlog*, II: 159.

9. *Broad Advice*, 161, 162.

10. Van Balen, *Holland aan de Hudson*, 127.

11. *Ibid.*

12. *New York Historical Society Quarterly Bulletin* 10: 3–12.

13. Stokes, IV: 105.

14. Stuyvesant Fish, "Peter Stuyvesant," 5, 6.

15. NYHS, I: 175–178; New Netherland Papers, 1221.

16. NYHS, I: 455.

17. E. B. O'Callaghan, *History of New Netherland*, II: 20; NYHS, I: 504.

18. NYHS, I: 504.

19. NNN, 342.

20. *Ibid.*

Chapter 15 A Bad Start

1. NYHS, I: 205.

2. NNN, 333.

3. DCH, XIV: 52, 53.

4. NYHS, I: 206.

5. DCH, XIV: 69–71.

6. *Ibid.*, 71, 73; NYHS, I: 206; Ellis Lawrence Raesly, *Portrait of New Netherland*, 243; NNN, 335.

7. NNN, 342.

8. NYHS, I: 204.

9. *Ibid.*, 207, 208.

10. NNN, 342.

11. NYHS, I: 349, 350, 214.

12. NNN, 342, 328; *Broad Advice*, 165.

13. NNN, 343; *Broad Advice*, 165.

14. NNN, 343.

15. NYHS, XIV: 82, 83; Hist. Gen., XXV: 487.

16. *Broad Advice*, 167.

17. NNN, 234.

Chapter 16 New Brooms

1. A. de Wicquefort, *Histoire des Provinces-Unies des Pais-Bas*, I: 2; P. J. Blok, *Geschiedenis van het Nederlandsche Volk*, V: 4, 5.

2. NYHS, I: 236; J. G. van Dillen, *Van Rijkdom en Regenten*, 158, 159; J. E. Elias, *Het Voorspel van den Eersten Engelsche Oorlog*, II; 145; Blok, *Geschiedenis van het Nederlandsche Volk*, IV: 352, V: 13, 14.

3. DCH, XIII: 22; Stokes, IV: III; NNN, 330.

4. E. B. O'Callaghan, *History of New Netherland*, I: 395; E. T. Corwin, ed., *Ecclesiastical Records, State of New York, 1621–1800*, I: 233 (hereafter cited as Eccl. Rec. N.Y.).

5. DCH, XIII: 23.

6. Stokes, IV: III, 113.

7. RNA, I: 4; DCH, XIV: 105.

8. NNN, 330.

9. *Ibid.*, 339.

10. *Ibid.*, 340, 341.

11. A. C. Flick (ed.), *History of the State of New York*, I: 262, 263.

12. O'Callaghan, *History of New Netherland*, II: 37–39.

13. NNN, 331.

14. New Netherland Papers, 1222; DCH, XIII: 21.

15. NNN, 345.

16. *Ibid.*

17. DCH, XIII: 23.

18. NNN, 344.

19. *Ibid.*, 369.

20. Ibid., 227, 228.

21. *Broad Advice*, 168.

22. Hist. Gen., XXV: 487.

23. NYHS, I: 249; DCH, XIV: 87.

24. DCH, XIV: 104, 105.

25. Winthrop Papers, V: 287.

Chapter 17 The Freedom Fighters

1. NYHS, I: 321.
2. *Ibid.*, 348, 352.
3. *Ibid.*, 352.
4. *Ibid.*
5. NNN, 345.
6. *Ibid.*
7. *Ibid.*
8. DCH, XIV: 110–112.
9. *Ibid.*, 112–114.
10. *Ibid.*, 110–119; NNN, 348–351; DCH, I: 211.
11. DCH, XIV: 104, 105; NYHS, I: 358.
12. NYHS, I: 321–333.
13. *Ibid.*
14. DCH, XIV: 114.
15. NYHS, I: 259; DCH, I: 262–270; NNN, 285–352.
16. DCH, XIV: 120, 121.
17. DCH, XIV: 120, 121.

Chapter 18 The Duke of Muscovy

1. NNN, 395–374.
2. NYHS, I: 401–406.
3. *Ibid.*
4. DCH, XIV: 122, 123; NYHS, I: 448.
5. *Ibid.*, I: 386; RNA, I: 13, 14; DCH, XIV: 108.
6. NYHS, I: 445, 446, 438, 439.
7. DCH, I: 445, 447, 452.
8. NYHS, I: 452.
9. *Ibid.*, 439.
10. *Ibid.*, 453.
11. DCH, XIV: 122.
12. *Ibid.*, 159–161.
13. *Ibid.*, 157.
14. NYHS, I: 514–517.
15. *Ibid.*, 438, 439, 453, 498.
16. DCH, XIV: 132.–
17. *Broad Advice*, 172; NNN, 340.
18. E. B. O'Callaghan, *History of New Netherland*, II: 181; NYHS, I: 510.
19. DCH, XIV: 164; NYHS, I: 510, 512, 513.

NOTES

20. NYHS, I: 471.
21. DCH, XIV: 178; NYHS, I: 475.
22. NYHS, I: 454, 476–478.
23. DCH, XIV: 204.
24. *Ibid.*, 211, 212; NYHS, I: 532, 533.

Chapter 19 Trouble in the North

1. NNN, 261, 262.
2. DCH, XIV: 92.
3. Bowier Mss., 652; E. B. O'Callaghan, *History of New Netherland*, I: 331; NNN, 262.
4. DCH, XIV: 55, 56.
5. *Ibid.*, 57, 58.
6. *Ibid.*, 59.
7. *Ibid.*, 92.
8. O'Callaghan, *History of New Netherland*, II: 71.
9. S. G. Nissenson, *The Patroon's Domain*, 215.
10. DCH, XIV: 93.
11. *Ibid.*, 95.
12. *Ibid.*, 96.
13. NYHS, I: 256, 325.
14. DCH, XIV: 120.
15. *Ibid.*, 135.
16. O'Callaghan, *History of New Netherland*, II: 174.
17. DCH, XIV: 149, 150, 161.
18. O'Callaghan, *History of New Netherland*, II: 177.
19. *Ibid.;* Nissenson, *The Patroon's Domain*, 229.
20. Nissenson, *The Patroon's Domain*, 229.
21. NYHS, I: 525.
22. O'Callaghan, *History of New Netherland*, II: 178.
23. NYHS, I: 522–525; O'Callaghan, *History of New Netherland*, II: 184.
24. DCH, XIV: 187, 191, 192; NYHS, I: 522–525.

Chapter 20 Losing Ground

1. DCH, I: 262–270.
2. *Ibid.*, II: 156.
3. DCH, XIV: 85.
4. Winthrop Papers, V: 170, 171.
5. *Ibid.*, 175, 176, 185.
6. DCH, I: 199, 200, XIV: 80, 81.
7. New Haven Col. Rec., I: 508–511; NYHS, II: 5.

8. New Haven Col. Rec. I: 521.
9. *Ibid.*, 328, 356.
10. *Ibid.*, 521.
11. E. B. O'Callaghan, *History of New Netherland*, II: 56.
12. NNN, 346, 370; New Haven Col. Rec., I: 363, 364, 333, 413.
13. Winthrop Papers, V: 211.
14. DCH, XIV: 82.
15. *Ibid.*, 105, 106.
16. NYHS, I: 201, 202, 206.
17. DCH, XII: 52.
18. *Ibid.*, 50.
19. Winthrop Papers, V: 361.
20. *Ibid.*, 347, 348.
21. *Ibid.*, 355.
22. Plymouth Col. Rec., IX: 148; NYHS, I: 208, 209.
23. DCH, XIV: 124.
24. *Ibid.*, 126.
25. NYHS, I: 210.
26. *Ibid.*, 211–214.
27. *Ibid.*, 218–233.
28. DCH, I: 457–461.
29. *Ibid.*
30. NYHS, I: 236, 237.
31. Massachusetts Archives, II: 327 (hereafter cited as Mass. Arch.)
32. NYHS, I: 548, 549.
33. DCH, I: 457–461.
34. NYHS, I: 450, 451; DCH, I: 457–461.
35. Plymouth Col. Rec., II: 21.
36. NYHS, I: 344; Plymouth Col. Rec., IX: 212; NYHS, II: 7.
37. NYHS, I: 486, 541, II: 7.
38. DCH, XIV: 172, 173.
39. *Ibid.*, 185, 186.

Chapter 21 Total War

1. Charles H. Wilson, *Profit and War*, 18.
2. *Ibid.*, 60.
3. L. van Aitzema, *Saken van Staet en Oorlog*, III: 324.
4. Henri and Barbara van der Zee, *William and Mary*, 5, 6.
5. Jan Wagenaar, *Vaderlandsche Historie*, XII: 208–210.
6. *Ibid.*, 211.
7. Harleian Misc. IV, 209 (British Museum); J. E. Elias, *Het Voorspel van den Eersten Engelsche Oorlog*, II: 127; Thomas Mun, *England's Treasure by Fforaign Trade*, 72–75.

8. Michiel Adriaensz de Ruyter, *Journaal, 1664–1665*, LXII: 7.

9. P. J. Blok, *Geschiedenis van het Nederlandsche Volk*, IV: 15, 282.

10. Elias, *Voorspel*, II: 40–42.

11. *Ibid.*, 99.

12. Wagenaar, *Vaderlandsche Historie*, XII: 212, 213.

13. Mun, *England's Treasure by Fforaign Trade*, 78.

14. NYHS, I: 484.

15. *Ibid.*, 483, 487.

16. DCH, XIV: 197, 198.

17. A. C. Flick (ed), *History of the State of New York*, I: 308.

18. New Netherland Papers, 1217; E. B. O'Callaghan, *History of New Netherland*, II: 211–214.

19. Schuyler van Rensselaer, *History of the City of New York in the 17th Century*, I: 329.

20. DCH, XIV: 197, 198.

21. *Ibid.*, 201–203; Van Rensselaer, *History of New York*, I: 333–335.

22. RNA, I: 90–104.

23. DCH, XIV: 206; H. T. Colenbrander, *Koloniale Geschiedenis*, I: 71, 74.

Chapter 22 Turncoats

1. DCH, XIV: 179, 180.

2. Plymouth Col. Rec., X: 424–427.

3. DCH, XIV: 186.

4. Plymouth Col. Rec., X: 3; E. B. O'Callaghan, *History of New Netherland*, II: app. G, 571.

5. Plymouth Col. Rec., X: 12.

6. *Ibid.*, 5–9.

7. *Ibid.*, 13–22.

8. NYHS, I: 250–254.

9. *Ibid.*, 254–260.

10. *Ibid.*, 261–267.

11. *Ibid.*

12. Thurloe State Papers, I. 565 (British Museum).; New Haven Col. Rec., II: 37.

13. DCH, II: 151.

14. Stokes, IV: 139; O'Callaghan, *History of New Netherland*, II: 234; RNA, I: 91.

15. New Haven Col. Rec., II: 44.

16. DCH, XIV: 226–229.

17. *Ibid.*, 216.

18. NYHS, I: 551–553.

19. DCH, XIV: 233.

20. *Ibid.*, 233–236.

21. *Ibid.*

22. *Ibid.*, 241.

23. RNA, I: 145–147.

24. DCH, XIV: 246; Schuyler van Rensselaer, *History of the City of New York in the 17th Century*, I: 353.

25. DCH, XIV: 261–262.

26. *Ibid.*

27. RNA, I: 158.

28. DCH, XIV: 254–256.

29. *Ibid.*, 254–256, 267.

Chapter 23 Danger from Abroad

1. Jan Wagenaar, *Vaderlandsche Historie*, XII: 243.

2. J. E. Elias, *Het Voorspel van den Eersten Engelsche Oorlog*, II: 220.

3. *Ibid.*, 221.

4. DCH, XIV: 216.

5. Schuyler van Rensselaer, *History of the City of New York in the 17th Century*, I: 354–357; E. B. O'Callaghan, *History of New Netherland*, II: 259.

6. New Haven Col. Rec., II: 107, 108; O'Callaghan, *History of New Netherland*, II: 259–261.

7. RNA, I: 200, 201.

8. DCH, XIV: 267, 268.

9. *Ibid.*, 269–271.

10. *Ibid.*, 272, 273; RNA, I: 209–211.

11. O'Callaghan, *History of New Netherland*, II: 264, 265.

12. Wagenaar, *Vaderlandsche Historie*, XII: 365, 366.

13. William Smith Jr., *The History of the Province of New York*, I: 14; Elias, *Voorspel*, II: 212, 213.

14. DCH, XIV: 250, 251; RNA, I: 215, 216.

15. O'Callaghan, *History of New Netherland*, II: 265.

16. NYHS, II: 10–12.

17. RNA, I: 232.

18. *Ibid.*, 271; Van Rensselaer, *History of New York*, I: 365.

19. Stokes, IV: 154.

20. E. B. O'Callaghan, *Voyages of the Slavers* St. John *and* Arms of Amsterdam, *1659, 1663*, p. vii.

21. A. C. Flick (ed.), *History of the State of New York*, I: 340–342.

22. DCH, XIV: 304–305.

23. RNA, I: 354, 362, 363.

24. Stokes, IV: 97; NNN, 364.

25. J. G. van Dillen, *Van Rijkdom en Regenten*, 160, 161.

26. Thomas J. Wertenbaker, *The First Americans, 1606–1690*, 61, 62; Carl Bridenbaugh and Roberta Bridenbaugh, *No Peace Beyond the Line*, 224.

27. Charles H. Wilson, *Profit and War*, 45; Bridenbaugh and Bridenbaugh, *No Peace Beyond the Line*, 65–68.
28. O'Callaghan, *History of New Netherland*, II: 285.
29. Van Rensselaer, *History of New York*, 366.
30. New Haven Col. Rec., II: 131.
31. DCH, XIV: 312, 313; O'Callaghan, *History of New Netherland*, II: 280, 281.
32. DCH, II: 161.
33. *Ibid.*, XIV: 317.

Chapter 24 Exit Nueva Suecia

1. DCH, XII: 85.
2. *Ibid.*, XIV: 317.
3. Israel Acrelius, *A History of New Sweden*, 61.
4. DCH, XII: 21.
5. Acrelius, *A History of New Sweden*, 32–34.
6. Ibid.
7. Winthrop Papers, II: 160–179.
8. E. B. O'Callaghan, *History of New Netherland*, I: 374, 375.
9. DCH, XII: 58.
10. *Ibid.*, 36.
11. *Ibid.*, 37.
12. *Ibid.*
13. *Ibid.*, 58; NYHS, I: 593.
14. DCH, XII: 43, 594.
15. *Ibid.*, XIV: 133.
16. Amandus Johnson, *The Swedish Settlements on the Delaware*, I: 435.
17. *Ibid.*, I: 596–599.
18. Israel Acrelius, *A History of New Sweden*, 412; Stokes, IV, 123.
19. DCH, XIV: 172.
20. O'Callaghan, *History of New Netherland*, II: 274–276.
21. DCH, XII: 73.
22. Johnson, *The Swedish Settlements on the Delaware*, II: 694.
23. NYHS, I: 601.
24. *Ibid.*, 601–603; DCH, I: 605, 606.
25. DCH, XII: 76, 77, XIV: 390.
26. New Haven Col. Rec., II: 112; Johnson, *The Swedish Settlements on the Delaware*, II: 579.
27. NNN, 383–386; DCH, XII: 101–103; New Netherland Papers, 1216.
28. DCH, XII: 106.
29. *Ibid.*, 108.
30. NYHS, I: 578, 583; DCH, XII: 119.

Chapter 25 The Peach War

1. DCH, XII: 98, 99.
2. *Ibid.*, 101–103.
3. NNN, 386; DCH, XIV: 98; Stokes, IV, 155; NNN, 386.
4. DCH, XIII: 70.
5. *Ibid.*, 49, 50.
6. *Ibid.*, XII: 98.
7. *Ibid.*, XIII: 50.
8. Stokes, IV: 155; NNN, 386.
9. RNA, I: 365–367; New Netherland Papers, 1222.
10. A. W. Trelease, *Indian Affairs in Colonial New York in the 17th Century*, 141–143.
11. DCH, XIII: 50.
12. *Ibid.*, 51.
13. Schuyler van Rensselaer, *History of the City of New York in the 17th Century*, I: 353.
14. DCH, II: 400.
15. *Quarterly of the New York State Historical Association* 1: 100, etc.
16. New Netherland Papers, 1215.
17. *Ibid.*, 1214.
18. *Ibid.*, 1214, 1222; DCH, XIV: 342.
19. DCH, XIII: 55–57.
20. *Ibid.*, 58.
21. RNA, II: 17, 18, I: 19, 20; NYHS, I: 498.
22. RNA, II: 41.
23. DCH, XIV: 342.
24. DCH, XIV: 342, XIII: 70.
25. RNA, II: 109, 121.
26. Van Rensselaer, *History of New York*, I: 375, 376.

Chapter 26 Pastoral Problems

1. NNN, 399.
2. *Ibid.*, 126–128.
3. *Ibid.*, 50.
4. Eccl. Rec. N.Y., I: 434.
5. Schuyler van Rensselaer, *History of the City of New York in the 17th Century*, I: 200.
6. A. Eekhof, *Bastiaen Jansz Krol*, 23, 24; Van Rensselaer, *History of New York*, I:

200; A. Eekhof, *De Hervormde Kerk in Noord-Amerika*, I: 213, 214.

7. NNN, 130.

8. Gerald F. de Jong, "The Ziekentroosters" . . . , in N.Y. Hist. Soc. Quarterly, vol. 54, no. 4, 340, 341.

9. NNN, 129.

10. DCH, XIV: 69–73.

11. *Ibid.*

12. *Broad Advice*, 157.

13. Eccl. Rec. N.Y., I: 151.

14. Acta Classis Amstelodamensis XX, fol. 36, 84, 85 (Church-Archives, Amsterdam).

15. Eccl. Rec. N.Y., I: 233–237.

16. DCH, XIV: 14.

17. *Ibid.*, 116.

18. Bowier Mss., 653.

19. NNN, 172.

20. Eccl. Rec. N.Y., I: 438.

21. DCH, XIV: 174.

22. *Ibid.*, 173.

23. *Ibid.*, 241, 242.

24. Charles Weiss, *History of the French Protestant Refugees*, 292.

25. Eccl. Rec. N.Y., I: 335.

26. *Ibid*, I: 350.

27. Eekhof, *De Hervormde Kerk in Noord-Amerika*, I: 188–205; Ellis L. Raesly, *Portrait of New Netherland*, 227.

Chapter 27 Heretic Confusion

1. Stokes, IV: 152.

2. Eccl. Rec. N.Y., I: 335, 336.

3. RNA, I: 240–244.

4. *Ibid.*, 249.

5. Herbert I. Bloom, *The Economic Activities of the Jews of Amsterdam in the 17th and 18th Centuries*, 166, 167.

6. Eccl. Rec. N.Y., I: 335, 336.

7. DCH, XIV: 315; RNA, I: 291.

8. DCH, XIV: 341.

9. Stokes, IV: 956; RNA II: 63, 262; DCH, XIV: 351.

10. DCH, XIV: 351, XII: 96.

11. Bloom, *Economic Activities of the Jews of Amsterdam*, 169.

12. Samuel Oppenheim, *The Early History of the Jews in New York, 1654–1664*, 4, 53–57, 77–86.

13. Eccl. Rec. N.Y., I: 399, 400.

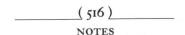

14. *Ibid.*
15. NNN, 400; Eccl. Rec. N.Y., I: 400.
16. NNN, 400; George Bishop, *New England Judged, Not by Man's, but the Spirit of the Lord,* 214.
17. Bishop, *New England Judged,* 214.
18. RNA, I: 20, 21.
19. DCH, XIV: 369, 370.
20. *Ibid.,* 403–405, 409.
21. Bishop, *New England Judged,* 47–62; RNA, II: 346.
22. DCH, XIV: 526.
23. Eccl. Rec. N.Y., I: 317, 318, 322.
24. DCH, XIV: 418, 421.
25. *Ibid.,* 351; A. Eekhof, *De Hervormde Kerk in Noord-Amerika,* II: 14–23.
26. NNN, 394; Stokes, IV: 181.
27. NNN, 402, 400; Eekhof, *De Hervormde Kerk in Noord-Amerika,* II: 14–23.
28. DCH, XIV: 418, 421.
29. NNN, 253.
30. *Ibid.,* 405.
31. NNN, 396, 397.
32. *Ibid.,* 401, 402.
33. DCH, XIV: 418, 421.

Chapter 28   *The Failure of Amsterdam*

1. NNN, 395.
2. *Ibid.,* 396.
3. DCH, XII: 113, 114, 120.
4. *Ibid.,* 125–129.
5. *Ibid.,* 128; NYHS, 2nd ser., I: iv, 106, 107, 614.
6. NYHS, 2nd ser., I: 619, 620.
7. E. B. O'Callaghan, *History of New Netherland,* II: 328–333.
8. DCH, XII: 131; NYHS, 2nd ser., I: iv, 106, 107; DCH, XII: 163.
9. NYHS, I: 643, 646.
10. DCH, II: 5–8.
11. *Ibid.*
12. *Ibid.,* XII: 163.
13. *Ibid.,* II: 5–8.
14. *Ibid.,* 17.
15. A. Eekhof, *De Hervormde Kerk in Noord-Amerika,* I: 259, 265.
16. DCH, II: 4, 17.
17. *Ibid.,* 21.
18. *Ibid.,* XII: 222, 225, 227, 231.
19. *Ibid.,* II: 49–51.

NOTES

20. *Ibid.*, XII: 222, 231.

21. *Ibid.*, 212, 213.

22. *Ibid.*, 219.

23. *Ibid.*, II: 69; O'Callaghan, *History of New Netherland,* II: 377.

24. DCH, XII: 249, 242.

25. *Ibid.*, 242.

26. *Ibid.*, 247, ii, 70.

27. *Ibid.*, 250–252; New Netherland Papers, 174–204.

28. DCH, II: 74, 75.

29. *Ibid.*

30. *Ibid.*, XII: 259, 260.

31. *Ibid.*, 254, 261, 262.

32. *Ibid.*, XIV: 80–83.

33. *Ibid.*

34. *Ibid.*, II: 88–98.

35. *Ibid.*, 116–119.

36. *Ibid.*, XII: 347.

37. *Ibid.*, II: 78, 112.

38. *Ibid.*, 110.

39. *Ibid.*, 115, 116, XII: 289.

Chapter 29 Clash with Boston

1. DCH, XII: 302.

2. New Netherland Papers, 1223; DCH, II: 163.

3. Schuyler van Rensselaer, *History of the City of New York in the 17th Century,* I: 383, 384.

4. Plymouth Col. Rec., X: 173–175; RNA, II: 180.

5. DCH, XIII: 107, 108.

6. *Ibid.*

7. Plymouth Col. Rec., X: 220, 221.

8. *Ibid.*, 443, 444; DCH, XIII: 126.

9. Winthrop Papers, XVI: 136; DCH: XIV: 446, 447.

10. Van Rensselaer, *History of New York,* I: 387.

11. DCH, XIII: 150, XIV: 465–467.

12. *Ibid.*, XIV: 465–467.

13. *Ibid.*, XIII: 163, 150, XIV: 469.

14. *Ibid.*, XII: 163.

15. *Ibid.* XIV: 481.

16. *Ibid.*, XIII: 146, 147, 163.

17. William Smith Jr., *The History of the Province of New York,* I: 18.

Chapter 30 The Esopus War

1. DCH, XIII: 146, 147, 163.
2. *Ibid.*, 80.
3. NNN, 398.
4. DCH, XIII: 77.
5. *Ibid.*, 79.
6. *Ibid.*, 80, 81.
7. *Ibid.*, 84–86.
8. *Ibid.*
9. *Ibid.*
10. E. B. O'Callaghan, *History of New Netherland*, II: 368.
11. *Ibid.*, 369.
12. A. J. F. van Laer, ed., *Correspondence of Jeremias van Rensselaer, 1651–1674*, 100, 156, 159, 160 (hereafter cited as Corr. JVR).
13. DCH. XIII: 109.
14. *Ibid.*, 112, 113.
15. O'Callaghan, *History of New Netherland*, II: 394, 395.
16. DCH, XIII: 116, 117.
17. *Ibid.*, 114, 115.
18. *Ibid.*, 119.
19. *Ibid.*, 124–126.
20. O'Callaghan, *History of New Netherland*, II: 400.
21. DCH, XIII: 124–126.
22. *Ibid.*, 131.
23. NYHS, II: 13, 14.
24. DCH, XIII: 135–142.
25. *Ibid.*, 142, 143.
26. *Ibid.*, 148.
27. *Ibid.*, 151, 152.
28. *Ibid.*, 152, 155.
29. *Ibid.*, 162, 163, 169, 178.
30. O'Callaghan, *History of New Netherland*, II: 411–412.
31. DCH, XIII: 181–184.
32. O'Callaghan, *History of New Netherland*, II: 397.

Chapter 31 Here to Stay

1. DCH, XIV: 444; Stokes, IV: 193.
2. F. C. Wieder, *De Stichting van New York in 1625*, 75–79; Stuyvesant Fish, "Peter Stuyvesant," 14, 31, 32.

3. NNN, 406, 407.

4. A. Eekhof, *De Hervormde Kerk in Noord-Amerika*, I: 156, 160; Schuyler van Rensselaer, *History of the City of New York in the 17th Century*, I: 469.

5. E. B. O'Callaghan, *History of New Netherland*, II: 350; Van Rensselaer, *History of New York*, I: 487, 273.

6. Van Rensselaer, *History of New York*, I: 487.

7. DCH, XIV: 518.

8. RNA, II: 329, 330.

9. Stokes, IV: 225, 226.

10. Corr. JVR, 157.

11. DCH, XIII: 279.

12. P. J. Blok, *Geschiedenis van het Nederlandsche Volk*, IV: 284–288; H. Brugmans, *Geschiedenis van Amsterdam "Bloeitijd," 1621–1696*, 8, 9; *Encyclopedic van Nederlandsche Oost-Indie*, 742, 3; *Quarterly of New York Historical Association* 44: 211.

13. NNN, 321.

14. DCH, XIV: 391, 392, 315, 322, 104, 105, 420, 235, 300, 301; RNA, III: 15.

15. DCH, XIV: 420.

16. *Ibid.*, 444.

17. Van Rensselaer, *History of New York*, II: 93, 94.

Chapter 32 *A Brave Place*

1. New Netherland Papers, 1791; DCH, II: 124; Stokes, IV: 163, 231.

2. DCH, XIV: 486, 489.

3. Stokes, IV: 125; NYHS, II: 1–3.

4. NNN, 421–423.

5. Stokes, IV: 192.

6. NNN, 423.

7. E. B. O'Callaghan, *History of New Netherland*, II: 544; DCH, XIV: 444.

8. DCH, XIV: 439.

9. *Ibid.*, 415.

10. RNA, III: 19, 74, 75, 78, 81, IV: 230; DCH, XIV: 415.

11. DCH, XIV: 431.

12. *Ibid.*

13. *Ibid.*, 427; New Netherland Papers, 1222(9).

14. DCH, XIV: 427.

15. RNA, II: 286, 287.

16. *Ibid.*, VII: 232–235.

17. *Ibid.*, I: 15–17; DCH, XIV: 135; RNA, III: 16.

18. DCH, XIV: 386, 428; RNA, I: 40, 41, III: 13, 17.

19. J. W. de Forest, *The De Forests of Avennes and of New Netherland*, I: 119.

20. RNA, I: 38, 39.

21. *Ibid.*, 300.

22. *Ibid.*, VII: 166, 167; Stokes, IV: 190.

23. RNA, I: 31, 33, VII: 215; Stokes, IV: 220.

24. RNA, I: 34, 35, VII: 191, 192, 207–209, 228.

25. B. Fernow, ed., *Minutes of the Orphan Masters Court of New Amsterdam, 1655–1663,* II: 110 (hereafter cited as MOC).

26. RNA, VII: 216, 217; MOC, II: 163.

27. DCH, XIII: 171, 172, XIV: 186.

28. MOC, II: 75–81; RNA, IV: 81.

29. RNA, I: 23, II: 169, I: 42; DCH, XIV: 143; RNA, VII: 230.

Chapter 33 Law and Disorder

1. RNA, VII: 208, I: 158.

2. DCH, XIV: 462, 463.

3. RNA, I: 51–65.

4. *Ibid.*, II: 201.

5. *Ibid.*, 407.

6. *Ibid.*, I: 192.

7. Corr. JVR, 37; New Netherland Papers.

8. RNA, II: 23.

9. E. B. O'Callaghan, *Calendar of Historical Manuscripts in the Office of the Secretary of State of New York,* I: 64 (hereafter cited as Cal. Hist. Mss.).

10. DCH, XIII: 144, 145.

11. RNA, I: 35, 36.

12. *Ibid.*, II: 263, 264.

13. *Ibid.*, 205.

14. *Ibid.* I: 172.

15. DCH, XIV: 249, 250.

16. RNA, I: 18, 19.

17. *Ibid.*, II: 37, 38, 304.

18. Cal. Hist. Mss., I: 203, 204.

19. *Ibid.*, 258, 259.

20. Stokes, IV: 218; RNA, IV: 231, III: 327.

21. Cal. Hist. Mss., I: 74.

22. *Ibid.*, 211, 213.

23. RNA, V: 93.

24. *Ibid.*, 95.

25. *Ibid.*, II: 289, 294–296, 355.

NOTES

1. Henry C. Murphy, *Anthology of New Netherland*, 32–35; Jacob Steendam, *De Distelvinck* (transl. by E. Raesly, Portrait of New Netherland), I: 173, 123.

2. Steendam, *De Distelvinck*, III: 108.

3. RNA, I: 276.

4. *Ibid.*, I: 261, II: 53.

5. *Ibid.*, II: 64–72.

6. David Pietersz de Vries, *Korte Historiael ende Journaels*, III: 272.

7. E. B. O'Callaghan, *Voyages of the Slavers* St. John *and* Arms of Amsterdam, *1659, 1663*, 140–182; Stokes, IV, 214.

8. Murphy, *Anthology*, 32–35.

9. DCH, II: 440.

10. *Ibid.*, I: 633.

11. Ibid., I: 413ff.

12. RNA, III: 90; Murphy, *Anthology*, 187–189.

13. RNA, III: 90.

14. Murphy, *Anthology*, 191–193.

15. A. Eekhof, *De Hervormde Kerk in Noord-Amerika*, I: 205–222; NNN, 389.

16. NNN, 408, 409.

17. Eccl. Rec. N.Y., I: 525.

18. E. L. Raesly, *Portrait of New Netherland*, 101.

19. Murphy, *Anthology*, 148, 149.

20. *Ibid.*, 136–144.

21. NNN, 409, 413.

22. Eekhof, *De Hervormde Kerk*, I: 225.

23. Winthrop Papers, XIII: 79.

24. NNN, 353.

25. *Ibid.*, 391, 392.

26. RNA, II: 219, 220.

27. NNN, 398, 399.

28. Eccl. Rec. N.Y., I: 401.

29. Schuyler Van Rensselaer, *History of the City of New York in the 17th Century*, I, 441–443

30. RNA, II: 348.

31. DCH, XIV: 169; RNA, III: 15, 16.

32. DCH, XIV: 419, 436, 437.

33. *Ibid.*, 443, 445.

34. *Ibid.*, VII: 224.

35. MOC, II: 76.

36. RNA, III: 344; Stokes, IV: 213.

37. E. L. Raesly, *Portrait of New Netherland*, 353.

NOTES

Chapter 35   Reconnaissance

1. DCH, III: 37–39.
2. *Ibid.*
3. E. B. O'Callaghan, *History of New Netherland,* II: 444, 445.
4. DCH, XIV: 429, 430, 469, 475.
5. *Ibid.,* 484, 486, 487, XII: 332.
6. *Ibid.,* XIV: 484.
7. Connecticut Historical Society Collections, XXIV: 6.
8. CSP Col., XIV: 495.
9. Schuyler van Rensselaer, *History of the City of New York in the 17th Century,* I: 400.
10. Earl of Clarendon, *Life and Continuation of the Same,* 21, 75–77; *Calendar of State Papers and Manuscripts Relating to the English Affairs,* XXXIII: 87 (hereafter cited as CSP Venetian).
11. CSP Venetian, XXXIII: 23, 24; Thomas J. Wertenbaker, *The First Americans, 1606–1690,* 1; P. L. Kaye, *English Colonial Administration under Lord Clarendon, 1660–1667,* 9; James Adams, *The Founding of New England,* 286.
12. CSP Col., XIV: 492-etc.; DCH, III: 30–36.
13. DCH, XIV: 486, 487, II: 125, 164.
14. *Ibid.,* XII: 350, XIV: 506.
15. *Ibid.,* III: 42, 43, XIV: 504.
16. *Ibid.,* XIV: 508.
17. Thomas Hutchinson, *The History of the Colony of Massachusetts Bay,* II: 104.
18. *Ibid.*
19. Lilian T. Mowrer, *The Indomitable John Scott,* 60–62; E. B. O'Callaghan, *History of New Netherland,* II: 497, 498.
20. Mowrer, *The Indomitable John Scott,* 70–82; DCH, XIV: 504, 506.
21. Conn. Col. Rec., I: 582, 583.
22. Winthrop Letters, VIII: 73.
23. DCH, II: 334.
24. Winthrop Letters, VIII: 73; Dingman Versteeg, *The New Netherland Register.*
25. NNN, 421–424.
26. NYHS, II: 21, 36.
27. *Ibid.,* 25–27.
28. Versteeg, *The New Netherland Register.*
29. DCH, XIV: 578.

Chapter 36 Annexation on Paper

1. Journal, cited in Robert C. Black, *The Younger John Winthrop*, 211; Dingman Versteeg, *The New Netherland Register*.
2. Black, *The Younger John Winthrop*, 114–115.
3. T. H. Lister, *Life and Administration of Edward, First Earl of Clarendon*, II: 50, III; 134, 135n.
4. John Beresford, *The Godfather of Downing Street*, 149; Winthrop Letters, 5th ser., IX: 34–35.
5. Lister, *Life of Clarendon*, II: 50.
6. DCH, II: 416–418.
7. John Beresford, *The Godfather of Downing Street*, 119, 120; Clarendon, *Life*, 52.
8. Clarendon, *Life*, 52.
9. *Ibid.*
10. Lister, *Life of Clarendon*, III: 229, 277.
11. Charles H. Wilson, *Profit and War*, 103.
12. Lister, *Life of Clarendon*, III: 135; N. Japikse, *De Verwikkelingen tussen de Republick en Engeland, 1660–1665*, app. V, pp ix, x.
13. Lister, *Life of Clarendon*, III: 170.
14. CSP Venetian, XXXIII: 33, 34.
15. Clarendon, *Life*, 336, 337.
16. CSP Venetian, XXXIII: 123, 131, 133, 137, 138.
17. *Ibid.*, 147, 148.
18. *Ibid.*, 161, 162; Lister, *Life of Clarendon*, III: 217.
19. CSP Venetian, XXXIII: 190; Jan Wagenaar, *Vaderlandsche Historie*, XIII: 45–49.
20. CSP Venetian, XXXIII: 19; Black, *The Younger John Winthrop*, 224.
21. CSP Col., 1661–1668, 87, 88.

Chapter 37 Twice Tricked

1. DCH, XIV: 515.
2. Conn. Hist. Soc. Coll., XXIV: 8, 9; DCH, XIV: 517.
3. DCH, XIV: 516, 517.
4. *Ibid.*, 518.
5. *Ibid.*, 520.
6. *Ibid.*, 525.
7. *Ibid.*, 526, 527.
8. E. B. O'Callaghan, *History of New Netherland*, II: 446, 447; Charles H. Levermore, *The Republic of New Haven*, 114–116.
9. DCH, XIII: 239.
10. *Ibid.*, XII: 416, 417.

11. *Ibid.*, 417.
12. O'Callaghan, *History of New Netherland*, II: 461, 462.
13. *Ibid.*, 464, 465.
14. DCH, II: 176.
15. Pieter Cornelisz Plockhoy, *Kort en klaer ontwerp . . .* ,
16. Henry C. Murphy, *Anthology of New Netherland*, 68, 69.
17. DCH, II: 200.
18. *Ibid.*
19. *Ibid.*, XII: 440–444; NYHS, 2nd ser. I: xiv, 443.
20. DCH, XII: 437, 438.
21. NYHS, 2nd ser., I: xiv, 423.

Chapter 38 War at Wiltwyck

1. Jerome Lallemant, *Relation . . . de la Compagnie de Jésus en la Nouvelle France, des années 1662 et 1663*, 1, 2.
2. *Ibid.*, 17, 18; Henry C. Murphy, *Anthology of New Netherland*, 175, 178; Corr. JVR, 325.
3. Corr. JVR, 307.
4. *Ibid.*, 325; E. B. O'Callaghan, *History of New Netherland*, II: 483.
5. Corr. JVR, 325; DCH, XIII: 224; O'Callaghan, *History of New Netherland*, II: 451, 452.
6. DCH, XIV: 487, XIII: 223.
7. *Ibid.*, XIII: 256, 257, 245.
8. A. Eekhof, *De Hervormde Kerk in Noord-Amerika*, I: 234–237; DCH, XIII: 373.
9. DCH, XIII: 245; Eekhof, *De Hervormde Kerk*, I: 234–237.
10. Murphy, *Anthology*, 136–138.
11. DCH, XIII: 245.
12. *Ibid.*, 256, 257.
13. *Ibid.*, 283.
14. *Ibid.*, 259, 260.
15. *Ibid.*, 283, 271.
16. *Ibid.*, 328, 330.
17. *Ibid.*
18. *Ibid.*, 335, 336.
19. *Ibid.*, 332, 340, 329.
20. *Ibid.*, 329.
21. *Ibid.*, 338.
22. O'Callaghan, *History of New Netherland*, II: 480.
23. *Ibid.*, 481.
24. *Ibid.*
25. DCH, XIII: 294, 295, 297.
26. *Ibid.*, 344.

27. *Ibid.*

28. *Ibid.*, 299.

29. *Ibid.*, 314.

30. *Ibid.*, 321.

31. *Ibid.*

32. *Ibid.*, 354.

Chapter 39 Desperate Diplomacy

1. DCH, XIV: 527.

2. *Ibid.*, XIII: 62–65.

3. *Ibid.*, 66.

4. *Ibid.*, 391.

5. Winthrop Letters, 5th ser. IX 48, 49.

6. *Ibid.*, 49; E. B. O'Callaghan, *History of New Netherland*, II: 456.

7. Winthrop Letters, 5th ser., IX 57, 58.

8. DCH, XIII: 294, 295.

9. John Josselyn, *An Account of Two Voyages to New England*, 195; NNN, 411, 412.

10. Josselyn, *Account of Two Voyages*, 161, 162; John Josselyn, *New England's Rarities Discovered* 137; Thomas J. Wertenbaker, *The First Americans, 1606–1690*, 292; Charles M. Andrews, *The Colonial Period in American History*, I: 514, 515.

11. DCH, II: 384; NYHS, I: 283, 284.

12. NYHS, I: 285.

13. *Ibid.*, 285, 286, 287; Plymouth Col Rec., V: 299–304.

14. NYHS, I: 288.

15. *Ibid.*, 289, 290; Plymouth Col. Rec., V: 304.

16. DCH, II: 384.

17. *Ibid.*, XIV: 533.

18. *Ibid.*, 532.

19. *Ibid.*

20. *Ibid.*

21. *Ibid.*, XIV: 535.

22. *Ibid.*, 536.

23. *Ibid.*

24. NNN, 432–445.

25. DCH, II: 484.

26. Robert C. Black, *The Younger John Winthrop*, 267.

27. DCH, XIV: 536–540.

28. RNA, IV: 325.

29. Stokes, IV: 230.

30. Schuyler van Rensselaer, *History of the City of New York in the 17th Century*, I: 505.

31. DCH, III: 488.

Chapter 40 President Scott

1. T. H. Lister, *The Life and Administration of Edward, First Earl of Clarendon,* III: 259.
2. *Ibid.*
3. DCH, III: 46.
4. *Ibid.*
5. E. B. O'Callaghan, *History of New Netherland,* II: 498, n.3.
6. DCH, III: 47, 48.
7. O'Callaghan, *History of New Netherland,* II: 499, n. 1.
8. Lilian Mowrer, *The Indomitable John Scott,* 128–130.
9. *Ibid.;* DCH, II: 393.
10. *Ibid.*
11. O'Callaghan, *History of New Netherland,* II: 500, 501.
12. Schuyler van Rensselaer, *History of the City of New York in the 17th Century,* I: 507.
13. RNA, V: 18–24; 28–33.
14. O'Callaghan, *History of New Netherland,* II: 503.
15. DCH, II: 232–234, 506, XIV: 546, 547.
16. *Ibid.,* XIV: 544, 545.
17. CSP Col., 226, 227.
18. DCH, II: 407; Conn. Col. Rec., I: 416.
19. Lilian Mowrer, *The Indomitable John Scott,* 128–130.
20. O'Callaghan, *History of New Netherland,* II: 552, 553.
21. Conn. Col. Rec., I: 430.

Chapter 41 Mad for War

1. DCH, II: 216.
2. H. T. Colenbrander, *Bescheiden uit vreemde Archieven omtrent de groote Nederlandsche Zee-oorlogen, 1652, 1676,* II: 125, 126.
3. T. H. Lister, *Life and Administration of Edward, First Earl of Clarendon,* III: 276.
4. Schuyler van Rensselaer, *History of the City of New York in the 17th Century,* I: 494.
5. CSP Venetian, XXXIII: 283.
6. Lister, *Life of Clarendon,* III: 277, 278.
7. Samuel Pepys, *The Diary of Samuel Pepys,* IV: 31, 49, 52.
8. *Ibid.,* 18, 19, 31.
9. *Ibid.,* 95, 98.
10. Lister, *Life of Clarendon,* II: 258, 259; Clarendon, *Life and Continuation of the Same,* 13–15.

11. CSP Venetian, XXXIII: 288; Lister, *Life of Clarendon*, II: 288, 289.

12. Pepys, *Diary*, IV: 93; Lister, *Life of Clarendon*, III: 299–300.

13. Lister, *Life of Clarendon*, III: 287, 305.

14. Pepys, *Diary*, IV: 114; Charles H. Wilson, *Profit and War*, 124.

15. Lister, *Life of Clarendon*, II: 254, 255; Pepys, *Diary*, IV: 123; CSP Venetian, XXXIV: 11, 12, 18.

16. DCH, XIV: 549–550.

17. *Ibid.*, XIII: 363.

18. *Ibid.*, II: 232, 233.

19. RNA, V: 33, 34, 45.

20. Corr. JVR, 353; DCH, II: 229, XIV: 549–550.

21. DCH, XIV: 549–550.

22. *Ibid.*, II: 228.

23. *Ibid.*, XIII: 372.

24. *Ibid.*, 375–377.

25. DCH, XIV: 549.

26. *Ibid.*, II: 407, XIV: 551–554.

27. *Ibid.*, XIV: 551, 552.

Chapter 42   The Duke's Invasion

1. Earl of Clarendon, Clarendon Papers, 1660–1667, 19–22 (hereafter cited as Clarendon Papers); John Josselyn, *An Account of Two Voyages to New England*, 153.

2. NYHS, II: 1–3; Clarendon Papers, 38, 43, 19.

3. DCH, III: 47.

4. Clarendon Papers, 57, 32; CSP Col., 603, 622, 647.

5. William Smith Jr., *The History of the Province of New York*, I: 22.

6. "Duke of York's Instructions," 1662–1666, Public Record Office, London. Adm. 2: 1733; DCH, III: 51–65.

7. Clarendon Papers, 21, 22.

8. Robert C. Black, *The Younger John Winthrop*, 271.

9. *Dictionary of American Biography*, XIII: 515, 516.

10. DCH, II: 243.

11. H. T. Colenbrander, *Bescheiden uit vreemde Archieven omtrent de groote Nederlandsche Zee-oorlogen, 1652, 1676*, I: 130; Comte d'Estrades, *Lettres, Mémoires et Négociations*, III; 459, 460.

12. NNN, 461.

13. DCH, III: 51–63.

14. *Ibid.*, 65, 66.

15. Smith, *History of the Province of New York*, I: 23, 24.

16. Winthrop Papers, VII: 189.

17. Stokes, IV: 838.

18. *Ibid.*, 237; RNA, V: 88.

19. DCH, II: 447.

20. RNA, V: 89; E. B. O'Callaghan, *History of New Netherland*, II: 518.

21. DCH, XIV: 551, 554, II: 505.

22. *Ibid.*, XIII: 390, 391.

23. Corr. JVR, 358.

24. DCH, XIII: 389.

25. Stokes, IV: 238.

26. *Ibid.*

27. DCH, XIII, 390.

28. Stokes, IV, 242.

29. Black, *The Younger John Winthrop*, 274; O'Callaghan, *History of New Netherland*, II: 523; Daniel Denton, *A Brief Description of New York*, 40.

Chapter 43 The Fall of the City

1. RNA, V: 104–106: DCH, II: 495.

2. RNA, V: 105, 106.

3. DCH, II: 376.

4. *Ibid.*, XIII: 392.

5. E. B. O'Callaghan, *History of New Netherland*, II: 521.

6. William Smith Jr., *History of the Province of New York*, I: 24, 25.

7. DCH, II: 447.

8. *Ibid.*, 504, 474.

9. *Ibid.*, 410–415.

10. *Ibid.*, XIV: 555, II: 469.

11. Smith, *History of the Province of New York*, I: 26–29.

12. DCH, II: 410–415.

13. RNA, V: 107, DCH, II: 508.

14. DCH, II: 476.

15. Winthrop Papers, 4th ser., VI: 295–297.

16. DCH, II: 476.

17. *Ibid.*

18. *Ibid.*, 508.

19. *Ibid.*, 476.

20. *Ibid.*

21. O'Callaghan, *History of New Netherland*, II: 527–529.

22. DCH, II: 476.

23. *Ibid.*, X: 251, 252.

24. *Ibid.*, XIII: 392, 394.

25. Winthrop Letters, 5th ser., VIII: 92.

26. RNA. V: 114–116.

Chapter 44 The Birth of New York

1. DCH, II: 276; R. B. Nye and J. E. Morpurgo, *The Birth of the USA*, 79; NYHS, 2nd ser., I: iv, 112, 113.
2. DCH, II: 253.
3. Samuel Pepys, *Diary of Samuel Pepys*, IV: 254; Schuyler van Rensselaer, *History of the City of New York in the 17th Century*, II: 3.
4. DCH, III: 67, 68.
5. *Ibid.*, XII: 457, 458, III: 68, 69.
6. *Ibid.*, III: 69.
7. Van Rensselaer, *History of New York*, II: 13; RNA, V: 160, 161.
8. T. H. Lister, *Life and Administration of Edward, First Earl of Clarendon*, III: 346, 347; DCH, II: 276; CSP Venetian, XXXIV: 49; Lister, *Life of Clarendon*, III: 348.
9. Lister, *Life of Clarendon*, III: 350, 351.
10. DCH, II: 278.
11. CSP Venetian, XXXIV: 51, 52, 56.
12. Pepys, *Diary*, IV: 360–363.
13. CSP Venetian, XXXIV: 48, 44.
14. *Ibid.*, 61, 45; Pepys, *Diary*, IV: 237.
15. Pepys, *Diary*, IV: 215–221; H. T. Colenbrander, *Bescheiden uit vreemde Archieven omtrent de groote Nederlandsche Zee-oorlog*, I: 138.
16. DCH, II: 302.
17. *Ibid.*, 324.
18. Michiel Adriaensz de Ruyter, *Journaal, 1664–1665*, 21; Lister, *Life of Clarendon*, III: 352–356.
19. Colenbrander, *Bescheiden uit vreemde Archieven omtrent de groote Nederlandsche Zee-oorlog*, I: 155.
20. CSP Domestic, 214.

Chapter 45 Return of a Patriot

1. RNA, V: 208, 160.
2. *Ibid.*, 143.
3. *Ibid.*, 144.
4. *Ibid.*, 145.
5. *Ibid.*, 214; Schuyler van Rensselaer, *History of the City of New York in the 17th Century*, II: 33.
6. RNA, V: 248, 249; William R. Shepherd, *The Story of New Amsterdam*, 191.
7. DCH, II: 361.
8. NNN, 458–466.
9. DCH, II: 490–503.
10. *Ibid.*, 472.

11. *Ibid.*, 447.

12. NYHS, 2nd ser., I: iv, 112, 113.

13. Henri and Barbara van der Zee, *William and Mary*, 43.

14. Winthrop Letters, 5th ser., VIII: 96, 97.

15. NYHS, XXV: 139.

16. Henry C. Murphy, *Anthology of New Netherland*, 160, 161.

Epilogue

1. New Netherland Papers, Moore Collection.

2. Cornelis Evertsen de Jonge, *De Zeeuwsche Expeditie naar de West, 1672–1674*, 39, 40.

3. DCH, III: 62.

4. Stokes, IV: 288.

5. Evertsen, 42.

6. Stokes, IV: 288.

7. Evertsen, 42.

8. *Ibid.*, 166.

9. *Ibid.*, 43, 44.

10. Plymouth Col. Rec., V: 386–389; Winthrop Letters, 5th ser., VIII: 150.

11. Evertsen, 44, 45.

12. *Ibid.*, 44, 109.

13. *Ibid.*, 144.

14. Winthrop Letters, 5th ser., VIII: 150; DCH, II: 660, 661.

15. Evertsen, 149.

16. Winthrop Letters, 5th ser., VIII: 157.

17. Daniel Denton, *A Brief Description of New York*, 40, 41; John Josselyn, *An Account of Two Voyages to New England*, 153, 154.

18. Stokes, IV: 300.

19. Ronald Cohen, "The New England Colonies and the Dutch Recapture of New York, 1673–1674," New York Hist. Soc. Quarterly 16, no. 1, 69–73.

20. Mass. Arch. LXI: 15; Conn. Col. Rec., II: 20.

21. Mass. Arch. LXI: 31, 32, 186.

22. Schuyler van Rensselaer, *History of the City of New York in the 17th Century*, II: 111, 116; John R. Brodhead, *History of the State of New York*, II: 242, 243

23. New Netherland Papers, Moore Collection; Evertsen, 168.

24. Stokes, IV: 293.

25. DCH, II: 529.

26. *Ibid.*, 530, 534.

27. DCH, II: 544

29. Van Rensselaer, *History of New York*, II: 123, 124.

30. Corr. JVR, 464.

31. DCH, II: 548; Evertsen, 200.

32. Van Rensselaer, *History of New York*, II: 125.

BIBLIOGRAPHY

Abbott, John, S. C. *Peter Stuyvesant, the Last Dutch Governor of New Amsterdam.* New York: 1873.

Acrelius, Israel. *A History of New Sweden, or the Swedes on the Delaware.* Stockholm: 1759.

Adams, James T. *The Founding of New England.* Boston: 1921.

Aitzema, L. van. *Saken van Staet en Oorlog.* The Hague: 1669.

Algemeen Handelsblad. Tercentenary Supplement commemorating the three hundredth anniversary of the City of New York. Amsterdam: 1926.

American Antiquarian Society. *Transactions and Collections of the American Antiquarian Society,* Vol. IV. Boston: 1860.

American Historical Magazine. New York: 1859.

American Historical Review. New York: 1906–1974.

Andrews, Charles M. *Colonial Self-Government 1625–1689.* The American Nation, Vol. V. New York: 1904.

———— *The Colonial Period in American History.* 4 vols. New Haven: 1934–1938.

Andrews, W. L. *New Amsterdam, New Orange, New York.* New York: 1897.

Arnold, Samuel Greene. *History of the State of Rhode Island,* Vol. I. Providence: 1899.

Asher, G. M. *Dutch Books and Pamphlets Relating to New Netherland and to the Dutch West-India Company.* Amsterdam: 1854.

Ashley, M. *Charles II: The Man and the Statesman.* London: 1971.

———— *England in the Seventeenth Century.* London: 1968.

Associated Authors. *Algemene Geschiedenis der Nederlanden,* Vol. VI. Utrecht: 1953.

Bachman, Van Cleaf. *Peltries or Plantations: The Economic Policies of the*

    Dutch West India Company in New Netherland, 1623–1639. Baltimore: 1966.

Bailyn, Bernard. *The New England Merchants in the Seventeenth Century.* Cambridge, Mass.: 1955.

Balen, W. J. van. *Holland aan de Hudson, een verhaal van Nieuw Nederland.* Amsterdam: 1943.

Barbour, Violet. *Capitalism in Amsterdam in the 17th Century.* Ann Arbor: University of Michigan Press, 1963.

Baylies, Francis. *An Historical Memoir of the Colony of New Plymouth.* 2 vols. Boston: 1830.

Beer, George L. *The Origins of the British Colonial System, 1578–1668.* New York: 1908.

Belloc, Hilaire. *James II.* London: 1928.

Bense, J. F. *Anglo-Dutch Relations.* The Hague: 1925.

Beresford, John. *The Godfather of Downing Street.* London: 1925.

Bilderdijk, W. *Geschiedenis des Vaderlands,* Vols. IX and X. Amsterdam: 1836.

Bischoffshausen, Sigismund von. *Die Politik des Protectors Oliver Cromwell, in der Auffassung und Thätigkeit seines Ministers des Staatssecretärs John Thurloe.* Innsbruck: 1899.

Bishop, George. *New England Judged, Not by Man's, but the Spirit of the Lord.* London: 1703.

Black, Robert C. *The Younger John Winthrop.* New York: 1966.

Blok, P. J. *Geschiedenis van het Nederlandsche Volk,* Vols. IV and V. Groningen: 1899.

Bloom, Herbert I. *The Economic Activities of the Jews of Amsterdam in the 17th and 18th Centuries.* London: 1969.

Bolton, Herbert E, and Marshall, Thomas M. *The Colonization of North America, 1492–1783.* New York: 1920.

Bouton, Nathaniel. *Documents and Records Relating to the Province of New Hampshire, 1623–1686,* Vol. I. Concord: 1867.

Bowen, Clarence W. *Boundary Disputes of Connecticut.* Boston: 1882.

Boxer, C. R. *The Dutch Seaborne Empire, 1600–1800.* 2nd ed. London: 1966.

——— *The Portuguese Seaborne Empire, 1415–1825.* London: 1969.

Bradford, William. *History of Plimoth Plantation.* Boston: 1898.

Brakel, S. van. *De Hollandsche Handelscompagnieen der Zeventiende Eeuw.* The Hague: 1908.

Brakell, H. de Vaynes van. "Vrijmoedige gedachten omtrent de Nederlandsche Zeemagt in de West-Indien," in *Verhandelingen Zeewezen.* 1957.

Breeden Raedt Aende Vereenichde Nederlandsche Provincien. Antwerp: 1649.

Bridenbaugh, Carl, and Bridenbaugh, Roberta. *No Peace Beyond the Line: The English in the Caribbean, 1624–1690.* New York: 1972.

Brodhead, John Romeyn. *History of the State of New York,* Vols. I and II. New York: 1853, 1871.

———. and O'Callaghan, E. B., eds. *Documents Relative to the Colonial History of the State of New York,* Vols. I–II and IX–XIV. Albany: 1856–1858.

Bromley, J. S., and Kossmann, E. H. *Britain and the Netherlands.* 3 vols. London: 1960, 1964, 1968.

Brouwer, H. *The Foundation of New York.* Amsterdam: 1945.

Brown, Alexander. *Genesis of the United States.* Boston: 1890.

Bruce, Philip A. *Economic History of Virginia in the Seventeenth Century.* 2 vols. New York/London: 1896.

———. *Social Life of Virginia in the Seventeenth Century.* Richmond, Va.: 1907.

Brugmans, H. *Geschiedenis van Amsterdams "Bloeitijd," 1621–1696,* Vol. III. 2nd ed. Utrecht: 1973.

Bryant, William C., and Gay, Sydney H. *A Popular History of the United States,* Vols. I and II. London: 1878.

Calendar of State Papers and Manuscripts Relating to the English Affairs, existing in the Archives and Collections of Venice and in other Libraries of North Italy, Vols. XXXIII and XXXIV. London: 1933.

Calendar of State Papers—Colonial Series, 1574–1660. Preserved in the State Papers Department of the Public Record Office. London: 1860.

Castell, William. *A Short Discoverie of the Coasts and Continents of America.* London: 1644.

Cheyney, Edwards P. *European Background of American History, 1300–1600.* The American Nation, Vol. I. New York: 1904.

Clarendon, Earl of. *Clarendon Papers, 1660–1667.* New York Historical Society Collection, 1869.

———. *Life and Continuation of the Same,* Vols. I and II. Oxford: 1760.

Clarke, Rev. J. S., ed. *James II: Memoirs.* London: 1816.

Cohen, Ronald D. "The Hartford Treaty of 1650." *New York Historical Society Quarterly* 53, no. 4 (1969).

———. "The New England Colonies and the Dutch Recapture of New York, 1673–1674." *New York Historical Society Quarterly* 16, no. 1 (1972).

Colenbrander, H. T. *Bescheiden uit vreemde Archieven omtrent de groote Nederlandsche Zee-oorlogen, 1652, 1676.* 2 vols. The Hague: 1919.

———. *Koloniale Geschiedenis.* 3 vols. The Hague: 1925.

Colman Hall, Clayton. *Narratives of Early Maryland.* New York: 1910.

Condon, Thomas J. *New York Beginnings: The Commercial Origins of New Netherland.* New York: 1968.

Connecticut Historical Society Collection, Hartford, 1860 etc.

Corwin, E. T., ed. *Ecclesiastical Records, State of New York, 1621–1800.* 6 vols. Albany, N.Y.: 1901–1905.

———. *Manual of the Reformed Church in America.* New York: 1902.

Court, Pieter de la. *Interest van Holland ofte Gronden van Hollands Welvaren.* Amsterdam: 1662.

De Forest, J. W. *The De Forests of Avennes and of New Netherland.* 2 vols. New Haven, Conn.: 1900.

Denton, Daniel. *A Brief Description of New York, Formerly Called New Netherlands.* Cleveland: 1902.

Dictionary of American Biography. 22 vols. London/New York: 1928–1940.

Dillen, J. G. van. *Van Rijkdom en Regenten.* The Hague: 1970.

Dilliard, M. E. *An Album of New Netherland.* New York: 1963.

Dunn, Richard S. *Puritans and Yankees: The Winthrop Dynasty of New England, 1630–1717.* Princeton, N.J.: Princeton University Press, 1962.

Earle, A. M. *Two Centuries of Costume in America, 1620–1820.* 2 vols. New York: 1903.

Edmundson, Rev. George. *Anglo-Dutch Rivalry during the First Half of the Seventeenth Century.* Oxford: 1911.

Eekhof, A. *Bastiaen Jansz Krol.* Leiden: 1910.

——. *De Hervormde Kerk in Noord-Amerika.* 2 vols. The Hague: 1913.

——. *Jonas Michaëlius.* Leiden: 1926.

Eerdmans, Martha. *Peter Stuyvesant: An Historical Documentation.* Grand Rapids, Michigan: 1957.

Elias, J. E. *Het Voorspel van den Eersten Engelsche Oorlog.* 2 vols. The Hague: 1920.

——. *Schetsen uit de geschiedenis van ons zeewezen, 1568–1654,* Vol. I. The Hague: 1916.

Elting, I. *Dutch Village Communities on the Hudson River.* Baltimore: 1886.

Encyclopedie van Nederlandsch Oost-Indie. 8 vols. The Hague: 1917–1938.

Estrades, Comte d'. *Lettres, Mémoires et Négociations de Monsieur le Comte d'Estrades,* Vol. III. London: 1748.

Evelyn, John. *The Diary of John Evelyn.* London: Everyman's Library, 1973.

Evertsen, Cornelis de Jonge. *De Zeeuwsche Expeditie naar de West, 1672–1674.* Linschoten Vereniging, Vol. XXX. The Hague: 1928.

Farmer, D. L. *Britain and the Stuarts.* London: 1965.

Farrand, Livingston. *Basis of American History, 1500–1900.* The American Nation, Vol. II. New York: 1904.

Fernow, Berthold, ed. *Minutes of the Orphan Masters Court of New Amsterdam, 1655–1663.* New York: 1907.

——. *The Records of New Amsterdam.* 7 vols. New York: 1907.

Fish, Stuyvesant. "Peter Stuyvesant." Address delivered at the annual meeting of the Order of Colonial Lords of the Manor in America. Baltimore, 1930.

——. *1600–1914.* Privately printed. New York: 1942.

Fiske, John. *The Dutch and Quaker Colonies in America.* 2 vols. London: 1899.

Flick, Alexander C., ed. *History of the State of New York.* 10 vols. New York: Columbia University Press, 1933.

Fox, Dixon Ryan. *Yankees and Yorkers.* New York: 1940.

Freyre, Gilberto. *The Masters and the Slaves: A Study in the Development of Brazilian Civilization.* New York: 1956.

Gardyner, George. *A Description of the New World, or America, Islands and Continent.* London: 1651.

Gedenkboek: Curaçao, 1634–1934. Amsterdam: 1934.

Gerard, James W. *The Old Stadt Huys of New Amsterdam.* New York: 1875.

Geyl, Pieter. *History of the Low Countries,* Vols. III and IV. London: 1964.

——. *The Netherlands in the 17th Century,* Vol. II. London: 1964.

Goodwin, Maud Wilder. *Dutch and English on the Hudson*. London: 1919.

Gorges, Sir Ferdinando. "A Brief Narration" in *America Painted to the Life* (*1659*). Massachusetts Historical Society Collections, 1837.

Graaf, Nicolaus de. *Reysen van Nicolaus de Graaf na Asia, Africa, America en Europa*. Hoorn: 1701.

Grant, Andrews M. *History of Brazil*. London: 1809.

Griffis, W. Elliot. *The Story of New Netherland: The Dutch in America*. New York: 1909.

Groce, George C., and Wallace, David H. *The New York Historical Society's Dictionary of Artists in America, 1564–1860*. New Haven, Conn.: 1957.

Haan, J. G. de and van Winter, P. J. *Nederlanders over de zeëen: 350 Jaar Nederlansche Koloniale Geschiedenis*. Utrecht: 1940.

Hakluyt, Richard. *A Discourse Concerning Western Plantations*. Maine Historical Society Collections, Vol. II.

Haley, K. H. D. *The Dutch in the Seventeenth Century*. London: 1972.

Harder, L., and Harder, M. *Plockhoy from Zurickzee*. Newton N.J.: 1952.

Hart, Simon. *The Prehistory of the New Netherland Company*. Amsterdam: City of Amsterdam Press, 1959.

Hershkowitz, M. J. "The Troublesome Turk: An Illustration of Judicial Process in New Amsterdam." *Quarterly of New York History* 46, no. 4 (1965).

Hill, Christopher. *The Century of Revolution, 1603–1714*. London: 1961.

————. *God's Englishman: Oliver Cromwell and the English Revolution*. London: Pelican Biographies, 1972.

Hinte, J. van. *Geschiedkundige atlas van Nederland*. The Hague: 1934.

Historische Genootschap. *Bijdragen en mededelingen van Historische Genootschap*, Vols. III and XXI. Utrecht: 1880, 1900.

Hoadley, Charles J., ed. *Records of the Colony and Plantation of New Haven*. 2 vols. Hartford, Conn.: 1857, 1858.

Hoboken, W. J. van. "Een troepentransport naar Brazilië in 1647." *Tijdschrift voor Geschiedenis* (1949).

Hoefman, J. W. *Oudste Nederlandse Nederzettingen*. Amsterdam: 1914.

Hoevenberg, A. R. van. "The Stuyvesants in the Netherlands." *New York Historical Society Quarterly Bulletin* 10, no. 1 (1926).

Hubbard, Rev. William. *General History of New England*. Massachusetts Historical Society Collections. 2nd Series, Vols. V and VI (1815).

Huizinga, J. H. *Dutch Civilisation in the 17th Century*. London: 1968.

Hutchinson, Thomas. *The History of the Colony of Massachusetts Bay*. 2 vols. London: 1760.

Irving, Washington. *A History of New York by Diedrich Knickerbocker*. New York: 1880.

Jameson, J. Franklin, ed. *Narratives of New Netherland, 1609–1664*. New York: 1909. Containing:

Meeteren, E. van. *On Hudson's Voyage*. 1610.

Juet, Robert. *The Third Voyage of Master H. Hudson*. 1610.

Laet, Johannes de. *New World*. 1625, 1630, 1633, 1640.

Wassenaer, Nicolaes van. *Historisch Verhael*. 1624–1630.

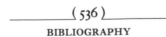

De Rasières, Isaack. *Letter to Samuel Blommaert.* 1628.

Nicaelius, J. *Letter of Rev. J. Nicaelius.* 1628.

Narrative of a Journey into Mohawk and Oneida Country. 1634–1635.

Megapolensis, Rev. Johannes. *Short Account of the Mohawk Indians.* 1644.

Vries, David Pieterz de. *Korte Historiael ende Journaels Aenteyckeninge.* 1655.

Jogues, Father Isaac. *Letter and Narrative of Father Isaac Jogues.* 1643, 1645.

———. *Novum Belgium.* 1646.

Journal of New Netherland. 1647.

Representation of New Netherland. 1650.

Tienhoven, Cornelis van. *Answer to the Representation.* 1650.

Bogaert, Johannes. *Letter of Johannes Bogaert to Hans Bontemantel.* 1655.

Dutch Ministers. *Letters of Dutch Ministers to the Classis of Amsterdam.* 1655–1664.

Description of the Towne of Mannadens. 1661.

Ruyven, Cornelis van. *The Journal of Cornelis van Ruyven.* 1663.

Town Council of New Amsterdam. *Letter of Town Council.* 1664.

Stuyvesant, Peter. *Report on the Surrender of New Netherland.* 1665.

Japikse, N. *De Verwikkelingen tussen de Republiek en Engeland, 1660–1665.* Leiden: 1900.

Jessurun, J. S. C. *Kiliaen van Rensselaer, 1623–1636.* The Hague: 1917.

Johnson, Amandus. *The Swedish Settlements on the Delaware.* 2 vols. New York: 1911.

Jong, Gerald F. de. "Dominie Joh. Megapolensis, Minister to New Netherland." *New York Historical Society Quarterly* 52, no. 1 (1968).

———. "The Ziekentroosters or Comforters of the Sick in New Netherland." *New York Historical Society Quarterly* 54, no. 4 (1970).

Jonge, J. C. de. *Geschiedenis van het Nederlandsche Zeewezen,* Vol. II, parts 1 and 2. Haarlem: 1835.

Josselyn, John. *An Account of Two Voyages to New England.* London: 1674.

———. *New England's Rarities Discovered.* American Antiquarian Society: 1860.

Juet, Robert. *Henry Hudson's Reize.* Linschoten Vereninging, Vol. XIX. The Hague: 1921.

Kaye, P. L. *English Colonial Administration under Lord Clarendon, 1660–1667.* Baltimore: 1905.

Kemperink, J. H. P. "Pieter Stuyvesant. Waar en wanneer werd hij geboren?" *De Navorscher, Nederlands Archief voor Genealogie en Heraldiek* 98, no. 3 (1959).

Kennet, White. *History of England: Charles I–William III.* London: 1706.

Kenyon, J. P. *The Stuarts.* London: 1972.

Kessler, Henry H., and Rachlis, Eugene. *Peter Stuyvesant and His New York.* New York: 1959.

Knuttel, W. P. C. *Catalogus van de pamflettenverzameling, berustende in de Koninklijke Bibliotheek.* 9 vols. The Hague: 1889–1920.

Kort Verhael van Nieuw-Nederlants Gelegentheit, Deughden, Natuerlycke Voorrechten en byzondere bequamheidt ter Bevolkingh. 1662.

Kupp, Jan. "Aspects of New York–Dutch Trade under the English." *New York Historical Society Quarterly* 58, no. 2 (1974).

Laer, A. J. F. van, ed. *Correspondence of Jeremias van Rensselaer 1651–1674*. New York: 1932.

———. *Van Rensselaer Bowier Manuscripts, Being the Letters of Kiliaen van Rensselaer, 1630–1643*. Albany: 1908.

Laet, J. de. *Iaerlyck Verhael van de Verrichtinghen der Geoctroyeerde W.I.C. in dertien boeken*. Linschoten Vereniging, 5 vols. The Hague: 1931–1937.

Lallemant, Jerome. *Relation de ce qui c'est passé de plus remarquable aux missions des pères de la Compagnie de Jésus en la Nouvelle France, des années 1662 et 1663*. Paris: 1664.

Lamb, Martha J., and Harrison, Constance C. *History of the City of New York*. 6 vols. New York: 1896.

Lambrechtsen van Ritthem, N. C. *Korte beschrijving van de ontdekking en der verdere voorgevallen van Nieuw-Nederland*. Middleburg: 1818.

Levermore, Charles H. *The Republic of New Haven*. Baltimore: 1886.

Ligtenberg, Catherina. *Willem Usselinx*. Utrecht: 1914.

Lionello and Suriano. *Brieven van Lionello and Suriano uit Den Haag in de jaren 1616–1618*. Werken van Historische Genootschap, Nieuwe Serie, no. 37. Utrecht: 1883.

Lister, T. H. *Life and Administration of Edward, First Earl of Clarendon*. 3 vols. London: 1838.

McManus, Edgar J. *A History of Negro Slavery in New York*. Syracuse, N.Y.: 1966.

Massachusetts Archives. State House, Boston.

May, Jan Cornelisz. *De reis van Jan Cornelisz May naar de IJszee en de Amerikaanse kust, 1611, 1612*. Linschoten Vereniging, Vol. I. The Hague: 1909.

Menkman, W. R. *De West-Indische Compagnie*. Amsterdam: 1947.

Morison, Samuel E. *Builders of the Bay Colony*. Rev. ed. London: 1936.

———. *The Puritan Pronaos*. New York: 1936.

Morton, T. *New English Canaan*. London: 1632.

Mountague, William. *The Delights of Holland*. London: 1696.

Mowrer, Lilian T. *The Indomitable John Scott, Citizen of Long Island, 1632–1704*. New York: 1960.

Muir, Ramsay. *A Short History of the British Commonwealth*, Vol. I. London: 1922.

Muller, Samuel. *Mare Clausum (bijdrage tot de geschiedenis der rivaliteit van Engeland en Nederland in de 17ᵉ eeuw)*. Amsterdam: 1872.

Mun, Thomas. *England's Treasure by Fforaign Trade*. London: 1664.

Murphy, Henry C. *Anthology of New Netherland, or Translations from the Early Poets of New York*. New York: 1865.

———. *Henry Hudson in Holland*. The Hague: 1909.

Myers, Albert C., ed. *Narratives of Early Pennsylvania, West New Jersey and Delaware, 1630–1707*. New York: 1912.

Netscher, P. M. *Les Hollandais au Brésil*. The Hague: 1853.

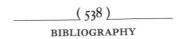

BIBLIOGRAPHY

New Netherland Papers. New York Public Library Brevoort Collection and Moore New York Papers.

New York Historical Society Collections. Vol. I and 2nd series, Vols. I and XXV. New York: 1811, 1841, 1892.

Nieuw Nederlandsch Biografisch Woordenboek. 10 vols. Leiden: 1911–1938.

Nissenson, S. G. *The Patroon's Domain*. New York: 1937.

Notenstein, Wallace. *The English People on the Eve of Colonization, 1603–1630*. London/New York: 1954.

Nye, R. B., and Morpurgo, J. E. *The Birth of the USA*. A History of the United States, Vol. I. Baltimore: Penguin Books, 1970.

O'Callaghan, E. B. *Calendar of Historical Manuscripts in the Office of the Secretary of State of New York*. 2 vols. Albany: 1865, 1866.

——. *The Documentary History of the State of New York*, Vol. IV. Albany: 1851.

——. *History of New Netherland, or New York under the Dutch*. 2 vols. New York: 1846.

——. *Voyages of the Slavers* St. John *and* Arms of Amsterdam, *1659, 1663*. Albany: 1867.

Oldmixon, T. *History of the Stuarts*. London: 1730.

Oppenheim, Samuel. *The Early History of the Jews in New York, 1654–1664*. New York: 1909.

Paltsits, V. H. "The Founding of New Amsterdam in 1626." *Proceedings of the American Antiquarian Society, 1924*. Worcester, Mass.: 1925.

Pearson, J., ed. *Early Records of the City and County of Albany, and Colony of Rensselaerswyck, 1656–1675*. Albany: 1869.

Pepys, Samuel. *The Diary of Samuel Pepys*, Vol. IV. Edited by Henry B. Wheatley. London: 1894.

Peyster, J. Watts de. *The Dutch at the North Pole and the Dutch in Maine*. New York: 1857.

Phelps Stokes, I. N. *New York, Past and Present: Its History and Landmarks, 1524–1939*. New York: 1939.

Phelps Stokes, I. N., ed. *The Iconography of Manhattan Island, 1489–1909*, Vols. IV and VI. New York: 1922, 1928.

Plockhoy, Pieter Cornelisz. *Kort en klaer ontwerp, dienende tot een onderling accoort, om den arbeyd, onrust en moeyelyckheyt van alderley hand-werckluyden te verlichten door een onderlinge Compagnie ofte Volck-planting aan de Zuyt-revier in Nieuw-Nederland op te rechten*. Amsterdam: 1662.

Plooy, Daniel. *The Pilgrim Fathers from a Dutch Point of View*. New York: 1932.

Pomfret, John E. *Founding of the American Colonies, 1583–1660*. New York/London: 1970.

Pope-Hennessey, James. *Sins of the Fathers: A Story of the Atlantic Slave Traders, 1441–1807*. London: 1967.

Powys, Llewelyn. *Henry Hudson*. New York: 1928.

Purchas, Samuel. *Hackluyt's Posthumus or Purchas His Pilgims*, Vol. XIX. Glasgow: 1906.

Quarterly of New York State Historical Association. 1931–1974.

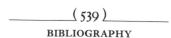

BIBLIOGRAPHY

Raesly, Ellis Lawrence. *Portrait of New Netherland*. New York: 1945.

Rees, O. van. *Geschiedenis der Nederlansche Volksplantingen in Noord-Amerika*. Tiel: 1885.

Renier, G. J. *The Dutch Nation*. The Hague: 1944.

Roever, Nicolaas de. "Killiaen van Rensselaer and His Colony of Rensselaerswyck." *Oud Holland VIII*. (1890).

Roosevelt, Theodore. *New York*. New York/London: 1895.

Ruyter, Michiel Adriaensz de. *Journaal, 1664–1665*. Linschoten Vereniging, Vol. LXII. The Hague: 1961.

Schuyler, George W. *Colonial New York, Philip Schuyler and His Family*. 2 vols. New York: 1885.

Seguy, Jean. *Utopie, Cooperative et Oecumenisme*. Paris: 1968.

Seymann, Jerrold. *Colonial Charters, Patents, and Grants to the Communities, Comprising the City of New York*. New York: 1939.

Shepherd, William R. *The Story of New Amsterdam*. New York: 1926.

Shurtleff, N. B., ed. *Records of the Colony of New Plymouth, in New England, 1620–1692*. 12 vols. Boston: 1855–1861.

Sille, Nicasius de. "History of the First Beginning of the Town of New Utrecht." *Documentary History of the State of New York*, Vol I. Albany, N.Y.: 1855.

Singleton, E. *Dutch New York*. New York: 1909.

Smith, William Jr. *The History of the Province of New York*. Edited by Michael Kammen. 2 vols. New York: 1972.

Spooner, Walter W. *Historic Families in New York*, Vol. III. New York: 1908.

Steendam, Jacob. *De Distelvinck*. 3 vols. Amsterdam: 1645–1650.

——. *Noch Vaster: A Memoir of the First Poet in New Netherland*. The Hague: 1861.

Temple, Sir William. *Observations upon the United Province of the Netherlands*. Cambridge: 1932.

Timmers, G. *Schetsen uit de nautische geschiedenis van Curaçao*. Curaçao: 1965.

Trelease, A. W. *Indian Affairs in Colonial New York in the 17th Century*. New York: 1960.

Trevelyan, G. M. *England under the Stuarts*. Rev. ed. London: 1946.

Trevor-Roper, H. R. *Archbishop Laud, 1573–1645*. London: 1940.

Trumbull, J. H., ed. *The Public Records of the Colony of Connecticut, 1638–1678*. 3 vols. Hartford: 1850–1859.

Tuckerman, Bayard. *Peter Stuyvesant, Director-General for the West India Company in New Netherland*. London: 1893.

Turner, F. C. *James II*. London: 1948.

Tyler, L. G. *England in America, 1580–1652*. The American Nation, Vol. IV. New York: 1904.

Underhill, John. *History of the Pequot War*. Massachusetts Historical Society Collections, 3rd Series, Vol. VI, 1825.

——. *Newes from America*. London: 1838.

Vail, R. W. G. "The Case of the Stuyvesant Portraits." *New York Historical Society Quarterly Bulletin*. 42, no. 2 (1958).

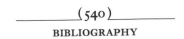

Valentine, David T. *History of the City of New York.* New York: 1853.

Van der Zee, Henri and Barbara. *William and Mary.* New York: 1973.

Van Laer, Arnold J. F. *New York Historical Manuscript.* Edited by Kenneth Scott and Kenn Stryker-Rodda. 4 vols. Baltimore: 1974.

Van Loon, H. W. *The Life and Times of Peter Stuyvesant.* New York: 1928.

Van Rensselaer, Mrs. John King. *The Goede Vrouw of Mana-ha-ta, 1609–1760.* New York: 1898.

Van Rensselaer, Kiliaen. *The Van Rensselaer Manor.* 1929.

Van Rensselaer, Schuyler. *History of the City of New York in the 17th Century.* 2 vols. New York: 1909.

Versteeg, Clarence L. *The Formative Years, 1607–1763.* London: 1964.

Versteeg, Dingman. *The New Netherland Register.* 8 vols. New York: 1911.

Versteeg, Dingman, ed. *New Netherland's Founding.* New York: 1924.

Verster, J. F. L. de Balbian. *Holland-America: An Historical Account of Shipping and Other Relations between Holland and North America.* Amsterdam: 1921.

Vries, David Pietersz. de. *Korte Historiael ende Journaels, Aenteyckeninge van verscheyden voyagiens in de vier deelen des werelts-ronde, als Europa, Africa, Asia ende America, 1618–1644.* Linschoten Vereniging, Vol. III. The Hague: 1911.

Vrijman, L. C. *Slavenhalers en slavenhandel.* Amsterdam: 1937.

Vroom. U. E. E. "Het pakhuis van de West Indische Compagnie." *Uit het Peperhuis* (1972).

Waal, C. de. *Zeeuwsche expeditie naar de West.* Linschoten Vereniging, Vol. XXX. The Hague: 1928.

Wagenaar, Jan. *Vaderlandsche Historie,* Vols. XI–XIII. Amsterdam: 1793.

Ward, Christopher. *The Dutch and the Swedes on the Delaware, 1609–1664.* Philadelphia: 1930.

Wassenaer, Nicolaes van. "The Description and First Settlement of New Netherland." *Wassenaer's Historie van Europa* in *Collectanea Adamantea XXVII,* Vol. II. Edinburgh: 1888.

Weiss, Charles. *History of the French Protestant Refugees.* London/Edinburgh: 1854.

Wertenbaker, Thomas J. *The First Americans, 1606–1690.* New York: 1927.

Weslager, Clinton A. *Dutch Explorers, Traders and Settlers in the Delaware Valley, 1609–1664.* Philadelphia: 1961.

Whitehead, William A., ed. *Documents Relating to the Colonial History of the State of New Jersey, 1631–1687,* vol. 1. Newark: 1880.

Wicquefort, A. de. *Histoire des Provinces-Unies des Pais-Bas.* 4 vols. Amsterdam: 1861.

Wieder, F. C. *De Stichting van New York in 1625.* Linschoten Vereniging, Vol. XXVI. The Hague: 1925.

Williams, Eric. *From Columbus to Castro: The History of the Caribbean, 1492–1960.* London: 1970.

Williams, Sherman. *New York's Part in History.* New York/London: 1915.

Wilson, Charles H. *Profit and War: A Study of England and the Dutch Wars.* London: 1957.

Wilson, James Grant, ed. *The Memorial History of the City of New York*. 4 vols. New York: 1892.

Winthrop, John. *Winthrop Papers*. Vols. I–V. Massachusetts Historical Society, 1925–1947. And Massachusetts Historical Society Collections, 4th series, vol. VI. Boston: 1863.

———. *Winthrop Letters*. Massachusetts Historical Society Collections, 5th series, Vols. VIII and IX. Boston: 1882.

———. *The History of New England from 1630–1649*. 2 vols. Boston: 1853.

Winthrop, Robert C. *Life and Letters of John Winthrop*. 2 vols. Boston: 1864, 1867.

Wright, L. B. *Everyday Life in Colonial America*. London: 1965.

———. "Local Government and Central Authority in New Netherland." *New York Historical Society Quarterly* 42 no. 1 (1973).

Wuorinin, John H. *The Finns on the Delaware, 1638–1655*. New York: 1938.

Zwierlein, Fred J. *Religion in New Netherland*. Rochester, N.Y.: 1950.

INDEX

Abrams Offrande, 252, 267
Acadia, 256, 403
Additional Observations, 187, 188
Admiralty: in Amsterdam, 471, 483, 491; English, 437; of Zeeland, 483
Adriaensen, Jacob, 321
Adriaensen, Maryn, 113, 117, 283; imprisoned, 121–22; leads freemen in Indian War, 118, 120
Aesop, 208
Africa, 6, 8, 20, 49, 77, 80, 162, 190, 247, 252–54, 338, 360, 362, 390, 426, 437, 467, 469
Albany, 5, 211, 466, 486. *See also* Beverwyck
Albany county, 50
Albert, Jan, 405
Albertsen, Jan, 405
"Albion knights for the conversion of the twenty-three Kings," 88
Algonquin nation, 103, 110, 117, 125. *See also* under names of tribes
Allerton, Isaac, 125, 126, 248
Allyn, John, 421
Allyn, Matthew, 421
Alphen aan de Rijn, 154
Alrich, Jacob, 302–308, 311, 398
Altona, 305, 306, 307, 352, 398–99, 408; acquired by Amsterdam, 401–402
"Amazon of North America," 83
Amboina, 229–30, 236, 239, 240, 449, 469
Amersfoort. *See* New Amersfoort
Amsterdam, 4, 6, 10, 14, 33, 48, 50, 58, 72, 74, 76, 79, 80, 94, 99, 125, 169, 171, 174, 175, 198, 205, 260, 275, 280, 283, 313, 334, 341, 342, 348, 353, 360–61, 365, 368, 369,

388, 470, 471, 482, 483, 491; acquires Company land on Delaware, 301, 400–402, 432; and Burgher Right, 345; East India Company in, 3, 5; effect of Anglo-Dutch war on, 246, 250; financial center of Europe, 22; Jewish community of, 292; and New Amstel, 301–302, 304–305, 307, 309, 311, 338, 370, 398–402; opposes renewal of Spanish war, 190; prominence of, 21–22, 151, 359; religious tolerance in, 21, 37, 67, 140, 281, 291, 292; republican sentiment in, 226, 246, 438; West India Company in, 1, 2, 7, 8, 17, 22, 28, 34, 49, 53, 56, 59, 71, 77, 150, 155, 157, 163, 176, 183, 190, 202, 210, 216, 218, 227, 233, 244, 259, 267, 268, 278, 286, 331, 333, 338, 344, 371, 375, 396, 423, 443, 464, 494; Winthrop in, 385
Andrews, Charles, 36
Andringa, Joris, 491
Andros, Edmund, 493
Anglican Church. *See* Church of England
Anglo-Dutch War (1652–1654), 201, 224, 225, 230–31, 232, 233–34, 235, 246–47, 276, 287, 312, 336, 337, 380, 470; background of, 226–30; concluded, 250; of 1665–1667, 472, 475, 477, 478–79; of 1672–1674, 482–83, 491–92
Angola, 77, 169, 254, 283, 338
Anna, 224, 231
Answer to the Remonstrance (Van Tienhoven), 193
Anthony, Allard, 231, 352, 473
Anthony, Christiaen, 353
Anthony, Mrs. Christiaen, 353
Anticosti, 344

Antilles, 82, 158, 252
Antonissen, Lysbeth, 356
Antwerp, 6, 21, 74, 191
Arent, 382, 385
Arminianism, 145
Arms of Amsterdam, 1
Arnhem, 275
Aruba, 150, 157
Aspinall, William, 260
Avesnes, 38
Ayscue, Sir George, 233, 255
Azores, 6

Backer, Jacobus, 335
Backer, Margriet, 335
Backerus, Dominie Johannes Cornelis, 166, 170, 284; and education in New Amsterdam, 369; supports rebels, 186–87, 190, 285
Baeck, Anthony, 358
Bahamas, 25
Bailey, Captain, 37
Baltic Sea, 32
Baltic trade, 20, 32–33, 301, 377, 401
Baltimore, 1st Baron. *See* Calvert, George, 1st Baron Baltimore
Baltimore, 2nd Baron. *See* Calvert, Cecilius, 2nd Baron Baltimore
Bank of Exchange (Amsterdam), 22
Bantam, 228
Baptism, as crux between Dutch church and Lutherans, 296–97, 298
Barbados, 22, 254–55, 386, 471; Stuyvesant to, 252, 255, 258, 267, 337, 343
Barendt, Gerrit, 176
Barents Sea, 3
Barrabas, 335

Barren Island, 204
Barsimon, Jacob, 290
Batavia, 228
Baudartius, Dominie, 14, 26
Baxter, George, 93, 128, 135, 147, 172, 218, 220, 241; agent for Rhode Island, 392, 427; commissioned to investigate New Netherland, 427, 445; turns against Stuyvesant, 242, 244, 256
Baxter, Thomas, 240, 245, 336
Bay Agreement, 146
Bay Colony: See Massachusetts Bay Colony
Bayard, Anna. See Stuyvesant, Anna
Bayard, Judith. See Stuyvesant, Judith
Bayard, Nicholas, 336, 461, 487
Bayard, Samuel, 335
Bear's Island, 308
Beaver Street, 14
Beaver trade, 1, 11, 12, 41, 147, 166, 262, 297, 323, 343, 346, 446
Beaver's Path, 354
Beck, Vice Director, 330, 362
Bedford, 448
Bedloo, Isaack, 352
Beeckman, Willem, 231, 305, 307–308, 352, 379, 398–99, 402, 408, 462
Beeckman, Mrs. Willem, 352
Beemstermeer, 7, 9
Beer, 302, 353
Beeren Island, 204
Begijnenstraat, 199
Bennet, Henry, 426, 427, 447
Bennet, Richard, 287
Benoni, 335
Bergen, 424
Berkeley, Sir John, 446
Berkeley, Sir William, 318–19, 320, 446
Berlikum, 151
Bermuda, 25, 134, 483
Beschryvinge van Nieu Nederlandt, 202
Bestevaer, Captain, 382, 384
Beversfuyck, 204, 206
Beversreede, 261–62
Beverwyck, 320, 369, 403, 452, 456; Boston visitors to, 314; established by Stuyvesant, 210–11; and Indians, 324, 325, 326, 404; rechristened Albany, 466; retaken by Dutch, 486. See also Albany; Willemstad
Bicker, Gerrit, 265
"Big Sachima with the Wooden Leg," 175
"Big Tub," 259
Binckes, Jacob, 483, 487, 491
Birthday Garland (Selyns), 366–67
Black Tulip, 22
Blacks, 49, 75, 97, 113, 245, 252–54, 294, 326, 330, 357, 362, 364, 366, 368, 370, 408, 457, 458
Blake, Robert, 224, 230, 233
Blaue Haen, 132, 133, 153
Blessing of the Bay, 64, 70, 146
Block, Adriaen, 5–6
Bloemaerts, Samuel: among

Heeren XIX, 9, 13, 79; domain in New Netherland, 50–51, 81; and Swedish encroachment in New Netherland, 79–81
Blom, Dominie Hermanus, 366, 405
Blue Dove, 349, 354
Board of Account (West India Company), 98, 131, 156
Board of Nine Select Men. See Nine Select Men
Bock, Arien, 199
Bogaert, Johannes, 267, 268
Bogardus, Annetje, 353–54
Bogardus, Dominie Everardus, 135, 187, 285; assails Kieft, 162–63, 166, 283–84; and church, 99; opposes Indian War, 117, 118; quarrels with Van Twiller, 58, 59, 72, 283
Bombay, 389
Bonaire, 150, 157, 331
Bonnie Bess, 10
Bontemantel, Hans, 267, 268, 276
Book of Resolutions of the Council of New England, 35
Boot, Nicolaes, 253
Boston, 24, 69, 83, 88, 95, 137, 144, 182, 217, 239, 260, 368, 371, 376, 377, 381, 384, 386, 447; Commissioners meet at, 236–37, 415–19, 422; compared to New Amsterdam, 416–17; and Connecticut River settlement, 64, 65, 66, 68; Duke's invasion and, 449–50, 451, 462; English fleet at, 245, 248, 249, 251; founding of, 146; fugitives from, 92, 138; Kieft communication to, 140; lays claim on Hudson, 314, 315–16, 396; and New Orange, 489–90; Stuyvesant to, 415–19, 420, 424, 475; Underhill in, 125, 126. See also Massachusetts Bay Colony
Boswell, Sir William, 71, 95
Boswyck, 380, 424
Bout, Jan Evertsen, 125, 175, 186, 187, 194
Boweries, 49, 77, 79, 242, 272, 273; of Stuyvesant, 271, 334, 337, 370, 457, 462, 474, 480
Bowery, the, 15
Bowne, John, 296
Boyer, Alexander, 262
Bradford, William: and Connecticut River settlement, 63–64, 66; relations with Dutch, 41–47, 57, 63–64
Bradstreet, Simon, 220, 418
Brazil, 15, 22, 60, 77, 150, 152, 191, 247, 286, 300; Dutch exodus from, 131–32, 133, 153, 154, 169, 190, 288, 290, 338; given to Portugal, 389; Jews from, 290–92; slaves in, 254
Breda, 155, 181, 478
Breeden, Thomas, 404
Breeden Raedt, 191. See Broad Advice
Bressani, Father, 286
Bret, Claes, 465
Breukelen, 93, 174, 241, 248, 288–89, 380, 424, 429–30; dominie

of, 334, 365–66, 368, 406; English troops at, 456, 458, 463
Brewster, Jonathan, 66
Bridal Torch (Selyns), 367
Bridge Street, 14, 357
Brief Narration of the English Rights to the Northern Parts of America, A, 313, 446
Bristol, 35
Bristol Channel, 166
British West Indies, 255
Broad Advice, 74, 108, 129, 154, 162, 191–92, 193, 284
Broad Street, 14, 342, 372
Broadway, 15, 233, 272, 354, 485
Bronck, Jonas, 97, 114
Bronx, 97
Brooke, Baron, 69, 391
Brookhaven, 487
Brooklyn, 93. See Breukelen
Brouwerstraat, 100, 348
Brown, Samuel, 255
Brownists, 42, 44, 139, 140. See Pilgrims; Puritans
Brussels, 357
Buckingham, George Villiers, 1st Duke of, 42
Burgher guard, 115, 195, 241, 248, 328, 349, 407
Burgher-recht, 345–46
Burgomasters, of Amsterdam, 301, 304; of New Amstel, 301; of New Amsterdam, 231–32, 240, 241, 243, 244–45, 249, 250, 251, 278, 292, 293, 297, 308, 320, 328, 330, 331, 336, 348, 349, 350, 351–52, 354, 355, 369, 371, 372, 404, 411, 421, 424, 441, 451–52, 455, 457–62, 464, 473, 474; of New Orange, 489, 491, 492
Burnett, Dr. Gilbert, 386
Buteux, Father, 298
Buzzards Bay, 41, 43, 46

Cabo Corso, 437
Cabot, Jean, 35
Cabot, Sebastian, 35
Calvert, Cecilius, 2nd Baron Baltimore, 306–10, 398, 402, 466
Calvert, George, 1st Baron Baltimore, 306
Calvert, Philip, 309–10, 398
Calvinism, 7, 21, 98, 106, 145, 151, 199, 247, 254, 281, 289, 338, 343
Cambridge, 386
Canada, 5, 88; Dutch trade with, 343
Canarsie Indians: and Indian War of Dutch, 119–20, 122, 128–29; and origin of Peach War, 272; sell Long Island, 86; sell Manhattan, 2, 103
Cape Charles, 33
Cape Cod, 33, 36, 38, 169, 442
Cape Cod Bay, 5
Cape May, 88
Capito, Mattys, 405
Caribbean Sea, 25, 150, 258, 344, 472
Carleton, Sir Dudley, 31, 33, 34, 35, 38
Carlisle, 1st Earl of. See Howard, Charles, 1st Earl of Carlisle

Carnarsee Indians. *See* Canarsie Indians
Carolina, 35
Carr, John, 466, 484, 485
Carr, Sir Robert, 447, 462, 466
Carrying trade, 156, 226, 227, 388
Cartwright, George, 447, 462, 466
Casimir. *See* Fort Casimir
Castle Island, 5, 11, 182
Castlemaine, Lady. *See* Villiers, Barbara, Lady Castlemaine
Catherine of Braganza, 379, 389, 390, 426
Cats, Jacob, 42, 229, 230
Catskill, 208, 209
Caughnawagah, 325, 326
Cavaliers, 470, 480
Chamber of Amsterdam (West India Company), 8, 13, 130, 178, 194, 201, 253
Chamber of Assurance (Amsterdam), 22
Chambers, Thomas, 321, 326, 405
Champlain, Samuel de, 108
Charles I, King, 380, 413; and Civil War, 93–94, 95, 216; and *Eendracht* incident, 29–31, 35, 47, 48; and English rights to North America, 31, 35, 38, 47, 230, 316; execution of, 218, 225–26, 377; and New England Puritans, 68; and Plowden patent, 88; and Spanish match, 34, 42; and Walloon petition to England, 38
Charles II, King: demands satisfaction of commercial complaints, 439; and diplomacy over New Netherland, 378, 435; and Dutch Republic, 378–79, 387, 388, 389–91, 426, 438, 439–40, 448, 465, 467–69, 471; and Dutch wars, 472, 479, 491–92; and New England, 375, 376–77, 379, 381, 391, 447, 449; New Yorkers' oath of allegiance to, 473–74, 489; orders fleet to Guinea coast, 469; refuge in Dutch Republic, 216, 219, 226, 250, 387, 438; relations with Duke of York, 446; Restoration of, 317–18, 374, 377, 378, 380, 391, 397; Scott representation of, 428–30, 432; and 1674 peace terms with Dutch, 491–92; title to New Netherland, 427, 446–47, 449–50, 456, 460, 463, 464, 465–66, 467, 468, 470, 473, 487, 493; treasury exhausted, 438, 471, 479, 491, 492
Charles River, 62, 88. *See* Delaware River; South River
Charlestown, 248
Chatham, 479
Chatham Square, 293
Cheassepeake Bay, 308
Chinatown, 293
Christiaensz, Hendrick, 5–6, 13
Christina, Queen, 81, 82, 259–60, 263, 264, 265, 269
Christina Kill, 301
Christy, James, 419–20

Church of England, 68, 139, 377, 384
City Council (Amsterdam), 399
City Council (New Amsterdam), 231–33, 251, 348, 455. *See also* Council (New Netherland)
City Court (New Amsterdam), 231–32, 279, 291, 351–58, 361. *See also* Court of New Amsterdam
City Hall (New Amsterdam, New York), 100, 233, 241, 248, 250, 251, 291, 330, 342, 348, 349, 358, 369, 371, 383, 424, 459, 460, 461, 463, 473, 474
City Tavern, 100, 232
Civil War, English, 91, 92, 93–94, 95–96, 138, 168, 216, 218, 225, 254
Clarendon, Edward Hyde, 1st Earl of: and Dutch Republic, 386, 388, 389–90, 426, 439, 471; and New England, 377–78, 383–84, 447; and New Netherland, 391, 436, 445, 447, 448, 464, 467, 468
Clarke, John, 392
Clarke, Thomas, 462
Classis of Amsterdam, 48–49, 280, 282, 283, 284, 286, 287, 288, 291, 296, 297, 298, 299, 366, 368, 369, 405
Claverack, 208
Cleves, 5
Cloth Counties, 141
Cloth trade, 32–33, 145
Cock, 84
Coe, John, 419–20, 424, 458
Coen, Jan Pietersz, 22, 228–29
Coerten, Geurt, 352
Coerten, Mrs. Geurt, 352
Coke, Sir John, 65
Colen Donck, 181, 201, 202
Cologne, 286
Colonization, Dutch: attitude toward, 19, 23, 34, 339, 494; fails under Minuit, 17–18; of New Amstel, 301–304, 399; of New Netherland, 2, 10–18; in patroon project, 49–51, 79, 204; Plockhoy scheme for, 399–400; and 1639 resolution, 78–79; Usselinx urges, 6–7, 49–50. For other countries and growth of New Netherland see under names of colonies; *see also* Connecticut River; Delaware River
Columbia county, 50
Columbus, Christopher, 35
Colve, Antony, 485; governor of New Orange, 486–90, 493
"Combination" (of English towns on Long Island), 428, 440
"Comforters of the sick," 48, 282
Commercial College, 264
Commission for Regulating Plantations, 68–69
Commission of Four, 447–49, 462–63, 466; fleet of, 448
Commissioners of the United Colonies: and Connecticut charter, 392; and Evertsen, 487; and Kieft, 147–49; mediate in York's invasion, 459–60; and

Stuyvesant, 213–14, 216–17, 218, 219–21, 223, 235–37, 248, 313, 314–15, 415–18, 459–60; and Westchester, 414, 415
Committee of Four, 220
Commonwealth of England, 223, 306, 317; Dutch relations with, 225–27, 229, 246–47, 250, 312–13, 413, 470. *See also* Cromwell, Oliver
Commonwealth of New Plymouth. *See* New Plymouth
"Complaint of New Amsterdam" (Steendam), 359, 362
Coney Island, 454
Coninck Salomon, 249
Connecticut, 139, 141, 218, 256, 376, 379, 384, 459; charter to include Dutch territory, 381–83, 391–92, 394–96, 398, 422, 426, 427–28, 432, 440, 443–44; claims annulled by Duke of York, 440, 447, 451, 454, 480, 486–87; designs on New Haven territory, 381, 392–93, 396–98, 417; and Dutch invasion of New York, 486–88, 489, 492; Indian uprising in, 124; occupies Westchester, 413–15, 417–18, 421, 422, 423, 432; Scott and, 397–98, 427–29, 432–33; trouble with Dutch, 89–91, 95, 138, 146, 147, 148, 220, 221, 236, 237, 238, 248, 251, 315, 335, 375, 402, 413–15, 417, 419–23. *See also* Connecticut River; Hartford
Connecticut River, 2, 5, 11, 213; Anglo-Dutch rivalry on, 63–67, 68, 70–71, 78, 89–91, 94, 95, 140, 146, 148, 169, 206, 219, 220, 240, 312, 314, 378, 381, 432, 442; Bay and Plymouth colonies vie for, 66–67, 68
Connecticut Valley, 84
Contra-Remonstrants, 7–8
Convention (of States' deputies, 1651), 226
Coorn, Nicholaes, 204–205
Copenhagen, 448
Corlaers Hook, 118
Cornelissen, Hendrick, 321
Cornelissen, Laurens, 284
Corsen, Arent, 262
Cortelyou, Jacques, 341
Council (Maryland), 307, 309
Council (Massachusetts), 450
Council (New Netherland), 42, 50, 74–75, 86, 90, 115, 121, 131, 165; De Sille added to, 275–77; of Stuyvesant, 172–73, 174, 177, 181, 183, 184, 185, 187, 189, 193, 196, 200, 207, 219, 222, 231, 240, 245, 248, 256, 258, 259, 275–77, 285, 286, 295, 297, 320, 321, 330, 345, 352, 395, 407, 411, 412, 419, 420, 452, 455. *See also* City Council (New Amsterdam); Provincial Council
Council for Foreign Plantations, 377–78, 379, 381, 427, 445–46
Council for Trade, 378, 388, 438–39
Council for Trade and Plantations, 491

Council of Amsterdam, 6, 304
Council of New England, 31, 33, 36, 42–43, 46, 47, 65, 67
Council of Plymouth, 57
Council of State, English, 223, 229
Court of Hartford, 392
Court of Holland, 198, 275
Court of New Amsterdam, 76, 102. See also City Court (New Amsterdam)
Court of Wards and Liveries, 145
Court tennis, 321
Cousseau, Schepen, 462
Couturier, Hendrick, the Younger, 337
Coventry, Sir William, 439, 450
Cow Neck, 86
Coxwell, Robert, 85
Crailo, 406
Crailo marshland, 49
Cregier, Catharina, 364
Cregier, Martin, 238, 356, 364; burgomaster, 231–32, 245, 407, 462; commands burgher guard, 241, 248, 407; envoy to Scott, 429; in Landtag, 241, 244; leads forces in Wiltwyck war, 407–12, 443; and soldiers to New Amstel, 302, 308; tavern of, 232, 354
Crieckenbeeck, Daniel, 16
Cromwell, Oliver, 95, 144, 216, 226–27, 229, 239, 246–48, 250, 256, 306, 312–13, 317, 318, 376, 378, 380, 386–87, 388, 391, 399, 413, 438, 470
Cromwell, Richard, 317
Crown Council (Sweden), 264
Culville, Adrienne, 129
Curaçao, 25, 77, 149, 157, 166, 186, 266, 330, 339, 349, 457; center of slave trade, 152, 252–54, 362; Esopus prisoners to, 331, 332, 335, 404–405; New Amsterdam trade with, 343; Stuyvesant at, 131, 150, 152–54, 155, 156; Stuyvesant visits, 252–53, 255, 258, 266, 337; and Stuyvesant voyage to New Netherland, 158–59, 161, 284–85
Curtius, Alexander Carolus, 371–72

D'Acosta, Joseph, 293
D'Ailleboust (Canadian deputy viceroy), 343
Dam Square, 58
Damen, Jan, 100, 113, 117, 120, 124, 125, 129, 174, 187
Danes, in New Amsterdam, 97, 113, 399
Darmstadt, 113
Dartmouth, 4
Davenport, Rev. John, 83, 316
David, William, 237
De Backer, Joost Theunis, 176
De Decker, Johannes, 406, 462, 466
De Ferrera, David, 293
De Forest, Isaack, 458, 462
De Forest, Jesse, 38, 75
De Koningh, Frederick, 268
De la Court, Pieter, 21
De la Mothe, Jacques, 290–91

De Laet, Johannes, 5, 8, 16, 281
De Pré, Jean, 343–44
De Rasières, Isaack, 15, 16, 17, 41–42; on Indians, 106; visits New Plymouth, 43–46, 63, 141
De Rosschou, Sarah, 361
De Ruyter, Claes Jansen, 354
De Ruyter, Michiel Adriaensz: defeats English and French fleets, 482; ordered to retake New Netherland, 471–72, 478, 479–80; to Guinea coast, 467, 469, 478
De Sille, Laurens, 275, 364
De Sille, Nicasius, 25; as Councilor, 275–77, 363–65, 412; and English on Long Island, 420, 424; as poet, 26, 363, 365, 366; and siege of Fort Christina, 268; and siege of New Amsterdam, 460, 461; succeeds Van Tienhoven as schout-fiscaal, 278–79, 363, 371
De Sille, Walburga, 364
De Visser, Jan, 273
De Vos, Matthew, 352
De Vries, David Pietersz, 28, 100, 136; and church in New Amsterdam, 98–99; and English on Connecticut River, 89; and Indian troubles, 111, 112, 113, 116; on Indians, 104, 105, 110, 116, 119, 122; on "Israelites," 141; leaves New Netherland, 123; negotiates with Indians, 120, 123–24; in New Haven, 83; in New Sweden, 260; opposes Indian War, 113, 117, 118–19, 123, 167; plantation burned, 112; and Swanendael massacre, 51–52; and Van Twiller, 53–54, 56–58, 72–73, 112; in Virginia, 61, 62, 123
De Wilda (Secretary of Admiralty), 471
De Witt, Johan: and diplomacy over New York, 467–68, 470; and Downing, 387, 390, 435, 438, 448, 467–68; ends Anglo-Dutch War, 246, 250; and English commercial complaints, 439–40; meaning of New Netherland to, 493–94; plans autonomy for New Netherland, 436, 494; and 1665 Anglo-Dutch War, 479
Declaration Set Forth, A, 255
Deduction of the West India Company, 30
Delaware Company (of New Haven), 84, 222
Delaware River, 2, 5, 11, 25, 33, 50, 107, 213, 305, 306, 337, 375, 452, 485; Amsterdam acquires Company land on, 301, 400–402, 432; Amsterdam colony on, 301–306, 308–309, 338, 370, 398–402, 466; and Connecticut claims, 381, 392; English subjection of Dutch and Swedes on, 466–67, 477; Fort Nassau on, 61, 62, 81–82, 84–85, 169, 259–61; Jews forbidden to trade on, 292; Maryland claims Dutch land on, 306–11, 312, 398, 402,

466; and New Haven colonists, 82, 83–86, 87, 138, 140, 217, 221, 222–23, 255–56, 266, 381, 397; Plowden palatinate on, 88; Swedish fleet to, 441; Swedish settlement on, 81–82, 84, 85–86, 88, 185, 257, 258–70, 276, 300–301, 400; and Virginia colonists, 61–62, 125
Delftshaven, 38
Democracy, first steps to in New Netherland, 113, 133, 173
Denmark, 401, 435, 479
Denton, Richard, 298–99
Deputati ad res Indicas, 282
Derby, 147
Dermer, Thomas, 33, 36
Dertienen, 27
Description of New Albion (Plowden), 88
Description of New Netherland (Van der Donck), 12, 202
Description of the Founding or Beginning of New Utrecht (De Sille), 364
Description of the Towne of Mannadens, 342, 383
Deutels Bay, 112
D'Hinoyosa, Alexander, 302, 311, 398–99, 401–402, 466
Dickop, 56
Diemen, 343
Dikes, 20, 151, 482
Dircksen, Gerrit, 113
Dircksen, Pieter, 321
Dirreck, Lichten, 405
Discourse on Westerne Planting (Hakluyt), 35
Distelvinck (Steendam), 361
Djakarta, 228
Dolfyn, 252, 267
Dorchester, 66
Doughty, Rev. Francis, 92, 137, 163, 182, 298
Dover, 25
Downing, Emmanuel, 65, 145–46, 380, 386
Downing, Sir George, 32, 386–89, 390, 391, 426, 435–39, 448, 467–71
Downing, Lucy, 386
Drake, Sir Francis, 228
Drisius, Dominie Samuel, 280, 287–88, 296, 297, 299, 366, 368, 371
Duckings, Evert, 89
Duke's Charter, 447, 451, 452. See also James II, King (as Duke of York)
Dunkirk, 125
Dutch Calvinist Church, 7. See Reformed Church
Dutch East India Company, 8, 22, 389, 472; and Hudson voyage, 3–5, 30; and spice trade, 3, 20, 33, 228
Dutch Republic, passim. See Dutch West India Company; Holland; Netherlands; United Provinces
Dutch West India Company, 5, 22, 50, 53, 288, 360; advertises New Netherland, 374–75, 397; and Anglo-Dutch War, 230, 236, 250, 312; Brazilian setback

of, 131, 153, 154, 169, 190, 338; in Caribbean, 8, 32, 60, 77, 150, 152–54, 159, 252–54, 266, 338; and charter for New Netherland, 425, 435, 442; and colonization, 9, 17, 19, 23, 34, 77–79, 339, 494; commissary at Fort Orange, 54–55; commissions Minuit, 2, 79; complaint of Eight to, 133–34, 155, 163, 164; concern with trade over government, 173; and Connecticut charter, 395–96; construction economies of, 59, 77, 98; crisis of, 169; decline of, 131, 169, 338, 467, 491; De Witt plans for, 436; dismisses Van Tienhoven, 278–79; encourages religious tolerance, 173, 291–93, 296, 297, 298, 299; encourages town organization, 93, 277; and English, 29–30, 34, 56, 71, 78, 95, 149, 212–13, 223–24, 242, 310, 312, 317, 378, 379, 381, 394, 395–96, 397, 413, 415, 426, 431, 435, 442, 444, 472; and English on Delaware, 85; and English Separatists, 37; formation of, 6, 7, 8–9, 20; and freeing of trade in New Netherland, 78, 156, 344; governmental principle of, 111; insolvency of, 130–31, 338; and James, Duke of York, 426; and Jews in New Amsterdam, 291–93; and Latin School, 371; and loss of Connecticut River trade, 71, 89, 95; monopoly abolished, 78, 109, 156, 157, 203, 204, 344; Negro slaves of, 77, 113, 252–53, 357; and New Amstel, 301, 302, 310, 311, 338, 398–99, 401; and New Netherland, 1, 2, 8–9, 10, 11, 12–13, 15, 16–18, 19, 27–28, 30, 34, 37, 46, 48, 49, 52, 54, 56, 57, 58, 59–60, 72, 73, 75, 77–79, 95, 110, 123, 130–31, 132, 142, 155, 169, 172, 177–78, 183, 186, 187–90, 194, 195, 200, 203–204, 212, 222, 223–24, 250, 277, 281, 291–93, 296, 297, 301, 312, 317, 338–39, 340, 341, 344–46, 351, 378, 397, 424–25, 431, 435–36, 442, 475–77, 493; North American failure of, 493–94; North American object of, 12; North American profits of, 17, 60; and orders of States General, 78, 193–94, 196, 201; orders Stuyvesant home, 474; organization of, 8; and patroons, 49, 51, 52, 58, 79, 81, 204–11; and pay to Indians, 102–103, 105; Portuguese pamphlets against, 191–92; recalls Kieft, 149; recalls Minuit, 18, 51; responsibility to defend New Netherland, 431; and reversal of Stuyvesant sentences, 178; sells land to Amsterdam, 301, 338, 401; 1644 report to, 131, 156; 1650 *Remonstrance* against, 187–90, 193, 231, 275, 339; 1663 petition to, 424–25, 435, 441; and slave trade, 49, 252–54, 338, 362; Stuyvesant and, 28, 131, 150, 152–54, 155–56, 159, 163, 175, 178, 183,

190, 192, 193–94, 197, 200–201, 202, 208, 216, 218–19, 222, 223–24, 233, 241, 242, 244, 247, 250, 258, 264, 270, 278, 292–93, 296, 297, 298, 316, 317, 320, 333, 337, 338–40, 344, 379, 397, 425, 431–32, 443–44, 452, 474–78; supports renewal of Spanish war, 190; surrenders Delaware to Amsterdam, 401; and Swedish settlement, 79–82, 258, 263–64, 265, 267, 269–70, 300, 301; and trade in firearms, 101, 176; trading grounds of, 8, 20, 77, 131, 150, 169, 190, 252–55, 338; upholder of Reformed Religion, 98–99, 173, 281–82, 286, 287, 475; vessels of, 23; and Walloon refugees, 38–39; and wampum currency, 346; and wars with Indians, 113, 118, 127, 130–31, 175, 320, 329, 330, 331, 339, 404; and York's invasion, 448–49, 452, 464, 465, 467, 468, 474, 476; zenith of, 77, 130. *See also* Fur trade; Heeren XIX; Trade

Duycking, Evert, 351
Dyckman, Johannes, 210, 211

Earthquakes, 403
East Anglia, 141, 143, 145
East India Company, English, 247, 250
East Indies, 22, 32, 52, 80, 113, 285, 391, 478; Dutch monopoly in, 33, 227–28, 246, 247, 389
East River, 53, 98, 100, 125, 165, 171, 231, 232, 252, 256, 262, 274, 284, 334, 336, 342, 344, 384, 432, 463, 482
Eaton, Samuel, 256, 266
Eaton, Theophilus, 83, 126, 139, 142, 222, 256; Kieft letter to, 147; and Stuyvesant, 214–15, 216, 217, 237, 245, 248
Eeckhoorn, 52, 53, 56, 57
Eelkens, Jacob, 53, 54, 55
Eendracht, 18, 29–31, 35, 47, 48, 55, 59
Eglise Wallon, 155
Eight Select Men, 124–28, 130, 132; complaint against Kieft, 133–34, 155, 163, 164, 174
Elb River, 315, 316
Electuarium lenitium (Wrightes), 24
Elfsborg. *See* Fort Elfsborg
Elft, 27
Elias, 448, 450
Elizabeth I, Queen, 4, 32, 35, 36, 43, 228
Elmer, Edward, 217
Elmina, 254
Endicott, John, 67, 145, 248; and Dutch-Indian threat, 235, 237; and Restoration, 376, 377; and Stuyvesant, 217, 221, 235
England, 32*n*, 349; accord with Dutch Republic, 389–91, 396, 471; alliance with Dutch, 42; and charter for Connecticut, 381–82, 384, 391–92, 396, 422; charter to Warwick, 69–70, 94,

391; Civil War in, 91, 92, 93–94, 95–96, 138, 168, 216, 218, 225, 254; claims first rights on Manhattan, 30–31, 33–35, 42–43, 45–46, 47, 54, 230, 313, 315, 445; claims first rights to Connecticut River, 64, 89; and colonial boundaries with Dutch, 140, 146, 219, 221, 223, 250, 312–13, 375, 378, 391, 395, 396, 415, 418, 422, 435, 452, 454; Commonwealth of, 223, 225–27, 229, 246–47, 250, 306, 312–13, 317, 374, 413; and confederation with Dutch Republic, 227; contrast with Puritan New England, 141; and Delaware settlement, 81, 82, 83–86, 87, 88–89, 217, 222–23, 312; and Dutch capital, 22; and Dutch colonists, 10, 25, 28, 29–31, 33–35, 68, 78–79, 94–96, 140, 223, 230, 247, 309, 313, 316, 318–19, 374, 378–79, 412, 415, 426–32, 435–36, 446, 447–54, 455–64, 466–67; and Dutch fishing rights, 32, 42, 226, 227, 229–30, 391; and Dutch mercantile competition, 19–20, 31–33, 42, 145, 226–29, 388, 389, 390, 426–27, 437–39, 448, 469, 471; fleet of, 469–70, 479, 482; grant of New England, 36; and Henry Hudson, 3–5; invasion of New Netherland, 447–54, 455–64; and Long Island, 86–87, 239–45, 256, 313, 346, 378–81, 391, 394–95, 412, 415, 419–25, 426, 427–34, 440, 441, 442, 443–44, 447, 448, 449, 452, 454, 456, 477, 486–88; "mad for" Dutch war, 437–39, 469–71; and New Netherland recruitment, 91–93, 374–75; New Netherland surrenders to, 463–64, 465–67; and New Netherland's thwarting of Navigation Act, 318, 389, 391, 436, 446; New World exploration by, 33, 35–36, 43; and New York, 465–72; New York restored to, 491–93; and North American colonies, 3, 4, 28, 29, 30, 33–37, 38, 59, 61–71, 78, 81, 94, 138, 139, 142, 144, 183, 219, 223, 239, 247, 306–10, 313, 316, 317, 320, 375–78, 384, 391, 416, 446, 447; patent to Baltimore, 306; and Portuguese alliance, 379, 389; Puritan emigration from, 37–38, 67–69, 141–42, 145–46, 374; Restoration in, 317, 374–78, 380, 383, 384, 386, 388, 391, 397, 398; seizes *Eendracht*, 29–31, 35, 47, 48; 1652 Dutch War, 201, 224, 225, 230–31, 232, 233–34, 235, 246–47, 250, 276, 287, 312, 336, 337, 380, 470; 1665 Dutch War, 472, 475, 478–79; 1672 Dutch War, 482–83, 491–92; and Spain, 34–35, 36, 41–42, 247, 255; trade on Hudson, 53–56, 312, 314–15; Walloons' petition to, 38; and West Indies possessions, 254–55. *See also* New England; and under names of colonies

England's Treasure by Fforaign Trade (Mun), 227, 229
"Errorists," 109, 126, 299, 400
Esopus, 273, 320–24, 326–32, 337, 366, 404, 407, 412, 440. *See also* Wiltwyck
Esopus Indians, 272, 320, 322–24, 326–32, 335; attack Wiltwyck, 404–12, 413; peace treaty with, 442–43; plot with Westchester, 440–42; truce with, 412, 430, 440
Esopus Kill, 332, 411
Esopus War, 320, 330–32, 343, 477; background of, 320–24, 326–30
Established Church. *See* Church of England
Evertsen, Cornelis, the Younger, 490, 492; appoints government of New Orange, 486, 488–89; conquers New York, 483–85; recaptures provinces, 486; receives Hartford envoys, 487
Expectation, 489, 491
Eyckenboom, 380

Fables (Aesop), 208
Fagel, Caspar, 490
Fairfax, Thomas, 216
Fairfield, 256
Fairfield Harbour, 240
Farming: and conflict on Connecticut River, 89–90; in New Amstel, 302, 303, 304, 305, 311; in New Netherland, 13, 17, 49, 73, 77, 78, 79, 189, 194, 195, 201, 204, 274, 321, 350, 408; in New Orange, 492; and patroons, 49–50; by Pilgrims, 44; and slaves, 49, 252, 253, 334; by Stuyvesant, 334, 457; in United Provinces, 7, 20
Farret, John, 152–53, 154
Farrett, James, 86–87
Feake, Tobias, 295
Fendall, Josias, 306–10
Fernando Noronha, 152
Fez, 76
Fifth Street, 334
"Figurative Map on Vellum," 6
Fishing: Dutch industry of, 32, 33, 226, 229, 391; in new world, 27, 194, 374
Flatlands, 73
Florida, 35, 82, 194
Flushing, 138, 236, 238, 239, 242, 287, 379, 394–95, 419, 433, 443; and Quakers, 295, 298
Flyboats, 13
Fogel Grip, 81
Folkestone, 225
Fort Albany, 486
Fort Amsterdam (Curaçao), 152, 153, 154
Fort Amsterdam (New Netherland), 56, 90, 114, 136, 159, 176, 180, 198, 203, 240, 276, 283, 330, 341, 430; building of, 14–16, 59, 76–77; as bulwark against English, 451–52, 455, 456, 457, 460, 461; church inside, 99, 284, 457; conflicts within, 16–18, 52, 56–59; defenselessness of, 98, 127, 134, 170, 189, 249, 455; English troops occupy, 463–64; meet-

ing of the Twelve at, 113; and New Plymouth, 41, 43–45, 57; rechristened, 464; refuge in Indian wars, 119–20, 124, 127, 134, 272–73, 321, 327; repair of, 77, 98, 175, 188, 224, 231, 232, 233, 249; strength of, 383; and taxation of Indians, 110; treaty with Indians concluded at, 443; Virginia prisoners to, 62. *See also* Manhattan Island; New Amsterdam; New Netherland
Fort Casimir, 263, 264, 300, 369; bought by Amsterdam, 301, 304; captured by English, 466; captured by Swedes, 258, 265–66; Dutch recapture of, 267
Fort Chemnitz, 259
Fort Christina, 82, 84, 85, 260, 263, 267; siege of, 268–70, 271, 272; under West India Company, 300, 301, 305
Fort Elfsborg, 260, 262, 263, 267
Fort Grange, 27
Fort James, 464
Fort Nassau (on Delaware River), 61, 62, 81–82, 84–85, 169, 259–61, 263
Fort Nassau, 5–6, 11, 206, 486. *See also* Fort Albany; Fort Orange
Fort New Gotheburg, 260
Fort Orange, 11, 16, 17, 41, 49, 50, 51, 52, 54, 56, 103, 108, 117, 118, 124, 135, 147, 149, 169, 176, 203, 243, 261, 286, 292, 297, 321, 325, 330, 335, 337, 343, 406, 407, 456, 459; dispute with patroons over, 204–10; Massachusetts lays claim to, 314–16, 396; Stuyvesant to, 203, 207, 210, 337, 404, 452–53, 455, 478; surrenders to English, 466
Fort Trefaldighet, 266. *See* Fort Casimir
Fort Van Nassoueen. *See* Fort Nassau
Fort Wildmeet, 327, 328, 330
Fortuyn, 5
Fourth Avenue, 15, 334
Fowler, Robert, 294
Fox, Dixon R., 23
France, 3, 5, 6, 19, 20, 21, 52, 74, 190, 247, 269, 321*n*, 343, 344, 387, 401, 416, 440, 469; and Dutch capital, 22; Dutch treaty with, 390; enters Anglo-Dutch War, 479; and Hudson River, 10–11; and Indian wars, 108, 324, 329, 404; missionaries of, 97, 281; privateers of, 290, 342; and slaves in New World, 254; supports Dutch against Spain, 168; war with Dutch Republic, 482, 491, 492
Franeker, 151, 152
Frederick III, King (of Denmark), 435
Frederick Hendrick, Stadtholder, Prince of Orange, 407
Fredericks, Crijn, 14–15, 171
French, 170, 403; in New Amsterdam, 97, 271; on Staten Island, 288
Friesland, 48, 150–51, 177, 338

Frisian Islands, 25
Fulton Street, 93
Fur trade: of Dutch, 1, 2, 3–5, 6, 10, 11, 12, 16, 17–18, 28, 29, 31, 33, 34, 41, 45, 49, 53, 63, 71, 73, 78, 79, 84, 97, 101–102, 108, 147, 171, 203–204, 206, 305, 312, 314, 321, 323, 343, 344, 375, 401, 456; of English, 53, 55, 314, 446, 466; in New Sweden, 258, 261, 262. *See also* Trade
Fuyck, the, 206, 210

Gabry and Company, 175
Gardiner, Lionel, 70, 86
Gardiner's Island, 450
Gelderland, 49, 151
Geldersche Blom, 302
General Assembly (Hartford), 487, 488
General Assembly (New Netherland), 243, 441. *See* Provincial assembly
General Court of Connecticut, 90, 381, 392, 394–95, 415, 421, 427, 433, 443
General Court of Massachusetts, 66, 91, 315, 316, 376, 386, 450, 487, 489, 490
General Court of New Haven, 84, 85, 126, 215, 248, 266
Geoctroyeerde West Indische Companie, 8, 191. *See* Dutch West India Company
Geraerdy, Marie, 354
Geraerdy, Philip, 100, 354
Germans, in New Amsterdam, 97
Germany, 21, 80, 145, 168, 401; and beaver trade, 12; New Netherland compared to, 26
Gerritsen, Adriaen, 100
Gerritsen, Manuel, 357
Gerritsen, Philip, 100
Giavarino, Geronimo, 377, 389, 390, 391
Gibbs, Mr. (Bostonian), 416
Gideon, 457, 463
Gilbert, Jonathan, 421, 433
Gilbert, Mathew, 397
Glauber, Johann, 385
Gloucester, 11
Goderis, Joost, 352
Godyn, Samuel, 50, 51
Goedenhuyzen, Samuel, 214, 215
Goetwater, Dominie Johannes Ernestus, 296–97
Goffe, William, 376–77
Gold Coast, 77, 360, 437, 467
Gonzaga, Saint Aloysius, 298
Good Hope, 205
Goodyear, Samuel, 214, 215, 266
Gorges, Sir Ferdinando, 44; and Council of New England, 33, 47, 67; land patents to, 36, 47, 139, 384; and Puritan colonists, 67–68
Gorges, Robert, 67
Gosnold, Bartholomew, 35
Governor's House, 118, 185, 233, 336
Governor's Island, 13, 73, 273, 457
Grain Exchange (Amsterdam), 22

Grand Committee (Hartford), 487
Gravesend, 92, 127, 241, 242, 256, 299, 313, 353, 371, 379, 394, 419–20, 443, 486; Nicolls comes ashore at, 454, 455–56. *See also* s'Gravesande
Gravesend Bay, 454
Great Burghers, 345–46
Great Council (New Amsterdam), 184
Great Fire of London, 479
Great House, 336–37, 350
Great Puritan Emigration, 67, 92
Great River of the Mountain, 4, 5, 10. *See* Hudson River
Great Yarmouth, 32
Greenbush, 204, 206
Greenland, 33
Greenwich, 91, 126, 128, 129, 137, 220, 256
Groote Burgher-recht, 345
Groote Gerrit, 157, 158, 159
Grootstede. *See* Megapolensis, Johannes
Groton Manor, 145
"Gualter of Twilley," 65. *See* Van Twiller, Wouter
Guiana, 7, 15, 25
Guinea, 58, 80, 253, 254, 360, 427, 469, 471, 472, 478
Guinea, 448, 450, 454, 455, 456, 459, 460, 463, 466
Guns: acquired by Indians, 101, 108, 110, 126, 127, 175–77, 203, 213–14, 217, 220, 235–38, 274
Gustavus Adolphus, King, 80, 259
Gyllene Hay, 266

Haarlem, 100, 151
Haarlemmerdijk, 338
Habsburg, House of, 35
Hackensack Indians, 116, 118, 122, 177, 272, 331, 411
Haen, 330
Haerlemse Saterdaghse Courant, 385
Hague, The, 1, 8, 38, 127, 157, 178, 181, 185, 186, 191, 199, 233, 265, 469; and England, 29, 31, 33, 34, 71, 95, 218, 226, 229, 230, 255, 378–79, 386–87, 388, 389, 426, 438, 467; Winthrop in, 385–86, 388–89
Hakluyt, Richard, 35
Hall, Thomas, 62, 124–25, 174, 187, 458
Hallett, William, 295
Halve Maen, 3–4
Hap, Willem, 405
Hardenstein, Margaret, 151
Haring, 74
Harlingen, 151
Harmensen, Marten, 405
Harmsen, Hendrick, 357
Hartford, 66, 216, 223, 316, 376, 381, 447, 462, 486; and annexation of New Netherland, 392, 394–96, 398, 428, 435; arrests Scott, 433–34; claims Long Island, 394–95, 419–23, 427–29, 432–33, 440, 442, 443–44, 477, 486–88, 492; confiscates House of Good Hope, 240; Dutch-

English conference in, 216, 219–23, 230, 315, 337, 422, 475; Dutch envoys to, 421–23, 424; and Dutch neighbors, 67, 89–90, 140, 146, 148, 149; protests Dutch conquest of Long Island, 486–88, 492; Varleths in, 335–36; and Westchester, 414–15, 417, 421, 422, 432, 477. *See also* Connecticut; Treaty of Hartford
Hartford Assembly. *See* General Assembly (Hartford)
Hartford Committee, 421–23
Harvard College, 386
Harvey, Sir John, 61, 62
Haversack Indians, 110
Haverstraw Indians, 112, 124, 331
Hawley, Jerome, 81
Hawthorne, William, 315–16
Haynes, John, 89, 95
Heckemack, 88
Heemstede, 92, 128, 135, 137, 212, 242, 428. *See also* Hempstead
Heeren XIX, 166, 200, 231, 241, 304, 333, 341, 359, 371; accuse Stuyvesant, 477–78; and Amsterdam acquisition on Delaware, 301, 401; appoint De Sille, 275, 278–79; appoint Kieft, 74; appoint Stuyvesant to New Amsterdam, 156, 170, 338; Board of Account report to, 131, 156; and Brazil, 169; burgomasters' motion to, 244; constitution of, 8–9; cumbrousness of, 183; direct settlers into Fort Amsterdam, 15; and English, 29, 30, 71, 72, 78, 95, 149, 212–13, 216, 218, 223–24, 230, 242, 247, 310, 312, 314, 317–18, 375, 378, 395, 397, 401, 415, 424, 426, 431, 435–36, 448–49, 452, 467; and Esopus War, 329; expenses in New Netherland, 73, 77, 131, 301, 338–40, 493; and Indian War, 127, 130, 175; and loss of New Netherland, 467, 474, 493; and Melyn, 177–78, 198; offices of, 18, 155, 338; and opening of foreign trade to New Amsterdam, 344; and patroons, 49, 79, 207, 208, 209; plea of the Eight to, 133, 155; and religion, 173, 281–82, 287, 292–93, 296, 297, 298, 299; reproached by City Fathers, 431, 464; and St. Martin expedition, 153, 154; and slaves for New Netherland, 49, 252–53; and smugglers, 344–45; and States General, 78, 156, 157, 161, 178, 195, 201, 230, 442, 448, 467; and Swedish encroachment, 79, 258, 263, 270; Van der Donck indictment of, 189–90, 202; welcome Restoration, 317–18; and Wiltwyck war, 404. *See also* Dutch West India Company
Heerengracht (Amsterdam), 18, 155, 338
Heerengracht (New Amsterdam), 342, 348

Heerenstraat, 350, 354
Heerenweg, 233, 272
Heerman, Augustine, 175, 181, 201, 238, 308–10, 318, 335, 341, 398
Hellgate, 13, 73, 169, 342, 413, 454
Hempstead, 92, 238, 239, 242, 287, 294, 298, 379, 394–95, 419, 428, 432, 443. *See also* Heemstede
Hendricksen, Jan, 409
Hendricksen, Willem, 100
Henri IV, King (of France), 108
Henrietta Anne, Duchess of Orleans, 466, 469
Henrietta Maria, Queen, 42, 94, 426
Henry VII, King (of England), 35
Herring trade, 32, 42, 226
Het Gekruyste Hart, 475
Het Houte Paerd, 100
Het Y, 25
Hill (Connecticut delegate), 90
Historisch Verhael (Van Wassenaer), 10
Hobocan Hacking, 51
Hoboken, 51, 411
Hodgson, Robert, 293–95
Hoerekill, 51, 107
Hog Creek, 260
Holborn, 31
Holland, 153, 185, 249, 267, 285, 287, 296, 305, 335, 345, 353, 362, 370, 374, 400, 413, 416, 441, 457, 463, 470, 481; agreement with England, 389–91, 396, 471; appealed to in Peach War, 274–75, 277; attitude toward colonization, 19, 23; colonists return to, 18, 109, 165–67, 186–87, 276, 431; conditions in, 19–21; diplomacy over New York, 467–71; Downing ambassador to, 386–89, 424, 435–39, 448, 467–71; and English claims in America, 28, 29–31, 33–36, 38, 42–43, 45–47, 56, 89, 94, 140, 212, 309, 310, 316, 378–79, 396, 424, 435–36, 442, 443, 445, 467–69; English commercial competition with, 31–33, 42, 145, 226–29, 388, 389, 390, 426–27, 437, 438, 439, 448, 469, 471; and English desire for war, 437–40, 469–72; financial empire of, 22, 80; and Hudson voyage, 3–5; Jews from, 290; and loss of New Netherland, 465, 467–69, 476–78, 491–92; Melyn in, 178–79, 190, 191, 197; merchant navy of, 19–20, 31–32, 80, 151, 226–27, 439; North American failure of, 494; and North American settlements, 1–2, 5, 6, 7, 10–18, 23, 26–28, 30–31, 33–34, 36, 43, 48, 58–59, 61, 72–74, 89, 94, 109, 110, 122, 130, 133, 134, 140, 156, 165, 178, 195, 212, 267, 274–75, 286, 309, 351, 368, 424, 446, 465, 467; Portuguese pamphlets in, 191; postal service to, 349; public interest in New Netherland, 192, 193; and purchase of Manhattan, 1–2; Puritans in, 37, 41, 94, 139, 140, 419; religious tolerance in, 21, 37, 281, 292, 335; relinquishes

New Netherland in Peace of Westminster, 491–94; 1652 war with England, 201, 224, 225, 230–31, 232, 233–34, 235–36, 246–47, 250, 276, 287, 312, 336, 337, 380, 470; 1665 war with England, 472, 475, 477, 478–79; 1672 war with England, 482–83, 491–92; and slave trade, 252–54; struggle with English for Guinea Coast, 390, 427, 437, 467, 469; Stuart refuge in, 216, 226, 317, 387, 438; Stuyvesant returns to, 474–79; to aid colony against English, 446; trading posts of, 2, 7, 20, 77, 150, 156, 171, 228, 261, 286, 301, 343, 437; treaty with France, 390; treaty with Portugal, 389; Van der Donck in, 187, 189–90, 194, 195, 198, 199, 201–202, 211; Van Tienhoven in, 193, 195–96, 198–99; war with Spain, 7, 8, 19, 21, 35, 42, 150, 151, 152, 153, 168, 181, 190; West India Company chartered, 8–9; zenith of, 168–69. *See also* Amsterdam; Dutch West India Company; States General
Hollantse Tuyn, 267
Holmes, George, 62
Holmes, Sir Robert, 390, 427, 437, 469
Holmes, William, 64
Hoogh, Pieter de, 21
Hooke, Rev. William, 239
Hooker, Rev. Thomas, 66
Hoop, 267, 382, 385
Hoorn, 5, 10, 123, 283
Hopkins, Edward, 89, 220
House of Commons, 387
House of Good Hope, 64, 65, 94, 169, 371; Hartford confiscates, 240; squeezed by English, 66, 71, 89, 91, 138, 140, 146, 148, 206, 220, 221; Underhill occupies, 240
Howard, Charles, 1st Earl of Carlisle, 386, 387
Howard, Frances, 386
Howe, Daniel, 86–87
Hubbard, James, 256
Hudde, Andries, 260–62, 300, 305
Hudson, Henry, 2–5, 30, 54, 189, 445, 463
Hudson Bay, 41, 88
Hudson River, 1, 6, 33, 45, 53–54, 59, 88, 94, 110, 117, 124, 128, 149, 203, 206, 223, 230, 266, 272, 273, 321, 336, 342, 347, 359, 382, 404, 411, 412, 440, 445, 456, 483, 486; Boston encroachment on, 312, 314–18; exploration of, 3–5; settlement along, 2, 10–11, 14, 37, 46, 50, 81, 146
Hudson Valley, 28, 36, 125
Huguenots, on Staten Island, 288
Hulft, Pieter Evertsen, 13, 14
Humble Remonstrance and Petition of the Colonies and Villages in this New Netherland Province (Baxter), 242–44
Humphrey, John, 146
Huntington, 487
Huron Indians, 108, 324, 329

Hutchinson, Anne, 92, 126, 127, 137, 138
Hutchinson, Susanna, 137
Hutson, David. *See* Hudson, Henry
Hutson, Hendrick. *See* Hudson, Henry
Huygens, Hendrick, 261–62
Huygens, Jan, 282, 283
Huys, Jacob Jansen, 311, 341
Hyde, Anne, 377
Hyde, Edward. *see* Clarendon, Edward Hyde, 1st Earl of

Independents, 291, 298, 299
India, 229
Indian Ocean, 229
Indian War, 109, 117–22, 124, 126–34, 137, 138, 140, 146, 154, 161, 164, 166, 169, 173, 189, 191, 193, 196, 198, 236, 248, 272, 329; background of, 109–17; peace concluded, 135–36, 162, 175, 272
Indians: and alcohol, 101, 116, 171, 204, 321, 322, 324–27, 355; alleged plot with Dutch, 235–39, 247; alleged plot with English, 453; and Baltimore patent, 309; brought to England, 36, 44; childbirth among, 107; and Connecticut River settlement, 63–66; conversion of, 69, 280–81, 286, 375; and Delaware settlements, 84, 261, 262, 263, 264; dress of, 103; and Dutch-English confederacy, 418, 419; and Dutch explorers, 3–4, 5, 6; Dutch peace treaty with, 442–43; Esopus War with, 320–24, 326–30, 477; example to colonists, 102, 142; and Fort Orange, 11, 16, 17, 50, 54–55, 56, 103, 108, 110, 117, 118, 135, 203, 207, 208, 324, 404, 406, 452–53; and French, 108, 324, 404; grievances against Dutch, 110; help to capture Scott, 433; marriage among, 106; and miscegenation, 75, 106–107; and New Netherland, 1–2, 15–16, 27, 45, 51–52, 54–55, 56, 84, 86, 90, 97, 101–108, 109–20, 122, 123–36, 137, 138, 164, 169, 170, 171, 175–77, 181, 187, 195, 198, 203, 204, 207, 208, 235–36, 261–62, 263, 271–78, 280–81, 286, 293, 303, 308, 320–31, 338, 339, 349, 355, 359, 375, 404–12, 413, 440–43, 452–53, 475; and New Plymouth, 44; "Peach War" with, 271–75, 276–79, 293, 413; plot with Westchester, 440–41; praise Dutch for payment, 262; and religion, 104–105; and sale of Manhattan, 1–2, 30, 103, 463; sell land to New Haven, 147, 149; sell land to patroons, 50, 206; sell Long Island to Dutch, 86; sell Long Island to Scott, 380; Swanendael massacre by, 51–52; and trade in firearms, 101, 108, 110, 127, 175–77, 203, 213–14, 217, 220, 235–38, 274; trade with Dutch, 2, 11, 12–13, 41, 73, 101–102, 105, 108,

109, 263, 321, 325, 401; trade with English, 55, 56, 445; trade with Swedish, 80, 81, 82; and Treaty of Hartford, 221; and treaty with Cartwright, 466; and treaty with d'Hinoyosa, 402; villages of, 104; Vriesendael massacre by, 112; wampum currency of, 45, 346–47; war with Kieft, 109, 117–20, 122, 124–36, 137, 138, 140, 146, 154, 161, 162, 164, 173, 189, 191, 193, 196, 198; war with New England, 84, 102; Wiltwyck war with, 404–12, 413, 430, 442–43, 477
Indies, 3, 391
Indonesia, 228
Interest of Holland (De la Court), 21
Ireland, 95, 97, 154, 226
Iroquois, 97, 103
Islip, 303
"Israelites," of New England, 141, 396
Italy, 97, 116, 168, 344

J. R., 227
Jacquet, Jean Paul, 300–301, 305
Jacobsen, Herman, 321
Jamaica, 255
Jamaica (Long Island), 379, 419, 422, 424, 443
James I, King, 4, 5; charters colonies, 30, 36, 215; and Dutch claims in America, 33–34, 230, 313; and Dutch mercantile competition, 32–33, 227
James II, King (as Duke of York), 216, 377, 390; charter to, 447, 451, 452; designs on New Netherland, 427, 440, 446–47; hostility to Dutch merchants, 426–27, 437; and invasion of New Netherland, 448–52, 464; leads war faction, 437–38, 440, 469, 470; and New York, 467, 473–74, 480, 483, 487; oath of obedience to, 473–74; relations with King, 446; Scott representation of, 427, 428, 432
Jamestown, 61, 62, 81, 318
"Janikens," 140
Jans, Elisabeth, 198
Jans, Hilletje, 353
Jansen, Geesje, 356
Jansen, Jan, 76
Jansen, Michiel, 175
Jansen, Ytie, 356
Jansz, Anneke, 99
Java, 228
Jean Baptiste, 343
Jesse de Forest's Journal, 75
Jesuits, 107, 203, 281, 286, 298, 306, 343
Jews, 362, 400; in Amsterdam, 281, 292; in New Amsterdam, 290–93, 334
Joachimi, Albert, 29–31, 38, 55–56, 94, 95, 140, 226
Jogues, Father Isaac, 97–98, 107–108, 170, 203, 286, 298
Jonker's Manor, 181
Jorck. *See* New York (English province)

(550)

INDEX

Joris, Hillegond, 349
Jorise, Arien, 11
Josselyn, Henry, 415
Josselyn, John, 24, 415, 416, 488
"Journal of My Voyage" (Winthrop), 385
Journal of New Netherland, 109, 110, 113, 116, 117, 128, 166
Juet, Robert, 2, 4
Jutland, 314

Kalckhoeck, 358
Kalmer Nyckel, 81, 82
Kennebec, 404
Keyser, Adriaen, 172
Kieft, Willem, 27, 169, 172, 174, 176, 181, 189, 191, 213, 334, 379; and Adriaensen, 120–22, 283; and Bogardus, 162–63, 166, 283–84; builds church, 98–100; contrasted with Stuyvesant, 177, 203, 261, 272; corresponds with Commissioners, 147–49; corresponds with Winthrop, 140, 146, 149; death of, 166–67, 284; dismisses mercenaries, 132; and English on Connecticut River, 89–91, 140, 146; and English on Delaware River, 85, 88, 140, 146; and English on North River, 147, 148; gains confidence of Stuyvesant, 163–65; governs New Netherland, 73–77, 79, 96, 97, 101, 106, 108, 132–34, 161–63, 166, 171, 175, 204, 283–84, 344; Indian troubles of, 109–14, 115–17, 322; Indian War of, 117–21, 122, 123–24, 127–29, 131, 132, 133–36, 137, 138, 147, 154, 161, 164, 166, 173, 248, 272, 329; manumits slaves, 253; protests against, 132–34, 155, 163–66; and purchase of Long Island, 86–87; recalled, 149, 159, 183; and Swedes on Delaware, 82, 260–61; taxes Indians, 110; taxes settlers, 132–33; terms to English settlers, 91–93; and the Twelve, 113–15, 118, 120
Kierstede, Hans, 99, 135, 349
Kierstede, Sarah, 99, 135
Kievitts Hook, 70
King's Memorial, 34
Kip, Hendrick Hendricksz, 175
Kip, Jacob, 231
Klacht van Nieuw-Amsterdam (Steendam), 359
Kleyne Burgher-recht, 345
Klingh, Moens, 262
Krol, Bastiaen Jansz, 49, 56, 282; buys land for Van Rensselaer, 50; commander of New Netherland, 48, 51–52; pursues English traders, 54–55
Kuffler, Abraham and Johann, 385
Kuyter, Jochem Pietersen, 97, 113, 124, 128, 132, 163–67, 177–78, 181, 184, 185, 245, 272

La Chair, Solomon, 313, 354, 361
La Montagne, Dr. Johannes, 74–75, 90, 111, 117, 118, 121, 128, 129, 133, 161, 162, 172, 185, 238, 262, 276, 277, 287, 314, 324, 326, 329, 371, 406
La Montagne, Rachel, 75, 407–408
Lallement, Father Hierosme, 403
Lamberton, George, 84–86, 260
Landtag, 241–43
Landtpoort, 233
Langdon, Thomas, 144
Latin School, in New Amsterdam, 371–73, 458
Laud, William, 68–69, 83, 95, 141, 145, 377
Laurence, John, 420–21, 429, 458
"Laurens the Norman," 297
Lawrence, William, 395
L'Esperance, 267
Le Grand, Pierre, 150
Le Moyne, Father Simon, 281, 286–87, 298, 343
Leete, William, 381, 392
Leeuwarden, 151
Leiden, 13, 37, 38, 67, 75, 125, 140, 202, 283, 337, 419
Lesser Antilles, 82
Leverett, John, 237, 248, 376
Levy, Asser, 291
Lewes, 50
Liefde, 158, 267
Lisbon, 191, 389
Lithuania, 314, 371
Little Book, 166
Livestock, in New Netherland, 13, 52, 78, 90, 110, 115, 323, 350
Lokenius, Lars, 300
London, 3, 4, 29, 36, 37, 38, 41, 42, 46, 55, 56, 62, 67, 68, 83, 87, 88, 95, 109, 139, 140, 143, 145, 146, 216, 218, 223, 225, 226, 227, 229, 247, 248, 251, 254, 255, 270, 287, 310, 317, 342, 375, 376, 378, 380, 381, 383, 384, 386, 390, 396, 398, 415, 416, 427, 428, 436, 437, 438, 445, 446, 450, 465, 467, 469, 471, 479, 491; Winthrop in, 69–70, 389, 391–92, 394
London Company, 36
Long Island, 6, 45, 76, 124, 169, 214, 236, 238, 303, 327, 328, 337, 344, 347, 353, 361, 450, 461; Baxter agitation on, 256; and Connecticut charter, 394–95, 422, 427–28, 440, 443–44, 454, 477, 480, 486–88; Connecticut-Dutch encounter on, 488, 492; Cromwell urges rebellion on, 313; De Sille on, 364; Dutch acquisition of, 86; Dutch-Indian negotiations on, 120; and Dutch invasion, 484, 486–88, 492; Dutch losses on, 220–21, 379; English claims to, 86–87, 346, 378, 379–81, 391, 394–95, 412, 415, 419–25, 426, 427–33, 440, 441, 442, 443–44, 447, 448, 449, 452, 454, 456, 477, 486–88; English settlers on (in New Netherland), 92, 137–38, 212, 238, 239–43, 249, 256, 287, 289, 313, 371, 379, 394–95, 412, 419–24, 428, 432, 441, 442, 443, 458, 484; first settlement on, 73; Hartford calls for rising on, 394–95, 419–21; Indian rampage on, 273–74; Indians of, 86, 119, 125, 128, 272, 277, 407; nucleus of York's province, 447, 452; piratical raids on, 240–41, 245; protests York's "usurpation," 480; Quakers on, 294, 295; Scott and, 380–81, 391, 394, 426, 427–34, 440, 443, 465; Underhill calls for liberation of, 239–40; Winthrop to, 443–44, 450, 453–54; York's forces arrive at, 454, 455–56
Long Island Sound, 5, 70, 87, 139, 380, 430
Long Peter, 409
Loockermans, Govert, 111, 133, 174, 205, 238, 321
Loper, Jacobus, 185
Lords Directors (of West India Company). *See* Heeren XIX
Louis XIII, King, 42
Louis XIV, King, 387, 390, 401, 469, 479, 491
Lourissen, Andries, 326–27
Lovelace, Sir Francis, 480, 483, 486
Lovelace, Thomas, 484, 486
Low Countries, 145, 156, 197
Lower Manhattan, and design of Fort Amsterdam, 14–15
Luanda, 254
Lubbertsen (Landtag petitioner), 244
Lubbertus, Sybrandus, 151
Lucassen, Pieter, 252
Lupolt, Petronella, 125
Lupolt, Ulrich, 75, 76, 125
Lutherans, in New Amsterdam, 291, 296–98, 335; in New Sweden, 300
Luyck, Dominie Aegidius, 367, 368, 372–73, 458
Lynn, 86

"Machidam" River, 98
Madoc ao Owen Gwyneth, 35
Madrid, 42
Magdeburg, 99
Mahikanders, 11
Maine, 36, 139
Maize, 44, 102, 142, 323
Manadoes. *See* Manhattan Island
Manahata. *See* Manhattan Island
Manahatin. *See* Manhattan Island
Manathans. *See* Manhattan Island
Manchester, Edward Montagu, 2nd Earl of, 391
Manhates. *See* Manhattan Island
Mahattan, 14–15, 100n, 334, 342
Manhattan Island, 114, 121, 124, 127, 128, 132, 169, 174, 188, 208, 214, 239, 253, 255, 261, 262, 267, 285, 288, 301, 305, 306, 343, 344, 353, 369, 398, 413, 414, 427, 450, 454, 459, 461, 464, 465, 475; and Anglo-Dutch War, 231; becomes New York, 467; climate of, 26; dawning of popular government on, 113–15; discovery of, 2–6; Dutch retaking of, 485–86; English resume government of, 493; English view of, 28, 30–

31, 41, 46, 54, 70, 342, 445; and Esopus War, 327, 328, 329; expansion of, 100*n*, 341; farms on, 13, 17, 49, 77, 334, 457; Fort Amsterdam erected on, 14, 16–17, 59, 77, 170; harbor of, 59–60, 97, 342, 347, 493; Indian rising on, 271–79, 293; Indians flee to, 117, 118; Indians of, 101, 110, 135–36, 272, 330; and New Plymouth, 41–46, 63–67, 220–21, 237, 248, 251; and patroon land purchases, 50–51; purchase of, 1–2, 30, 79, 86, 103, 463; Quakers arrive at, 294; schools on, 368–73; 1645 peace negotiations on, 135–36; Westchester-Indian plot against, 440; and Wiltwyck war, 411, 412. *See also* Fort Amsterdam (New Netherland); New Amsterdam; New Netherland; New York (English Province)

Manhattes. *See* Manhattan Island

Manitou, 105

Manna-hata. *See* Manhattan Island

Manning, John, 483–86

Manomet, 43, 45

Manuel the Giant, 357

Maranhão, 153, 154

Marcktveldt, 100

Maria, Infanta, 34

Maria Theresa, Infanta, 479

Martin, 448, 450

Martinique, 483

Mary (wife of Willem II). *See* Stuart, Mary

Maryland, 335, 376, 396; claims Dutch land on Delaware, 306–310, 329, 375, 398, 466; and D'Hinoyosa diplomacy, 398, 401–402; Dutch colonists flee to, 306, 307; Stuyvesant embassy to, 308–10

Mason, John, 125

Massachusetts Bay, 450

Massachusetts Bay Colony, 86, 91, 145, 149, 215, 218, 220, 237, 342, 383, 386, 392, 422, 445; character of, 69, 141, 143; Charles I and, 68; and Connecticut River settlement, 64–67, 71, 206; delegation to Europe, 95; desires peace with Dutch, 221, 248, 251; discovery of, 35–36; and Duke's invasion, 450, 458, 459; and Dutch-Indian "conspiracy," 235–39; and Dutch-Indian War, 138; and Dutch invasion of New York, 487, 489–90, 493; Hudson expansion of, 312, 314–18, 329, 375, 396; and origin of New Haven colony, 83; position among colonies, 139; religious intolerance in, 92, 137, 138, 143–44, 251, 296, 384; and Restoration, 376, 377; rivalry with New Plymouth, 66–67, 68; and Saye-Brooke charter, 69–70; settlement of, 64, 145–46; and Stuyvesant, 213, 216, 221, 235, 236, 238,

239, 314–18, 329, 375, 415–19, 459; Underhill and, 125; and Winthrop Jr., 69–70, 95, 385. *See also* Boston; Winthrop, John, Sr.

Massachusetts Bay Company, 67, 145

Massacres: at Amboina, 229–30, 236, 240, 449, 469; by Dutch in New Netherland, 118–19, 128, 129, 130, 132, 410; by Indians, 51–52, 127, 137, 138, 271, 273, 275, 277, 278, 293, 321, 327, 334, 343, 405–406; rumored on Guinea coast, 469

Mather, Rev. Cotton, 368

Mathews, Samuel, 318

Mattehoorn, 82, 261

Matteno, 411–12

Mauritius River, 1, 5, 30, 54. *See* Hudson River

Maurits, Prince (Maurice of Nassau), 8, 38

Maurits, Prince Johan (van Nassau-Siegen), 169

Maverick, Samuel: advises subjection of New England, 383–84, 391, 447; in Commission of Four, 447–48, 450; in New Amsterdam, 138, 342, 383; urges English takeover of New Netherland, 383, 427, 445–46, 447

Mayflower, 38, 125

Maypoles, 356

Mayn Mayano, 128

Medemblik, 82

Medicine: of Indians, 102; and voyages to America, 24–25

Medway River, 479

Meeuwken, 2

Megapolensis, Dirrick, 287

Megapolensis, Hillegont, 287

Megapolensis, Jan, 287

Megapolensis, Johannes, 298, 299, 346, 369–70, 461; aids Jewish refugees, 290; on Indians, 103–104, 105, 106, 107, 108, 280, 281; and Lutherans, 296–97, 300; negotiator with English, 456, 462; on New Netherland, 26, 291, 296, 321; pastor of New Amsterdam, 280, 285–87, 366; pastor of Rensselaerswyck, 103, 163, 204, 285, 286; on Quakers, 294

Megapolensis, Machteld, 286, 287

Megapolensis, Samuel, 287, 456, 461

Melyn, Anneke, 195

Melyn, Cornelis, 190, 192, 194, 492; appeals to States against Kieft, 133, 155; and *Broad Advice*, 191; captured by Indians, 273; delivers writ to Stuyvesant, 180–81, 184; in group of Eight, 125, 132, 133–34, 163, 164; sentence reversed, 178–79; and Stuyvesant enmity, 185–86, 197–98, 210, 273; Stuyvesant sentences, 164–65, 184; survives wreck, 166–67, 177

Melyn, Isaac, 492–93

Mennades. *See* Manhattan Island

Mennonites, 291, 399, 466

Mercurius, 301, 343

Mespath, 92, 137, 138, 361. *See also* Newtown (Long Island)

Meulen, 296

Mey, Cornelis Jacobsz: and settlement of New Netherland, 10–11, 13, 39

Meyndertsen, Meyndert, 116

Miantonimo, 115, 138

Michaëlius, Dominie Johannes, 15, 16–18, 58, 104, 107, 280, 282–83, 286

Michielsen, Stoffel, 351

Middelburg, 33, 157

Midwout, 241, 248, 288–89, 366, 380, 424, 429, 430, 456

Milkmaid, 154

Mills, Richard, 414–15

Minerals, 27

Minnewit, Peter. *See* Minuit, Peter

Minquas Kill, 82

Minuit, Peter: and acquisition of Manhattan, 2, 30, 79, 86, 97, 103, 463; governs New Netherland, 2, 15, 16–17, 28, 42–43, 58, 111, 159, 189, 282, 283, 334; leads Swedish expedition, 79–82, 258, 261, 262; and patroons' purchase of land, 50; recalled, 18, 29, 48, 51; relations with New Plymouth, 42–43, 46

Mohawks, 65, 97, 216; attack Algonquin tribes, 117; castle of, 325–26; claim English plot, 453; and Fort Orange vicinity, 16, 17, 50, 103, 108, 110, 117, 118, 135, 203, 207, 208, 324, 404, 406, 452–53; and French, 108, 324, 404; friendship with Dutch, 324–26, 329; Kieft treaty with, 135; Megapolensis on, 103–104, 286; sell land to patroons, 50; Stuyvesant receives captives of, 404; treaty with York's commissioners, 466; war with Hurons, 108, 324, 329; war with Mohicans, 16, 17, 63, 108, 110, 203, 453; war with Onakoques, 452–53

Mohicans, 16, 17, 56, 108, 110, 203, 236, 453; attack Canarsie Indians, 272; Dutch treaty with, 135; and English on Connecticut River, 63–64; sell land to patroons, 50

Molemaecker, Francis, 15

Moline. *See* Melyn, Cornelis

Monchonock, 86. *See also* Gardiner's Island

Monck, George, 317

Montreal, 404

Monument Beach, 43

Moody, Lady Deborah, 92, 93, 127, 137, 371

Morocco, 76

Morris, Rutger, 27

Muley Zidan, Sultan, 76

Mun, Thomas, 227, 229

Munster, 168, 169

Muscovy Company, 3

"Muscovy Duke" (Stuyvesant), 196, 202

Myggenborg, 263

Nantasket, 450, 451
Nantucket, 489, 491
Narragansett Bay, 94, 392
Narragansett Indians, 115, 138, 235
Narragansett River, 70
Narrows, the, 457
Nasaump, 142
Nassau, 43, 45
Navigation Acts, 229, 247, 252, 318, 378, 388, 389, 391, 416, 427, 436, 446
Nayack Bay, 454, 456–57
Neale, James, 310
Neptune, 111
Netherland Glorified by a Restoration of Commerce, 436
Netherlands, 23, 74, 79, 123, 164, 168, 176, 177, 185, 223, 288, 290, 297, 309, 313, 338, 353, 355, 386, 414, 426. *See also* Holland; Spanish Netherlands; States General; United Provinces
Nevis, 386
Nevius, Johannes, 351
"New Albion," 87–88
New Amersfoort, 73, 174, 205, 241, 245, 248, 288–89, 366, 380, 424, 430
New Amstel, 379; amalgamation with Altona, 401–402; clashes with West India Company, 398–99, 402; English conquest of, 466; flight from, 306, 307; and Maryland, 306–11, 398, 401–402; misfortunes of, 304–306, 311; Plockhoy scheme for, 399–400; purchase of, 301, 338; school in, 304, 370; settlement of, 303–304; voyage to, 302–303, 304
New Amstel, 311, 341
New Amsterdam, 25, 26, 75, 81, 108, 166, 205, 302, 334, 335, 377, 404, 420, 494; and Anglo-Dutch wars, 224, 230, 231, 232, 235, 247, 250–51, 287, 312, 336, 337, 380, 478–79, 482–93; Boston contrasted with, 416–17; Brazilian Dutch to, 132, 133, 154, 290–91; buildings in, 14, 59, 76, 98–100, 170, 171–72, 336–37, 341, 347, 431; celebrates peace, 250–51; as center of colonial trade, 156, 342–44, 475; church in, 15, 59, 98–100, 134, 143, 170, 171, 175, 180, 278, 284, 296, 334, 347, 350, 367, 417, 457; conditions at Stuyvesant's arrival, 170–72, 341, 476; conditions in 1660, 341–50; and Connecticut River settlement, 63–67, 68, 70–71, 78, 89–91, 94, 140, 146, 206, 219, 220, 312, 314; De Sille to, 275–79; defense against York's fleet, 451–52, 455–61, 465, 478; drinking in, 53, 54, 55, 57, 58, 59, 72–73, 75, 76, 99, 100–101, 111, 116, 170–71, 172, 200–201, 349, 354–55, 356, 364; Dutch character of, 347; duties in, 59, 86, 171, 214, 217, 301, 318, 339, 343, 344, 346, 431, 478; education in, 368–73; and the Eight, 124–25, 126, 127, 128, 130, 132, 133–34, 163, 164; and English

colonies, 28, 30–31, 33–35, 41–47, 61–66, 71, 78, 83–84, 85–87, 89–90, 94–96, 101, 126–27, 138, 140–41, 144, 146–49, 171, 182–83, 197, 213–24, 230, 235–40, 245, 248–49, 250, 251, 255–56, 287, 308–10, 312–19, 320, 329, 342, 346, 360, 375–76, 378–79, 381–83, 391–92, 394–98, 402, 412, 413–15, 417–25, 427–29, 435–36, 440–44, 453, 458, 459–60, 462, 463; English commission in, 237–39; and English on Delaware, 85–86, 88–89, 140, 217, 219, 221, 222–23, 256, 260, 266, 306–11, 312, 398; and English traders, 53–55, 63–65, 147, 314–15, 342–43, 346; Esopus skirmishes and, 320–24, 326–30; Esopus War of, 330–32, 343, 477; fire prevention in, 348–49; fleet of, 266–67; gives Delaware to Amsterdam, 401–402; Indian skirmishes of, 16, 109–14, 115–17; Indian tribes around, 103, 108, 110, 112, 271–79, 330; Indian War of, 109, 117–22, 124, 126–36, 137, 138, 140, 146, 154, 161, 164, 166, 173, 189, 193, 196, 198; invites English settlers, 91–93; law in, 351–58; and Long Island, 86–87, 220–21, 313, 378–81, 391, 394–95, 412, 415, 419–24, 426, 429–30, 432, 435, 440, 441, 442, 458; markets of, 350; and Massachusetts claims on Hudson, 312, 314–18; municipal government for, 194, 201, 231–32, 244, 349, 369; nationalities in, 97, 113; negotiations with Maryland, 308–10; and New Amstel, 303, 305, 306, 308–10, 398–99, 400–402; and New Haven settlement, 83, 140, 148, 214–15, 216, 237, 238, 239, 247, 248, 251; Nicolls' terms to, 454, 456–57, 459–61, 463, 473–74; and the Nine, 172–75, 180, 181, 182–84, 186, 187–89, 196, 200, 210; opening of foreign trade to, 344; pastors of, 15, 17–18, 58, 59, 72, 99, 162–63, 166, 170, 186–87, 280, 282–89, 296, 297, 366; and patroons, 50, 56–57, 205–11; paved streets in, 348; and "Peach War," 271–75, 276–79, 293, 320, 413; petitions Stuyvesant to surrender, 461–62; port of, 59–60, 97, 156, 159, 171, 278, 283–84, 342, 347, 350, 383, 388, 493; potential of, 28, 494; prosperity of, 59, 341–42, 475; provincial assembly in, 241–43, 424, 441–42; religious Babel of, 291; shrunken population of, 136, 431; and Stuyvesant authoritarianism, 164–65, 177, 195, 196, 222, 231, 242, 243, 340, 475; surrenders to English, 462–64, 476–77; and Swedes on Delaware, 81, 82, 169, 257, 258–70, 271, 272; tradesmen in, 59, 346, 349, 459; treaty with Nicolls, 462–63; and the Twelve, 113–15, 117, 118, 120, 124; wall of, 231, 232, 240, 293, 344, 451, 455, 461; and Wilt-

wyck war, 404–12, 424, 430, 477; Winthrop in, 382–84, 416. *See also* Manhattan Island; New Netherland; New Orange; New York
"New Belgium," 435, 436
New Canaan, 397
New Castle, 263
New England, 62, 73, 102, 125–26, 129, 242, 253, 255, 294, 337, 346, 355, 375, 387, 403; articles traded with Dutch, 342–43; and borders with New Netherland, 95, 140, 146, 188, 216, 218, 219, 220–21, 223, 250, 312, 314, 375, 378, 391, 395, 396, 415, 418, 435, 452, 453–54; character of, 140–45; Charles I and, 68–69; Charles II and, 375, 376–78, 379, 381, 391, 447, 449; churches contrasted to New Netherland, 98, 143, 280–81; confederation of, 138–40; Cromwell fleet to, 248–49, 251; delegation to Europe, 95; and Dutch capital, 22; and Dutch-Indian threat, 235–39, 247; and Dutch-Indian trade in firearms, 101, 176, 213–14, 217, 220, 235–38; first settlement of, 37–38; fragile unity of, 251, 393, 417–18; Gorges and, 33, 36, 47, 67–68, 384; government contrasted with New Netherland, 183; grant of, 36; Indians of, 84, 102, 115, 138; and Kieft's war, 126–27, 138; as market for England, 377–78, 388; Maverick on, 384, 391, 447; and New Amsterdam, 28, 30–31, 33–35, 41–47, 63–67, 68, 70, 71, 78, 82, 83–91, 94, 95, 101, 126–27, 138, 140–41, 144, 146–49, 169, 171, 182–83, 186, 188–89, 197, 213–24, 230, 235–40, 245, 248–49, 250, 251, 255–56, 287, 312–18, 329, 342, 375–76, 378–79, 381–83, 391–92, 394–97, 398, 402, 413–15, 417–25, 427–29, 435–36, 440–44, 453, 458, 459–60, 462, 463; and New Orange, 486–88, 489–90; persecutes Quakers, 296; and Plowden "palatinate," 88–89; Puritan emigration to, 67–69, 95, 141–42, 145–46; refugees from, 91–92, 137–38, 215–16, 251, 335; refugees from New Orange in, 489; and slave trade, 254; standard of living in, 182; and Stuyvesant, 179, 213–24, 235–40, 245, 248–49, 313–18, 337, 375–79, 382–84, 394–97, 402, 413–20, 423–25, 435, 440, 441–42, 443, 453, 459–60; Stuyvesant in, 219–22, 337, 415–19, 420, 475; villages contrasted with New Netherland, 92–93, 143, 171, 277; war with Pequots, 84, 102, 125, 126; whipping in, 356; Winthrop missions for, 69–71, 95, 381, 385, 389, 391–92; witchcraft in, 336; and York's invasion of New Netherland, 447, 449–51, 452, 453, 454, 459–60, 462, 463, 465. *See also* United Colonies of New En-

gland; and under names of colonies

New England Company, 67

New England Confederation, 138–40. *See also* United Colonies of New England

New France, 6

New Guinea, 8

New Haarlem, 411, 424

New Haven, 221, 245, 273, 315, 316, 361, 375, 421, 426, 486; and *Beninjo* incident, 214–15, 216; and Connecticut charter, 381, 392–93, 396–98, 417, 427, 433; and Delaware settlement, 84–86, 87, 138, 140, 146, 217, 219, 222–23, 255–56, 266, 397; desires war with New Netherland, 247, 248, 251; and Dutch-Indian plot, 237, 238, 239; and Dutch smugglers, 214, 344; included in Duke's charter, 447; and Long Island, 87, 379, 381; and New Canaan under Dutch, 397; and North River settlement, 147–49; position among colonies, 139; Puritan conditions in, 139, 143, 144, 396–97; and Restoration, 376, 377; settlement of, 83–84, 141; and war appeal from Dutch, 126–27, 138

New Holland, 169

New Jersey, 88

New Jorcke. *See* New York (English Province)

New London, 102, 217

New Netherland: charter from States General, 425, 435, 442, 459; conditions of voyage to, 23–25, 158; and Connecticut charter, 381–84, 391–92, 394–97, 398, 422, 426, 440, 443–44; contacts with New Plymouth, 41–46, 57, 63–67; courts of, 76, 102, 164–65, 173, 174, 176, 198, 202, 208, 231–32, 253, 279, 289, 291, 294, 345, 349, 350, 351–58, 361, 372, 380, 382, 397; De Ruyter ordered to retake, 471–72, 478, 479–80; Duke's charter for, 447, 451, 452; and English, 28, 29–31, 33–35, 41–47, 54, 56, 61–67, 68, 70, 71, 78, 79, 83–91, 94–96, 126–27, 138, 140–41, 144, 146–49, 169, 182–83, 186, 188–89, 206, 212–24, 230, 235–40, 245, 248–49, 250, 251, 255–56, 287, 306–10, 312–19, 320, 329, 338, 360, 374–76, 378–83, 391–92, 394–98, 399, 402, 412, 413–15, 417–25, 426–30, 431–32, 435–36, 440–44, 445–52, 453, 454, 455–64, 465–67; English fleet to, 448–52, 453, 454, 455–64, 465; English Separatists appeal to, 37–38; English settlers in, 91–93, 137–38, 144, 146, 174, 212, 218, 239–43, 249, 256, 287, 298–99, 300, 313, 335, 342, 371, 375, 394–95, 397, 412–15, 419, 421, 424, 428, 432, 441, 442, 443, 449, 458; extent at Stuyvesant's arrival, 169–70; failure of, 23, 71, 493–94; farming in, 13, 49, 73, 77, 78, 79, 194, 195, 201, 204, 274, 321, 334,

350, 408, 457, 492; first steps toward democracy in, 113, 133, 173; flogging in, 356–57; founding of, 2, 6, 10–18, 39; government contrasted with New England, 183; government officers of, 2, 13, 15, 16, 48, 51, 52–53, 58, 59, 72, 73–75, 113, 115, 124–25, 131, 133, 155–56, 161–63, 172–75, 194, 200, 231–32, 242, 243, 275–79, 349, 407, 424; heretics in, 290–99, 334–35; and Indians, 2, 15–16, 17, 27, 45, 51–52, 54–55, 56, 73, 84, 86, 90, 101–108, 109–14, 115–20, 122, 123–36, 137, 138, 140, 146, 154, 161, 162, 164, 169, 170, 175–77, 187, 195, 198, 203, 204, 207, 208, 235–36, 261, 262, 263, 271–79, 280–81, 286, 293, 320–32, 338, 339, 359, 404–12, 413, 440–43, 452–53, 475; internal troubles of, 16–18, 46–47, 52, 56–59, 72–73, 120–21, 132–34, 161–66, 180–90, 194–98, 200–201, 202, 204–11, 212, 233, 242, 283–85; Kieft governs, 73–77, 79, 82, 85, 86–93, 96, 97–101, 106, 108, 109–14, 115–22, 123–24, 127–29, 131, 132–36, 140, 146–49, 160, 161–63, 166, 175, 204, 283–84, 344; Krol and, 48–52, 54–56; lack of villages in, 92–93, 277, 321–22; living conditions in, 14–15, 26–28, 46, 59, 76–77, 97–101, 134, 170–72, 195, 341–43, 346, 347–50; London campaign against, 427, 445–46; makes news in Europe, 192; Minuit and, 2, 15, 16–18, 42–43, 46, 50, 51, 79, 81–82, 97, 189, 282, 283, 334, 463; morals in, 75–76, 141, 352–54, 356, 357; natural resources of, 14, 26–28, 347, 363, 374, 493; and Navigation Acts, 229, 318, 388–89, 391, 436, 446; New Haveners apply to, 397; patroon project in, 49–51, 52, 58, 79, 204–11, 242, 286, 324; petition for government reform in, 115; poetry in, 25–26, 359–63, 365, 366–68, 406; provincial petition in, 242–44; publicity for, 374–75, 397; recaptured by Dutch, 483–90; reconstruction of, 170–75; religious freedom in, 91–92, 97, 173, 251, 292, 296–97, 299, 397; returned to English, 491–94; and 1649 appeal to States General, 187–90; 1650 provisional order reforming government of, 194, 195, 196, 201; and slave trade, 252–54; soldiers to, 52–53; Stuyvesant appointed to, 156–60, 161, 163, 169–70, 476; surrender of, 463–64, 465–67; Swedish encroachment on, 79–82, 169, 257, 258–70, 271, 272, 297; trade in, 1–2, 6, 8–9, 11, 12–13, 17, 19, 29, 43, 47, 78, 84, 101, 105, 108, 109, 110, 134, 156, 171, 173, 175–77, 203–204, 213–14, 217, 220, 223, 235, 263, 305, 312, 342–44; Van Twiller in, 52–59, 61–65, 70, 71, 72–73, 76–77, 97, 98, 112, 162, 283, 334; Walloons to, 38–39. *See also* New Amster-

dam; New Orange; New York (English Province); Stuyvesant, Peter

New Orange, 485; Dutch character of, 488; fortification of, 490; government of, 486, 488–89; and Hartford, 486–88, 489; and Massachusetts, 487, 489–90; restitution to England, 491–93. *See also* New York

New Plymouth, 16, 38, 92, 125, 135, 269, 376, 392, 433; conditions in, 44; and Connecticut River settlement, 63–67, 68; position among colonies, 139; Puritan laws of, 141, 143; relations with Dutch, 41–46, 57, 63–65, 67, 68, 220–21, 235, 237, 248, 251, 419, 459, 487, 490; rivalry with Bay Colony, 66–67, 68

New Sweden: background of, 79–81; birth of, 82; capitulation of, 269–70, 272, 297, 300, 301; and New Haven, 84–86, 260, 266; and New Netherland, 185, 257, 258–70, 271, 276; under Dutch, 300–301, 466, 477

New Utrecht, 364, 365, 380, 424, 454

New York (English province), 466; Dutch-English diplomacy over, 467–71; Dutch invasion of, 482–87, 492; Dutch origin of, 1, 14–15; government of, 464, 467, 473–74, 489, 491; marks end of Dutch Golden Age, 494; prosperity of, 488; rechristened New Orange, 485; restored to England, 491–93. *See also* New Amsterdam; New Orange

New York City, 100n. *See also* Manhattan

New York State, 51

Newes from America (Underhill), 125

Newesingh Indians, 412

Newfoundland, 5, 52, 194, 416, 480, 486

Newman, Francis, 237

Newmarket, 29, 30

Newton, Brian, 157, 172, 318, 320

Newtown (Long Island), 92, 137, 242, 298, 379, 394, 419, 420, 422, 443

Newtown (Massachusetts), 66

Niantic Indians, 235

Nicolls, Matthias, 489

Nicolls, Sir Richard: arrives at Long Island, 454, 455–56; conquers provinces, 466–67; governor of New York, 464, 467, 473–74, 480, 489; leads expeditionary force, 447–48, 449, 476, 478; raises support from Long Island, 458; requests troops from Boston, 450; terms to Stuyvesant, 454, 456–57, 459–60, 461, 462–63, 473–74; troops occupy New Amsterdam, 463–64; and Winthrop, 451, 454, 460

Niessen, Christiaen, 406

Nieu Nederlandt, 10, 39, 63

Nieu Nederlandt (2nd ship), 17, 189
Nieu Nederlandts Fortuyn, 197
"Nieu Pliemven." *See* New Plymouth
Nieuwpoort (ambassador in London), 270
Nijkerk, 205
Nine Select Men, 172, 173, 180, 181, 200; composition of, 174–75, 182; conflict with Stuyvesant, 183–84, 186, 187–90, 196, 210; powers of, 174; suspended, 210
Ninigret, 235, 237
Nonconformists, 83, 94, 141. *See* Puritans
"Norrogancett Bay." *See* Narragansett Bay
North River, 29, 38, 50, 147, 148, 208, 231, 232, 273, 312, 315–17, 331, 411, 413, 460.
North Sea, 20, 25, 29, 31, 226, 480
Northern Indians, 452–53
Nottingham, 93
Nova Anglia. *See* New England
Nova Bohemia, 310, 335, 398
Nova Scotia, 404
Nova Zembla, 3, 5
Novum Belgium (Jogues), 97
Nueva Suecia, 258. *See* New Sweden
Nut Island. *See* Governor's Island

Oakey, John, 386
Observations, 471
Ogden, John, 99
Ogden, Richard, 99
Oldham, John, 64
Olim Jacatra, 228
Onakouques Indians, 452–53
Onrust, 5
Oostdorp, 299, 414. *See* Westchester
Op't Water, 336
Orange, Princes of, 19, 28, 33, 34, 54, 91, 93, 119, 125, 133, 205, 226, 227, 246, 250, 261, 407, 482, 484, 487
Orangists, 226, 387
Orantinim, 177
Oratamy, 411–12
Ordinances and Code of Procedure before the Courts of the City of Amsterdam, 351
Örn, 264, 265
Orson, 6
Overtoom, 198
Overzee, Simon, 308
Oxenstierna, Count Axel, 80, 259, 264
Oyster Bay, 169, 220, 487

Pacham, 112, 124
Paerelstraat, 354. *See* Pearl Street
Palatinate, 288
Palmer, Barbara. *See* Villiers, Barbara, Lady Castlemaine
Pampus, 25
Papegoia, Armegot, 268
Papegoia, Johan, 264
Papoquanaehem, 410
Parcel, Jan, 356
Paris, 11, 100, 234, 436, 466
Park Row, 15

Parliament, 94, 95, 145, 218, 226, 229, 239, 245, 247, 250, 254, 255, 376, 390, 437, 439, 447, 472, 491
Patroons, 49–51, 52, 56, 58, 242, 286, 324; clash with West India Company, 204–11; and 1640 liberalization, 79; and slaves, 49, 253
Patuxent, 308–10
Patuxent Bay, 310
"Paugussett River," 147
Pauw, Adriaen, 225
Pauw, Michiel, 50
Paving, in New Amsterdam (New Orange), 348, 488
Pavonia, 51, 72–73, 117, 118, 124, 125, 174
Pawcatuck River, 392
Peace of Breda, 478–79
Peace of Munster, 168, 169
Peace of Westminster, 250, 251, 307, 313; of 1674, 492
"Peach War," 271–79, 293, 320, 413
Pearl Street, 14, 59, 100*n*, 232, 350, 354, 362
Pelham Neck, 92
Pell, Thomas, 256, 413
Pels, Evert, 332
Penhawitz, 86, 120, 128
Penn, Sir William, 255
Peperga, 150–51
Pepys, Samuel, 386, 390, 437, 439, 465, 469, 470
Pequot Indians: and New Haven colonists on Delaware, 84; sell Connecticut land to Dutch, 63, 65; treaty with English on Connecticut, 65; war with Puritans, 84, 102, 125, 126
Pequot River, 217
Pequot War, 126
Pereboom, 252, 253
Perkins, Edward, 361–62
Peter, Rev. Hugh, 69, 70, 94–95, 126
Petition, 187–88, 193
Petraeus, 385
Philadelphia, 306
Philip IV, King, 34
Pieter (hangman), 357
Pietersen, Evert, 303–304, 370, 371
Pietersen, Jan, 336
Pietersen, Styntjen, 151
Pietersz, Cornel, 110
Pilgrims, 38, 92, 125; and Dutch colonists, 41–46, 67; oppose Dutch on Connecticut, 64–67; rivalry with Bay Colony, 66–67. *See also* New Plymouth
Pinnaces, 23
Piracy: and Dutch-English accord, 471; of New Netherland turncoats, 240–41, 245, 248, 336; of Royal African Company, 437, 469; Scott and, 380; Turkish, 52
Plague, 470, 479
Plancius, Dominie, 3
Planck, Abram, 113, 117, 120
Planters' Plea, 46
Plimoth. *See* New Plymouth
Pliny, 12
Plockhoy, Pieter Cornelisz, 399–400

Plowden, Sir Edmund, 88
Plumb, J. H., 21
Plymouth, 29, 31, 36, 47
Plymouth (colony). *See* New Plymouth
Plymouth Company, 36, 86
Pocahontas, 252
Point Comfort, 62
Poland, 28, 258, 259, 401
Polder building, 9, 20
Polhemius, Catherina, 288
Polhemius, Dominie Johannes Theodorus, 288–89, 290, 366
Portsmouth, 448, 450
Portugal, 6, 20, 77, 97, 150, 168, 247, 292, 293, 298, 399, 416, 436; Dutch lose Angola to, 169, 338; Dutch treaty with, 389; English alliance with, 379, 389; reconquers Brazil, 288, 290; and slave trade, 254; sponsors pamphlets against West India Company, 190–91; supports Brazilian insurgents, 169
Pos, Lodewyck, 349, 354
Pos, Simon, 16–17, 47, 52
Potomac River, 306
Poughkeepsie, 314
Prague, 175
"Praise of New Netherland, The" (Steendam), 362
Prence, Thomas, 220, 433
Presbyterians, in New Netherland, 298–99
Preummaker, 331
Prince, Thomas. *See* Prence, Thomas
Princess Amalia, 157–58, 165–66, 177, 187, 284
Princess Royal, 267
Prins Maurits, 302, 303
Printz, John, 80, 260, and New England, 85–86; and New Netherland, 259–64
Printz, Maria van Linnestau, 259
Privateers, French, 290, 342. *See also* Piracy
"Privies," in New Amsterdam, 347–48
"Privileges and Exemptions of Patroons, Masters, and Private Individuals," 49
Privy Council, 68
Prostitution, in New Netherland, 76, 107, 173, 353
Protectorate, 319, 438. *See* Commonwealth of England
Provincial assembly: in New Netherland, 241–43; called by Stuyvesant, 424, 441–42
Provincial Council, 330, 355, 356, 369, 371, 397
Provost, David, 148, 238, 371
Puerto Rico, 15, 153
Pulu Run, 229, 391
Puritans, 45, 65, 66, 149, 214, 218, 355, 386, 391, 398, 400, 416, 428, 447, 448; character of, 141–46; churches of, 98; Dutch view of, 140–41; emigration of, 67–69, 70, 141–42, 145–46; in Holland, 37, 139, 140; and Indians, 84, 102; of Massachusetts Bay, 64, 69, 139, 296; in New Haven settle-

ment, 83, 84, 396–97; and New Netherland's freedom of religion, 91–92, 251, 291, 335, 397; to New Plymouth, 38; and Underhill, 126, 138. *See also* New England; and under names of colonies

Pynchon, John, 453, 462

Quakers. *See* Society of Friends
Quebec, 108, 343, 403
Quinnipiac River, 83, 381

Rademaker, Claes, 112, 113, 115
Raet, 158
Raleigh, Sir Walter, 31, 35
Rampjaar, 483
Rapenburg, 338
Rappelje, Joris-Janes, 113
Rappelje, Sarah, 113
Raritan Indians, 198; enmity to Dutch, 110–11, 112–13, 114
Raritan River, 111
Rayon, Deborah, 380, 434
Reade, Elizabeth, 69, 94
Real, 85
Red Hill, 147
Reformed Church, 98–99, 145, 173, 281, 296, 299, 480. *See also* Calvinism
Rekenkamer (West India Company), 131
Religion: Dutch, 7–8, 21, 98, 151, 280–89, 295, 296–97, 334–35; freedom of in New Netherland, 91–92, 97, 173, 251, 286, 291–92, 295, 296, 297, 397; Independent, 291, 298, 299; and Indians, 104–105, 280–81; Lutheran, 291, 296–98, 300, 335; Presbyterian, 298–99; of Puritans, 37–38, 91–92, 137, 138, 140–41, 143–45, 251, 291, 296, 335, 396–97; Quaker, 293–96, 335, 400; and slaves, 366, 368; tolerance in Amsterdam, 21, 37, 67, 140, 281, 291, 292. *See also* Jews; Mennonites; Roman Catholics
Remonstrance of New Netherland to the States General of the United Netherlands, 187, 189–90, 193, 196, 198, 202, 231, 241, 242, 275, 285, 339, 369
Remonstrants, 7
Rensselaer county, 50
Rensselaers Stein, 204–205
Rensselaerswyck, 52, 103, 135, 147, 163, 166, 176, 181, 285, 286, 324, 412; conflict with New Amsterdam, 204–11, 441; and creation of Beverwyck, 210–11; founding of, 50; pastor of, 103, 163, 204, 285–86
Restoration, 317, 374, 375–78, 380, 383, 384, 386, 388, 391, 397, 398
Reyniers, Griet, 76, 353
Reyntgen, Jacob, 176
Rhine River, 315, 316
Rhineland, 22
Rhode Island, 92, 109, 119, 139, 179, 197, 218, 294, 295, 376, 427; and Connecticut charter, 392, 487; haven for privateers, 240
Rhode Island Sound, 43

Rich, Robert, 2nd Earl of Warwick: and Connecticut patent, 70, 94, 95, 391; and patent to Massachusetts colony, 67
Richards, John, 315, 316
Ridder, Peter, 84
River Indians, 11, 119, 120, 125, 277, 278, 326, 331
River of Canada, 169
Riviere van der Vorst Mauritius. *See* Mauritius River
Robinson, Rev. John, 37
Rochelle, La, 74
Roelantsen, Adam, 59, 368–69
Rolfe, John, 252
Roman Catholics, 95, 168, 400; in Amsterdam, 21, 281; in Maryland, 306, 398; in New Netherland, 286, 291, 298. *See also* France; Jesuits; Spain
Rotterdam, 70, 94, 123, 154
Rouen, 5
Roy, Jacob, 135
Royal African Company, 426, 437, 469
Royal Charles, 479
Royal Company of Adventurers, 390, 426. *See also* Royal African Company
Royal Commission, 447. *See* Commission of Four
Royal Secretariat, 447
Royal Swedish General Trading Company, 80, 81, 259, 264, 269
Rupert, Prince, 469
Russia, 12, 22
Rysingh, Johan, 264–69, 272

Sagredo, Alviso, 436, 439, 469
St. Charles, 288, 290
St. Christopher, 82, 154, 158
St. Helena, 483
St. John, Oliver, 226, 227
St. Joseph, 490
St. Mark's-in-the-Bouwerie, 334, 480
St. Martin, 153–55, 158
St. Martyn, 52, 54–55, 85
St. Mary's, 308, 310
St. Nicholas Church, 99, 170, 171, 180, 284, 296, 328, 334, 347, 367
St. Stephens Church, 83
Salem, 67, 126, 145, 380, 386
Salt trade, 20, 32, 343, 416
Sandy Hook, 88
Sauna, Indian, 104
Saxony, 99
Saybrook, 70
Saye and Sele, William Fiennes, 1st Viscount, 69, 94, 140, 391
Scandinavia, 168
Schaefbanck, Pieter, 351, 358
Schaets, Dominie Gideon, 335
Schepens: in New Amsterdam, 231–32, 243, 244–45, 250, 251, 278, 297, 305, 336, 349, 351–52, 369, 371, 372, 379, 424, 441, 458, 474; of New Amstel, 301; of New Orange, 489
Schermerhorn, Jacob Jansen, 176
Scheveningen, 317
Schiedam, 158
Schools: in New Amstel, 304, 370;

in New Amsterdam, 59, 175, 194, 282, 285, 368–73
Schouts Bay, 86
Schreierstoren, 25
Schreyer's Hoeck, 171
Schriftelicke Examinatien ofte Confessie (Megapolensis), 286
Schüte, Sven, 265, 267
Schuyler, Philip, 210
Schuylkill, 259, 261
Scotland, 32, 229, 317
"Scots and Chinese," 187, 345
Scott, Deborah. *See* Rayon, Deborah
Scott, John: arrested, 433–34, 440; career of, 380; claims Long Island, 380–81, 391, 394, 426, 427–32, 435, 440, 443; commissioned to investigate New Netherland, 427, 445; and Connecticut commission, 427–29, 432–33; joins York's forces, 456; and New Haven, 397–98, 427, 433; as "President," 428–32, 433; and Stuyvesant, 394, 429–32, 440
Scurvy, 24, 154
Seawan, 45, 346. *See also* Wampum
Second Part of the Amboyne Tragedy, The, 236, 247
Secoutagh, 303
Sedgwick, Robert, 248
Seeley, Nathan, 433
Seely, Lieutenant, 223
Selyns, Dominie Henricus, 334, 363, 365–68, 406, 481
Senecas, 466
Separatists, 37–38. *See* Puritans
Sephardic Jews, 292
Setauket, 427, 428, 433
Seven Provinces, 190. *See* United Provinces
Seventeenth Street, 334
Seweckenamo, 411–12, 443
s'Gravesande, 76, 212, 241. *See also* Gravesend
Sharpe, John, 484, 485, 489, 492, 493
"Ship fever," 24
Shipbuilding, 17, 64, 146
Short Account of New Netherland's Situation, A, 436
Short Account of the Mohawk Indians (Megapolensis), 103, 286
Short and clear plan . . . (Plockhoy), 399–400
"Short Notes," 244
"Sieckentroosters," 48, 282
Silk, 28
Sint Beninjo, 214–15, 216, 218
Slave trade, 152, 252–54, 338, 362, 437
Slaves: African, in New Netherland, 49, 77, 97, 252–54, 283, 326, 330, 334, 356, 357, 362, 366, 455, 457, 458; Dutch soldiers sold as, 466, 477; Indian, 102–103, 148, 254
Sluyter, Hendrick Janzen, 353
Small Burghers, 345–46
Smallpox epidemic, 65–66
Smit, Dirck, 267, 323, 326–27, 329–31

Smit, Hendrick Jansen, 357–58
Smith, John, 3
Smith's Island, 88
Smoutius, Adrianus, 283
Smuggling, 73, 75; at Fort Christina, 305; Stuyvesant deals with, 171, 172, 344–45
Society of Adventurers, 95
Society of Friends, 293–96, 335, 380, 400
Sole Bay, 482
Soutberg, 52, 53, 58, 76
South America, 77, 190. *See* Brazil
South River, 11, 29, 51, 62, 84–85, 140, 243, 258, 259, 263, 300, 301, 303, 312, 317, 375, 398, 400, 401, 459. *See also* Delaware River
Southampton, 38
Southampton (Long Island), 87, 380
Southern Netherlands. *See* Spanish Netherlands
Southold, 87, 380, 394; English-Dutch encounter at, 488, 492
Spain, 2, 6, 32, 290, 292, 342, 344, 389, 416; and Dutch capital, 22; Dutch church and, 21, 98; Dutch commercial precedence over, 19–20; and Dutch in Caribbean, 8, 150, 152, 153, 247, 255; and English in Caribbean, 247, 255; and marriage negotiations with England, 34–35, 41–42; missionary zeal contrasted with Dutch, 280–81; New World claims of, 7, 35, 36, 309; and slaves, 254, 362; treaty with United Provinces (1648), 168; truce with Dutch, 7, 8; war with Dutch, 7, 8, 19, 21, 35, 42, 80, 150, 151, 152, 153, 168, 181, 190
Spanish Netherlands, 38, 190, 479
Specht, Machtelt, 366–67
Speculation, Dutch, 22
Speedwell, 38
Spice Islands, 3, 33, 229, 230
Spice trade, 3, 20, 33, 42, 228
Spitzbergen, 33
Springfield, 89, 453, 462
Squanto, 44
Stadt Huys: of Amsterdam, 169, 250; of New Amsterdam, 244, 347, 351
Stadt's Herberg, 100, 101, 135, 171, 232
Staets, Abraham, 453
Stamford, 126, 127, 128, 129, 137, 220, 422
Stangh, Jacob, 121
Staple Act, 388, 446
"Staple right," 59
State Street, 336
Stated Baai, 5
Staten Island, 100, 128, 181, 278; Dutch invasion forces at, 482, 486; English claim of, 313; Huguenots on, 288; Indian depredations on, 110, 111, 112, 116, 272, 273; Indians of, 411; Melyn fortification of, 198, 210; Nicolls on, 456; patroon of, 125, 163, 185, 197
States General, 19, 87, 95, 202, 484, 487, 490; abolishes West India

Company monopoly, 78, 109, 156, 157; and acquisition of Manhattan, 1; addresses Long Island towns, 442, 443; and Anglo-Dutch War, 225, 230, 234, 250; appealed to against Kieft, 133; appealed to against Stuyvesant, 165, 178, 187–90, 193–95, 197; appealed to in Indian War, 127, 130; and Brazil, 169; commissions Stuyvesant, 157; and Commonwealth, 226, 312–13; and Downing, 387, 388, 435; and Duke of York, 438–39; encourages slave trade, 252; and English claims in North America, 29–30, 33–35, 43, 64, 78, 85, 91, 94, 95, 146, 149, 219, 223, 312, 316, 378, 391, 413, 414, 432, 435, 443, 448, 463, 467, 471, 491; and English invasion of New Netherland, 448, 463, 465, 467, 471, 476; New England Confederation compared to, 139; and New Netherland, 1, 6, 17, 29–30, 37, 43, 46, 50, 55–56, 70, 72, 73, 77–78, 109, 127, 130, 132, 133, 146, 149, 156, 157, 163, 178, 185–87, 193–95, 197, 201, 219, 222, 295, 316, 339, 351, 374–75, 378, 391, 413, 414, 432, 435, 441, 442, 443, 448; New Netherland reforms of, 78–79, 157, 194, 201; and New Sweden, 265, 269, 270; and New York, 467; patent for New Netherland, 425, 435, 442, 459; and patroons, 50, 78–79, 208; questionnaire on New Netherland, 78; and restitution of New Orange, 491–92; reverses sentences of Melyn and Kuyter, 178–79, 180; Separatists apply to, 37–38; 1650 provisional order of, 194, 196, 201; 1652 order of, 201; and 1665 English war, 472, 478; Stuyvesant addresses, 185–86; Stuyvesant defense before, 476–77, 478; Stuyvesant remonstrance to, 274; summons Stuyvesant, 178, 180–81, 186, 194, 195, 201; and West India Company, 1, 8, 17, 29–30, 34, 46, 56, 77–78, 156, 157, 161, 169, 178, 183, 193, 198, 201, 223, 230, 339, 378, 467, 476
Stede Amsterdam, 321
Steen, Hans, 118
Steendam, Jacob, 25, 351, 359–63, 365, 368, 400
Steenwyck, Cornelis, 352, 424, 460, 462, 473, 488, 489*n*
Stevensz, Jan, 369
Stilwell, Nicholas, 407, 419–20
Stirling, Earl of, 86
Stirling, 4th Earl of, 379, 380, 447
Stock Exchange (Amsterdam), 22
Stockholm, 79, 264
Stoll, Jacob Jansen, 327
Stone, Captain, 57, 65
Stone, Rev. Samuel, 383, 385
Stone Street, 14, 100, 348, 361
Strand, the, 336, 348, 350, 357, 480
Strickland, Walter, 226, 227
"Strongheaded Peter," 213

Stuart, Mary, 94, 226, 387, 438
Stuart family, 35, 226, 250, 313, 391
Student Club, 151
Stuyfsant, Balthasar. *See* Stuyvesant, Balthasar
Stuyvesant, Anna, 151, 154, 155, 294, 335, 336
Stuyvesant, Balthasar, 150–52
Stuyvesant, Balthasar Lazarus, 334, 368, 462
Stuyvesant, Judith, 155, 157, 159, 185, 254, 271, 333–34, 474, 480
Stuyvesant, Nicholas Willem, 334, 368, 475
Stuyvesant, Peter (or Petrus), 24, 28, 166, 203, 212, 287, 288–89, 299, 348, 350, 353, 357, 358, 365, 487; achievement of, 475; and Anglo-Dutch War, 224, 231, 232, 235–36, 247, 250–51, 337; appearance of, 159, 337; appointed to New Netherland, 156–60, 161, 163–65, 169–79, 284–85, 338, 341; and arms sales to Indians, 175–77, 195, 235–38; attacked by West India Company, 477–78; authoritarianism of, 163–65, 177, 195, 196, 207, 222, 231, 242, 243, 292–93, 297, 340, 475; blow to authority of, 177–79, 180–81; in Boston, 415–19; bouwery of, 271, 334, 337, 370, 457, 462, 474, 480; and Brazilian exodus, 131–32, 153–54, 291–92; and City Council, 231–33, 251–52, 455; concludes peace treaty with Indians, 442–43; critics of, 178–79, 180–89, 192, 193–98, 200–202, 210, 218, 239, 242–44, 276, 285; at Curaçao, 131, 150, 152–54, 155, 156; and De Sille, 275–78, 363–64; death of, 480–81, 482; declares war on Esopus Indians, 330–32; defense before States General, 476–77, 478; and Duke's charter, 447, 449, 452; early life of, 150–52; and Eaton, 214–15, 216, 217, 237, 245; and English invasion, 451–52, 455–64, 465, 476–78; and English privateers, 240–41, 245, 248, 336; foresees war with New England, 423–25; and Hartford conference, 216, 219–24; hosts Winthrop Jr., 382–84; impoverished administration of, 424; and Indians, 271–75, 277–78, 320–32, 338, 339, 404–407, 408, 410, 412, 418, 419, 440–41, 442–43, 452–53; and Jews, 291–93, 334, 362; and Kieft, 163–65; loses leg, 153; and Lutherans, 296–98, 335; marriage of, 155; and New Amstel colonists, 302, 303, 305, 308, 310, 398–99, 401–402; and New Amsterdam trade, 342–47; and New England, 179, 212–24, 235–39, 245, 248–49, 313–18, 337, 375–79, 382–84, 394–97, 398, 402, 413–20, 423–25, 435, 440, 441–42, 443, 453, 459–60, 475; New Haveners apply to, 397; and New Sweden, 257, 258, 261–70, 271, 272, 276, 300, 301, 441; in

New York, 473, 474, 480; officials of, 172–75, 182–83, 199–201, 231–32, 242, 275–79, 349, 407, 424; orders settlers into villages, 277–78, 321–22; ordinances of, 170–72, 177, 206, 209–10, 215, 274, 345, 347, 348, 355–56; and patroons, 206–11; personal life of, 333–38; petitioned to surrender city, 461–62; and provincial petitioners, 242–44; puritanism of, 354–56, 382; and Quakers, 294–96, 335; returns to Republic, 474–79; and schools, 368, 369, 370, 371, 372–73; and Scott, 394, 429–32, 440; sentences Melyn and Kuyter, 164–65, 178; and siege of Fort Christina, 268–70, 271, 272; and slaves, 252, 253–54, 362, 457; summoned by States, 178–79, 180–81, 186, 194, 195, 201; summons provincial assembly, 424, 441–42; surrenders city, 463–64, 476–77; to West Indies, 252–53, 255, 256, 258, 266, 267, 276, 343; travels of, 203, 219–22, 252, 255, 261, 337, 404, 415–19, 432, 443, 452, 455, 475, 478; as versifier, 152–53; and Virginia, 287, 318–19, 320; and West India Company finances, 338–40; and Westchester, 413–15, 417, 440; and Winthrop, 213, 216, 217, 382, 383; and Winthrop Jr., 217–18, 336, 382–84, 394–96, 415, 417–18, 423, 424, 440, 443–44, 453, 454, 459–60, 461

Sugar, 22, 254, 416
"Sunk Squaw," 433
Supreme Court of Holland, 182
Suriano, Cristofore, 8
Surinam, 478, 491
Surinam, 487
Swaenenburgh, 483–85
Swanendael, 50, 53, 81; massacre at, 51–52, 61
Swannekens, 102, 112, 113, 116, 118, 120, 124, 322
Swansea, 166
Swarte Beer, 6
Sweden, 9, 20, 343, 401; colony under Dutch, 300, 301, 466, 477; *Mercurius* colonists from, 301; North American settlement of, 79–82, 84, 85, 88, 169, 217, 257, 258–70, 271, 272, 400, 441; war with Poland, 258, 259
Swits, Claes Cornelissen. *See* Rademaker, Claes
Synod of Dort, 295, 296

T Lof van Nieu-Nederlandt (Steendam), 362
Taden, Michiel, 354
Talcott, John: and Long Island, 419, 421, 428; and Westchester, 413, 415, 417, 421
Tangier, 389
Tappan Indians, 110, 117, 122
Taxes: beer and wine excise, 132–33, 171, 233, 241, 244; and fortification of New Amsterdam, 233; imposed by burgomasters, 349; imposed by Kieft, 110, 132–33;

imposed by Stuyvesant, 171, 172, 189, 249, 293, 441; and New England, 182; in New Orange, 489; as object of *Remonstrance*, 187, 188, 189; and patroons, 49
Terreneuf, 471, 480
Texel, 2, 3, 10, 25, 81, 157, 302, 385
Thames, 316, 470, 479
Thienpont, Adriaen Jorisz, 11
Thirty Years' War, 168
Thomassen, Ielmer, 158
Three Little Doves, 199
Throckmorton, Rev. John, 91
Ticonderoga, 108
Tidön, 264
Timber: in New Amstel, 301, 303; in New England, 377; in New Netherland, 26, 28
Tinicum Island, 260
Tobacco, 27–28, 62, 63, 81, 82, 102, 188, 201, 204, 254, 260, 262, 318, 343, 374, 381, 416, 446
Tobago, 75
Tolck, Jacob Pieters, 150, 153
Tonneman, Pieter, 352, 357, 462, 473
Tortuga, 380
Towerson (English agent on Amboina), 229
Town Hall (Amsterdam). *See* Stadt Huys
Town Hall (Boston), 417
Town Hall (Hartford), 421, 422
Trade: and Anglo-Dutch War, 225–30, 246; Boston as center of, 416; and Burgher Right, 345–46; on Connecticut River, 63–65, 71; on Delaware River, 81–82, 84, 258, 260, 261, 263, 264, 266, 305; of Dutch and New England, 342–43, 346, 418; of Dutch and Pilgrims, 42, 45; Dutch-English rivalry on Guinea coast, 390, 427, 437, 467, 469; of Dutch in Barbados, 252, 254–55; Dutch monopoly in slaves, 254; and Dutch peace with Spain, 169, 190; Dutch precedence in, 19–20, 22, 32–33, 42, 77, 80, 226–29, 254, 388, 389, 390, 437, 439, 448; and Dutch truce with Spain, 7, 8; emphasized over agriculture, 189; emphasized over religion, 281, 292; of England and New England, 377–78, 388, 416, 446; of English on Hudson, 53–56, 59, 312, 314–16, 445; in firearms, 101, 108, 110, 127, 175–77, 203, 213–14, 217, 220, 235–38; foreign trade opened to New Amsterdam, 344; fosters colonization, 6–7; freedom promised in Dutch surrender, 460, 463; freeing of in New Netherland, 78, 156, 157, 188, 203–204, 344; on Hudson's voyage, 3–5; of Jews in New Netherland, 292–93; of liquor with Indians, 101, 116, 171, 204, 321, 322, 324, 325, 326, 327; in Massachusetts Bay, 35–36; and Navigation Acts, 229, 252, 254, 318, 378, 388, 389, 391, 416, 427, 436, 446; New Amsterdam as center of,

156, 342–43, 475; New England boycott of Dutch, 217, 220; in New Netherland, 1, 2, 6, 10, 11–13, 17, 19, 28, 29, 30, 34, 41, 43, 60, 73, 78, 84, 101, 105, 108, 109, 110, 134, 156, 171, 173, 175–76, 189, 203–204, 217, 223, 263, 305, 312, 314, 321, 342–47; and New York, 466; patroons vs. Company in, 78–79, 204–206; between Virginia and New Netherland, 63, 318–19, 343; West India Company chartered for, 8–9, 20; West India Company monopoly abolished, 78, 109, 156, 157, 203–204; in West Indies, 8, 32, 60, 77, 150, 152, 157, 158, 223, 247, 252–55. *See also* Dutch East India Company; Dutch West India Company; Fur trade; Slave trade
Trades Increase, The (J. R.), 227
Trantveersjes, 152–53
Treat, Robert, 397
Treaty of Hartford, 221–24, 248, 312, 315, 378, 395, 417–19, 422, 442
Treaty of Southampton, 42
Treaty of Tordesillas, 35
Treaty of Utrecht, 275, 281. *See also* Union of Utrecht
Treaty of Westminster. *See* Peace of Westminster
Treaty of Westphalia, 168
Trekschuiten, 156–57, 191
Trevisano, Girolamo, 20, 21
Trevor, William, 53–54
Trico, Caterina, 11
Trinity Church, 485
Tromp, Maarten Harpertsz, 224, 225, 230, 233
Trouw, 382, 384, 385
Tulips, 22
"Turk, The," 76, 353
Turks, 52, 74
Turner, Captain, 84
Turtle Bay, 112, 125
Twaalft, 27
Twelve, the, 113–15, 117, 118, 120, 124, 174
Tyger, 5

Underhill, John, 451; accuses Van Tienhoven, 236, 239; calls for English rising, 239; dismissal of, 132, 134–35; and Dutch-Indian War, 125–30, 132, 138, 236, 248; piracy against Dutch, 240; and Scott, 432
Union of Utrecht, 139. *See also* Treaty of Utrecht
United Colonies of New England, 147, 213, 218, 222; army of, 238, 248–49, 251; boycott Dutch merchants, 217, 220; formation of, 138–39. *See also* Commissioners of the United Colonies; New England
United New Netherland Company, 6, 13
United Provinces, 8, 31, 38, 42, 51, 151, 230, 246, 275, 281, 345, 359, 388, 438, 479, 482, 487, 490; commercial empire of, 19–20; model for New England

confederation, 139; recognition of independence of, 168. *See also* Holland; Netherlands
Universal Friend, 199
University of Leiden, 181
Usselinx, Willem, 20, 21; promotes Swedish colonization of America, 79–80; urges Dutch colonization, 6–7, 9, 49–50
Utie, Nathaniel, 307–309
Utrecht, 50, 139, 366, 367

Valkenier, 194
Van Arnhem (delegate to Heeren XIX), 29
Van Bergen, Adriaen Jansz, 181
Van Brugge, Carel, 206–208
Van Brugh, Johannes Pietersz, 424
Van Cortlandt, Maria, 404
Van Cortlandt, Oloff Stevensen, 189, 348, 404, 412, 420, 421–22, 429, 432, 462
Van Couwenhoven, Jacob Wolfertsen, 175, 181, 186, 187, 194, 231
Van Couwenhoven, Pieter, 231, 407, 440–41
Van Curler, Arent, 204–205, 325
Van Curler, Jacob, 63–64, 65, 73, 200, 371
Van der Capellen van Ryssel, Jonkheer Hendrick, 197
Van der Donck, Adriaen, 135, 147, 191, 192, 211, 440; as ambassador of New Netherland, 195, 196, 198, 199, 201, 218; authors *Remonstrance,* 187, 189–90; on Indians, 101, 104, 105, 106–107; mutiny against Stuyvesant, 181–85, 186, 187–90, 193, 194, 212, 218; and Rensselaerswyck troubles, 209; returns to colony, 202; secretary of the Nine, 182; writes *Description of New Netherland,* 12, 202
Van der Donck, Mary, 182
Van der Grift, Paulus Leendertsen, 172, 231, 232, 244, 252, 273, 337, 412, 420, 460, 462, 473
Van der Huygens, Cornelis, 75, 111, 162, 166
Van der Linde, Jan Quisthout, 357
Van der Linde, Pieter, 369
Van Dincklage, Lubbertus, 59, 210; assails maladministration, 72–73; killed by Indians, 273–74; proposed as Kieft's successor, 131, 155; resists Stuyvesant, 184, 185, 186, 196–97, 198, 200; Stuyvesant Vice Director, 156, 157, 172, 197, 262
Van Dyck, Hendrick, 114, 199, 253; in Indian War, 129, 272; and origin of "Peach War," 272, 273, 275; and Stuyvesant, 156, 157, 158–59, 196, 200–201, 211
Van Eeda, Margaret, 199
Van Elslandt, Claes, 244, 250, 256, 350, 351
Van Elslandt, Claes, Jr., 350, 351, 443
Van Elswyck, Hendrick, 266, 268
Van Gheel, Max, 231

Van Gogh (ambassador in London), 448, 465, 467, 468, 469–70
Van Hardenbergh, Arnoldus, 174, 180–81, 185
Van Hattem, Arendt, 231, 241, 244
Van Hoboken, Harmen, 369–70
Van Hoogvelt, Elisabeth Jansen Croon (Liesbeth), 198–200
Van Hoossett, Gillis, 50, 51
Van Houten, Hans Jorissen, 54–55, 56
Van Ilpendam, Jan Jansen, 85, 260
Van Imborgh, Gysbert, 407
Van Isendooren, Judith, 367
Van Meeteren, Emanuel, 3, 4, 5, 7
Van Notelman, Coenraed, 57, 59
Van Oldenbarneveld, Johan, 7–8, 228
Van Opdyck, Gysbert, 89–90
Van Remunde, Jan, 16–18, 57, 58
Van Rensselaer, Jan Baptist, 210, 211, 324
Van Rensselaer, Jeremias, 211, 324–25, 337, 353, 403–404, 406, 441, 453, 493; carries petition to Amsterdam, 424, 435
Van Rensselaer, Johannes, 205, 206
Van Rensselaer, Kiliaen, 113, 210; argues for patroon system, 79; fort of, 204–205; as patroon, 49–50, 51, 52, 60, 79, 81, 182, 204–206, 286; and Swedish expedition to Delaware, 81; and Van Twiller, 52–53, 58–59, 72, 73, 205; warns against English settlers in New Netherland, 93; and West India Company, 8–9, 16, 27–28, 47, 49, 52, 54, 60, 79, 204
Van Rensselaerswyck, 75
Van Ruyven, Cornelis, 278, 308, 330, 411, 491; consoles Stuyvesant, 478; in embassy to Hartford, 420–22; envoy to Scott, 429
Van Ruyven, Mrs. Cornelis, 459
Van Salee, Anthony Jansz, 76, 353
Van Schagen, Peter Jansen, 1
Van Slechtenhorst, Brandt Aertsz, and patroon-Company dispute, 205–11
Van Slechtenhorst, Gerrit, 209–10, 453
Van Stoffelsen, Jacob, 77, 113
Van Sweeringen, Gerrit, 398, 401–402
Van Tienhoven, Adriaen, 263, 265
Van Tienhoven, Cornelis, 75, 114, 129, 161, 166, 192, 204, 210, 256, 263, 292, 353; burgomasters oppose, 244; defends Stuyvesant, 193, 197; dismissal of, 278–79, 363; and Dutch-Indian "conspiracy," 236, 238, 239; leads soldiers against English settlers, 86–87; leads soldiers against Raritan Indians, 111, 112; leads troops in Indian War, 118; and "Peach War," 271, 272, 273, 275,

277, 279; prepares war petition, 117, 173, 189; and States General, 195–96, 198–99; Stuyvesant retains, 172–73, 181, 184, 200, 201, 214, 232, 245, 276–77; to Holland, 186, 193
Van Tienhoven, Janneken, 199
Van Tienhoven, Johannes, 199
Van Tienhoven, Lucas, 199
Van Tienhoven, Rachel, 199, 346
Van Twiller, Wouter, 131, 162, 176, 283, 334; administers Van Rensselaer estate, 205–206, 208, 209; arrives in New Netherland, 52–53; and English, 53–55, 57, 61–62, 63–65, 70, 71, 146; on fort, 77; and growth of New Amsterdam, 59, 76–77, 97, 98; misgovernment of, 56–59, 72–73, 112; supports New Netherland rebels, 190, 209
Van Vees, Anthony Jansz. *See* Van Salee, Anthony Jansz
Van Vorst, Cornelis, 73
Van Vorst, Gerrit Jansz, 116
Van Walbeeck, Johannes, 150
Van Wassenaer, Nicolaes, 10–11, 13, 14, 15; on Indians, 101, 103, 104, 105
Van Werckhoven, Cornelis, 337
Van Wieringen, Jan, 42–43
Varevanger, Dr. Jacobus, 349
Varleth, Caspar, 335
Varleth, Jenny, 335
Varleth, Judith, 336
Varleth, Nicholas, 318, 320, 331*n*, 335–36, 337, 415, 462
Vastrick, Gerrit, 176–77
Vaudois, 401
Venice, 8, 20, 32, 377, 389, 390, 436, 439, 469
Vergulde Bever, 305, 366
Verhulst, William, 13, 15; chooses Manhattan as site of fort, 14
Vermeer, Jan, 21
Vermuyden, Sir Cornelius, 246
Verrazano, Giovanni da, 3
Vertoogh (Usselinx), 6, 7
Vertoogh van Nieu-Neder-Land. See *Remonstrance of New Netherland to the States General of the United Netherlands*
Vestiensz, Willem, 369
Victoria, 229
Villages: in New England, 92–93, 171, 277; urged on New Netherlanders, 93, 277, 321–22
Villiers, Barbara, Lady Castlemaine, 389–90
Virginia, 3, 4, 6, 10, 25, 27, 28, 30, 57, 81, 84, 88, 123, 214, 215, 223, 249, 298, 313, 342, 349, 375, 376, 396, 416, 458, 480; conditions in, 62; and Delaware River, 62, 125, 308; Dutch colonists flee to, 306; Dutch prisoners sold as slaves in, 466, 477; and Maryland, 306; and New Netherland, 43, 61–63, 171, 287, 310, 318–19, 320, 335, 381, 446; Puritan view of, 141; settlement of, 35, 36; and slaves, 252, 254; Walloons seek emigration to, 38, 75
Virginia Company, 37, 38

Vliegende Hert, 82
Vlissingen, 138, 241–42. *See also* Flushing
Vondel, Joost van den, 28, 168
Vrede, 110, 111
Vreedenland, 92, 256, 414. *See also* Westchester
Vriesendael, 111, 112, 116

Waegh, 259, 267, 268, 269, 304, 413
Wagenaar, Jan, 246
Waldensians, 401
Waldron, Resolved, 308–10, 395, 414, 443
Wales, 165–66, 284
Wales, Prince of. *See* Charles II, King
Wall Street, 231, 232
Walloons, 10, 38–39, 74–75, 97, 113
Wampum, 45, 103, 105, 106, 116, 124, 195, 221, 323, 325, 347, 489; devaluation of, 346
Wappinger Creek, 314, 315
Wappinger Indians, 124, 130, 409, 411, 440
Warwick, Robert Rich, 2nd Earl of. *See* Rich, Robert, 2nd Earl of Warwick
Warwick Charter, 69–70, 391
Waterhont, 199, 210
Waterpoort, 232
Watertown, 66
Waugh, Dorothy, 294
Waymouth, George, 36
Weatherhead, Mary, 294
Wecquaesgeek Indians: forts of, 128; trouble with Dutch, 16, 110, 111–12, 113–14, 115, 117, 128, 130, 132
Weeping Tower, 25
Weesp, 100
Welius, Dominie Everardus, 304, 311
Welysburg, 182
Wesel, 2
West, John, 62
West Africa, 390. *See also* Gold Coast; Guinea
West India Company, English, 250
West Indies, 8, 32, 38–39, 60, 77, 81, 157, 223, 230, 247, 257, 288, 338, 374, 386, 416; as market for New Amsterdam, 156; and slave trade, 252–54; Stuyvesant in, 150, 152–55, 158–59, 252, 255, 256, 266, 267, 276. *See also* under names of islands
Westchester: Dutch sacrifice of, 423, 432; occupation by Connecticut, 413–15, 417–18, 421, 477; plots with Indians, 440–41. *See also* Vreedenland

Westchester county, 92, 181
Westerhuyzen, Willem, 214–16
Weytinge. *See* Whiting
Whale fishery, 33, 42
Whalley, Edward, 376–77
Wheeler, Thomas, 414
Whitehall (Great House), 336, 480
Whitehall Palace, 437, 470, 480
Whitehall Street, 14, 100, 336
Whiting (Connecticut delegate), 90
Whore's Creek, 107
Wickendam, William, 295, 298
Wicquefort, Abraham de, 435, 448
Wilbore, Miriam, 126
Wilden, 101, 110, 117, 274, 320, 328, 330, 405. *See also* Indians
Willem II, Stadtholder, 94, 178, 190, 219, 226
Willems (New Amstel citizen), 398
Willemstad, 486
Willett, Thomas, 135, 220, 248, 294, 381, 418, 420, 421, 443, 451–54
William, 53, 55–56
William III, King (as Prince of Orange), 246, 250, 387, 438, 482
William and Nicholas, 448, 466
Williams, Roger, 109, 119, 138, 142, 179, 218
Williamson, Sir Joseph, 427, 428, 447
Willoughby, Lord, 254
Willys, Samuel, 454, 462
Wilmington, 82
Wilson, Charles, 388
Wiltwyck: war at, 404–12, 413, 415, 419, 424, 430, 442–43, 477. *See also* Esopus; Esopus Indians
Winckelstraat, 162
Windmills, 20
Windsor, 66, 67, 89
Windsor Castle, 216
Winslow, Edward, 419; on Jamaica expedition, 255; and Plymouth claims on Connecticut River, 63–64, 68
Winslow, Josiah, 419
Winthrop, John, 144, 260, 386; character of, 145–46; and Connecticut River settlement, 64, 65–66, 140, 146; and delegation to Europe, 95; on Dutch-Indian War, 138; and emigration, 24, 25, 142–43, 145–46; governs Bay Colony, 64, 145; on Kieft, 149; letters to Kieft, 140, 146, 148; and New Haven settlement on Delaware, 84, 86, 140; and Plowden, 88–89; and Stuyvesant, 213, 216, 217, 382,

383; and Underhill, 125, 126, 138
Winthrop, John, Jr., 179, 316; appeals for charter, 381–82, 384, 391–93, 426; Bay Colony envoy, 69–70, 95, 385; character of, 69, 218, 382; and Downing, 386, 388–89; and Duke's charter, 447, 450–51, 453, 454, 480; and Dutch invasion of New York, 486–88, 489; and fleet of De Ruyter, 479; governor of Connecticut, 335, 336, 381, 391; mediator in Duke's invasion, 454, 459–60, 461, 462; and Mohawks, 453; and New Haven, 217, 381, 392; and New Netherland, 70–71, 217–18, 381–84, 391–92, 394, 395, 396, 415, 417–18, 421–24, 426, 427, 440, 443–44, 453, 454, 459–60, 464; reconnaissance of New Amsterdam, 382–84, 416; and Saye-Brooke patent, 69–70, 94, 391; and Scott, 427–28, 429, 433–34, 443; sends troops to Long Island, 488, 492; to Long Island, 443–44, 450, 453–54
Winthrop, John (Fitz-John), 453, 486, 488, 492
Winthrop, Mrs. John (Jr.). *See* Reade, Elizabeth
Winthrop, Margaret, 213
Winwood, Sir Ralph, 33
Witchcraft, in New England, 336
Witte Paert, 253
Woerden, 70
"Wooden Horse, The," 100, 354
"Wooden Leg," 208, 324
Woodhouse, 293–94
Worcester, 229
Worsley, Benjamin, 391
Woutersen, Aryan, 361
Woutersen, Catalyntie, 361
Wrightes, Doctor, 24

Yonkers, 181
York, Duke of. *See* James II, King (as Duke of York)
Young, Captain John, 380, 394–95, 415, 428
Young, Rev. John, 87
Young, Thomas, 62

Zeeland, 7, 9, 20, 157, 399, 483, 490
Zeeland Chamber (of West India Company), 157
Zierickzee, 399
Zutphen, 14, 26
Zuyder Zee, 25
Zwoll, 158, 214

INDEX